Free Trade and Social Conflict
in Colombia, Peru and Venezuela

ALSO BY RENÉ DE LA PEDRAJA
AND FROM MCFARLAND

The United States and the Armed Forces of Mexico, Central America and the Caribbean, 2000–2014 (2014)

Wars of Latin America, 1982–2013: The Path to Peace (2013)

Wars of Latin America, 1948–1982: The Rise of the Guerrillas (2013)

Wars of Latin America, 1899–1941 (2006)

Free Trade and Social Conflict in Colombia, Peru and Venezuela

Confronting U.S. Capitalism, 2000–2016

René De La Pedraja

McFarland & Company, Inc., Publishers
Jefferson, North Carolina

Library of Congress Cataloguing-in-Publication Data

Names: De La Pedraja Tomán, René, author.
Title: Free trade and social conflict in Colombia, Peru and Venezuela : confronting U.S. capitalism, 2000–2016 / René De La Pedraja.
Description: Jefferson, North Carolina : McFarland & Company, Inc., Publishers, 2016 | Includes bibliographical references and index.
Identifiers: LCCN 2016034271 | ISBN 9780786499298 (softcover : acid free paper) ♾
Subjects: LCSH: Colombia—Economic policy. | Peru—Economic policy. | Venezuela—Economic policy. | Colombia—Foreign economic relations. | Peru—Foreign economic relations. | Venezuela—Foreign economic relations. Social conflict—Colombia—History—21st century. | Social conflict—Peru—History—21st century. | Social conflict—Venezuela—History—21st century. | Colombia—Politics and government—1974– | Peru—Politics and government—2000– | Venezuela—Politics and government—1999–
Classification: LCC HC125 .D37145 2016 | DDC 338.9861—dc23
LC record available at https://lccn.loc.gov/2016034271

British Library cataloguing data are available

ISBN (print) 978-0-7864-9929-8
ISBN (ebook) 978-1-4766-2640-6

Printed in the United States of America

McFarland & Company, Inc., Publishers
Box 611, Jefferson, North Carolina 28640
www.mcfarlandpub.com

To Beatriz and Jaroslav

Table of Contents

Preface 1

1. Venezuela: From the Fourth Republic to Hugo Chávez 3
   The Failure of the Fourth Republic 3
   PDVSA: A State Within a State 8
   The Emergence of Hugo Chávez 11
2. Peru: The Return of Dictatorship 22
   The Partnership with Vladimiro Montesinos 22
   The Alberto Fujimori Dictatorship 25
   The First Reelection 32
3. The United States and the Crisis in Peru 39
   The Second Reelection of Alberto Fujimori 39
   The Last Battle of Vladimiro Montesinos 44
   The Unraveling 51
   The Transition 55
4. Initial Attempts at Transformation 60
   Venezuela: New Constitution and Task Forces 60
   Peru: The Start of the Alejandro Toledo Presidency 68
   Decentralization in Peru Under Alejandro Toledo 71
5. Venezuela: The Coup of April 2002 77
   The 49 Decree Laws 77
   The Coup Attempt of 11 April 2002 81
   Peter the Brief 90
6. Two Decisive Turns in 2002 96
   Colombia: The Rise of Álvaro Uribe Vélez 96
   Peru: From the Arequipazo to the Andahuaylas Revolt 100
7. Venezuela: The Second Attempt to Overthrow Chávez 110
   Missed Opportunity 110
   The Petroleum Strike: December 2002–February 2003 114
8. Colombia: The Álvaro Uribe Vélez Presidency 120
   The War Against Guerrillas 120
   The Challenge to the Political Class 122
   The Problem of the Paramilitaries 124

9. Venezuela: The Best Years of the Chávez Presidency 131
The Third Effort to Oust Chávez: The Recall Election of 2004 131
The Opposition in Disarray 136
Attempts to Transform Venezuela 141

10. Peru: Ups and Downs of the Alejandro Toledo Presidency 149
Reaching for the Sky 149
The Agony of the Alejandro Toledo Presidency 155

11. Blows Against the Left 160
Colombia: The Reelection of Álvaro Uribe Vélez 160
The 2006 Presidential Campaign in Peru 164

12. Venezuela and Peru: From Success to Setback 170
The Bolivarian Revolution: From Euphoria to Repudiation 170
Peru: From Honeymoon to Social Conflict 179

13. Peru: The Self-Destruction of the Alán García Presidency 186
New Outbreaks of Violence 186
The Scandal of the Petro Audios 190
The Final Blow: The Bagua Massacre 193

14. The Bolivarian Revolution on the Offensive, 2008–2011 203
PSUV, Nationalizations and Elections 203
2009: The Decisive Year 210
The Struggle to Safeguard Society 215
Food Scarcity and Agriculture 222
The End of the Offensive 227

15. The Álvaro Uribe Presidency in Distress 231
The Twilight of the Uribe Presidency 231
Three Scandals 236
The Third Term and the Presidential Election of 2010 245

16. Peru: The Nationalist Reaction 251
The Presidential Campaign of 2011 251
Ollanta Humala: Defining the Presidency 254
The Ongoing Struggle Over the Conga Mining Project 256

17. Transitions in Venezuela and Colombia 260
The Agony of the Hugo Chávez Presidency 261
Course Corrections in Colombia 264

18. The Closing of a Period 272
Colombia: The Struggle for Peace 272
Peru: Trapped in Conflicts 279
Venezuela: The Bolivarian Revolution on the Defensive 284

Chapter Notes 297

Annotated Bibliography 333

Index 335

Preface

Starting in the late 1980s the U.S. government and Wall Street intensified their earlier efforts to impose capitalism and free trade on Latin America. Foreign aid, technical assistance, and educational cooperation sank to insignificant levels and often vanished completely, while free trade and foreign investment became the magic formula for all of Latin America's economic problems. And as the countries of Latin America increased their participation in the U.S. economy, these trade links enlarged the political influence of Washington. U.S. embassies gained considerable leverage to shape both domestic and international policies of individual countries. However, the adoption of free trade and the entry of foreign capital did not always proceed smoothly, and resistance sometimes turned into violent clashes.

Fulfilling its historical role, the onward rush of capitalism destroyed many existing practices, customs, and institutions. Not unexpectedly, groups and individuals suffering harmful effects struggled to stop the march of capitalism, and their resistance produced social conflict of varying degrees of intensity and violence. The purpose of this book is to examine the responses of Colombia, Peru, and Venezuela to the intensification of economic links with the United States and with international capital from 2000 to 2016. Colombia welcomed these closer ties while Venezuela tried to reject them. Located between these two extremes was Peru, which in spite of having entered into a free trade agreement with the United States in 2007, in many cases has continued to block the entry of foreign capital.

The struggle over free trade in the three countries assumed diametrically opposed dimensions. In Colombia and Peru, the opposition tried to soften the free trade agreements and also to delay their entry into force. In direct contrast, in Venezuela the opposition took the most extreme form of aiming to overthrow the government of Hugo Chávez as the only way to create strong economic ties with the United States through a free trade agreement.

The central goal of this book is to show that the different outcomes in the three countries originated in their history, an explanation naturally very appealing to historians. Thus the first two chapters present those historical experiences most pertinent to the twenty-first century. Starting in the late 1980s when the U.S. government and Wall Street intensified the pressure to impose the free market, the result has been recurrent social conflict, as the remaining chapters of this book narrate.

Readers have received major insights into the period from my previous book *The United States and the Armed Forces of Mexico, Central America, and the Caribbean 2000–2014*, but its military perspective left many issues unexplored. Although the armed forces are far from out of the picture in this new book and readers can expect some revelations, a new cast of characters and a broader set of issues occupy most of this narrative. Politicians, policemen, and opposition groups hold center stage, while elections, referendums, foreign investment, and free trade comprise the principal topics. And while the struggle sometimes took place peacefully through elections and civil debate, the more usual way to decide an outcome was through the social conflict that has gripped the three countries until today.

As I have stated in my previous publications, this new book again is possible only thanks to the Wikileaks revelations of the diplomatic cables of U.S. embassies. Considerable information in the cables did not fit into my previous studies, and I felt that a scholar could still extract many valuable insights from the once-in-a-lifetime discovery of priceless materials. These cables substantiate my text because they chronicle the goal of Washington and Wall Street to impose free trade on Latin America.

My wife was enthusiastic about this project the very first time it crossed my mind. Without her support, I could not have finished the manuscript. As always, she drew the maps, made suggestions to the many drafts, and helped in countless ways. I am truly blessed to have a person who throughout an entire lifetime has remained a firm believer in my writing endeavors. In his own way, my son Jaroslav provided crucial insights at the right moment. It is my sincere hope that all these efforts to create a coherent and readable narrative will provide readers with a deep understanding of the forces shaping three South American countries during the initial decades of the twenty-first century.

CHAPTER 1

Venezuela: From the Fourth Republic to Hugo Chávez

The economic organization of Venezuela combined [...] the worst elements of both socialism and capitalism without the redeeming features of either system.—David Eugene Blank[1]

The Failure of the Fourth Republic

When Raúl Leoni completed his presidential term of office in 1969, Venezuela seemed to be on the right track to become a prosperous and peaceful country. Although early signals of difficulties were already appearing, elections took place in an orderly manner, the insurgency was faltering, and many guerrillas returned to civilian life. As part of the policy of Import Substitution Industrialization (ISI) the government generously financed the establishment of new factories to manufacture items previously purchased abroad. And, thanks to vigorous official support, even agriculture experienced a strong 6 percent annual increase in output.[2]

The improvement in agriculture was misleading, and structural defects hampered production. The contrast with Colombia enjoying similar and often identical conditions of climate and soil was a cause for serious concern, because in the bordering country its farmers with inadequate government support were able to produce abundant surpluses of almost all the tropical food crops. And inside Venezuelan cities other deficiencies were also starting to appear. Public education was showing the first signs of deterioration in quality, and the expansion of schooling was proving to be harder than originally expected. The quality of health care also began to decline, and Venezuela was having enormous difficulty creating a network of social welfare for its citizens. This last point was not just a Utopian ideal but also was a central element of the campaign to attract guerrillas and more importantly to dissuade citizens from joining the insurgency. It was imperative to demonstrate to the country that armed struggle was not the way to obtain a better quality of life for the population.[3]

The situation deteriorated under Rafael Caldera (1969–1974) as his administration proved incapable of sustaining the industrialization of Venezuela. Critics have pointed out that Latin American countries reached a dead end once they exhausted the possibilities of manufacturing under ISI. Venezuela never reached that ceiling and continued to import items that it should have been able to produce in its factories. The same was true for agriculture, because for the first time the country experienced food shortages and frequent jumps in the price of meat and other produce. The situation might have become explosive had not a quick fix been available.[4]

The popular perception has been that the rise in oil prices began in 1973 with the energy shock, but in reality for Venezuela oil prices began moving upwards with the Libyan crisis of 1970. The Caldera administration, enjoying higher than expected oil revenues, unwisely decided to solve the food shortages by importing meat and many other foodstuffs from abroad. The United States and the European Union with its heavily subsidized agriculture were the chief beneficiaries of this buying spree by Venezuela. And enjoying ample oil revenue, the government did little to halt the import of manufactured items, thus undermining the previous attempts at industrialization. And once the energy crisis of 1973 confirmed the duration of high oil prices for nearly a decade, there was no turning back, and the government continued to spend its way out of its problems by wasting the oil revenue. Without a decisive commitment to change the nature of the economy, "Dutch Disease," the tendency of oil to stun if not destroy all other economic activities, solidly took root in Venezuela. This disease, which had been only a weed in the 1960s, became an invasive species in the early 1970s; mitigation has occasionally had some success, but all attempts to eradicate it completely have failed right down to the present.[5]

When Carlos Andrés Pérez took office in 1974, he was the first president to realize that petroleum rather than a benefit, was turning into a curse for Venezuela. Oil revenues had become an addiction for the country, and because of the "Dutch Disease" nothing else could thrive. The acute fear also existed that the country's oil reserves would run out in the 1980s, and this anxiety—which turned out to be false—gave an additional urgency to find replacements for petroleum exports during his presidency. "The Pérez government argued that the 1975–1980 period could be Venezuela's last chance to stimulate economic diversification and to consolidate electoral democracy."[6] Although his party AD had won ample majorities in both houses of the Venezuelan congress, in a wise precaution he insisted on receiving enabling authority from congress to issue decrees with the force of law. A lifetime in politics had taught him the lesson that powerful interest groups could block or emasculate any major bills during the long and cumbersome legislative process. When the congress gave him this authority in May 1974, he set the precedent that Hugo Chávez later followed in 2001.[7]

Pérez knew that only extraordinary measures could save Venezuela from its exclusive dependence on petroleum, and as a first major step, he used his decree authority to nationalize iron mining on 26 November 1974. He then converted the small Orinoco Steel Company (SIDOR) into a massive state owned enterprise with the capacity to export large amounts of steel. To make Venezuela a major exporter of aluminum, he also supported the expansion of another state enterprise to transform the abundant ore deposits into finished aluminum. Because electricity is the major cost in the smelting of aluminum, Pérez began in 1976 the final phase of the Guri hydroelectric project. The dam was completed in 1986, years ahead of schedule. By providing abundant and cheap electricity, Guri supported the expansion of the state aluminum company.[8]

Iron, steel, aluminum, and electricity were among the most important projects Pérez promoted to diversify the economy and to turn the country into a modern industrial power. He realized that industrialization required abundant oil revenues to cover the large start-up costs of these vast economic projects. Although both major parties had kept the nationalization of petroleum out of the presidential campaign of 1973, Pérez had already concluded that nationalization was indispensable for Venezuela to extract the maximum amount of revenues before the expected depletion of oil reserves.

In another wise political move, Pérez, partially inspired by the successful nationalization of copper in Chile, decided not to use his enabling power to issue laws and instead sought congressional legislation. A full debate ensued in both chambers, and after all the leading personalities had expressed their views, the congress passed the bill nationalizing petroleum. Pérez duly signed the bill into law on 29 August 1974, and the next day he issued the decree creating PDVSA, a state-owned petroleum company, to administer the nationalized properties. As part of the negotiations to secure the acquiescence of the U.S. government, the foreign companies received compensation for the value of all their properties. The foreign companies had grudgingly accepted nationalization mainly because they realized that this was the best way to prolong their influence in the petroleum sector.[9]

And President Pérez had concluded that the only way to prevent disruptions in the oil industry was to preserve the administrative structures of the foreign companies. Thus initially PDVSA was more like a holding company supervising 14 affiliates. In 1978 the state enterprise consolidated them into four main units, three of which had been the subsidiaries of Exxon, Shell, and Mobil. To highlight the continuity, President Pérez retained all the Venezuelan personnel trained by the foreign oil companies. Nationalists had called for firing all this skilled personnel because it was too brainwashed with foreign ideologies to serve the needs of Venezuela, but the president wisely rejected those calls and ratified the skilled personnel in their positions. In what at first did not seem controversial, he granted PDVSA virtual autonomy from the rest of the government and respected its right to enforce secrecy over proprietary information. PDVSA was on its way to becoming a peculiar if not unique oil company in the world.[10]

Curiously when dealing with foreign companies and the U.S. government, Pérez had not encountered strong resistance to his policies. In contrast, the reaction was completely hostile when he attacked some privileges of the Venezuelan economic oligarchy, as happened when he tried to break the oligopoly existing in the cement industry. Two firms controlled almost all the cement production in Venezuela, but when they requested government financing to expand their output, Pérez instead decided to support the creation of new plants under different ownership. His goal was to introduce the supposedly holy concept of competition into the sector, but the cement oligopoly was determined to preserve its privileged position.[11]

In attacks anticipating the ones hurled against Hugo Chávez after 2000, many business leaders began a ferocious campaign against President Pérez, accusing him of fostering "crony capitalism" for a few favored friends. The media campaign was not as effective as later was the case against Chávez, because the governments of the Fourth Republic traditionally subsidized lavishly the press and also made generous payments to individual reporters. Shielded from the worst media coverage, the Pérez administration was able to complete the expansion of cement plants and to break the oligopoly in that sector. But the struggle proved politically exhausting, so his presidency avoided additional confrontations with existing economic groups. One sector of the economic oligarchy had been weakened, but the rest of the powerful business conglomerates remained intact and even more determined to preserve their privileged position against any future government daring to challenge them.[12]

The first presidency of Carlos Andrés Pérez foreshadowed the obstacles Chávez encountered in the early years of his rule but the latter inherited a country in a much worse situation. The modifications under Pérez renewed the optimism about Venezuela, and the high oil prices generated tremendous expectations for the future. During the 1970s many citizens believed that the country was on the way to becoming prosperous and self-sustaining, and the mega projects in areas such as steel, electricity, and petroleum certainly created the impression of moving forward in a dramatic way. But even in the boom years of the 1970s with the record high oil prices, ruinous habits became widespread. The country's ports collapsed with the massive surge of imports, and the conspicuous consumption of foreign goods devoured a disproportionate share of oil revenues. The government could not balance its budget and covered its deficits with foreign loans. Foreign banks were eager to lend, because the price of oil was expected to remain high forever, and the government supposedly could pay its foreign debt out of future oil revenues.[13]

The orgy of spending in the 1970s and the spread of a "new rich" mentality among many citizens were the principal expressions of the boundless optimism that so many Venezuelans came to espouse. But when the oil prices tumbled after 1980, Venezuela lacked a safety net to face a grim scenario. Declining oil revenues could no longer cover the budget deficits, and the government had no choice but to make drastic cuts in spending. Meeting the payments on the foreign debt contracted during the previous decade became increasingly harder, and to conserve dwindling reserves, the Fourth Republic for the first time imposed controls on the currency in 1983.[14]

Social programs suffered the worst budget cuts, and gradually the government dismantled the public welfare network. After 1980 the health care system deteriorated and many citizens lost access to medical services. The decline in social programs was most evident in public education. From 1980 to 1999 the middle class gradually displaced the lower class from most public schools. As the population increased, the number of students attending private schools remained stable, because many members of the middle class could not afford the high tuition of private institutions. But because the public educational system was also suffering from budget cuts, principals and teachers began to collect fees and to charge parents for many school services. Although the fees were not an excessive burden for the middle class, they were prohibitive for most parents of the lower class. Not only did enrollments from lower class children decline, but those who entered suffered high dropout rates in both primary and secondary education. And even for those students who graduated, the quality of their education usually had deteriorated considerably.[15]

The decline in public education was just one of many manifestations of the fall of a large segment of the population into misery. Thirty-three percent of the population lived in poverty in 1970, and that share increased to 70 percent in 1995. Such a dramatic jump in the level of poverty was unheard of in Latin America, where the usual pattern has been for the population either to remain poor or to make small incremental steps to improve its condition. And this sharp reversal in the standard of living fell particularly hard on the people who had experienced the elation of rising expectations in the 1970s. The economic oligarchy continued uninterrupted its lavish lifestyle and if anything loved even more than before to flaunt its wealth in the face of the increasingly impoverished masses in Venezuela.[16]

Corruption was the link between the economic oligarchy and the government. Private business groups maintained their monopolies or oligopolies by lobbying government officials for privileged policies. Bribes and gifts were the indispensable tools to make sure that the legislative and executive branches at all levels strongly supported private business. Having business leaders occupy high positions in the government, such as cabinet appointments, facilitated enormously crafting measures favorable to private business. The favors that firms secured were of a wide variety depending on the specific sector, and could range from lax inspections to speedy approval of questionable permits. Four stood out as very important for private business. The first and most important was protection from foreign competition so that Venezuelan businesses did not suffer from cheap and possibly better imports. Second, firms tried to obtain favorable exchange rates to purchase foreign currency. Another was to try to block state investment in possible competitors. Last was direct support for private business, rarely in the form of subsidies, more frequently in low taxes and preferential state purchases of local goods and services.[17]

To encourage economic growth, the Fourth Republic tried to reduce the power of the oligopolies by opening the country to direct foreign investment, because the Venezuelan elite was not ideologically opposed to their entry. But the same rule applied to investment as to competition, and if any Venezuelan firm existed in that area of activity, then the private business formed a united front to block the entrance of foreign companies. That left new products or services using cutting-edge technology as the only acceptable areas for direct foreign investment, and in those cases firms from abroad could expect a hearty welcome. Yet this type of foreign investment could not weaken the fundamental grip the economic oligarchy had over the country.

In Venezuela not all areas of economic activity were appealing either to private business or to foreign investment. To fill this gap, the government established many public enterprises either in the form of state ownership or "mixed" state and private investment. Creating these new enterprises was easy during the boom years of the 1970s and seemed a great way to make oil revenues contribute to the economic diversification of the country. These public enterprises proliferated so rapidly that soon not even the government was sure how many actually existed. An estimate of 1979 put their number at around 226, and as could be expected with this rapid expansion, corruption and fraud plagued almost all these public enterprises.[18]

Perhaps corruption was an inevitable part of the start and expansion of these companies, but the bigger problem was that even when they were fully operational, the firms could not cover their expenses. In effect, either after creation or nationalization, the new state firms became sink holes for treasury funds. Only a few of these firms could survive without massive and constant infusions of subsidies, and whenever the government lagged behind in providing funds, those companies ran up huge debts to cover operating expenses and in the process added the costs of repaying the loans to their already staggering losses. Independent of the function of the specific state enterprise, throughout all of them emerged the pattern of a small elite inside the firm milking the state to enjoy the great life and usually not sharing the benefits with the rank-and-file employees. The direct knowledge Hugo Chávez had of the failed state sector made him most reluctant to embark on the path of nationalizations as the solution to Venezuela's problems. During his entire rule he struggled to find alternatives to state ownership, because he knew very well that simply repeating the path of the Fourth Republic meant heading to another failure.

Why were these state enterprises such dismal failures? The simple explanation that the state is inherently inefficient reveals an ideological basis and does not account for the failure of the private sector to enter and to operate in those fields. After the initial capital investment had taken place in state firms, the biggest operating expense was the inflated payroll, because these firms tended to hire more personnel than they actually needed. And unlike private companies, state enterprises had little flexibility to dismiss employees when they were no longer needed. But the huge burden of a bloated payroll brought the societal benefit of providing employment otherwise unavailable, and this need to preserve jobs was a powerful political consideration pressuring the government to find funds to cover the operating deficits. Related to the excessively large work force was the defect of not being able to impose discipline and order on workers and employees; unlike private companies, state firms rarely had the opportunity to demote and much less fire deficient or poorly performing employees. Instead the frequently cited reason of bad management decisions adversely affecting state enterprises did occur but not more frequently than in the private sector.

The blatant failure of state enterprises to operate efficiently and without permanent subsidies created widespread disenchantment and sparked calls for their privatization. Public pressure to take drastic action remained weak, however, because the inefficiency of the state enterprises brought benefits to many private businesses. The inability of the treasury to continue providing funds to cover the massive losses finally imposed privatization on the state enterprises. While in some instances foreign investors and Venezuelan private business proved very eager to acquire state enterprises, most of the time nobody was interested in acquiring them even at give-away prices. The accumulated debts were too high, the operating expenses so crushing, and the assets so low that liquidation was the only realistic alternative, as happened with the airline VIASA and the shipping company CAVN. The reality that private businesses were not willing to step in to fill the void strongly suggested that a lot more than the supposed inherent inefficiency of state enterprises had been at play.[19]

Another much more persuasive explanation for the failure of state enterprises was the "Dutch Disease" that blights all non-petroleum productive activities whether in private or public ownership. One direct confirmation of the "Dutch Disease" came from the extraordinary success of the state-owned PDVSA in sharp contrast to "the utterly dismal performance of the other Venezuelan state enterprises."[20] Several reasons help to explain the divergent results. All the other state enterprises needed official funding to begin and expand operations, but PDVSA was always self-financing. The other companies, accustomed to government largesse, were never able to break the umbilical cord of subsidies and cash transfers. PDVSA always earned massive profits, unlike other state enterprises that rarely could cover operating expenses. Yet even those few well-managed state enterprises could never match the extraordinary profits of the oil business, a very lucrative activity that put PDVSA in a preferential position.

PDVSA: A State Within a State

PDVSA seemed destined to repeat the pattern of Mexico's oil monopoly, PEMEX, but instead it took a surprising turn. As mentioned earlier, the first decisive step came under the Pérez presidency when PDVSA obtained autonomy from the government and the right to secrecy, in particular of proprietary information. Secrecy in state institutions inevitably leads to corruption, as frequently happened to PEMEX, but in Venezuela the company instituted such strict internal controls that no scandal ever became public. Instead management used its freedom and resources to transform the autonomy into virtual independence until the company became a state within the state. The management culture turned to contempt toward politicians, and in the most extreme case of an elite seeking only its own benefit, the company deliberately set out to weaken the government.[21]

By law the company was supposed to hand over profits and royalties to the treasury, but upper management decided to reduce the transfer of funds. A number of partial steps in the 1980s culminated in 1989 with the entrenchment of an accounting system that automatically transferred costs to Venezuela and kept profits in subsidiaries abroad. The goal of this system was to reduce the amount of oil revenue the government received. In a revealing comparison, the payment that PDVSA gave the treasury in 2001 for each barrel of petroleum exported was only one-fourth of the sum that PEMEX handed over to the Mexican government for the same barrel. The most visible aspect of the transfer of profits abroad were the many refineries, pipelines, and even distribution companies that PDVSA acquired, yet these accounted for only a fraction of the funds upper management stashed away in many foreign financial institutions and offshore banks.[22]

The details of these transactions became known only during the Chávez years, even though occasional leaks suggested the need to examine thoroughly the operations and goals of the state enterprise, but that never happened during the Fourth Republic. The Ministry of Energy supposedly was supervising PDVSA, but the oil company zealously deprived that agency of the essential information. Salaries at PDVSA were generally at least three times higher than in the public sector, so routinely the company lured officials away from the Ministry of Energy. PDVSA also secured the loyalty of officials at the Ministry of Energy by paying them bonuses or a second salary.[23]

As far as the Venezuelan congress, timely campaign contributions made sure that the legislature never sponsored any bills threatening the privileges of PDVSA. The company had ample clout to repeal laws requiring the transfer of funds to the government, and managers correctly concluded that the existing laws helped protect the image of the company as a vital element in Venezuela. The media also helped to create a positive public image, and just like the government subsidized newspapers and gave payments to reporters, so PDVSA did the same to assure not just favorable publicity but also to make sure that TV stations and newspaper headlines never reported any damaging accusations.

Upper managers, however, could not resist flaunting their wealth, and many lived a luxurious lifestyle comparable to the economic oligarchs of the private sector. Mansions, flashy automobiles, yachts, private airplanes, and wild parties characterized the life of upper managers much in the same way as had been the custom under the foreign subsidiaries. Money kept this lavish lifestyle out of the media except for the social pages, but the conspicuous consumption of PDVSA management and of the upper class gradually became public knowledge and fueled mounting resentment among the increasingly impoverished masses in Venezuela.[24]

The only inefficiency in the company was the large number of administrators, generally estimated at twice the number PDVSA required for its operations. This excessive number of administrators was the key to understanding the protest movements against

Chávez in 2002 and 2003, because those employees formed the backbone of the opposition. In 1997 when PDVSA president Luis Giusti merged the last three operating subsidiaries, he did not fire white collar employees who kept their generally unnecessary jobs. And because these employees earned at least three times the salary of government officials, this very lucrative remuneration for doing very little work earned tremendous loyalty to the company and gave them plenty of time to engage in scheming. The passion and commitment of these employees were responsible for the determination to embark on the violent protests of 2002 and 2003.[25]

The company drew the line at administrators and adopted different policies toward blue-collar workers. PDVSA paid higher wages than in the private sector to its workers, thereby guaranteeing labor peace. But unlike for administrators, the company constantly strove to reduce the number of workers. It pioneered techniques for measuring output and constantly sought ways to reduce the labor force through automation, computer systems, and organizational rearrangements. PDVSA was intent on avoiding the bloated bureaucracy of PEMEX, and although the decision was sound from a business perspective, in the highly political environment it was not a wise move. Hiring more workers was political insurance because in the classic patron-client relationship, each additional hire gained loyalty among a large group of relatives and friends for the company. This type of political calculation had doomed the other public enterprises, but a company devoting huge efforts to hide profits could certainly afford hiring many more workers. Upper management, if it wanted to preserve its privileged position during the Chávez years, had to increase its labor force to at least 100,000, a number comparable to PEMEX's at that time. But greed made upper management sacrifice political insurance, which was not needed during the Fourth Republic—only when rising waters threaten properties do homeowners rush to buy flood insurance but then it is too late.

One other policy of PDVSA during the Fourth Republic was of even greater importance to understand the Chávez years. Venezuela had been the real founding member of OPEC (Organization of Petroleum Exporting Countries) in September 1960 and that institution had been instrumental in keeping world market prices high during the 1970s. But the collapse of oil prices in 1981 forced OPEC to reevaluate its policies and to draw two main conclusions. First, it was most important for the growth of the world economy, including both consumers and producers of oil, to have stability in prices. Secondly, OPEC members realized that they needed to use their market power not to raise but to *lower* world oil prices. The reason for this remarkable turnaround came with a changed understanding of world petroleum reserves. Conventional wisdom and alarmist articles in the 1940s and even earlier claimed that the earth would soon run out of petroleum. The energy crisis of the 1970s debunked that myth and proved that the earth possessed much more petroleum in various forms than anyone had ever suspected. The experience of later decades confirmed that extracting petroleum depended on production costs at a particular location and the application of new technologies.

OPEC consequently had to keep the price of oil down to prevent other countries from expanding their production and developing new extractive processes; consumers needed to be kept away from alternate sources of energy. However, OPEC members could not reach unanimous agreement on how far to reduce the price of oil. The Venezuelan government joined the majority of OPEC members in wanting to keep oil prices sufficiently low to prevent the appearance of competitors and still generate important oil revenues. PDVSA using its own calculations concluded that the OPEC price was too high, and the Venezuelan company, on its own, and in defiance of its own government, continued to flood the world market with cheap crude for the rest of the twentieth century. By selling at a low price the company reduced its profits and made easier the task of hiding them from the government.[26]

The Chávez administration harshly condemned PDVSA for having undermined OPEC production quotas, but the historical experience, particularly after 2014 has amply confirmed the validity of the analysis and practice of the Venezuelan company during the twentieth century. OPEC had control over the oil market as long as prices remained below the production costs of alternate suppliers of oil. A momentary surge in prices was not going to unleash new sources of oil, but as the years of high oil prices turned into a decade, countries, companies, entrepreneurs, and inventors could not resist the opportunity to enter perhaps the most lucrative activity in the world.

The low price policy of PDVSA was actually the best thing possible for Venezuela, and had the oil company also shared more of its profits with the people, probably not even Chávez would have attempted radical changes during his rule and the Bolivarian Revolution might not even have occurred. But in the last decades of the twentieth century the failure of PDVSA to hire more Venezuelans and to share more benefits left the Fourth Republic irreversibly marching to its doom. Many regions in Latin America were considerably poorer than Venezuela, but no other country had experienced such a dramatic fall from prosperity. It was not being poor but the return to poverty after having experienced a better material life that made the social situation so explosive in the last two decades of the twentieth century. The safety valve of presidential elections was losing its calming effect as voters became increasingly bitter and angry with each succeeding ruler. Venezuelans regained their illusions when Carlos Andrés Pérez became the first person to win a second term to the presidency in December 1988. Voters associated him with the most prosperous period in the history of Venezuela and believed that he was sure to alleviate the increasingly desperate situation of the majority of the people.[27]

The Emergence of Hugo Chávez

The most important legacy of the second presidency of Carlos Andrés Pérez was making possible the political career of Hugo Chávez. Years before taking office Pérez had already taken the fateful steps that made his presidency so decisive for Venezuela's history. During the 1980s he succumbed to the siren calls of capitalism and attended tutorials at the International Monetary Fund (IMF) and the World Bank. Quietly he also recruited an economic team among free market zealots who were not affiliated to his political party (AD).[28] At some moment he experienced a profound almost mystical conversion to capitalism, and thus he joined the ranks of former left-leaning rulers such as Salinas de Gortari in Mexico and later Alán García in Peru, who ditched any remaining socialist notions in their passionate embrace of the free market.

Pérez was too astute a politician to announce his conversion during the electoral campaign, and he limited himself to stating the need for a drastic change but without giving any specifics. To maintain the candidate's popularity, the outgoing administration helpfully supported his campaign by imposing price controls on basic necessities in particular on foodstuffs. After the election in December 1988, merchants hoarded edible goods and even appliances because the prevailing belief was that the new government would lift the price controls after the inauguration on 2 February 1989. Empty shelves became routine in many grocery stores, and already sporadic food riots had broken out in provincial towns and even in Caracas.[29]

Warning signs were obvious to the public and no sophisticated spying agency was needed to detect the discontent. But Pérez callously had already factored social conflict into his reform package and he felt no need to alter his plans. On 16 February 1989 in an extraordinary turnaround or the "Great Betrayal" as Venezuelans later called it, the president announced a typical IMF austerity program designed to enrich the wealthy and to exploit the poor. Because Venezuela as an oil-rich country had kept the price of gasoline at perhaps the lowest level in the world, even a slight increase at the pump provoked intense anger. Pérez went to the extreme, and his shock package doubled the price of gasoline and stipulated more increases in future years. To try to minimize the expected backlash, the government raised bus fares only by 30 percent, a precautionary measure that paradoxically came to ignite riots.[30]

The first full day of operation of the austerity program was Monday, 27 February, and neither he nor his economic team of free-market enthusiasts expected any initial reaction. The president went away to Barquisimeto, leaving the government leaderless at a crucial moment. A wage dispute had crippled the city police force, so that an inadequate number of policemen were available to respond to disturbances. Soldiers could not fill the gaps because the army normally stationed few units inside Caracas.[31]

The countless commuters coming to work every day in the capital were very angry about the 30 percent increase in bus fares. When the first passengers arrived at the bus station of the bedroom community of Guarenas to the east of Caracas to buy their tickets at dawn on 27 February, drivers greeted them with the news that the fares had doubled. The bus owners did not need a Ph.D. in economics to calculate their losses when gasoline prices doubled and their fares went up only by 30 percent. The failure to make adequate arrangements to compensate the bus owners was the government's big mistake that triggered the disturbances. Angry crowds of passengers gathered at Guarenas, hurled stones at the buses, and by 0730 had set vehicles on fire. By then similar violent incidents had erupted at other bus terminals both in Caracas and in 19 towns of the interior.[32]

Students had previously scheduled for noon that day a large rally at the Central University of Venezuela to protest the austerity package of Pérez, but when they heard the news of the initial disturbances, the emboldened students set up barricades in nearby avenues of the capital. By 2:00 p.m. residents joined the students in blocking most of the main avenues of Caracas, and in a decisive escalation, the demonstrators stopped all trucks carrying food and distributed the cargo to neighbors. All this time the weak police response showed that the authorities were rapidly losing control of the streets.[33]

After the seizure of the food trucks, the next logical step was to begin looting the grocery stores and supermarkets in central Caracas. Merchants had delayed these assaults by locking their stores and closing the metal gates early in the morning, while demonstrators were not too eager to break in because they expected to find mostly empty shelves. But when the protestors smashed the doors of the first grocery stores around 4:00 p.m. and discovered that the stock rooms in the rear contained vast quantities of food items the merchants had hoarded over the previous weeks, the news spread like wildfire. Hungry residents desperately broke into supermarkets and then turned their attention to furniture stores and appliance outlets.[34] The rampage swept central Caracas, and "the looting took on an almost festive air as television news crews followed crowds of men, women and children carting off sides of beef and stereo sets."[35]

By nightfall the sacking of stores reached the barrios in the hills overlooking Caracas, but the poor neighborhoods offered slim pickings. Many residents hesitated to loot corner stores because the owners were usually almost as poor as the neighbors; the larger stores in the barrios simply opened the doors and let residents take away the meager contents thus sparing the premises from damage. During the morning of February 28 the looting died down and was practically over by noon. Caracas virtually shut down, with the people largely hiding inside houses and buildings. The demonstrators had not attacked any official buildings, so this was not a political insurrection. The looters also had not entered the wealthy neighborhoods, so the disturbances did not even qualify as a revolt of the poor against the rich.[36] The moment was ideal for the authorities to return the police to the streets, with the occasional participation of army patrols. A modest show of force was sure to restore order gradually to the city, and the government could have speeded up the process by announcing a partial repeal of the harshest of the austerity measures.

International organizations, with more experience in dealing with the social conflict they were responsible for having caused, stood ready to offer a stand-by loan to Venezuela to help ease the transition into the austerity program. But Pérez did not want to take this route and instead he wanted to prove to the country and to the world that he was not a weak president. The machismo or maleness tradition was certainly an influence in his decision, but his determination stemmed mostly from the new found passion of a recent convert to the free market. If socialist regimes had used force to impose state ownership of the means of production, why should capitalist rulers not impose the free market by force? Capitalism in its historic role was bound to smash all pre-capitalist practices, customs, and institutions, so why could not the state use its powers to speed up the process for completing the transition to a full free market economy? But only a strong government could impose capitalism on the impoverished masses, and a decisive action was the best way to impose respect and obedience from its terrified citizens.

After Pérez completed his scheduled events in Barquisimeto, he returned to Caracas around 8:00 p.m. on 27 February, and by that time the situation did not seem to require drastic action. The next day the looting was dying down, yet the president suddenly decided to send the army to make a dramatic show of force. In a televised speech on 28 February at 6:00 p.m., he announced a curfew during the night, the suspension of constitutional guarantees, and the imposition of martial law. The army had in place a contingency plan called Ávila, but this was inadequate because it merely called for securing government installations in central Caracas; army trucks carrying soldiers rolled unopposed and secured without firing a shot all the objectives of Plan Ávila. Pérez needed a more dramatic show of force, and the soldiers received orders to go into the barrios in the hills starting that night and to shoot at anything that moved. Pérez saw a class warfare dimension to the riots more clearly than the looters, and he was determined to teach the lower class in the barrios a lesson about the dangers of ever challenging his free market formula. During three days the army went on a rampage of shooting, and at least 534 died and many more citizens were wounded.[37]

The army repression had resulted in the worst massacre in the history of Venezuela, yet not until Saturday, March 4, did the government finally recall the troops from their gruesome mission. Nearly a week of social conflict and repression had changed fundamentally the country. Even the economic team of Pérez proposed softening some of the harshest measures of the austerity program as a way of erasing the wounds from this bloody episode. But the president haughtily rejected all suggestions of compromise on his sacred capitalist agenda, and he pushed full steam ahead with the austerity package. In doing so, he gained deep and lasting resentment if not hatred not just for his regime but for the Fourth Republic. He never wavered in his free market convictions, and he soon was gloating when the economy of Venezuela seemed to be improving.[38]

In effect what had happened was that when Saddam Hussein invaded Kuwait in August 1990, this action triggered a rise in the price of petroleum because markets feared that the war might disrupt supplies from Saudi Arabia. For both Pérez and PDVSA, the Venezuelan petroleum company, the Kuwait war was a sudden and unexpected benefit. As explained in the previous section, PDVSA had a complex strategy to keep oil prices low, but rather than seeing the rise as a permanent threat, the oil company saw it as a temporary bonanza that had to pass soon. PDVSA found new ways to hide its profits from the government and reluctantly accepted giving more oil revenues to the Venezuelan treasury. With these oil revenues Pérez covered the payments for the foreign debt, and the country attained supposedly high levels of growth.[39]

This temporary prosperity did not trickle down to the people, because the austerity program Pérez had imposed in February 1989 made sure that the upper class became wealthier and the mass of population continued to suffer. Income inequality became worse than ever, while the rich could not stop flaunting their wealth in flashy cars, huge mansions, and conspicuous consumer spending. The oil revenues flowed out of the country in an orgy of luxury imports, and in the most telling example, Venezuela came to have the highest per capita consumption of Scotch whiskey in the world. The bonanza of 1990–1991 once again confirmed the truth that unless the government was constantly applying strong measures to redistribute the oil wealth, inevitably the free market system pushed income into the upper class.[40]

The relatively easy and swift Iraq War in 1991 proved that the threat from Saddam Hussein had been vastly exaggerated, and reflecting this realization, world market prices for oil returned to their customary low levels in 1992. PDVSA knew that it was indispensable that prices drop, because if high oil prices continued for a long stretch of years, then new producers would appear to increase output from existing and untapped sources. Once oil prices declined, the austerity program of Venezuela remained firmly anchored because the fall in revenues prevented any large scale social spending, something that in any case Pérez refused to do.

The discontent among the lower class was spreading to the middle class even during the brief bonanza. Demonstrations multiplied across the country and already by January 1992 nearly half of street protests in Venezuela under Pérez had turned violent. Not surprisingly large segments of the population were totally disenchanted with the Fourth Republic and its entire system of corrupt politics. The public was waiting for someone to lead them out of the economic suffering and to give them hope for a better tomorrow.[41] By a series of coincidences, the leader who at last offered that opportunity was Lieutenant Colonel Hugo Chávez.

During the bloody repression of February 1989 or Caracazo as it came to be known, Chávez had been stationed in Caracas to carry out desk duties, and he had been a silent spectator to the unfolding massacre. Given his fiery personality, in all likelihood he would have joined the crowds and tried to convert the riot into an insurrection, but his time had not yet arrived. He had come down with a bad case of chicken pox, and his superiors, to prevent the contagion from spreading to fellow workers, had confined him to his home. After he recovered, soldiers and officers came to tell him how anguished they felt for having to follow orders to fire on the defenseless population and were so disgusted with Pérez that they wanted to quit the army. Chávez persuaded them to stay in the ranks, and the Caracazo served as a great tool for recruiting more conspirators. Since 1982 he and several officers had been planning a coup to overthrow the Fourth Republic and not just Pérez.[42]

The assumption behind the coup was that the population was so desperate and so angry at Pérez that people were just waiting for a spark or excuse to take to the streets and to demand the removal of the government. Luis Miquilena, a radical leader who had become a wealthy rancher, was one of the civilians who tried to persuade leftist groups and labor unions to mobilize residents of the Caracas slums. Inside the army the lack of salary raises made personnel very receptive to a coup attempt, and the air force with its F-16 jets seemed very determined, but the navy much less so. Suspicion lurked over Chávez and other key plotters in the ranks such as Lieutenant Colonel Francisco Arias Cárdenas for having supposedly sympathized with the Caracazo, but authorities could not find incriminating evidence to halt the careers of these officers. Thus, late in 1991 as required under army rules, the conspirators duly assumed command of combat units. But the routine deployment of many soldiers to training missions depleted the ranks of their units, and the conspirators realized that only from late January to early February 1992 could they count on having the full complement of troops in their units to make an attempt against the regime.[43]

When sympathizers inside the presidential palace Miraflores reported that Pérez was going away to the international conference at Davos, Switzerland, Chávez sensed an opportunity to seize the president upon the latter's return on the night of 3 February 1992. The civilian groups were wavering and the air force wanted a delay, but Chávez felt the plotters had to act before their window of opportunity closed. Starting at 1900 on 3 February, fellow conspirators seized four cities in Venezuela; the greatest success came in Maracaibo, where Arias Cárdenas in a flawless operation gained control of every important installation in the second most important city in Venezuela. However, in barracks in other parts of the country, the officers adopted a wait-and-see attitude of not taking sides until a clear winner emerged.[44]

The success of the coup depended on Chávez taking control of Caracas, but he had assumed the double role of leading operations in the capital and being the national leader of the uprising. Worse, he had trapped himself in the military museum on a hill overlooking Caracas in the mistaken assumption that from that isolated point he could contact all rebel units. But the lack of communications equipment prevented him from giving orders to cope with any changes, and consequently the rebels failed to secure all the necessary objectives in the capital. Meanwhile bad luck and quick response by the president's security team foiled the several attempts to capture Pérez. Starting at 0115 on 4 February the president made the first of several announcements about the failure of the coup, and these broadcasts rallied loyal troops and finished demoralizing the rebel units in the capital.[45]

During years of conspiring Chávez had been unable to learn the basics of staging a coup, but as a commander who cared deeply about saving his soldiers' lives, he knew that he had to act promptly. By 0700 he agreed to surrender and only asked that under guard he be driven around the city to tell all the rebels to surrender. By 1000 this task was finished, but the high command was still worried about the rebels in the other four cities who showed no willingness to abandon the revolt. The major fear of the generals was a civil war, and to calm them Chávez offered to make a broadcast over radio calling on his fellow conspirators to lay down their arms. The generals proposed broadcasting both over radio and television, and President Pérez authorized taping a message and then editing out any inflammatory comments before transmission over television and radio. When news came that a rebel column was heading for Caracas, the generals, who wanted to avoid any bloody clash at all costs, promptly put Chávez in front of the TV cameras to make a one-minute appeal.[46]

Instinctively he put on his red beret of the paratrooper unit and straightened his uniform to make an imposing appearance. Chávez revealed his political genius when he used this brief opportunity to convey to the rebels the message that any further bloodshed was useless and at the same time to inspire the feelings of the people. Speaking impromptu and knowing that any inflammatory appeal meant being cut off the air, he stated without realizing it that "for now" the rebels were not able to achieve their objectives. He also assumed responsibility for the failure of the coup attempt. The speech had an electrifying effect on the Venezuelan population and instantly launched his political career. In giving one of the most famous speeches in the history of Latin America, he turned a military disaster into a political victory.[47]

The February 1992 coup attempt had been the equivalent of the Moncada attack in Cuba in 1953. Although the two schemes ended in failure, the media messages from Chávez and Fidel Castro converted both leaders into heroes if not celebrities. The events also revealed the permanent characteristic of both men to be risk takers. But a significant difference was that Castro generally avoided making so many mistakes in future operations whether military or civilian. Preparation, planning, and micromanagement usually prevailed in Cuba, but improvisation, haste, and lack of direct supervision became the norm in Venezuela. In many ways, the February 1992 coup attempt foreshadowed the difficulties Chávez later created for himself while trying to govern Venezuela.

After his surrender Chávez, besides the end of his military career, faced many years in prison, just as had happened to Castro after the Moncada attack. But later that same day on 4 February as the Venezuelan congress was roundly condemning the coup attempt, former president Rafael Caldera gave a speech that practically endorsed the coup. By this one speech he revived his flagging political career, and not surprisingly, in the elections of December 1993 he was elected for another term as president. After taking office in February 1994, one of the first acts of Caldera was to release all the participants in the February 1992 coup from prison. Chávez refused to leave until all the other prisoners were free, and his turn finally came on 26 March 1994. His confidant Luis Miquilena had remained in close contact, and during the prison visits they planned the return of Chávez to political life.[48] The U.S. Embassy recognized him as an individual with real potential to govern Venezuela and stated that "he is clearly charismatic and articulate, and deft at using his status as a hero."[49]

Miquilena had been carefully making the preparations for his candidate to run in the December 1998 presidential elections. After his release from prison Chávez embarked on a 100-day tour through every region of Venezuela. The trip was a tremendous logistical feat given that his campaign lacked any resources and personally he was broke. He and Miquilena realized that they had only the term of the Caldera presidency to prepare a winning campaign. Any longer delay meant risking the fading of the hero's prestige. Even more dangerously, President Caldera initially was softening the austerity measures of Carlos Andrés Pérez and seemed to be abandoning privatization and other free market solutions. The January 1994 financial crisis, when the government had to bail out half of the country's banks, was a healthy reminder about the dangers of relying on the free market. The level of protests declined by half compared to the Pérez years, and the possibility existed that if another moderate candidate such as Caldera won in 1998, then the momentum for a dramatic transformation might well dissipate.[50]

Chávez embarked on several more tours of every corner of Venezuela over the coming years, and he used these domestic travels to increase his appeal among citizens. This personal contact with large numbers of sympathizers made him tremendously popular with the masses and earned him an inexhaustible supply of political capital. Although he was a gifted speaker who could whip a crowd into a frenzy, generally all he had to do was raise his arms to receive rapturous applause. His red beret and camouflage uniform became trademarks for his followers who dressed accordingly, and it became common for children and even babies, to appear in this military attire. Joining the civilian masses to the military in the pursuit of social goals was becoming a realistic possibility.[51]

To improve his international credentials, in July 1994 he went on a tour of most of South America reaching as far as Argentina and Chile. He returned via Colombia where he spend considerable time talking to former guerrillas of the demobilized M-19. Many Colombian leftists were so rabidly anti-military that they refused to even meet with him, because they could not conceive of an officer leading a popular movement. But a lasting influence came from Colombia, where he learned in detail why the attempt to reform the rigid political system through the Constitution of 1991 had ended in merely confirming the status quo. In all the South American countries he had moved about freely as a private citizen, because the authorities did not care about him and practically ignored him; nobody had any interest in talking to him. Nevertheless, because the U.S. government had banned all participants in the February 1992 coup from receiving visas, Chávez always took the precaution of checking with the embassies of Latin American governments to see if they had objections to his trip, but none seemed to care and in many cases were not even aware of his problems with the U.S. government.[52]

Because the traditional parties were hopelessly corrupt, the only opportunity to start a political movement lay with the fragmented leftist groups. Leftists, many of them former guerrillas who had fought against the army, were most reluctant to embrace a career officer, but without their support, his campaign could not get off the ground. The initial attempts to gain the support of Venezuelan leftist groups failed, and Miquilena decided that the only remote chance of success lay in appealing to a higher authority. He organized a trip to Havana in December 1994 for Chávez who was supposed to use his personal charm to try to secure the approval and perhaps even the blessing of the Cuban government for his candidacy. This seemed to be a mission impossible, because Fidel Castro had been among the first foreign leaders sending a message condemning the coup attempt of February 1992 and offering support for President Pérez. As Chávez had done with the South American embassies in Caracas, he visited the Cuban embassy to learn if any objections existed to his trip. For the first time the consular officials of any country warmly greeted him, and they told him that by all means he should proceed with his travel plans to visit Revolutionary Cuba.[53]

In effect, a close study of the Venezuelan reality and of the character of Chávez had already persuaded Castro to make a complete turnaround, and this was not the first time the Cuban Revolution had made drastic reversals in policy. Chávez was unaware of the changed situation and, as he flew to Cuba with an associate, he was surprised when upon landing at Havana the commercial jetliner was detoured to an area of the airport reserved for foreign dignitaries. Chávez and his companion were told to disembark and, as they descended the steps, he saw an honor guard and military band in the tarmac. Even greater was his shock when he realized that at the foot of the stairs was none other than the great Fidel Castro himself waiting to welcome the Venezuelan visitor. After a review of troops and other ceremonies usually reserved only for heads of state, Chávez, just a private citizen, went for long discussions with Castro lasting into early in the morning.[54]

A magical whirlwind tour followed of the island over the next days as an honored guest of the Cuban state, and Castro was doing everything possible to impress Chávez. Photographers and TV cameras followed him usually in company of the Castro brothers and other Cuban leaders as they traveled throughout Havana. The newspapers put the story into headlines, while the television networks broadcast extensive live coverage of the visit. Chávez was welcomed as a long-lost family member returning home, and he struck up friendships for a lifetime with many Cuban personalities, and of course with the Castro brothers. As a final memento of the trip, Castro gave him an album with the best photos of the trip to Cuba. As the accounts of the smashing success of the visit to Cuba reached Venezuela, most leftist groups had no choice but to bow before the unquestioned authority of Castro and to support the candidacy of Chávez once he had decided to run for the presidency.[55]

Chávez struggled for years with the issue of whether to participate in elections. He shared with the majority of Venezuelans the well-founded belief that the Fourth Republic and its two main political parties were so corrupt, that radical outsiders could never win elections. As concrete proof that a peaceful way was not possible, government agents harassed his movement and tried to intimidate his followers. Wiretaps and intercepts of their conversations became routine occurrences. In a favorite tactic, the secret police stole the cars from his close collaborators so that they could not get around quickly. In an early preview of his life-long nemesis, the national media boycotted his events; the fawning coverage he had enjoyed as a novelty after the February 1992 coup attempt gave way to oblivion. The private media outlets, both television stations and newspapers, had detected his radical streak, and although mistakenly labeling him a traditional socialist, they correctly realized that he intended to carry out major transformations in the country. Yet all was not lost completely with the media, because the provincial press and the local radio stations loved Chávez, and his visits to their usually ignored editorial offices brought massive favorable publicity in the interior of the country.[56]

After his release from prison, Chávez called for a boycott of elections, but this refusal to participate soon caused deep rifts among his supporters. The most visible sign was the split with Francisco Arias Cárdenas, who until then had been the second most important person in the Chávez movement. Relations between the two military conspirators had always been tense, but his departure took on an additional importance when he decided to run for office. To everyone's surprise, Arias Cárdenas won the elections for governor of Zulia state in December 1995, and the former plotter peacefully occupied the same governor's palace in Maracaibo that he had taken by force during the February 1992 coup.[57]

The stubborn refusal of Chávez to participate in elections left him with no obvious alternative to reach power in Venezuela. Occasionally he hinted at returning to guerrilla warfare, but that was not a valid option and even he had criticized former guerrillas as having lost touch with the masses over the long years of the campaign in remote jungle areas. A combination of coup and popular uprising similar to what had overthrown General Marcos Pérez Jiménez in 1958 seemed the best alternative. But the generals who commanded army units had a vested interest in preserving their privileged position in the Fourth Republic, and they persecuted any officers suspected of pro-Chávez tendencies. Because the first two years of the Caldera administration seemed to have calmed the country as indicated by the drop of social protests in half, the task of mobilizing a huge popular demonstration to overthrow the government looked impossible. As the months of 1995 ticked by without any signs of a popular insurrection, Chávez realized that his popularity could fade unless he kept his name out in front of the public.[58]

The opportunity came in April 1996 when Caldera caved in to the pressure of the IMF and imposed an austerity program very similar to the one that had doomed Pérez in 1989. Once again the Venezuelan voters had been duped, because they had voted for Caldera hoping to restrict the free market policies. Clearly the old president was too weak and frail to say no to foreign financial institutions, and Venezuelans realized that they needed a forceful champion to oppose international capital. Seeing the political winds shifting, Chávez took a partial step by authorizing the professionals of his movement to conduct in late 1996 and early 1997 perhaps the most widespread survey to have ever taken place in Venezuela. His educated volunteers, many of them university students, scattered throughout the country to interview nearly 100,000 citizens on their political preferences. The two key questions in the survey instrument asked voters whether Chávez should participate in the December 1998 elections and whether they would vote for him.[59]

Experts poured this data into computers, but even after correcting for possible errors and running different simulations, the results were very conclusive. According to the survey, 70 percent of the people wanted Chávez to run, and 57 percent would vote for him. It should be kept in mind that as the survey was taking place, Chávez was carrying out tours of all the regions in Venezuela, so that these two double efforts were giving him maximum exposure to the majority of the population. The only exception might be Caracas where the national media continued to ignore him, but in reality the residents of the slums, who comprised the majority of the population of the capital, could not afford to buy the national newspapers and instead learned about Chávez through his frequent visits and those of his collaborators. With this overwhelming evidence that he was sure to win, Chávez could no longer delay the inevitable, and in a national convention of his followers on 19 April 1997, he announced his decision to be a candidate for the presidential election of 6 December 1998.[60]

By the end of 1997 almost all the leftist parties had endorsed Chávez as their candidate, but securing this support was not as easy as it might seem. Even inside his movement some militants insisted on armed struggle and resigned in protest over the decision to participate in elections. The military dictatorships of South America cast such a heavy shadow, that many leftists could not accept change through a career officer. Also, Venezuela had the longest tradition of army regimes in Latin America, and the memories of the Marcos Pérez Jiménez dictatorship, overthrown in January 1958, were still in the minds of many Venezuelans. Even though the fears about a possible military dictatorship were understandable, in reality they were pretexts to hide the swing of many leftists toward the free market. Even former guerrilla leaders had embraced capitalism, and during the last decades of the Fourth Republic the leftist parties had assumed the comfortable role of playing the loyal opposition to the corrupt regimes. The more material benefits the leftists received from the capitalist system, the more their commitment to socialism cooled. This subtle change taking place explained not just their reluctance to embrace Chávez but also the many defections of leftists from his movement during later years.[61]

In a last united show of force almost all the left rallied behind Chávez for the December 1998 elections. Because he already had an extensive organization of volunteers across the country and also was a household word, he certainly was a serious contender for the presidency. As usual, the national media was the first to sound the alarm about the threat Chávez posed and began a vicious offensive to smear him with every possible accusation. To scare the upper class, the most obvious line of attack was the trip to Cuba graphically portrayed in television footage and his personal links to Fidel Castro. Other more scurrilous accusations followed, but the general drumbeat was that Chávez intended to nationalize all private property, both foreign and domestic, and to convert Venezuela into another Cuba.[62]

The smear campaign was effective among the upper class and less so among the middle class; in reality the majority of the population was not scared by his links to Cuba and actually admired Fidel Castro. Chávez did promise major changes in Venezuela and he caught the public mood when he denounced the entire Fourth Republic and its political parties. To achieve this transformation, he had been calling for the convocation of a constituent convention to write a new constitution for the country. He was well aware of the failed attempt in Colombia to effect major change through the 1991 Constitution, and he promised not to let privileged groups hijack the convention as had happened in the neighboring country. In all his campaign events he insisted on Venezuela's desperate need for a new constitution to create a completely different political system to be known as the Fifth Republic.[63]

With the general theme of structural change and the specifics of a constitutional convention, Chávez, who was turning out to be a charismatic speaker, was a formidable campaigner. Venezuelans could not remember any other political figure who had generated such tremendous enthusiasm among the crowds, and he quickly became a celebrity. Curiously, except for the media, the upper class was not violently opposed to him and at times seemed amused by his colorful antics. Better than anyone else in Venezuela, he knew how to put on a show, and even upper class members found the entertainment to be captivating. Around 30 businesses even made campaign contributions as a way to assure access to the new government. Sensing an opening, Chávez had gone to great lengths to reassure the upper class that he did not intend to confiscate their properties. As a matter of fact, in conversations with business leaders and with the U.S. ambassador, he announced his commitment to the ongoing privatization. Chávez knew very well the failures of state enterprises, and he had no intention of embarking upon a massive campaign of nationalizations. In an additional reassurance, he talked to foreign bankers and even stated publicly that he welcomed foreign investment in Venezuela.[64]

Chávez had succeeded in driving a wedge between the upper class and the traditional politicians. The upper class did not see the elections as a life-and-death matter, but the traditional politicians realized that their survival was at stake. Corruption and patronage had been the lifeblood of the traditional parties, and they could not exist without access to public funds. Seeing this mortal threat to their existence, the politicians strove to find a candidate able to block Chávez.

The first rival was more appropriate for a fairy tale than for a campaign. Irene Sáez, a former Miss Universe pageant winner, had won election as mayor of Chacao, one of the rich municipalities of metropolitan Caracas and was reelected because by all accounts she had done a great job in reducing crime and cleaning the streets. Many politicians and a part of the public became infatuated with her, and polls showed her as the favorite to win the presidency, even though she did not formally declare her candidacy until May 1998. By then her earlier popularity was fading and her soft and rather vapid campaign style turned off many voters. In her statements she did not want to antagonize any one and she avoided speaking on the burning issues of the day. The final blow to her campaign came when one of the traditional parties nominated her as its candidate, an endorsement equivalent to the kiss of death because the public held an abysmally low opinion about the traditional parties. The other candidate came from another traditional party, and he was so drab that nobody took him seriously.[65]

As the campaigns of Sáez and the other candidate floundered, the career politicians desperately sought a solution. A minor party had put Henrique Salas Römer as its candidate, and the emerging "Stop Chávez" movement turned to him as a savior. Although the new candidate climbed to second place in the polls, he still could not prevent the traditional politicians from panicking as they realized that Chávez might win in a landslide. Fearful for their privileged positions, the politicians first divided the electoral calendar by moving up the congressional and provincial elections a month ahead to 8 November 1998. Such a last minute change in the electoral calendar had never before occurred in Venezuela's history and testified to the panic rapidly spreading among the career politicians. And in a more surprising decision, the two main traditional parties dumped their candidates just a week before the elections and put all their institutional support behind Salas Römer in a desperate last minute attempt to stop Chávez. But Sáez and the other candidate did not retire gracefully and very angrily fought to remain on the ballot and urged their supporters not to follow the party line.[66] These bizarre twists bordered on the comical, and "the opposition's efforts were turning into a circus."[67]

In the 8 November 1999 regional elections, the supporters of Chávez did not win a majority in either house of congress. The strategy of politicians to block him seemed to have been effective and without a congressional majority he could not obtain legislative approval for any dramatic agenda. But the attempt to keep his margin of victory below a simple majority failed. Electoral authorities declared him the winner on 6 December 1999 barely three hours after the polls had closed. Chávez received 56 percent of the vote, while his nearest rival, Salas Römer received 40 percent.[68] The landslide victory validated the conclusions of the survey of 1996–1997, but the 40 percent his main opponent received foreshadowed troubles in the future. If with a weak candidate the politicians had been able at the last minute to rally considerable support, what could they do under more favorable circumstances? The opposition had to learn from its mistakes as it prepared for future electoral battles, yet for 1999 being on the lookout for opportunities to attack the Chávez presidency seemed the best strategy. No one doubted that a sea change was about to take place in Venezuelan politics.

CHAPTER 2

Peru: The Return of Dictatorship

The Fujimori-Montesinos regime has been the most corrupt in the history of Peru.—Alfonso W. Quiroz[1]

The Partnership with Vladimiro Montesinos

It might seem odd to begin a chapter on the dictatorship of Alberto Fujimori not with him but with his associate Vladimiro Montesinos. In reality, the Fujimori presidency existed only thanks to Montesinos, who early on became known as the Peruvian Rasputin in recognition of his concealed power. The white-skinned Montesinos was a native of Arequipa, just as Shining Path leader Abimael Guzmán. Both men suffered the same complex of provincial inferiority and craved acceptance from the Lima elite. In another striking coincidence, Montesinos and Guzmán suffered satyriasis, and this need for obsessive sexual gratification proved decisive in their careers.[2]

For a poor provincial in Peru, only the army made possible rapid social advancement, so Montesinos entered the Chorrillos military academy in Lima and graduated in 1966. This was a very favorable time to enter the officer corps, because the military, in power since the bloodless coup of 1968, needed many enthusiastic officers to implement revolutionary transformations in the country. Montesinos, a quick learner with a prodigious memory, soon caught the eye of his superiors; when he was just a captain he became an aide to senior officers. But in the fierce competition for promotion inside the army, his meteoric rise triggered the envy of many rivals. Eventually he was tried, imprisoned, and expelled from the army under unclear circumstances, presumably for having sold military secrets to the United States. When released after a few years, he was prohibited from entering army installations.[3]

Apparently crushed, actually he learned invaluable lessons from the struggle. He became a master at striking fast, unexpectedly, and deviously, so that never again did he lose a bureaucratic battle. A new Montesinos emerged who "was extraordinarily cunning and had no moral scruples."[4] The consummate insider who operated best in the shadows, he made his comeback as an attorney. Too often in Latin America legal education has consisted solely in the rote memorization of clauses in legal codes, an easy task for Montesinos who while still in the army attended night school to obtain his law degree in 1972. The career shift from officer to lawyer was not his only change, because during these years he also became a strong supporter of capitalism. The Revolutionary Military had vastly increased state intervention in the economy, and Montesinos, although just an aide, had diligently supported those policies. The argument can well be made that as long as he had the opportunity to wield power, he did not have an ideological commitment to any system. By the late 1980s he fervently embraced private enterprise and had even become an admirer of the savage capitalism of Chilean dictator Augusto Pinochet, in spite of the traditional enmity of Peru with Chile.[5]

The possibility of personal enrichment may well have tipped the balance away from socialism, and even in his legal career he did not always practice profit maximization, that fundamental axiom of capitalism. But Montesinos did not want to become one more among the many starving lawyers in Peru, and to avoid falling into poverty he sought out wealthy clients. He knew that the only way a young lawyer could earn large sums of money in Peru was by defending drug traffickers, and without any hesitation he took on their cases. Endowed with a remarkable memory, he certainly was a very competent attorney who could put together an impressive legal argument. Because he knew that his clients were guilty, he realized that if he wanted to accomplish more than simply reduce their sentences, he had to manipulate the system.[6]

Good defense lawyers always know which judges are more sympathetic to the accused and who are the most aggressive prosecutors. Montesinos used that knowledge to have his clients assigned to judges and prosecutors most susceptible to bribes, so settling the case preferably out of court was usually an easy matter. The drug traffickers at this time came only from the remote Amazon region, and they appreciated having a suave, cultured, and white Montesinos as the Lima insider who could fix any case. The deference and sometimes reverence they showed him was also psychologically pleasing to his ego.[7]

He easily became a trusted confidant who was offering more than legal advice to clients such as "Vaticano" (Demetrio Chávez), Peru's first major drug lord. Everything indicated that he could have remained the attorney and counselor for the drug traffickers for the rest of his life. But the drug trade was too narrow a field of action to satisfy his need for power. Thus, even as he continued to earn big money by defending drug traffickers, he was more interested in taking on cases that would give him the opportunity to regain that power he had indirectly savored as an advisor to the Revolutionary Military in the mid–1970s. The insurgency of Shining Path, the Maoist terrorist group, had been raging since 1980, and already several officers faced criminal charges for violations of human rights. In 1988 a massacre of peasants took place in Cayara, Ayacucho, and General José Valdivia, the commander of that military region, was accused of having ordered the massacre. Montesinos eagerly assumed the defense and soon had the charges against the general dismissed. His success in this and in other similar cases restored his standing among many army officers, and as a first step the prohibition on entering army bases was lifted.[8]

Montesinos also gained easy entrance to the office of the attorney general, and he used that access to make disappear the case files of accusations against army officers. As a recognition of his valuable services, he received an appointment as civilian advisor to the National Intelligence Service (*Servicio de Inteligencia Nacional*) or SIN in 1989, an agency that was to become his home for the next 11 years. Although the espionage agency was technically under the presidency, in practice the military funded and staffed SIN. As part of Montesinos's strategy to worm himself back into the army's good graces, he continued to defend its personnel from legal accusations. Of these cases, the most decisive for his future was the one of Matilde Pinchi Pinchi, a wealthy female merchant from the Amazon region. This attractive woman who had a child with a married army officer, faced a prison sentence for having smuggled Chinese jewelry into Peru without paying the customs duties in May 1986. This astute woman possessed a sharp business sense and had been among the first to realize that smuggling Chinese merchandise could be a lucrative business; she rapidly amassed a small fortune and moved her base of operations from the Amazon to Lima.[9]

Pinchi Pinchi used to bribe custom officials at Lima international airport to avoid paying duties on the merchandise, but once in a major error, three suitcases full of Chinese merchandise remained unclaimed at the luggage belt. Authorities traced the shipment back to her, and she panicked at the possibility of having to spend time in prison. Upon taking on the case, Montesinos promptly hospitalized her to delay her court appearance. She stayed in the hospital until the day a corrupt judge was on duty; it was then an easy matter to reduce her punishment to the payment of a fine and the customs duties. She was extremely grateful to the white knight who had saved her from prison.[10]

As a sufferer from satyriasis, it was not uncommon to find Montesinos having sex with one of his many secretaries, and soon he added Pinchi Pinchi to his list of sexual partners. With her more than a purely sexual relationship emerged. She realized that her emotional options were rather limited, because he was already married and supported at least one full-time mistress, yet a powerful bond blossomed between Pinchi Pinchi and Montesinos, as each one saw something in the other that proved irresistible. She became his full-time confidant, executive assistant, and occasional sex partner. For over 12 years the two spent more time with each other than with anybody else, but for him the relationship was fraught with danger, because she was a fiercely independent and intelligent woman. She maintained her thriving business and did not depend on him for money as did all his other women, including even the sister of his official mistress. As a native of the Amazon who loved to wear tiger and animal prints, Matilde conveyed a sense of wild danger irresistible to Montesinos.

Only in 2000 did the perils of the relationship with Matilde appear, but until then they enjoyed a mutually satisfactory partnership. At the end of the 1980s Montesinos confronted a more immediate problem. He had prospered under the Alán García administration, but once the attempt to extend that presidency failed, Montesinos was in real danger of losing access to power. His livelihood was no longer a concern, because the drug lords generously rewarded his legal services. He had developed very useful personal contacts both inside and outside SIN, but his influence was sure to crumble if he did not secure support from the next ruler of Peru. Because a clear favorite had not emerged among the many candidates in the presidential campaign of 1990, ruthless personalities such as Montesinos could provide the margin of victory by swaying politicians and influencing votes. As an astute political observer, he concluded that the candidate with the highest possibility of winning was the internationally renowned Mario Vargas Llosa. Montesinos approached the campaign of the literary figure, but because of overconfidence, his offer of services was rejected.[11]

Mario Vargas Llosa seemed to have a winning coalition: his absolute embrace of capitalism had made him the darling of the business class, while the middle classes were dazzled by having as president the most famous Peruvian in the world. With the collapse of the Soviet Union, the left and socialism in particular were totally discredited, and the winds sweeping the globe did not stop proclaiming the wonders of capitalism. Ideological fanatics mechanically repeated the simplistic cliché that socialism had failed and that capitalism had triumphed. Even more damaging was the contrived linking of capitalism with democratic regimes, an obvious distortion even in Latin America where the business class had enthusiastically cooperated closely with brutal tyrannies. No doubt Soviet socialism had been a failure, but to conclude that the state had failed as Vargas Llosa claimed in his campaign was simply wrong. When the candidate announced an economic shock program to get rid of state enterprises and to liberate all the market forces, such was the excitement in the immediate post–Cold War years that few felt threatened, and the novelist coasted to a first-place finish in the 8 April 1990 presidential election.[12]

The 1979 Constitution required a majority of votes to win the presidency, and thus Vargas Llosa faced a runoff election on 10 June 1990. Because the second-place winner had been the unknown Alberto Fujimori, a professor and college president of Japanese origin, the prevailing wisdom was that the favorite Vargas Llosa would win easily. Fujimori lacked campaign funds, and actually his wife Susana Higuchi and her wealthy merchant family had financed his candidacy, yet he saw a chance to win by putting himself squarely against the free market views of Vargas Llosa. In public statements Fujimori warned that the economic shock of his rival would cause immense harm to the lower and middle classes, and he showed deep respect for the state-driven economic initiatives of the previous decades. The message began to resonate among those citizens who had to shift their votes from one of the leftist defeated candidates to either Fujimori or Vargas Llosa. Actually the most decisive convert was President Alán García who still was in his socialist phase. But the outgoing president could not publicly express his support, so he ordered SIN to use all its resources, including its own secret polls, to support the candidacy of Fujimori.[13]

This blanket authorization from the president increased immensely the influence of Montesinos who on his own had approached the candidate. The reputation of Montesinos as a "fixer" of tough cases was well known, and a mutual acquaintance asked him whether he could solve an accusation of tax evasion facing Fujimori. As expected, Montesinos easily solved the dispute by shifting the case to a sympathetic judge; more importantly, in his dealings with Fujimori a common attraction or sympathy emerged between the two men. A symbiotic relationship was born, including a dose of mutual affection, with Fujimori the politician being the public face, and Montesinos the manipulator lurking behind the scenes.[14]

Montesinos discovered how paranoid Fujimori was about the risk of a military coup and easily obtained the support of the candidate for the struggle against the military commanders. The immediate danger came from the navy, which was openly supporting Vargas Llosa; to escape its wiretaps and surveillance, Montesinos moved Fujimori from the Hotel Crillón in downtown Lima to the Círculo Militar, the club for senior officers at the Chorrillos army base. The new location also had the advantage of allowing Montesinos to control access to the candidate. In strategy sessions he showed himself to be the indispensable associate as the two men plotted the electoral campaign. Wielding the full resources of SIN, Montesinos converted the second place finish in the first election into an overwhelming victory in the 10 June 1990 runoff. Fujimori won the election with 62.5 percent of the popular vote compared to the 37.5 percent of the former favorite Vargas Llosa.[15]

The Alberto Fujimori Dictatorship

Before his inauguration on 28 July, Alberto Fujimori made the trip—mandatory for Caribbean banana republics—to Washington, D.C., and to Wall Street to receive instructions for his presidency. The U.S. government, the World Bank, the International Monetary Fund (IMF), and Wall Street told him to impose extreme free market measures as the only way to save Peru. Not surprisingly, scarcely had he taken office that on 8 August 1990 his finance minister stunned the country by announcing an austerity package remarkably similar to what defeated candidate Mario Vargas Llosa had promised during the presidential campaign. The avowed reason for this complete turnabout was the need to stop the hyperinflation that had appeared in the last years of the failed Alán García administration. By applying harsh austerity measures, Fujimori's finance minister reduced inflation to acceptable levels and in the process bolstered the popularity of the president.[16]

Simultaneously with the measures against hyperinflation, Fujimori was taking dramatic steps to counter the threat from Shining Path. This Maoist-inspired group had turned to terrorist acts to spread its control over the country and had intensified its attacks on Lima. The García administration had seemed powerless to stop Senderistas (the militants of Shining Path), while the frequent bombings and attacks gave the impression that the terrorist organization posed a real threat to the government. Fujimori shared the collective fear about the danger, and in one of the worst decisions of his presidency, in August 1990 he authorized Vladimiro Montesinos to organize a death squad called the "Colina Group" to kill and torture any suspected Senderistas. He was merely legalizing a practice dating back to the mid–1980s when army death squads had appeared to eliminate terrorists because judges and prosecutors were afraid to bring charges even against known Senderistas.[17]

In contrast to the García administration, under Fujimori the Colina Group enjoyed presidential blessing and was directly controlled by Montesinos. Although army personnel comprised this unit, operational control was through the rapidly expanding National Intelligence Service (*Servicio de Inteligencia Nacional*) or SIN. The Colina Group carried out its first massacre on 3 November 1991 when faulty intelligence led to the slaughter of innocent residents of the Barrios Altos neighborhood in Lima. The press learned about this botched operation and the reporting provoked the first human rights crisis of the Fujimori administration. International groups and the U.S. government demanded the punishment of the soldiers involved in the massacre, but incredibly, SIN did not even disband this team of assassins, so that the Colina Group remained free to carry out new atrocities as later happened.[18]

Governing Peru was turning out to be much more difficult than Fujimori had ever imagined, and he was soon reaching the limits of what he could do by relying only on the powers of the executive branch. He wanted to apply free market principles even more widely in the economy, but he needed the approval of congress to repeal many of the laws favoring state intervention. His electoral victory had been such an unexpected event, that he had never seriously considered running a complete slate of candidates for the congress; therefore, his deputies won only 17.8 percent of the seats in the house and 22.6 percent in the senate. As a partial remedy, he promised former president García not to investigate the corruption in his administration in exchange for the votes of his party, but APRA controlled only 29.4 percent of seats in the house and 27.4 percent in the senate.[19]

Because of defections and splits within the political groups, the legislature was unable to pass laws. In an implicit admission of its failure, congress delegated to Fujimori the authority to issue decrees with the force of law; however, a simple majority vote in both houses sufficed to repeal these decrees. In September and November 1991 Fujimori issued decrees covering several topics, including privatization and measures against Shining Path. The new measures against Senderistas immediately provoked an outcry because citizens in many regions of Peru lost almost all their rights and even their properties. A legislative backlash led to the repeal of 16 of these decrees and the substantial modification of many others. But it was not so much the rights of citizens as the profits of foreign speculators that most concerned Fujimori, and he was furious when congress began the proceedings to repeal the decrees on privatization.[20]

An increasingly exasperated Fujimori repeatedly stated that he could not fix the problems of Peru with this congress that let him do nothing. The tension between both branches of government became so acute, that in December 1991 the senate declared that he was morally unqualified to be president, a motion that just barely failed to pass the house. Approval of the motion was the equivalent of removing the president from office, and this hostile act turned the anger of Fujimori into fear about his political survival. The fear of the president turned into panic when on 2 April 1992 a committee of the senate decided to investigate accusations of corruption about foreign aid. Because the accusations came none other than from his wife Susana Higuchi, the congress was sure to uncover enough evidence to remove him from office.[21]

A desperate Fujimori frantically searched for a way out, when in reality he did not need to worry at all, because his trusted associate Montesinos had all along been quietly preparing for just such an eventuality. Starting from the day of Fujimori's inauguration on 28 July 1990, Montesinos had used his broad mandate from the president to create a power base in SIN which he soon converted into his home when he installed secret living quarters inside the headquarters building. Although military personnel comprised the overwhelming majority of SIN personnel and its head had always been a high-ranking officer, the spy agency reported to the presidency and many civilians worked there, so that the presence of Montesinos was not an anomaly. In less than a year he replaced the head of SIN with a very pliable general, but of course the real boss was Montesinos himself.[22]

His reputation as the person who enjoyed the complete trust of the president made him extremely influential, and he enhanced his authority by extending the network of SIN informants throughout the government and in particular in the military. As the agency grew in size, he drew on its resources to spy on suspected rivals and to bribe officials. Large monthly payments from the drug lords for immunity provided additional funds to finance his realm of corruption. By using drug money, spying, and the network of informants, Montesinos had no difficulty rigging the promotion process in the army to bring generals suitable for his purposes to the highest positions.[23]

The intricate process of promoting loyal generals and retiring or reassigning independent officers advanced relentlessly and reached a culmination with the appointment of General Nicolás Hermoza as army commander on 19 December 1991. Besides being incompetent, pompous, and vain, he was hopelessly corrupt, the last characteristic being indispensable for Montesinos.[24] To maintain control he carefully adhered to the practice of selecting the new commanders from "the most corrupt and inept generals and admirals."[25] The appointment of Hermoza also completed the formation of a triumvirate to govern Peru, with the general being the weakest of the three members. At the beginning rumors surfaced about his rivalry with Montesinos, but soon the two men reached an accommodation. Just as Montesinos appointed a pliant general to do the daily work of running SIN so he placed Hermoza to do the same in the army.[26]

As Montesinos moved his pieces across the chessboard of the military, he made it clear that loyalty to him and to Fujimori had to be absolute and required defense of the regime not just by words but also by force. Written plans for a military coup had been circulating during the García administration, and Montesinos adapted them to the new circumstances. The overwhelming electoral victory of Fujimori on 10 June 1990 seemed to rule out the need for a military coup, but as the relations of the administration with the congress reached a crisis point in December 1991, Montesinos prepared to orchestrate a revolt. By then senior commanders had been bribed and threatened into submission, and the appointment of Hermoza had not triggered any backlash.[27]

With the army firmly under the grip of Hermoza, Montesinos was confident that he could save the Fujimori administration, provided that both men acted fast before the opposition could begin congressional proceedings to remove the president from office. The time frame narrowed down to less than a week: on 2 April a senate committee had decided to launch an investigation into the corruption accusations of Higuchi and on 7 April the congress was scheduled to open its legislative session. Fujimori and Montesinos calculated that they could pull off the coup without triggering any popular resistance, and at 10:30 p.m. on 5 April, television stations broadcast a previously taped message in which the president announced that he was assuming complete power, suspending the 1979 Constitution, and dissolving national and regional institutions. Before the announcement, troops had occupied key places in Lima including newspapers, while police arrested congressional and party leaders. Of political figures, only Alán García evaded capture and sought asylum in the Colombian embassy. Among other measures in the self-coup, the president announced a complete reorganization of the judiciary branch and the Attorney General's Office. As a first step towards gaining control over the legal system, trucks arrived at the Palace of Justice and carted off thousands of case files, including those of the Barrios Altos Massacre.[28]

The army patrolled the streets, but the absence of any disturbances allowed almost all of the troops to return to their barracks on 7 April. The lack of protests was not surprising when opinion polls soon showed that as many as 82 percent of the population approved the self-coup; popular opinion blamed congress for not letting Fujimori solve the country's security crisis. The acceptance and in some sectors the enthusiasm with which the population greeted the dictatorship was extraordinary: Montesinos and Fujimori had calculated correctly because they realized that most citizens were more than willing to sacrifice a lot for very little. However, the two men had failed to gauge the intensity of the negative international reaction. The U.S. government, supposedly for altruistic but in reality for practical reasons, had decided to keep Latin America as a "coup-free zone," and Fujimori's action clearly threatened to inspire a wave of military revolts across the region. When foreign lending agencies threatened to cut off the financial assistance that Peru desperately needed to end the threat of hyperinflation, Fujimori agreed to negotiate a compromise solution.[29]

The U.S. government demanded a return to constitutional rule and in particular the restoration of the congress. Fujimori countered by the novel proposal of merging the two key demands into the single one of convoking a convention to have simultaneously the authority to draft a new constitution and to perform legislative functions. The U.S. government hesitated, because while Washington wanted an immediate return to the old constitutional system, Wall Street was salivating at the prospect of huge profits from privatizations in Peru. Finally the Clinton administration caved in, and as soon as Fujimori

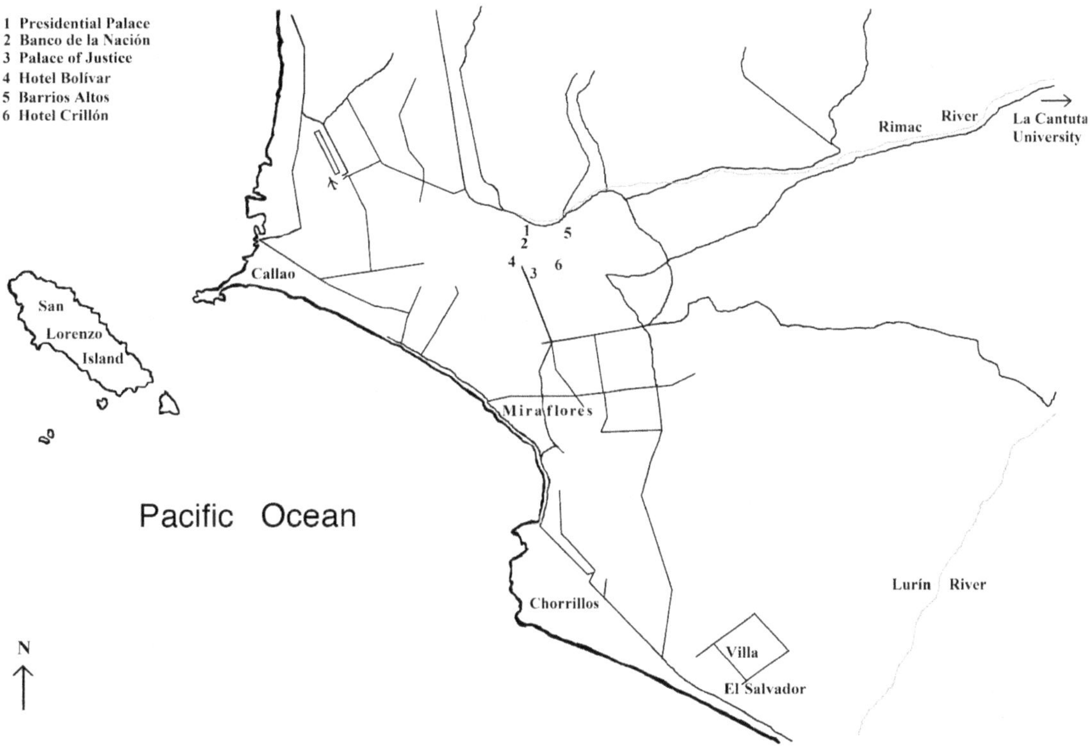

Metropolitan Lima, Peru

scheduled elections in November for the constitutional convention, international organizations resumed their financial assistance to Peru.[30]

The unexpected foreign hostility proved to be the biggest stumbling block to consolidating the internal dictatorship. The international pressure once again confirmed to Fujimori what rulers of banana republics had long known: they could stay in office only as long as they remained in the good graces of Washington. But for the rest of 1992 Fujimori was free to act as a dictator with no check on his actions, and in a blatant abuse of power, he carried out purges of officials in the executive and judiciary branches of government; Montesinos was the hatchet man firing and replacing employees both in the courts and in the Attorney General's Office. Tens of thousands of employees lost their jobs in the largest purge ever seen in the history of Peru. Not even the Foreign Ministry escaped his drive to fire all officials who were not unconditional supporters of the regime.[31]

This absolute power needed spectacular results to justify its existence, and no better target existed than the terrorist group Shining Path. But once again the Colina death squad blundered, when on 18 July 1992 in cold blood it killed nine university students and one professor at La Cantuta University east of Lima. This new massacre could have caused considerable difficulty for the Fujimori administration had not Montesinos carried out damage control. As a lawyer, he had always taken a personal interest in the legal system, and he had been extremely active after the April self-coup in purging judges and prosecutors and replacing them with pliant officials. His master stroke was putting on his payroll Blanca Nélida Colán who became the attorney general of Peru. From her position she squashed any investigation against the Fujimori regime and carried out her task with a fanatical devotion and complete disregard for the law. For the rest of the Fujimori administration, she remained the best insurance against any hostile prosecution.[32]

The La Cantuta massacre was soon overshadowed by the most dramatic blow against Shining Path in the history of this terrorist movement. Since January 1991 when the police had made public the "Zorba the Greek" video showing Abimael Guzmán frolicking with his female followers, the Fujimori administration had been predicting that this terrorist movement was nearing its end. Shining Path tried to discredit the official propaganda by mounting a series of dramatic raids after the self-coup of April; the most spectacular was a car bomb explosion that killed many civilians in the exclusive Miraflores neighborhood of Lima on 16 July 1992. The police had been tracking Guzmán quietly for years and finally arrested him on 12 September 1992.[33] Fujimori believed that the capture of the leader of Shining Path had vindicated the self-coup of April and also guaranteed his reelection. In reality the gratitude of the public lay less with the government and more with the dedicated detective who masterminded the operation.

If Fujimori had any doubts about the immense power he had delegated to Montesinos over the army, they completely vanished when rebel officers tried to stage a counter coup on 13 November 1992. Ever since the two men had meet at the Hotel Crillón in April 1990, Montesinos had fed Fujimori's paranoia about the danger of a military revolt. The real motivations of the rebel officers have remained murky, and perhaps unwittingly they served the purposes of Montesinos; even after an informant had revealed the conspiracy, he still allowed part of the operation to proceed. The most likely explanation was that advisors of Fujimori, probably his younger brother Santiago, were trying to convince the president to rein in the Peruvian Rasputin. By letting the attempted coup start to unfold, Montesinos gained the opportunity to appear as the savior of the regime; after giving his reassurances that everything was going to come out fine, he had Fujimori abandon the presidential palace and seek safety temporarily in the Japanese embassy. The failed 13 November 1992 counter coup left as its main legacy an even closer relationship between the two men. As a secondary benefit, the coup attempt allowed Montesinos to finish purging the army of disgruntled senior officers, who either were expulsed or retired from the service, while the principal ring leaders ended up in prison.[34]

A major reason why the 13 November army revolt failed and why the country had already accepted the dictatorship after the April 1992 self-coup was the attitude of the business class. The early commitment to capitalism erased any fears about a Fujimori administration, and after the self-coup business leaders enthusiastically embraced the regime as an ally. The total shift from initial skepticism in 1990 to passionate support was so extreme in the business class, that even the defeated candidate Mario Vargas Llosa could not understand this total submission to Fujimori. The novelist began to suspect that the widely proclaimed dogma after the fall of the Soviet Union that capitalism equaled democratic regimes was seriously flawed.[35]

Without any congress to block him, Fujimori raced ahead with privatizations, the real test of total commitment to capitalism. Between 1991 and 2000, he privatized 150 state-owned companies, with the proceeds from these sales largely disappearing; only years later was it discovered that most of the money had ended up in the foreign banks accounts of high officials.[36] The belief in the miraculous powers of the free market brushed aside any objections: "transparency was not considered necessary as opposed to the need to privatize as quickly and expeditiously as possible."[37] The policy applied also to government services, in particular the privatization of the social security system and its replacement by private pension funds operated for the benefit of investors and not of pensioners. What was more remarkable was that foreign investors largely took over the key sectors of the Peruvian economy, and this transformation accounted for the determination of Wall Street to support the Fujimori dictatorship.

Privatization was supposed to open up the Peruvian economy to the free market, but once again foreign investors rather than Peruvians were the real beneficiaries. While Chilean businesses spent over $4 billion in the country, Peruvians were able to invest a mere $25 million in Chile. As one scholar concluded, "national capital (state enterprise and domestically owned power groups), has therefore been displaced from its commanding position in the economy."[38] Put more directly, Peruvians no longer owned the country they lived in.

The biggest exception was the state-owned oil company PetroPeru, which by a miracle escaped privatization. A major reason for the lack of foreign interest was that PetroPeru no longer extracted crude from the ground and operated only as a distributor and refiner. Part of the legacy of the military regime of 1968–1980 included a network of gas stations scattered throughout the countryside; outside the main cities PetroPeru usually was the only provider of fuel. These retail outlets in distant corners of Peru were money-losers, and traditionally the state-owned company covered the losses with the profits from its lucrative urban operations. Foreign investors insisted on PetroPeru dumping its rural gas stations as a prerequisite for privatization, but the political cost of such a divestiture was too high for the government.[39]

The danger of antagonizing rural or any other voters became clear when the previously scheduled elections for delegates to the constitutional convention took place on 22 November 1992 just nine days after the failed coup attempt. Although APRA and several other political parties had boycotted the elections, Fujimoristas won only 44 seats and the remaining 36 seats went to new political groups. The small margin occasionally forced the regime to modify its proposals and to accept some opposition input for the new constitution. On a deeper level, the failure to sweep the elections of 22 November 1992 was an early indication of the weak foundations supporting the Fujimori regime.[40]

The convention began its sessions on 29 December 1992 and soon was busy writing the new constitution and also serving as a provisional legislature. More pliable than the previous congress dissolved on 5 April 1992, the convention was not totally submissive. What Fujimori wanted most from the constitutional convention was a path to perpetuate his rule, but the delegates refused to abolish presidential term limits and only authorized one consecutive reelection. The simplest solution was for him to run for office after the new constitution went into effect and then to seek reelection for one term, thus prolonging his rule until 2004; this was the formula Hugo Chávez later followed in Venezuela. Instead, because of the intense resistance in the convention to abolishing term limits and his reluctance to engage in an exhausting campaign, Fujimori opted for the formula Chávez had originally preferred: complete his original five-year term in 1995 and then run for another five-year term. The disadvantage of this alternative was that later he had to contrive a way to extend his presidency beyond the expiration of the second term in 2000. In both the Venezuelan and Peruvian constitutional conventions, the failure to solve certain issues completely in the president's favor led to considerable turmoil and complications in a not too distant future.[41]

These later confrontations seemed very remote in 1993, and a much more pressing issue was the congress, which Fujimori and Montesinos correctly regarded as their Achilles' heel. A related problem was the shortage of candidates willing to run for office from the provinces; the president's refusal to create any party or organizational group limited sharply the recruitment of politicians into the ranks of Fujimoristas. A structural solution was to reduce the number of elected positions, and the simplest way was to combine the senate and the house into a single assembly. This unicameral legislature, the most important contribution of the constitutional convention, also made it easier to pressure and bribe deputies into supporting the official line. The regime still did not have sufficient candidates, so it turned to the quick fix of filling the electoral slates with natives from the provinces who were permanent residents of Lima.[42]

Ideologically the Constitution of 1993 was the direct opposite of the 1979 Constitution largely drafted by the then still socialist APRA party, in the same way as the self-coup of April 1992 was the reaction to the leftist military coup of October 1968. Consequently, the 1993 Constitution eliminated all references to the social function of property and to socialist values and in their places substituted an unapologetic defense of capitalist principles. Although socialist verbiage of the old constitution had largely become meaningless under the free market policies of Fujimori, a clear statement of the supremacy of private property and capital was immensely reassuring to the business class and pleased international financial institutions such as the World Bank and the IMF.[43]

Because the official propaganda constantly repeated that capitalism and democracy were inseparable, the regime had to make some token concessions to the other political groups in the convention. The most important of these was the creation of a national ombudsman or *Defensoría del Pueblo* to listen to citizen complaints. The government was not eager about this possible new check on its actions but felt that it could contribute to the democratic appearance. And because the director of the *Defensoria del Pueblo*, just as the national controller (*Contralor*) who supposedly audited all official expenses, were both appointed by the unicameral legislature, the government believed that the new ombudsman would be as compliant as the national controller.[44]

The government expected an easy approval of the 1993 Constitution in the referendum of 31 October 1993 but was shocked when only 52 percent of the electorate supported the proposed text while 48 percent were opposed. The Fujimori administration should not have been surprised because the poor showing in the election for constitutional delegates on 22 November 1992 had been the first warning. Legalizing one presidential reelection and codifying capitalistic principles had aroused the skepticism if not the hostility of many voters. His election for a second presidential term was far from assured, but he still continued to rule with few constrains because the largely compliant constitutional convention remained as a passive legislature until the elections of April 1995.[45]

The First Reelection

Alberto Fujimori had laid the groundwork for his reelection with the creation of FONCODES (National Fund for Compensation and Social Development) in August 1991 under the prodding of the IMF and the World Bank. The latter institution in particular was receiving feedback from many countries that the rush to capitalism was inflicting enormous suffering on vast sectors of the population. Consequently these financial agencies wanted governments to create "social investment funds" to help soften the negative impact from the supposedly temporary blows of rapidly adopting a free market system.

The World Bank and other international institutions provided some funding, but after the disappointing electoral results of the October 1993 referendum, Fujimori concluded that he had to channel some of the proceeds from privatization away from favorites and into social programs. Fujimori had created the Ministry of the Presidency in May 1992 precisely to spend funds on generating political support for his regime. FONCODES was put under the vastly enlarged Ministry of the Presidency and along with other social programs such as the previously existing soup kitchens, these agencies began spending substantial sums of money among slum dwellers and the rural poor always with the goal of garnering electoral support.[46]

The contrast with the goals of international financial organizations could not have been greater, because while the World Bank wanted a temporary prop until the free market could effortlessly lift Peru out of its crushing poverty and income inequality, for Fujimori these social programs were simply a way to win reelection. "The government confined itself to instituting targeted social-assistance programs, which sought to benefit many people at relatively low cost."[47] Among other electoral benefits, "targeting guarantees a high marginal return because a few dollars can make a significant difference to the destitute [and] targeted programs give the government discretion over whom to favor and whom to exclude." The extensive social spending regained popularity for Fujimori, who perfected the technique of visiting places across the country to inaugurate projects while he appeared in local dress. He and the Ministry of the Presidency were very careful to direct the funds only to his supporters in districts essential for electoral victory. By distributing a small share of the proceeds from the sale of state enterprises, (the majority of the funds ended up as corruption in overseas accounts), Fujimori felt that he was well prepared to face any challenger in the 1995 election.[48]

As the 1995 elections approached, many well-informed citizens looked for an alternative to the flawed Fujimori. The two most prestigious Peruvians then alive were the novelist Mario Vargas Llosa and the former UN secretary general Javier Pérez de Cuéllar. Vargas Llosa, who had already learned the mechanics of running a presidential campaign, seemed the best choice, but he declined. Thus, the road was open for Pérez de Cuéllar to launch his candidacy. Very astutely the former UN secretary general returned from Paris not by flying into Lima but by driving from Bolivia into bordering Puno, and from there he went on a campaign tour through the Andean regions of Peru such as Cuzco and Arequipa. When he finally made his way to Lima it was through slums such as Villa El Salvador. His electoral efforts were off to a good start, and in a crowded field of precandidates, he shot up to a close second to Fujimori in the preference polls. Because he had always openly defended free market views, the business community did not fear him but was still hesitant to abandon Fujimori.[49]

The unexpected initial popularity of the suave and sophisticated Pérez de Cuéllar caught Vladimiro Montesinos off guard, and his SIN went on overdrive to neutralize the challenge that this candidacy posed for the reelection of Fujimori in the first round. Anything less than a resounding victory meant a repudiation of the regime, and winning less than 50 percent of the votes mandated a runoff election. Montesinos knew that the rise of Pérez de Cuéllar had to be stopped, and the best way was by undermining his support among the dark-skinned lower classes. The Indian-looking Alejandro Toledo, who claimed to have taught at Harvard University, offered the best alternative to stop the Pérez de Cuéllar steamroller, but Toledo as an unknown figure and without a political movement did not seem capable of mounting an effective challenge. SIN stepped in to make his candidacy viable, and the first step was to secure the required number of signatures for his inscription as a presidential candidate. Not surprisingly Toledo failed to deliver the signatures, but just a few hours before the inscription deadline on 11 October 1994, a minor party declared him its candidate; later it was learned that Montesinos had bribed the leader of that political movement to switch its support to Toledo. The next step was to provide television coverage for Toledo until he became a household word. SIN, by pressuring media outlets, obtained unusually extensive TV and press coverage vastly exceeding that of the minor candidates. Soon Toledo was among the top three in the polls, and he started to regard himself as the equal of Pérez de Cuéllar and Fujimori.[50]

A three-way race was not at all what Montesinos had in mind; the Toledo tree had grown too wildly and it was time for some drastic pruning. SIN leaked to the press information unmasking the claim of having taught at Harvard University and more seriously about his involvement in scandals of the Alán García administration. Even more easily, SIN cut off the candidate's access to television. In reality, the precautions proved unnecessary, because Toledo was his own worst enemy as he made one mistake after another during the campaign. He lost any chance of winning a decent percentage of the vote when his presentation in front of a business roundtable turned into an embarrassing flop. He had not bothered to learn about the issues, and he came across as ill-prepared to business leaders, who however, did not dismiss him completely. Clearly he was not ready for prime time, but Latin American business leaders know that disciplined and hard-working government officials can be just as dangerous to profits as radical leftists. Perhaps Toledo could be useful under other circumstances in the future, but in his presidential debut of 1995 he stood no chance of winning, and he finished in the next to last place with only 3.2 percent of the popular vote.[51]

The fears of Montesinos about Pérez de Cuéllar proved unfounded, and the weak campaigner was struggling to connect with the lower classes. Fujimori with his simplistic yet seductive style was once again wooing voters as he had done in the 1990 elections, and Pérez de Cuéllar could not escape his image as a cosmopolitan diplomat. Incredible as it may now appear, Fujimori seemed more authentically Peruvian than his rival.[52]

The Ecuadorian invasion of Peru in January 1995 provided the last opportunity to reverse the momentum of the presidential election. Not only did the invasion catch the Fujimori administration and the vaunted SIN by surprise, but the army struggled to expel the Ecuadorian invaders. Inadequate armament, lack of planning, and logistical difficulties in the Amazon region hampered the Peruvian effort. But worst of all was the micromanagement of the war by Fujimori, who secretly strove to turn the conflict into an opportunity for his international prestige and possibly also for a Nobel Peace Prize. Fujimori placed crippling restrictions on the actions of Peruvian forces; for example, Ecuadorian artillery shelled Peruvian territory almost continuously but the Peruvian cannon were forbidden to reply, and similar restrictions applied to warplanes. Although eventually Peru expulsed the invaders, victory came at an excessively high cost of lives. As news of the blunders in the conduct of the war leaked out, Pérez de Cuéllar had the opportunity to win the election by appealing to Peruvian nationalism. More than in any other Latin American country, nationalistic feelings have been extremely intense among the population.[53]

By wrapping himself with the Peruvian flag and promising to redeem the honor of the country at all costs, he would have ridden if not to victory in the election at least to a runoff. But here his prior experience as UN secretary general proved to be crippling baggage, and although he criticized the mismanagement of the military campaign, he could not bring himself to demand a war against Ecuador. His refusal to stir Peruvian nationalism lost him the last chance to win the election; nearly 15 years had to pass before another presidential candidate dared to appeal to nationalism. But in 1995, the outcome was a foregone conclusion, and on 9 April 1995 Fujimori won reelection in the first round by 64 percent of the vote, a figure higher than his 62 percent victory in the runoff against Vargas Llosa in June 1990. Even more unexpectedly, the president won a majority of delegates in the unicameral legislature.[54]

The months after the smashing electoral victory of April 1995 were the high point of the Fujimori administration. Such was the confidence of the president that he asked congress to pass an amnesty not only for all military and police personnel accused of human rights violations but also for the participants in the 13 November 1992 countercoup attempt. He had waited until after his April 1995 electoral victory before presenting the amnesty bill to congress. The other two members of the triumvirate, Montesinos and Hermoza, had been pressing for this law to reward the loyalty of the military and also to avoid incriminating prosecutions in particular about the Colina death squad. When he signed the bill into law on 14 June 1995, Fujimori rewarded not only the military supporters of his regime but also showed the country that his position was so strong that he did not fear the former coup plotters. The Amnesty Law also was the earliest indication that he intended to run again for president, yet the result was precisely the opposite. Public opinion was outraged about granting blanket immunity to human rights violators, and the Amnesty Law widened the gap between the people and the regime.[55]

Fujimori dismissed the outcry about the Amnesty Law as just a passing thing, and he was sure that he could shore up his support by another round of pro-business measures. Fujimori knew that he needed the continued support of private business to govern, but as a precaution, he had held off on the next package of benefits for corporations until after his electoral victory. Because the privatization of social security had not been completed, he gave even more advantages to the private pension funds in 1995 and 1996; the goal had been to favor the owners of these pension funds and not the pensioners as could be expected from regulations written and advocated by industry leaders. The tax reform of the first presidency unexpectedly had turned out to be a big burden for large corporations, and finance minister Jorge Camet mitigated these effects by granting companies exemptions and tax cuts. The demands of large corporations for tax exemptions coincided perfectly with the views of the World Bank that resolutely condemned progressive tax system and urged the adoption of value added taxes. In accordance with the prescriptions of the World Bank, the government finished transforming Peru's tax system into one that extracted revenue from the majority of the population to benefit a privileged minority.[56]

Fujimori also announced another round of sales of state enterprises, and here too Minister of Finance Camet and his advisors had a direct stake because they reaped illegal fees and benefits from these transactions. But the well of lucrative privatizations was running dry, and the remaining state enterprises enjoyed the support of strong constituencies and usually were not attractive to foreign investors. The administration's last major effort was the attempt to privatize PetroPeru, but the outbreak of the first massive demonstration against the regime made Fujimori desist from the proposal.[57] The PetroPeru protests sparked a backlash against privatization as many Peruvians realized that the much heralded sale of state assets was not helping the vast majority of the population. In the cutthroat business world, future benefits are much more important than past favors, and after practically having given away the store, Fujimori had little left to offer the private sector in the future.

The need to shore up his support among business was only one of several hurdles the second Fujimori presidency faced. "In 1996 Fujimori began a slow decline in popularity as his constituency among the rural and urban poor started to tire of austerity measures that seemed to yield no appreciable benefits."[58] The signs were clear that Fujimori needed to use his second term to make a graceful exit that spared him from prosecution over illegal activities. His brother Santiago and a small group of Japanese-origin advisors had been warning for years of the danger of the unhealthy reliance on Montesinos, but after the resounding electoral victory of April 1995, their fate was cast. Exactly a year later in April 1996, Fujimori dismissed his brother and other long-term associates from government service. The last voices of sanity and reason disappeared from the inner circle of the president who increasingly fell into illusions, lost touch with reality, and placed blind faith in the Peruvian Rasputin.[59]

Montesinos was not all-powerful, however, and he could not get two-thirds of the deputies to amend the 1993 Constitution to allow a second consecutive reelection. As may be recalled, Fujimori had been unable to abolish term limits during the 1993 Constitutional convention, and the failure to muster a two-thirds majority in congress should have persuaded him to drop the bid for a second consecutive election. Instead, his deputies rushed through congress in the dawn hours of 23 August 1996 a bill entitled "The Law of Authentic Interpretation of the Constitution," and it essentially authorized Fujimori to run a second time for president in 2000. Judicial challenges to this law were inevitable because congress lacked authority to interpret the constitution. More significantly, this law marked the start of the unraveling of the Fujimori presidency.[60]

No less damaging for the regime was the first revelation confirming the corruption of Montesinos. Up to this moment the Peruvian Rasputin had successfully kept hidden his ties with drug traffickers, but on 16 August 1996 the Peruvian drug lord Vaticano exposed their relationship. He had controlled the drug trade in the Amazon region of the upper Huallaga River but had fled to Colombia after a dispute with Montesinos over immunity payments. Diligent Colombian police officials captured Vaticano, and assuming that Peru wanted to try him, had deported him back to his native country. Fearing damaging declarations, Montesinos initially succeeded in keeping the drug lord out of public. But it was simply impossible to prevent a public hearing for the accused, and Vaticano then openly and in detail described the long-standing relations with Montesinos.[61]

These statements triggered a mini crisis in the government, and Montesinos frantically tried to silence his accuser. Electroshocks and sundry tortures forced Vaticano to recant his accusations publicly, but his appearance in a near-zombie condition undermined the credibility of his reversal. Simultaneously the regime launched a media offensive as one high ranking official after another went on television to vouch for the honesty of Montesinos. Even General Hermoza came out strongly in favor of the Peruvian Rasputin, so close had become the relationship between these two members of the triumvirate. Attorney General Blanca Nélida Colán and the very conservative Bishop Luis Capriani added their voices to the many officials denouncing the accusations of Vaticano as complete lies.[62]

In spite of the damage control, the Vaticano accusations hurt Fujimori, whose approval ratings continued to decline during 1996 until an unforeseen event came to restore his popularity. On 17 December 1996 a commando team of the guerrilla group

MRTA seized the Japanese ambassador's residence and took a large number of hostages. This kidnapping caught the authorities by surprise and was particularly embarrassing because previously the government repeatedly had announced the nearly complete destruction of MRTA. Initially the guerrillas released most of the hostages, but when negotiations failed to obtain the release of the rest, Fujimori planned a bold rescue operation. After miners excavated tunnels under the ambassador's residence, specially trained soldiers, who had rehearsed in a duplicate site, liberated the hostages and killed the guerrillas on 22 April 1997.[63]

The rescue operation temporarily improved the approval ratings of Fujimori but in reality the crisis marked the beginning of the end of his regime. The regained popularity emboldened the president to set in motion the steps for his reelection. On 29 May 1997 he used his rubber-stamp congress to remove from office the three judges who earlier had issued the ruling that he was ineligible to run for reelection in 2000. The arbitrary action by the congress triggered the largest protests so far against Fujimori, and students for the first time joined in the demonstrations. The regime was clearly losing its appeal among the population, but a determined president pressed ahead and did not stop until a compliant Supreme Court invalidated the previous ruling by the three deposed judges and declared him eligible to run a second time for election in 2000.[64]

The diminishing popular support complicated enormously the reelection, but just when the regime needed to show the greatest unity, a crisis erupted inside the triumvirate. General Hermoza was accustomed to performing an awkward balancing act to maintain his reputation inside the army. Of course, only a handful of insiders knew that this was all for show because he was stashing away millions of ill-gotten dollars into foreign bank accounts. His latest stunt was to present himself as the organizer of the rescue operation of the Japanese embassy. Almost as a rookie reporter, he went around interviewing the soldiers involved in that operation and even asked their permission to tell their stories in a book that he published a few months later.[65]

The problem was that in his book and in press conferences, General Hermoza reduced Fujimori to the role of a spectator, when the president in long interviews had described himself as the architect of the rescue operation. The vanity of both men clashed as they struggled to take full credit for the success. In previous decades an attempted military coup would have been the outcome, with either Fujimori or Hermoza emerging as the ruler of the country. But the presence of the Peruvian Rasputin changed the equation. After the triumvirate had first emerged in 1991, Montesinos had tried to remove General Hermoza, but soon both men reached a meeting of the minds; although Montesinos was the more powerful partner, he found the not very bright general to be a very useful tool, and a mutually beneficial modus vivendi emerged between both men. But the situation was different when Hermoza threatened the president and by implication the power of his associate. The officer corps had long been divided into pro–Hermoza and pro–Montesinos factions, and once Fujimori asked for the support of his associate, the outcome was predictable. On the morning of 20 August 1998 Fujimori convoked an unsuspecting Hermoza to a defense meeting in the presidential palace; in his only inkling of what was coming, the general could not contact his subordinates when he tried to telephone them as he drove to the palace. When Hermoza saw ranged before him the commanders of the five military regions of Peru at the meeting, along with the heads of the air force and navy, at last he sensed that something was not right. Before he could speak, Fujimori effusively thanked him for his services and then showed him the door.[66]

Behind the scenes Montesinos, a masterful choreographer, had orchestrated the entire scene and had even placed army tanks around the presidential palace. General Hermoza went into a comfortable retirement, and his millions in foreign banks prevented him from speaking against the dictatorship. His dismissal had come as a complete surprise to the country that did not realize that the end of the triumvirate had dangerously weakened the Fujimori regime. The apparently tireless Montesinos assumed the exhausting burden of running the army, in addition to his existing duties of managing the political world, the legal system, and the network of corruption. Inevitably Montesinos devoted less attention to the details of the military, and he only partially compensated for this void by appointing his brother-in-law General Luis Cubas Portal to be the commander of the second military region, which included Lima.[67]

Increasingly the regime was vulnerable, not the least because its survival depended on preserving a harmonious relationship between Fujimori and an overburdened Montesinos. Both men were locked in an inseparable embrace almost like Siamese twins, and the fall of either one was sure to put the survival of the other at serious risk.

CHAPTER 3

The United States and the Crisis in Peru

In spite of having been born independently, Alberto Fujimori and Vladimiro Montesinos became Siamese twins of the type that science cannot separate without causing the death of both.—Carlos Iván Degregori[1]

The survival of the Alberto Fujimori presidency depended on the support of the U.S. government. The privatization program and the massive imposition of free market principles created common ideological values and guaranteed the support of Washington as long as the regime never undermined vital U.S. goals in other parts of the continent.

The Second Reelection of Alberto Fujimori

During the first presidential term of Fujimori, Peruvian participation in U.S counter narcotics operations had been rife with contradictions for Vladimiro Montesinos. On the one hand the U.S. government needed his support to carry out drug interdiction but at the same time he received payments from noted drug lords, in particular Vaticano (Demetrio Chávez). As Mexican drug cartels had learned to do when buying protection from corrupt officials, Montesinos solved the dilemma by arresting drug traffickers who were the rivals of his drug lords. The decline of cocaine production during the mid–1990s also helped to mitigate the inherent contradiction between supporting U.S. counter narcotics operations and protecting the drug trade. Not surprisingly, the DEA (Drug Enforcement Agency) was pleased with Montesinos and considered him a valuable ally.[2]

As additional insurance to buttress his reputation in Washington, he also became a steady source of information for the CIA. Since Montesinos already had stashed away millions of dollars in overseas accounts, it was highly improbable that the CIA was paying him to be an informant or "asset." The most likely explanation was that he gave the CIA information to solidify the alliance with the United States. For the CIA he was a treasured source who opened a window into the activities and ideas of the Lima government in the late 1990s, at a time when American diplomats, including the ambassadors, had almost no access to senior Peruvian officials. He also shared with U.S. officials some of the information flowing into the National Intelligence Service (*Servicio de Inteligencia*

Nacional) or SIN coming from its agents in neighboring countries. He boasted of having the largest number of informants infiltrated in FARC, the main Colombian guerrilla organization.[3]

In Washington his principal advocates had been the CIA and the DEA, but the relationship with the latter agency started to deteriorate when on 14 May 1998 drug czar Barry McCaffrey made negative public comments about the Peruvian Rasputin. As a sinister figure operating in the dark, Montesinos avoided publicity but did lash out against negative press coverage, especially when it threatened to undermine his claim that he enjoyed the unconditional support of Washington. In retaliation for the hostile comments of McCaffrey, Montesinos shut down several counter narcotics operations; over the next 12 months American diplomats were able to soothe his ruffled feelings and gradually DEA resumed its campaign to interdict cocaine coming from Peru.[4]

Maintaining good relations with DEA became easier in the second half of the 1990s as cocaine production declined in Peru. However, the smaller the amounts of cocaine exported, the less money the drug lords could afford to pay Montesinos. The shrinking amount of drug money created a major problem for a Fujimori regime dependent on widespread corruption for its survival. Not only were all senior officials receiving illegal payments, but it seemed that almost everyone of importance in Peru was on the payroll of Montesinos, including deputies, judges, district attorneys, and generals. And in the private sector, almost all media organizations received generous sums to assure favorable television coverage, and most journalists accepted payments for reporting only favorable news. The Fujimori regime operated as a vast distribution machine sucking money from the drug trade and corrupt deals and then paying out the funds as bribes and as deposits in overseas bank accounts.[5]

As the drug trade entered into a temporary slump, Montesinos sought alternate sources of funds in the lucrative arms deals he negotiated after the 1995 war with Ecuador. As chapter 2 mentioned, Peruvian soldiers went to battle "poorly armed and undernourished,"[6] and Montesinos cleverly twisted the popular demand for the proper outfitting of the military into secret purchases of useless or obsolescent weapons. The most egregious violation was the acquisition of MIG-29s; although they were great warplanes, without a service contract they soon ceased to be airworthy. Needless to say, the MIG-29 transaction yielded millions of dollars in commissions to Montesinos and to favored generals such as Nicolás Hermoza.[7]

Outrageous as was the cynical manipulation of Peruvian nationalism to enrich a handful of individuals, these criminal deals did not bother U.S. officials who were extremely pleased with the free market polices of the Fujimori regime. But not everyone shared the complacency of Washington, and soon rumors of the shady deals began to circulate. Once Peru reached an agreement with Ecuador in 1999 on an apparently permanent peace treaty, it became impossible to justify additional arms purchases. Unable to use nationalism to extract more cash, Montesinos saw his income declining right when the 2000 presidential campaign was promising to cost a lot more than the 1995 election. Montesinos had already accumulated around a quarter of a billion dollars, and his safest course of action would have been to tap these funds to cover the expenses of the 2000 reelection.

Instead greed won out, and Montesinos, in the fatal error of his career, took the decision that doomed the Fujimori presidency. The Revolutionary Armed Forces of Colombia (*Fuerzas Armadas Revolucionarias de Colombia*) or FARC was trying to upgrade and standardize the rifles of its combatants. Traditionally smuggled weapons and those captured from government forces had armed the Colombian guerrillas, but the bewildering array of brands created a logistical nightmare and limited combat effectiveness. Finding modest quantities of any small arms has been easy in the black market, but stocks numbering in the thousands of the same rifle have been available only to governments.

In the last quarter of the twentieth century, many armies were shifting to rifles firing a smaller caliber cartridge, and the conversion left army arsenals clogged with the previous large caliber weapons. For the Colombian guerrillas usually travelling on foot, the longer range and hitting power of the large-caliber rifles were very appealing. When Jordan put on the market 10,000 unused Kalashnikovs rifles, FARC wanted to acquire the lot, but the purchase seemed impossible because only governments could submit bids. Through his network of informants inside the Colombian guerrilla organization, Montesinos learned of the situation and saw the opportunity to participate by using the Peruvian government as a dummy buyer for the transaction.[8]

The Peruvian government provided the end-user certificates stating that these weapons were only for the exclusive use of its armed forces. But the rifles never reached Peru, because in separate flights the cargo planes dropped the crates by parachute over prearranged sites in the Colombian jungle. FARC deposited a large sum in Montesinos's accounts right after each air drop had reached the guerrillas. The deal was successfully concluded, and with these powerful rifles a well-armed FARC intensified its attacks against Colombian forces. From a military perspective, the procurement of these new Kalashnikovs was a major reason why the guerrilla war dragged on in Colombia until the second decade of the twenty-first century.[9]

The FARC transaction had given Montesinos fresh funds to spend on the campaign of 2000 without having to draw on the quarter of a billion dollars he had stashed away in foreign accounts. He established a command post at SIN to coordinate the reelection efforts. His forte was bribing politicians, and first order of business was to support the proliferation of presidential candidates. The goal was to fragment the opposition so that Fujimori would emerge with at least 50 percent of the popular vote, thereby eliminating the need for a runoff election.[10]

A special case was Alejandro Toledo, who already was looming as a dangerous contender, yet in another miscalculation, Montesinos felt that just as in the 1995 election, he had him under his thumb because of damaging personal information. Montesinos concentrated on knocking out the two serious contenders, but he waited too long to release the incriminating video of Toledo cavorting with prostitutes in sexual orgies. As the other candidates fell by the wayside, Toledo continued to rise in the polls, and in February for the first time he broke beyond single-digit numbers in voter preferences. He exploited his Indian features to increase his appeal to the mass of Peruvians, and taking a page from the Fujimori playbook, he too wore native dress and local garments during his tours across the country. The turning point came in the first week of March 2000 when voters rather suddenly made him the leading opposition contender. This accomplishment was all the more remarkable, because Fujimori had been stepping up social spending much as he had done before the 1995 campaign, but the failure of privatization and his free market policies to improve the lives of the majority of Peruvians had diminished his popularity.[11]

Trying to salvage a victory in the 9 April election, Montesinos threw the armed forces into the campaign. The commanders of all five army regions received the order to make the reelection of Fujimori their highest priority; when two generals hesitated about carrying out such blatantly partisan activity, Montesinos promptly replaced them with two loyal officers from his graduating class at Chorrillos military academy. Huge Fujimori billboards appeared in all bases and in nearby hills, while soldiers went out in the streets to glue posters and to paint over opposition messages. Military trucks also routinely transported people to rallies and other campaign events.[12] As the U.S. Embassy reported, "not only has the military performed the basic personnel and organizational services for Fujimori that normally would be realized by a political party, it has signaled loudly and clearly to Peruvians that Fujimori is the candidate of the armed forces and, hence, of stability."[13]

In Peru active-duty personnel may not participate in elections, unlike in Venezuela where the 1999 Constitution gave soldiers the right to vote. Many in uniform found Toledo to be an appealing figure, although Fujimori remained popular among junior officers and soldiers. The military carried out the orders to support Fujimori, but he could expect only so much from an institution increasingly restless under the control of Montesinos. The mounting discontent with Fujimori became clear when in the election on 9 April 2000 he received only 47 percent of the popular vote, while Toledo edged out the other opposition candidates to receive 40 percent of the vote.[14]

The results stunned Montesinos, who after a lifetime operating successfully in the dark, had lost the ability to function effectively out in the open. To make things worse, for a brief moment on 9 April early returns showed Toledo winning more votes than Fujimori. No political genius was needed to predict that if the opposition voters united behind Toledo, Fujimori would lose the election. The adverse results were unexpected even for the president, who briefly considered withdrawing from the runoff. By 1999 at the latest he started to lose enthusiasm for his reelection but had kept his doubts hidden largely because of the optimism of Montesinos who claimed to have the 2000 reelection wrapped up. The motto of the Peruvian Rasputin was that everything can be fixed with money in Peru, but an increasingly moody Fujimori became despondent and began to consult a witch to predict his future. Montesinos repeatedly talked with Fujimori to restore the president's confidence, and the associate claimed to have several scenarios to guarantee victory in the runoff election scheduled for 28 May 2000.[15]

The most fantastic scenario called for having SIN hire individuals to start disturbances that would serve as a pretext to launch a military coup. Presumably Fujimori would remain in office, but this revival of the 5 April 1992 self-coup opened up the possibility that Montesinos would become president, because as a civilian he did not suffer from the U.S. veto on generals running Latin American countries. At the 12 April meeting with army commanders, the coup option was not completely ruled out, but all present agreed that the best solution for the moment was that Fujimori continue actively campaigning for an electoral victory on 28 May.[16]

Montesinos seemed to be consulting the generals, but in reality he had already taken his decision beforehand on 10 April, and the real purpose of the 12 April meeting was to prepare the generals for a military coup should his latest maneuver prove unsuccessful. On 10 April, the day after the election, he had sent copies of the video showing Toledo participating in a drunken orgy with prostitutes to the candidate. The images must have been shocking, so that same day his outraged wife Eliane Karp declared to the press that Toledo had been twice kidnapped and drugged and then videotaped performing lewd acts on top of prostitutes. Toledo did not speak about the topic, and when asked by reporters simply referred them to his wife who made no additional comments.[17]

To maintain the credibility of the runoff and to prevent a substitute candidate from entering the race, Montesinos could not have Toledo drop out immediately from the campaign. Toledo, who knew how the game was played, continued to campaign for over a month. Whether on his own or in collusion with the regime, he waited until 18 May to announce just ten days before the election that his movement was halting its participation in the runoff and that it had requested a postponement until 28 June. Two days later he explained that he had not withdrawn and that the campaign was continuing on the assumption that the government would agree to postpone the election. These imprecise and contradictory statements served adequately the purpose of confusing his bewildered supporters who did not know what to make of his statements.[18]

Not surprisingly, Fujimori won the 28 May 2000 election with three-quarters of the popular vote, and once again Montesinos demonstrated that he was capable of overcoming any obstacle standing in the way of his ambitions. But the victory of Fujimori in the runoff was only half the battle, and simultaneously Montesinos had been coping with the second major problem that emerged from the 9 April election. Voters had also elected deputies, and the nine opposition parties had gained a majority of the seats in the congress; this weak electoral result reflected not just the declining approval of the president but also the refusal of the regime to create solid political organizations in the provinces. Although the Fujimoristas with 52 representatives were the single largest group in the assembly, the real threat existed that the opposition parties could unite to vote into office legislative leaders and chairs of congressional committees who were sure to start investigations into the many abuses of the regime. To avoid this danger, Montesinos launched a campaign that he cynically called "Operation Recruitment."[19]

As a wise precaution, Montesinos traditionally had maintained good relations with many opposition deputies even when Fujimori had a congressional majority. Through personal favors and by facilitating their congressional tasks, he helped to soften the hostility of opposition deputies. He intensified these contacts in the months before the 9 April 2000 elections, because the private polls the SIN contracted—the most extensive in Peru—early on revealed that the Fujimoristas had no chance of retaining control of the congress. As a hunter after his prey, he zeroed in on the weakest and most vulnerable deputies who were most likely to accept his illegal proposals. Once again he validated his motto that in Peru everything can be arranged with money, and he gave cash payments to members of the opposition to switch their party affiliation. At least one deputy demanded a million dollars for betraying his party, but he had priced himself out of the market and Montesinos kept on looking. Other deputies asked for more reasonable prices; more typical was Alberto Kuori who received a down payment of $15,000 in bills counted in front of him while being unaware that he was been secretly videotaped.[20]

Through bribery Montesinos persuaded 12 deputies to switch to the Fujimorista bloc, which originally had numbered only 52 and now rose to 64, a comfortable majority to prevent any serious inquiry into the criminal acts of the regime. The legislative branch had reached perhaps the lowest points in its history, and once the 12 legislators announced that they were betraying their party colleagues, the sense of outrage was tremendous. As the deputies entered the chambers on 24 July to begin the new legislative session, furious deputies hurled coins at the 12 traitors. On 25 July the 64 deputies of the majority bloc elected loyal Fujimoristas to the leadership positions of the congress.[21] Once again the president was grateful to Montesinos who had been able to convert the congress into a compliant body.

Fujimori seemed to have the third presidential term securely in his grasp, but because he had made it clear that the third term would be his last, Montesinos was already preparing for both the 2005 election and the next presidential term. The 2005 election might have another new twist, however, if Montesinos decided to become president, but he was more likely to retain all power and rule through a puppet, as Plutarco Elías Calles had done in Mexico from 1929 to 1936.[22]

Before Montesinos could concentrate on planning for the 2005 election, he first had to fend off one final challenge from defeated candidate Alejandro Toledo. Using the inauguration of Fujimori on 28 July as a reason to protest, Toledo, who did not stop repeating that the government had stolen the 9 April 2000 election, scheduled the "March of the Four Corners," a series of mass demonstrations simultaneously occurring across the country over four days. The largest march by women ever in Lima began the cycle of protests on 26 July and the next day even bigger crowds filled the street in anticipation of the massive rally on 28 July, the day of the presidential inauguration.[23]

Montesinos immediately saw an opportunity to discredit not just Toledo but the entire opposition as irresponsible fanatics bent on returning the country to the terrorism of Shining Path. According to a plan carefully prepared days before, SIN sent undercover operatives into the crowds on 28 July in order to instill in the demonstrators a desire to loot and destroy. Already in previous days the media, almost all controlled by the government, had been warning that the real purpose of these four days of marches was to unleash mayhem and chaos. Undercover agents enraged the crowds and launched incendiary bombs at many government buildings, including the Palace of Justice. The culminating act of the orchestrated campaign came on 28 July when SIN operatives set on fire the Banco de la Nación, in an action reminiscent of the Nazis burning the parliament building or Reichstag in February 1933 to solidify their control over Germany. Whether part of the plan or not, the fire trapped 16 security guards inside the building where they suffered horrible burns, and six died from suffocation.[24]

The government-controlled media was ready with a well-prepared campaign applying that classic theme in Latin American history of "civilization versus barbarism." The news outlets accused Toledo of trying to set Lima on fire as the mad emperor Nero had done in ancient Rome. Television news repeatedly portrayed Toledo and his wife Elaine Karp as leading Vandal hordes of savages to loot, destroy, and torch the buildings of Lima. The media increased the number of wounded in the disturbances to over 300 and played up the agonizing deaths of the security workers burned alive. In contrast to this image of desolation and destruction stood the Fujimori administration, the only possible guardian of stability, order, and prosperity for peaceful citizens.[25]

The Last Battle of Vladimiro Montesinos

The staged events of 28 July 2000 and the media manipulation totally discredited the opposition. Once again Vladimiro Montesinos had overcome seemingly impossible odds and emerged victorious. As he gloated over his extraordinary maneuvers, he did not realize that his days in power were already numbered. Blissfully unaware of the implications of a seemingly harmless decision, early in August he went on a trip to Russia supposedly to acquire new electronics equipment for intercepting communications and recording conversations.[26]

He had always prided himself on having good relations with the United States, but perhaps remembering that Washington took the Peruvian generals of 1968–1980 more seriously when they turned to the Soviet Union for weapons and trade deals, he saw no harm in flirting with the Russians as a way to enhance his position with the United States. Perhaps in earlier more quiet years this strategy could have been mildly successful, but in the critical months of 2000 the timing could not have been worse. He also absented himself from the country when his keen eye might have detected how shaky were the foundations of the Fujimori presidency.

Yet it was not the political costs of the trip to Russia but the personal ones that triggered the rapid unfolding of events. As chapter 2 mentioned, he suffered from satyriasis and needed to have sexual relations several times each day to quiet his addiction. Until 2000 he had been able to keep compartmentalized the many women at his disposal, so that they rarely saw each other. In the second biggest blunder of his career, he decided to bring along for the Russian trip not just his official mistress but also Matilde Pinchi Pinchi, his confidante since the late 1980s. During the trip a violent altercation and shouting match took place between the two women as they insulted each other, and Matilde, who was financially independent, felt humiliated. The always suave and diplomatic Montesinos appeared to have calmed them down, and too confidently he believed that peace had returned to his domestic household. But the failure of Montesinos to support her in the clash with the official mistress had aroused the wild jungle feelings of this native of the Amazon jungle, and she secretly began plotting revenge.[27]

After his return from Russia, Montesinos received the first confirmation of the worst blunder he had committed during his entire career in the Fujimori administration. On 11 August 2000 three American agents came to the headquarters of the National Intelligence Service (*Servicio de Inteligencia Nacional*) or SIN to present irrefutable evidence that Montesinos had masterminded the sale and delivery of Kalashnikov rifles to the Revolutionary Armed Forces of Colombia (*Fuerzas Armadas Revolucionarias de Colombia*) or FARC. The U.S. government usually has been very tolerant of abuses inside an allied country, but much as a sultan becomes outraged when outsiders try to enter his harem, so a cardinal principle since 1898 in American foreign policy in Latin America has been that no country can interfere in the affairs of another without first obtaining prior permission from Washington. The delivery of a large quantity of weapons to rebels was in itself also an act of aggression and under international law Colombia could well consider the transaction a reason to declare war on Peru. But it was the United States and not Colombia that first reprimanded Montesinos over the arms sale.[28]

The official explanation was that the Colombian army had captured the new Kalashnikovs in combat and had traced them back to Peru with the assistance of U.S. intelligence agencies. But in 1999 and 2000 FARC was still on the offensive, and it seemed highly unlikely that victorious guerrillas would easily lose their new rifles; at the same time, even if a few rifles had been captured, their appearance fit into the pattern of the guerrillas using a bewildering array of weapons.[29] Only U.S. intelligence agencies had the means to uncover the arms delivery by reconstructing the paper trial through Jordan and then to Peru. Once no doubt remained about the guilt of Montesinos, the U.S. government regretfully concluded that this very valuable intelligence source had to go. His many American contacts had failed to alert him about the imminent scandal, but they wanted to give him the opportunity to make a graceful and quiet exit. The 11 August 2000 visit to SIN was his "severance offer" or an advance warning that he could no longer remain in the Peruvian government and needed to start preparing his departure preferably by the end of the year and no later than early 2001.

Removing Montesinos could never be an easy matter, especially when the U.S. government wanted to keep Fujimori as president until he finished his third term in 2005. American officials were entering the treacherous waters of "dictator disposal" and were optimistically assuming that an orderly and gradual departure of Montesinos was possible. His foreign bank accounts bulged with at least a quarter of a billion dollars in ill-gotten gains, and he could still use his position of power to leverage a golden exile in a foreign country.[30] But although greed had been a strong motivation behind his actions, his unquenchable lust for sex and his need for power were even stronger driving forces. He could not conceive abandoning all possibility of wielding power for the rest of his life, and in another disastrous decision, he rejected the severance offer of the U.S. government.

Rather than going quietly and leaving matters well arranged for Fujimori, Montesinos mistakenly saw the FARC arms deals as one more challenge to overcome. Because he could neither obtain the return of the Kalashnikov rifles nor much less defeat FARC, it was beyond his abilities to undo the damage he had done, and consequently he could not convince the U.S. government to reverse its determination to remove him from power. He decided instead to stage a sham show with Fujimori at his side on 21 August 2000. At this press conference, the two men, flanked by generals, claimed that an operation was underway to halt the flow of arms to FARC; the implied message was that Peru could help destroy the Colombian guerrillas. Years before such a gesture would have helped Montesinos ingratiate himself with U.S. officials as an active ally in the struggle against FARC, but not after he had sold the weapons that condemned Colombia to over 15 more years of guerrilla insurgency. The 21 August press conference backfired completely; immediately the governments of Colombia and Jordan refuted the statements and accused Peru of being the real culprit in the delivery of arms to FARC.[31]

The scandal was out in the public, and the pressure was mounting on Fujimori to do something soon. The earlier severance offer of having Montesinos gradually fade away was no longer acceptable. To press the message home, on 8 September 2000 at a United Nations meeting in New York, Secretary of State Madelaine Albright told Fujimori that Montesinos had to be removed from office; she even specified that Fujimori could complete his term but only if he got rid of his associate. This must have been the lowest point in the Fujimori presidency as he was reduced to receiving orders from the United States about whom to have in his administration. The ability to decide who could hold high public office has been a fundamental characteristic of U.S. control over its informal empire in the Caribbean. The fiercely independent and nationalistic legacy of the 1968–1980 military regime was nothing but a distant memory as Fujimori completed the transformation of Peru into a banana republic.[32]

During the twenty-first century Peruvian nationalists tried to find any avenue to loosen the U.S. grip over their country, but in September 2000 the only concern of Fujimori was how to make as painless as possible the departure of his associate. The pledge of U.S. support was reassuring, but in an inexplicable lack of self-confidence, he did not feel capable of ruling without Montesinos. The immediate task was to keep under control the armed forces and the congress, the only two institutions that could remove Fujimori from office.[33]

As Fujimori struggled with the problem of how to survive without Montesinos, a parallel but independent process emerged to force his hand and to send Peru hurling into the next state of its turbulent history. After the return of Montesinos from the trip to Russia, his confidante Matilde Pinchi Pinchi was plotting revenge against him because of the humiliations she had suffered at the hands of his official mistress. She fooled him into believing that everything was normal again and she resumed her normal daily routine of being the personal assistant who shared all his secrets, including guarding at SIN headquarters his collection of nearly 3000 videos of taped conversations with most of the leading personalities of Peru. She decided to leak a video of Montesinos bribing a deputy, but on the mistaken assumption that she could not trust opposition journalists to keep her identity secret, she naively asked her chauffeur to use an intermediary to make the video public.[34]

The chauffer turned to small-time builder Germán Barrera, another individual with ties to the Amazon region, for assistance in getting the video out to the media. Barrera promptly pointed out that the deputy in the video was an insignificant figure unable to arouse any public indignation, and instead a video of Montesinos bribing Deputy Alberto Kouri was of immense interest to the media. Kouri had just filed a defamation suit of one million dollars against Alejandro Toledo when the latter had accused the deputy of receiving a bribe to join the Fujimorista bloc. The chauffeur went back to Pinchi Pinchi with the request, and she duly complied and submitted two videos of the same Kuori meeting where Montesinos counted $15,000 in bills in front of the deputy as the hidden camera recorded the scene. Barrera knew that he had dynamite in his hands and saw the opportunity to make the deal of a lifetime by selling this video to the highest bidder.[35]

No deep thinking was required to regard defeated presidential candidate Alejandro Toledo as the most likely buyer for the video. Given the lawsuit of a million dollars against him, Barrera conservatively priced the video at $300,000 but was totally surprised when Toledo declined to acquire the video. The refusal has provided additional evidence for those who claim that the former presidential candidate had always been under the control of Montesinos. However, in Toledo's defense, he did not rush to alert SIN that this highly damaging video was on the market. The refusal of Toledo to buy the video disappointed Barrera who saw the value of his merchandise fall precipitously. As he peddled the video around Lima, nobody seemed interested until a private contributor of another political group offered to purchase the video but only for $100,000. Seeing that each passing day lowered the value of his asset, Barrera took the low offer.[36]

The political group convoked reporters to a press conference in the Hotel Bolívar of downtown Lima at 4:00 p.m. on 14 September 2000; as a precaution, just in case SIN tried to sabotage the electricity, an emergency generator stood ready to provide the current to run the projectors so that the journalists could see the video. The one television station still outside the control of Montesinos also received a copy with instructions to broadcast the video at 7:00 p.m. Early that morning a textile manufacturer (who presumably had been contacted about its purchase) telephoned Montesinos to state that a political group had acquired the video and was going to release it that afternoon at 4:00 p.m. Although the press conference was delayed until 5:00 p.m., the journalists had their story, and at 7:00 p.m. television viewers tuned in to see with their own eyes the video of Montesinos counting the bills of the $15,000 bribe for Deputy Kuori.[37]

Because of a failure to understand the underlying circumstances, it has become conventional wisdom to conclude that the broadcast of this video on 14 September doomed Fujimori and Montesinos. In reality the release of the video was the trigger rather than the cause of the subsequent events. The content of the video was so graphic, that it has been correctly labeled as pornographic, or more exactly the visual depiction of what everyone knew was occurring on a daily basis. In Peru revelations about the corruption of politicians evoke as much surprise as the sun setting every day. Traditionally scandals about domestic political dealings have entertained the public but soon faded and things returned to business as usual. For his part, Montesinos had as his unconditional ally the attorney general, and Blanca Nélida Colán quashed any investigation into the contents of the leaked video. The Fujimorista majority in the assembly prevented any congressional inquiry. Only the independent Ombudsman Office persisted in pursuing the matter, but without any access to the evidence its efforts could not be more than a temporary nuisance.[38]

U.S. opposition to Montesinos was the real reason for his fall; the video merely triggered the acceleration of his inevitable departure. The U.S. government could not forgive his sale of weapons to FARC in Colombia, and it was time for Montesinos to pay for his colossal blunder. However, Fujimori hesitated and was looking for a graceful way to ease out his associate in a slow and gradual manner. The release of the video on 14 September forced the president's hand, and he finally telephoned Montesinos that same day to demand his resignation. As was his usual response in times of crises, the associate explained that he would take care of this matter that had been blown up out of proportion.[39]

The next day the president repeated the pleas for the resignation and reiterated the message through third parties. The dilemma for Fujimori was agonizing in the extreme, because he needed both his associate and the U.S. government to survive, "but to fire Montesinos he had to fire himself."[40] Montesinos refused to budge and insisted that everything would soon blow over and even threatened to use troops under his command to stage a coup against the president. Fujimori was left with no choice but to act on his own to try to salvage his political career and most importantly his legacy. On Saturday, 16 September 2000, at 9:00 p.m., he went on national television to announce that first of all he was deactivating SIN and secondly that he was also convoking new elections for president and for congress. He specified that he was not running again for office and that he was reducing his presidential term to one year. Some have criticized Fujimori for being a coward and not renouncing immediately, but actually he was taking a large risk by staying in Lima, a decision that revealed courage under adversity.[41]

The president benefited from strong U.S. support, and American diplomats diligently strove hard to implement the formula of a Fujimori administration without Montesinos. For the U.S. government, this variation on "dictator disposal" promised to deliver an orderly transition and above all to avoid a messy coup attempt. Fear that a cornered Montesinos would engineer a military revolt was the primary motivation behind U.S. actions. Other Latin American countries, most notably Brazil, also shared this fear about a coup, and the secretary general of the Organization of American States, César Gaviria, expressed the continent's collective repugnance against any return to military regimes.[42]

The clock was ticking for Montesinos because he had to act before the congress approved the president's request to dissolve SIN. As incentives for departure, Fujimori gave him a severance payment of $15,000,000. Meanwhile the Peruvian Foreign Ministry worked overtime to find him refuge in a foreign country. The United States, Brazil, and Spain, and Secretary General Gaviria were likewise contacting countries willing to provide safe haven for the disgraced associate. Almost all countries gave negative responses, and only Panama with its traditional open policy of welcoming all foreigners under tourist visas said that he could come. The U.S. government and Secretary General Gaviria did claim that the Panamanian tourist visa could be transformed into political asylum and urged Montesinos to go to Panama as a first step. Montesinos foolishly abandoned his position of power in SIN and flew to Panama on 23 September with his official mistress.[43]

The consummate gambler had miscalculated, because once he left Peru, he no longer posed a threat and consequently ceased to be an urgent priority for the U.S. government. Panama, as one of the oldest client states of the United States, was sure to grant asylum, but only at a price. Long experience in dealing with Washington had taught Panamanian rulers not to do anything without receiving something in return, because Great Powers have a bad habit of forgetting past favors. While Montesinos was in Lima, Washington was willing to reward Panama much more splendidly than after he left Peru. After his departure his value to the U.S. government dropped so much that for Panama the sharply reduced benefits were no longer worth the bad press of harboring a known criminal. Simultaneously Spain had obtained safe haven for him in Morocco, but for unclear reasons, either the offer collapsed or Montesinos refused to go to spend the rest of his life in that Arab country; if the latter was the case, he made another big mistake.[44]

Fujimori still needed Montesinos even if he was in Panama. The immediate task was to complete his last year, but to do so, he required a congress that would not undertake investigations or threaten to remove him from office. As will be recalled, Montesinos created the Fujimorista majority in the National Assembly by bribing 12 deputies to switch parties, but already on 17 September, the day after Fujimori's speech shortening his presidential term to one year, a first deputy bolted from the government coalition. Discontent was spreading inside the Fujimorista majority, and Montesinos made repeated telephone calls from Panama to the wavering deputies to keep them loyal to the regime. The line held firm, and when on 12 October the opposition made the first attempt to censure the congressional leadership, the motion failed.[45]

Everything indicated that Fujimori was going to be able to complete his last year as president and to save his political legacy by shifting all the blame for any misdeeds on his former associate. But this idyllic scenario came crashing down when Montesinos reappeared in Peru on 23 October, almost a month after his departure. When Panama refused to grant asylum, Montesinos belatedly realized the error of having left Peru without a firm guarantee of safe haven in any foreign country. To try to correct the error, he decided to return to Peru to use his surviving power base to negotiate a more advantageous deal. When the president closed the Lima airport to the private plane of Montesinos, the airplane landed in Guayaquil, Ecuador. During a long and heated telephone conversation with the president while the plane sat on the tarmac, Montesinos reminded Fujimori that they were Siamese twins, and if one fell the other inevitably dragged down the other; the former associate may have also threatened the president with revealing videos of their criminal activities. The two men failed to reach any understanding in their final conversation, which marked their final and complete break. A defiant Montesinos took off on his plane and through his contacts secured permission to land in a practically deserted military air strip at Pisco in southern Peru.[46]

Montesinos immediately went undercover but did not disappear from view. Up to this moment the conflict with the president had generated many rumors but had largely stayed behind closed doors until on October 24 Montesinos appeared on national radio to accuse Fujimori of being a coward for hiding behind his geishas and not assuming personal responsibility for his presidency. This insult added to injury was too much for Fujimori, who putting on a bullet-proof vest and a helmet, led commando teams of soldiers and policemen to search for Montesinos in Lima neighborhoods and in the SIN complexes; dozens of journalists and many camera crews accompanied the president in this television extravaganza. The raids lacked judicial standing, because no arrest warrant existed for Montesinos, and legally he could not be detained. The main purpose of these operations lasting from October 25 to October 27 was to locate the incriminating videos concerning the president. Although no videos were found, the arrest of Colonel Roberto Huamán, the officer in charge of taping the conversations, may well have provided some leads. Another reason for these highly publicized raids was to serve as a rebuttal to the cowardice charges and to ratify the image of a brave president not afraid to face bullets in the pursuit of his mission.[47]

Once Fujimori was persuaded that he had sufficiently proved his courage to the public in the television broadcasts, he halted the raids to give himself time to take care of another pressing problem. When the president confirmed that in defiance of his strict order the military had allowed Montesinos to land on October 23 in Pisco, he was livid with fury. Throughout his presidency he refused to tolerate the slightest dissent from any subordinate, and in the case of the generals, their disobedience revived his latent paranoia about a military coup. At the time of the first departure of Montesinos on 23 September to Panama, the understanding was that almost all officials, including the military high command, would remain at their posts for the last year of Fujimori's term in office. On the part of the generals, this required shifting their alliance to the president, but when they betrayed his trust by allowing Montesinos back into the country on October 23, he felt that he needed to act decisively.

Using his authority as commander in chief, he dismissed officers from key command positions and sometimes he had them taken away in handcuffs. Knowing that he had the full support of the U.S. government, Fujimori then demanded the resignation of the entire military high command. Such an ultimatum in previous decades meant triggering a military coup, but this time the generals hesitated. U.S. officials had been repeatedly emphasizing to the officers that a military coup was unacceptable and would trigger sanctions against the Peruvian economy. Even the commander of the U.S. Southern Command came to Lima to deliver this message personally to any doubting Peruvian generals. The choice for the generals was clear: stage a coup or resign. The past preference of Montesinos for appointing mediocre and submissive generals without any independent spirit backfired on him. Not surprisingly, the generals capitulated and the president appointed new commanders on 28 October.[48]

Senior commanders were afraid to act, but mid-level and junior officers had been looking for an opportunity to rescue the army from the abusive manipulation by Fujimori and Montesinos. A nationalistic and Catholic movement had gained many followers inside the officer corps, and after several aborted attempts in previous years, Lieutenant Colonel Ollanta Humala felt that he could no longer wait for generals to join the plot. The time for striking was slipping away, and to restore the honor and prestige of the army, he and his brother Antauro, a former army major, decided to stage a revolt. Ollanta was stationed at Locumba in Moquequa Department, and Antauro came to join his brother and to be the second in command of the uprising.

On Sunday, 29 October 2000, Lieutenant Colonel Ollanta Humala launched a revolt against the Fujimori dictatorship. At 1:00 a.m. he led his anti-aircraft unit of 62 soldiers out of the army base and to the nearby mining camp of Toquepala. He had friends among the former army officers who provided security at the site, so his unit effortlessly secured control of the mining camp by 5:00 a.m. After attending Sunday mass with his soldiers, Colonel Humala spoke to the inhabitants in the public square and asked them for his support; he also read a manifesto urging the country to rise up in revolt against the Fujimori dictatorship. The officials at the mine faxed the manifesto to Lima, and as soon as the country heard about the uprising, hundreds of ex-servicemen began coming to Locumba. The local population strongly supported the movement, and in the face of this popular sympathy, the army officers who had been sent to arrest Humala desisted from the pursuit; in reality they secretly sympathized with him. During the next few weeks several thousand ex-servicemen came to join the movement, and not surprisingly Humala easily eluded capture. His name became a household word in Peru as he periodically surfaced from hiding to grant interviews to reporters. In that bloodless uprising a promising political career was born.[49]

At the time the Humala uprising seemed inconsequential and instead Fujimori with the removal of the military high command had seemed to gain a great victory. The reality was more complex, because once Fujimori removed those army loyalists ready to repeat the self-coup of April 1992, the president lost the option of using the military to remain in power for his last year in office. The newly named commanders, under heavy U.S. influence, remained idle spectators as the political drama of the Fujimori presidency unfolded. For Montesinos it was also the end of the road, and on 29 October, the day after the president appointed new military commanders, the former associate this time without his mistress secretly fled aboard a sailing vessel and set a course for the Galápagos Islands. He succeeded in keeping his departure a secret, and nobody knew about his whereabouts for over six months.[50]

The Unraveling

Because Peruvian authorities believed that Vladimiro Montesinos was still in Peru, Alberto Fujimori continued desperately to search for his former associate and the collection of incriminating videos. Once again the witch he relied on as a fortune teller revealed that the fugitive was hiding in a Lima neighborhood. Fujimori let all government officials know that his highest priority was the capture of his former associate, but this time the president desisted from another round of spectacular raids until he first obtained an arrest warrant for Montesinos. However, Attorney General Blanca Nélida Colán stood in the way. As one of the last die-hard followers of Montesinos, she refused to ask a judge for an arrest warrant. Under the Peruvian system, a judge cannot order an arrest until the district attorney first made a formal request, and this initial step Attorney General Colán always blocked with legalistic technicalities that no layman could fathom. Fujimori then remembered the principle that the only way to defeat a lawyer is to hire a better attorney, and he asked his minister of justice to find a candidate.[51]

The search for a suitable attorney led to José Ugaz, one of the most respected lawyers in Lima. As an incorruptible individual who had earned the wrath of Montesinos, he was above any suspicion of being biased toward the fugitive. On 1 November 2002 the minister of justice gave Ugaz the immediate task of pushing the request for a search warrant through the labyrinthine criminal system and more importantly around the hostile Colán.

For Fujimori hiring Ugaz was doubly advantageous: if the attorney obtained the arrest warrant, then the path was clear to track Montesinos both in Peru and in foreign countries, but if Colán blocked the legal process, then the president at last had a valid and publicly acceptable reason to fire her from the position of attorney general.[52]

Ugaz realized that he was entering treacherous political waters, and fearing reprisals from Montesinos's followers, he delayed accepting until he consulted an American diplomat. U.S. influence had so permeated Peru that just like in the banana republics of the Caribbean, no major change could take place without first receiving the green light from the U.S. Embassy. Ugaz agreed to assume the specific task of obtaining the arrest warrant, but when the next day the news broke that Swiss authorities had uncovered secret bank accounts of Montesinos, the government decided to expand the functions of Ugaz. The minister of justice announced that same day on 2 November the appointment of the attorney as a special prosecutor to investigate and seek punishment for the crimes of Montesinos.[53]

News of the Swiss bank accounts came to have another unexpected consequence. On November 3, the day after the revelation of the Montesinos accounts in Switzerland, Colán resigned as attorney general; later it was learned that she had been receiving monthly payments in the tens of thousands dollars from Montesinos, and she realized that tracing some of the money from the Swiss bank accounts back to her was going to be easy.[54] But even with Colán out of the way, the supporters of Montesinos in both the Attorney General's Office and in the judiciary branch were still a majority of the officials, so Ugaz had to craft a careful strategy to shepherd the request for an arrest warrant. The special prosecutor was successful, and on 6 November a judge issued the long-coveted arrest warrant for Montesinos, who promptly went on the most wanted lists of Peru and of Interpol.[55]

Barely had the judge issued the arrest warrant when that same day the police sent an intelligence report arguing that Montesinos was probably hiding in one of four likely places in Lima, including the condominium of his estranged wife. With the precise coordinates, it was a simple matter for the police to enter those places seeking to detain the fugitive; at first glance other than prodding the police to execute the arrest warrant promptly, no additional action seemed necessary. However, the special prosecutor and his staff thought otherwise, and they reacted to the intelligence report with misdirected diligence. Perhaps expecting to find traces of his whereabouts in any of those four places, and perhaps fearing that Montesinos might destroy incriminating evidence, the special prosecutor presented to the same judge a formal petition for a search warrant for the four places on 6 November.[56] Without realizing it, Ugaz and his staff were creating the opportunity Fujimori had long been looking for to save his political reputation, and they could not have imaged that their hasty response was going to change the history of Peru.

When the judge received the request for the search warrant, he quite naturally hesitated, and either he or informants may have begun to alert higher officials about what the special prosecutor was planning to do. After nightfall on that day the judge issued the search warrant but also included the disclaimer that the search was being carried out under the sole responsibility of the special prosecutor. This qualification was frequent in civil cases where the court wanted to shift legal responsibility for any property damages occurring during the search to the plaintiff, but was most unusual in criminal cases. The judge sent copy of this search warrant to the special prosecutor but by the time it arrived the next day on 7 November, this action had been overtaken by a surprising turn of events.[57]

On the night of November 6 as soon as Fujimori received from his informants a copy of the search warrant, he jumped into action. As a hunter patiently waiting for the only favorable moment to strike his prey, he knew that he had only until sunrise on November 7 to execute his master maneuver. In Peru search warrants are elaborate affairs cloaked in formality unlike in the United States where normally a few cops arrive with a crumbled piece of paper and begin to rummage through the residence or business to secure any evidence. According to Peruvian law, the judge issuing the warrant comes personally attired in his robes to direct the search, and he is accompanied by assistants, secretaries, and usually district attorneys all dressed in suits and wearing a special medallion hanging from a colored ribbon around their necks. All these officials set up a temporary office at the place and recorded on paper all the steps in the search.

On short notice Fujimori organized teams to enter the four places, but they were not under the direction of a judge and instead were under military lawyers who were not even district attorneys. And because the president could not locate loyal policemen in sufficient numbers, he completed the contingents with soldiers from the three armed branches. The whole operation was totally illegal with gross violations of established criminal procedure. Three of the sites (including the one the witch had seen in her paranormal visions) yielded nothing, and an exhaustive search of the wife's apartment likewise turned up empty. This should have been the end of the procedure, but under circumstances never cleared up, the team learned that Montesinos owned another condominium in the same building, but it was heavily bolted and unoccupied.[58] Did the estranged wife, constantly humiliated by the incessant sexual escapades of her husband, see an opportunity for revenge against Montesinos? Or was she trying to protect her small children by getting the horde of intruders out of her home?

According to legal procedure, the most that the authorities could do was to put a guard around the other apartment and then return the next day with a different search warrant for the new address. But Fujimori was not about to let his sole opportunity slip away, and by telephone he ordered the team to smash the heavy bolts and break into the apartment. The jackpot was immense: inside the apartment were 63 large suitcases, 75 boxes, and five small suitcases. Again following orders from Fujimori, the team promptly took the large hoard to the presidential palace. Morning newspapers were reporting the spectacular and illegal raid at dawn on 7 November, but nobody knew yet what was inside all those boxes and suitcases.[59]

Fujimori tried to delay, but the public clamored for an explanation. With pressure mounting in congress, on 9 November he and the minister of justice convoked the media to a press conference in the presidential palace. On live television the president showed reporters 120 designer suits, hundreds of Italian ties, and 1200 dress shirts from the exclusive wardrobe of his associate; heaps of precious jewelry and gold watches encrusted in diamonds gave a glimpse into the life of luxury Montesinos had been leading with his looted fortune. But this ostentatious display did not dazzle the reporters who insistently asked about the hundreds of videos the officials claimed to have found. Under this relentless questioning, the president and the minister of justice finally promised to hand over the videos to the legal authorities.[60]

Stating that videos numbered in the hundreds was deceptive, because at least 3000 recordings of conversations originally had existed. The reason why officials announced a low number was to disguise the frantic attempts to eliminate those videos most harmful to Fujimori, who was not going to repeat the mistake of Richard Nixon of failing to destroy the Watergate tapes. After Fujimori removed almost all the incriminating videos, the remaining secret recordings still numbered almost 2500. Because a few videos harmful to his reputation had slipped through, Fujimori must have worked under tremendous time constraints while he was desperately trying to "clean" or sanitize the collection. It is not clear whether he destroyed the incriminating videos or whether he smuggled them out to Japan. Without the missing videos, he could make a more convincing case to salvage some of his image and to bolster the explanation that Montesinos and not Fujimori was responsible for all the crimes and abuses committed during his administration.[61]

Once the videos were in the hands of judges and prosecutors, leaks to the media were inevitable, and even more so when congress demanded a copy of all the videos for its own investigations. However, the broadcast of a second video on 13 November was far from accidental. Unlike the first video showing deputy Alberto Kuori accepting a bribe, this second video exposed the slavish submission of the military high command to Montesinos. The release of this second video shattered the reputation of the generals and ended completely any military involvement in the unfolding political crisis. Clearly the video had been leaked to the media to guarantee that the military stayed in their barracks.[62]

Implacable as were the judges and prosecutors in exposing the flaws of the military, they were much more lenient with themselves. Ever since he had been a private lawyer, Montesinos used corruption to undermine the legal system, and among the videos Fujimori submitted to the criminal justice system were many recording the bribing of attorneys and judges. Yet afterwards several of the most incriminating videos containing conversations with judges and prosecutors mysteriously vanished. This blatant perversion of justice revealed once again the dangers of lacking an effective solution to an ancient question: who will judge the judges?[63]

Fujimori failed to realize the intensity of public outrage over his illegal raids of November 7. Throughout his presidency the numerous human rights violations had taken place in isolated regions and usually against suspected Shining Path terrorists; the public, eager for a return to peace and order, had granted him considerable benefit of the doubt. But the four raids at dawn of November 7 revealed a dictatorial president acting without any legal authority. If Fujimori on his own could order soldiers to break into private homes to seize property and possibly to threaten lives, then no citizen was immune from such outrageous violation of the most basic civil rights of Peruvians.

With the military out of the game, the decision on the fate of the Fujimori presidency fell to the congress largely by default. Since the failure on 12 October to censure the Fujimorista congressional leadership, the national assembly outwardly appeared in no rush to challenge the regime. By an almost unanimous vote on 5 November 2000, the congress approved the constitutional amendment proposed by Fujimori to have his presidential term end on 28 July 2001. The amendment also prohibited the reelection of a presidential incumbent, and the Fujimorista congressional leadership believed that this concession sufficed to appease the opposition parties. But when several deputies demanded the creation of a special commission to investigate the crimes of Vladimoro Montesinos, the Fujimorista leadership delayed and blocked the presentation of the motion before the full congress.[64]

The refusal to create the special commission triggered a revolt among the deputies. Montesinos from his exile saw an opportunity to obtain revenge, and he persuaded the swing deputies to vote against the Fujimorista congressional leadership. One deputy publicly stated that Fujimori was planning to flee the country and had already loaded baggage aboard the presidential airplane, but official spokesmen vigorously denied the accusations. On November 13 by a vote of 64 to 51 the deputies voted no confidence in their congressional leadership and later that same day unanimously approved the creation of a special commission to investigate the crimes of Montesinos. The prediction about being Siamese twins was turning out to be true, and Fujimori could only watch helplessly as the life flowed out of his mortally wounded presidency.[65]

Fujimori had staged a big public event at noon that same day in a distant part of Lima. As the media gathered to report on his statements, it soon became clear that he was a no show; hours later it was learned that he had secretly gone in the opposite direction to the international airport. That same 13 November he left aboard the presidential plane at 11:30 a.m. and flew to Brunei to participate in a previously scheduled Asian economic summit. He carried a huge amount of luggage with him, and some of the suitcases were later identified to have been among those seized in the illegal raid on the condominium of Montesinos. Official spokesmen continued to deny that Fujimori had fled, and business continued as usual at the presidential palace under the assumption that he was returning after completing his Asian trade tour.[66]

The Transition

By leaving precipitously on 13 November 2000, Alberto Fujimori preferred to err on the side of caution, but his hasty and secret flight did open him up to charges of cowardice. He was afraid that if he stayed in Peru, after the congress impeached him, he might be sentenced to imprisonment. Yet his removal from office was far from a foregone conclusion, and with his remaining congressional bloc he could delay impeachment proceedings. And if he could procrastinate into early 2001, the U.S. Embassy was sure to urge the deputies to let the president reach the end of his term on 28 July 2001. But having to deal with a congress in the hands of the opposition during all that time was highly unpalatable to a dictator who did not tolerate any questioning of his authority; the thought of returning to the independent congress existing before his self-coup of April 1992 was simply unacceptable. The previously scheduled trade trip to Asia provided good cover to make his escape and still left open the slight possibility of a return as he watched events unfold in the congress from a safe distance.

As expected, the congress was slow to react; the easy part had been to vote out the Fujimorista congressional leadership on 13 November, but to get the deputies to agree on a new slate proved much harder. After extensive discussion and negotiation, the deputies settled on Valentín Paniagua to be the next chair of the congress. He was a good compromise candidate for the political establishment, because he lacked an individual power base and his political party was one of the smallest in Peru. His election on 16 November was revealing in another sense, because Paniagua received 64 votes in favor and 51 against, the same numbers of the no confidence motion of 13 November.[67] The vote on 16 November confirmed that the Fujimorista congressional bloc was still standing together; although the president had lost control of the legislative agenda, he still could block any attempt to remove him from office. And the 51 deputies were on his side not just out of loyalty but also out of self-interest, because they knew that any extensive inquiry into the president inevitably was sure to expose their criminal misdeeds.

This optimistic analysis of his congressional bloc might have persuaded Fujimori to tough it out and try to come back to hang on until the end of his term on 28 July 2001, but a second vote later that same 16 November dampened any last hopes. By a vote of 54 in favor, the assembly retroactively restored to their positions the three judges the Fujimorista assembly had removed from office in May 1997 when they had declared that the president was ineligible to run for a second reelection in 2000. The vote of 54 was actually smaller than the 64 who had voted in the elections for chair of the congress, but on the nay side the results were terribly disappointing. Rather than the expected 51 votes against the bill, only six voted no and five abstained: where were the rest of the Fujimorista deputies?[68]

The absence of the president certainly demoralized the deputies, and Fujimori hastily concluded that his congressional bloc was too weak a reed to save his presidency and even to keep him out of prison. The next day, on 17 November, he ordered the presidential airplane to fly from Brunei to Tokyo, Japan. Deep contemplation in the Japanese capital with the spirits of his ancestors persuaded him after a few days that he had taken the right decision. On 19 November he telephoned the Peruvian prime minister to say that the next day he was faxing his resignation as president. The prime minister was shocked, and his first reaction was to telephone the U.S. ambassador before contacting any Peruvian official; the submissiveness of Peru had fallen to such a low point that no change in high-level personnel could take place without first obtaining the approval of the U.S. Embassy. On 20 November Fujimori faxed from Tokyo his resignation as president of Peru to the assembly in Lima. The next day seven deputies bolted his party, reducing his congressional bloc to 45 seats.[69]

Also on 21 November the assembly rejected his resignation on the legal technicality that in Peru any presidential decision to be valid required the signature and seal of a cabinet minister. Instead the deputies declared the presidency to be vacant because of the moral incapacity of Fujimori. Intense negotiations and bargaining had been taking place since the arrival of the faxed resignation of Fujimori to determine who would serve as interim president of Peru. According to Alejandro Toledo, the congress had resolved to elect a deputy from his congressional bloc to be the next president, but he felt that having one of his followers occupy this position might actually hurt his chances to win the presidential election of April 2001. After consultation with former presidents and candidates, the choice to fill the interim position fell on the recently elected chair of the assembly, Valentín Paniagua, who was acceptable to all parties. By a vote of 62 in favor, nine abstentions, and only nine opposed, the assembly elected him the interim president on 21 November, and the next day he formally took the oath of office. News of the change of government persuaded Lieutenant Colonel Ollanta Humala to end his revolt. Surrounded by throngs of protective civilians who prevented the police from arresting him, he slowly made his way to Lima from southern Peru. Only when he reached the capital did he surrender to military authorities who arrested and charged him with criminal insubordination.[70]

Paniagua was supposed to fill out the unfinished part of Fujimori's shortened presidential term until 28 July 2001 when he would hand over the office to the candidate who won the 8 April elections. The general expectation was that with the fall of the dictatorship Peru was entering a period of prosperity, honesty, openness, and democratic practices. Rooting out the corruption of the past was the highest priority for the interim government, and Paniagua appointed to key positions the most respected and capable Peruvians in the country; as one example, he picked Javier Pérez de Cuellar, the former UN secretary general and defeated candidate of 1995, as his prime minister. Theoretically Paniagua had extraordinary powers, because in a constitutionally questionable move, the assembly refused to elect a new chair, so simultaneously he occupied the two positions of president of Peru and chair of the congress. Not wishing to antagonize the trust of his colleagues by a noisy resignation, he quietly delegated the vast majority of legislative duties to the vice chair of the congress, and Paniagua wisely stayed away from most congressional events during his interim presidency.[71]

In spite of heading simultaneously the legislative and executive branches, everyone knew that he lacked major political support to undertake substantial changes either in the economy or inside the government. Panigua strongly supported the congressional investigations into the crimes of the Fujimori administration, and he kept José Ugaz as special prosecutor. Another easy measure was passage of a bill granting amnesty on 22 December 2000 for all the civilian and military participants in 29 October uprising against the Fujimori dictatorship. Around the congressional building crowds numbering in the thousands had gathered to demand approval of this amnesty. The law releasing the rebels from prison also reinstated in the army all the military personnel, including its leader Lieutenant Colonel Ollanta Humala, thereby clearing the path for a very promising political career in the future.[72] But what the congress did not even consider was the need to extend terms of office for at least another year, because the seven months of the Paniagua administration (including the long holiday season of Christmas and New Year's when the whole country shut down) were clearly insufficient to dismantle the Fujimorista system of corruption.

It was in the political interest of the deputies to prolong their terms at least for another year to prepare their reelection campaigns. Everyone agreed that the corruption under Fujimori had been rampant and needed to be pruned but the same consensus did not exist about destroying its root causes. Corruption has been the lubricating oil that drives the Peruvian political system, and just like too much oil damages the engine as happened under Fujimori, inadequate lubrication leads to a halt. Seven months of honest government under Paniagua was the maximum that the political establishment could tolerate without having to make fundamental changes, while for his part candidate Toledo did not want to see dissipate his status as the favorite for the presidential election.

The failure to extend the terms by another year to 2002 meant that the highest priority for the deputies became not starting the process of transforming Peru but obtaining their reelection. Frantically deputies campaigned in their districts, and the instinct of political survival displaced any interest in adopting long-overdue structural reforms. During November 2000 congress for the first time had played a decisive role in shaping the history of the country, but perhaps the responsibility had been too much a burden to bear, and the legislature gradually returned to its more traditional passive role. When on 23 January 2001 the attorney general began handing copies of the videos of Vladimiro Montesinos to the assembly, astute deputies saw the opportunity to gain political cover for their inaction. Over the next months the assembly selectively released the videos to the media and thus provided graphic entertainment to the public. The expectation about discovering the next person implicated in future video releases created a sense of suspense that not even the best television soap operas could match. As the deputies joined citizens in effusively expressing their shock at the blatant corruption depicted in the videos, nobody seemed to care that the congress was doing very little to prevent the reoccurrence of those criminal acts.[73]

Voters easily deluded themselves into believing that the elections on 8 April 2001 would eradicate the corrupt legacy of the Fujimori dictatorship. They did not realize that the three main candidates held the same extreme free market views of Fujimori that had already brought so much suffering to many segments of the Peruvian population. On the right Lourdes Flores openly espoused capitalism, while on the center the favorite Alejandro Toledo promised to put a human face on the free market and even pledged a presidency for the poor. Supposedly on the left was Alán García the nominee of the political party APRA. He was trying to make a political comeback after his disastrous presidency of 1985–1990 and his forced political exile of nine years.[74]

The most misleading of the three was former president García, who although running on a leftist populist platform was leaning toward the United States and was far advanced on the path to become a free market zealot. The dark-skinned Toledo was only slightly less misleading when he claimed to have the magic formula to make capitalism work for the improvement of the poor, but his campaign style exposed the hollowness of his promises. When in Lima, he usually appeared attired as a businessman eager to reassure international investors of his capitalist credentials, but in the countryside he normally dressed in the local native garments, as part of his campaign strategy to become the first president of Indian features. Blatantly he played the race card against the white Flores, and the election of 8 April was shaping out to be a contest between white and dark-skinned Peru.[75]

Polls showed that the vote was fragmented among the three main candidates and the other minor contenders. Because nobody could obtain the constitutional minimum of 50 percent of the votes on 8 April 2001, a runoff election was inevitable. The illegitimate daughter of Toledo surfaced at this time to demand that the candidate recognize his paternity, and this personal issue hurt his poll numbers. More serious was the circulation of a hospital document reporting his intoxication with cocaine; this leak was maliciously motivated and the report formed part of the materials Montesinos had accumulated to keep Toledo under control. The videos showing Toledo engaged in sordid sex acts with prostitutes while consuming cocaine were sure to destroy his candidacy, but why did the media receive only the dry medical report? Once Peruvians had become accustomed to the graphic Vladivideos of people caught doing shameful acts, formal written reports no longer generated the same sense of outrage: they could convict a person in judicial trials but not in the court of public opinion.[76]

Clearly the intent of leaking the cocaine report had been to weaken but not to destroy the Toledo candidacy. As Flores struggled to escape her image as a privileged white girl of Lima high society, the ranking of García in the polls rose, and on of 8 April he was able to snatch the second place position away from her. His political recovery was far from complete, and the business community remembered with dread the disastrous economic policies of his presidency. He was a consummate speaker and easily won the presidential debate on 19 May, where he did not hesitate to bring up the charge of cocaine consumption by Toledo. However, the eloquence of García could not compensate for his forced absence from the movement to drive out Fujimori. In contrast Toledo, by his participation in the March of the Four Corners in July 2000 and other anti-government rallies, had become the face of the opposition movement. Perhaps inevitably, Toledo won the runoff election on 3 June 2001 with 53 percent of the vote to 47 percent for García.[77]

What was remarkable was not that Toledo had won by the comfortable margin of 6 points but that García in spite of all the baggage of his failed presidency, had succeeded in receiving such a large percentage of the popular vote. More significantly, he had regained his position as the undisputed leader of his party and his name had increased significantly the number of APRA deputies elected to the national assembly.[78] Not surprisingly, the business community decided to take a second look at García, and a growing number of CEOs began to regard him as a viable alternative to occupy the presidency in the future.

Days before the election, interim president Paniagua came to the conclusion that irrespective of who won, little was going to change in Peru. Perhaps regretting that he had not done more during his brief term to push for at least the start of a process of transformation, he decided in his last full month in office to make one last gesture. Because none of the congressional commissions slowly investigating the crimes of Fujimori and Montesinos were directly studying human rights violations, Paniagua decided to fill this void by using his executive powers to create a Truth and Reconciliation Commission (*Comisión de la Verdad y de la Reconciliación*). Human rights activists had been lobbying him intensively for months, but perhaps not wishing to turn this into an issue during the presidential campaign, he had held off action until the day after the elections; on 4 June the interim presidency published the decree creating the Truth and Reconciliation Commission and charging it with investigating the political violence during the 20-year-long war against Shining Path. The primary function of the commission was to collect testimonies from the victims of political violence across the country. Without congressional authorization, the commission lacked subpoena powers to summon witnesses and to collect evidence from the armed forces and other government agencies. But in an interesting innovation, the Truth Commission had the authority to recommend cases for prosecution to the Attorney General's Office whenever the evidence uncovered revealed criminal acts.[79]

Paniagua was the creator of the Truth Commission, but it was up to the incoming Toledo administration to determine its future. For the president-elect, his highest priority was to follow in the tradition of rulers of banana republics in the Caribbean, whose first step before taking office has been to visit Washington to receive instructions. Senior American officials were particularly interested in meeting him, because he represented in one way a break with past rulers in Peru and in the Caribbean. Traditionally the U.S. government relied on dictators and members of the white elite to keep the masses submissive and exploited in their countries, but a purely white formula was not bringing the same favorable results as before. Already the example of Fujimori of Japanese descent had shown that non-whites could be as effective if not more so than traditional white rulers, and in 2001 with Toledo Washington was experimenting with the formula of having a dark-skinned person of Indian factions ruling for the benefit of Wall Street. Toledo hit it off wonderfully with U.S. officials and in particular with President George W. Bush. Toledo justified his pre-inaugural visit to the United States and then to European countries as a way to secure financing, investment, and assistance for Peru.[80] Although these promises largely turned out to be hollow, Toledo proved no less diligent in trying to meet the requests of the global financial community once he took office as president.

Chapter 4

Initial Attempts at Transformation

For it is proper to consider not only what is the best constitution but also what is the one possible of achievement, and likewise also what is the one that is easier and more generally shared by all states.—Aristotle[1]

Venezuela: New Constitution and Task Forces

The landslide victory of Hugo Chávez on 6 December 1998 was a turning point in the history of Venezuela. The president-elect wanted to make drastic transformations, but the opposition's maneuver of separating the presidential from the legislative elections left him without a majority in congress, while the judiciary branch could well block his agenda. To bypass these institutional barriers, he had made the convocation of a constitutional convention his highest priority. As president-elect he issued an ultimatum on 5 January 1999 that if the congress did not convoke a constitutional convention by 15 February, he would do so on his own. And to stress his determination, on his inauguration on 2 February he swore "on this moribund constitution" to give Venezuelans a new governing charter.[2]

The political opposition never forgave him for the insulting reference to the 1961 Constitution, for the Fourth Republic had raised and fed generations of traditional politicians. After his election the two largest parties were busily organizing coalitions to block the calling of a constitutional convention, but Chávez had already anticipated this dilatory move. Later in the afternoon of the same day of his inauguration he issued a decree calling for a referendum to decide whether the people wanted a constitutional convention. This audacious move also showed the country who was in charge and revealed a president willing to lead even in the grey areas of questionable constitutionality. By this brilliant political stroke, Chávez turned the tables on the opposition in Congress. The political coalitions that had been adequate to block the bill convoking a constitutional convention could not muster the votes necessary to repeal the president's decree, while the ecstatic crowds of Chavistas milling around the Capitol building after the inauguration made the legislators hesitant to react. An ambiguous clause in the 1961 Constitution did grant some legal cover for this referendum, and Chávez adroitly maneuvered to obtain the acquiescence of the Supreme Court, itself mired in many controversies of its own making.[3]

Popular enthusiasm guaranteed the approval on 25 April 1999 of the referendum authorizing the convocation of a constitutional convention. The next step was the election of delegates on 25 July, and in a major break with past practice, Chávez prohibited party lists. Candidates retained their affiliation but won only as individuals and not because of their ranking in a party list. Popular enthusiasm had exceeded all expectations, and a large number of candidates ran for the 131 seats in the convention. Because 96 percent of the winning delegates claimed to support Chávez, the election seemed to be another resounding success, but in actual practice they operated as an independent body. When its sessions began on 3 August, Chávez, in what later turned out to be a mistake, delegated most of the task of composing a new constitution to his trusted confidant Luis Miquilena who was elected chair of the convention. The president concentrated on running the machinery of government while the delegates carried an open process of consulting large segments of the population in open meetings.[4]

As the delegates worked on writing a new text, Chávez was already far advanced in his goal of changing the political landscape of the country. Just a few weeks after his inauguration, an examination of finances confirmed that he had few or no resources to work with. He soon began taking steps to increase the revenue from oil production, but he knew that at least a year if not longer was required to see any significant results. He wanted right away to show the people that the government was doing something for them and that his presidency was not just business as usual. And politically, he knew that he had to sustain the popular momentum for change if he was to secure approval of the new constitution.

He had always planned to give the military a prominent role in his government, and since his inauguration he had appointed retired officers or those on leave to hold important civilian positions. He had great trust in the military, because after a life spent in the army, he believed that the institution embodied all that was best, noble, and patriotic in Venezuela. Yet ever since the Caracazo massacre of 27 February 1992, the people looked at the army as an occupying force existing only to repress poor people. Inspiring himself on the example of the Revolutionary Military of Peru under General Juan Velasco, he took the anniversary of the Caracazo to launch Plan Bolívar 2000, a vast civic action program on a scale never before seen in Venezuela.[5]

When Chávez launched Plan Bolívar in a formal ceremony on 27 February 1999, he ordered all army garrisons to find ways to meet the needs of the population in the surrounding areas. Rather than a centrally planned and directed operation, he delegated maximum authority to the local commanders. In the process he established the practice of dealing directly with these officers rather than relying exclusively on the chain of command. This personal relationship with the unit commanders—many of whom he knew from his army career—later proved instrumental in shaping the outcome of the April 2002 coup.

Each senior officer surveyed the resources at his disposal, whether personnel, machinery, materials, or otherwise, and then tried to direct them to the most crying needs of the local communities. Many poor villages desperately needed medical and dental care which the garrisons provided. Army engineers directed soldiers in construction crews to repair or build hospitals, schools, and other structures. Road building, whether clearing routes for new roads or paving the existing ones, was a frequent job for the troops. At the request of residents, soldiers removed garbage piles from lots and streets. To help reduce hunger in poor areas, every two weeks the military ran popular markets selling foodstuffs at vastly discounted prices.[6]

Plan Bolívar emphasized increasing civilian participation, and as a first step, soldiers took a census of the unemployed and then directed those individuals to jobs. Chávez gave priority to joint military-civilian projects, for example in some construction sites local residents and soldiers worked together under the direction of military engineers. The same was true for combined projects with Indians and other marginalized groups of society.[7] The local communities that had expected the army to come to repress and kill them were pleasantly surprised to see military personnel come to inquire about their needs. Soldiers, who generally were from the lower classes, had a natural affinity with the underprivileged, and this effective cooperation made possible that close military-civilian alliance that Chávez aspired to create. The army uniform, rather than a source of fear, became a symbol of pride and respect for the vast majority of civilians. In a capstone of the emerging military-civilian alliance, Chávez at many public events wore his uniform, often topped with his signature red beret of the paratroopers. Even more significantly, civilians at rallies also began to don partial uniforms or at least the red berets in a demonstration of unity with the new military.[8]

As Plan Bolívar was generating popular momentum for his movement, Chávez was taking the first steps on his economic program. The ideological triumph of capitalism after the collapse of the Soviet bloc had been so great, that the superiority of the free market was the supreme and unquestionable dogma reigning even in the remotest areas of Venezuela. And among privileged groups, their belief in capitalism reached fanatical levels. Chávez, in spite of his sympathies with the Cuban Revolution, could not be immune from the intoxicating fascination with the free market. He accepted the basic notions of private ownership and the free market, although he had never become a capitalist convert such as Carlos Andrés Pérez and other formerly leftist Latin American leaders. Not surprisingly, his initial economic policy continued that of his predecessor Rafael Caldera.[9] And it could not be otherwise, because his electoral campaign had been based on changing political institutions, and he had not yet grasped the realization that specific economic groups had formed the Fourth Republic.

He had placed limits on privatization but had not ruled out that policy as a valid alternative for failing government enterprises. His new cabinet contained many new faces and excluded almost completely the old political class, but it was far from revolutionary. For minister of finance and for director of the Central Bank he reappointed the officials of the outgoing Rafael Caldera presidency, while to head PDVSA he appointed one of its high executives.[10] And even more encouraging to fiscal conservatives, he was "in the process of shrinking the number of ministries from 26 to approximately 15."[11] He still seemed committed to keeping his campaign promise of reducing the number of bureaucrats but had not yet announced any job cuts. He was enthusiastic about welcoming capital into Venezuela and already as president-elect he was making personal appeals for foreign corporations to come and invest in the country.[12]

Wall Street demands caressing, and not until he made the mandatory trip to New York City would foreign investors be assured of his free market credentials. In a pre-inaugural trip to Washington he had a friendly conversation with President Bill Clinton in the White House, but after that auspicious beginning twice he postponed trips to the world financial center. Finally in June 1999 he made the mandatory visit to New York City; in long-forgotten episodes, he attended meetings with investors and even brought down the gavel to close a session of the Stock Exchange. His attendance at the Mets baseball game was a hit with the public, and he appeared to have enticed many businessmen to invest in Venezuela. And as additional insurance, before returning to Venezuela he stopped at Houston to obtain the blessing of former president George H.W. Bush and of his son George W. The photographs captured the smiles and friendship during the meetings with the Bush family, and nobody could have imagined their diametrically divergent path in the future.[13]

By the time Chávez returned from his U.S. trip, Venezuela was in the midst of the excitement of drafting a new constitution. Although 96 percent of the delegates claimed to be Chavistas, in reality many were former politicians of the Fourth Republic. These opportunist individuals simply wanted to retain a hold on political power, and Chávez later admitted that his movement should have looked more carefully at their credentials and not included them so quickly in their movement. Not surprisingly, shortly after the convention began sessions on 3 August, these traditional politicians started negotiating their votes with powerful business groups. The original expectation was that the convention would last at least a year if not two, and Chávez had set 5 January 2000 as the deadline to present a text to the Venezuelan people. The government sought maximum popular input by establishing toll-free telephone numbers so that common citizens could communicate their views. The Chavista delegates returned each week to their districts to hold town hall meetings, and this experiment in participatory democracy thrilled large segments of the population.[14]

Citizens held traditional politicians in such low repute that the proposal to combine both chambers into a single National Assembly easily passed. Reformist army officers bitterly resented the partisan influence on promotions, and in response the constitution deprived the new National Assembly of any role in military careers; henceforth promotions remained under the exclusive authority of the executive branch. The civil-military alliance received a powerful boost when the constitution extended the suffrage to soldiers. The military vote remained a fundamental element in the electoral coalitions supporting the Chavista administration. Another blurring of the distinction between the military and civilian sectors took place when the constitution left open the possibility that active duty (and not just retired) personnel could hold any civilian appointment and even run for elected positions with the approval of their superiors.[15]

However, strong disagreements behind the scenes were threatening to tear the convention apart. Miquilena supported the free market advocates who wanted to insert clauses to facilitate the privatization of certain services, such as social security, and of government enterprises such as the aluminum industry. In contrast, leftists wanted the constitution to prohibit privatizations and to expand the role of the state. The outcome was a text ambivalent about capitalism and socialism. An equally fierce struggle raged over the future of the labor confederation, the CTV, and here radical reformists such as Nicolás Maduro wanted to abolish this corrupt labor organization, but Miquilena once again blocked them. In one very damaging consequence for the soon-to-be-named Bolivarian Revolution, the convention failed to launch an investigation into the corrupt practices of the Fourth Republic. Many of the delegates were merely following the instructions of Chávez who in his inaugural speech magnanimously had called on Venezuelans to forgive the errors of the past and focus instead on the future.[16] Opposition politicians did not reciprocate the generous gesture and in contrast were avidly if not desperately looking for any opportunity to attack the president. Letting the traditional corrupt politicians walk away scot free gave an image of official weakness and also emboldened opposition figures to launch increasingly vicious attacks over the coming decade.

When the convention lost focus, Chávez personally intervened to obtain his minimum requirements of the extension of the presidential term from five to six years and the right to one immediate reelection. The reelection proved a hard pill for delegates to swallow, and they consented only when the convention adopted a mechanism to recall the president after half the term had elapsed. It took another impassioned personal appeal from Chávez to secure changing the official name of the country from Republic of Venezuela to Bolivarian Republic of Venezuela. In spite of these successes, he concluded that traditional politicians threatened to gain control of the convention, and he decided to bring it to a close by November.[17]

Chávez had failed to realize that the convention was his immediate political battleground and that not dealing with pending issues merely postponed the confrontation to a later time when he might be in a less advantageous position. His failure to insist on more dramatic changes and clearer language in the new constitution was his second biggest mistake after the failure to investigate the corrupt politicians of the Fourth Republic. A few more months sufficed to eliminate the ambiguities in the text, and with popular enthusiasm for the new constitution at an all-time high, no better moment could have existed to complete a text making possible drastic changes in Venezuela. Instead the many vague platitudes in the text later gave the opposition plenty of ammunition to sabotage his efforts to transform Venezuela.

Chávez and most citizens still held the simplistic view that changing the political institutions was all that Venezuela needed; not surprisingly, under this assumption the voters overwhelmingly approved on 15 December the new 1999 Constitution.[18] That day turned out to be emblematic for the government, because torrential rains triggered the biggest mud slides in history on the slopes of Mount Ávila next to the Caribbean Sea. The slums on the slopes of the mountains were ravaged, with shacks and larger structures swept away; the number of deaths will never be known exactly, but the numerous mass graves suggests that as many as 20,000 died buried under the water and mud. The government mobilized on a massive scale to cope with the catastrophe, and soon it was bringing effective assistance to the survivors of the disaster. The opposition tried to blame the government for the calamity, and even some in the Catholic Church called it divine punishment. Confirmation by experts that these floods were unpredictable and at most occurred once a century soon dissipated the accusations. The catastrophe literally had thrown mud on what should have been a joyful celebration of one of the great victories of the Chávez presidency and served as an omen that the great successes in the future inevitably would come paired with unexpected setbacks.

The natural disaster of the mud slide was merely a prelude to a political bombshell from former army collaborators of Chávez. At a press conference on 4 February 2000, the anniversary of the coup attempt of 1992, three fellow plotters publicly broke with him; one of them, Francisco Arias Cárdenas, went on to become the standard bearer for the opposition in the mega-elections scheduled for 31 July 2000. These elections were to select individuals for the positions that the 1999 Constitution had created. Chávez initially had stated that he wanted voters to exempt him from having to run again for the presidency, in the same manner that in Peru Alberto Fujimori had completed his existing term rather than run again under the new Peruvian Constitution of 1993. Chávez was preparing to insert a proposition in the 15 December 1999 referendum that would retain him as president for the rest of his original term, but wisely he listened to good advice and agreed to be a candidate in the mega-elections.[19]

He had been hesitant to run again because campaigning took a lot of time away from the task of governing the country, and also because as a politician he feared not being able to equal the percentage of votes he had received on 6 December 1998. He did not have to worry, because he won on 31 July 2000 by 59.8 percent, a margin higher than the 56.2 percent he had attained in his first presidential election. He had won by attracting voters not just of the lower classes but also of the middle class. In the mega-elections of 31 July 2000, his supporters also won 105 of the 165 seats in the Assembly, a percentage just shy of the two-thirds majority needed to pass budgets and to confirm appointments.[20] But no matter how many elections he won, the opposition, sometimes joined by human rights activists, constantly repeated the accusations that he was a military dictator.

After his reelection he concentrated his efforts on petroleum policy. Ever since his inauguration he had been working through Minister of Energy and Mines Alí Rodríguez to persuade Mexico and Saudi Arabia to reduce their output of oil, and those efforts raised the market price of oil from the previous $8 a barrel to $34 in March 2000. As Venezuela's oil revenue increased, Chávez decided to consolidate these gains by revitalizing the formerly weak OPEC (Organization of Petroleum Exporting Countries). In reality, Venezuela, and specifically PDVSA, the state oil company, had been responsible for breaking the oil production quotas for decades and thus keeping oil prices low. Chávez decided to enforce the quotas, and this was why Saudi Arabia and Mexico (a non–OPEC member) had agreed to reduce their output starting in 1999.[21]

Chávez wielded the common sense argument that the price of all imported goods had been going up, yet since the 1980s oil prices had remained stagnant except for brief spikes such as during the Gulf War in 1990. To build a consensus among oil exporters, Chávez proposed to host in Caracas the second summit in the history of OPEC. And to enhance the prestige of the event, he decided to visit each of the OPEC members to convey the invitation personally to the heads of state. He went on his whirlwind tour in August, but he unwisely decided to visit Saddam Hussein's Iraq to deliver the invitation. He had persuaded the big players, in particular Saudi Arabia and Iran to attend the Caracas summit, but going to war-ravaged Iraq with its crippled oil industry did not have any practical justification. The visit was a needless slap on the United States, and even though the Bill Clinton administration wisely decided not to dramatize the event, later the Bush administration used the photographs of Chávez effusively embracing Hussein as very effective propaganda in the campaign against the Venezuelan president.[22]

The OPEC summit in Caracas of September 2000 was a resounding success for Venezuela, because Saudi Arabia could no longer deny the argument that oil prices had been frozen for too long at very low levels. Even then, Chávez had to propose a flexible system to allow oil prices to fluctuate between $22 and $28 a barrel. The reluctance of Saudi Arabia to increase prices was well founded, because it shared the concern of PDVSA executives that prolonged high prices inevitably meant luring into the market new and marginal producers of petroleum. But the evidence was so persuasive that exporters were long overdue for an upwards readjustment in oil prices, that OPEC agreed to maintain the quotas in production. With the certainty of at least a decade of high oil prices, Chávez was guaranteed ample revenue to finance transformations in the Venezuelan economy.[23]

A less well-known consideration was that PDVSA seemed to be softening its hostility to the Venezuelan state. As explained in chapter 1, the state oil company had developed a great contempt for the Fourth Republic and utilized many evasive maneuvers to reduce the oil revenue flowing into the hands of corrupt politicians. But the Chávez phenomenon was something too big and powerful to ignore, and sharing some of the oil revenue with the government seemed a natural way to seek an accommodation that would preserve the independence of the company. At least this was the view of the moderates within PDVSA management, who were willing to respect the new OPEC oil quotas and also to share a greater part of the oil revenue with Chávez.

After the successful summit of OPEC in Caracas, Chávez at last could tap into funds to pour into his many social programs and could afford to phase out Plan Bolivar 2000. This program had succeeded in forging strong bonds between the soldiers and the majority of the population, and the army could return to the barracks as it handed over many of its civic-action programs to the newly elected Chavista officials who received funding from the growing oil revenue.

It was also time for Chávez to repay an old debt and to enjoy the friendship of the living person he most admired. He had never forgotten the extraordinary hospitality he had received during his visit to Cuba in 1994, and as president of Venezuela he felt obligated to reciprocate. In response to a formal invitation, on 26 October 2000 Fidel Castro arrived to a hero's welcome in Caracas. A whirlwind tour of Venezuela followed over the next days, and the two men tremendously enjoyed each other's company; both chatted for over five hours in a special edition of the TV talk show renamed *Aló Presidentes*. The culmination of the visit was the signing of agreements that supplied the island nation with one-third of its fuel in exchange for goods and services. Venezuelans went to Cuba for training, education, and medical treatment, while Cuban medical and technical personnel provided a wide range of services across Venezuela. The agreements were beneficial to both countries, and for the island nation the alliance meant full recovery from the economic devastation caused by the collapse of the Soviet bloc in 1991.[24]

A U.S. government still determined to overthrow the revolutionary government in Cuba was most upset with these agreements. Instead, inside Venezuela the visit helped Chávez because the majority of the population held Castro in high esteem as the only Latin American leader who had successfully defied Washington. The opposition incessantly condemned Chávez for wanting to replicate the Cuban model, when in reality his personal admiration for Castro did not mean ideological affinity. But the supposed imitation of Cuba soon gave the opposition the first chance to strike a blow against Chávez.

As discussed in chapter 1, public education in Venezuela had become the preserve of the upper middle class because poor families could not afford the mandatory fees. One of the first acts of Chávez after taking office was to prohibit the charging of these fees in public schools, a prohibition later included in the 1999 Constitution. Admirable as was the decision to open education to the masses, the move was very risky, and by 2000 at least one million new students had registered to attend classes. The real danger was that without the revenue from the fees the public schools could either collapse or turn into disguised holding centers with little or no teaching taking place. Chávez had to replace the revenue from the fees with subsidies, but only if world oil prices rose sufficiently could he obtain funds to keep the public schools running at adequate teaching levels.[25]

Unlike many educational reforms that unfairly blamed teachers, the central elements of the new school policy were the doubling of salaries and the hiring of new instructors to cope with the increased enrollment. As part of Plan Bolivar 2000, already the military had repaired and built many schools in city slums and rural areas. As the soldiers faded after 2001, government spending covered the costs of new construction and the outfitting of teaching facilities with equipment and libraries. Because poverty and not just registration fees had kept many students out of schools, Chávez from his first year in office decided to establish military-style "Bolivarian Schools" that supplied not only education and books but also meals and uniforms for the students. Increased revenue and the arrival of more Cuban personnel allowed many of the Bolivarian Schools to provide medical and social services to both students and their families.[26]

The larger government expenditures on education did not eliminate many of the defects the schools retained from the Fourth Republic. Politicians routinely had given jobs in schools as rewards, with the result that many teachers, staff members, and principals worked sporadically and many showed up only to collect their paychecks. In other cases, teachers abused children or coworkers with impunity. A cleaning out of the corrupt system seemed in order, and in October 2000 Chávez issued Decree 1011 giving supervisors the right to recommend the firing of unworthy personnel in the public schools. The decree also authorized inspection visits to private schools to see if they were in compliance with academic standards. However, the absence of a clear prohibition on firing private school teachers exposed a weak flank and gave the opposition the opening to launch its first major attack against the Bolivarian Revolution.[27]

On 19 January 2001, parents and teachers numbering 5000 led the first protest march against the Chávez government in Caracas. The well-orchestrated demonstration received extensive publicity from the private media that had already become a bitter enemy of the Bolivarian Revolution. Another protest march two weeks later asked the Supreme Court to strike down the decree as unconstitutional, and although Chávez organized counter-demonstrations and pledged to enforce the decree, clearly he and his followers had been caught off guard.[28] Parents, drawing upon the recent visit of Castro, claimed that the decree aimed to Cubanize the schools, and the catchy slogan of "Don't mess with my children's education" caught the attention of the public and of the hostile media.[29] Chávez decided to back down from the reform of the public schools, and his presidency suffered its first public political defeat.[30]

Chávez made the mistake of not realizing that this was not an isolated issue that could be defused but rather was just the first of many actions whose real aim was to remove him from office. Even worse, the inauguration of George W. Bush as president in the United States on 20 January 2001 marked the start of bitter hostility toward Chávez. In a sharp reversal from the Bill Clinton administration, right-wing hardliners and Neo-Conservatives occupied the principal positions in the intelligence, defense and foreign policy agencies of Washington. These ideologically driven officials were determined to display U.S. power across the globe and regarded Chávez as a mad dictator and a Communist.[31]

It was really the links with Cuba that most angered the new Bush administration. The U.S. government had gradually learned to tolerate the relatively harmless links of Latin American countries with the island, but Venezuelan oil shipments were an entirely different matter. The Bush administration was passionately committed to the overthrow of Fidel Castro and regarded generous Venezuelan assistance to the island as nothing less than an insult and a direct challenge to U.S. hegemony in the Western Hemisphere. Sometime during its first semester the Bush administration reached the consensus that Chávez had to go, and secretly U.S. agencies such as the CIA and the Defense Department began to prepare the ground for the removal of the Venezuelan president from office. The Bush administration carried out a significant percentage of its activities through publicly funded agencies such as the National Endowment for Democracy. These organizations provided a fig leave to deny U.S. involvement but were sufficiently authoritative to inspire in opposition leaders the confidence that Washington supported their efforts.[32]

The effort to overthrow the regime took on an added urgency when on 28 October 2001 Chávez publicly condemned the U.S. bombing of Afghanistan. Bush officials were indignant and outraged that a Latin American leader had dared to criticize the morality of the U.S. bombing campaign. Washington pulled all the levers at its disposal to try to remove Chávez from power and also pressed hard to secure the senate confirmation of an ambassador violently hostile to the Venezuelan regime. But the task of overthrowing a leader who had just won a landslide election in an oil-rich country was not going to be easy unless local proxies were able to do the dirty work.[33]

The education strike of 19 January 2001 had been a good starting point, because for the first time Chávez backed down and unintentionally gave an image of weakness. A separate festering issue offered the possibility of vastly enlarging the ranks of the pro–U.S. opposition. In accordance with his general principles, Chávez had wanted to increase popular participation in labor unions through honest elections and secret ballots. Not surprisingly, the corrupt labor leaders opposed inserting a clause to this effect in the draft of the Constitution of 1999. Rather than having a showdown, the constitutional convention, just as it had done with other crucial topics, deferred the matter until another confrontation in the future.[34]

Predictably, finding an agreement with the corrupt labor leaders proved impossible, so the government included a referendum to remove all leaders holding union offices in the 3 December 2000 local elections. The referendum easily passed, but quite naturally the CTV, the labor confederation, refused to abide by the outcome. It took intense negotiations and mediation by the International Labor Organization to reach an agreement to schedule new union elections on 25 October 2001. The results of the elections were mixed, with Chavistas winning the leadership positions for many of the unions, in particular FEDEPETROL, the most important workers' union of the state oil company PDVSA. However, oil worker Carlos Ortega, although he lost the presidency of FEDEPETROL, was elected head of CTV in bitterly disputed elections. Chavistas made charges of extensive fraud in the CTV elections, and in the ensuing struggle to remain CTV president, Ortega became one of the most ferocious enemies of the Chávez presidency.[35]

Organized labor was fractured along the lines of supporters and opponents of Chávez, and thus it was too weak to try to overthrow the government, even counting with U.S. support. Originally business groups with a degree of snug satisfaction had watched the divisive struggle inside the labor movement as necessarily benefitting management in its dealings with workers. As long as the Chávez administration undermined the unions and confined its reformist efforts to altering government structures, private business saw no reason to modify its traditional policy of cooperating with officials on specific economic issues. As 2001 was heading toward its final months, the Chávez presidency seemed to have completed another successful year, and the possibility of bitter confrontations in 2002 seemed very remote.

Peru: The Start of the Alejandro Toledo Presidency

No sooner had Alejandro Toledo won the runoff election on 3 June 2001 than he made preparations for a trip to the United States and Europe prior to his inauguration in July. In the manner of Caribbean proxies whose first foreign trip is to Washington, D.C., to receive instructions from the master, so the president-elect headed for personal meetings with high government officials including President George W. Bush. Toledo created a very favorable impression on jaded U.S. officials accustomed to dealing with old white oligarchs. Here was a dark-skinned Toledo of Indian features faithfully reciting as if by rote memory all the cherished free market principles the Bush administration was trying to impose on the world. The U.S. government offered to extend every possible assistance to its new ally and instructed the World Bank to grant loans because Toledo had become "our man in Peru."[36]

Similar success accompanied Toledo in the European leg of his trip, and his aides later claimed that he had racked up over one billion dollars in offers of financial assistance for Peru. Even assuming that the country had received these sums, it goes without saying that the international community does not promise such large investments without expecting a much larger material compensation in return. But independent of the exact amount of the delivered assistance, Toledo through privatizations, profits, mining contracts, and free trade delivered a Return on Investment (ROI) exceeding the expectations of the international financial community.

Special conditions fueled the interest of foreign investors in Peru. International capital is tirelessly searching for profit opportunities across the world, for as the saying goes, money never sleeps. Since the late nineteenth century foreign investors had found in certain products and sectors the opportunity to reap profits, but starting with the last quarter of the twentieth century, a much larger variety of profitable opportunities appeared in Peru, particularly in minerals. The situation resembled the one of Venezuela in the middle of the twentieth century, but unlike that country, petroleum never became the sole driving force of the economy.

The crucial decision for Toledo, just as it had been for his infamous predecessor Alberto Fujimori, was to decide if the public sector, foreign capital, or local investors should develop the resources of Peru then in demand in the world economy. The emerging modus vivendi was that agricultural exports were primarily the purview of private Peruvians, while foreign capital predominated with extractive industries. But for this arrangement to work, both the Peruvian government and foreign capital had to make their own separate contributions. Capital had to flow easily and rapidly to those projects most likely to generate large profits. International lending agencies, such as the World Bank, channeled the appropriate resources to improve the infrastructure and in at least one case (Yanacocha gold mine) even became an investor. Several foreign corporations poured their funds into developing the projects on the expectation of favorable ROI. It thus came as no surprise that in his first foreign trip Toledo received all these pledges about fantastic sums for investing in Peru.

For its part, the Peruvian government had to clear and facilitate the path for international capital inside the country, and this was the task that the Toledo administration was trying to perform. The new president was mostly continuing the policies his disgraced predecessor had begun of being completely in favor of foreign investment. In many ways the entire Toledo administration was largely an attempt to have Peru deliver the compromises acquired under the Faustian bargain with international capital. As a down payment to foreign investors, he appointed Roberto Dañino as his prime minister and Pedro Pablo Kuczynski as minister of finance, both individuals who enjoyed strong ties with Wall Street and the World Bank.[37]

The appointment of these free market zealots was a surprise to a public expecting Toledo to deliver on his populist campaign promises to increase public sector salaries and pensions. The surprise turned to anger when the press revealed that these cabinet ministers were receiving high salaries of nearly U.S. $20,000 a month when nearly half of the Peruvian population lived below the poverty line and earned around U.S. $20 a month. Toledo ranked among the highest paid presidents of Latin America, and in an attempt to dampen the controversy over excessive compensation to high officials, he reduced his own salary to U.S. $12,000. The pay cut failed to improve his image because "the bon vivant lifestyle of a president often seen dining and drinking into the early morning hours in some of the best restaurants in Lima"[38] meant the inevitable decline in approval polls.

In an effort to reverse his fall in popularity and also to deliver on campaign promises to raise the salaries of public sector employees, Toledo agreed to a stimulus package for a sluggish economy in the fall of 2001. To increase consumer spending and create jobs, the government reduced the payroll tax and increased public sector wages and pensions. The treasury paid for these expenses by ending the cuts on personal and corporate income taxes that Fujimori had adopted in a desperate attempt to retain the popularity of his crumbling regime. Because Toledo kept the stimulus package within a balanced budget, this achievement impressed international institutions, and they pledged additional sums to Peru.

Toledo hastily concluded that his stimulus package had gained him adequate political cover to pursue free market principles aggressively. He was trying to complete the drive toward capitalism that his predecessor had left unfinished. But Toledo was too smart a politician to know that the stimulus package had only a short-term effect and that he needed to distract the population from his real goals. The words "democracy" and "freedom" were on everyone's lips after the fall of the Fujimori dictatorship, and little did the average Peruvian realize that the business definition of "democracy" really meant freedom to exploit the poor and defenseless people. It was easy to start a national dialogue on the need for constitutional changes in Peru, and soon congress was absorbed in endless debates over how to reform the structures of government. The framework for the discussions was actually quite simple, and meant either keeping the pro-capitalist Constitution of 1993 or returning to the pro-socialist Constitution of 1979. The overwhelming popular rejection of the Fujimori dictatorship seemed to guarantee the immediate abolishment of the 1993 text, but not surprisingly, business groups rallied to its defense and prevented any wholesale repeal.[39]

Another aspect of constitutional reform dealt with the role of political parties, and this topic fascinated professional politicians who constantly discovered new dimensions and unsuspected nuances on an otherwise boring topic. The endless debates over bills could not change the structural weaknesses of Peruvian political parties, which other than the APRA, have lacked any real substance and have struggled just to survive. The Peruvian public had lost any interest in the topic long before congress unanimously passed a meaningless law on 1 October 2003.[40] Toledo, anticipating that something else was needed to capture the public imagination, had already settled on decentralization as the topic most likely to provide cover for his real agenda of imposing savage capitalism on Peru.

Decentralization meant shifting authority and funds from the national government in Lima to officials in the regions. The campaign to decentralize government functions also could create territorial jurisdictions better suited to facilitate profits for international capital in the Peruvian countryside. Attempts to decentralize Peru had repeatedly ended in dismal failure during the twentieth century, but Toledo believed that when capitalism performed its historic role of smashing existing political and economic structures for the sake of profits, Peru at last would attain not just that elusive prosperity but also that previously unattainable decentralization.

Decentralization in Peru Under Alejandro Toledo

> *And what does Lima think about this issue?*—Perennial final question of provincial Peruvians[41]

Since independence from Spain in 1824, two ingrained attitudes have remained almost innate for Peruvians living in the provinces. The first has been a near fanatical attachment to their locality, a passion that has driven them to defend their village, town, and district at all costs from outside control. The second and seemingly contradictory attitude has been a fascination if not obsession with Lima. The country's capital has captivated the imagination of provincial Peruvians to a degree bordering on the irrational. Any excuse is a good reason to visit Lima, and as the epigraph of this section states, the discussion of any policy question ends when provincial Peruvians receive the answer to their inevitable question: "what does Lima think about this issue?"

Since the establishment of the Republic, these two attitudes of provincial Peruvians have resulted in the concentration of political power in Lima under centralism and the fragmentation of the rest of the country into ever smaller territorial jurisdictions. The departments, the basic geographical units of Peru, increased in number to 25. Although the creation of additional departments cannot be ruled out in the future, their number seems to have stabilized at 25 in the twenty-first century. On average, each department contains seven provinces, while the number of municipalities inside each province likewise fluctuates around seven. But unlike for the departments, the pressure to create new provinces and new municipalities out of existing ones has been fairly constant. As an example, while the number of provinces has inched up from 194 in 2002 to only 196 in 2015, a stronger increase has taken place in the number of municipalities. Any politician knows that the easiest way to win nearly all the votes of an area has been to support proposals to create a new province or municipality.

Major decentralization efforts have taken place at least seven times during the country's history, the last one under the first presidency of Alan García (1985–1990). Because earlier attempts invariably called for merging the existing departments into larger territorial units, decentralization directly clashed with the passionate desire of provincials to rule their own local affairs. Not surprisingly all these proposals failed, and although the specifics of each experiment varied, an accurate generalization has been that the provincials preferred to be ruled by a distant Lima rather than a nearby rival city.

In spite of the many failed attempts, economists, intellectuals out of touch with reality, and idealistic Non-Governmental Organizations (NGOs) argued for decentralization as a key instrument for increasing the prosperity of the country. During the first round of the presidential election of 2001, candidate García, trying to stay away from the disastrous record of his first presidency, seized upon decentralization as a major campaign issue. This emphasis forced candidate Toledo to pay attention to the topic, but he made it a central part of his campaign only after García emerged as the rival in the runoff election of 3 June 2001. The decision to emphasize decentralization as part of a return to democratization after the dictatorship of Alberto Fujimori seemed to have paid off as a campaign strategy when Toledo won the second round with 53 percent of the vote.[42]

Had decentralization really been the determinant factor in pushing Toledo over the finish line in the race against García? As discussed in chapter 3, the desire for change and for new personalities seemed to have been the primary motivation driving Peruvian voters rather than any one issue or even group of issues. Once the election was over, Toledo could have safely abandoned his decentralization promises, but instead he saw an opportunity to squeeze more political benefits. As chapter 6 shows, his real agenda called for privatization, foreign investment, and the dismantling of legal protections for employees; this rapid imposition of free market principles upon the economy could only lead to massive disruptions and waves of protests. As a genuine believer in the beneficial effects of savage capitalism, Toledo knew the advantages of disguising his true intentions as long as possible to postpone the inevitable resistance.

Among several issues he tried, decentralization proved to be the most effective to distract public opinion from his real free market agenda. In his inaugural speech of 28 July 2001 he made a passionate plea against centralism and announced the creation of a National Decentralization Commission as a first indication of his commitment. The main task of this commission was to shepherd legislation through congress to make possible decentralization. Any real change meant amending the centralist Fujimori Constitution of 1993. The process for adopting an amendment required passage by two separate sessions of the unicameral congress in separate years, and consequently the Toledo administration was in a rush to secure the first approval before the session of congress ended in November 2001.[43]

The original proposal called for combining the existing 25 departments into 4 or 5 mega regions. However, the Toledo administration could not find the votes in congress, and with the clock ticking against the November 2001 deadline, it accepted the compromise of beginning decentralization with the existing departments, which were renamed regions; the merger into larger territorial units was left for voters to decide in a referendum several years afterwards.[44] The impossibility of obtaining congressional votes for the original constitutional proposal was an early warning about the obstacles facing decentralization. It should have been obvious that provincial Peruvians were vehemently opposed to sacrificing their hard-won self-rule.

The congress approved the amendment first in November 2001 and then as required by the constitution a second time in a different session in March 2002. It was up to the government to convoke elections for the 25 regional governors (the 24 departments plus Callao), and Toledo wanted to set an early date as a way to halt the declining popularity of his administration. As his desire to privatize and to push for extreme free market solutions became clear, large segments of the population became disenchanted with his presidency; as a quick fix to restore his popularity, he hoped to regain public opinion by focusing on decentralization. Elections for the regional governments took place on 17 November 2002, but in another slap at Toledo, his party won only in Callao, while the single largest winner was the opposition party APRA, which gained 12 of the 25 regional governorships.[45]

After the approval of the constitutional amendment in March 2002, the Toledo administration not only organized the first regional elections but also on 26 June 2002 created a National Council of Decentralization to replace the ineffective National Decentralization Commission, which had been mainly a study group. An official of cabinet rank headed the new Council in its task of carrying out the transfer of functions and funding to the new regional authorities. On 1 January 2003 most of the elected officials took office in what many supporters hailed as a turning point in the construction of democratic practices in the new Peru. Many candidates had competed for each office, and with no requirement for a runoff to obtain a majority, few of the winners received more than 30 percent of the vote. Without a clear mandate from the voters, it did not seem clear how they could govern effectively, and not surprisingly the approval ratings of most newly elected regional officials soon dropped to single digit numbers. The sole exception was Yehude Simón of Lambayeque, who was emerging as the only success story of decentralization.[46]

President Toledo correctly stated that international pressure from foreign governments and agencies such as the World Bank had not been responsible at all for his decision to embark on decentralization. However, once the process began, international organizations and foreign governments sensed an opportunity and funded programs to facilitate decentralization. This generosity and sudden discovery did seem suspicious and in reality reflected the hope that the new regional authorities would be easier to manipulate than sophisticated officials in Lima. The extraction of mineral resources, whether petroleum, gas, copper, and gold, was proving to be the major draw for foreign corporations to come to Peru, and CEOs had incorrectly assumed that they could obtain better terms from local authorities than from Lima.[47]

Transfers of funds were indispensable to put the new regional authorities on a firm footing, and their share of government budgets steadily grew from zero under Fujimori to 18 percent in 2007. But a better indicator was the share of the municipal budgets, which only in 2007 reclaimed the level (13 percent) under the last year of the Fujimori dictatorship in 2000. At the regional level the statistics about budget transfers were either inflated or meaningless. In a major distortion, the government padded the figures by counting the expenses of district civilian offices of cabinet ministries as part of the budgets of the regional governments. The money did flow through the latter, but all the decisions about money and about the activities of those officials still were made in Lima.[48]

Another major distortion came from funds already allocated to infrastructure projects in the departments. Of the sums the central government transferred to the regional authorities, 89 percent went to infrastructure projects, such as roads, irrigation, and sundry buildings. Lima sometimes acting alone and usually in conjunction with the World Bank, the Inter-American Development Bank or other international lending agencies had already taken the decisions about these expenditures, and the regional governments lacked any discretionary authority. That left only 11 percent of the budget available for debate, and this seemed too small an amount to excite a lot of public attention. A major goal of decentralization had been to expand popular participation in the budgetary process, and the creation of a complex set of procedures was supposed to make possible extensive consultation with residents and with both private and public local institutions. Not surprisingly, the bulk of the public input came from individuals with lots of free time and institutions with a direct stake in the projects. Average citizens lacked either the time or money to attend the many long meetings, and peasants generally lived too far away to make more than rare appearances.[49] As one frustrated citizen exclaimed, "Participation can make you poor!"[50]

Yet the limited amount of funds flowing through the regional governments was not too small to escape the reach of grasping hands. Already by 2005 many regional governors faced criminal accusations, and corruption charges drove four from office. Corruption spread unabated at this new level of government as officials channeled funds to create personal fiefdoms. The resurgence of local political bosses (*caciques*) who gained control of many electoral campaigns was another unexpected consequence of decentralization. The new regional authorities, rather than being spreaders of democratic practices, revived the corruption and abuses that centralism had labored to keep in check.[51]

As some had warned would happen, the new regional authorities began to defy the authority of the national government. Routinely the elected officials supported general strikes and opposed the activities of foreign mining companies. The most blatant defiance came when coca growers (*cocaleros*) persuaded the regional government to legalize the drug trade, as happened at Cuzco in August 2005. At Trujillo a movement was gaining force to prohibit the eradication of coca plants, and similar initiatives were at work in other coca producing areas of Peru. The many candidates running for each office meant that all the regional governors had been elected with a small minority of votes; consequently, the winners were very vulnerable to pressure from any powerful group such as the coca growers. This issue was too important for the U.S. Embassy to ignore, and expert lobbying by American diplomats proved decisive in convincing Alán García to tell APRA regional governors to stop trying to legitimize the drug trade. Soon after the Peruvian Supreme Court confirmed that only Lima had jurisdiction over the drug trade, yet the decision put into doubt the authority of regional governments to legislate on any major issue.[52]

In spite of the mounting evidence about the adverse actions of regional officials, the U.S. Embassy during the Toledo presidency continued to support decentralization as a useful means to extend American interests. The U.S. government, ably seconded by the European Union, was at the forefront of financing programs to make decentralization work. The U.S. Embassy did not just support innocuous sounding training programs but also lobbied at times to move forward decentralization. When politicians made one final push to restore the upper house in the Peruvian congress, American diplomats wholeheartedly supported the proposal. The United States, as a very conservative country, traditionally opposes major changes, and having two chambers in its congress has been very effective in slowing down to a crawl the legislative process. Latin American countries cannot afford the luxury of delay, and because the need for drastic changes has been obvious for many decades, unicameral legislatures have emerged in both leftist and conservative regimes as a way to speed up transformations and thus avoid costly and bloody domestic turmoil and possibly even the outbreak of civil wars.[53]

The U.S. Embassy tried again with García to get his APRA party to support the reestablishment of the senate. Because this action required changing the Fujimori Constitution of 1993, two sessions of the legislature had to approve the amendment in two separate years. The specific motivation of the U.S. Embassy was to cast in concrete the privileges and benefits that the Peruvian government had granted to foreign corporations, so that no future congress could revoke those laws. Any initial sympathy provincial Peruvians might have had towards a senate vanished when they learned that the bill for the amendment had been cleverly drafted so that the proposed senators could only be elected in a single nation-wide election the same as for the president. In practice, this meant that the candidates running from Lima would automatically gain more votes than any rival from outside the capital; the provinces would be lucky to win a few of the proposed 50 seats for senators. Even the Lima public perceived these 50 senate seats as plum jobs for parasitic politicians. Not surprisingly, the bill to restore the senate failed to receive the required number of votes, and the proposal gradually faded away.[54]

The obstacles with trying to restore the senate suggested a tremendous discontent with decentralization. The Toledo administration, rather than heeding the warning signs, decided to push ahead with the final test, the referendum of 30 October 2005. On that day, voters were supposed to approve the merger of 16 departments into five supposedly efficient macro-regions. In reality the government felt it had no choice but to push forward, because the collapse of its approval ratings was putting in doubt the completion of Toledo's term in office. In May 2005 the president had barely survived the struggle over the forged signatures scandal (see chapter 10), and he was hoping to turn his prestige around with a big win in this referendum. For Toledo this was also an ideological test, because his reading of economics textbooks made him a fervent believer in the administrative efficiency of the larger geographical units. Originally the proposal was supposed to be for all 25 departments in Peru, but foot-dragging and latent resistance reduced the number of those ready to be merged to just 16. The Toledo administration disregarded this additional warning that the proposal faced massive opposition and decided to hold the referendum for just the 16 departments.

Polling is very different in the provinces than in sophisticated Lima. Pollsters better versed in survey techniques and statistical methods rather than in the history of Peru were not interpreting correctly the results from their surveys and were often asking the wrong questions. Provincial Peruvians overwhelmingly were enthusiastic about the transfer of funds and authority to departments, provinces, and municipalities. But this type of decentralization was different from the one that international agencies and Peruvian economists were proposing. In the last week of October 2005, the most trustworthy polls predicted that only seven of the 16 departments were sure to approve the referendum. But because the forecasts had only one department rejecting the proposal, many politicians and analysts easily fell into repeating the cliché that the election was too close to call. As many observers prepared for a photo finish with the outcome not clear until days after several vote recounts, the Toledo administration sought insurance by trying to change the definition of votes. Toledo with the support of former president Valentín Paniagua and opposition leader Lourdes Flores tried to obtain congressional passage for a bill that stipulated that only yes and no votes would be counted in the referendum. But in a heated session on 27 October, the bill failed to pass just short of one vote of the required 61 votes in the congress. Consequently the electoral board continued to count null and void notes in the totals, thereby making it harder for the referendum to gain the required majority of voters in each department.[55]

In contrast APRA leader Alán García from the start had told his party's congressional delegation to vote against the constitutional amendment. His action was part of a difficult balancing act he was trying to perform. He could not turn against the issue that he had so strongly supported both in his presidency of 1985–1990 and during the electoral campaign of 2001, but as a better student of Peruvian history than Toledo, García sensed that the merger proposal was doomed. In a Solomonic decision, he declared that APRA was remaining neutral on the referendum, but at the same time he urged voters to go to the polls on 30 October 2005.[56]

Party officials in the departments did not always heed García's call to remain neutral, and five of seven APRA regional governors switched their position from support of the merger to active opposition. Two other regional governors also stated their opposition, and it seemed that at last local politicians realized that the safest course was to run away from the decentralization proposal. Although some still clung to the hope of a narrow victory, almost nobody had expected the stunning results. In the referendum with very high turnout, only 24 percent of voters supported the plan to merge the 16 departments into 5 macro regions. The proposal went down to defeat in 15 of the 16 departments, and only in a few cases did the plan receive more than 30 percent of the votes. Because the blank or null ballots amounted to only 7 percent of votes, the failed congressional proposal to ignore them did not change the scale of this landslide defeat for the Toledo presidency.[57]

The overwhelming rejection of the proposal was so obvious, that the government dropped plans to carry out the referendum in the remaining departments. The idea died so completely that later presidents have not dared revive the proposal to merge existing territorial units. In a rush to bury this failed attempt, almost nobody bothered to provide a deeper analysis to explain the victory margin in the single department where the referendum passed. What was surprising and in need of explanation was not that the referendum passed in Arequipa but that the margin of 50.4 percent was so narrow. Because Arequipa, the largest city in the 16 departments, was slated to become the capital of one of the five new regions, supposedly a large vote in favor of the referendum seemed natural, perhaps as high as two-thirds. But attachment to a province or department is not a simplistic principle and hides lurking meanings; the U.S. Embassy to its credit tried to probe deeper. Party stalwarts explained the narrow victory because the APRA regional governor had opposed the referendum, but the APRA mayor of the city had supported it. The business community claimed all the credit for its efforts to win approval, but the most likely explanation was that many residents felt that Arequipa would suffer if it was saddled with the problems of bordering departments.[58]

APRA leader García cleverly left an opening to exploit the issue in the future, but he always avoided tampering with existing departments and provinces. In another example of his superior political abilities, García had shown himself to be more knowledgeable about the history of Peru than Toledo who had preferred to follow the macroeconomic textbooks written in the United States. But it was not clear for how long the leaders of the country would remain committed to working within the history of Peru rather than trying mechanically to impose the economic models preferred by foreign countries and international agencies.

CHAPTER 5

Venezuela: The Coup of April 2002

And it ought to be remembered that there is nothing more difficult to take in hand, more perilous to conduct, or more uncertain in its success, that to take the lead in the introduction of a new order of things.—Niccolò Machiavelli[1]

The 49 Decree Laws

The failed educational reform, the struggle with organized labor, and the break with the United States had been the most visible signs during 2001 of a deeper struggle inside the Bolivarian Revolution. The 1999 Constitution had gone far in transforming the political system of Venezuela but had done little about the economic and social structures. Even privatization, the signature issue of the last two decades of the twentieth century, had not received a definitive response in the 1999 Constitution. Hugo Chávez was at a crossroads: he could be content with primarily bureaucratic changes or he could try to modify the economy and the society. The constitutional convention, lacking clear guidance from the president, had largely avoided the tough decisions and left the issue for the new government to resolve at a later date.

A first inkling that Chávez was preparing to tackle economic and social issues came on 10 June 2001 when in his television program *Aló Presidente* he called on citizens to organize Bolivarian Circles to support major changes. In size they usually numbered around 12 citizens, and many eager volunteers flocked to take part in their activities and discussions. The Bolivarian Circles held their first parade under the watchful eyes of Chávez in Caracas on 17 December 2001 and eventually came to have over a million participants. These grassroots organizations, besides helping to mobilize masses, inadvertently also became the final line of defense for the Bolivarian Revolution.[2]

The call to join the Bolivarian Circles received such an enthusiastic response that Chávez by October 2001 believed that he was in a strong position to challenge some of the entrenched and privileged elites in the economy of Venezuela. Because he lacked a two-thirds majority in the National Assembly, he knew that he could not get any radical agenda through the legislature. Fortunately for him, even when he had a smaller legislative majority in 1999, the president had received enabling authority to issue decree laws subject only to reversal with a two-thirds majority vote. Both in 1999 and again in 2000 he had used this enabling authority to deal with really pressing issues that could not wait for a protracted legislative debate; because the measures were generally of a technical nature and received considerable input from affected economic groups, the decree laws had become a routine and largely unnoticed element in keeping the Venezuelan government operating.

His political acumen told him that because the opposition in the National Assembly could never muster a two-thirds majority to overturn his executive actions, he could use the enabling authority to legislate fundamental changes in the economy and the society. However, for this political maneuver to be successful, he had to move quickly and quietly, because any premature revelations threatened to torpedo his efforts at economic and social reform. The opposition did not have warning of what Chávez was up to, so when shortly after 9:00 p.m. of 13 November 2001 he announced on national television a package of 49 decree laws, the news fell like a bombshell. The first thing he did was to take a final stand against privatization. The 1999 Constitution had defended a state-run pension system but left the details to subsequent laws that the National Assembly had still not passed. One of the decree laws firmly rejected the privatization of the social security system, and the implicit message in the rest of the measures ruled out privatization as an economic tool of the government. The debate about selling off state enterprises was over, but unlike what the opposition immediately charged, this did not mean a headlong rush into nationalizations of private property as had happened in Cuba starting in 1959.[3]

In the minds of the opposition the Cuban cloud hung heavily over the package and in particular over the Land Law, one of the most controversial of the 49 decree laws. The Agrarian Reform Law of May 1959 had marked the real beginning of the Cuban Revolution, and free market zealots insisted on seeing the decree law of November 2001 as the confirmation that Chávez was an avowed Communist. In reality, the decree law targeted properties only over 5000 hectares and then only if they were untilled and unexploited. Many landless peasants wished to grow crops but the owners of large properties generally kept them underutilized or fallow. In particular the obligation to plant crops on lots used only for cattle grazing angered large ranchers who became bitter enemies of the regime. Although the law sent the clear social message of redistributing land to those who wanted to grow crops, the government's main intention was to expand agricultural production and make the country self-sufficient in food.[4]

Venezuela was the only Latin American country that imported the majority of its food. The contrast with Colombia was striking, because the bordering country with similar soils and climate easily feed its larger population and exported substantial surpluses. As one solution to the food deficit in Venezuela, landowners with more than 5000 hectares had a grace period of two years to put their properties under production before they faced any risk of nationalization. Even partial compliance gained extensions, and in practice not until 2005 did the Chávez administration finally began proceedings to expropriate a handful of large estates. Until that year the government confined its activities mainly to distributing public properties to landless peasants, in a manner similar to the Homestead Act in the United States. But the only historical analogy the opposition embraced was the paranoid fear that another Cuban Revolution was coming to confiscate all the properties of large landowners as fast as possible.[5]

The inclination to favor the underprivileged was also evident in the decree law extending the ban on commercial trawlers from five to ten kilometers off the seacoast. This Fisheries Law intended to help the poor seashore fishermen who in small boats struggled to earn a living to feed their families, yet the opposition promptly condemned it as a violation of the sacrosanct principles of the free market.[6] In spite of the uproar, the direct confrontation with Chávez came not from the rather modest Fisheries Law or even the Land Law but from the Hydrocarbon Law. The two key provisions in the Hydrocarbon Law required at least a 51 percent state participation in all joint ventures with foreign oil corporations and increased from 16.7 to 30 percent the amount of royalties PDVSA (the state petroleum company) paid to the national treasury. By raising the percentage of royalties the government obviously was trying to increase its revenues, but here too the effect was not as drastic at it might seem at first sight because the decree law also reduced the income tax rate of PDVSA from 67.7 to 50 percent. The message to management was that the company should have the income to support its operations, but that the government wanted a greater share of the profits.[7]

As was explained in chapter 1, PDVSA management had mastered the art of reducing payments to the national treasury. When the Chávez administration discovered many of the subterfuges for evading payments, it did not launch a major attack on the independence of the corporation and merely asked for a greater percentage of the oil wealth. And even the requested percentage share was not an ultimatum, because the hydrocarbon law, like the rest of the 49 decree decrees, were initial bargaining positions for Chávez. He always remained open to discussing the implementation of the decree laws, and he welcomed input from affected economic groups. As a politician he was ready to compromise and modify, and it was not out of the question that he might repeal or suspend some of the decree laws in order to obtain firm support for the rest.

If business groups had welcomed the decree law as great ideals, they could have requested delays to elaborate careful procedures for a successful implementation. But the political climate in Venezuela has rarely been conducive to calm and rational debate. Passionate and highly emotional attacks have been the norm since the Fourth Republic, and any attempt to introduce even the most modest structural reforms immediately provoked fiery and outrageous responses lacking any empirical base. Even groups not directly affected by proposals joined the condemnations. Could it be that the hot tropical climate makes residents naturally prone to extreme passions and fiery outbursts?

The opposition had been roundly defeated in one election after another and was desperate to find anything to shatter the appeal of the Chávez administration. The 49 decree laws of 13 November became the casus belli to trigger the start of a movement to remove him from power, but the corrupt politicians of the Fourth Republic knew that their reputation was so low that they could not lead any credible movement against Chávez. The first person to realize that the opposition needed an untainted leader was Pedro Carmona, the president of FEDECAMARAS, the most powerful business group in Venezuela. He immediately saw in the 49 decree laws the means to propel himself to prominence and to destroy the Chávez presidency. Promptly seizing the moment before the opportunity slipped away, already the next day after the promulgation of the 49 decrees he announced that FEDECAMARAS was breaking all contact with government officials. The reason he gave was that the Chávez administration had failed to consult with business groups prior to the promulgation of the decree laws, yet ominously he also raised the possibility of calling for a national work stoppage.[8]

Such a strong response went beyond the views of many in the business sector, and manufacturing companies actually welcomed the nationalistic policies in the 49 decree laws. Out of a total of 257 affiliates, Carmona had to recur to extreme pressure and personal appeals to create a majority consensus for his harsh position. Thirty-one affiliates of FEDECAMARAS still refused in a vote on 28 November to participate in the work stoppage that Carmona called for 10 December 2001. What finally swayed business leaders to accept the hard line of Carmona was their meeting with Chávez on 21 November. The conversations began well when the president stated his willingness to discuss the regulations affecting the implementation of the 49 decree laws. However, he then explained that after the bitter words of condemnation he had received in the media, he could no longer consider any changes in the texts of the decree laws. The president felt that since the opposition had made the 49 decree laws a struggle not over content but over control and power, this time, unlike what had happened with the educational reform in January, no turning back was possible.[9]

Chávez had underestimated the force that the business groups could bring, and at first he easily smeared the proposed 10 December work stoppage as a management strike. He began to discover the strength of the opposition when on 4 December the Confederation of Venezuelan Workers (CTV) voted to support FEDECAMARAS. As explained in chapter 4, Carlos Ortega had remained very bitter with the attempts of Chavistas to oust him from the presidency of CTV, and he saw in the alliance with FEDECAMARAS the means to maintain his position and seek revenge. This joint action between the leading labor and business groups set off alarm bells among Chavista officials who feared that the work stoppage of 10 December might resemble those mass mobilizations that had occurred in the past to try to overthrow governments. Minister of Interior Luis Miquilena detected that not all the private companies were solidly behind this work stoppage, and in negotiations with bankers, he offered them a lucrative deal to stay out of the work stoppage. Apparently Minister Miquilena had exceeded his authorization to negotiate, and Chávez was not pleased with the agreement. A falling out occurred between the two men, and Miquilena left office quietly in January of 2002; his departure was a big loss for the government, because he had been effective in coordinating activities. Chavistas wishfully assumed that because of his old age Miquilena was retreating peacefully into a well-earned retirement.[10]

The deal with the bankers had only caused minor divisions within the opposition, and as an additional response the government organized a massive counter rally that same day in Caracas. The work stoppage of 10 December "was a resounding success. Caracas became practically a ghost town, with businesses of all sizes closed and traffic probably the lightest here since the dawn of the automobile age."[11] However, the counter rally showed that Chávez still remained popular, and that same day Chávez went to Barinas to promulgate the Land Law, one of the 49 decree laws he had issued on 13 November. In a fiery and passionate speech, he proclaimed his determination to press ahead and even "to tighten the screws" against the oligarchs and to denounce the business class as parasites of the government.[12] These aggressive statements fired up his base but could only scare business leaders who became more willing to adopt extreme measures against the president.

Despite the limited success of the work stoppage of 10 December 2001, the alliance between FEDECAMARAS and CTV marked the start of the offensive against the government. The opposition prepared a campaign to take control of the streets away from Chavistas and carried out a second work stoppage on 23 January 2002. This second action had the novelty of trying to have the protestors march either to Miraflores Palace or to the Capitol, the two buildings respectively the seat of the executive and legislative branches. But the participation although substantial was not as massive as for the 10 December 2001 work stoppage, and Chavista crowds were easily able to block the protestors from reaching the key installations in downtown Caracas. And the government regained the initiative when its supporters came out in even greater numbers for a counter march on 4 February 2002. It seemed that the tide of protest against the 49 decree laws was ebbing, and the opposition was losing the battle for control of the streets. Soon high Chavista officials were concluding that they had survived the worst of the campaign and that the country was returning to normal.[13]

Two reasons accounted for the apparent calm after the 23 January work stoppage. First of all, the backlash against the 49 decree laws was losing its intensity. Large segments of the middle class learned that the 49 decree laws did not threaten their interests and on the contrary actually helped them. Many business groups realized that the nationalistic policies of the government countered any ill-effects that the 49 decree laws might have; discussions and negotiations with cabinet ministries seemed a more productive way to deal with concerns about policies rather than open and violent street confrontations. Once again, the business coalition was starting to fracture, and Pedro Carmona knew that FEDECAMARAS had to inject oxygen into the fire to keep the hostility burning at a fever pitch.

Secondly, intransigent business leaders had channeled their efforts to inciting disgruntled generals to stage a coup d'état against Chávez. Rumors of a military coup had predated his election on 6 December 1998, and a first attempt to prevent him from taking office had actually taken place before his inauguration on 2 February 1999. Officers during the Fourth Republic had risen through the ranks thanks to deals with corrupt legislators whose approval was required for all high promotions, but once the 1999 Constitution put the authority exclusively in the president's hands, Chávez began to promote candidates dedicated to transform the country. The old officers had opposed the use of troops for Plan Bolívar 2000, and senior officers in particular resented that Chávez bypassed the chain of command and gave orders directly to army units. The haughty generals could never accept having to obey a former lieutenant colonel (the highest rank Chávez reached in his army career) and were outraged to have the president parading across the country in uniform and in the red beret of the paratroopers.[14]

The Coup Attempt of 11 April 2002

As soon as FEDECAMARAS concluded that the government was not even going to modify the 49 decree laws, contacts with disgruntled generals intensified, and by January 2002 the principal plotters were already deeply engaged in preparing the coup. The commanders faced an unsurmountable obstacle in that both international and domestic opinion did not approve of a coup. The memory of the abominable military regimes in South America was too fresh in everyone's mind, and the firm international condemnation of the coup in Haiti of 1991 made the generals hesitant to become outcasts. So it quickly became clear that although the generals were willing to carry out the coup, they needed civilians to preside over a provisional government. The generals and the civilians needed each other, but while the former believed that they could gain control of combat units, the civilians did not seem likely to deliver on their side of the bargain. The weakness became public when the population largely ignored the convocation by FEDECAMARAS and CTV to stage another work stoppage in March, and the organizers with great embarrassment retracted the appeal.[15]

The lack of popular enthusiasm for a new work stoppage left the coup plotters in a dilemma by the end of March. The generals insisted on a massive demonstration before launching any military coup, but the civilians knew that they could not deliver the human wave in the streets. To try to encourage demonstrators to pour into the streets, the generals tried to create the impression that enormous discontent existed inside the military institution, and that the officers were just waiting for a sign of popular unrest to overthrow the government. Having retired officers announce discontent has been a favorite ploy of armies throughout the world, but public opinion required more direct evidence. In a calculated maneuver, the generals began to sacrifice some of the conspirators, either by having active duty officers publicly state their disagreement with the government or by having commanders resign after taking a blast at Chávez. These signs of disaffection within the ranks surprised Chavista officials who failed to take strict measures against active duty personnel. Chávez and Minister of Defense José Vicente Rangel with excessive confidence believed that the government enjoyed such overwhelming support among officers that it could safely ignore these protests.[16]

Because these signs of military discontent still failed to spark a mass response from civilians, the generals stopped sacrificing their players, and the resignation of secret police chief Ovidio Poggioli in January 2002 was the last major step in this strategy. The coup plotters effortlessly fell into two main categories: (1) active conspirators who among other activities strove to confirm the participation of key officers; (2) "quiet" conspirators who expressed their sympathy for overthrowing Chávez, but who carefully avoided taking any action that might make them look suspicious. It was this second most insidious group that posed the greatest risk because while professing loyalty, they shared information with the active conspirators to push the coup plotting forward while suppressing or sidelining accusations threatening to expose the active conspirators.

In spite of the best efforts of the silent conspirators, Chávez and Defense Minister Rangel began to receive many reports of coup plotting. Because the president had a personal relationship with the majority of generals, he naively believed that he knew whom he could trust. He placed in command of troops those officers that he considered most trustworthy. Officers of doubtful loyalty he sent abroad as military attachés and left many others doing nothing and sometimes just sitting in their homes collecting their salaries. Unfortunately for Chávez, he was not as great a judge of character as he believed himself to be, and in the name of an imagined friendship he ignored too easily reports questioning the loyalty of certain generals. Nevertheless, by late March the conspirators realized that confirmed loyalists were in command of the vast majority of army units and that the likelihood of any coup succeeding was very slim.[17]

Coup plotters decided to use tricks to remove loyal generals at least temporarily from command of their troops. Because Chavez had made sure that the commanders at Fort Tiuna, the largest army base near Caracas, were completely loyal, the conspirators on 4 April ordered the troop commanders to attend long war gaming exercises in another region of Venezuela. When reports were already swirling of possible clashes in Caracas, the gaming exercises were too obvious a ploy to leave the troops without leadership, and wisely the loyal generals secured permission to delay participating in these fake exercises. Army commander Efraín Vásquez Velasco had been one of the quiet conspirators who fed information to coup plotters and by early April was actively diverting reports of disloyal officials away from Chávez presidency. The paratroop brigade in Maracay was the most prestigious unit in the army, but the coup plotters considered its commander, General Raúl Baduel to be an unconditional loyalist because of close ties with Chávez dating back to the 1980s. As an alternative solution, Vásquez Velasco contrived a plan to invite General Baduel to come to Caracas in the first days of April and then force him to stay to answer questions about his supposed participation in a conspiracy. General Baduel became suspicious that he was being framed and decided to stay in Maracay, thus depriving the coup plotters of control over the crucial paratroop brigade.[18]

As April started, neither the military coup plotters nor the civilian conspirators were having any luck and their plans for a coup seemed to have reached a dead end. Minister of Interior Rodríguez Chacín believed "that the opposition was weak and running out of options [... and] has been grasping at straws."[19] Clearly the alliance of FEDECAMARAS with CTV did not seem capable of overthrowing Chávez, but the considerable support from the George W. Bush administration might just improve the opposition's chances. Ever since his arrival, the new U.S. ambassador had been touching base with civilian conspirators with the message that Washington wanted regime change. When Assistant Secretary of State Otto Reich visited Caracas, he again gave reassurances about U.S. support, provided that the coup was not messy and did not bring generals to power. At all costs the U.S. government did not want another military dictatorship, so although a coup outwardly similar to the overthrow of popularly elected Salvador Allende in 1973 seemed the example to follow, in reality the model was the 1992 Fujimori coup in Peru.[20]

The likelihood of any coup of whatever model seemed very remote until the mounting crisis over PDVSA provided the conspirators the opportunity that they had been desperately looking for. One of the 49 decree laws of November 2001 brought a larger percentage of the oil revenue to the government, and quite naturally the management of the petroleum company had been violently opposed. Because PDVSA president Guaicaipuro Lameda rather than opposing had passionately taken the side of the managers, Chávez appointed on 9 February 2002 a new CEO, Gastón Parra Luzardo, a university professor and expert on the oil industry. The senior managers still refused to budge, and to try to break their power Chávez replaced the old Board of Directors with new loyal members on 25 February. Only two of the previous directors were reappointed, and the new members were outsiders with substantial knowledge of the oil industry. The appointments outraged senior managers who traditionally regarded a seat in the Board of Directors as the exclusive domain of company insiders who climbed to that position as the final step in their career ladder. That same day at least 68 percent of the executives signed a petition "Let's Save PDVSA" (*salvaguardemos* PDVSA) demanding the return of control of the company back to senior management; a few days later over 13,000 blue-collar workers had also signed the petition. The managers wielded the argument of preserving "meritocracy" against political criteria, but in reality the struggle was over the independence of the company and whether PDVSA would continue to operate as a state within a state. The independence of upper management became so extreme that the government made the oil company the primary intelligence target of the secret police.[21]

The protests did not stop the new appointed officials from trying to implement the decree law of November, and their diligence provoked the anger of upper management. In open defiance of the government, senior managers staged slowdowns, walkouts, and even encouraged random acts of sabotage. As the situation worsened inside the company, Carmona and labor leader Ortega saw in the crisis the perfect opportunity to rally Venezuelans against Chávez. On 5 March in a large auditorium the leading opposition figures gathered to announce their intentions to create a post–Chávez government. The assembly took place in an environment of self-righteousness, as if the participants were the only ones who knew what was best for Venezuela. And to sanctify the gathering, the Roman Catholic Church joined FEDECAMARAS and CTV in proclaiming the "Bases for a Democratic Accord" consisting of ten principles that a transitional government should follow. Since December of 2001 the Catholic hierarchy under the leadership of Cardinal Ignacio Velasco had been publicly clashing with Chávez and at the 5 March assembly openly joined the opposition. CTV president Ortega in a fiery speech brazenly announced the intention to establish a new government. Such a blatant statement of rebellion resembling the manifestoes of the Mexican Revolution seemed an incredible act of open defiance against legally constituted authorities.[22]

Carmona knew that the crisis of PDVSA was reviving the opposition, and to keep the flames burning, in his speech of 5 March to the assembly he made an impassioned call for the resignation of the entire new Board of Directors of the oil company. This conspicuous support emboldened the rebel managers who pressed harder their actions to paralyze the company. Political opponents and company managers were mutually reinforcing each other, and to try to break this deadly grip, on 22 March CEO Parra forced two senior executives into retirement. At first FEDEPETROL, the workers' union, backed the demand to reinstate the two executives, but because the leaders of the blue collar workers were still negotiating with the government, the opposition could not take their support for granted.[23]

The tense situation became even more critical when CEO Parra went on national television on 4 April to announce additional retirements and also the firing of senior managers. This announcement touched off a firestorm, and to show the country that he was solidly behind the decision of the CEO of PDVSA, Chávez on 7 April ratified the dismissals in one of the most memorable episodes of his Sunday morning television talk show *Aló Presidente*. But in what he later admitted to have been a mistake, he went on to read the names and titles of the fired managers on live television. By these actions, the government had fired, retired or demoted most of the executives who had signed the "Let's Save PDVSA" petition. In his speech Chávez also contrasted the high salaries of the managers with the low pay of the oil workers. The good life that these privileged managers enjoyed had always irritated the average Venezuelan, and many viewers applauded the tough talk of Chávez; however many citizens found this behavior not just rude but repugnant. Irate employees shortly after gathered in front of company headquarters to protest the president's actions.[24]

The firing gave the opposition a perfect incident to begin the process of toppling the government. The military plotters had demanded a mass popular mobilization before they started any coup attempt, and the crisis at PDVSA provided the opportunity. As tensions rose, a confrontation seemed inevitable. FEDECAMARAS and CTV seized the moment to convoke a national work stoppage for Tuesday, April 9, and left open the possibility of its extension and even its transformation into a general strike. The defiance was so blatant that even the government could no longer ignore the seriousness of the crisis. Frantically Chavista officials sought ways to counter the announced work stoppage and in the process neglected the bigger danger from the armed forces. The work stoppage of 9 April was serving the double purpose not only of providing the big show of public support the generals wanted but also of diverting the attention of the government away from generals of doubtful loyalty. As his advisers came up with ways to neutralize the effects of the work stoppage, Chávez overestimated his strength and concluded that this

Venezuela

popular mobilization could not be worse than the previous ones his government had weathered. Had he known about the extent of the conspiracy within the military, almost certainly he would have capitulated to the demands of PDVSA senior managers to remove the Chavista Board of Directors. But when his closest civilian officials were confident that the opposition was on its death throes, any reasons for worry seemed groundless.[25]

After his *Aló Presidente* television broadcast, Chávez met with civilian and military advisors at Miraflores Palace on Sunday, April 7, to review the government response to the work stoppage. All agencies received orders to dismiss any employees who failed to show up for work. Very significantly, Chávez approved the agreement CEO Parra and labor leader Nicolás Maduro had made with FEDEPETROL, the blue collar labor union of PDVSA. The speeches of Chávez denouncing the disparity between the lavish lifestyles of senior managers and the low wages of the workers had resonated with FEDEPETROL members, so in exchange for a generous bonus, the workers agreed to remain at their posts. Building upon the populist theme, Chávez decided to announce later that evening a 20 percent increase in the minimum wage, a figure much higher than his advisors thought was economically feasible. Lastly, populist leaders were preparing to call the Bolivarian Circles to come out in the streets to demonstrate support for the government. Already Chavistas were gathering around the presidential palace, but the 7 April Miraflores meeting ended without the participants agreeing on where to send all the supporters.[26]

After the conclusion of the strategy session at Miraflores, Chávez returned to live television to announce the 20 percent increase in the minimum wage effective on 1 May. He continued to monitor developments over the next day, and nothing suggested to him that the announced work stoppage of 9 April posed a threat to his presidency. While the opposition busily continued preparations for the work stoppage on Tuesday, Carmona was already deeply engaged in a different type of planning. In a trip to Spain the week before, Carmona had obtained a presidential sash, and while in Madrid he had also secured support from the Conservative government of José María Aznar for any regime change in Venezuela. Apparently the recognition by Spain was intended to provide the cue for the Bush administration to accept the new regime. Carmona had been circulating drafts of decrees for the new government, so that he would be ready to govern as soon as he was in power. The text of the new decree to rule a post–Chávez Venezuela was making the rounds of sympathetic lawyers and received its final substantive revision on 10 April. The civilian conspirators were leaving nothing to chance, but they knew that everything hinged on the success of the work stoppage of April 9.[27]

U.S. diplomats estimated that the work stoppage of Tuesday, April 9, was 80 percent effective in shutting down Caracas, and emboldened by this very high compliance, the civilian conspirators extended the protest for another 24 hours through Wednesday, April 10, but this second day the compliance dropped below 70 percent. As was usual with this type of protests, the popular mobilization was losing steam, and the government strove to bring this disruptive event to a close. The epicenter of the work stoppage was the headquarters of PDVSA in the Chuao neighborhood, and the proposal surfaced to bring large numbers of Chavistas to this site to counter the protesting employees. Such a deployment meant triggering a probably bloody clash between sympathizers on both sides, and the government wisely took the decision to send its supporters to Miraflores Palace a considerable distance away in downtown Caracas.[28]

The "quiet" conspirators promptly reported this decision to Carmona and Ortega who were reaching a crossroads and probably a dead end. The military plotters from the start had demanded a mass demonstration as a prerequisite to launching a coup, but the 9 April work stoppage proved inadequate to push most officers into open rebellion. The generals raised their demands and before taking action wanted a bloody clash to demonstrate that the government had lost control of a volatile situation of its own making. Dutifully before noon on 10 April FEDECAMARAS and CTV at a joint televised news conference announced a march to begin on Thursday, April 11, at 9:00 a.m., from Parque del Este and to conclude at PDVSA headquarters at Chuao for a mass rally. But the real intention was to take the marchers all the way to Miraflores Palace to present a petition for the resignation of Chávez, and the westward march from Parque del Este to Chuao was just the first segment of the longer trip to downtown Caracas.[29]

Carmona counted on the middle and upper class neighborhoods in eastern Caracas to provide many of the participants for the march from Parque del Este. As an additional source of demonstrators, FEDECAMARAS and CTV urged many sympathizers from outside Caracas to come and support the march, and after nightfall on 10 December the roads leading to the capital were clogged with vehicles bringing volunteers to participate in the march. Carmona and Ortega dispelled any doubts that the real purpose of the march was to topple the government when at the auditorium of FEDECAMARAS they announced in the afternoon of 10 April the creation of a "Coordinating Committee for Democracy and Liberty" to direct the opposition. Unlike the 5 March assembly when FEDECAMARAS and CTV had elegantly used the Roman Catholic Church to clothe their opposition to the government, on 10 April these two groups joined with all the corrupt traditional political parties to make a united front. The intention to restore the debased Fourth Republic with its privileged elites was clear, and this Coordinating Committee provided the blueprint for any post–Chávez government.[30]

When agents of the secret police confirmed the intention of Carmona and Ortega to take the march from PDVSA headquarters to Miraflores Palace, officials had the first indication that the movement went beyond a work stoppage and its real intention was to overthrow the government. The outbreak of violence in the capital seemed inevitable, and how could the authorities minimize the clashes between the marchers and the Chavista crowds near Miraflores Palace? At non-stop meetings in Miraflores Palace late at night on 10 April and stretching into the early hours of 11 April, the "quiet" conspirators suggested as the solution most favorable to their goal that the government order all the Chavistas to return to their homes. Because the Caracas Metropolitan Police was on the side of the coup plotters and only small detachments of the National Guard were still loyal to Chávez, the marchers would be able to reach the Miraflores Palace unopposed and push their way into the presidential palace to demand the resignation of Chávez. Because the presidential guard was not trained in crowd control methods, should the soldiers open fire on the marchers, the resulting massacre gave the perfect pretext to start the coup; and if the soldiers did not open fire, the marchers by force would seize Chávez and force him to resign.[31]

Loyalists immediately rejected any idea of removing the Chavista crowds and proposed instead choking the approaches to PDVSA headquarters so that no more demonstrators could enter the zone. This was the best solution to defuse the march, because if the army set up roadblocks at key avenues and checkpoints at the city's outskirts, neither participants from the surrounding neighborhoods nor visitors from outside the capital would be able to join the march. And without sufficiently large numbers the rally at PDVSA headquarters could not reach the critical mass that the military conspirators demanded. The "quiet" conspirators delayed taking a decision on this solution by wielding legal and practical arguments until late at night on 10 April the government concluded that the time to implement that operation had passed.[32]

As Thursday, 11 April, dawned, few realized that the most decisive day of the Chávez presidency was beginning. Starting at 9:00 a.m. a column stretching for miles wound its way from Parque del Este to the massive rally at Chuao. For several days the Metropolitan Caracas Police had deployed most of its personnel at PDVSA headquarters without incident because the police sympathized with the demonstrators. Around 11:00 a.m. most of the marchers had arrived and speakers such as the previous CEO Lameda whipped up the crowds numbering several hundred thousand persons into a frenzy. When Carmona and Ortega spoke, it was easy to persuade the demonstrators to take the march all the way to Miraflores Palace to demand the resignation of Chávez. By 11:30 a.m. the marchers had set out on their trek, and shortly after as a first sign of panic among Chavistas, CEO Parra and the new Board of Directors offered their resignations to the president as a way of pacifying the crowds and bringing the crisis to an end.[33]

As the marchers set out for the grueling trek toward downtown, many dropped out as the column left the middle class neighborhoods. By then it was noon, and the scorching tropical heat and the fierce sun sent many marchers scurrying away for cover in shady places for lunch or to return home. The defections weakened the column and reduced the chance of reaching Miraflores just as had happened in the 23 January attempt. A few choke points along the avenues provided great opportunities for small police units or National Guard personnel to set up effective road blocks, but this never happened. The army could easily man those choke points without provoking confrontations, but the government never sent out the orders to have soldiers fill the gaps left by the absence of the Metropolitan Police and the National Guard. The loyalist General Wilfredo Silva did take the initiative and readied his units to enter the city, but as soon as army commander General Vásquez Velasco learned through informants of this alert, he promptly ordered his subordinate Silva to keep the troops inside the barracks.[34]

By the time the unopposed column made the last turn north from Bolivar Avenue toward Miraflores Palace around 2:00 p.m., the protesters numbered barely several tens of thousands. The still loyal small National Guard detachment fired gas canisters to keep the approaching vanguard of the marchers away from the Chavistas who had previously gathered near the presidential palace, and it looked like the column was sputtering out of existence. Anti-climactic as the march seemed, it was just the last act of the whole day of protests, and because word had spread rapidly through the TV stations about the resignation of the PDVSA Board of Directors, the demonstrators were certainly justified in considering the day to have been a great success.[35]

In reality the day was just beginning as the center of gravity shifted from the people in the march to the generals in the bases. Massive TV coverage of the march persuaded the military conspirators that this was their best chance to carry out their coup. At a meeting at 2:00 p.m. in Fort Tiuna, eight generals were saying that the president had lost control and was going away. Shortly after 2:00 p.m., when just the first marchers were entering the Miraflores area, rebel soldiers began seizing some installations at the vast military complex of Fort Tiuna to the south of Caracas. To prevent loyal troops from leaving the base, rebel soldiers detoured civilian vehicles at 2:30 p.m. into the base, creating monumental traffic jams inside Fort Tiuna, and also set up roadblocks in the highway leading to the capital. General García Carneiro, one of the loyalists the coup plotters had tried to send away to practice exercises, regained control of Fort Tiuna by 3:30 p.m. but it was not yet clear to the government what exactly was happening.[36]

As a precaution, Chávez decided to activate Plan Ávila, a contingency plan to have the army secure key installations throughout Caracas. He also wanted two squadrons of tanks sent to Miraflores from Fort Tiuna to reinforce the soldiers of the presidential guard who lacked any heavy weapons and were armed only with assault rifles. When Chávez sent the order around 5:30 p.m. by radio through the normal channel to the commandant of the armed forces, General Manuel Rosendo, the later did not answer. When General García Carneiro overheard the order in his radio, he answered that he would promptly send the two squadrons of nine tanks each to Miraflores even though he did not know why General Rosendo was not answering the radio message. Because of the road blocks in the highway, the tanks took longer than usual to make the trip and only arrived by 7:30 p.m. García Carneiro had come separately and he immediately reported to President Chávez that the tanks were ready at the garages of the presidential guard. The president felt reassured and said that he would talk to the tank commander after a meeting with generals among whom were some of the "quiet" conspirators. General García Carneiro returned to his command at Fort Tiuna, and some hours later when Chávez emerged from his meeting with his commanders, he learned that the tanks were no longer at Miraflores: an officer of higher rank had ordered them back to Fort Tiuna.[37]

Chávez had requested the tanks because of the deteriorating situation around Miraflores. A last group of marchers from the column arrived around 3:00 p.m. and made one final attempt to get close to the presidential palace, but their leaders took them not through the most direct route but through a street that ended in a set of stairs. Before the marchers reached the dead end, shots rang out and soon the protestors, the Chavistas, and innocent bystanders began to suffer dead and wounded. The origin of the shots has never been cleared up, but no evidence has ever surfaced linking any of the shooters to the government. Because the secret police was already in the hands of the rebels, not even that agency could be suspected of having started the shooting. A rogue group loosely linked to the opposition seemed to be the most likely culprit, but the exact identity of the shooters will likely never be known.[38]

The opposition at last had the bloody incident it needed to justify the coup. The hostile TV media promptly jumped on the shooting and accused the government of massacring innocent citizens. The conspirators had not just a march but a massacre to justify their military coup, and in the face of incessant television provocations by the private TV owners who loathed Chávez, most generals at Fort Tiuna turned against the government. But the coup needed to disguise its military nature and had to hide behind civilians. The first leader to declare rebellion was none other than Luis Miquilena who appeared in front of TV cameras at 7:00 p.m. to urge the overthrow of the government. This statement coming from the former mentor of Chávez was an unexpected betrayal that shocked many officials. And the airing of a video (later proven to be manipulated) at 7:30 p.m. purportedly showing Chavista militants firing with pistols at protestors was the coup de grace that seemed to doom the regime.[39]

At 7:30 p.m. General Carlos Alfonzo went in front of the TV cameras to announce to the country that he had just taken control of the National Guard; because the Caracas Metropolitan Police had from the start been in rebel hands, the loss of the National Guard meant that only the army still remained loyal to Chávez. And the army support started to crumble when unit commanders began parading through television to announce their revolt against the government. The definitive blow came at 9:00 p.m. when army commander General Vásquez Velasco stated that in good conscience he could no longer support a regime that massacred its own people, and he urged all officers to follow his example. At 10:15 p.m. opposition figures began the first raids on the offices of Chavista leaders, and in the early hours of the 11th these raids spread across the capital and led to the arrests of those government officials who did not quickly go into hiding.[40]

After 10:00 p.m. the coup generals had taken control of Fort Tiuna but had failed to arrest several loyal commanders in particular García Carneiro and Silva. The coup generals celebrated wildly and congratulated themselves on having pulled off the coup as they exclaimed excitedly words to the effect "that we did it."[41] But Chávez was still in Miraflores Palace and no coup was complete as long as the deposed president was present in his office. As one key installation after another in Caracas fell under the control of rebels, Chávez felt abandoned and isolated, although he still had not heard from the commanders of the garrisons outside the capital. At the moment that he did not know what to do, his best friend Fidel Castro miraculously was able to get a phone call through to Miraflores Palace. The Cuban leader explained to Chávez, who was thinking of making a suicide defense like the Chilean leader Salvador Allende had done in 1973, that the vast majority of the army was loyal and that he needed to save his life to lead the struggle against the coup plotters. Chávez, who had been walking around the palace in his combat uniform with a pistol strapped to his leg and carrying an assault rifle, had no hesitation about sacrificing his life as Allende had done, but he did not want to endanger the lives of the soldiers of the presidential guard who were determined to die for him.[42]

In the first hour of 12 April, Chávez received a phone call from General Raúl Baduel, the commander of the paratroop brigade in Maracay, who pledged total loyalty to the president. When Chávez explained his desperate situation, Baduel was ready to order his unit to head to Caracas. Because the paratroop brigade enjoyed the reputation of being the best combat force of the Venezuelan army, its support meant guaranteeing the survival of the government. However, fear of provoking unnecessary bloodshed made the president order Baduel not to move. Other garrison commanders (but not the navy and the air force) were pledging support, and Chávez accurately concluded that he had to gain time to allow his superior forces to regain control of the capital.

The coup plotters had underestimated the depth of support for Chávez among the army and simplistically believed that once the deposed president was out of the way the rest of the garrisons in the country would passively accept the events in Caracas. General Rosendo, the commandant of the armed forces, assumed the task of forcibly removing Chávez from the presidential palace. The rebel generals were demanding the resignation of Chávez, but because he kept playing for time, then shortly before 3:00 a.m. General Rosendo accepted the suggestion to threaten Miraflores Palace with attacks and bombing. Chávez, not wanting to inflict needless bloodshed on the presidential guard and the neighborhood, agreed to resign provided he and his family were given safe passage to Cuba. The generals wanted to keep him away from the television, so he authorized General Rincón (who secretly remained a loyalist) to read a communiqué announcing on live television that Chávez had resigned the presidency. At 4:15 a.m. Chávez left Miraflores Palace and arrived at Fort Tiuna as a prisoner shortly after 4:30 a.m.[43]

A first act of vengeance was to humiliate Chávez by making him change into civilian clothes; the generals had always felt insulted whenever the president wore his military uniform. The coup plotters believed that taking the uniform and television access away made him powerless. The generals reversed their position on letting Chávez leave for Cuba, because they wanted to bring him to trial immediately on charges of having ordered the supposed massacre near Miraflores Palace. Meanwhile loyal soldiers were already trying to rescue him, and when coup plotters heard about the plan, naval pilots flew him out of Caracas. The navy shuttled him across its installations until he finally ended up a prisoner in La Orchila Island off the coast of Venezuela.[44]

Peter the Brief

The Chávez presidency had still not ended when already the process was underway to organize the regime of Pedro Carmona, whom that perspicacious Caribbean sense of humor soon dubbed "Peter the Brief" (*Pedro el Breve*). Late in the afternoon of 11 April he went to the studio of Venevisión and on live television repeatedly denounced the Chávez presidency. The venomous statements seemed to be having an effect because, as mentioned in the previous section, civilians and officers joined him in condemning Chávez, and by 11:00 p.m. the intention of the president to negotiate his resignation seemed real. At midnight Carmona left the television studio for a good night's rest at a hotel, but he was just entering the lobby when his cell phone rang with a call summoning him to the fifth floor of army headquarters at Fort Tiuna.[45]

When he reached Fort Tiuna, two other civilians had preceded him: his future attorney general Daniel Romero and the wealthy businessman Isaac Pérez Recao who had been an instrumental figure in coordinating the events leading to the coup. In the lobby of the fifth floor they engaged in a heated discussion arguing that under no circumstances could Chávez leave the country and that he must face trial. The generals in a nearby suite on the same floor were simultaneously carrying out the two tasks of completing the removal of Chávez from the presidency and creating a new transitional government; until they made up their minds, they kept Carmona pacing in the lobby without officially telling him anything. The generals had left nothing to chance, and they kept waiting another candidate in his car in the parking lot just in case Carmona should decline to accept.[46]

Even before the phone call to Carmona at the hotel lobby, he was already the favorite of the coup generals. All plotters agreed that he should have a major role in the new government, but his exact status remained unclear, because the commanders preferred a civilian-military junta composed of two civilians and one general. Carmona would be one of the civilians, but the plotters regretfully concluded that the presence of any senior officer in the junta would look too much like a military coup and was sure to cause problems with the international community as temporarily happened to Alberto Fujimori after his 1992 self-coup. The generals accepted having as their replacement Cardinal Ignacio Velasco, who had given his blessing and encouragement for the coup, but when he declined because the Vatican was sure to object, any lingering support for a junta of only two civilians vanished. An additional consideration was that Carmona had let it be known days before that the alliance of FEDECAMARAS with CTV had been predicated on the agreement that Carmona would assume the presidency while labor leader Ortega would become the vice president. In a vote among the coup generals, a majority approved having Carmona lead the civilian junta, but Ortega failed to receive even a single vote.[47]

By then Chávez had arrived as a prisoner to Fort Tiuna, but the generals still had not communicated their decision to an exhausted and sleepy Carmona who told a military assistant that he was leaving. The generals told him to wait a bit more, and then later they appeared to confirm his appointment as the new president of Venezuela. Reporters congregated to hear statements and to take photographs of this historic moment, and shortly afterwards, Carmona left Fort Tiuna just as the first yellowish gleams of dawn were starting to appear in the tropical skies.[48]

Neither exhaustion nor the high drama of the exciting moment could detract Carmona from the real purpose of his regime. At 6:30 a.m. on 12 April his first phone call went to Guaicaipuro Lameda to tell him to return to his old job of CEO of PDVSA and that he was reinstating the Board of Directors that Chávez had fired in February. By his first action Carmona clearly stated his intention to return Venezuela to the status quo ante Chávez or more specifically to restore the Fourth Republic. As is normal in Latin America, family ties remain of paramount importance, and Carmona's next phone call was to his cousin Rafael Arreaza Padilla, a distinguished doctor, to ask him to accompany him on his entry into Miraflores Palace and also to announce his appointment as the new minister of health. Many in the staff considered Arreaza a dangerous leftist and even a Chavista, but he enjoyed Carmona's full trust. At 6:30 a.m. the two men entered Miraflores Palace and the honor guard performed a formal welcome ceremony; at the presidential suite the new attorney general Romero was already starting to set up the transitional regime.[49]

The complex of Miraflores Palace gave the sensation of having been suddenly abandoned by its occupants and was deserted except for the presidential guard. The soldiers were letting into the palace anybody who presented an identity card, and among the first arrivals were several officers demanding promotions and one general asking to be appointed commander of the army. All these officers insisted that their decisive participation in making the coup possible had earned them these rewards. Civilians were pouring into the building and were pressing Carmona and his aides for appointments, contracts, and other favors from the new president. Disguised in the form of congratulations, letters and petitions were already arriving proposing candidates for jobs. This unsolicited correspondence continued to reach the mail room for many days afterwards, and to try to reduce the flow of job seekers, Carmona gave orders to restrict the entry of citizens into the building. The restriction was only partially effective, and the throngs of ecstatic people roaming in the hallways of the palace as if on a non-stop festival seemed impossible to stop.[50]

Among the people were the politicians of the Fourth Republic who besides appointments to positions also wanted to safeguard their quota of influence inside the new government. Actually, the most important visit that morning came from labor leader Ortega, who was furious that Carmona had violated their agreement to make him vice president. Nothing that Carmona said could calm down Ortega who did not want anything to do with the new regime and promptly left Caracas to stay at his home town. Without his presence, the support from organized labor for the new regime evaporated. On a more optimistic note, the congratulations were pouring into the palace, and around noon Prime Minister José María Aznar of Spain extended his best wishes to Carmona who already could share the good news that PDVSA was not sending one more barrel of petroleum to Cuba, their mutual enemy.[51]

After the Aznar phone call, Carmona returned to finish working on the two most pressing issues facing the transitional regime: a constitutive decree and the appointment of high officials. As mentioned earlier, the decree creating the new government had been circulating for days before, and although Carmona made small changes, its essential purpose was to abolish the institutions of the state and to replace them with the provisional regime. As if abolishing the Supreme Court and all other appointive positions was not enough, the decree also eliminated the National Assembly and all elected offices. Around 2:00 p.m. some insiders, such as his cousin Arreaza, pointed out that the decree was a legal monstrosity, and for a moment Carmona hesitated to issue it without major changes. The sticking point was the National Assembly, but the persuasive argument came from one attorney who claimed that if Carmona did not abolish this legislative body, then it would declare the transitional regime to be illegal. Any doubt about the possibility that the National Assembly would oppose the change of government ended when at 3:00 p.m. the Chavista attorney general Isaías Rodríguez announced on national television that what happened in Venezuela was a coup d'état. This statement was totally unexpected, and the TV stations did damage control by refusing to repeat the video containing the declaration of the attorney general. But hearing this legal opinion was all that was needed to rally many wavering Chavista militants who up till this moment could not make sense of the departure of Chávez and his supposed resignation.[52]

Carmona decided to push forward with the constitutive decree as drafted in previous days. Finding individuals to appoint to the cabinet and other high positions proved relatively easy, because here too he had been compiling a list of names days in advance. Everything was going well as his secretaries tracked down the candidates and Carmona obtained their acceptance, but when he showed his staff the list of citizens willing to hold office, a few advisers complained that the names came exclusively from the white, wealthy elite of Caracas and that most belonged to ultra-conservative groups and some were even members of the Catholic Opus Dei lay fraternity. In desperation one associate begged Carmona to include at least one black person among the appointments, but with the inaugural ceremony scheduled to be broadcast live starting at 4:00 p.m. it was too late to confirm any different appointments.[53]

The parking lots of the Miraflores complex were clogged with the chauffeured automobiles of the businessmen and wealthy citizens who had come to attend the swearing-in ceremony. At 4:00 p.m. Attorney General Romero summoned the elegant guests to the Ayacucho auditorium, the largest public space in the Miraflores complex. In the standing room only ceremony broadcast on live television, officers in their gala uniforms alternated with society ladies in refined hairdos, and the air inside reeked with the mixture of expensive perfumes. In an indication that the Bolivarian Revolution was over, the portrait of Simón Bolívar, the liberator of the country, was quietly removed from the Ayacucho auditorium. Romero began by reading the decree constituting the new Republic of Venezuela, which no longer included the title "Bolivarian," and also announced key appointments, including the return of Guaicaipuro Lameda as the CEO of PDVSA. After the reading of what became known as the "Carmona decree" had finished, the new president took the oath of office by himself and not in front of any judge and did not even bother to place his hand on the 1999 Constitution. Romero then called many of those present by their full name to come and sign an affidavit ratifying the decree, and Cardinal Ignacio Velasco was the first to sign. In the reception following the ceremony, Romero worked the crowd trying to secure more signatures from skittish guests, and his secretaries also roamed around the auditorium cornering persons to make sure that everyone present had put their signatures into blank sheets; afterwards those individuals claimed that they had believed that they were signing only attendance sheets and not the Carmona decree itself. By 9:00 p.m. most of the guests had gone home and Miraflores Palace seemed to have regained its usual quiet.[54]

In reality the ceremony had unleashed a backlash that threatened to overwhelm the fledging regime of Carmona. Even the Bush administration considered the Carmona decree to be an unacceptable way to overthrow a government. The abolishment of the National Assembly generated a firestorm, and immediately pleas appeared to restore this legislative body. Many measures in the decree of 12 April were not only authoritarian but also openly favored the wealthy. Organized labor and many members of the middle class lost their enthusiasm for the new regime and were no longer willing to go out on the street to demonstrate in favor of Carmona. The crowds that had demanded the overthrow of Chávez on 11 April disappeared, and in their place came growing numbers of Chavistas who had been emboldened by the statement of the deposed Attorney General Rodríguez. The rising momentum on the street was evident as Bolivarian Circles took their members to the street to clamor for the return of Chávez even in the face of brutal and bloody repression by the Caracas Metropolitan Police. Unarmed Chavistas risked wounds and in some cases even death to face the formations of the rebel police, while other sympathizers gathered in Fort Tiuna and around Miraflores Palace.[55]

The coalition supporting the Carmona regime was disintegrating but still could count on the support of the wealthy, the PDVSA management, the media, and less surely on the military. In reality, army backing had never been solid, for example only a quarter of the generals supported the coup, and no garrison commander had pledged loyalty to the Carmona regime. But when General Vásquez Velasco, who considered himself entitled to the position of minister of defense, saw that Carmona had appointed an admiral for the position, the general felt betrayed. All coup generals felt insulted because they would never accept any navy officer as their superior. In a public statement at 4:37 p.m. General Vásquez Velasco stated on live television that the military could support the new regime only if it made 12 major changes, including the reestablishment of the National Assembly. The public appearance of Vásquez Velasco demoralized the coup plotters, and the most astute rapidly began to take evasive action to deny their involvement in the coup.[56]

As many officers tried to distance themselves from the coup, the presidential guard was preparing to strike a counter blow. Ever since the entry of Carmona into Miraflores Palace the soldiers had wanted to take him hostage, but their commander explained that it was best to feign loyalty and to wait for the most propitious moment to strike. The soldiers were disgusted with the ceremony inaugurating the Carmona regime and right after its conclusion had begun to plot to take back control of the palace. The commander obtained authorization from General García Carneiro to begin the operation around noon of the next day.[57]

On Saturday morning, April 13, Carmona and his advisers were back in Miraflores Palace trying to cope with the rising tide of discontent. At 10:00 a.m. Carmona had an appointment with Ovidio Poggioli, the new head of the Secret Police, who had come to give warning of the many mortal dangers facing the transitional regime. Already Carmona had appointed a general to be the new minister of defense, but this measure came too late to appease army plotters. Other officials joined the discussion which unexpectedly degenerated into a silly argument over the appointment of a female journalist to a high position. About noon several officers approached Carmona to tell him that he was no longer safe in Miraflores Palace and that General Baduel intended to rescue Chávez at all costs.[58]

In effect what had happened at Miraflores was that starting at 11:00 a.m. on 13 April the presidential guard began quietly seizing control of the complex. The goal was to capture all the officials of the new regime, but after the first detentions, reports of the action preceded the soldiers, and most officials succeeded in fleeing. The soldiers did capture Romero, against whom they had a special grudge because they had seen him reading the infamous Carmona decree the day before. The commander of the presidential guard, once he had assured full control of the complex, then knew that it was extremely important to announce the news publicly to finish rallying the Chavistas. All the Venezuelan TV stations had abandoned the palace while trying to keep up with the fleeing Carmona. Only CNN, Caracol of Colombia, and Española of Spain still had camera crews on the site, so a link-up through those countries, and in particular to CNN Atlanta, finally allowed the news to reach Venezuela.[59]

Carmona fled to Fort Tiuna and from the fifth floor of the army building he continued to issue orders and messages through the Venezuelan television channels. He still believed that he was president and did not want to accept the reality that his hasty escape from Miraflores Palace at noon had marked the effective end of his reign as Peter the Brief. That afternoon the rebel generals saw their authority wasting away as one garrison commander after another pledged support to restore Chávez to power. Much as the hostile TV had tried to hide the news about the fall of Carmona, even the garrison at Fort Tiuna realized that Chávez was coming back. After nightfall loyal soldiers asked Coronel José Gregorio Montilla Pantoja to lead an operation to detain Carmona.

The coronel agreed, and when soldiers reported that Carmona was in the Inspector General's suite, he went to arrest him. The first attempt failed because Carmona was no longer in that suite, but loyal soldiers quickly detected his presence in a nearby office in the fifth floor of army headquarters. Coronel Montilla approached Carmona, tapped him on the back, and stated that he was under arrest. Carmona asked under whose authority, and the general snapped back under that of the 1999 Constitution. As Carmona was being led away, General Manuel Rosendo made one last attempt to have him released, but it was useless, and Pedro the Brief remained under arrest.[60]

The only missing piece was Chávez himself, and the coup attempt could not come to a final end without his return to power. Luis Miquilena was still orchestrating a last minute effort to prevent Chávez from returning to office on the argument that the president had abandoned his office. A substantial number of delegates in the National Assembly were sympathetic to the idea of having a third person fill the interim presidency, but the formula of neither Chávez nor Carmona quickly fizzled as the crowds demanded the return of Chávez. The presidential guard had finally located the captive prisoner at La Orchila Island in the Caribbean, and soon a commando team was on its way to rescue him. His guardians at the island had always opposed the coup and they enthusiastically transferred Chávez to the rescue team that flew him back to Caracas to greet the crowds anxiously awaiting him.[61]

The stay at La Orchila, however, had not been without disastrous long-term consequences for the Bolivarian Revolution. Chávez, a man of deep Catholic convictions who was given to outbursts of mysticism, had fallen under the spell of Cardinal Ignacio Velasco. The president did not know that the Cardinal had been the first to sign the decree establishing the Carmona regime and that the coup plotters had sent the Cardinal to La Orchila in a last ditch attempt to persuade Chávez to sign the resignation as president. Obviously the Cardinal failed in his assigned mission but he did not come back empty handed and obtained something almost as good. In long walks on the tropical beach praying together with the cardinal, Chávez experienced a mystical born-again conversion. He asked forgiveness from the cardinal and promised to do everything possible to reconcile the Venezuelan people in one big happy family. As an indication of his profound conversion, he carried a crucifix on his return trip back to Miraflores Palace. When he landed on 14 April at 4:30 a.m. to the roars of the cheering crowds anxiously waiting for him, he held a crucifix in his hand, and the ecstatic followers believed that an avenging angel had arrived to give just punishment to all those who had betrayed him and had brought so much suffering and turmoil to the Venezuelan people.[62]

CHAPTER 6

Two Decisive Turns in 2002

For Colombia and Peru 2002 turned out to be a decisive year when the policies in both countries turned in different directions. In Colombia Álvaro Uribe Vélez came to power, moved the country even farther to the right, and imposed the most authoritarian regime in the country's history. Instead in Peru a nationalistic backlash marked the start of a still ongoing process to limit policies favoring the free market and free trade.

Colombia: The Rise of Álvaro Uribe Vélez

> *If Colombians feel they are at war, and want a war leader, Uribe will be the man.*—U.S. Ambassador Anne W. Patterson[1]

Public frustration at the seemingly endless insurgency raging in Colombia since the 1960s was responsible for the emergence of Álvaro Uribe Vélez in 2002. During the twentieth century Colombian governments tried different formulas to bring peace to the country, and in the presidential campaign of 2002 Uribe promised to end the conflict. Previous administrations had successfully demobilized several rival guerrilla groups, most notably M-19 and the People's Liberation Army (*Ejército Popular de Liberación*) or EPL. But the Revolutionary Armed Forces of Colombia (*Fuerzas Armadas Revolucionarias de Colombia*) or FARC, the largest guerrilla group, refused to lay down its arms until basic structural changes in the Colombian economy first took place. Likewise the oldest guerrilla group, the National Liberation Army (*Ejército de Liberación Nacional*) or ELN, although only a tenth of the size of FARC, also refused to demobilize.[2]

In one of the many contradictions of their national character, Colombians, in spite of having experienced almost constantly record levels of violence, have traditionally preferred negotiations and legal solutions to the brute use of force. But as the twentieth century came to a close, it was becoming obvious that negotiations alone were inadequate to reach a peace settlement with FARC or ELN.[3] Candidate Andrés Pastrana believed that he could succeed where his predecessors had failed. He won the presidential election of 1998 by campaigning on a platform to bring peace to a war-weary Colombia. To induce the guerrillas to negotiate, he withdrew the army and the police from five municipalities in the Caguán valley in southern Colombia on 7 November 1998. He did not require any cease fire or impose any other preconditions, so FARC leadership saw no harm in resuming still another round of negotiations with the government.[4]

After an auspicious start with well-publicized photo shoots of President Pastrana and high government officials meeting with famous guerrilla leaders, the negotiations soon bogged down and failed to tackle any substantive issues. When procedural questions came to dominate the discussions, Pastrana should have cancelled or at least threatened to end the FARC safe haven if the negotiations did not shift to substantive issues. The guerrillas were in no rush, because the safe haven gave them the opportunity to strengthen their forces for new offensives. FARC was still riding high on a wave of successful military campaigns and saw the negotiations as one more step along the path toward the eventual acquisition of power in the country.[5]

Even more than its other military offensives, the entry of FARC into Arauca proved instrumental in turning public opinion against the Caguán negotiations. Arauca was the site of the Caño Limón oil field, which had converted Colombia from an importer into an exporter of petroleum, while national and local budgets came to depend on oil royalties for a substantial part of their revenue. Until 1997 Arauca had been one of the last surviving strongholds of ELN, and protection payments remained its main source of income. Occasional attacks on the pipeline of 778 kilometers linking Arauca to the Caribbean Sea convinced the oil companies that paying money to the guerrillas was the cheapest way to keep the underground pipeline operational. For its survival ELN needed the oil revenue as much as the government and always made sure that the damage to the pipeline never seriously interrupted the export of crude.[6]

In 1996 FARC wanted financial assistance for its military offensive, but when ELN refused to share its oil wealth, the rival guerrilla group entered Arauca in mid-1997. FARC made a large deployment in February 2001 and soon its units were clashing with those of ELN, while the number of pipeline attacks increased from 96 in 2000 to the record-high of 170 in 2001 (Table 1). These attacks were threatening to strangle the Colombian economy, so the Pastrana administration prepared to cut the national budget and to reduce the cash distributions to local governments in May 2001. The exchange rate for the Colombian peso was declining, and the danger of an economic downturn was real.[7]

Because the sabotage of petroleum exports was taking place at the same time as the Caguán negotiations, public opinion increasingly resented Pastrana's approach of negotiating without a cease fire. Álvaro Uribe Vélez, a former governor of Antioquia department, had sensed the public anger caused by the safe haven and with considerable political acumen saw in this issue an opportunity to reach the presidency. Because the official candidate of the Liberals, then the majority political party of Colombia, intended to continue the Pastrana policy of negotiating and fighting, Uribe bolted from the Liberals and launched his candidacy as a supra-party movement. By rising above any one political party, he could claim to run as an "anti-politics" candidate, much in the tradition of his Peruvian predecessor Alberto Fujimori. Uribe's reputation as a tough and efficient administrator during his governorship gave him the credentials to mount an effective campaign. The decaying Conservative Party realized that its only chance of survival was with Uribe, and rather than running its own candidate, it joined the Uribe movement and nominated him to be its candidate for the May 2002 presidential elections.[8]

Table 1
Colombia: Attacks on Arauca Pipeline, 1986–2015

Year	*Number of Attacks*	*Year*	*Number of Attacks*
1986	23	1988	50
1987	11	1989	28

Year	*Number of Attacks*	*Year*	*Number of Attacks*
1990	23	2003	34
1991	60	2004	17
1992	62	2005	25
1993	38	2006	24
1994	45	2007	8
1995	46	2008	5
1996	47	2009	7
1997	64	2010	2
1998	77	2011	24
1999	79	2012	44
2000	96	2013	40
2001	170	2014	40
2002	82	2015	22

NOTE: Petroleum exports from Arauca began in 1986, the year of the first attacks on the pipeline to the Caribbean coast.

Sources: Government Accountability Office, *Security Assistance: Efforts to Secure Colombia's Caño Limón-Coveñas Oil Pipeline Have Reduced Attacks, but Challenges Remain*, September 2005, p. 15; Diego Otero Prada, *Las cifras del conflicto colombiano*, 2d ed. (Bogotá: INDEPAZ, 2007), pp. 212–213; José Saul Triviño Gualdrón, "Medidas de seguridad física en prevención y acciones de reparación de los atentados terroristas al oleoducto en la región del Sarare-Arauca (Colombia)," Bogotá, Universidad Militar Nueva Granada, 2013, pp. 14, 19; "Boletín Agora Consultorías," April 2015, 2016. Divergences exist in the figures for some years.

Uribe campaigned across the country on a platform of "democratic security," and he promised in his speeches that his first action in office would be to abolish the save haven for FARC in the Caguán valley. He already enjoyed the support of business groups and did not have to seek their approval, and consequently he enjoyed the freedom on the campaign trail of not having to emphasize his capitalist credentials. He thus avoided antagonizing the middle class with talk of pursuing privatization and dismantling social services; in many ways he was the perfect candidate for the rich who knew that their interests were very well protected. Instead he campaigned against the political establishment, a safe topic that tapped into the public's resentment against the corruption and incompetence of Colombian politicians. In early January 2002 polls showed him ahead of the official candidate of the Liberal Party, so Uribe seemed certain to force the election into a runoff because no candidate appeared likely to gain more than the 50 percent required by the Constitution of 1991.[9]

Already the front-runner in the polls, his candidacy received an additional boost when President Pastrana, in a desperate attempt to salvage the peace process, extended the safe haven for FARC on 20 January 2002. The decision caused public outrage, because citizens were expecting a cancellation rather than a prolongation of a failed process. Uribe's promise to end the safe haven resonated with citizens, and his poll numbers rose even more. FARC did not realize that its last best chance to negotiate the most favorable peace agreement was rapidly slipping away. On the contrary, the guerrillas decided to make the most of the safe haven and carried out violent attacks across the country and also interrupted the Arauca pipeline for months. The breaking point came when in a brazen hijacking of an airplane, guerrillas kidnapped Senator Eduardo Gechen Turbay. President Pastrana could no longer deny that the peace process was irremediably doomed, and on 20 February 2002 he announced the end of the safe haven for FARC. He still left open the possibility of continuing negotiations in other settings, but this was a forlorn hope.[10]

The biggest winner was Uribe, and his poll numbers shot up to 60 percent in early

March. The public accepted his claim that the safe haven had been a mistake and that his approach of a tough offensive against the guerrillas was the only sound policy. Analysts confidently predicted that he would win without a runoff. And this time the predictions were correct: facing a large field of candidates, Uribe won the presidential elections on 26 May 2002 with 53 percent of the vote, a comfortable margin to avoid a runoff.[11]

Right after his inauguration on 7 August, he took his first decisions to confront the guerrilla threat. He began securing resources for a massive offensive against FARC and ordered the military to prepare plans for victory. However, Uribe knew that he had to take immediate action against FARC to show the public that he was capable of safeguarding the vital interests of Colombia. The Pastrana administration during its last months in office had made its highest priority the reestablishment of authority over the former FARC safe haven in Caguán valley. Troops easily occupied the five municipal capitals, but the deep support FARC enjoyed among the rural population made reestablishing government authority a long and difficult task. Uribe sympathized with the efforts of the outgoing administration, but as soon as government had established at least the outward appearance of control in the Caguán valley, he shifted the immediate focus to Arauca.[12]

As was mentioned earlier, the attacks on the petroleum pipeline had done the most to turn the Colombian public against the peace negotiations. FARC had Colombia by the jugular in the pipeline, and Uribe realized that before he could engage in his grand offensives against the guerrilla group, he first had to protect the oil revenue. The situation in Arauca not only had worsened during the presidential campaign but had also became more complicated with the entry of the paramilitaries of AUC (*Autodefensas Unidas de Colombia*) in September 2001. The paramilitaries had not done well in combat with skilled FARC guerrillas and turned instead to their usual tactics of threats, extortion, and murders. AUC began targeting anyone suspected of ties to guerrillas and carried out high-profile assassinations including that of one political figure while visiting in Bogotá. The paramilitaries also targeted for elimination independent voices such as community organizers, labor leaders, and school officials.[13]

As was the pattern with paramilitary actions, innocent civilians suffered the bulk of the casualties, while the guerrillas escaped with their units relatively untouched. The Uribe administration had no illusions about the capabilities of the paramilitaries in Arauca and intensified official efforts to protect petroleum exports. Oil royalties were so important for financing national and departmental budgets, that the outgoing Pastrana administration had made protecting the Arauca pipeline its second highest priority and had actually put into motion the most promising strategy.

U.S. and Colombian officials understood that stationing soldiers along the pipeline required transferring almost the entire Colombian army to that region and thus could not be a solution. Patrols were not the answer either, because soldiers had to travel in large numbers to avoid falling into guerrilla ambushes. The shooting down of a helicopter by FARC on 6 June 1997 eliminated the use of that risky transport and reduced the mobility of soldiers. The government also stopped using air power against the guerrillas after 18 innocent civilians (including seven children) died on 13 December 1998 in a Colombian Air Force bombing of the town of Santo Domingo just 20 kilometers from Arauca City. The 18th Brigade was clearly insufficient to meet the threat, and the Pastrana administration had been organizing a new unit, the 5th Mobile Brigade of 1,100 soldiers, to bolster the army presence. Uribe hastened the preparations, and shortly after his inauguration the first detachments of the 5th Mobile Brigade began arriving in Arauca. The creation and deployment of this mobile brigade was the first part of the bigger strategy to deploy similar units against FARC in other parts of the country.[14]

Indispensable as were additional troops to safeguard the pipeline, the doubling of the police presence was no less important. For the first time in history, the government had established a strong presence in Arauca, and the availability of adequate numbers of soldiers and policemen provided the resources to shape a successful strategy to reduce the damage to the pipeline. Close analysis of the attacks since their start in 1986 revealed that they all had taken place in the flat plains at a distance no farther than 100 kilometers from Arauca City. Although attacks were not impossible at higher altitudes toward the west as the pipeline snaked its way through the Andes Mountains, guerrillas had stayed away from those distant areas. On the working assumption that urban networks of both ELN and FARC were perpetrating the attacks, ECOPETROL and Oxy petroleum funded a special group of detectives, investigators, and prosecutors to track down the culprits; the new task force began operations in January 2002.[15]

Whenever an attack occurred, a team from this task force went to inspect the site. A rapid army response forced the guerrillas to flee in a hurry leaving behind incriminating evidence that the task force soon traced back to the urban cells of the guerrillas. The results surprised everyone, because while only three persons had been arrested on charges from 1988 to 2001, over 100 were arrested for the pipeline attacks in 2002. With timely intelligence the task force was able to frustrate 47 intended attacks. The number of pipeline attacks that had reached the record high of 170 in 2001 dropped to less than half in 2002 and again to less than half of the previous year in 2003. The reduction had been so dramatic because the prosecutors were able to identify and arrest the principal makers of bombs; without the explosive experts the attacks not only dropped in number but also were less destructive as desperate guerrillas tried to jerry-rig any type of bomb.[16]

Uribe visited Arauca with key cabinet officials in October 2002 to provide personal leadership for a strategy that was already proving successful. As the pipeline attacks declined in effectiveness, the Colombian government could count on receiving its oil royalties. The threat of disrupting the country's economy eased, and the president could claim his first major victory for "democratic security." For Arauca, the success against the guerrillas had been so great, that ranchers and wealthy citizens began returning to the department in 2003 to enjoy the benefits of peace and personal security for their activities.[17] For the Uribe administration, Arauca had been a quick fix to one part of a much larger problem. Simultaneously the government was preparing a comprehensive plan to end the guerrilla problem in Colombia once and for all, as chapter 8 will narrate.

Peru: From the Arequipazo to the Andahuaylas Revolt

> *In many ways, the Toledo government reproduced the authoritarian ways of the Fujimori regime.*—Moisés Arce[18]

While Colombia marched towards an intensification of its capitalist system, Peru for the first time experienced fierce resistance to free market policies. During the Alberto Fujimori dictatorship the repressive intelligence apparatus of Vladimiro Montesinos had prevented the outbreak of violent protests, and his bribes to the media largely kept the mounting discontent out of the news. But after the fall of the dictatorship, the repressed tensions started to come out in a mounting wave of social explosions. Sensing the looming cracks in society, the Valentín Paniagua interim government was careful not to do anything to antagonize the Peruvian people and wisely concentrated on diligently exposing the horrendous abuses and the rampant corruption of the Fujimori regime.

When Alejandro Toledo took office on 28 July 2001, prudence indicated that he should follow closely the cautious example of his predecessor Paniagua, but instead the new president was already deeply committed to plunging forward with the free market policies of the totally repudiated Fujimori dictatorship. As explained in chapter 4, in his pre-inauguration trip to the United States and Western Europe, he had assumed obligations to make Peru as friendly and open to foreign investment as possible. His cabinet appointments of Pedro Pablo Kuczynski as finance minister and Roberto Dañino as prime minister reflected these commitments to bring savage capitalism to Peru. Toledo passionately shared those capitalist ideas, but in the Latin American tradition of unscrupulous politicians, during his presidential campaign he had promised to oppose privatizations.[19]

The decision before Toledo was whether to fulfill his campaign promises or to honor the commitments he had assumed with international financial organizations. The first meant serving the people of Peru, the second serving Wall Street. As no man can have two masters at the same time, Toledo, irrespective of his campaign promises, had all his life been a faithful servant of international capital. But he was too clever a politician to plunge directly into free market policies, and to gain political cover, he distracted the country during the fall of 2001 with an economic stimulus package. His macroeconomic policies were very conservative, but the real litmus test for Wall Street was privatization. Admittedly, after the orgy of selling off state firms during the Fujimori dictatorship, not much remained to be privatized. In order to feed the insatiable demands of Wall Street, Toledo's fanatical cabinet ministers searched frantically for new targets to privatize. Although rumors of privatization had already sparked isolated protests across the country since August 2001, the ideologically driven Toledo administration paid little attention to these early warnings. On 3 January 2002 the government made a call for bids to privatize EGASA (*Empresa de Generación Eléctrica de Arequipa*) and EGESUR (*Empresa de Generación Eléctrica del Sur*), the utility companies providing electricity to most of southern Peru and to Arequipa, the second largest city in the country.[20]

News of the bid to privatize provoked the first spontaneous protests in Tacna on 4 January. Demonstrations would have spread across all of southern Peru had not popular leaders persuaded the residents to channel the popular outrage into a 48-hour work stoppage in Arequipa on February 26 and 27. Conventional wisdom has seen the unfolding events as being local in origin and primarily a response to excessive centralization in Lima, but those explanations miss the mark. Even when these protests occurred mostly in southern Peru, their nature was essentially national. The criminal investigations under the interim Paniagua presidency had confirmed that privatizations resulted in the classic capitalist outcome of illicit enrichment of a privileged few and the loss of employment for many individuals. These two characteristics had started to become evident during the latter years of the Fujimori dictatorship, but the conclusive proof appeared only with the revelations during the Paniagua presidency.[21]

The privatizations of the 1990s had occurred while most citizens were still dazzled by the collapse of the Soviet Union and the supposed triumph of capitalism. But by the start of twenty-first century the savage side of capitalism was creating many doubts about the benefits of this economic system. The cupboard of state-owned firms was almost empty when the Toledo administration took office, and it had to scourge the countryside to find new sacrificial victims to satisfy the insatiable hunger of Wall Street for quick and easy profits. During the 1990s privatization had impacted mostly Lima, yet even in the capital former employees usually fell into the ranks of the unemployed or at best became underemployed. In the interior of the country, where the state-owned enterprises provided the majority of salaried jobs and sometimes were the sole large employer in a region, privatization meant the permanent elimination of jobs.

The mayor of Arequipa, Juan Manuel Guillén, emerged as the leader of the protest movement. A philosophy professor and former head of the state university in the city, he originally had been an enthusiastic supporter of the president. In 2001 when Toledo campaigned in Arequipa, he had solemnly promised not to privatize the state-owned utilities and even subscribed in public a document to that effect. Toledo felt that he had covered the political angle by bringing Guillén to Lima to head the decentralization campaign, but when the latter realized that the president intended to betray his campaign promises, Guillén, true to his principles, returned to Arequipa to become mayor and to spearhead the campaign against privatization.[22]

The free market cabinet ministers of Toledo pressed on with plans for privatization and ignored the 24-hour work stoppage in 12 southern departments on 21 March. But a second work stoppage, this time of 48 hours on 16–17 April finally forced the government to announce on 18 April the postponement of privatization. On 10 May Toledo delayed the sale until 15 June, but because residents wanted a cancellation and not just a delay, the protest organizations called for a massive work stoppage for 14 May. As a show of force the demonstration was sufficiently strong to persuade the last remaining American company to withdraw its offer to purchase the state-owned utilities. Previously the initial mobilizations had scared away another American corporation, and thus only Tractabel, a Belgian firm, remained as the sole bidder, and just this absence of competition argued decisively for cancelling the sale of the two state-owned utilities.[23]

Having only a single bid did not in the least erode the faith of Toledo and his finance minister in the workings of the market through supply and demand. But the president knew that he had to do something to secure the acquiescence of Arequipa, and in the tradition of divide and rule, he cut a deal with business groups and wealthy residents of the city. Fifty-two years earlier all of Arequipa had united behind a movement to overthrow the government, but by 2002 the growing concentration of wealth made business groups abandon their previous loyalty to the region. For the price of some additional funding for construction projects likely to benefit only developers, on 24 May Toledo obtained the support of wealthy residents for the privatization of the electric utilities. As soon as the agreement was announced, that same day the protestors denounced this new betrayal and promised to continue the struggle.[24]

On Thursday, 13 June, Arequipa carried out its fifth work stoppage, and when that same day a judge accepted the petition of Mayor Guillén to declare null and void any sale of the electric utilities without the approval of the local authorities, the demonstrators went wild with joy and believed that the struggle was over. But the celebrations were premature, because on 14 June the residents could only watch with shock as a high government official congratulated the Belgian firm for having become the proud owner of the two electric utilities.[25] A triumphal Toledo proclaimed that the privatizations would continue, and to add insult to injury, Interior Minister Fernando Rospigliosi was quoted as

Southern Peru

supposedly saying that "only some deadbeats were opposed to the privatizations in Arequipa."[26]

While the protest organizers pondered what to do next, the residents took matters into their hands and spontaneously mobilized in the streets on the afternoon of 14 June. As huge crowds formed, the demonstrators shouted that they were not deadbeats. Soon barricades emerged in many southern cities and protestors burned tires and blocked streets. The massive scale of the demonstrations persuaded the police not to attempt to stop the mobilization, and in return the protestors did not hinder the police from performing its duties of protecting public buildings and preventing any looting of stores. But the Toledo administration wanted a crackdown, and when the minister of the interior ordered police reinforcements from Lima to Arequipa, the protestors seized the airport and blocked the runways, leaving stranded hundreds of passengers. The simultaneous demonstrations in other southern cities of Peru prevented the minister of the interior from sending police reinforcements by land. In barely one afternoon the problem of public order had exceeded the capacities of the police to control disturbances.[27]

The protestors remained in control of the streets, and tempers rose on Sunday, 16 June, when local radio stations put on the air leaders who called for ex-servicemen and all able-bodied men to report for the defense of the city, while other speakers demanded the resignation of Toledo. A few extremists went so far as to demand the independence of Arequipa. Already two students had died in the clashes, and any further escalation of violence was sure to result in more deaths and considerable destruction.[28]

The only option left was to call on the army to crush the revolt, and numerous battalions were readily available near the Chilean border. Toledo declared a state of emergency thus clearing the path for the use of force, but the army high command showed the greatest reluctance to carry out this operation.[29] While not openly defying the president, the generals explained that most of the recruits of the nearby battalions came from this area and would refuse to fire on the protestors and might even join them. A more reliable military alternative was to turn heavy artillery on Arequipa to obliterate the barricades at a high cost in lives and property. Possibly because of humanitarian reasons but more likely because the image of a city reduced to rubble was not at all attractive to foreign investors, Toledo realized that he had been checkmated.

The government turned to the Roman Catholic Church to negotiate a solution to the uprising in Arequipa. Archbishop Fernando Vargas Ruiz arrived on Monday, 17 June, to seek an agreement, but while he negotiated with the protest leaders, demonstrations intensified across southern Peru. Finally, even Iquitos in the Amazon joined the movement, because the state-owned electric utilities in the north were the next ones in line for privatization. With the protest threatening to spread across the entire country and putting in risk the survival of the Toledo presidency, the government had no choice but to capitulate and to accept the conditions of the protestors. On Wednesday, 19 June 2002, the negotiators signed the Declaration of Arequipa, essentially cancelling any attempts to privatize the two electric utilities; in a separate message the government also suspended any plans to sell off the remaining state-owned electric utilities in northern Peru.[30]

The political fall-out for the Toledo administration was not long in coming. Everyone expected the two free market ministers to resign over their failed policy, but instead the first one to resign three days later was Rospigliosi because of his supposed "deadbeat" comment. However, the attempt to make him the scapegoat for the Arequipa uprising failed, and three weeks later another cabinet shuffle finally brought the resignation of the real culprits, Prime Minister Dañino and Finance Minister Kuczynski. Toledo replaced the later with the finance minister of the Paniagua presidency, and this measure helped to reassure the country that the stage of privatizations was over in Peru. With premature optimism, Toledo expected that he could continue his presidential term without any additional upheavals.[31]

Had he avoided privatization altogether he might have enjoyed a relatively tranquil presidency, but after the Arequipazo (as the revolt came to be known) merely making a promise not to sell state-owned enterprises was no longer adequate. Critics accused him of weakness, when in reality his real blunder had been to trap himself into a situation that he could not win. Ideological zeal and stubbornness rather than weakness had almost cost him the presidency, and once other groups realized that he was vulnerable, protests and strikes spread across Peru during the second half of 2002 and throughout 2003. Any one of them could easily mushroom into an uprising, so the Toledo administration spent its time "putting out fires" or trying to defuse a conflict before it spun out of control. This soft approach was already evident in the strike by over 250,000 teachers in May 2003. After six weeks without classes for the students, angry parents pressured Toledo to grant a wage increase to end the strike.[32]

Likewise, the Toledo administration decided to bring the "Lime War" in Tambogrande to an end. The Canadian firm of Manhattan Minerals Corporation had been trying since 1999 to extract gold and copper through open-pit mines in the fertile lands of Piura Department. Mining meant leaving fertile soils contaminated with toxic chemicals for centuries and the project also required the relocation of at least 8000 residents. The local population united in a Defense Front in August 1999 to halt the mining project, and after the government ignored peaceful petitions, the group shifted to rallies and road blocks to slow down company operations. On 27 and 28 February 2001 the protests turned violent when the demonstrators destroyed the installations of the Manhattan Minerals Corporation. The campaign to drive out the Canadian company intensified when the president of the Defense Front, riding a massive wave of anti-mining sentiment in the locality, was elected mayor of Tambogrande in 2002. Under his direction, the Defense Front very cleverly combined protests with an astute publicity campaign that resonated with Peruvians in the capital. Lime juice was an essential ingredient in the national dish of ceviche, and because the region was the largest producer in Peru, the Defense Front was able to frame the campaign as an effort to save a symbol of national identity from destruction at the hands of a foreign corporation.[33]

To sacrifice the agricultural wealth of the region for centuries if not forever, in exchange for no more than a couple of decades of mining was an outrageous proposition impossible to defend. As the Lime War escalated in early 2003 with a combination of targeted protests and popular mobilizations, citizens in Lima and foreign NGOs added their support to the anti-mining movement. Under immense public pressure, the Toledo administration examined the credentials of the Manhattan Minerals Corporation. It turned out that this supposedly mid-size company was largely a shell organization lacking the resources to conduct a project of this magnitude. To disguise its inadequate capital, the Canadian company in 1996 had associated itself with a state-owned entity, and in this way the assets of the latter helped met the requirements for the mining venture. This trick of associating a sham company with a state-owned enterprise reappeared in the infamous case of the Petro Audios several years later. But in 2003 it was clear that foreign speculators had once again duped the Peruvian state, and on 12 December the Toledo administration revoked the mining concession and brought the Lime War to a close.[34]

Because of the Lime War, the capital for the first time began to pay close attention to conflicts not just in large cities as had been the case with the Arequipazo in 2002 but also in distant and small provinces. The relatively peaceful protests in Tambogrande had gradually awakened the curiosity of Lima, while the subsequent bloody events in the town of Ilave in the Department of Puno intensified the interest. The story began in a typical manner: Cirilo Robles had been elected mayor on the promise of repairing a damaged bridge and paving an access road to Ilave, but once in office he did nothing. Anger mounted against the mayor, and to lower the rising tension, he held an open forum to explain the situation on 2 April 2004. The meeting turned out badly, ten persons were injured, and over 20,000 Indians poured out into the streets to demand his resignation. The next day local residents organized a Struggle Committee, and it promptly declared a work stoppage in the town. Mayor Robles fled to the city of Puno where he should have stayed, and after conversations he agreed on 8 April to ask for a leave of absence from his position.[35]

The Indians were outraged with this incomplete response, because they demanded his resignation from the position. Clearly the mayor was counting on the storm blowing over and then being able to return home to resume his political career. But the discontent continued to increase, and on 8 April the Struggle Committee set up roadblocks in the highway to Bolivia and welded steel beams on the bridge in the international crossing. In a deadly miscalculation, mayor Robles returned to Ilave and convoked town councilmen in his home at 9:00 a.m. on 26 April. As soon as news of this meeting became known, a crowd numbering at least 2000 residents appeared in front of the mayor's house and broke through the windows and doors to try to take him prisoner. The frightened mayor fled to a nearby house, but the furious crowds broke into the surrounding houses until they had seized him and dragged him through the streets. By noon the number of demonstrators on the streets had risen to nearly 10,000, while another 5000 demonstrators kept the 30-man detachment trapped in the police station. Television cameras filmed the angry crowds rampaging through the streets, and these shocking images created a huge impression on the public. The demonstrators dragged the unfortunate mayor through the streets and not only beat him savagely but began stripping the skin from his body. In a painful agony the mayor slowly bled to death, and at 2:30 p.m. the protestors dumped his lifeless body outside the town near the bridge he had failed to repair. Over the next few days the government sent police reinforcements from Lima until the force came to number 600 officers who gradually restored order, and by then the fury of the crowds had passed, apparently satiated with the death of the mayor.[36]

The television images of the savage killing shocked the Peruvian public and created the impression that the country was on the verge of a massive social explosion similar to bloody revolts occurring during the colonial period. Although those fears were exaggerated, several other disturbances in the provinces during the rest of 2004 reinforced the image of a Toledo presidency unable to control the country. Nationalist and environmentalist concerns coincided in the next test of strength, the Mount Quilish episode of the Yanacocha gold mine not far from the city of Cajamarca in the Andes Mountains.

Mining in Peru had taken place since colonial times primarily in the southern half of the country but in the late twentieth century the quest for profits brought foreign corporations to northern Peru. The Lime War had prevented open-pit mining on the fertile fields of Tambogrande in Piura Department, but in the high mountains of Cajamarca farming seemed too weak to pose an obstacle to mining companies. The extraction of gold began in Yanacocha in 1993, and the free market dreams after the collapse of the Soviet bloc created illusions of great wealth for Cajamarca. The start of mining operations had not provoked major resistance, although minor difficulties already arose during the 1990s over the purchase of lands from peasants. Initially the most serious obstacle to mining was the struggle among foreign corporations for control of the project. The dispute only ended when Vladimiro Montesinos obtained a Supreme Court ruling giving majority control to the Denver-based Newmont Mining Corporation in 1998. The incriminating transaction was recorded in one of the infamous videotaped conversations of Montesinos, but not even these revelations persuaded the Peruvian government to withdraw its enthusiastic support for gold mining in Yanacocha.[37]

In 2000 the unfulfilled promises of bringing wealth to Cajamarca were creating enormous discontent; in a predictable result, capitalism had brought prosperity to hundreds at the high cost of keeping tens of thousands in poverty. Just one spark was needed to galvanize the population, and this came on 2 June 2000 when a truck overturned and spilled 151 kilograms of mercury. Because the truck belonged to a subcontractor, Newmont refused to assume any responsibility and kept the incident quiet. Nearby peasant residents, thinking that the substance contained gold, scooped up the mercury and took it to their shacks. At least 1000 persons became ill because of mercury contamination and over 300 suffered permanent health disorders. Once the news of the toxic disaster came out, this event created an intense public awareness of the health and environmental dangers that the mining operations posed to the entire area.[38]

Because the Fujimori dictatorship was doing everything to minimize this incident, inhabitants realized that they were alone in the struggle to protect their environment. Hearing that Yanacocha was planning to expand operations to Mount Quilish, only a few kilometers from the water intakes of Cajamarca City, the inhabitants organized a Mount Quilish Defense Front of local associations to advocate for the safety of the community. In a major victory, Cajamarca issued a municipal ordinance on 5 October 2000 declaring Mount Quilish a natural reserve. Not only was the water supply of the city at risk because of the mining activities, but the rural inhabitants considered Quilish to be a sacred mountain and believed that any tampering with its surface meant bringing ruin to Cajamarca.[39]

Newmont, one of the largest mining enterprises in the world, had been doing everything possible to sabotage the anti–Yanacocha movement and had even threatened the government to halt foreign investment in Peru. The rich company was a true Goliath and enjoyed the support of the powerful U.S. government, unlike the small Canadian firm of the Lime War in Tambogrande. The price of gold was rising, and the corporation in true capitalist tradition was not going to let talk of a sacred mountain stand in the way of earning record profits. The company lost the two initial judicial appeals, but then on 7 April 2003 the Constitutional Court ruled in an ambiguous decision that although the municipal ordinance was valid, Yanacocha could carry out the expansion because its authorization from the national government was of a previous date, provided that an environmental study concluded that the extraction was not harmful.[40]

The Constitutional Court should have shown more courage and simply ratified the municipal ordinance, but instead it passed the final decision back to the national government. The pro-business Toledo administration, after its defeat in the Arequipazo, was determined to repair its reputation among foreign investors and even without the threats from Newmont was going to do everything possible to break the barriers holding back foreign investment. On 16 July 2004 the Ministry of Mines and Energy gave full authorization to Newmont to carry out the planned expansion into Mount Quilish, and none of the desperate pleas from the affected citizens of Cajamarca could budge the Toledo presidency from its ideological commitment.[41]

The Mount Quilish Defense Front vainly tried to persuade the government to retract its decision, but the arrogance of officials was so great that they simply did not show up for a decisive meeting on 26 August 2004. The peasant leaders were so outraged that after several days of consultations they announced on 1 September that the next day they intended to block the road leading to Yanacocha. When nearly 3000 peasants arrived on 2 September to impose the blockade, the company was waiting with security forces and police reinforcements but was able to keep open only some segments of the road. As more and more peasants arrived, the road block became solid and the protestors established a tent camp to remain living right next to the road. Because so far only peasants had dared to clash with the private guards and the police, the company believed that it could shatter a purely rural movement that lacked support from the urban residents. But any idea of crushing supposedly primitive peasants vanished on 3 September when large number of university students joined the protest movement. The company was desperately trying to infiltrate the movement with provocateurs and was making all types of threats by phone calls and other means to those city residents suspected of sympathizing with the movement.[42]

The Mount Quilish Defense Front took decisive action when it declared a general strike on 8 September, and nearly 20,000 protestors gathered in the central plaza. The next day the university students blocked the road leading from Cajamarca to the coast, in effect isolating the city from the rest of the country. Many politicians had been slow to grasp the magnitude of the protest movement against Yanacocha, but finally on 9 September they agreed to form a newly created United Civic Struggle Committee, This steering entity represented nearly all the private, public, and party institutions in Cajamarca, but because leadership of the new organization remained in the hands of the Mount Quilish Defense Committee, the non-negotiable demand remained cancelling the expansion of Yanacocha.[43]

Actually the United Civic Struggle Committee had become the de facto ruler of Cajamarca, and on 13 September it made a call for a second general strike to take place on 15 September. The population was even more outraged than before, because national government officials were taunting them for foolishly trying to imitate Arequipa; the insult that Cajamarca did not have the courage of Arequipa really angered locals who were determined to prove their determination. The strike of 15 September was a total success, and nearly 40,000 persons marched from the central plaza to support the protestors blocking the road to Yanacocha. Newmont, in a vain attempt to keep operations going, had rented two helicopters to fly in critical personnel, but after a few days shortages of supplies and chemicals gradually shut down the mining operations.[44]

The Toledo administration had on its hands another insurrection no less serious than that of Arequipa in 2002. The last recourse was to turn to the army, and all the time from inside the barracks the soldiers attentively watched the struggle unfold. But just as during the Arequipazo, the generals were most reluctant to crush the revolt, particularly because the army did not want to antagonize the inhabitants of strategic Cajamarca near the border with Ecuador. Not just the generals but also high civilian officials realized that the Toledo presidency was in danger of collapsing. In an attempt to restore calm to Cajamarca, the Ministry of Mines and Energy on 16 September rescinded its earlier authorization to mine Mount Quilish. The protest movement had won another major victory against the capitalist zealots in the Toledo administration; gradually Cajamarca returned to its daily routine and Yanacocha was able to resume its usual operations. But Newmont had lost only one major battle in the war for gold, and the mining giant was sure to seek a rematch in the future.[45]

The defeats over Yanacocha, Arequipa, and the Lime War had weakened the Toledo administration. These protest movements were really directed against policies rather than the government itself, although inevitably someone was bound to conclude that the government was ready to be overthrown. The temptation to strike a blow against the Toledo presidency was irresistible, and a revolt openly stating this intention finally broke out in Andahuaylas province on 1 January 2005.

Ever since the Ilave uprising of April 2004, members of the nationalist movement of Antauro Humala had actively participated in the disturbances occurring throughout Peru. Meanwhile, the nationalist movement was splitting into two branches, the radical one of Antauro urging the use of violence and the moderate branch of his brother Ollanta Humala who was seeking to become president through peaceful elections. Ollanta was already a national figure because of his courageous revolt on 29 October 2000 against the Fujimori dictatorship. Antauro felt that he needed to gain similar exposure and concluded that the moment was right to strike against the Toledo presidency. However, lacking the national standing of his brother, Antauro falsely told his followers that Ollanta, who then was military attaché in South Korea, had ordered him to launch the revolt.[46]

In an action reminiscent of the Moncada attack of Fidel Castro in Cuba, Antauro picked dawn of New Year's Day to seize the central police station in Andahuaylas province. Just as in the attack in Cuba, Antauro had picked this hour because the personnel was either on holiday leave or too intoxicated to mount any real resistance. The nationalists, who were mostly ex-servicemen, arrived at dawn on 1 January 2005; they gained control of the central police station, took 14 policemen as hostages, and captured the modest arsenal. The plan had been more successful than Fidel's failed attempt to capture a large army base in the second largest city of Cuba, but it was not clear at all what Antauro could do with this small police station in a remote corner of Peru. Antauro promptly issued a manifesto demanding the resignation of Toledo, but Peruvians, partly suffering from the hangovers of the New Year's parties, failed to respond at all.[47]

On January 2 a police unit tried to enter the town to regain control, but two rebels and four policemen died when the nationalists repulsed the attack. The residents sympathized with the revolt and hundreds of young males supported the rebels. When reinforcements arrived and surrounded the town, a tense faceoff ensued and bloodshed seemed imminent. A timely telephone call from brother Ollanta in South Korea proved decisive in ending the revolt. But once again Antauro twisted his brother's words and told his followers that Ollanta had ordered him to surrender. On 4 January 2005 Antauro Humala and 159 of his nationalist followers gave up their arms and were imprisoned.[48]

For Toledo the revolts were merely the growing pains of capitalism as it spread its beneficent effects throughout every corner in Peru. His political strategy of transferring authority from Lima to the provinces had failed to prevent turmoil, and if anything decentralization had facilitated protests without being the real cause of the discontent. Toledo did not want to accept the reality that the disturbances had crippled his presidency. The survival of the regime was in doubt, and long before he realized it, his administration was struggling to complete its presidential term. He did not want to recognize the gravity of the situation, because he expected rapid economic growth to improve drastically the lives of the great majority of the population. He was certain that once the people received the benefits of capitalism, his free market policies were sure to become hugely popular, and under these idyllic assumptions Toledo pressed forward confidently with the task of transforming Peru.

CHAPTER 7

Venezuela: The Second Attempt to Overthrow Hugo Chávez

He who neglects what is done for what ought to be done, sooner effects his ruin than his preservation. For a man who wishes to act entirely up to his professions of virtue soon meets with what destroys him among so much that is evil.—Niccolò Machiavelli[1]

Missed Opportunity

Scarcely had Hugo Chávez landed in Miraflores Palace when he began to proclaim the ideas that Cardinal Ignacio Velasco had planted in the president's mind. The exuberant crowds, expecting an avenging angel to lash out against the traitors and the criminal rebels, heard instead these startling words: "therefore no reprisals, there will be no reprisals of any kind, here we will not have a witch hunt because I do not come with a desire for vengeance."[2] The justification for this attitude was that "we are humanists, we respect the human being," but the comments created great frustration among his followers, emboldened the opposition, and weakened his presidency. In his speech he even related how he had asked forgiveness from the same Cardinal who had been the first to sign the Carmona decree ratifying the overthrow of the president, an action that Chávez still did not know. Cardinal Velasco during this stay with Chávez at La Orchila Island had performed the invaluable service of gaining time for the opposition to mount another attempt to overthrow Chávez.

After the fiasco of the coup attempt of April 2002 the Roman Catholic Church prudently kept a low profile and only occasionally criticized the government. However, by this near withdrawal from any public role the Catholic Church let slip perhaps the last best opportunity to end the social strife in Venezuela. In his same 14 April speech, the president called for the start of a national dialogue with all sectors of the country. The opposition remained interested in the conversations as long as he was granting concessions, but when the government asked something in return, the national dialogue faded away.[3]

In his speech of 14 April Chávez also accepted the resignations of the PDVSA Board of Directors and of CEO Gastón Parra. As a previous chapter narrated, it was precisely the attempt to appoint new trustees and a CEO from outside the state petroleum company that triggered the chain of events leading to the 11 April coup attempt. By withdrawing all his appointees and also reinstating the fired managers, Chávez again reinforced the impression of acting out of weakness.[4] He highlighted his vulnerability even more when the next day on 15 April in another speech he publicly apologized for having read the names of the fired executives on his TV show *Aló Presidente* of 7 April. "That was an error, I admit it, and I ask forgiveness" were the words reflecting an abject capitulation.[5]

Sensing a fundamental weakness, the opposition decided to press hard to see what else the president was willing to give up without a struggle. In prior years FEDECAMARAS, the confederation of business groups, had been the normal channel to present requests to government officials, but its participation in the April coup had tarnished the institution. The Venezuelan-American Chamber of Commerce temporarily filled this gap and communicated the requests of the private sector to the government. In a message of 26 April, this business group requested that Venezuela adhere to the Free Trade Agreement of the Americas, respect foreign investment, and reconsider the Hydrocarbon decree law; the Chamber also indirectly requested a revision of the 49 decree laws of November 2001. As chapter five explained, the 49 decree laws were the real cause of the clash with economic groups, and although the request of the Venezuelan-American Chamber of Commerce was diplomatic and did not openly demand the outright repeal of the 49 decree laws, the real intention was clear. The business groups were willing to give Chávez an easy way to reverse himself, and they slyly suggested that in negotiations the president rely on those officials who were well-versed in economic issues and sympathetic to private business. The implicit assumption was that technocrats would modify or partially repeal the 49 decrees in a gradual process mostly out of view of the public.[6]

Very astutely the Chávez administration decided to use the message of the Venezuelan-American Chamber of Commerce as an opening wedge to start negotiations separately with key sectors of the economy. Industrialists were generally very sympathetic to the nationalistic message of Chávez, and soon sectors such as textiles, chemical, and pharmaceutical signed agreements with the government. Many small businesses also received preferential treatment, and as the number of defections from the anti–Chávez coalition increased between June and October, the opposition leaders felt under pressure to strike before the government became solidly entrenched.[7]

The only area where Chávez could not avoid some housecleaning was in his beloved military. The treason of so many high-ranking officers had shaken him profoundly, particularly when he had considered many of the coup plotters to have been not just loyal but also friends. The easy part of the task was to ratify loyal commanders in their positions and to remove from posts the traitors. Loyal commanders could expect promotions and rewards, while the coup plotters should then have expected at least demotion and most likely expulsion from the institution. Because the coup plotters fell into the two categories of active participants and sympathizers, an excessive purge of the ranks risked firing many competent officers, but in practice the housecleaning did not even affect all the active participants. In the months following the coup attempt the high command fired around 100 officers, but even such well-known plotters as military attaché General Enrique Medina Gómez remained on active duty. Many coup sympathizers stayed in the ranks receiving their salaries and, deprived of any duties, passed the time in their homes. Forgiveness for those who had flirted with the coup and then turned against it seemed advisable, but clemency to inveterate haters of the government bordered on recklessness. In particular, although Chávez made sure that no officer suspected of disloyalty ever commanded troops again, the housecleaning did not reach far into the ranks of brigadier generals and colonels.[8]

Chávez never again faced the danger of military coup, but a minority of bitter enemies still remained in the officer corps. The difficulties he had with the military raised the deeper question of whether a radical transformation is possible in a Latin American country without first destroying the old army. This seemed to be the lesson from the Mexican, Cuban, and Nicaraguan revolutions and from the tragedy in Chile when Salvador Allende failed to neutralize the existing armed forces. A more perceptive assessment reveals that the experience of Chávez validated the precedent of the revolutionary military in Peru. The real lesson was not that the old army had to be disbanded, but that most of the generals—and not just senior commanders—had to be dismissed.[9] Handpicking loyalists for key command posts starting in 1999 allowed Chávez to survive the coup attempt of April 2002. Had he dismissed, retired, and replaced more generals, the April 2002 coup attempt could not have taken place. The housecleaning he carried out after the coup was not as complete as was needed but at least guaranteed that the Chávez presidency never again faced another army revolt.

One casualty of the coup attempt was the experiment with a civilian as minister of defense. No more loyal and dedicated figure existed that José Vicente Rangel, but as a civilian he simply was not an insider in the high officer circles. Rangel became vice-president in May 2002, and because of his strong following among the middle class, he remained a vital figure in the government, in a sense partially filling the shoes of the disloyal Luis Miquilena. But as far as the military, the rule became of having uniformed personnel occupy most of the positions in the Defense Ministry.

Civilians enjoyed exemption from dismissal or even demotions. On 12 April many high officials in the Central Bank had joyfully feasted with champagne and whiskey the fall of Chávez, and similar celebrations on a less lavish scale took place in many government offices; other officials rushed to take down and throw in the trash the portraits of the fallen president. Although the courageous attorney general had declared on television the removal of Chávez to have been a coup d'état, 300 of his attorneys signed a petition supporting the removal of the president. All the bureaucrats went back to work on 14 April as if nothing had happened, and those who had openly supported the coup quietly waited for another opportunity. The lack of reprisals certainly emboldened the opposition leaders and in particular the managers of PDVSA.[10]

Hostile critics denounced the judicial branch as tools of the Chávez administration, when in reality Chávez had made the same mistake with judges as he had with his appointments of military officers. He was always too trusting of individuals and he had the bad habit of taking their word at face value. So when candidates for judges went before the National Assembly for confirmation, he was too quick to accept names proposed by the corrupt political parties of the Fourth Republic. The errors in selecting judges came to hurt the government when on 15 August 2002 the Supreme Court in a shocking decision declared that no coup d'état had taken place in April, a blatantly false statement of fact. Only in March 2005 did the Supreme Court overturn this ruling and finally admit that a coup d'état had actually taken place, but by then the window of opportunity to strike a decisive blow against the plotters and to send a warning to the opposition had passed.[11]

The legal consequences of the 15 August 2002 decision were immense and resulted in dropping the majority of charges against all persons involved in the coup attempt of April 2002. Without being able to use the claim of a coup d'état, the attorney general had to undertake the laborious task of proving a variety of criminal charges against individuals for having violated the laws. Because the legal system in Venezuela has been notoriously incompetent, slow, and corrupt, the prosecution of the great majority of conspirators became almost impossible. In the most obvious example, military officers avoided criminal prosecution and only had to worry about administrative sanctions inside the institution. The most favored, however, were the civilians who signed the affidavit proclaiming the Carmona presidency on 12 April; the simple list had sufficed to convict them on the charge of supporting the coup attempt, but the Supreme Court decision blocked that path for prosecution.

Opposition figures who evaded prosecution were not going to let Chávez escape unscathed. In a bizarre mockery of justice, hostile politicians repeatedly tried to have the National Assembly bring Chávez to trial as the real culprit in the coup attempt. When than maneuver failed, the next step for the opposition was to try to shorten the presidential term in order to anticipate the date of the next elections. Such a change required a constitutional amendment, and when Chávez firmly stated that the 1999 Constitution was not on the table for negotiation, that strategy also failed. Finally, the opposition turned to the recall provision in the constitution and began the first steps to hand to the voters the authority to remove Chávez from office. The political maneuver of a recall vote faced a long and difficult road ahead as a later chapter explains and could only begin after the president had completed half of his term.[12]

Parallel to the political initiatives to keep Chávez on the defensive, the opposition was trying to wreck the economy as a way to bring down the government. The goal was to have the economic situation deteriorate to the point that the people would turn out in the streets to demand the departure of Chávez, as had happened in Chile against Allende in 1973. The economic indicators did decline in 2002 and the population suffered some hardships but the government was never in any danger of facing a popular insurrection. Because many private businesses were cutting deals with the Chávez administration, the weapon of trying to wreck the economy was losing its effectiveness, and the opposition began to realize that to bring economic pressure it was going to have to turn to the "nuclear" option of launching PDVSA into the battle.

As rumblings of a coming clash with the opposition were becoming stronger in the first days of October, the administration decided to settle one pending item from the failed coup attempt of April 2002. The Caracas Metropolitan Police, an agency of the municipal government, had been an important player in the movement to overthrow Chávez, and its refusal to stop the marchers heading to Miraflores had been instrumental in making the coup possible. The Metropolitan Police tried to prove its innocence and to appease the national government by handing over for prosecution about a dozen policemen as scapegoats. It turned out that these policemen had not even been involved in the events, so their imprisonment was a smokescreen to cover the real culprits in the coup activities. The patience of the government ran out when a strike by key elements inside the force weakened its policing functions. When on November 12 a clash of military police with striking officers resulted in two deaths and many civilian injuries, the government could no longer delay acting and on 16 November 2002 army and National Guard units took over the Metropolitan Police. During the raid the soldiers confiscated a large number of assault weapons and machine guns supposed to be only in the army arsenals.[13] By this preemptive move, the government neutralized the Metropolitan Police and deprived the opposition of a powerful ally once the final struggle for control of PDVSA began.

The Petroleum Strike: December 2002–February 2003

The alliance between FEDECAMARAS, the most important business group, and the labor confederation CTV survived the failure of the April 2002 coup attempt. In an apparent contradiction, the political bonds linking these two organizations having diametrically opposed economic goals actually became stronger. The fierce hatred against the Chávez administration provided the glue to sustain this alliance. The vacancy left by the arrest and subsequent flight into exile of Pedro Carmona was filled by new FEDECAMARAS president Carlos Fernández, but leadership in the struggle against Chávez passed to Carlos Ortega, the head of CTV. As will be recalled from chapter 5, Ortega had abruptly left Caracas at the start of the coup attempt of April, and in response to many criticisms, he was determined in this new round to make up for his previous weakness. The vehicle for directing the struggle remained the "Coordinating Committee for Democracy and Liberty," which also included the corrupt politicians of the Fourth Republic.[14]

On 5 October 2002 FEDECAMARAS at its annual convention ratified its support for a massive protest march in Caracas to take place on 10 October and for a subsequent general strike on as yet unspecified date. By all accounts the march of 10 October was a resounding success, although claims that the protestors numbered over half a million were clearly exaggerations. The crowds were more than ample to persuade Ortega to state at the end of the march that the Coordinating Committee was threatening a general strike on 21 October unless Chávez resigned or moved forward the presidential elections. Quite naturally the president rejected the demands, and the Coordinating Committee called for a one-day general strike on 21 October.[15]

The general strike of 21 October paralyzed the country as most businesses did not open and people stayed home to watch the non-stop coverage on the hostile television channels. The Coordinating Committee again called the general strike a huge success, when in reality many retail stores and small businesses had closed not out of sympathy with the movement but out of fear that they might suffer looting. The next day activities went back to normal, but before the Coordinating Committee could organize additional protests, it was upstaged by an unexpected event. Fourteen disgruntled military officers suddenly set up a camp at Altamira Plaza on 22 October in an open sign of defiance to the government. As the previous section explained, after the coup Chávez had removed all disloyal officers from any command or influential position, but he had been slow to dismiss all the coup plotters from the ranks and many were getting away with nothing more than a written reprimand. But with no chance at a promotion, their military careers were effectively over, so these officers with nothing to do and still receiving their salaries had decided to go out with a bang.[16]

The officers issued a manifesto explaining their disobedience, and already on 25 October their numbers grew to around a hundred disgruntled military personnel. The uniformed protestors camped out in tents and raised signs declaring Altamira Plaza to be liberated territory, to the immense fascination of the residents in this upper-class neighborhood of Caracas. FEDECAMARAS and CTV promptly endorsed the military's open defiance as did the traditional political parties. Many sympathizers came after work hours and joined the officers in speeches and music denouncing the Chávez administration as hopelessly totalitarian and Cuban inspired. In reality, the Altamira Plaza defiance was the last attempt of the military to retain a place inside the opposition. For the April coup both civilians and generals had operated along parallel but interconnected paths, and the disloyal officers were trying to create the image of deep divisions within the military.[17]

As the month of November wore on, it was becoming clear that the opposition could not expect much more than this show in Altamira Plaza from the military. Worse, as mentioned before, the drive for profits was weakening the resolve of private business to put economic pressure on the government. The opposition had one last major card to play if it was going to have any chance of removing Chávez from office before his term ended. Success in the April coup had seemed so certain, that the opposition had felt no need to push for a PDVSA lockout. But the situation was so desperate in November that the Coordinating Committee threw PDVSA into the final battle. At first sight this struggle seemed bizarre to observers across the world and not just to socialists, because never before had a state-owned corporation tried to overthrow a government in Latin America.

The bitter hostility of PDVSA managers turned into passionate hatred for Chávez. They had been the driving force behind the October 2002 general strike and were eagerly looking for any opportunity to overthrow the government. In their arrogance they dismissed all conciliatory gestures as signs of weaknesses, and the managers regarded themselves as indispensable and irreplaceable. In an attempt to placate upper management after the April 2002 coup, Chávez wisely chose as the new head of PDVSA the renowned Alí Rodríguez. A dedicated nationalist and a former guerrilla of the 1960s insurrection, he had struggled throughout his life to make the petroleum wealth benefit all Venezuelans; he had worked well both with Chávez and the presidents of the Fourth Republic. However, in spite or perhaps because of his credentials in the field, private oil company officials considered him to be just another Communist. Entering the mine field of PDVSA, Rodríguez went out of his way to placate the dissidents, who did not appreciate the salaries and many benefits that they were enjoying. The CEO granted all the requests of the executives and protected them from political pressure, but nothing seemed to satisfy the managers who openly plotted their participation in the next general strike.[18]

As FEDECAMARAS and CTV had feared, the response to the call for a general strike on Monday, 2 December 2002, was less enthusiastic than on 21 October, and the traditional east-west divide in the city was becoming even more marked than in the past. In the western more densely populated part of poor Caracas, most activities operated normally, while in the eastern and wealthy part of the city most businesses shut down. But even in the eastern part of the capital, the compliance with the general strike was more apparent than real, because stores and shops had closed not out of sympathy with the strike but out of fear that their valuable inventories of expensive goods might be damaged. Small businesses had been opposed to the call for the general strike because they were looking forward to record sales for the upcoming Christmas season. The real strike began when PDVSA executives declared a lockout and forced installations to shut down throughout the country because of lack of personnel. At Maracaibo 70 percent of employees did not report for work that first day, and at Caracas, the epicenter of the PDVSA strike, 90 percent of the personnel were absent.[19]

The participation of PDVSA employees was the clearest warning sign that the government faced a titanic struggle over the future of Venezuela, yet officials optimistically expected the general strike to dissipate after a day or two as had happened in the past. As will be recalled, during the April 2002 coup attempt, the oil workers' union, FEDEPETROL, had refused to participate in the general strike, and the government confidently believed that without the workers no general strike could succeed. In reality, PDVSA managers for months had been waging a relentless propaganda campaign among workers to persuade them to support the strike and to undermine the authority of the union leaders of FEDEPETROL. Consequently on 2 December many workers decided to participate in the general strike, a decision they afterwards came to regret.[20]

By Wednesday, December 4, the general strike was weakening, and many observers expected activities to return to normal in a day or two. Suddenly late that evening the captain of the PDVSA tanker *Pilín León* announced on television that he and his crew were joining the general strike. The ship, named after a Venezuelan beauty queen, cast anchor outside the entrance channel to Lake Maracaibo and refused to take its cargo of gasoline to the docks. The rest of the 13 PDVSA tankers (most also named after beauty queens) joined the general strike and either stayed offshore or refused to leave port. Because the port teams also joined the general strike, those chartered tankers with foreign crews could not dock to load or unload cargoes. It was obvious that if the tankers did not export crude abroad the economy of Venezuela would collapse, but why was the *Pilín León* bringing gasoline? PDSVA executives, as part of their strategy to hide profits from the government, had for decades imported most of the gasoline for domestic consumption from abroad. By exporting crude and buying refineries in foreign countries, PDSVA could entangle transactions and generate fake losses to offset the real profits.[21]

The five refineries in Venezuela lacked the capacity to cover the domestic demand for gasoline and their production dropped precipitously because of personnel shortages. Any long interruption of the gasoline supply meant paralyzing the country because the cheap gasoline had eliminated other forms of transportation to a greater degree than in other countries still operating railway networks. At that time in Venezuela, other than the subway in Caracas, almost all goods and passengers relied on gasoline for movement. CEO Rodríguez had anticipated disruptions in gasoline supply and previously had stockpiled reserves estimated at between a 20 to 30 days' supply, but without gasoline the trucks could not resupply the service stations and on December 6 the first lines of waiting cars appeared at the pumps.[22]

In response, on December 5 Chávez turned to the military to break the bottlenecks. Troops used army trucks and requisitioned private ones to take gasoline to the service stations, and soldiers stayed guarding the pumps, but it was clear that once the existing reserves ran out, the entire country would be paralyzed. Seeing an opportunity to topple the government, the opposition organized protests and marches almost every day to make a critical situation become even worse. Actually, schools and businesses were closing not in anger at Chávez but because gasoline shortages impeded the movement of people. The hostile television gave extensive coverage to every demonstration and tried to create the expectation that at any moment the government might fall. The opposition had a colorful new ally in the former wife of Chávez; after a nasty divorce she was lashing out at her ex-husband on television. A familiar figure from the past could not miss this opportunity to please the right, and just a few months before his death, Cardinal Ignacio Velasco joined the chorus of voices putting the blame for the country's difficulties exclusively on Chávez. For their part, Ortega and Fernández, the two moving forces in the Coordinating Committee, issued triumphal bulletins every day proclaiming the imminent collapse of the government.[23]

So far no individual business sector had come out solidly behind the PDVSA general strike, even though the bank employee union closed private banks on 10 December and afterwards reopened them for only half a day of service. By making it harder for customers to access their accounts, the decline of money in circulation aggravated the problems already caused by the shortage of gasoline. After the appearance of the first lines of waiting cars on 6 December, the government announced its intention to operate service stations if necessary, but in practice its intervention at the retail and wholesale level did not go beyond stationing soldiers to protect the facilities and to make sure that customers did not become disorderly. Because senior management at PDVSA refused to lift the lockout, CEO Rodríguez on 12 December fired a small number of company executives; his hope was that this first round of dismissals would persuade the rest of the managers to return to their jobs.[24]

The call to return to work went unheeded, and as the five refineries ground to a halt, tankers emerged as the decisive battleground to decide the fate of the general strike. On land extensive sabotage by the striking employees delayed returning the refineries to normal operation for months.[25] But if the government could not provide gasoline to keep the country running, then the possibility existed that a frustrated population might take to the streets to demand that Chávez resign, and this was the maneuver that the Coordinating Committee was counting on. With the crews aboard the merchant ships on strike, and the owners of tugboats refusing to dock the tankers, the option of importing gasoline from abroad disappeared, because it would take time to charter new tankers on the world market and have them deliver the gasoline to the ports. Obviously if the crude oil tankers did not take Venezuela's main export abroad, the country was headed to economic bankruptcy, but this could happen only months after the gasoline shortage had paralyzed the country.

The Chávez administration took a two-fold approach to the looming gasoline shortage. First, it appealed to friendly countries to make emergency deliveries of gasoline to Venezuela. Secondly, the government tried to regain control of the private tugboats and of the PDVSA tankers lying idle off the coast. Almost from the first day port authorities had prevented food and fresh water from reaching the striking vessels, but this proved inadequate to break the will of the crews. Chávez ordered naval personnel to board the ships including the tugboats, but even then the civilian crews refused to abandon the tankers until certified personnel arrived. The argument of the strikers was not without some foundation, because fully-loaded tankers, especially those filled with gasoline, were disasters waiting to explode at any moment. PDVSA called loyal personnel out of retirement, and on 19 December Captain Carlos López and a replacement crew of loyalists climbed aboard the *Pilín León*, the tanker that had triggered the supply bottleneck. The naval personnel had arrested and removed the original crew members who had been quietly sabotaging the machinery aboard to make it look normal when in reality it no longer functioned properly.[26]

The hostile television promptly launched a massive campaign accusing PDVSA of bringing Cubans to operate the *Pilín León*, and these false accusations made Captain López and his Venezuelan crew more determined to prove that they could operate the giant tanker. The major step was to get the ship under the bridge traversing the entrance to Lake Maracaibo. Soldiers were already guarding the longest bridge in Latin America, but the danger existed that the tanker might accidentally ram into one of the piers supporting the massive structure. Everyone knew that this was the crucial battle in the strike, and the whole country was glued to live television watching the drama unfold. Shortly before noon on December 21 Captain López decided that the *Pilín León* was ready to make the run into Lake Maracaibo. The huge ship began heading toward the entrance channel, but when the Diesel engine mysteriously overheated, the captain took the precaution of having the tanker circle rather than crash into the bridge. The opposition had won the first round of the saga of the *Pilín León*.

The engineers cooled down the engine, and around noon Captain López decided to make another attempt at entering the shipping channel. This time the vessel plowed forward, and when it was 300 meters from the bridge, the crew members on the deck jumped up in cheers, because they knew that even if the engine stopped again, the momentum of the huge tanker sufficed to enter Lake Maracaibo. The engine stayed running smoothly, and on live television viewers could watch the soldiers guarding the bridge who wildly waved their arms in excitement as the *Pilín León* crossed safely underneath the huge structure. Tugboats under navy control brought the tanker safely to the dock, and loyal port teams promptly pumped the gasoline out to a thirsty Maracaibo city which had practically run out of the vital fuel. The empty tanker then set out on a voyage abroad to bring another cargo of gasoline to Venezuela.[27]

The image of ships at sea fascinated Venezuelans, and Chávez instinctively exploited the media opportunity by staging an event for his next *Aló Presidente* television broadcast at a gasoline shipping center on the coast of Carabobo State. Military and civilian personalities, including CEO Rodríguez, paraded before the TV cameras, and the crowning moment came when Chávez spoke to the nation against a backdrop of tankers sailing away in the sea. The shipping strike was over, and PDVSA resumed the export of crude oil, although production levels did not return to normal until the middle of January.[28]

Putting the refineries to produce was a lengthier and much more complicated issue, so that even with the PDVSA tanker fleet operating at full capacity, gasoline shortages were inevitable. An important stopgap measure was the assistance that friendly countries provided to Venezuela. Brazil was the first country to send an emergency supply of gasoline, and soon after Trinidad and Tobago provided additional cargoes. These emergency shipments helped bridge the gap in supply until PDVSA could charter additional foreign tankers and until the refineries in Venezuela went back on line with the help of army engineers. The distribution of the gasoline inside the country remained under military control, and soldiers drove tanker trucks to refill the pumps. The people proved very patient with the gasoline shortages, and the waiting lines at the service stations turned into an opportunity for socializing, playing games, and snacking on treats sold by the walking vendors so frequent in Latin America.[29]

The government had remained very vigilant to prevent the shortage of gasoline from provoking a scarcity of foodstuffs for the population. Previously supermarkets had increased the inventories at their warehouses, and although some items occasionally ran out, the main problem was getting the goods from the central warehouses to the individual supermarkets. Once again, if private deliveries were inadequate, troops stepped in to guarantee the supply for the supermarkets. In the poor neighborhoods, the government organized popular markets and trucked in large amounts of food to feed people whose local corner stores had long exhausted their small stocks. Because Venezuela relied heavily on imported foods, neighboring Colombia provided many emergency shipments; when scarcity of ships threatened to delay shipments, the Venezuelan navy loaded foods aboard its vessels for delivery at home ports. Colombia had traditionally supplied food to the bordering regions of Venezuela, but once again gasoline shortages limited the possibility of trucking Colombian products into the interior.[30]

The export of crude oil was returning to normal levels at the start of 2003 and PDVSA was so confident of its abilities that on 3 January it resumed deliveries of crude oil to Cuba on 3 January 2003. CEO Rodríguez decided to press home the advantage, and after making one more plea for workers to return to work, he began another round of firings on 8 January, with at least 4000 employees expected to lose their jobs at PDVSA. Partly to protest the firings and partly in opposition to the resumption of oil shipments to Cuba, the opposition intensified its protests and summoned crowds to march in defiance of the government. The outrage persuaded the bank employees' union to declare a two-day strike on January 9 and 10, but when this action failed to spark any strong demonstrations, the bank workers returned to the half-day workweek. The last chance for a significant number of workers to join the general strike came when the transportation union of Caracas considered participating. This labor organization represented the subway and bus drivers, and it could easily create chaos in the capital, but able lobbying by officials, and in particular by Deputy Nicolás Maduro, persuaded the union on 13 January 2003 to refuse to participate in the general strike.[31]

The opposition was fast running out of cards to play, and in desperation it called for a tax boycott and asked merchants to stop collecting the value added tax included in the price of the majority of items. When the supermarkets continued to collect the tax, this idea to reduce the revenue flowing into the treasury quietly faded. Even in wealthy eastern Caracas the majority of small businesses had not wanted the general strike; claiming hardship, many stores and shops began opening after New Year's, even if for shortened hours. Trying to breathe life into a faltering movement, the Coordinating Committee—itself torn by bitter infighting—authorized small businesses to adopt a "flexible" strike schedule of opening just enough hours to survive and then closing to bring pressure on the government, but this ploy proved ineffective. Even those parents who initially had sympathized with the general strike wanted their children to return to classes and not miss any more of the school year.[32]

The general strike had clearly failed, but the Coordinating Committee still hoped for a miracle to turn the people against Chávez. Consequently "during its final weeks the strike simple petered out without any official announcement that it had been called off."[33] A fitting end to the general strike came on 4 February 2003 when Chávez commemorated another anniversary of his failed çoup attempt of 1992. The fiery speech he gave to a large crowd confirmed that he was still in charge and even more determined to carry out the transformation of Venezuela. In an indication of changes to come, he accepted the suggestion to rename the tankers of the PDVSA fleet after famous women of the wars of independence and no longer after beauty queens. Thus the *Pilín León* became the *Negra Matea*, the governess of national hero Simón Bolívar, and another tanker was renamed *Manuela Sáenz* after his close confidante.[34] The name changes reflected a need to recognize women beyond their physical beauty and also was a slap at the beauty queens who had foolishly supported the general strike. And as chapter 9 shows, more reprisals were in store for the opposition.

CHAPTER 8

Colombia: The Álvaro Uribe Vélez Presidency

There is no solution without U.S. help.—Álvaro Uribe Vélez[1]

The intention to seek reelection was the paramount driving force for Álvaro Uribe Vélez even before he took office as president on 7 August 2002.[2] Essentially, he was trying to repeat the maneuvers of Alberto Fujimori who had cleverly manipulated Peru to secure two reelections as president. Uribe could draw on both the successes and the ultimate failure of Fujimori to try to craft a Colombian winning formula. By obtaining generous U.S. support from the George W. Bush administration, Uribe believed that in the long-running war against the guerrilla insurgency he could achieve a striking success that would make possible his reelection as president in 2006.

The War Against Guerrillas

The highest priority for the incoming administration was the war against the Revolutionary Armed Forces of Colombia (*Fuerzas Armadas Revolucionarias de Colombia*) or FARC. President Álvaro Uribe Vélez knew that U.S. assistance was indispensable to any government offensive. The U.S. government had been helping the Andrés Pastrana administration in the anti-drug campaign, but this aid had been clearly insufficient. By labeling FARC as a terrorist group, President Uribe cleverly used the fears after the 9/11 attacks to obtain substantial assistance from the George W. Bush administration to finance the campaign against the guerrillas. Both the Colombian and U.S. presidencies shared similar right-wing views, and this ideological affinity facilitated forging a strong alliance against FARC.[3]

The U.S. contributions came primarily in equipment, technology, advising, and training; eventually hundreds of American advisors joined the effort. The guarantee of generous support from Washington helped President Uribe obtain from the Colombian congress the passage of a "War Tax." All this additional revenue financed the expansion of the armed forces, which reached the largest size in the country's history. The 158,000 military personnel of 2002 increased to 260,000 in 2006. The national police of Colombia also increased from 104,000 in 2002 to 134,000 in 2006, but the preference of the military over the police openly reflected the priority of the Uribe administration and also was an early indication of a misplaced emphasis in the strategy against FARC.[4]

In 2002 when the guerrillas were interrupting oil exports in Arauca and were threatening Bogotá, nobody doubted the need for a vigorous military response. As explained in chapter 6, the government made securing the pipelines its highest priority in 2002, while at the same time gathering forces for the launching of a military offensive. The preparations were ready in June 2003 for the new offensive baptized with the name of *Plan Patriota*.

Phase 2 A of *Plan Patriota* began in June 2003 with the operation *Libertad I* in the areas around Bogotá. FARC had boasted of capturing the capital of the country, but the easy advance of the troops suggested that the guerrillas had merely been bluffing. The threat to capture Bogotá had merely been a feint to divert troops from the decisive theater of operations at Arauca; fortunately for the government, it had not fallen for the ruse and correctly deployed its troops first to protect the pipelines in 2002 and only the next year to the areas surrounding Bogotá. The large number of troops easily overwhelmed the small guerrilla detachments and killed many of its commanders. By December 2003 *Libertad I* came to a successful conclusion, and the operation not only had cleared the areas near the capital but also pushed deep to the east beyond the Andes Mountains into the Guaviare River basin.[5]

The easy victory in *Libertad I* boosted the morale of troops and created the illusion that *Plan Patriota* was capable of delivering complete victory over the guerrillas. The highly encouraging results both from *Libertad I* and the Arauca operation persuaded the government to proceed with the next stage of the offensive. The army duly launched Phase 2 B of *Plan Patriota* in February 2004, but just as the deployments were beginning, a totally unexpected event briefly put into doubt the optimistic assumptions. In one of the most daring actions of the war, on the night of 23 February 2004 guerrillas seized key points of the departmental capital of Neiva and attempted to kidnap wealthy citizens for later ransom payments. FARC remained in control of parts of the city until the next day because the commander of the army garrison had refused to send his soldiers to help the beleaguered police units.[6]

The Neiva attack was extremely embarrassing for the government and revealed that the transformation of the army into an effective combat force was going to be a lot more difficult than anyone had imagined. An angry President Uribe promptly removed the derelict officers from command, but this unexpected attack still remained as an inauspicious event to mark the beginning of Phase 2 B of *Plan Patriota*. The operation was certainly ambitious and called for sending over 17,000 soldiers to the southern Amazon regions of Colombia near the Andes Mountains. The deployment was the largest in the history of the military in Colombia and even exceeded in number the forces used in the victorious war against Peru of 1932–1933.[7]

The new mobile brigades took part in the offensive as did riverine task forces. Enjoying extensive air support, the troops blasted their way through the known FARC camps in the region and captured many supplies and considerable equipment. Phase 2 B rolled forward without encountering any significant resistance, and the government estimated that in a period ranging from 18 to 24 months the operation should complete ridding southeast Colombia of FARC guerrillas. As the army advanced, behind came the police to establish authorities in many towns previously without any state representatives. At the start of the Uribe administration, 158 Colombian municipalities had lacked any police presence, but by the first quarter of 2004 the government claimed to have established police stations in all the 1098 municipalities then existing in Colombia.[8]

As the year 2005 began, the gamble of President Uribe of concentrating resources on a military solution seemed to have worked. The police played only a secondary role in the offensive to destroy FARC. Not surprisingly, the public was extremely grateful to the president for having fulfilled his campaign promises to pacify Colombia. His efforts to improve the country went beyond dismantling the guerrilla threat, because President Uribe also had a very ambitious agenda to transform the political system in Colombia.

The Challenge to the Political Class

In the 2002 elections, the anti-politics and anti-party campaign had achieved extraordinary success, and not just because Álvaro Uribe Vélez won the race for president by defying the Liberal and Conservative parties. Neither of the two traditional parties won a majority in both houses, something that had never before happened in the history of Colombia. Blaming the problems of the country on the traditional politicians was extremely popular with citizens, and Uribe here was following the similar approaches first of Alberto Fujimori in Peru and then of Hugo Chávez in Venezuela. Not surprisingly, for the first time since the military rule of General Gustavo Rojas Pinilla in the 1950s, Colombia's political class feared for its existence.[9]

Uribe, confident of his mandate from the people to do away with traditional politicians, appointed technocrats and business leaders to his cabinet. The ministries had traditionally been sources of patronage for politicians, so the president, by cutting off access to public funds, hoped to starve the politicians out of power. He counted on the enthusiastic support from the private sector to wage his campaign against politicians. Business provided many key officials for his administration and the bulk of the contributions for his campaign. And, as an incalculable benefit, business conglomerates solidly lined up behind the president and had their media affiliates provide very favorable coverage to the government. The contrast with Venezuela was jarring, because while Hugo Chávez struggled throughout his presidency with vitriolic and hateful media, Uribe basked in flattering media press. And while local and international bodies routinely condemned Chávez for stifling freedom of the press, Uribe with few exceptions enjoyed accolades from the international press.[10]

The business conglomerates also deliberately blocked out any dissident voices. "Opposition found few spaces in either the written or oral press to voice complaints and to hold the government accountable for its actions, which helped the president maintain high levels of approval."[11] This almost propagandistic press coverage was an incredible boom for the government, and Uribe tried to repay this generosity by pursuing the most pro-business policies whenever possible. But more than favorable economic benefits were behind the enthusiastic support of the private sector for the government. Business leaders, just like the rest of the population, shared the intense desire to restore peace to the country by ending the insurgency and were determined to do everything to make sure that the government succeeded. As discussed in the first section, the willingness of the upper class to pay the war tax made possible the vast expansion of the military establishment.

In Venezuela Chávez had partially overcome the vicious attacks from the private media by reaching the people directly through his weekly televised talk show *Aló Presidente*. One of the appeals of his program usually lasting for many hours and taking place anywhere in the country was its spontaneous nature, as guests blurted out non-scripted comments and Chávez announced unexpected decisions. Uribe instead opted for the "town hall meeting" format (*Consejos Comunales de Gobierno*) or Communal Councils of Government for his television broadcasts. On most weekends he and a team of advisors traveled to a different region of Colombia to hear directly the concerns of the residents, and thus "creating the illusion of a direct relationship between the president and the people," but in reality the town hall meetings "were carefully staged and tightly controlled events."[12] Political operatives laid out the script to follow during the meeting, and security personnel carefully selected the participants to make sure that no one made awkward questions. On average each year Uribe held 35 of these meetings that proved highly effective propaganda opportunities to boost the popularity of his presidency.

Enjoying perhaps the highest popularity of any Colombian president, Uribe believed that with the support of business groups he could launch an attack to destroy the political class. During the electoral campaign he had already talked about the need to overhaul completely the political system and possibly also to combine the two houses of congress into a single chamber. In reality, lurking behind this maneuver was his desire to clear the way for a possible reelection in 2006. Even before taking office in 2002, he had begun saying that four years was too short a time to restore peace to Colombia. He saw the political class standing in the way of his ambitions, and he was determined to neutralize or push it aside. Congress was the bulwark of the political class, and Uribe concentrated his attacks on that often misunderstood institution. The not completely unfounded belief existed that many legislators and their assistants had very little to do, and Uribe tapped into that myth to begin a campaign to transform congress into a unicameral legislature.[13]

Abolishing the upper house was going to be a hard sell in Colombia, because its citizens had seen how in neighboring Peru a unicameral legislature had been one of the key instruments Alberto Fujimori had created to consolidate his dictatorship. Even Non-Governmental Organizations were worried about reducing the authority of the Colombian congress. As Uribe used the media to try to persuade the public that congress had to be sharply pruned, the political class felt mortally threatened and struggled to find a way to survive. In particular, the senators who were party leaders also headed the lists of candidates in the single nation-wide election for the senate, and they were not going to give up their guaranteed reelection. When Uribe formally presented a package of constitutional reforms, the legislators quietly dropped the unicameral proposal.[14]

The congress, suffering from record low approval rating, realized that rejecting too many of the proposals was very dangerous. A real possibility was that Uribe might be tempted to dissolve the congress in a "mini coup" imitating the action of Fujimori in April 1992. Whether the Colombian military might have supported a "self-coup" remains an open question. Although the president was very popular among the officer corps because of his increases of the military budget, he did not have a Vladimoro Montesinos to manipulate the armed forces. Any possibility of a coup passed when congress dutifully approved the rest of the proposals and sent them to the voters for their decision in a special election on 23 October 2003.

The remaining proposals threatened to cripple the congress under the guise of calling for a more open and responsive institution. It was hard to dispute the requirement that all elected officials had to hold town house meetings, but these legislators, without the resources of the presidency to stage and script the events, were sure to suffer merciless attacks from the large disgruntled sectors of the population. The referendum sharply reduced the authority of legislators to appropriate funds and took away the right to appoint assistants and employees. The proposal also lowered the number of seats from 268 to 218 for both houses, and even more seriously for the political class, eliminated alternative members of congress, a favorite source of patronage. By reducing the capacity of congress to distribute funds to regions and to clients, the referendum sharply limited the influence of the institution. But because power is not something that simply vanishes and instead reappears somewhere else, whatever the legislature lost necessarily passed to the executive branch. Consequently, the approval of the constitutional referendum meant laying the foundation for a dictatorship in Colombia similar to Fujimori's in Peru.[15]

The Supreme Court ruled that the 15 provisions of the referendum had to be presented separately, so that voters could express their preferences for each item. Although on 23 October 2003 the citizens voted overwhelmingly in favor of the 15 proposals, this was not the end of the story. The Constitution of 1991 in one of its more innovative clauses had stipulated that amendments required for approval not just passage by congress and a majority of the popular vote but also the participation of a minimum of 25 percent of the electorate. In the 23 October 2003 referendum, over three-fourths of the electorate had voted with their feet and stayed away from the voting tables. The political class, the group most threatened by the constitutional reforms, had also flexed its muscles by demonstrating its ability to refuse to deliver votes on Election Day.[16]

The failure of the referendum was the first major defeat for the Uribe presidency. So great was his business support, that conglomerates directed their media outlets to minimize and then bury the referendum defeat and instead to concentrate on the positive accomplishments of the government. The referendum was proving to be but a bump in the road for Uribe, but he knew that he had to find another way to secure his reelection. A direct confrontation with the political class had failed, and he wisely abandoned any efforts to change drastically the governing system of Colombia. But he still wanted to be reelected, and soon he was pleased to find that the political class was more than willing to accommodate his desires, as chapter 11 will explain.

The Problem of the Paramilitaries

In the 1980s ranchers and large landholders in the Sinú and San Jorge valleys had suffered kidnappings and extortion at the hands of guerrillas. The wealthy landowners sought protection by creating personal armies. These privately funded armed groups came to be known as paramilitaries, and besides protecting the wealthy, they came to provide other services such as threatening opposition figures and displacing peasants from valuable lands. This last function became so important, that paramilitaries were responsible for causing nearly half of the large number of internally displaced persons in Colombia; in contrast, the guerrillas were responsible for only a small percentage of these displacements. The business of forcing peasants, Indians, and blacks off their lands became so irresistible that soon not just large landowners but also foreign corporations were hiring the paramilitaries to expel inhabitants from lands valuable either for soils or minerals.[17]

When the paramilitaries expanded into the banana-exporting region of Urabá in

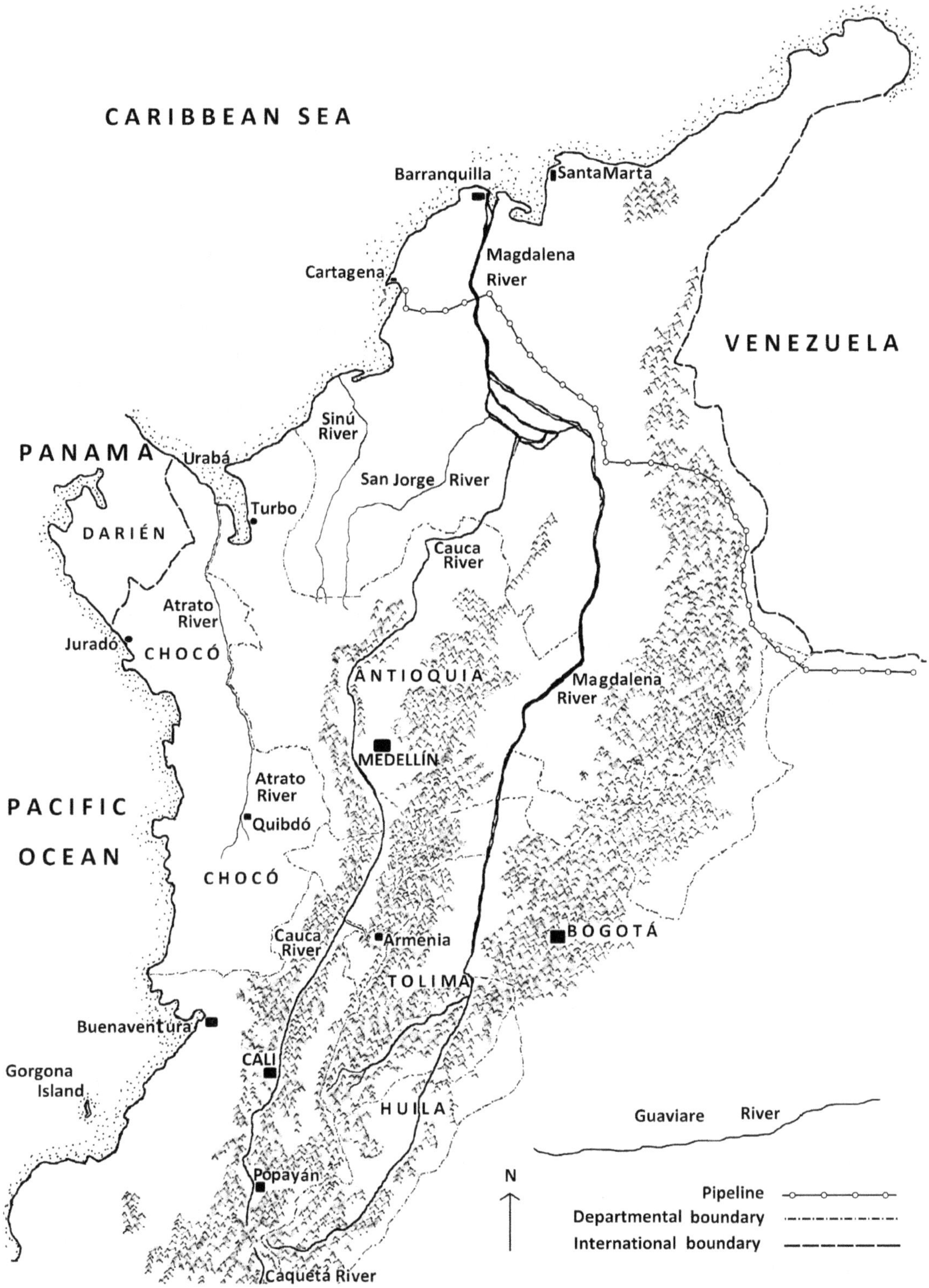

Northern Colombia

the 1990s, they gradually became autonomous as they adopted extortion as the normal way to finance their operations. The initial success with gaining autonomy led other individuals to try to create groups of paramilitaries in many other rural parts of Colombia, often in collusion with army or government officials. When paramilitaries arrived in a new locality, their first step was to demand money from large landowners in exchange for protection. Because paramilitaries fervently espoused an anti-guerrilla and procapitalist agenda, property owners under threat reluctantly made the payments.[18]

Once the paramilitaries had quietly established a base in a locality, they announced their presence by carrying out either a horrific massacre or the simultaneous assassination of suspected guerrilla sympathizers. The blowing up of buildings and community structures then followed, and was usually accompanied by public executions and the looting of the victims' properties. These savage actions terrorized the local population, but the killings did not stop after the opening rampage of violence. The paramilitaries continued to target labor leaders, peasant activists, and other community leaders for elimination. The repression of popular groups indirectly helped the wealthy who could extract more profits from their businesses and in this way defrayed the costs of their payments to the paramilitaries. And with this money the paramilitaries purchased properties in the region and also seized lands from any resident who refused to make the protection payments. Rapidly the paramilitaries were turning into a large criminal enterprise seeking to maximize profits from ill-gotten properties and funds.[19]

The paramilitaries claimed that the massacres and murders were weakening the guerrillas, but that was rarely the case. The small National Liberation Army (*Ejército Nacional de Liberación*) or ELN suffered the most from the paramilitaries because of its urban-based model of insurgency, but the rural-based FARC, which was responsible for 90 percent of guerrilla actions in Colombia, escaped largely unscathed. To disguise their inability to stop the guerrillas, paramilitaries constantly exaggerated their supposed successes. In a major example, paramilitary leaders such as Carlos Castaño claimed that keeping FARC out of the Urabá region in the 1990s had been their greatest initial success; in reality the guerrillas failed to gain control of that region because of local hostility and a strong army presence. Already in the Urabá campaign the paramilitaries confirmed that as soon as they left the protective mantle of the army, they suffered defeat in engagements with FARC. In two major battles in 1998 FARC destroyed the main base of Castaño and confirmed beyond a doubt that the paramilitaries were incapable of defeating the guerrillas in combat.[20]

Instead of being a group fighting the guerrillas, the paramilitaries, numbering about 3,000 in 1995, had become a vast criminal enterprise sprawling over many parts of Colombia and increasing in number to 8,000 armed members in 2000. Carlos Castaño succeeded in organizing the leaders into the umbrella organization *Autodefensas Unidas de Colombia* (United Self Defense Forces) or AUC on 18 April 1997. However, rather than contributing to the defeat of the guerrillas, the paramilitaries became a worse problem. Criminal groups, including those formerly associated with the dismantled drug cartels, reinvented themselves as paramilitaries to continue their illegal life style. The switch to relying on drug trafficking as the major source of income for the paramilitaries followed naturally. By the early years of the twenty-first century 70 percent of income for these criminal organizations came from zones involved in drug trafficking. The vast sums of money from the drug trade brought ample funds to lure into their ranks many members of urban gangs; the paramilitaries also recruited extensively among the unemployed youth in urban slums and in rural areas. The drug money also financed the acquisition of substantial arsenals more than adequate to terrify the local populations, but even with weapons comparable if not superior to those of the guerrillas the paramilitaries still avoided combat with FARC.[21]

The struggle against the guerrillas was the fig leaf disguising the multitude of sins of the paramilitaries, but the efforts of President Andrés Pastrana to secure a peace agreement with FARC threatened to leave the criminal enterprise without any political cover. As a first step, the president gave a safe haven zone for FARC in November 1998 and then pursued negotiations so vigorously that many members of the Colombia upper class started to fear that he was giving away too much to the guerrillas. When in response to demands from FARC negotiators Pastrana removed from command the generals with known ties to the paramilitaries, the latter lost the support they had occasionally received from army officers. Out of fear that the government might cave in to all the guerrilla demands, large landowners took a second look at the paramilitaries and began to consider them as possible counterweight. Fearful of losing their privileged positions, wealthy landowners increased their support for the paramilitaries as the best way to try to negate the harmful effects of any bad peace deal with the guerrillas.[22]

At this moment the leader Carlos Castaño had the insight to see an opportunity to legitimize the paramilitaries as an organization holding importance comparable to both FARC and ELN. He was also inspired in the negotiations of the early 1990s when drug cartel leaders such as Pablo Escobar had been able to cut deals with the government to keep most of their illicit gains in exchange for vastly reduced prison sentences. Castaño more than any other leader realized that the paramilitaries had degenerated into a criminal enterprise and that only by securing some sort of partial amnesty could its members hope to return to Colombian society.

On 1 March 2000 Castaño made his prime-time television debut in a 90-minute interview filmed a few days before. Previously in photographs and brief film clips he had always appeared in combat fatigues and a camouflage hat with its brims folded, but for this interview the 35-year-old looked almost decent wearing a tie, dress shirt, and nicely pressed slacks. In the interview he admitted that the organization normally relied on extortion and had carried out a number of massacres and murders as part of the relentless war against the guerrillas. His answers were remarkably polished for a high-school dropout, and the TV appearance turned him into a national celebrity. He followed this appearance with other interviews and soon his name had become a household word in Colombia. Shortly after he released his autobiography, and this book remained on the bestseller lists for months as it went through repeated printings.[23]

The upper class was closely scrutinizing Castaño who some might even consider to be presidential material. Although his much more modest goal was simply to obtain the return of members of his criminal organization into society, he clearly was pressuring the rural members of the upper class with having to take a decision about the future of Colombia. That same year, the former governor of Antioquia Álvaro Uribe Vélez was starting to generate momentum for his presidential campaign, and Castaño made it clear in his interview that the paramilitaries did not support the likely favorite. The explanation for the refusal of the paramilitaries to support Uribe was quite simple, because they knew that his promise to carry out a massive military offensive to destroy the insurgency meant eliminating the guerrillas as the pretext for the existence of the criminal enterprise.[24]

The last hope for the paramilitaries to gain support from rural members of the upper class was if the government signed a bad peace deal with FARC. But the decision of President Pastrana to order the occupation of the safe haven zone on 20 February 2002 marked the effective end to the negotiations. The paramilitaries no longer could take advantage of a bad peace agreement, and their repudiation became complete when Uribe Vélez won the presidential elections on 26 May 2002. His resounding victory over many candidates in the first round meant that the upper class had not just discarded the paramilitary alternative but also fully backed the new presidency. And the support meant a willingness to pay the higher taxes needed to finance the military offensive; wealthy ranchers and large landlords had made the calculation that it was better to pay the "wealth tax" that Uribe implemented than extortion payments to the paramilitaries. The transition from extortion payments to higher taxes was neither smooth nor ever complete, and certainly not immediate, but as the government found ways to demobilize the paramilitaries, the upper class increasingly could pay the higher taxes out of the previous protection payments.[25]

After the collapse of the peace negotiations in February, political analysts had predicted a huge electoral victory for Uribe Vélez; seeing the handwriting on the wall, Castaño turned to the Roman Catholic bishops to serve as intermediaries in contacts with the outgoing Pastrana administration. As soon as Uribe won the presidential election, Pastrana informed him of these secret talks, and the winning candidate urged the president to keep the conversations going. Once Uribe took office on 7 August 2002, he confirmed from army intelligence reports that the paramilitaries lacked any combat capabilities. However, he realized that these illegal armed groups had tremendous political value and could play a very useful role in satisfying his ambitions.[26]

Rather than denouncing the paramilitaries as a criminal organization and as a phantom force, he continued to exaggerate their importance to the public. He knew that the bigger the public believed the paramilitaries to be, the greater would be his political gain. The paramilitaries knew how the game was played, and they inflated their ranks by offering high wages to attract many last-minute recruits. Commanders traveled to the slums of Medellín and other poor areas of Colombia until they had increased their forces to around 13,000 paramilitaries. This large number panicked the public and persuaded the congress to pass on 26 November 2002 the law authorizing the president to negotiate a peace agreement with non-guerrilla groups. This law was a crowning achievement for Castaño, because he had succeeded in placing his criminal organization on the same level as the guerrilla groups. Uribe had taken part in the farce because he was certain of gaining political benefits fairly soon unlike in the long-term military offensive against the guerrillas.[27]

The public expected another long period of talks just to agree on the conditions for the negotiations as had been the case with the guerrillas in the past. Because almost all Colombian observers routinely neglected the military side of the problem, they were shocked to learn that just a few days after the passage of the law Castaño agreed to all the conditions laid down by the Uribe administration for negotiations. Even more startling for Colombian analysts, he announced a unilateral ceasefire to begin on 1 December 2002 of that same year. In reality he knew that he had to take advantage of the media image of the powerful paramilitaries before anyone could shatter the myth of an effective fighting force.[28]

Many paramilitary leaders initially did not accept the ceasefire. This public division revealed not only that Castaño was far ahead of the other commanders in understanding that a negotiated demobilization was their best possible alternative and also exposed the fragmented nature of the organization. Rather than a single centrally controlled structure, the paramilitaries were in reality a loose federation of autonomous regional groups. Only a few still considered the struggle against the guerrillas to be their main obligation, and almost all the others vigorously employed illegal means to pursue their highest priority of maximizing profits. Participation in drug trafficking had become rampant among the paramilitaries, and while they continued to kill innocent civilians, clashes over drug routes became the most frequent type of violence. Not surprisingly, the paramilitary commanders who had inherited personnel and routes of the defunct drug cartels were most reluctant to end their lucrative activities. The greatest fear of drug lords disguised as paramilitaries was extradition to the United States, but aware of their military weakness they joined the rest of the paramilitary leaders in accepting the unilateral cease fire by the end of December 2002.[29]

The delay in accepting the unilateral ceasefire persuaded the government to engage in separate negotiations across Colombia. In the early stages Castaño was urging other commanders to complete the negotiations with the government. The reasons for reaching an agreement were so compelling, that even after a personal rivalry over a beautiful woman resulted in Castaño's death, the negotiations continued. On 24 November 2003, almost a year after the passage of the law authorizing the government to negotiate with non-guerrilla groups, a first detachment of paramilitaries agreed to turn in their weapons.[30]

This first of 37 demobilizations took place in Medellín, Antioquia; this first group comprised 874 persons but only 30 percent were paramilitaries; the rest were petty criminals and gang members hastily recruited from the city's slums. As part of their process of returning to society, the men spent three weeks in training and education in a nearby camp. Afterwards the municipal government took over the task of returning these former militaries to their families and helping them find employment. The Medellín demobilization was one of the most successful, because the municipal government prosecuted as criminals only a very small number and insisted on giving the misled young men a second opportunity to rebuild their lives. Because Antioquia often operates as a large extended family and partly also because of experience with drug gangs and guerrilla groups, the demobilization in Medellín was not only the first but was among the most successful.[31]

Repeating the Medellín success proved harder in other regions, because financial assistance dwindled to insignificance. Former paramilitaries soon drifted into petty crime and even bank robberies; drug trafficking remained the most attractive employment alternative. Returning to legal pursuits the 31,670 paramilitaries who turned in their weapons between 26 November 2003 and 16 August 2006 was no easy task even under the best of circumstances. When the lack of opportunities persuaded some commanders to delay demobilization, the government either threatened or launched attacks against those reluctant paramilitaries to make them hand in their weapons. The government sparingly used force against the paramilitaries who soon after the attacks returned to conclude the negotiations. The rapid pace of demobilization continued to surprise observers in 2004 because they had not realized how militarily weak the paramilitaries had always been.[32]

The process received legislative approval when congress passed a law in June 2005 granting reduced prison sentences to paramilitaries who demobilized. President Uribe took full credit for the demobilization, and his initial calculation that this could bring political benefits proved accurate. As he was shaping the campaign to secure his reelection, he created the image that the dismantling of the paramilitaries had been a major success of his presidency. However, as mentioned earlier, his deliberate neglect of social programs meant that many former paramilitaries drifted into other types of illegal activities.[33]

In reality, the paramilitaries had simply been one more expression of the crime rampant in Colombia since the start of *La Violencia* in 1946. Throughout that long time, political parties, guerrilla groups, drug cartels, paramilitaries, gangs, and most recently "criminal bands" have inflicted waves of violence on many sectors of the Colombian population. And more disturbingly, as crime became such an integral part of society, individuals were free to move from one delinquent group to another without excessive difficulty. But the underlying structural problems of Colombia were not the concern of President Uribe who had gained in the demobilization one more argument to use in his campaign to secure his reelection.

CHAPTER 9

Venezuela: The Best Years of the Chávez Presidency

Chávez's steady rise in the polls can be attributed to rampant government social spending, the work Chávez is perceived to be doing for the poor, the economic recovery, and the image many have of the opposition as troublemakers.—Cable from U.S. Embassy, Caracas[1]

The Third Effort to Oust Chávez: The Recall Election of August 2004

After the failure of the petroleum strike of December 2002–February 2003, Hugo Chávez finally learned the lesson that he needed to take reprisals to avoid another similar outbreak. As mentioned previously, the revolt of the state-owned company (PDVSA) against its government was such a bizarre event, that any repetition was sure to cause enormous damage. CEO Alí Rodríguez launched a first purge of all hostile personnel, an action a private firm would have taken long before against striking employees. After the April 2002 coup a surge of Christian charity moved Chávez to rehire rebellious executives, but this second time around the company wisely fired all managers who had abandoned their jobs. CEO Rodríguez had begun the dismissals even during the petroleum strike, and in February he included in the firings all the white-collar employees who had participated in the attempt to cripple the economy. The task of identifying the defiant individuals was easy and accurate, because in October 2002 almost all of the employees on strike had signed the "Let's Save PDVSA" petition, which had been the opening salvo of the petroleum strike.[2]

Replacing these managers proved less difficult than expected, because as explained in chapter 1, a bloated bureaucracy of while-collar employees had characterized the excessively large office staff of PDVSA in Caracas. Before the strike the company had been saddled with many superfluous employees, and when CEO Rodríguez divided PDVSA into two operating entities, one in the western and another in the eastern part of the country, he eliminated the need for many positions in the staff of the Caracas offices. Gradually training, promoting, recalling retirees, and recruiting Venezuelans living abroad to come to work for the company sufficed to replace any gaps in the upper ranks in the company. Cutting the payroll from 40,133 employees before the strike to 22,924 in May 2003 also brought PDVSA important savings.[3]

The old managers had lured many workers to join the petroleum strike and to defy the pro–Chávez union leadership of FEDEPETROL. When tens of thousands of loyal Chavistas were clamoring to have any job in PDVSA, for the company to keep disloyal workers besides being unnecessary and risky also sent a message of political weakness. The petroleum strike was still raging when the company began on 9 January 2003 to publish in newspapers the first of successive lists of fired workers who also were easy to identify because they too like the white-collar employees had also signed the "Let's Save PDVSA" petition. In subsequent years the government rejected all attempts to reinstate the workers, who in addition became disqualified to work in any other government agency. The blacklisting might seem vindictive, but when the loyalty of workers in other state enterprises had been an indispensable element in the struggle to defeat the general strike, the government did not want to expose other institutions to the risk of subversion.[4]

In April 2002 the government had appeared weak by letting almost all the leaders of the coup attempt roam around freely to conspire and plot new schemes, but in 2003 the authorities were determined to avoid that mistake. Starting with the detention of FEDECAMARAS president Carlos Rodríguez on 19 February, the attorney general issued warrants for the arrest of all the members of the Coordinating Committee for Democracy and Liberty, the body that had directed both the April 2002 coup attempt and the petroleum strike. As soon as word spread of the government's unexpected intention to act tough, the majority of the suspects fled the country; a few, such as CTV president Carlos Ortega, sought asylum in embassies. The arrest warrants did not destroy the opposition but made many leaders reluctant to engage in illegal activities. Without dynamic personalities leading the opposition, it resembled an amorphous mass pulling in many directions and sharing only the common goal of overthrowing Chávez.[5]

The most serious challenge facing the government was not so easily solved. The two attempts to overthrow Chávez had wrecked the economy, indeed bringing the country down to its knees was an integral part of the opposition's strategy to drive him from office. The president had survived, but he faced the huge task of reconstructing the economy. Compliance with OPEC prices was keeping petroleum prices high, and the control of PDVSA for the first time gave the government ready access to large revenues, but these stimuli could not improve the economy immediately and required at least a year to make their effect felt. Meanwhile, the Chávez presidency was at a low point in approval ratings, as many people fell into the orchestrated trap of blaming the government for the economic damage the opposition had deliberately created.[6]

The government needed to gain time for prosperity from the oil wealth to reach most Venezuelans and entered into negotiations with the Organization of American States and the Jimmy Carter Center to seek a political solution. The government on 29 May 2003 accepted an agreement brokered by the Organization of American States and the Jimmy Carter Center to hold a recall election. In one of its flaws, the 1999 Constitution contained the provision that a sitting president could be recalled after the midway point of his term. During the petroleum strike the opposition had demanded that if the president did not resign, then the date of the elections had to be moved up, but those demands lacked any constitutional justification. Instead the recall clause provided a perfectly legal way to get rid of the president, provided that 20 percent of registered voters signed a petition requesting the election. The clause left open the possibility that even if voters approved the recall, Chávez could still run for president again.[7]

The opposition was delighted with the agreement, and the newly reconstituted Coordinating Committee was confident that the great majority of Venezuelans wanted to kick out Chávez. The optimism was well founded, because polls showed that Chávez would lose the recall vote. However, a first setback came in the fall of 2003, when the National Electoral Council ruled that the signatures the opposition had begun to collect during the petroleum strike were invalid because most had been gathered before the midway point of the presidential term. After complaining and griping as was usual for the opposition, the Coordinating Committee grudgingly launched a new campaign for signatures in November 2003; the recall was not just for Chávez but also for other elected officials, such as National Assembly deputy Luis Tascón.[8]

Even before the opposition accepted the need to collect signatures all over again, the president was busily preparing his first line of defense against the recall movement. In October 2003 Chávez stated in a speech that those who signed the petition were unpatriotic and would face consequences. It was not too late for signers to retract their signatures by filing appeals with the National Electoral Council. Because the names of many individuals were appearing on the petition without their permission, deputy Tascón posted and updated on his web site the names of individuals who supposedly had signed the petition, that way everybody had a chance to retract their signature if their name had been fraudulently used. And for those without access to computers, Chavista newspapers published special editions containing the identity numbers of all persons who had signed the petition. Having the names of the signers on the web site gave officials a great tool to check the loyalty of their employees, and when they could not be fired, they inevitably suffered loss of benefits, promotions, and other perks of the job. PDVSA retirees who signed the recall petition even received threats that their pensions were at risk. In reality, the government agencies were merely playing catch-up with many private firms that previously had coerced employees to sign the recall petition as a condition for keeping their jobs.[9]

The recall drive seemed to have failed when the National Electoral Council announced in late February 2004 that the valid signatures the opposition had turned in did not reach the number required to convoke the recall. However, the decision of the Council still left an opening for the opposition. 400,000 signatures had never existed, 375,000 were fake, and the handwriting of another 876,000 seemed remarkably similar as if the work of a small number of persons; if the citizens of this last group came forward and confirmed their signatures, then having 530,000 ratified signatures sufficed to reach the 20 percent threshold required by the 1999 Constitution.[10]

All that the opposition needed to do was to concentrate on tracking down those citizens to confirm their signatures, and then the recall process could proceed. Actually the opposition was the best ally of Chávez because it "seems prone to error and miscalculation."[11] As one anti–Chávez activist told U.S. diplomats "the opposition suffers from several asymmetries when it comes to political battle: they have lots of guts but few brains" and the Coordinating Committee "has tremendous operational capability (organizing marches and signature drives) but lacks strategic sense." A march to collect more signatures in Caracas on 14 February had gone off well, but the opposition went ballistic after the National Electoral Council announced that the number of signatures was inadequate to convoke the recall. A protest march on 27 February turned violent injuring dozens of demonstrators and killing one. Days of conflict followed lasting until March 4, as small groups of demonstrators engaged in disturbances.[12]

The violence seemed to subside after March 4, but in reality the large-scale demonstrations of February 27 to March 4 had been the official beginning of "Operation Guarimba," an opposition plan to shut down the city. The more violent protestors set up road blocks in key streets and hurled Molotov cocktails to delay the arrival of the police. The protestors who set tires and vehicles on fire vanished after clashing with police, and then they returned the next day to resume their violent protests. These acts of vandalism were supposed to reflect the desire of the majority of the residents to drive Chávez from office, but because almost all of the clashes and road blocks took place in the wealthy eastern parts of the city, many residents became tired of these professional demonstrators. Operation Guarimba rather that helping to bring the government down was actually discrediting the opposition as rabble rousers of an extreme fringe.[13]

Public opinion began to turn in favor of Chávez in early May. Although polls still said that he would lose the recall vote, he appeared as the likely winner in the presidential election that the recall triggered. His social spending and the recovery of the economy were making many Venezuelans, particularly of the middle class, more open to the idea of letting Chávez complete his presidential term. Chávez sensed an opening and decided to increase the margin of his popularity. To remind lower class Venezuelans of who was looking after their welfare, he announced two increases in the minimum wage, one of 20 percent effective on 1 May and a second of 10 percent on 1 August; these increases at a time of little inflation enhanced the purchasing power of many Venezuelans and boosted the president's popularity. The heavens seemed to favor Chávez when the early arrival of torrential rains dispelled the specter of outages in a country relying primarily on hydroelectric dams for most of its current. Up to the arrival of the providential rains, unusual drought in 2003 had depleted the reservoirs, and electricity shortages had threatened to make voters angry in 2004.[14]

Chávez the politician knew that ample electricity and rising income were essential elements but by themselves could not guarantee electoral victory. Voters are moved by emotions and not just by material interests. To take the initiative, on his *Aló Presidente* TV program of 9 May he announced that earlier that day 53 Colombian paramilitaries had been arrested and that the authorities were tracking down many more who had been involved in another coup attempt to overthrow him. According to later claims, apparently thousands of Colombian paramilitaries working in conjunction with disgruntled Venezuelan army officers were preparing to launch a coup to overthrow the government. Over a hundred Colombians were eventually arrested, but the figure of thousands was an exaggeration. The whole episode seemed murky, and although many of the detained persons were paramilitaries, they and the other civilian Colombians under arrest seemed to have been misled about job opportunities in wealthy Venezuela. But something had been going on, and Chávez used the paramilitary episode for its propaganda value and as an excuse to expose any remaining disgruntled military officers.[15]

The paramilitary episode regained the initiative for Chávez just when the likelihood of holding a recall increased. The opposition had expected the National Electoral Council to refuse to approve the recall, but anti–Chávez sympathizers in its staff reported that it was just doing its job. The Coordinating Committee learned by late May that the Council had received confirmations of signatures in a number just barely adequate to reach the required threshold of 20 percent of voters. Obviously the government had good informants in the Council and soon Chávez received irrefutable proof that the petition drive had reached the required number of signatures.[16]

The margin was small, and more careful scrutiny could well invalidate signatures, but Chávez was reluctant to declare the results void. International media generally regarded him as a dictator, while human rights activists were constantly hovering and ready to pounce on any supposed abuse. In a speech on 1 June Chávez hinted at his decision when he announced that the opposition might have reached the required number of signatures to convoke a recall election. Also, his campaign to have people retract their signatures had clearly failed. Briefly Chávez toyed with accepting a 2002 demand from the opposition to call early elections because polls were giving him a clear lead, but no constitutional justification existed for this solution. In an often overlooked reason, he had acquired a taste for elections, and waiting until the presidential contest of December 2006 seemed too far away to practice his campaign skills. When on 3 June the National Electoral Council announced that the number of signatures had reached the requirement, that same day Chávez welcomed the decision as another great example of participatory democracy in Venezuela. He looked forward to the recall as a way to ratify his mandate and to extend his support among the population.[17]

The National Electoral Council set the recall election for 15 August 2004, a date conveniently falling after his most recent increase in the minimum wage went into effect on 1 August. The opposition, believing that it still had the initiative, launched a "National Consensus Plan" on June 9 to make its views known in a coherent announcement. Chávez promptly named the document "the Plan for Bush" and labeled it an anti-Christian tract from the devil and warned that the Plan meant a return to the failed policies of the Fourth Republic. The opposition was slow to react effectively to the attacks on its plan and found itself on the defensive. The opposition still did not realize that it had been checkmated and sensed trouble only when polls in late June showed that the recall vote was tied.[18]

The verbal attacks of Chávez were a smokescreen for the real campaign. The president took direct control of the recall battle and established the special committee *Comando Maisanta* to coordinate all activities. Official agencies saturated the air waves, billboards, and walls with messages calling on people to vote "no" on the recall. The government naturalized as Venezuelan citizens hundreds of thousands of Colombians who received their voter registration at the same time as their naturalization certificates. At the center of the campaign were the electoral patrols composed each of ten Chavista militants. Although *Comando Maisanta* fell short of its goal of creating 130,000 electoral patrols, the nearly 100,000 established made extraordinary contributions to the campaign. The main tasks of the electoral patrols was to make sure that before the deadline of 10 July as large a number as possible of lower class Venezuelans and naturalized foreigners had registered to vote. After that date the electoral patrols shifted their efforts to voter turnout, and they carefully organized teams of volunteers to make sure that the newly registered voters were able to reach the polls.[19]

Slowly the Coordinating Committee was realizing that it was being outgunned in the publicity and the voter recruiting campaigns, while the failure to agree on an acceptable candidate to run for president if Chávez lost the recall perplexed many voters. A disastrous setback came when companies either made no contributions or at best offered only token sums to the recall campaign. The constant interruptions of Plan Guarimba hindered company operations and cooled business support for the opposition. Instead as profits increased, private firms gradually were becoming reconciled to the Bolivarian Revolution, and years of dealing with Chavista officials persuaded the private sector that negotiation rather than confrontation brought better results. By early August the U.S.

Embassy was completely sure that Chávez would win and decided to put the best face forward by declaring the campaign a victory for democratic institutions. The polls left no doubt about the defeat of the recall, but predicting the margin of victory was trickier.[20]

Somehow the opposition still deluded itself into believing that the recall would pass According to the law the campaign closed on 12 August, and when live election coverage resumed on 15 August, the hostile media sent the TV crews only to the wealthy neighborhoods in eastern Caracas to film the long lines of voters waiting supposedly to vote yes on the recall. But the cameras did not go to the western half of the city where the majority of the population lived. The lines of citizens were so long that the National Electoral Council repeatedly extended voting hours, and the last votes were cast only in the early morning hours of August 16.[21]

The results stunned almost everyone. The recall went down to defeat by a margin of 59 percent to 41 percent, and Chávez had won again and by a margin larger than in his previous presidential campaigns. International observers and foreign agencies certified that the election had been fair and honest, but once again the opposition refused to accept the result claiming massive fraud. Even the U.S. government grudgingly accepted the results but did not congratulate Chávez, an implicit admission that the recall had been just one more battle in a long war.[22] As the U.S. Embassy explained, "Identifying the strengths of Chávez campaign, the pressure points within the Venezuelan electoral system, and the weaknesses of the opposition's campaign and leadership is important, however, for the next electoral match against Chávez."[23]

The Opposition in Disarray

Even with ample funding from the U.S. government, a fragmented opposition needed a long time to recuperate before it could mount any serious challenge against Chávez. Venezuelans experienced great prosperity as the country entered the best years of the Chávez presidency, a period lasting until the referendum of December 2007. In spite of the constant accusations throughout his career that he was a Communist dedicated to replicating another socialist Cuba, one of his first phone calls after his victory was to the president of FEDECAMARAS Albis Muñoz. Chávez wanted to reach out the private sector, but she refused to take the call or to make a return call later. Her refusal added insult to injury to the president who did not take kindly to these personal affronts.[24]

In reality Albis Muñoz could not answer the phone because FEDECAMARAS was in the midst of an internal struggle to determine its attitude toward Chávez. This group belonged to the Coordinating Committee for Democracy and Liberty and had supported the recall drive. The previous president Carlos Fernández had actively supported the petroleum strike of December 2002–February 2003 and had fled to Miami to avoid imprisonment. As his replacement, Albis had been elected to head FEDECAMARAS. She had defeated rival candidate Alberto Cudemus, the head of the Federation of Pork Producers, who was a friend and supporter of Chávez. With unusual prescience for a member of the business community, Cudemos had sought collaboration with the government rather than confrontation, and Chávez rewarded his loyalty by prohibiting pork imports from the U.S. Under this protection, the pork industry thrived and this was one food item that has remained abundant in Venezuela. Chávez occasionally mentioned

Cudemos in his *Aló Presidente* broadcasts, and this public recognition guaranteed that all the properties of pork producers in Venezuela remained immune from the land reform law.[25]

Partly for psychological reasons and also because of economic convenience, Chávez wanted acceptance from the private sector. He could never understand why so many business leaders remained hostile to him when he was ready to shower them with privileges and benefits. Corporations run for profit rather than personal whim found the logic of Chávez compelling, and the pressure within FEDECAMARAS to enter into dialogue with the government mounted. A first half-baked attempt backfired on 30 August, when the business group issued a manifesto listing economic concerns but then suddenly veered off into questioning the validity of the voting results in the recall. Incensed officials broke off talks with FEDECAMARAS, arguing that no discussions were possible when the business group refused to accept the legitimacy of the government.[26]

Corporations moved to do damage control and soon obtained the removal or silencing of those persons in FEDECAMARAS most hostile to Chávez. They might not be ready to embrace fully the collaboration that Cudemos kept on urging, but FEDECAMARAS was moving down that path, partly because the business group risked being eclipsed by the Venezuelan-American Chamber of Commerce (VENAMCHAM). This Chamber of Commerce traditionally had been more prominent than even the ones in other Latin America countries with a greater American economic presence. With a membership consisting of American corporations and Venezuelan firms closely linked to the U.S. economy, its members fully embraced the principle of putting profits ahead of political considerations. Consequently VENAMCHAM rejected the highly emotional outbursts of impassioned Venezuelan businessmen who claimed that Chávez was a Communist determined to nationalize all private property. Except for the faux pas of having its president sign the Carmona decree of 12 April 2002, VENAMCHAM had not actively supported that coup attempt. Having learned its lesson, the Chamber of Commerce stayed away from the petroleum strike of 2002–2003 and declined to become a member of the Coordinating Committee. Its more moderate stance made VENAMCHAM an acceptable partner for dialogue with the government, and quite naturally the traditional discussions continued after the recall vote.[27]

The government saw an opportunity to drive a wedge inside the business community and began "to set up a dichotomy between a good Venezuelan-American Chamber of Commerce and a bad FEDECAMARAS."[28] The divide and rule ploy worked well, and business leaders, whether enthusiastically or grudgingly, saw no alternative but to make peace with Chávez. "Venezuela's businessmen have read the numbers and written off the prospects for Chávez departure any time within their planning horizon. [...] Under those circumstances, they have little choice but to find some accommodation with him if they are to get any help on specific issues and contain any surge towards more radical policies."[29] The attempts to have business speak as a unified bloc even on purely economic matters failed, and the government had clearly succeeded in removing from the opposition's camp a very powerful group.

The attempts to woo business groups formed part of the government's campaign to destroy the Coordinating Committee. The existence of this group claiming to represent the opposition and aiming to overthrow the government by any means had always irked Chavistas. With FEDECAMARAS gradually withdrawing its support, the organization entered a long agony. Chávez and Vice President José Vicente Rangel declared that it was time to bury the Coordinating Committee and refused to recognize it any longer as a valid representative of the opposition. The corrupt and discredited political parties of the Fourth Republic remained as its sole support, but they did not wish to risk their survival, and one by one they abandoned the sinking ship. Defeat is never pretty, and the political parties turned on each other in a mad dash to survive the disintegration of the opposition's principal institution. By October 2004 the Coordinating Committee was no longer holding regular meetings for its members, and one insider said that it "had become nothing," and was too fragmented to mount any real challenge in the regional elections of 31 October. The long slow agony of the organization lasted until the end of 2004 when it finally faded from view.

The disappearance of the Coordinating Committee, the last remaining symbol of a united opposition, was another victory for the government; simultaneously, another smashing success came in the regional elections of 31 October 2004. In the greatest sweep until then, Chavista candidates won 20 of the 22 governorships in the country and 270 of the 337 municipalities. The most dramatic gain was in the municipalities, because Chavistas had previously controlled only 115. An important consequence was that Caracas once again had a pro-Chávez mayor, thus making much more difficult any protests in the capital.[30] The regional election, more by default than design, also brought the unexpected result of boosting the prominence of opposition candidate Manuel Rosales. He became governor of Zulia, one of only two states to remain under opposition control. "Rosales appears to be the last man standing in the opposition," and thus enjoyed a preferential position to seek the candidacy for the presidential elections of December 2006.[31]

Rosales was already in the government's sights as a prominent opposition figure, and he was notorious for having signed the decree legitimizing the Pedro Carmona regime on 12 April 2002. In the wake of the recall vote, the government intensified its campaign against all the participants of the attempted coup as a way to weaken the already fragmented opposition. On 17 September 2004, barely a month after the recall vote, Prosecutor Danilo Anderson announced that on the orders of the attorney general, he was reopening the investigation into the 12 April 2002 illegitimate regime of Carmona. As explained in chapter 7, the government had been excessively and dangerously lenient with the coup plotters, and in a belated attempt to compensate for that deficiency, officials insisted on an aggressive prosecution as the best way to prevent the reoccurrence of similar events in the future.[32]

The Anderson investigation was "designed to shut down sources of financing and other support for opposition leaders by bringing the real threat of prison close to home [...] the government of Venezuela is turning to ensure that opponents understand there is a cost to participation in politics against the government."[33] Starting point for the prosecution was the list of the 360 citizens who had signed the so-called Carmona decree constituting the illegitimate regime on 12 April 2002; Anderson intended to supplement the infamous list with television footage of everybody who had attended the swearing-in ceremony on that day. The Anderson investigation touched a raw nerve in the Venezuelan upper class, which for the first time in recent history faced the real threat of spending time in prison. The 360 citizens who signed the Carmona decree belonged to the wealthiest families in the country, and their incarceration meant nothing less than a social revolution. Many of the signers were running scared and some were terrified just imagining having to stay in the dilapidated and hellish Venezuelan prisons.[34]

Anderson began using the traditional prosecutor's ploy of getting the suspects to turn on one another, but his investigation had been underway barely two months when a massive car bomb explosion at 2300 hours on 18 November mangled his body beyond recognition; it took crime experts over 12 hours to confirm that the charred remains did belong to Anderson. The news outraged Chávez who had proof that the opposition had no hesitation about using force to destroy his presidency. The public was shocked, because unlike neighboring Colombia, assassinations had been a very infrequent occurrence in the recent history of Venezuela. The authorities launched an extensive search, and soon the police detained three suspects and killed two assassins when they resisted arrest.[35]

The police had successfully killed or captured the triggermen (*gatilleros*) but tracking down the intellectual authors proved much more complicated. Any of the 360 signers of the Carmona decree could have ordered the assassination. Evidence surfaced that some of the lawyers working with Anderson had been selling immunity from prosecution to some of the Carmona signers; leads also suggested that the order to assassinate had come from exiled Venezuelans in Miami, Florida. But too many dead ends frustrated investigators, and although Chávez wanted to bring the assassins to justice, soon even he realized that this case was going to remain largely unsolved. As far as the resumption of the case against the Carmona signers, prosecutors were naturally jittery about an assignment that implied a death sentence. The government, mistakenly concluding that the political benefits from this investigation were diminishing, gradually lost interest in vigorously pursuing these charges against the upper class.[36]

The National Assembly did not give up so easily and continued its own investigation into the Anderson assassination but reached the same dead ends. As a partial substitute Chavista deputies passed a bill imposing harsh restrictions on the opposition and also punishment against the criminals starting to proliferate in Venezuela. Clauses in the bill were early indications that the public was tiring of the opposition protests and wanted them drastically reduced. The bill also sharply increased the prison terms for felonies, in particular for rape, kidnapping, murder, and crimes against property. The National Assembly approved the bill on 6 January 2005, but in one of the major blunders of his presidency, on 3 February Chávez vetoed the bill. His reluctance to sign this popular anti-crime and anti-protest bill surprised many, and the best explanation for his political error was that the prisons were again experiencing overcrowding and that he did not want to make their situation worse by incarcerating more people for longer sentences. Shortly after taking office in 1999, he had embarked upon a vast program to revamp the prison system. His efforts had been successful, but by 2004 the old vices at the prisons resurfaced. The real issue was the increase in crime, and the refusal of the government to tackle this problem created the conditions for the relentless deterioration of law and order in the streets and in the prisons in later years.[37]

One of the excuses given for vetoing the bill against crime was that any law increasing prison terms was meaningless until the judicial system was first reformed. It was well known that many judges, and possibly a majority, were corrupt and incompetent. The National Assembly had been working on changing the composition of the Supreme Court, because this body besides being the final court of appeals also had authority over the judges of lower courts. The process of reconstituting the Supreme Court was completed on 2 February 2004 when the justices elected former guerrilla Omar Mora as the Chief Justice. In the process of appointing new justices, Chávez obtained for the first time a real majority in the highest court of the country. The first urgent item of business was the reversal of the decision that falsely declared that no coup had occurred on 11 April

2002. This absurd sentence of 14 August 2002 had prevented the attorney general from bringing criminal charges against civilian and military coup participants who remained free to try again to overthrow the government. By 2005 almost all the military coup plotters had been dismissed, and although the reversal by the Supreme Court on 11 March 2005 made possible the criminal prosecution of the officers, the government wisely decided to keep this possibility as a threat thereby assuring good behavior among former officers.[38]

The new Supreme Court carried an active campaign against corruption: 53 judges had been removed from lower courts by May, and as the investigations proceeded, more dismissals took place. Curiously, it was not the firing of judges but their replacement that raised the most public controversy. The Supreme Court insisted on high academic credentials for the positions but also wanted individuals who would not be openly hostile to the Chávez presidency. Thus, any individual who had participated actively in the opposition was automatically excluded. Although the Supreme Court used a variety of sources to determine the political tendency of the candidates, the most important was the Tascón list, named after the deputy Luis Tascón who had gathered the names of signers of the different petitions for the recall vote and posted the list in his website to see if anyone's name had appeared by mistake in the petitions. After the recall vote, Tascón removed the list from his website, but the list had already been downloaded and soon was available for purchase in a convenient CD-ROM. Other shorter lists such as the "Let's Save PDVSA" petition were also available to determine the political affiliation of citizens, but any person appearing in the other lists almost certainly had also signed the recall petition and thus was also in the Tascón list. Already on April 15 Chávez had said in a televised speech in front of his cabinet to stop using the Tascón list to inflict reprisals on government employees and private contractors, but the Supreme Court went on using it to assure the political loyalty of all the new judges.[39] Whether other government agencies heeded Chavez's call to stop using the list remains unclear. Although its use certainly declined over the coming years the Tascón list became a major barrier to repeating another recall effort.

Chávez could afford to show compassion to the many citizens duped into signing the recall petitions because he sensed that his political steamroller was marching ahead practically unimpeded. After the resounding victory in the regional elections of 31 October 2004 came an even greater success in the National Assembly elections of 4 December 2005. Everyone had predicted a Chávez victory, but not even he had expected the complete sweep that occurred. The opposition was having a hard time fielding candidates and with so many uncontested seats, it could only win a small minority in the National Assembly. Then suddenly a cascade effect began on 28 November when a political party pulled its candidates out of the race and then another group did the same until no opposition candidates remained on the ballot by 3 December. Chávez could not have received a better Christmas gift.[40]

Quite naturally, MVR, Chávez's own party, increased the number of its deputies from 69 to 114 out of a total of 167. The president for the first time had a two-thirds majority in the National Assembly, but in reality his control over the legislative body was absolute, because the remaining deputies belonged to small pro-government parties. The boycott of the legislative elections was another of the many blunders the opposition made in its struggle to drive Chávez from power.[41] The U.S. Embassy struggled to find any silver lining in these dismal results and observed that "if this incident marginalizes the opposition's leadership dinosaurs and the grassroots retains its voice"[42] then perhaps in the next electoral contest the voters might at last turn against Chávez.

Attempts to Transform Venezuela

During the best years of the Chávez presidency Venezuela was enjoying great prosperity. At the simplest level, high petroleum prices were responsible for the record growth of the economy, but the causes were deeper. First of all, the government pressed OPEC (Organization of Petroleum Exporter Countries) to reduce oil output, while PDVSA, the state corporation, stayed within the production quota. Secondly, once PDVSA lost its independence the government could tap into its revenues for the benefit of the whole country. This access to petroleum revenues gave the Chávez presidency the means to finance a vast array of programs designed to improve the life of vast segments of the population.

Everyone understood that prosperity depended on exporting large amounts of crude at high prices, but the big unanswered question remained what would happen to the country if either output or prices declined. Petroleum exports had made Venezuela excessively dependent on imports and had also squeezed out other exports. The Fourth Republic had channeled large amounts of oil revenue into making Venezuela self-sufficient in foodstuffs and had also expanded heavy industry, in particular steel and aluminum. The Chávez administration was very sympathetic to domestic industry but curiously never got around to formulating nor much less to implementing a systematic long-term policy of industrialization. Working with private business groups, officials generally concentrated on trying to build a consensus on how best to help individual manufacturing firms. The most important decision was to halt the privatization of state enterprises, and this change in policy saved the state aluminum company (VENALUM) from falling into private ownership.[43]

Perhaps because industrialization was too technical a topic to be explained in simple terms or perhaps because only small segments of the population participated in manufacturing, industrial policy rarely entered into the debates of political campaigns. The same was not true for agriculture, because the population expected abundant and cheap supplies of foodstuffs. In 2005 Hugo Chávez was emphasizing the need for the country to achieve "food sovereignty" partly because of its strategic vulnerability. Officials realized that a blockade of the country's ports sufficed to reduce the population to starvation. By emphasizing food self-sufficiency he came to grips with the same conundrum that the Fourth Republic had vainly tried to disentangle: how could a country with abundant agricultural lands fail to feed itself? The contrast with Colombia made the riddle even more unexplainable, because the neighboring country with similar soils and climate easily feed a population twice as large and in addition supplied a significant percentage of the food consumed in Venezuela.

The Fourth Republic had failed to make Venezuela self-sufficient in food, yet many of its individual programs had succeeded in increasing agricultural output, so Chávez had a base to build upon. One reason behind the failure of the Fourth Republic was that many large landowners did not plant their fields. The Land Law of November 2001 had tried to address this problem by threatening expropriation if the owners of properties larger than 5,000 hectares did not put uncultivated lands under production. The opposition condemned the Land Law as a property grab patterned on the Cuban Revolution, but the first expropriations took place only four years later in 2005. Without additional incentives such as infrastructure and market access, large landowners did little to increase the amount of land under cultivation.[44]

After the sweep in the October 2004 regional elections, Chávez turned his attention not to agriculture but to the supposedly burning topic of land distribution. In November 2004 in a summit at Fort Tiuna with governors, mayors, and national officials, he made agrarian reform one of the ten major goals of the last two years of his presidential term. Although he placed first on the list of goals the strengthening of the 24 missions or special programs, in reality this first goal and eight of the other ten were mainly a reaffirmation of existing policies; only the strident call for a "war" on large landed estates (*latifundios*) gave a new urgency to an old proposal. Diplomats and observers have struggled to find the reasons why Chávez prioritized land reform over agricultural production as he shifted back and forth between fierce statements and ambivalent implementation.[45]

Land for the peasants had been a valid argument during the age of agrarian societies, but after the middle of the twentieth century when the majority of the population moved into the cities, the goal of redistributing land had lost its urgency. By the time Chávez first took office nearly 90 percent of the Venezuelan population lived in urban areas, and in a country with vast open frontiers of untapped public land a peasant protest movement did not exist. From a political perspective, the percentage of the population living in the countryside was so small that the rural vote did not seem crucial to win elections.[46]

Land for the peasants had been a rallying slogan so long that Chávez embraced agrarian reform as a way to satisfy leftist ideologues and bolster his radical credentials. During 2005 the so-called war against large landed estates boiled down to struggles over the nationalization and compensation of about a dozen large properties; because British and Spanish citizens owned several of these properties, lengthy diplomatic and judicial negotiations complicated any land expropriations.[47] Not satisfied with this modest start, early in 2006 Chávez decided to make a new push for agrarian reform. On his *Aló Presidente* television broadcast of 8 January 2006, he announced the ambitious goal of distributing one and a half million hectares during the coming year. This goal seemed beyond reach when the Venezuelan state simply lacked the capability to survey and register such a vast extension of land, and "Chavez has a history of announcing sweeping land transfers that peter out in a few months, as well as demanding surveys of idle land that are never carried out."[48]

When squatters inside large landed estates demanded a share of the harvest, speculators and swindlers soon realized that agrarian reform offered great opportunities for making profits. If squatters were not already inside the large estate, then speculators encouraged nearby peasants to invade or occupy illegally the private property. Then these peasants pressured the government to nationalize part or all of the large estate, and when accomplished, the land went into a cooperative. The speculators then bought the land at low prices from the members of the cooperative and sold the land at a high price to new private owners. In other cases the new owners of the land were former urban dwellers who then sold the land at a nice profit and moved back to the city. As one way to forestall these land invasions, property owners used Spain's generous citizenship laws to become Spanish citizens and thus gained immunity from these nationalizations.[49]

Speculators eager to make fast profits were creating havoc in the countryside and destroying any possibility of achieving that "food sovereignty" officials kept talking about. For the government "the utopian rhetoric of sweeping land reform serves both to bully wealthy landowners and to play to Chávez's political base."[50] In the tradition of the Cuban Revolution, Chávez assigned the task of taking physical control of any nationalized landed estate to a 19-person military team as the first step toward establishing cooperatives to administer the property. Chávez announced with great fanfare the deployment of these military teams when they really lacked estates to take over. The shortage of nationalized properties was making impossible staging a publicity stunt, so Chávez had his television cameras broadcast the triumphal entry of a military team into Hato Callejas in March 2007 to take control of the landed estate. In reality this was pure show: previously the owner had been glad to sell the property because its marshy soils were suitable only for raising water buffalo.[51]

Ranches tended to bear the brunt of the agrarian reform, and not surprisingly, the Cattleman's Association (FEDENAGA) became a bitter enemy of Chávez, although the exact origin of the animosity is not clear. The situation was the opposite with the pork producers, who became staunch supporters of the government. Loyalty to Chávez brought immediate practical benefits, such as complete immunity from expropriations and protection from imports for pork producers. Instead for the cattlemen, they not only remained out in the cold but feared the entry of Venezuela into MERCOSUR, the Latin American common market and the alternative to the U.S.-promoted Free Trade of the Americas. Venezuelan cattlemen correctly feared that they could not compete with Argentina and Brazil, two members of MERCOSUR who were respectively the third and the first largest exporters of beef in the world. Some ranchers had been proposing violent demonstrations and general strikes to force the government to follow more favorable policies.[52] As the opposition of the cattlemen to Chávez turned bitter, American diplomats correctly concluded that the eccentric and haphazard attempts at agrarian reform "offer opportunities for us to build coalitions among the agriculture, business, environmental, and political communities"[53] as steps toward first restraining and later destroying the Chávez presidency.

The ill-planned attempts at land reform needlessly complicated the task of meeting the two essential goals of providing food at low prices and trying to achieve self-sufficiency in foodstuffs. The clash between the two goals was already intense, because to increase domestic output, producers had to receive higher prices, but to satisfy the voter base food prices had to remain low. And whenever land reform affected significant producers such as cattle ranches, the confiscation disrupted supplies and inevitably led to increased food imports to avoid shortages at the shelves. During the Fourth Republic, high prices had kept many foodstuffs beyond the reach of the lower class, but with the transfers of income taking place during the Chávez presidency, the increased purchasing power of the masses increased the demand for foodstuffs that the country was not able to produce at least in the short run. The government imposed price controls on a list of basic food items to prevent inflation, and the inevitable result was shortages of those items and empty shelves on the stores.[54]

One example without the complicating variable of land reform illustrated the pitfalls of using price controls to try to reach simultaneously the two goals of low prices and high output. One of the rare positive legacies of the Fourth Republic had come when the country became self-sufficient in coffee in the last years of the twentieth century. The government was so confident that supply was more than adequate to cover domestic demand that in 2004 it lifted the prohibition on exporting coffee, and Venezuela resumed making modest shipments abroad for the first time in many decades. Yet in the last weeks of December 2004 ground coffee disappeared from the shelves of stores and the country was experiencing a near scarcity of this beverage.[55]

The government on its own had created this crisis by failing to coordinate its policies. In response to complaints from roasters that they were having to sell below production cost, one agency raised the price of ground coffee by 66 percent on 1 December 2004. This measure should have guaranteed a steady supply, but another agency nullified the benefits when it raised the price that roasters had to pay for coffee beans by 102 percent on 16 December. No Ph.D. in economics was necessary to calculate the loss to the roasters, who stopped buying beans and hoarded their remaining ground coffee. When news of the hoarding spread, the government briefly tried to pin the scarcity on greedy private merchants, but then it was learned that the state-owned roaster was doing the same thing. After much posturing by Chávez and other officials denouncing private greed and claiming that coffee belonged to all Venezuelans, the government on 17 January 2005 quietly raised the price of ground coffee by an additional 60 percent and soon after abundant supplies reappeared on store shelves.[56]

Similar problems dogged the supply of sugar, corn flour, and powdered milk, the latter being very important in tropical Venezuela where refrigeration often is not readily available. Consumers resigned themselves to the reality that occasional shortages of different good items were going to be a normal part of daily life. Most voters, however, seemed to prefer this less than ideal situation to the harsh reality of the Fourth Republic when stores were overflowing with every conceivable food item at prices beyond the reach of the vast majority of the population.[57] The ability to fix prices at a level not too low to discourage producers and not too high to deprive consumers of goods requires extensive knowledge and special skills; not surprisingly the difficulty of acquiring this talent has led most industrial countries to give up the task as hopeless and by default to leave the decisions to the blind market forces of supply and demand.

Venezuela never mastered the art of setting prices for agricultural products, but the most successful of the new missions, Mercal (*Mercado Alternativo*) succeeded in providing ample foodstuffs at low prices, extensive support for domestic producers, and not least, political cover for the Chávez presidency. The state had not intended to enter into the grocery business, and the official food distribution network emerged by accident. During the petroleum strike of December 2002–February 2003 the gasoline shortage prevented trucks from completing their routes. As chapter 7 mentioned, the government ordered the army to make the deliveries, and soon the supermarkets in the wealthy eastern part of Caracas were adequately stocked. The situation became critical in western Caracas and downtown where the small corner stores (*bodegas*) had exhausted their inventories and the residents faced hunger. It had been easy for army trucks to restock the several dozen supermarkets brightly visible in eastern Caracas but supplying hundreds of often unmarked small stores whose location was not always known was a more daunting task. Wisely army officers decided to organize "mega public markets" in open spaces of the western neighborhoods of Caracas. To offset the inconvenience of residents having to walk far to buy and carry back the food to their homes, the government slashed the prices on those products available at the open-air markets. The hungry residents did not complain and were so pleased with the low prices that they demanded that these mega markets continue even after the collapse of the petroleum strike in February 2003.[58]

The government responded by creating Mercal, and the distribution network began operating with a few warehouse style stores in April 2003. Its numbers rapidly increased until 15,000 stores existed in 2006 and Mercal was serving nearly half of the population and supplying half of the food to consumers in the country. Originally the army operated Mercal and it remained an important influence in the institution. However, Cuban advisors with their considerably experience in running government stores became the driving force in operating Mercal and adapting its functions to local conditions. Obviously this was a subsidized firm, but the sums of $144 million U.S. in 2004 and $166 in 2005 seemed a wise use of petroleum revenue and a small cost to pay to improve the standard of living of a majority of Venezuelans.[59]

Mercal at 92 percent approval ratings became the most popular mission or program of the Chávez presidency. What some might consider unfair government competition did not really happen. The small corner stores, whose existence had always been precarious, generally took the option of becoming franchises for Mercal. These franchises, generally known as "Mercalitos," combined the advantages of public and private ownership. The large supermarket chains catering to upper and middle class citizens actually saw their market share increase slightly, because these chains sold luxury and many imported items not available at Mercal stores. Thus although Mercal sold nearly half the foodstuffs by amount, by price it had between 20 to 30 percent of sales, reflecting its concentration on basic staples of the household basket. The supermarkets differentiated themselves by increasing their selection of products, making their facilities more attractive, and offering better personal service. Supermarkets encouraged credit card use while Mercal stores accepted only cash. Invariably supermarkets offered frozen and chilled products, but only the largest Mercal stores began in 2006 to set up cold storage facilities.

On the aftermath of the disruptive petroleum strike, Mercal had no choice but to rely heavily on imported goods to fill its shelves, and here it enjoyed the additional benefit of tax exemptions on food imports. However, Mercal resisted the temptation to become just an intermediary for foreign foods and strove hard to favor domestic producers. The subsidy covered the difference between buying high from producers and selling low to consumers. In 2005 the percentage of imported items dropped to 37 percent compared to 70 percent in 2004, and this big drop reflected the commitment to support the campaign for self-sufficiency in the country. As an added incentive to domestic producers, the discount chain provided free packaging materials, which brought the political advantage of putting messages supportive of the Chávez presidency in all the labels. On principle the upper class refused to shop at the discount chain and be exposed to the propaganda throughout the store and on food labels, but the middle class was not so squeamish. Admittedly few Mercal stores were near wealthy neighborhoods, but for many commuters working downtown, "picking up a few items" at the discount chain became an unspoken practice. Even upper middle-class Venezuelans could not resist taking advantage of some bargains at the Mercal stores whose appearance frequently resembled crowded warehouses stacked to the top with jumbled food items in contrast to the bright and well-ordered shelves of the spacious supermarkets.[60]

Mercal became so popular that even opposition candidates promised to preserve the discount distribution network. The other 23 missions did not attain that high level of success, but even if only moderately effective, they helped to sustain the perception that Chávez was the first president who really was working to improve the lives of average Venezuelans. These social programs and his growing international standing as a visible opponent of the George W. Bush administration were giving him tremendous boost as he prepared for the presidential election in December 2006. At the summit of November 2004 at Fort Tiuna he had formulated the ten main goals for his movement, but upon closer reflection, he concluded that they were too diffuse to be enunciated briefly. He needed a shorthand slogan to refer to his program, and after much hesitation he coined the term "twenty-first-century Socialism" in January 2005. He repeated this expression in countless speeches and in the *Aló Presidente* television broadcasts, so the slogan remained a foundation stone during the years of his presidency.[61]

The "twenty-first-century" part of the slogan was certainly timely, but after over ten years of practice "Socialism" seemed an unfortunate word choice. Constantly the opposition has used his proclamation of socialism as adequate proof to condemn him as an unrepentant Communist. Had he planned to nationalize vast sectors of the economy, the use of the word socialism certainly seemed warranted. But in accordance with his deeply held convictions, he repeatedly insisted that he had no intention of abolishing private property. At the other extreme he repudiated Soviet Communism, and in spite of all his admiration for Fidel Castro, he rejected replicating the Cuban economic system in Venezuela. In reality, he was trying to create a new economic model out of capitalism, the Cuban system, and popular participation. At the November 2004 summit at Fort Tiuna he had talked about pursuing an economic model that was social, humane, and egalitarian; and in this perspective his approach harked back to the attempt of General Juan Velasco to find a "third way" for Peru between capitalism and socialism.[62] The danger of that approach was of falling into the trap of leftist parties in Western Europe that slyly lure unwary voters into accepting the supremacy of privileged wealthy groups.

Chávez never found a concise and accurate expression to convey what he really wanted to do. What he tried to accomplish reveals more accurately the type of system that he desired for Venezuela. As a constant critic of "savage" capitalism that systematically and brutally exploits the masses for the benefit of a wealthy minority, he believed along with many other reformers that cooperatives were a more humane alternative for economic organization "since they buttress his vision of a more self-sufficient, non-capitalist, revolutionary society."[63]

As soon as he took office in 1999 the government provided generous financial backing for the establishment of cooperatives, and for their organization even one of the 24 missions offered free training and expert counseling. They spread rapidly, and by the end of 2004 around 50,000 had been registered, "but determining how many really existed was impossible because cooperatives tended to fold as fast as they formed."[64] About 90 percent were agricultural, and they received most of the land from nationalized estates. Personal quarrels plagued them, and sometimes violent clashes erupted between rival cooperatives. In an embarrassing episode in the unscripted *Aló Presidente* a peasant explained that sometimes rural residents hesitated to organize a new cooperative because they inevitably ended fighting bitterly among themselves. Not even this revelation could deter Chávez from changing course, and he returned to the pat answer of blaming capitalism for all the problems in the countryside. Meanwhile, astute scam artists were taking advantage of the land reform to persuade unsuspecting peasants to establish cooperatives on good private lands; when the operations were over, the swindlers made a nice gain and the peasants were left with nothing.[65]

The financial rewards for creating the new cooperatives were so great, that urban operators also wanted to cash in on the benefits. After the failure of the recall vote in August 2004, many small businesses and even larger companies converted into cooperatives and abandoned their legal status of private firms. 42,000 cooperatives appeared just in 2005, and their total number rose to 107,000 employing around 4.6 percent of the labor force. A central goal of these new organizations has been to blur the distinction between owners and workers; in the case of Venezuela, all workers after a trial period of six months were supposed to be given the opportunity to become partners if they also met additional conditions, the most common being that of making a monetary investment. By giving all employees a direct financial stake and by distributing profits equally among partners, the cooperatives were supposed not only to eliminate labor conflict but also to obtain a well-motivated and highly productive work force.[66]

In reality, the conversions of private firms into cooperatives had taken place in paper only, and the firms maintained their existing business model intact. Workers were denied the opportunity to become partners, and management continued to hire and fire at will. Because the minimum requirement to have a cooperative was only five employees, some sham outfits appeared as tax dodges only to avoid payments. Because the government also offered loans on very generous terms, some swindlers took the loan money, defaulted, and then vanished; these fraudulent activities frequently disrupted the production and distribution of food in the country. Although not all the attempts ended in failure, the more than a billion dollars the government poured into cooperatives were largely wasted.[67]

Some cooperatives through no fault of their own were facing bankruptcy, while many private companies were also in danger of closing. The workers, desperate not to lose their jobs, were clamoring for a bailout, and the government listened to their pleas and created the model of co-management. In all cases the government took over the failing company or cooperative and then injected capital until it owned 51 percent of the enterprise. The 49 percent share remained in the hands of the previous private owners, the cooperative, or workers, and in some cases a combination of those groups. The common origin of these failed enterprises was the petroleum strike of 2002–2003, and the government felt a moral obligation to save those firms weakened by the disruptions. This co-management model had saved many firms from bankruptcy, but the danger was that workers in other poorly managed companies might routinely turn to the government for a bailout. Whatever might be the exact economic benefits from keeping these companies functioning, the government had reaped considerable political popularity by demonstrating its determination to save jobs.[68]

Partly out of the co-management model and partly out of the experience with cooperatives, the government, and in particular PDVSA had come up with a third business model, the Social Production Enterprises (EPS). These enterprises were supposed to combine the best characteristics of private and state ownership. As with co-management, the government owned 51 percent of the company which supposedly was run as a cooperative in a non-hierarchical manner. In contrast with the co-management model that emerged as a response to failing companies, the government took the initiative to create EPS in many sectors of the economy, particularly in manufacturing and housing. All the EPSs were required to make substantial reinvestments in their community, most notably in building housing to help cover the growing shortage in the country. The role of PDVSA was crucial, because not only did it usually supply the 51 percent government share, but it also began favoring ESPs as suppliers to the company. Contractors learned that if they did not adopt the ESP model, they would have to invest 1 to 2 percent of their profits in community programs. Companies adjusted by raising their bids upward to accommodate the increased cost of getting contracts from PDVSA.[69]

Ingenious and intriguing as were many of the social experiments the Chávez presidency was attempting to carry out, even when not very successful they all helped to create the impression that here was a government that for the first time in the country's history was trying to improve the conditions of the majority of Venezuelans. The contrast with the Fourth Republic existing basically for the benefit of privileged economic and political elites was striking, and with the economy booming since the failed petroleum strike, Chávez remained extremely popular among the overwhelming majority of Venezuelans. But 2006 was a presidential election year, and by December the voters had to decide whether they wanted another six years of this exhilarating if sometimes chaotic system.

CHAPTER 10

Peru: Ups and Downs of the Alejandro Toledo Presidency

The president has made a habit of shooting himself in the foot politically just when his own prospects are brightening.—U.S. Ambassador Struble[1]

Four major issues amply illustrate the desire of Alejandro Toledo to push Peru in new directions. The achievements in these four areas were clear, yet their flaws and deficiencies eroded the reputation of his presidency. The limited successes helped to reduce but could not prevent the outbreak of the social conflicts such as those already narrated in chapter 6. Additional clashes and scandals sent the Toledo presidency in a downward spiral that threatened to topple the government.

Reaching for the Sky

Economic growth Alejandro Toledo considered the economic growth of Peru to be the greatest accomplishment of his presidency. The macroeconomic indicators revealed a steady increase in Gross Domestic Product (GDP), which rose from only 0.2 percent in 2001 to 7.6 percent in 2006. GDP growth averaged around 4.5 percent, and the gains were real because inflation stayed low (in the range of 1.1 to 1.5 percent). Balanced budgets helped to dampen inflation, while the tripling of exports during his administration boosted the foreign reserves of the country. But as his biographer noted: "the core problem was that economic growth was not translating into more jobs, reduced unemployment, and a higher standard of living for most Peruvians."[2]

Per capita income was rising, yet the economic expansion was not improving the lives of most Peruvians. Actually rival Chile consistently had higher per capita income figures and was widening its lead over Peru. Poverty was another troubling indicator. In 2001 54.3 percent of the population lived in poverty, and the Toledo administration in is initial years was unable to reduce the percentage below 50 percent. Improvement came in 2004 when the percentage of the population living in poverty fell to 48.6 and continued falling steadily to 39.3 percent in 2007. But the reduction was taking place mainly in the prosperous coastal areas and was generally bypassing the highlands and the Amazon region. Economists admitted that poverty reduction was inelastic with regard to GDP growth but never formulated the question of whether major sacrifices to achieve this unequal growth were really justified.[3]

Except for the agricultural exports from the coast, primarily the new crop of asparagus, most of the growth was driven by the extraction of minerals. The immense environmental damage and the disruption of native and non-native communities did not figure into the profit calculations of the foreign companies. And even assuming that the expansion of mining was the only way to achieve economic prosperity, leaving the extractive activities in the hands of foreign corporations deprived Peru of a substantial part of the benefits. As was usual in capitalist economies, growth was coming at the high price of income inequality. Public sector companies do a better job at keeping benefits inside a country and in minimizing income inequality, but the decision of Peruvian governments to hand over extractive activities to foreign corporations precluded this alternative. Not surprisingly many Peruvians felt largely bypassed and in desperation took to the streets to engage in violent demonstrations as the only way to try to reclaim at least crumbs from the economic system.

The Camisea Gas Project A major achievement of the Toledo administration was to bring into production the gas fields of Camisea in the Amazon region. The benefits from the extraction of this resource were so great, that in large part natural gas was the main factor responsible for the economic growth during the Toledo years. And this success with gas was also instrumental in preventing and reducing the social protests in many parts of Peru.

The discovery of natural gas deposits in the Amazon region dated back to 1931, but gas fields were considered a nuisance for the real business of extracting petroleum. The world and Peru became interested in natural gas after the energy shocks of the 1970s, and Petroperu, the state oil company, obtained from the first Alán García administration the concession to develop these gas fields in association with Royal Shell Petroleum.[4]

Gas, just like all mineral concessions, proved a tempting source of corruption for the Alberto Fujimori administration. Although the details of the maneuver have not yet been uncovered, the Fujimori team deprived Petroperu of its rights over gas deposits as part of the price for escaping complete privatization. In two separate contracts in 2000, the government granted two international consortia the concession to extract gas and ship it by pipeline to the coast. The gas from this part of the project was mainly for domestic consumption. The 212 kilometer pipeline built from the Amazon to the top of the Andes Mountains was built wider than necessary in anticipation of having to accommodate later volumes destined for export through additional segments running only in the Pacific coast.[5]

Camisea I, the name of this part of the gas project, entered into production in August 2004 when the first gas flowed from the Amazon to metropolitan Lima. The pipelines crossed Indian lands and vulnerable environments, yet the opposition to the project never reached the level of popular protests or much less of social conflict. The construction companies succeeded in allaying local concerns, and the Toledo administration seemed to have scored a big success without any glitches.[6]

The celebrations proved premature, because the supposedly new pipeline suffered four major ruptures in 2004. Building shoddy pipelines and charging full price has been a frequent source of profits and corruption in many underdeveloped countries, and Peru could not be the exception. The shady deals of the Fujimori administration were the cause of these defects in 2004, but the Toledo administration and the U.S. Embassy sought to minimize the damage by labeling the ruptures as mere "cracks." The public relations campaign fell apart on 4 March 2006 when a fifth rupture caused an explosion and injured at least three individuals. With headlines covering the newspapers, the government reluctantly engaged in a long overdue investigation. The findings were totally predictable and confirmed that the companies in a drive to cut costs, had recycled old and often corroded tubes into the pipeline and hired unqualified workers to perform faulty welding. And because the contracts stipulated large penalties for delays in completion, the companies rushed to finish the pipeline without observing the quality standards.[7]

Supplying gas for domestic consumption has never been a concern of foreign corporations whose essential goal has always been the extraction of mineral resources at the lowest price possible for export to industrialized countries. In the case of Peru, the foreign corporations had to placate nationalistic demands and accepted supplying the domestic market as a heavy price for obtaining the lucrative export concessions. The strategy was working, and President Toledo did not waver in his unflinching support for Camisea II, the export component of the gas fields. Already on 12 January 2006 the groundbreaking ceremony took place for the Liquefied Natural Gas (LNG) plant on the coast 169 kilometers south of Lima. This plant was the terminal for exporting the natural gas aboard LNG ships. Loans from international agencies and company expenditures in Camisea II, including additional pipelines, came to total $3.8 billion, making this the largest foreign investment project ever in the history of Peru.[8]

The thousands of jobs this construction project generated facilitated selling Camisea II to a skeptical public. The fear that most profits were flowing out with the LNG proved difficult to dispel, but the Toledo administration had more success reassuring the population that Peru possessed ample gas for domestic consumption. As the amount of proven reserves expanded through prospecting, Peru could count on at least a century of gas supplies. Already in an early indication, the companies reinjected gas back into the fields because the supply vastly exceeded the domestic demand.[9]

As a typical export project to take profits abroad, Camisea both under Fujimori and Toledo had given little attention to the domestic consumption of gas. The ill-prepared Toledo administration scrambled to find uses for domestic gas to try to satisfy the nationalists who had insisted on keeping some of the gas inside Peru. The most important and the most widespread positive effect was the reduction of electricity rates for both residential and industrial consumers. Until then about half of the electricity of Peru had come from Diesel plants and hydroelectricity supplied the rest. Utilities converted their power plants from petroleum to natural gas, thereby achieving huge costs savings. In anticipation of their lower costs, the electricity companies had been lowering their rates even before the first Camisea gas reached Lima. The cheaper electricity meant that consumers received a boost in their incomes and enjoyed greater disposable income to buy goods and services, in effect fueling the growth of the economy discussed earlier in the chapter. And because domestic gas was replacing expensive imports of petroleum, Peru also reaped substantial foreign exchange savings that contributed to the growing monetary reserves.[10]

Lower electricity rates were the most important benefit but far from the only one of Camisea gas. Vehicles in Lima, beginning with taxis and buses, began a steady conversion from gasoline to gas. The conversion would have taken place faster had the government from the start made provision for opening an adequate number of filling stations for the gas-powered vehicles. The government had also failed to prepare adequate number of workshops to carry out the conversions, and a huge backlog meant long delays in completing the process. Once the cleaner gas vehicles entered into service, they also helped to reduce the smog in the polluted air of the capital.

Many households wanted to take advantage of the cheap natural gas for cooking and heating water, but once again the government failed to make preparations. Prior to Camisea some households consumed imported gas in small cylinders, but the real opportunity was to construct a network of subterranean pipes to bring gas to households. An excessive number of restrictions hindered the process, while among middle class homes the fear of explosions, such as the rupture in the pipelines, made some households hesitant to rush into the conversion. Quite revealingly, the poor households were the most eager to adopt gas; as one utility official explained, "the poorer Peruvians are quicker to switch to natural gas because they value the cost savings more and have lower conversion costs."[11] Besides the conversion to gas of households, businesses, and vehicles released funds for consumption and investment, thereby contributing to fuel the economic growth of Peru.[12]

The rosy panorama from Camisea became even brighter because the taxes on the gas turned into an important source of revenue for the national government. Although the royalties for the new regional governments were supposed to be substantial, only departments with gas deposits qualified to receive the funds. And even for those that did receive royalties, contradictory information makes it hard to evaluate whether they were actually benefiting. In a revealing example, royalties were supposed to transform Cuzco, but in reality this department could not escape from its traditional poverty.[13]

The regional effect of the natural gas had another very important dimension. The highly populated coast received the bulk of the benefits from the cheap gas but areas lacking hydroelectricity or direct supplies of gas did not experience any reduction in the utility rates. The natural gas benefited most the Lima metropolitan area, which became more sympathetic to the free market orientation of Toledo. And when it came time for elections, the coast was most likely to vote for candidates with a free market orientation. Not surprisingly, social protests were much more prevalent in areas outside of Lima. A clear correlation existed between the savings from natural gas and the level of social protest.

But did Camisea validate the policy of handing over Peru's precious non-renewable resources over to private enterprise? The grip that foreign corporations have exercised over Peru's economy remains today as strong if not stronger than in any period of its history. The attempt of the military government of General Juan Velasco (1968–1975) to regain control over natural resources appears as a brief almost idealistic interlude, before Peru slipped back again under the control of foreign capital. But are these private foreign corporations really indispensable, especially when so much of their funding, such as for Camisea, came from international lending organizations?

And as far as technical expertise, why is Peru unable to produce engineers, technicians, and managers able to conduct the extraction of the vast array of minerals scattered throughout the country? A mining school seems a high priority, and when combined with graduate studies abroad, there is no reason why abundant local talent should not be available. And in the case of Camisea, the deliberate exclusion of Petroperu from the extraction of gas, was a missed opportunity. A large part of the profits going abroad would have stayed in Peru if the state oil company had been in charge. And the corruption that foreign companies inevitably sponsor would not have been as widespread.

Camisea was so lucrative, that the profits during the initial years were more than adequate to satisfy the government, foreign corporations, and many sectors of the population. In many ways Peru was following Venezuela's example of relying on foreign corporations to handle the export of mineral resources. That formula worked well for Venezuela in the early decades of the Fourth Republic but soon became harmful to the real interests of the country. It is too early to tell whether Peru, because of its extensive agribusiness, will follow a path resembling Venezuela's. Yet the exclusive dependence on foreign corporations to extract the non-renewal mineral resources of the country remains a troubling concern.

Free Trade Agreement with the United States To an even greater degree than for the Camisea Gas Project, President Alejandro Toledo can claim credit for the Free Trade Agreement with the United States. Initially both proposals dated back to the twentieth century, but the free trade proposal came to have a distinct identity because of unforeseen circumstances and thus gave President Toledo the opportunity to make his distinct imprint on the agreement.

The collapse of the Soviet Union in 1991 apparently confirmed the superiority of capitalism over socialism and set off a stampede across many parts of the world to adopt free market and free trade principles. An early example of this rush to free trade was the treaty signed by the United States, Mexico, and Canada to create a North American free trade area. NAFTA went into effect on 1 January 1994, and even during the previous year while its ratification process was working its way through the U.S. Congress, talks were underway to extend NAFTA across the entire Western Hemisphere. The proposal took firm shape in the First Summit of the Americas held at Miami Florida in December 1994 when the delegations of the attending countries pledged to negotiate a Free Trade Agreement for the Americas (FTAA) on the model of NAFTA.[14]

Because it was clear that the negotiation of FTAA among so many nations was going to be much more complex and lengthy than the relatively simpler NAFTA, the Clinton administration concluded that a gradual approach was needed to open the path to a final agreement. As a first major step, the United States granted trade benefits to countries in the area on a regional basis. The Andean Trade Promotion Act granted tariff reductions to Peru in August 1993 and the results far exceeded expectations. Peru's volume of exports increased greatly, and the U.S. share of Peru's exports "almost doubled from about 16.1 percent to 29 percent in 2004."[15] And when the Andean Trade Promotion and Drug Eradication Act (ATPDEA) increased the trade benefits for Peru in October 2002, exports to the U.S. increased at an even faster pace, particularly with the emergence of asparagus as the largest agricultural export of Peru.[16]

The considerable prosperity that these trade benefits brought to Peruvians in the coastal areas made the government determined to make the tariff reductions permanent. Unfortunately, in November 2003 the talks to create a FTAA reached a dead end. Because rhetorical fireworks by Hugo Chávez marked the fiery end of the FTAA proposal, it has become widespread to blame its collapse on the antics and hostility of the Venezuelan president. Chávez merely took the heat and became a convenient scapegoat, when in reality the quiet but firm opposition of Brazil had been primarily responsible for delaying and eventually destroying FTAA. The Brazilian objections were not frivolous or capricious, because its government realized that without additional measures, such as increased foreign aid, expanded training, and large incentives to local businesses, the one-sided nature of FTAA condemned Latin America to the role of supplier of raw materials and foodstuffs. At first Brazil was alone in its quiet resistance, but when the meltdown of the Argentine economy in December 2001 soured the country on the benefits of the free market, any FTAA without the participation of the two largest countries in Latin America was meaningless. However, the reluctance of the key countries to embarrass the United States by a public defiance kept the negotiations going until Chávez with his rhetorical excesses assumed the blame for killing FTAA at the Fourth Summit of the Americans on November 4 and 5 of 2004.[17]

American diplomats knew that FTAA was doomed, and long before its collapse, had been developing alternatives as partial substitutes. For the countries of Central America and the Dominican Republic, the United States devised CAFTA-DR, a free trade agreement that the member countries signed in 2004 and went into effect the next year. Because the countries were small in size and population and their economies were in a relatively incipient state of industrialization, the multilateral approach of CAFTA-DR seemed suitable and did not prove unduly difficult to negotiate. CAFTA-DR made possible expanding the free trade zone of NAFTA into most regions south of Mexico, but the multilateral formula proved unworkable for the large countries of South America.[18]

The hope of salvaging an agreement still remained alive when the United States began negotiations for an Andean free trade treaty with Colombia, Peru, and Ecuador in May 2004, with the participation in observer status of Bolivia as a possible later member. The U.S. government favored the multilateral approach as the easiest way to avoid envy by one country at the supposed better deal another country received, but in an early indication that this approach was doomed, Chile had previously negotiated with the United States a separate FTA, which entered into force on 1 January 2004. Gradually the possibility of signing a multilateral agreement with Colombia, Ecuador, and Peru faded.[19]

Peru was under pressure to sign a FTA because its tariff preferences in the U.S. market under the ATPDEA were set to expire in December 2006, while the other Andean countries did not seem to have the same urgency about concluding the negotiations. Peru had accepted the negotiation of a single multilateral treaty mainly as a legislative tactic to secure approval by the U.S. Congress, but the relative difficulty in securing U.S. congressional approval for the CAFTA-DR worried Peruvian officials who preferred to take their chances with a separate treaty. President Toledo concluded in June 2005 that Peru would have to go alone and negotiate its own separate FTA with the United States. Public opinion was on his side, and a poll showed that 68 percent of Peruvians supported the FTA; however, in a more perceptive view, 55 percent believed that the agreement would bring more benefits to the United States than to Peru.[20] But President Toledo had acted decisively to make sure that the momentum toward free trade did not dissipate, and he pursued relentlessly the opportunity to secure an agreement with the United States.

Truth and Reconciliation Commission The accomplishments of the Toledo administration were not limited to economic issues but also extended to the major political and moral issue of dealing with the country's turbulent past. The long struggle against the insurgency of the Maoist terrorist group, Shining Path (*Sendero Luminoso*) cried out for exhaustive scrutiny and for hearing the voices of the victims. The interim government of Valentín Paniagua established a Truth and Reconciliation Commission to carry out a two-year investigation, and most of its work took place under the Toledo administration which strongly supported and generously financed the search into human rights violations.

After extensive information gathering and the interview of over 17,000 witnesses and victims throughout the country, the commission issued its multi-volume final report on 28 August 2003.[21]

The commission had elaborated careful narratives about almost all the important events occurring in Peru from the 1960s to 2001, and these detailed accounts comprise the bulk of the report and remain of lasting value for understanding that violent period in the country's history. However, using flawed methods, the commission expanded the reasonable estimate of 20,000 deaths into the incredibly high number of nearly 70,000 as the number of fatalities from the insurgency. This excessive figure reflected the inability of the commission to understand the true reasons for the defeat of Shining Path. And this conceptual defect shaped its decision to assign responsibility for deaths in a "balanced" way almost equally between Shining Path and the official authorities. In those deaths perpetrated by government agents, the commission placed primary responsibility on the armed forces, although the police received ample blame as well.[22]

Upon receiving this massive report, Toledo rejected its estimates of the high number of casualties, and he did not agree with its hostility to the military. He easily could have shelved and ignored the report, but he felt that the country needed to hear the many riveting accounts of human rights abuses.[23]

Because the commission had made specific suggestions for action and had even recommended criminal prosecution against some perpetrators, Toledo felt that he could not ignore its findings and did entrust prosecutors with the task of bringing to trial the accused. To follow up on the recommendations of the final report, he created a new commission on November 2003. As a low-level group, it was not expected to exert any powerful influence, and gradually its activities faded from view. For Peru the Commission of Truth and Reconciliation had been a missed opportunity, even though President Toledo did the best that he could with its final report to try to get the country to recognize the violent past of the insurgency but without creating new complications in the present.[24]

The Agony of the Alejandro Toledo Presidency

Starting with the Arequipazo of June 2002, a wave of social conflicts spread across Peru. The intensity and frequency of the demonstrations undermined a government apparently incapable of halting the protests. The turbulence was baffling for President Alejandro Toledo, who naively believed that the improving economic indicators were the best antidote to defusing the protests. As has been typical of free market advocates, he failed to realize that if economic growth occurred at all, it always came at the high price of increasing the concentration of wealth. An intrinsic bias toward economic inequality has been the structural defect of capitalism, and absent strong government intervention can easily lead to extreme concentrations of wealth such as the emergence of a privileged class of billionaires in the countries of the former Soviet bloc. In a belated admission that his beloved free market was not going to lift large segments of the Peruvian population out of crushing poverty, Toledo proposed a program to distribute a monthly subsidy (equivalent to U.S. $30) to those living below the poverty level.[25]

The subsidy proposal depended on taxing the outrageous profits the privileged minority had effortlessly reaped, and not surprisingly, implementation of this redistribution plan proved practically impossible. As a public relations gimmick it might have fooled some Peruvians, but those with immediate needs could not afford to wait to see if they would ever receive their $30 monthly. A first outbreak occurred on 3 April 2005 when peasants in the conflict-prone province of Andahuaylas blocked highways and the airport as a way to pressure for better roads and for higher prices for potatoes, the most important crop in the region. Because the Antauro Humala revolt had taken place in the same locality a few months before in January, the government promptly responded by dispatching a large number of policemen to the region. The presence of 300 policemen, three times the size of the normal detachment, overawed the protestors who stopped their blockade and agreed to negotiate with a high-level government commission about their demands.[26]

The success with Andahuaylas was short lived, because the protest turned out to be only the forerunner of the large wave of protests that farmers began on 23 May 2005 in ten departments. Although the growers of rice, cotton, and potatoes had mainly concerns about their specific crops, what was most disturbingly for the Toledo administration was that the demonstrators were united in their opposition to the proposed Free Trade Agreement (FTA) with the United States. Fear of cheaper U.S. imports fueled the opposition among cotton and rice growers, when in reality most rice imports were coming from Uruguay under the terms of the MERCOSUR trade agreement. In the case of potato growers, they feared that massive imports of low-price wheat might drive Peruvian consumers away from the traditional staple diet of potatoes. The worry was not unfounded, because the U.S. Embassy under the guise of "foreign aid" had been offering free wheat shipments as the Trojan horse to entice Peruvians to eat more bread.[27]

The government went into high gear to divide and then to meet the demands of the protestors. In San Martín region the inhabitants agreed to end the road blocks in exchange for getting the construction of a new access road to Tocache. The offer to purchase modest amounts of rice, cotton, and potatoes for government granaries temporarily satisfied the peasants in the other departments, and these timely offers brought the last of the agricultural demonstrations to an end on 27 May 2005. The Toledo administration with clever evasive actions had pacified the country, but it was clear that FTA was in danger. President Toledo made the deliberate decision to concentrate his remaining political capital on concluding the FTA with the United States. This meant that other free market initiatives, such as privatizing the Talara refinery of Petroperu, simply had to be abandoned. Any attempt to reduce Petroperu (the state petroleum company) to being merely the owners of gas stations and pipelines meant provoking massive public protests and tremendous resistance from the army. A weakened government was in no shape to face this political firestorm and instead concentrated on cementing its legacy by securing the FTA.[28]

The Toledo administration was rushing to finish the negotiations by July 2005 but failed and then had to settle to urging the U.S. government to conclude the agreement by October. Peruvian negotiators pressed for the most favorable terms, particularly protection for agriculture and pharmaceuticals, although intellectual property rights were also a matter in dispute. No doubt remained that in the rush to conclude an agreement, the Toledo administration gave away too much to U.S. negotiators because of the ingrained dogma among Peruvian economists that the greater the access of private business to foreign markets, the larger the benefits for the country.[29]

In spite of its desire to concentrate exclusively on the FTA agreement, the Toledo administration found most of its efforts absorbed by a crisis that threatened its very survival. The privatization efforts of President Toledo and his failure to live up to his many campaign promises to improve the lives of the majority of Peruvians had generated widespread bitterness and occasionally even intense hatred. Some politicians sensed this strong mood, and indeed opinion polls consistently showed Toledo suffering from very low approval numbers. The challenge for the opposition consisted in how to translate the economic discontent into a political scandal that could at least cripple and perhaps even end the Toledo presidency.

Since the initial months of 2004 rumors had been circulating that Alejandro Toledo had been personally involved in the collection of false signatures so that he could qualify to run for the 2000 election. The "signature factories" of Alberto Fujimori had become infamous in Peru, and soon claims emerged that opposition candidates had likewise engaged in the same fraudulent activities. But to have a real scandal, irrefutable evidence needed to show that the candidate had been personally involved in inventing signatures for petitions.

The scandal began in July 2004 when Carmen Burga, an insider of the Toledo presidential campaign, announced that Toledo had authorized the fabrication of false signatures to qualify for the 2000 election. The public outrage was immediate, but before anything else could happen, she diffused a video reversing her earlier statements, and then she and her family conveniently disappeared from Peru so that no further questioning was possible. Later it was learned that because the Burga family did not have passports, government officials had the immigration office work after closing hours to issue their passports immediately. Toledo party officials then took advantage of the lax customs controls at the land border with Ecuador to slip her and her family members into the neighboring country and then flew them to Colombia and Peru. Officials of Toledo's party financed the residence abroad of Carmen and her family until the scandal blew over.[30]

With the disappearance of a potentially fatal witness, President Toledo seemed to have dodged the bullet, but in reality this was just the first act in the drama of the scandal. At first he succeeded in distancing himself from the accusations, but when a video of 1997 or 1998 surfaced in which he and his wife Eliane Karp appeared hosting a lunch for his sister Margarita in recognition of all her work in collecting signatures for registering the party, public opinion concluded that he had been involved in the false signatures scandal. The evidence against Margarita was sufficient for a judge to order her placed under house arrest, but the video and other testimonies still did not prove conclusively that President Toledo had ordered or even knew that this fraudulent activity was going on; he merely appeared as grateful to his sister and to the party workers for having collected so many signatures.[31]

The target was too tempting for some politicians who were seeking any pretext to remove the unpopular Toledo from office, and the Peruvian congress after considerable prodding established a five-member investigative committee under Edgar Villanueva in October 2004. Even then, the committee showed no rush and did not begin any substantive work until January 2005. The delay with the committee was not careless or accidental, and reflected the decision of former president Alan García, the real kingpin on this issue, to save the presidency of Toledo as being in the best interests of Peru. The game plan was to let the investigation be a forum for opposition figures to vent their frustration at the Toledo administration, and once that cathartic function was completed, then to file away the report of the committee. And to make sure that the committee did not narrowly focus on the Toledo campaign, it accepted a broad mandate to look at all cases of signature fraud in the elections during the Fujimori dictatorship.[32]

On 3 May 2005 the Villanueva Committee submitted its final report, but the two pro–Toledo members refused to accept its findings, while the three opposition members could not agree on making specific recommendations to the congress. As the U.S. Embassy reported, "The Villanueva Committee has been mired in controversy from the start, and it is not surprising that its final report should continue this trend."[33] Because committee reports required a quorum of at least four for its conclusions to be official, experts believed that the investigation would gradually disappear in some forgotten desk of the Peruvian congress.

A faux pas by Toledo prevented the Villanueva report from fading away. In two private meetings with the president, García, the head of APRA, stated that his party wanted Toledo to complete his term. Because the removal of the president required the votes in congress of both APRA and the other main opposition party under the control of Lourdes Flores, Toledo felt secure in his position. He took notes of the conversation with García, but somehow these notes fell into the hands of reporters and soon appeared in the press.[34]

The understanding between Toledo and García created a political problem for the latter, who had to relent on his earlier position to let the Villanueva report die quietly. APRA agreed to let two bills come to the whole congress for a vote. The first bill called for suspending Toledo temporarily from office while the criminal investigation was proceeding, and the second called for disqualifying him from holding office for ten years, a clear blow against any return to office in 2011. When news of this possible constitutional crisis reached Prime Minister Carlos Ferrero, he panicked and rushed over to the U.S. Embassy to ask for help in saving the presidency of Toledo. A worried ambassador set up appointments with both opposition leaders on 18 May to state the U.S. position against the removal of Toledo from office.[35]

García shared completely the U.S. view and he reassured the ambassador "that there was no need to worry as, everything will come out fine tomorrow."[36] García explained that APRA, his party, would vote for suspending the president, but the party of Flores would not, and thus the bill would fail. On the motion to disqualify Toledo for ten years the votes of the two parties were reversed and thus the bill likewise would not pass. On 19 May 2005, exactly as García had predicted, both bills failed in congress. After a session lasting 16 hours, the Peruvian congress voted 56 to 47 to send all the information collected by the Villanueva Committee to the Attorney General's Office for additional investigation. This decision left open the possibility that if the attorney general uncovered more evidence conceivably it could bring the matter back to the congress.[37]

With no new revelations of criminal actions, the public lost interest in the scandal, and by July 2005 officials of the Toledo administration were confident that they had put the matter behind them. The government could return its attention to concluding the free trade agreement with the United States and hoped to finish by November, but that date proved too optimistic. The most recent stumbling block was on whether to negotiate an extension to the Andean Trade Preference Act or to concentrate solely on the new FTA which among other clauses also made permanent the tariff preferences Peru enjoyed. On 7 December 2005 American and Peruvian representatives concluded the FTA agreement. Because the negotiations had taken much longer than expected, the presidential campaign was already in full swing, and a messy congressional struggle to ratify the treaty seemed unnecessarily risky. Wisely Toledo decided to postpone submitting the agreement to the congress at least until after the inevitable runoff in the presidential elections of 2006. His party lacked the votes to approve the FTA agreement without the support of at least one of the two major opposition parties, and he hoped to negotiate with the winner of the presidential election an arrangement to secure congressional approval in the last months of his term.[38]

Chapter 11

Blows Against the Left

Recent INR polling shows that Peru and Colombia, where 70 percent of the population has a favorable view of the United States, are the most pro-American countries in all of South America.—U.S. Ambassador Struble[1]

For the U.S. government, the spread of Chavismo across South America lurked as a serious threat. The George Bush administration wanted not only to overthrow Hugo Chávez but also to eliminate his influence across the continent. Would the socialist nationalism of Venezuela find imitators in the region? Two crucial tests were the elections in Colombia and in Peru; after leftist regimes came to power in Bolivia, Ecuador, and Nicaragua, it was imperative for Washington to prevent the rise of additional radical leaders who could then seriously weaken U.S. political and economic dominance over Latin America.

Colombia: The Reelection of Álvaro Uribe Vélez

Even before his inauguration on 7 August 2002, Álvaro Uribe Vélez was already laying the groundwork for his reelection. By constantly emphasizing that the defeat of the guerrillas was going to require more than a mere one four-year term, he cleverly planted in the minds of the population the need for his reelection. The support by business conglomerates made possible his attempts to extend his presidency into a second term. As expected, business provided generous funding and even more importantly favorable media coverage. This willingness to broadcast positive stories was indispensable for Uribe, because unlike in Peru, he lacked a Vladimiro Montesinos who used bribes to control television and radio reports. The business conglomerates made sure that their news subsidiaries provided an uninterrupted stream of sympathetic articles, television clips, and radio broadcasts. At the same time, critics and opposition voices deliberately were deprived of access to the mass media, and the public gradually became accustomed to a steady flow of news supporting the president and the armed forces while at the same time demonizing the guerrillas. The press remained open to moderate critics, but because the traditional policy of the country's main newspaper, *El Tiempo*, has been to rally behind the administration in office, its occasional reporting of inconvenient facts was not harmful and in any case reached an exclusive reading audience composed mainly of the Bogotá elite.[2]

In Colombia no less than in Peru, highly favorable media coverage had been instrumental in keeping both presidents Uribe and Fujimori in office. Instead in Venezuela the private television channels had constantly fueled the attempts of the fragmented opposition to overthrow Hugo Chávez. In Colombia the media campaign in favor of the Uribe administration generally was indirect and thus much more effective, because even the average citizen was not gullible enough to swallow propaganda openly in favor of the president. Television broadcasts reporting on the accomplishments of the government were frequent as were the many silences and omissions about its failures. The media message consisted of two closely related topics. First was the constant denigration and disparagement of the guerrillas as irrational evil forces bent on destroying Colombia. Second was the unrestricted praise for the armed forces as the saviors of the country. The military appeared as the most noble of Colombian institutions, and totally absent from the broadcasts were the human rights abuses of the army or even less of the growing similarities with the brutal military regimes of South America in the 1970s and 1980s. Put in simplest terms, soldiers were the angels who could do no wrong and the guerrillas were the evil monsters who could do no right.[3]

When the media praised the military as the instrument indispensable to crush the guerrillas, this message dovetailed smoothly with the "democratic security" campaign platform of candidate Uribe Vélez in 2002. Public revulsion against the failed strategy of negotiating a peace settlement with the Revolutionary Armed Forces of Colombia (*Fuerzas Armadas Revolucionarias de Colombia*) or FARC had propelled Uribe to prominence. Although Uribe won the elections in the first round, as president he had to show that the strategy of military victory was feasible. Chapter 8 showed that the military offensive called *Plan Patriota* had started out well and seemed likely to bring peace to Colombia.

According to the schedule of *Plan Patriota*, the army was supposed to finish Phase 2 B of its offensive against FARC in the Amazon region by the end of 2005, or roughly 18 months after its start. Then the army was supposed to shift the bulk of its forces to Antioquia to begin Phase 2 C of *Plan Patriota*. But a series of guerrilla attacks against police stations in February and May 2005 prevented adhering to this excessively optimistic schedule. And when FARC simultaneously carried out 12 raids in the Putumayo region on 25 June 2005, it became clear that any deployment of troops away from the Amazon to Antioquia was impossible. Army planners postponed Phase 2 C to an indefinite future because the units slated for that operation were bogged down in the Amazon jungle.[4]

Why had *Plan Patriota* run out of steam after its apparent early successes? FARC had practiced the classical guerrilla strategy of giving up worthless land and retreating in the face of overwhelming military force. The guerrillas were "highly adaptive to new tactics and terrains, an important advantage as they retreat to more difficult and remote locations."[5] Even more revealing was the contrast between the two opponents: "The guerrillas can operate nimbly in small mobile columns, invisibly in dense jungle, and silently with good discipline in communications," but instead the Colombian army only moved in large units of at least battalion size, was "slow to react to real-time intelligence of enemy movements and lax in keeping its attack plans quiet."

With the huge forces of *Plan Patriota* tied down chasing elusive guerrillas in the Amazon, FARC had quietly redeployed many of its units to other areas of Colombia, thus making possible the surprise attacks of June. The overemphasis on the military had deprived the police of the personnel to guard effectively many sites in Colombia. Having to place units in all Colombian municipalities had stretched thin the manpower of the national police. And without an extensive police presence, intelligence on impending FARC attacks was not always available in time to alert the targeted areas. Quietly the army shelved Phase 2 C of *Plan Patriota* as Utopian, and when the high command deployed units from the Amazon to protect other vulnerable areas in the country, the plan was receiving a tacit burial. *Plan Patriota*, no less than other attempts starting with the Marquetalia campaign of 1964, had ended in failure.[6]

The significance of shifting army units into guard duties was not immediately obvious. At least for the purpose of the presidential campaign of 2006, the surprising survival of FARC actually benefitted President Uribe's reelection bid, but only because he enjoyed the favorable media coverage the business conglomerates showered on his administration. With a straight face he could make the claim that the guerrilla menace had been much bigger than anyone had expected and that consequently he needed a second four-year term to complete the task of pacifying Colombia. But to allow him to run for president required amending the 1991 Constitution, and here Uribe faced serious obstacles.

Uribe had tried in the initial years of his presidency to weaken if not to destroy the traditional political class in Colombia; here he was imitating the approach that Alberto Fujimori had adopted to construct his dictatorship. Uribe had to weaken congress, the bulwark of traditional politicians, but his attempts to rig the political system in his favor faced delays and obstacles until the final blow came with the defeat of the constitutional referendum of 25 October 2003. Uribe insiders blamed the defeat of the referendum on a poor public relations campaign, but in reality the resemblance of the proposals to the Fujimori experience made them highly unpopular. Not surprisingly, Colombians voted with their feet by failing to turn out in the minimal numbers required to obtain approval of the constitutional referendum.[7]

Already anticipating the defeat of the referendum, Uribe had quietly reestablished links with traditional politicians. His public attacks on congressmen and on the legislature gradually faded, and while he knew that he could not openly praise politicians, the political class, usually devoid of principles or scruples, was quick to grab the olive branch. The life-blood of traditional politicians consisted of patronage and cabinet appointments, and these two overlapping resources Uribe began sharing with the political class. Although he made sure that officials representing the business class retained a fair share of appointments in the government, gradually the traditional politicians returned to occupy important positions from which they could dispense patronage to loyal followers. After an attempt in the initial years to break from the Colombia tradition of dispensing quotas of influence to selected groups, the political class once again confirmed its traditional role in the Colombian system.[8]

The quid pro quo that Uribe demanded from the political class was passage of an amendment to allow the consecutive election of presidents. The Constitution of 1991 had established a complex legislative process to pass any amendments, which then also required the approval of a special Constitutional Court. Consecutive reelection had never before existed in the country, and this dramatic change generated considerable opposition. The initial reaction was to consider reelection only for future presidents and not to the incumbent Uribe; in another limitation, the suggestion to allow more than one consecutive reelection was immediately rejected.

Two reasons finally persuaded the congress to authorize one consecutive reelection to the presidency. Assurances from Uribe that in his second term he would continue to share patronage and official appointments with the political class proved particularly persuasive. Traditional politicians thus spared themselves the hassle of having to maneuver frantically every four years to obtain quotas for jobs and funds in the new administration. In partisan terms, Uribe knew that if the two traditional parties, the Liberals and the Conservatives, supported his initiative, then he could obtain passage of the constitutional amendment authorizing his reelection. The Conservatives emerged as the swing vote, but the president, by courting them too assiduously, estranged some Liberals who resented any loss of patronage.[9] But besides the more cynical explanation of the crude buying of congressional votes for the constitutional amendment, a deep shift in public opinion had been taking place. For decades it was widely recognized in Colombia that a term of four years was vastly insufficient for presidents to accomplish their goals. When many Latin American countries either adopted a six-year term or one reelection, Colombian presidents with a mere four years seemed unable to match the continuity of most of their colleagues.

So when 14 December 2004 both houses authorized the reelection of the president, the move did not provoke any sharp protests, and on the contrary, the approval ratings of Uribe remained as high as before. The increasingly widespread idea that Colombia needed to have its presidents stay in office longer to function effectively also weighed very heavily with the Constitutional Court. Unlike a referendum that went into effect automatically if approved by a minimum number of registered voters, the 1991 Constitution specified that any amendment adopted by the legislative procedure also needed the approval of this special court to have validity. After ten months of deliberation, the court, by a 7 to 2 decision, concluded on 19 October 2005 that the amendment to establish consecutive reelection was valid. The judges may not have known that had they ruled in the negative, the Uribe administration was ready with contingency plans to put Uribe in the ballot for the 2006 election by devious means.[10] Fortunately for Colombia, these blatant attempts reminiscent of the maneuvers of Montesinos in Peru did not prove necessary, and the country was spared the dangers of falling into a dictatorship or chaos.

Uribe had seemed to pull off the impossible, and he had expertly navigated the reelection proposal so that he could appear on the ballot for the 28 May 2006 presidential elections. Because his approval ratings remained high, he was the favorite to win the first round. FARC was the spoiler when it resurfaced to launch raids starting in February 2005 and culminating in 12 simultaneous attacks on 25 June 2005. When the Colombian public had been fed a steady diet of broadcasts proclaiming the virtual defeat of FARC, the guerrilla actions came as a surprise, but the government was ready with a new propaganda campaign. Repeatedly the media broadcast the new official line that this was the last gasp of a dying insurgency that refused to accept quietly its inevitable demise. The implicit message was that with the guerrillas on the run and scrambling to survive, the public needed to give Uribe the extra years to bring to an end once and for all the insurgency that had tormented the country for decades.

Additional political insurance came with congressional approval of the law in June 2005 ratifying the demobilization process with the paramilitaries. Uribe's astute decision to utilize the paramilitaries to his political advantage had clearly paid off. He had exaggerated their military capability until he placed them on the same level as FARC, and then he could point to the demobilization of the paramilitaries as a preview to the inevitable disarmament of FARC. His campaign for reelection was more like a triumphal parade across the country, as he trumpeted the success with the paramilitaries and promised to bring FARC to an end. Not surprisingly, he won reelection on 28 May 2006 with 62 percent of the popular vote and carried 30 of Colombia's 32 departments. This percentage in the first round was higher than the 53 percent he had won in the 2002 election.[11]

The Liberals and the Conservatives, the two traditional parties in Colombia, had fared badly in the elections. The second runner up was the leftist Carlos Gaviria, who with 22 percent of the total, had received the highest number of votes of any leftist candidate in Colombian presidential elections. The fact that 22 percent of voters felt that Colombia needed a radical change should have given Uribe cause to reflect on what the policies of his second term should be.[12] But the excitement of winning 62 percent of the popular vote pushed aside any rational reflection on new directions, and Uribe confidently felt that more of the same was what the country needed and certainly wanted. Considering himself the indispensable person, barely had he won that he began thinking about the possibility of a third term. And if he could end the insurgency during his next four years, a grateful country was sure to grant him another four years in office.

The 2006 Presidential Campaign in Peru

The disintegration of the Alejandro Toledo administration guaranteed a wide open election for president in 2006 with no clear favorites. Over 20 candidates were vying for Peru's highest office, but only four were serious contenders. The best known candidates were the former presidents Alán García and Valentín Paniagua. Peruvians remembered fondly the interim presidency of the latter, and to any intelligent observer Paniagua stood out as an elder wise man. The same could not be said about García, and most Peruvians who had lived through his disastrous presidency recalled only his many failures.

Besides the ex-presidents, only two other candidates had any chance of winning the election. The public was familiar with Lourdes Flores from Lima because she had run previously for president in 2001. This white wealthy professional had risen to the top of the political world through sheer personal efforts, but in a male-dominated society where men are accustomed to see women as objects to be used and abused, her gender posed a real barrier. Those not taking her candidacy seriously were surprised to see her emerge as the front runner when the campaign season started in the last months of 2005. Wealthy Peruvians and the business class saw in her one of their own and enthusiastically backed her candidacy with funds. The Toledo administration saw her as the candidate most likely to continue the extreme free market policies of the outgoing administration and threw what little support it could still muster behind Flores.[13]

The least well known of the four serious contenders was Ollanta Humala. This former army officer had debuted on the national scene on 29 October 2000 when he staged a failed barracks revolt against the dictatorship of Alberto Fujimori (chapter 3). After the fall of Fujimori, congress amnestied the rebels and reinstated the military personnel in the army. However, the generals never forgave his revolt, and he finally was forced to retire from the army during the Toledo presidency. After his return into civilian life, he used his fame to organize former servicemen; the army however, was divided over his candidacy, because while most officers supported him, the generals were strongly opposed. As many Peruvians flocked to his movement, unofficially he became the candidate of protest voters and to a lesser degree of leftists.[14] A superficial resemblance with Hugo Chávez was hard to miss, because these two former army officers had led unsuccessful revolts against civilian presidents.

An early casualty in the election was the distinguished Paniagua. The grueling pace of the campaign trail proved too much for his frail body, and in spite of enjoying the highest favorability ratings, he failed to connect with voters. Sadly, Peru was no longer a country where wise old men had a place, and even he realized that his candidacy no longer suited the times. He wanted to withdraw from the campaign, but because his presence in the ballot guaranteed a minimal number of seats for his party in the National Assembly, he trudged on to the bitter end.[15]

The effective elimination of Paniagua and the insignificance of the rest of the candidates turned the campaign into a three-way struggle. Flores, the candidate of the wealthy, stood for continuity with the Toledo presidency. Commentators labeled Humala as leftist, and García, with nowhere else to go, tried to position himself as the centrist candidate. In reality, Humala knew that he had to avoid at all costs the label of leftist extremist, because the vast majority of the public still associated Marxism and any strain of socialism with the murderous Shining Path insurgency. Although a devout admirer of General Juan Velasco, Humala had never fully embraced many key aspects of the leftist agenda and remained essentially a fervent nationalist. It came as no surprise to learn that early efforts to unite Humala's movement with leftist groups failed in September 2005. Yet because many of his advisers were radicals, his campaign could never shake free completely from the image of leftist extremism, and business leaders saw him as a danger to their profits.[16]

When poll numbers in early November revealed that Humala was in fourth place with just 11 percent of voters and unlikely to qualify for the runoff election, he took firm steps to save his candidacy. His first action was to try to distance himself from Hugo Chávez by claiming that Venezuela's dependence on petroleum and its tensions with the United States made the experience of that country not applicable to Peru. He vigorously defended the rights of coca growers (*cocaleros*) and spouted strong anti–Chilean statements to bolster his nationalistic credentials. To show his independence, he rejected renewed attempts to make him the candidate of leftist groups, and as a final precaution he also avoided being pinned down to specifics on most issues. As the U.S. Embassy reported, "Ollanta is offering a Chávez-like slick package for a discontented electorate, staying deliberately vague about plans and proposals and adopting a moderate tone, even when promoting positions that are basically *cocalero* and statist."[17]

The U.S. Embassy had expected the shift in tone to improve the prospects for Humala, but the surge in December went beyond anyone's expectations. In polls taken in the first half of December, Humala shot up to second place and was within a hair's margin of taking the first place spot from the initial front runner Flores. And because the polls overrepresented urban areas and neglected the countryside, the U.S. Embassy reached the scary conclusion that "Ollanta Humala may actually be leading the presidential race at present."[18] Equally worrisome, businesses were making campaign contributions partly out of the bandwagon effect of wanting to be with the winner. Producers for the domestic market were also making large contributions in a last hope of derailing the Free Trade Agreement with the United States.

In the face of this new threat, the U.S. Embassy changed its tactics toward Humala. Before the surge of Humala, American diplomats were insistent on remaining neutral: "we have no/no intention of involving the Embassy in anti–Humala information or commentary campaigns: that is a task for the competing political parties."[19] But once it became clear that "the specter of Humala reaching the second round has to be taken seriously at this stage,"[20] in particular because many voters found his youthful image appealing, the attitude changed. The American ambassador reported that U.S. AID was channeling at least a million dollars to subject the candidate to intense public scrutiny. Later in the campaign a blogger hinted at U.S. involvement in the efforts to defeat the Humala campaign, and other U.S. agencies must have also contributed to undermine this candidate.[21] Surprisingly, even though the U.S. Embassy had unleashed hostile actions against Humala, it still did not exclude reaching an accommodation with the candidate. This attitude reflected not just the diplomatic tradition of securing an advantageous settlement after applying pressure but also the reasonable hypothesis that Humala had still not formulated a consistent set of ideas. Except for a rock-solid commitment to nationalism, the rest of his statements suggested an inchoate and shifting agenda. American diplomats sensed that this appealing candidate might be more pliable than his sometimes harsh rhetoric suggested.[22]

The rise to front runner status in December made Humala overconfident, and he decided to grasp at the elusive prize of a complete victory in the first round on 9 April 2006. According to the Constitution of 1993, a candidate needed to win more than 50 percent of the vote to avoid a runoff. All analysts had correctly predicted that the fragmentation of the votes among over 20 candidates made it impossible for any one person to win a majority in the election, but the unexpected upset victory in Bolivia of Evo Morales finished convincing Humala that victory was within reach. In a dangerous gamble, his campaign team imposed a news blackout on the whereabouts of the candidate. This silence heightened the curiosity of the press, which then was caught by surprise when unexpectedly on 3 January 2006 Humala and his wife Nadine appeared in Caracas next to a beaming Chávez and Evo Morales. Chávez publicly praised the Peruvian candidate, and in response to this near endorsement, President Toledo recalled Peru's ambassador.[23]

By this surprise appearance at Caracas, Humala crippled fatally his candidacy. His opponents had been repeatedly trying to link him to the Venezuelan president but had consistently failed, among other reason because the Peruvian public liked Chávez. But at the same time, Peruvians did not want the Venezuelan president interfering in their country's politics. As long as Humala kept his distance from Chávez, his campaign was safe, but the video and photographs showing him and his wife smiling next to the Venezuelan president sent chills through many segments of the Peruvian population. Morales did help Humala by increasing the latter's high popularity among the highlands and southern Peru, but at the heavy cost of driving away many voters in the more populous coastal region. Clearly Humala should have waited at least until he was president-elect before embarking on a trip to Venezuela.

The visit to Caracas actually gave Humala a bump in the polls so the harmful effects of this action were not immediately evident. The other presidential candidates tried to heap blame on Humala because of the close association with Chávez, but among the critics was not Alán García. Alone among the contenders, he defended the trip to Caracas because he wanted to appear more anti–U.S. than he really was. García, fighting to save his political career, was pursuing a strategy to take him into the runoff election of 4 June 2006 because he knew that he was in too weak a position to challenge the front runner. García saw that the only way that he could survive was by knocking Flores from her second place position. After a great start as a front runner, her poll numbers fell and her campaign floundered. To give gender balance to her ticket, she had to appoint a man to be her running mate, but her choice of an uninspiring white male from a very rich family hurt her candidacy. She and her wealthy running mate came across as two privileged candidates out of touch with the rest of the country.[24]

Flores boldly plunged into campaigning in rural areas and tried her best to be seen in public with people of the lower class and of dark Indian complexion, but try as she might, she was barely able to hold on to her second place. García was fast closing in but could not overtake her. In a desperate gamble, he decided to exploit her status as a single woman who had never married and did not have children or her own family. Anonymous and vicious attack ads spread the unfounded accusation that she was a Lesbian and undermined her campaign.[25] When the first round of elections took place on 9 April 2006, García succeeded in clawing his way to second place finish with 24.3 percent of the popular vote, barely a point ahead of Lourdes, and considerably behind Humala with 30.6 percent of the vote. As everyone had expected, a runoff election on 4 June was necessary because no candidate received more than 50 percent of the vote.[26]

The first part of the strategy of García had worked perfectly, and now he directed his batteries at the more formidable opponent. He already counted on strong support from the navy, particularly from its intelligence service, to offset the limited help Humala received from the army. García realized that his victory hinged on gaining concrete assistance from business leaders but to do so he needed to persuade them that the old socialist of his first presidential term had vanished long ago. Up to the first electoral round the business elite had concentrated on destroying Humala and still hoped that Flores would be the winner. As part of the campaign to discredit Humala, accusations had surfaced on 22 January 2006 that he had participated in horrible human rights violations during the struggle against Shining Path.[27] Human rights activists jumped at the chance to condemn a former army officer, and "the Peruvian elite suddenly discovered a concern for human rights, after years of ignoring or downplaying the findings of the Truth and Reconciliation Commission."[28] But as the weeks went by, no evidence appeared to substantiate the claims. Humala had been confused with a certain Captain Carlos González who had participated in massacres, and the accusation seemed a case of mistaken identity.

Humala weathered the accusations, and a management consultant firm hired by business leaders concluded that he was still likely to win the runoff in June. "The consultant is also involved in researching and publicizing skeletons in Humala's closet" but "said that the investigators had run out of adverse material."[29] The message was clear that the approach of stopping Humala by discrediting him had been inadequate and that the sole remaining option was for business groups to rally behind García as their savior. But García carried a lot of deadweight from his first presidential term, and he had to prove himself repeatedly to businessmen that his conversion to free market principles was sincere. And he had a trump card to play, because he already had the U.S. Embassy on his side. At first sight this American support seemed unexplainable, because as a campaign tactic, he had refrained from defending the Free Trade Agreement with the United States.

In reality García had been doing his homework, and as private business groups began to take a second look at him, he had already been assiduously cultivating the U.S. Embassy at least since 2004. In Central American and Caribbean countries the approval of the U.S. Embassy has been indispensable for a candidate to win, and since the Fujimori dictatorship Peru had been rapidly falling into that pattern. Years earlier García had realized that in a close election American support could tip the electoral outcome. Already in March 2005 the U.S. Ambassador believed that his conversion to free market principles was both sincere and also politically astute. The main electoral base of García's party, APRA, was in the coast, and these densely populated areas had already benefitted the most from the increase of exports to the United States because of the Andean Trade Preference Act. Although as late as October 2005 some embassy officials remained skeptical about his shift to the right, his repeated reassurances that he really had changed overcame the last misgivings of American diplomats. The U.S. Embassy finally came to understand that he did support the Free Trade Agreement enthusiastically but could not say so publicly.[30]

In contrast, Humala proved reluctant to express his economic views to U.S. diplomats, and he even cancelled abruptly a meeting scheduled for 19 March with the American ambassador. Not feeling slighted in the least, an unperturbed U.S. Embassy patiently tried to arrange another meeting but to no avail. American diplomats had to be satisfied with the surrogates the campaign deputized to explain the candidate's views on the issues.[31] Only after the first electoral round did Humala finally meet with the American Ambassador on 17 May 2006, but by then the U.S. Embassy had made up its mind to support García as its preferred candidate.[32] The U.S. Embassy explained that "our strategy is to influence the electorate indirectly,"[33] while keeping a safe distance from the organizations funded by U.S. dollars. However, the contacts helped to convince American diplomats that Humala should not be written off as completely hostile to U.S. interests and that he might even be a suitable candidate for the next presidential election in 2011.

García, even with the blessing of the U.S. Embassy, still faced a hard campaign ahead and realized that he needed the cooperation of Chávez to win. Humala now knew that to win the crucial votes in Lima and the coastal region, he had to distance himself from the Venezuelan president in the runoff election, and at first this approach seemed to be working. The situation drastically changed when on 28 April Chávez launched a verbal attack on García and called on Peruvians to vote for Humala. García saw a golden opportunity, and unlike in January when he had defended the visit of his rival to Caracas, now García responded in kind to the Venezuelan president and accused him of drinking too much rum and being a person of low social origin. An enraged Chávez shot back on 29 April, and President Toledo used the remarks as an excuse to recall again the Peruvian ambassador from Caracas.[34]

Humala could still stay in the ring by repudiating the blatant intervention of a foreigner in the domestic politics of Peru, but he remained silent. Belatedly his wife Nadine and his press spokesperson Carlos Tapia condemned the statements of the Venezuelan president, but this response was inadequate. Seeking to exploit a vulnerable spot, García prodded Chávez into making additional inflammatory comments and soon turned the campaign into a referendum under the new slogan "Either for Chávez or for Peru!" García astutely fed the fears of voters in metropolitan Lima that Humala as a puppet of Chávez would destroy the economic prosperity that exporters had achieved in coastal Peru. The reversal in the media was complete, and television stations previously hostile to García shifted their attacks toward a hapless Humala who still did not realize how rapidly his lead was shrinking.[35]

In many ways Humala made the mistakes of a rookie campaigner. On Election Day on 4 June 2006, García won with 52.6 percent of the national vote and carried every district in Lima where he received 62 percent of the vote compared to Humala's 38 percent.[36] Supposedly the contest had been over the voters of Lourdes Flores, but in practice "García won not only almost every vote that had gone to Flores in the first round, but considerable more votes as well."[37] Foreign observers interpreted the defeat of Humala as a setback not just for Chávez but for the left as well. It seemed that the rising wave of leftism in Latin America had crested in Peru, and that free market principles could again take the offensive. In reality, the blow that the left received in Peru was not the defeat of Humala, but his decision to conclude once and for all that in spite of some leanings, he had never been a socialist much less a Marxist and that his ideology did not stray far from a narrow conception of Peruvian nationalism.

CHAPTER 12

Venezuela and Peru: From Success to Setback

Whenever you emerge victorious after engaging an enemy in battle, you cannot become arrogant or lax but should undertake rigorous preparations night and day in order to await the enemy. [...] After a victory one should act as if victory had not been attained.—Chinese Classic[1]

The Bolivarian Revolution: From Euphoria to Repudiation

The electoral campaign for president began on 2 February 2006 when Hugo Chávez commemorated his seventh year in office. At a massive public ceremony he announced his intention to seek reelection and more ominously to remain in office until 2021; this later year meant amending the 1999 Constitution. At this moment he did not specify how he planned to legalize successive reelections, and instead he framed the campaign as a struggle against President George W. Bush. He repeatedly accused the U.S. government of wanting to stage an invasion similar to the one that overthrew Manuel Noriega of Panama in 1989. As proof, he announced on live television the expulsion of the U.S. naval attaché on charges of having tried to subvert the Venezuelan military. Because at that time President Bush was perhaps the most unpopular person not just in Venezuela but in the world, framing the campaign as a struggle against the U.S. president was a master move on the part of Chávez.[2]

No rival candidate had declared the intention to run, and the opposition was talking about another boycott as had happened with the legislative elections of 4 December 2005. In an attempt to persuade the opposition to run a candidate, Chávez threatened to include on Election Day a referendum to approve a constitutional amendment eliminating term limits. This was the second major announcement he made about extending his presidency beyond the existing two-term limit.[3] Everything indicated that he was going to win an overwhelming reelection, and it made sense to include the proposed amendment into the presidential election to remove this last barrier to the prolongation of his rule. He was trying to correct his error in the 1999 Constitutional Convention of having postponed the struggle over multiple reelections.

His followers welcomed the proposal to amend the constitution for the first time. The opposition hated the 1999 Constitution and had repeatedly offered many amendments and really wanted to abolish it. So nobody considered the flawed 1999 Constitution as a sacred text, even though it had captured the public's imagination and had become popular in a pocked edition that seemed to be available at almost every street corner in Caracas and other cities. The time to strike was in 2006 when the masses were solidly behind him, but precisely this feverish enthusiasm made him overlook the inevitable voter fatigue starting to set in among the population. Chávez had created a false dilemma: he believed that open elections were sure to solidify his image as a popularly elected ruler, but he failed to realize that as long as he continued to attack private property, the opposition and international capital would continue to condemn him as a mad dictator no matter how many elections he won. By March 2006 he made the fateful decision of not going for both reelection and constitutional amendment, but he made it clear that after the presidential election he would convoke voters to vote separately on a referendum approving multiple reelections.[4]

When in March 2006 Manuel Rosales, governor of Zulia state, began to emerge as the likely standard bearer of the opposition, Chávez very cleverly was ready with a plan to incorporate the governor into his anti–U.S. strategy. Rosales in April 2002 had signed the infamous Carmona decree in the name of all governors and was a traditional politician of the corrupt and discredited Fourth Republic. Because Rosales openly expressed his sympathy for the United States and frequently conversed with American diplomats, it was easy for Chávez to accuse him of wanting to make the oil-rich state of Zulia an independent country. An earlier Panama model, not the one of Noriega in 1989 but of Panama against Colombia in 1903 was supposed to provide the game plan to make Zulia independent of Caracas. Just as in Panama in 1903, American warships would intervene to support separatists in Zulia; no real fighting was expected, and all the U.S. Navy had to do was impose a blockade to drive Venezuela into starvation because of its huge dependence on food imports.[5]

The accusation of plotting independence for Zulia seemed hard to prove, and try as hard as it might, the secret police could not come up with incriminating evidence. Finding proof became irrelevant when the Bush administration in its recurrent pattern of blunders decided to send the aircraft carrier *George Washington* to lead a vast task force to the Caribbean. This visible display of gunboat diplomacy was supposed to terrify Chávez but merely played into his game of depicting the U.S. government as a big bully. Voters recalled that a similar carrier task force in 1983 had preceded the U.S. invasion of the island of Grenada near Venezuela, and the naval deployment in 2006 unleashed nationalistic frenzy as the population rallied behind their president to defend the country from the imminent invasion.[6]

Chávez had positioned himself to be the only Venezuelan candidate determined to defend the country. And just riding this nationalistic wave sufficed to carry him into the presidency. His operatives did not become complacent and, to guarantee victory, repeated the successful tactics of the 2004 recall campaign, in particular naturalizing and simultaneously registering vast numbers of Colombian immigrants as Venezuelan voters. His political machine also put a lot of effort into making sure that every possible native Venezuelan was also registered to vote. In contrast, Governor Rosales struggled to secure the support of all opposition groups, and his almost exclusive reliance on citizens from his native Zulia to run his campaign needlessly distanced likely allies. The only setback that Chávez suffered came in November when Venezuela lost its campaign to obtain a two-year term in the United Nations Security Council. This defeat actually fed into the anti–U.S. narrative, because Chávez fueled nationalistic feelings by immediately blaming the Bush administration for having blocked Venezuela's bid for the seat in the Security Council.[7]

Chávez did not even mention the name of his opponent Rosales and constantly told his supporters that he was running against Bush. Not surprisingly, the Venezuelan president won a landslide victory in the election of 3 December 2006. The margin of 63 percent to 37 percent was the largest he ever attained in his political career and abundantly confirmed the success of the strategy of running against Bush. The wide margin showed that had he put on the ballot the referendum for an amendment allowing multiple reelections, he would have effortlessly corrected the deficiency in the 1999 Constitution.[8]

Even more seriously than this lost opportunity to solve the reelection problem, Chávez at the moment of greatest triumph made the crucial mistake of confusing nationalistic feeling for approval of both his "Bolivarian Revolution" and his slogan of "twenty-first-century Socialism." He had used those terms constantly during the entire presidential campaign, but it was the nationalism that really resonated with voters. But once the fear of U.S. attack receded, it was not going to be as easy to bring voters to the polls to approve more of the rambling and often chaotic measures that were becoming the norm in the Bolivarian Revolution. And for their part, alarmed American diplomats intensified their hostile efforts and successfully secured a considerable increase in funds to support the opposition and in particular to "penetrate and divide Chavismo."[9]

Without realizing the dangers that lurked, the Chávez administration enthusiastically plunged into new areas to make drastic changes. Proposals proliferated rapidly, and no idea seemed too far-fetched in the euphoria following the electoral victory of 3 December 2006. Chávez fully partook of the enthusiasm and like his followers, he mistakenly concluded that the nationalistic vote had given him a resounding mandate to push forward his Bolivarian Revolution. But even he realized that the government could undertake only a small part of the proposals to transform Venezuela. His initial actions reflected a determination to tackle issues previously considered to have a high political cost.[10]

Whiskey had become the favorite alcoholic beverage during the Fourth Republic, and Venezuela came to have one of the highest per capita indexes of consumption in the world. Alcoholic beverages locally distilled from sugar cane and from grapes usually sufficed to quench the thirst in the rest of Latin America, but in another strange anomaly, Venezuelans, particularly of the upper class, could not live without this imported liquor which also became a status symbol. When on 5 December 2006 the government imposed a 15 percent tariff duty on whiskey and a host of luxury imports, a predictable howl went up from the inveterate drinkers. However, even the opposition admitted that whiskey consumption was excessive in Venezuela and grudgingly accepted the necessary measure.[11]

In what promised to be the start of a policy of industrialization, the government simplified and speeded up the process for importing raw materials and capital goods. Previously local factories needed to follow a cumbersome process to obtain foreign currency to pay for their imports. The incomplete industrialization of Venezuela, just like in many other parts of Latin America, forced firms to import components and other inputs not yet available inside the country. The U.S. Embassy worried that Venezuela was belatedly embarking on Import-Substitution-Industrialization, an older and by then largely abandoned policy that threatened to reduce the massive flow of imports from the United States.[12] But the government dampened expansion of capacity by imposing price controls on 47 construction materials, such as sand, bricks, wood, and stones. High oil prices were having an effect on many sectors of the economy and fueling a housing boom; the resulting shortages in building materials hindered the completion of both private and public infrastructure projects. The government had fixed prices for construction materials fairly high, so at least initially this measure should not have had an adverse effect.[13]

Close monitoring of the industrial and construction sectors was certainly indispensable but rather monotonous; "low ministerial competence and high turnover rates"[14] among high officials impeded continuity in policies. Indeed a reluctance to track the daily grind of details remained a structural flaw of the Chávez presidency, and its avowed penchant for dramatic moves rather than boring steady progress fairly soon shifted attention to more glamorous topics. Chávez traced out a bold agenda at the swearing-in ceremony of his new cabinet on 8 January 2007, when he announced his intention to nationalize strategic sectors of the economy. He singled out telecommunications and the joint petroleum ventures with foreign companies for acquisition. He also promised to take over other strategic sectors such as electricity and emphasized that everything that had been privatized under the Fourth Republic had to be renationalized. Presumably to hasten these acquisitions, he asked the National Assembly for enabling authority to legislate in many key areas; as will be recalled, he had received similar authorization from the legislature in previous years.[15]

At his inauguration on 10 January 2007 he repeated the call for nationalizations and added a passionate commitment by finishing his speech with the new slogan of "socialism or death." He gave the offensive against capitalism a religious air when he dedicated his speech to Jesus Christ, whom he considered the first true revolutionary. His impassioned pleas often reflected a strong messianic content and bolstered the religious aura of his movement. Not surprisingly, invoking heaven and earth against capitalism sent the Caracas stock market crashing as private business scurried to hide from the thunderbolts of nationalization.[16]

The ceremonies had electrified Chavistas but the government fell behind in delivering the promised nationalizations. In the telecommunications sector, the American company Verizon owned a minority stake in a television station, but this seemed too small a target to bother with, and soon the government lost interest. Through a Dutch off-shore subsidiary an American corporation owned 82 percent of Electricidad de Caracas, which had been the last major privatization of the Fourth Republic. The company operated Diesel plants to generate electricity and occasionally also purchased current from the state-owned Guri hydroelectric station, the largest dam in Venezuela. The American-owned utility had provided excellent service to Caracas and neighboring regions; its service had suffered only minor interruptions during the petroleum strike of 2002–2003 even when PDVSA failed behind with fuel deliveries. The government's decision to reduce industrial production in the factories near the Orinoco River during the strike had released ample hydroelectricity for transmission to Caracas and allowed the utility to maintain normal service.[17]

The American company had made good profits and wanted to stay in Venezuela, but the investors felt that this might be as good a time as any to pocket the gains and return to safer activities in the United States. Both the government and the company negotiated through New York law firms and followed New York law (highly favorable to corporations) in reaching an agreement on 5 February 2007. The price of nearly a billion dollars amply satisfied the owners who were also pleased with the government's decision to make one final dividend payment at the end of the first quarter. In spite of the amicable settlement, it still was not clear what benefit Venezuela had gained by nationalizing the utility company.[18] Admittedly, the Fourth Republic should not have privatized the electricity utility, but in 2007 the government could more effectively have used that billion dollars to bolster agricultural and industrial production. And by assuming control of this utility, the government opened itself up to charges of bad management if the electricity supply ever faltered. The early arrival of drenching downpours in 2003 had saved Venezuela from power outages, but if the rains were late, the government no longer could make the American company into a convenient scapegoat.[19]

When on 31 January 2007 the National Assembly unanimously approved granting enabling powers to the executive branch for 18 months, many expected a rash of nationalizations and a wave of radical measures. But as the months passed, the anticipated decrees failed to materialize. The final accomplishment for 2007 came on 30 April when with great fanfare Chávez announced that Venezuela was withdrawing from the International Monetary Fund and the World Bank. By this step it was joining Cuba that likewise had left those organizations in the 1960s, but unlike that country, Venezuela's withdrawal meant recuperating a deposit estimated at over a quarter of a billion dollars. With so much money flowing into the country from the high oil prices, this sum had not been a major consideration, and Chávez correctly explained that the real reason for the separation had been to reduce the ability of world powers to use those international institutions as instruments to coerce and exploit poor countries.[20]

As the months passed by, the authority of the enabling law remained largely unused as Chávez lost interest in economic issues and devoted increasing amounts of energy to international relations.[21] He had assumed the mantle of leading the world in the campaign against the Bush presidency, a crushing burden seemingly beyond the capabilities of a modest country like Venezuela. Ever since his first international travels, he had been fascinated with visiting foreign countries, and he fancied himself as the leader of an anti–U.S. coalition. In making foreign policy his highest priority, he neglected vital domestic issues inside Venezuela. Not surprisingly, the tedious and complicated details of agriculture and the economy bored him; assuming that the oil wealth would last forever, he saw no pressing need to immerse himself in the daily grind of keeping state firms running smoothly. Without realizing it, his attention gradually shifted away from economic issues to the apparently simpler to understand politics.

In another major error of his presidency, he decided to create a new political party. He had publicly announced his intention on 9 September 2006; any illusion that this was just another empty campaign promise ended when after his reelection he reiterated on 15 December his goal to merge the existing pro–Chávez parties into a single entity. This decision was all the more unexpected, because among the many requests that citizens, groups, and institutions were making, nobody had ever asked for a new political party or for merging the existing ones. The origins of this proposal remain murky, and although several personalities later claimed to have suggested the idea as early as 2004, this was the clearest example of Venezuela trying to follow the example of the Cuban Revolution. Fidel Castro had combined three parties into one in 1961, but Chávez had the harder task of having to merge 24 parties into one. The number was so large because the opposition's absurd decision to boycott the 4 December 2005 legislative elections artificially inflated the number of seats that minor pro–Chávez parties were able to win. Having these small parties around was convenient because Chávez could point to this diversity of voices in the National Assembly as proof of a democratic system. In reality his own party, the Movement for the Fifth Republic (MVR) controlled the majority of the seats and traditionally received the largest percentage of the popular vote.[22]

The MVR with its 23 allied parties had won every electoral contest since 1998, and no practical reason existed for dismantling this winning coalition. Why then did Chávez in late 2006 decide to create a single official party and why did he insist on carrying the consolidation in 2007? Here is where the example of the Cuban Revolution fails, because during his visits to Cuba he learned how the single-party system operated. But the Cuban leadership did not recount for him the "old" history of how the Cuban party had been created in the early 1960s and did not emphasize that merging the previous pro–Castro parties into a single entity besides being a traumatic experience also created a structural flaw in the political system in Cuba. Fidel Castro expressed to Chávez the fear that should anything happen to the Venezuelan leader, the Bolivarian Revolution might disappear unless a unified party existed to guarantee continuity into the future. These indirect reminders of his mortality and perhaps the first seemingly insignificant symptoms of declining health prompted Chávez to try to assure his legacy.

On 15 December 2006 the president announced his intention to combine the pro–Chávez parties into a single one whose name was supposedly still under discussion. In reality the name of Unified Socialist Party of Venezuela (*Partido Socialista Unificado de Venezuela*) or PSUV had already been decided upon. Because it was an obvious calque of the original name of the first unified party of the Cuban Revolution, Chávez wisely tried to hide the name as long as possible, but it soon leaked out. On 18 December the MRV promptly dissolved itself and by January 2007 almost all of the pro–Chávez parties had done the same and promised to join the new PSUV. However, the three largest allied parties, PODEMOS, PPT (*Patria Para Todos*), and the Venezuelan Communist Party, were most reluctant to merge. Government officials had not even bothered to explain the reasons for needing to make this shift to a single socialist party, and the simplistic assumption among loyal followers was that voters, by giving Chávez a massive victory margin in the presidential election of 3 December 2006, had already given their approval.[23]

The Communist Party was the oldest partisan group in the country, and by a strange coincidence, some of its members had been in Moscow when Russia formally abolished the Soviet Communist Party. The Venezuelan organization considered itself as the heir and one of the few remaining guardians of this political tradition. Not surprisingly, it completely refused to sacrifice its own identity but remained willing to endorse most PSUV candidates.

PODEMOS and PPT were understandably upset that they had not been consulted and had major reservations about merging with PSUV. Both political organizations had begun as dissident factions within the old corrupt parties of the Fourth Republic and traditionally resented having to follow the official leadership. PODEMOS and PPT both operated through tightly connected networks of highly dedicated militants. Unlike the Communist Party, they wanted to negotiate quotas of power and influence in the new PSUV. Chávez was outraged with this suggestion, because it smacked of the corrupt deals that traditional politicians had brokered during the Fourth Republic. He instead increased the pressure and in his statements tried to create a "political purgatory" between the government and the opposition for these recalcitrant parties, but they still refused to budge. In a final threat, on 18 March 2007 Chávez told these three parties either to merge into the PSUV or to join the opposition. The Communist Party ignored the threat, and the other two parties refused to dissolve. The situation was so critical, that the leadership of PPT put the matter to a vote, and 97 percent of its members voted against joining the PSUV.[24]

Bitter struggles raged inside the three parties, and "Chavez's ongoing dispute with leaders from the holdout parties is the biggest public fissure in recent years within his normally lock-step and hermetic camp."[25] The opposition watched with undisguised glee how for the first time Chavistas were attacking each other but still did not realize that an opportunity to strike was fast approaching. The many past electoral defeats had taught the opposition to be cautious and to continue leaving the initiative to Chávez who was trying to organize his new PSUV.

Chávez naively had believed that all MVR militants would automatically jump at the chance to join the new party, but registration proved sluggish. MVR consisted of a nucleus of card-carrying members and a much larger number of supporters who voted for this party at every election. The failure of the nucleus to migrate to the PSUV raised doubts about the likelihood of voters automatically shifting their loyalty from the MVR to the PSUV. The inscription of members originally took place only at schools, but the inadequate response forced party operatives to go into neighborhoods in western Caracas and to metro stops to collect signatures. Soon officials were coercing government employees, contractors, and the beneficiaries of the 24 missions (programs) into joining the new party. A surge in registration took place only after those citizens whose names were in the infamous Tascón list realized that their inscription in the new party was a great opportunity to redeem their reputation as loyalists. It was clear that anyone interested in jobs, contracts, and services from the government needed to join PSUV; without realizing it, Chávez for the first time was replicating the fatal mistakes of the failed Soviet party system.[26]

The basic unit of the new party were "battalions" of 200 to 400 citizens each. The goal was to have 22,000 "battalions," but only 14,000 existed by October, and many rarely did any work or even held meetings. "Opportunists and militants with bureaucratic interests" took over most of the "battalions" and even then organizers of the recruitment drive had to inflate the membership lists to meet their quotas. One deputy nearly committed political suicide when he publicly stated that PSUV was having such a hard time getting off the ground that it was time to "dust off" the tried and proven MRV for the next electoral contest.[27] The deputy was punished for this statement because an outraged Chávez did not want to hear defeatist talk when everything indicated that the Bolivarian Revolution was unbeatable: "still stinging from its tenth consecutive electoral defeat since 1998, the opposition is plagued by infighting, the need to rebuild, disillusioned supporters, and an inability to effectively confront President Chavez's plans to push his Socialist agenda."[28]

The opposition was having a hard time taking advantage of the clashes over the creation of PSUV when another controversy came to provide a great rallying point to whip up anti-government frenzy. After the April 2002 coup attempt, Chávez had failed to suspend constitutional guarantees and consequently had not confiscated the television stations that had been openly inciting the population to revolt. The television channels did not halt their non-stop anti-Chávez propaganda, and the most vitriolic was RCTV. After the landslide victory in the presidential election, Chávez in another mistake concluded that the moment had come to send a warning to the television owners, and on 28 December 2006 he announced that the government intended not to renew the station's authorization to broadcast on the air when it expired on May 2007. The opposition, and particularly groups of university students, were expected to protest vigorously against the closure, all in the name of freedom of the press. Similar demonstrations had flared and fizzled out in the past but never before had they occurred so close to an important electoral contest.[29]

The size and intensity of the demonstrations and the extensive international media coverage over the refusal to renew RCTV's broadcast license counseled letting the issue cool down before attempting any major initiative. Sensing trouble ahead, Chávez wisely announced in May that he did not plan to introduce constitutional amendments in 2007. The obstacles and delays in organizing the new PSUV counseled against using this untested party in an electoral contest any time soon. Chávez could still solve economic and social problems either by using his enabling authority or by securing legislation from the National Assembly. Instead he increasingly devoted his efforts to foreign affairs and was away for long periods in official trips abroad. By leading the anti–Bush global coalition Chávez neglected the many issues inside Venezuela, and gradually he started to lose touch with the political reality. For the only time in his electoral career, the illusion of victory gripped him and his party officials. This dangerous overconfidence made him change his mind again in late June 2007 when he reversed his earlier decision about the constitutional amendments. He now promised to bring the proposed changes before the voters by the end of the year. The key amendment was the elimination of term limits on the president so that he could run for office again in 2012.[30]

The off-again, on-again statements about presenting a referendum created a degree of confusion in the public's mind about what really the president considered important. The uncertainty increased because not until 15 August did he finally propose the specific text for the changes. American diplomats, much more acute observers than local politicians, were the first to realize that Chávez, by calling for the constitutional referendum, had exposed a vulnerable flank at a moment of weakness. The U.S. government promptly channeled additional funds and resources to bolster the opposition, although at this stage the U.S. Embassy had no illusions about defeating Chávez. The more modest goal of American diplomats was to reduce his victory margin so that the opposition could claim that the regime was losing popularity because of the move to socialism and the closing of RCTV; just making Chávez have to struggle to win kept him from stirring up problems for the U.S. government in Venezuela and elsewhere in the world.[31]

The Roman Catholic Church was leading the public denunciations of the constitutional reform, and soon after other institutions, such as the business group FEDECAMARAS, joined in condemning the constitutional amendments, as did leading opposition figures such as Luis Miquilena. But so far only the old coalition that had supported the Pedro Carmona regime had come out against the referendum, and the U.S. Embassy correctly concluded that without defections from inside the ranks of Chavismo, the referendum necessarily had to pass by a large margin. Almost as if on cue, PODEMOS, one of the parties Chávez had ostracized for not joining PSUV, publicly came out questioning but not attacking the constitutional amendments. The party's secretary general explained on 7 September that its membership was divided over the merits of the 33 amendments but was united on demanding that voters get to vote on each of the amendments and not just on the entire package. Chávez refused to compromise, and PODEMOS, after being rebuffed, was left with no choice but to oppose the constitutional reform. For the first time a pro–Chávez group had joined the opposition in trying to block the government.[32]

In a close vote PODEMOS could tip the election, but only if millions of voters either voted NO or abstained. Yet the fragmented opposition was unlikely to mount any serious resistance because it could not agree on the right tactics. The electoral invincibility of Chávez was so great, that many critics believed that abstention was the only possible alternative to remove some of the luster from the inevitable government victory; the university students were particularly insistent on urging people not to participate in the referendum scheduled for 2 December 2007. And as for the traditional politicians "opposition parties appeared to spend as much time criticizing each other as Chavez's constitutional proposals."[33]

Frustrated American diplomats once again struggled with the recurrent challenge in U.S. foreign relations of putting together a winning coalition of allies willing to fight enemies either in the ballot box or in the battlefield. The opposition unexpectedly gained an additional advantage when Chavez sent the proposed amendments to the National Assembly for final approval. The legislature resented being labeled a rubber-stamp body, and in an act of independence, added 36 new amendments to the original 33 to produce a hodgepodge of measures. The 1999 Constitution stipulated the procedure to replace a small number of clauses but implied that many changes required the convocation of a constitutional convention; 33 amendments already seemed too many and adding another 36 clearly exceeded any reasonable limit.[34]

Clearly the constitutional referendum had gotten out of control and threatened to inflict damage on the Bolivarian Revolution. As a runaway missile in a space launch, Chávez had no choice but to press the self-destruct mechanism, but because of his concentration on foreign affairs, he failed to realize the danger threatening both the specific proposal and his entire political movement. As a minor correction, he persuaded the National Assembly to group the amendments into a first group of his 33 and a second group of the legislature's 36, thus giving voters more of a choice. On 2 November 2007, the National Assembly approved the two packages, but this time the vote although overwhelming, was not unanimous. The PSUV and the Communist Party voted for the packages, but PODEMOS abstained; one deputy of PPT also abstained. This break in the formerly united ranks of Chavismo encouraged an opposition that was soon to receive an additional boost from a totally unexpected quarter.[35]

The reluctance of some pro–Chávez parties to endorse the amendments intrigued many citizens who for the first time began to examine the complex maze of proposals contained in the 69 proposed amendments. Except for lifting the prohibition on reelection to the presidency, most of the proposals were hard to understand; constitutional experts had complained from the very beginning that the language of most the amendments was more confusing than many of the ambiguous clauses in the 1999 Constitution. Public interest increased dramatically when on 5 November 2007, three days after the National Assembly approved the two packages of amendments, retired general and former defense minister Raúl Baduel urged all Venezuelans to vote "NO" on the referendum. This bombshell declaration, coming from a famous general who had saved Chávez during the April 2002 coup attempt, had a great impact on the country. For Chávez this betrayal was a major political loss and also a psychological blow. Baduel had shown signs of discontent if not disloyalty during his term as defense minister, but Chávez was so grateful for his actions during the April 2002 coup that he refused to act on the many warnings that Baduel was quietly undermining the Bolivarian Revolution. When the discontent became public before the presidential election of 3 December 2006, Chávez should have promptly fired Baduel. However, an exaggerated sense of gratitude persuaded Chávez to let the general complete his term as defense minister; the president also naively believed that Baduel intended to remain quiet during his retirement.[36]

Instead, Baduel called on Venezuelans to vote NO and also joined opposition figures in loudly condemning the proposal. By the middle of November polls showed that Chavistas were increasingly turning against the constitutional amendment. Chávez too read the polls and made last minute efforts to turn the tide. In many public rallies he tried to frame the vote as a referendum on him and not on the constitution, but it was too late in the campaign to change the message. He also ordered PSUV members to make frantic efforts to get the vote out; the previous MVR had been a superb organization for delivering the voters on elections day, but the PSUV was having trouble matching the performance of its predecessor. For the first time the opposition sensed that victory was within grasp, even if only by a slim margin.[37]

On 2 December 2007 51 percent of the electorate voted NO and 49 percent YES: "the stunning defeat of the constitutional referendum is President Chavez's first electoral loss since he won the presidency in 1998."[38] As a defeated general, Chávez bravely recognized the opposition's first victory. The need for damage control was obvious, and on his *Aló Presidente* broadcast of 6 January 2008, he announced that he was putting on the brakes on the Bolivarian Revolution to give his presidency time to "Review, Rectify, and Re-launch" his "twenty-first-century Socialism." He insisted on consolidating the PSUV, but in contrast to the disdainful attitude before the election, a more humble president welcomed creating electoral alliances with minor parties. Whether these measures sufficed to save his presidency was uncertain; as the year 2008 began, it remained to be seen whether the defeat of the constitutional referendum marked the start of the irreversible decline of Chavismo or whether the electoral loss had been merely a bump in the road.

Peru: From Honeymoon to Social Conflict

A rarely mentioned concern in the long presidential campaign of 2006 was the near universal desire for peace and stability in Peru. Whether wealthy investors trying to expand private business or average citizens exhausted from the constant political mobilizations of the last years of the Alejandro Toledo presidency, the desire for a government able to reduce tensions and maintain a fair degree of order was the one goal unifying the Peruvian population.

A major divisive issue remained the Free Trade Agreement with the United States. While candidate Ollanta Humala had openly opposed the agreement, Alán García had urged renegotiating many of its clauses. Actually, García was a passionate supporter of the Free Trade Agreement, but as a very astute politician, he was trying to distance his campaign from this highly emotional issue. To avoid having to deal with this hot topic during his presidency, he instructed the congressmen of his party APRA to vote with other parties to approve the treaty prior to his inauguration. As he told the U.S. Embassy in Lima, García "wants the Free Trade Agreement signed, sealed, and delivered before he takes office."[39] The Peruvian unicameral assembly complied and by a vote of 79 to 14 approved the treaty in the last days of June; lame-duck President Alejandro Toledo duly signed the bill into law as his final major action in office.

By this preemptive maneuver, García could claim that the Free Trade Agreement was already a done deal. He thus rid the country, at least temporarily, of a very divisive topic and cleared the deck for launching his own initiatives. Already in his inaugural speech of 28 July 2006 he announced a laundry list of measures he wanted his government to undertake during his five-year term. Avoiding the usual tradition of speaking in generalities, he enumerated concrete programs and created the impression that he really meant to address the problems of most segments of the population. As one example, he singled out "Water for Everyone," a construction project to deliver drinking water to the majority of the population. Particularly seductive was his linking of austerity in government with budget allocations to new social programs: without having to impose new taxes, the government claimed to have found the funds to pay for the costs of bringing much needed services to the underprivileged. García also tried to deliver on his campaign promises to accelerate decentralization by channeling these funds through the new municipal and regional authorities. And to show that he had not forgotten the Free Trade Agreement with the United States, he inserted in his inaugural speech a reference to attracting investment as the best way to create jobs in Peru.[40]

The reference to foreign investment did not seem particularly significant, but in reality he was trying to disguise his new economic policy in a long list of apparently populist measures. He had become a convert to free market and free trade, but he did not want to reveal the complete change from the socialistic tendencies of his 1984–1990 presidency. He was following the career path of Venezuelan President Carlos Andrés Pérez who in his first term of 1974–1979 had been nationalizing foreign properties only to revert to extreme free market policies in his second presidency of 1989–1992. But in the Peru of 2006, García carefully hid his adoption of extreme free market principles and, by pretending to straddle both the left and the right, he seemed well-positioned to take the country out of the turmoil of the final years of the Toledo presidency.[41]

His biggest test in 2006 was to persuade the U.S. Congress to ratify the Free Trade Agreement. Nobody expected the American legislature to approve the treaty in 2006, but vigorous Peruvian lobbying was indispensable to prevent the proposal from languishing and even falling into oblivion. However, the fear existed that if the García administration pushed too hard in Washington, Peruvian opponents of the Free Trade Agreement might gain the opportunity to refight the struggle over the treaty against a backdrop of renewed protests and disturbances. A determined García constantly spoke in his speeches about the need to obtain U.S. ratification of the treaty. Starting in August he appointed high-level emissaries, such as the famed economist Hernando de Soto, to win over key American legislators, while the president and cabinet officials travelled regularly to Washington to lobby for the treaty. His repeated claim that seeking approval of the treaty was a matter of national honor seemed to resonate with Peruvians, and as a testament to his careful presentation of the issue, his efforts on behalf of ratification did not spark any major backlash.[42]

The constant clashes in the last years of the Toledo situation had been so serious that not just the U.S. Embassy in Lima but members of García's own team assumed that the honeymoon period after his inauguration on 28 July 2006 would be very brief. To everyone's surprise, Peru calmed down as master politician García traveled across the country reassuring the population. An accomplished speaker with a gift for words, he created the impression of being sincerely interested in helping the people. Protests either failed to materialize or soon fizzled out, and the tense confrontations of the Toledo presidency seemed a thing of the past.[43]

A large part of the favorable image of the initial year of the new presidency came from his deft handling of the explosive situation in the gold mines of Cajamarca Department. Since the ill-begotten inception of the project under the Fujimori dictatorship, Yanacocha had provoked nearly endless conflict and turmoil, most recently under the Toledo administration. The parent company, Denver-based Newmont, reaped huge profits from its open-pit mine but created only a small number of jobs for the local community; this was the usual pattern for extractive activities across the globe. In a pathetic scene, at the entrance gate throngs of locals gathered every day waving their résumés in a usually hopeless attempt to land any type of employment. The company was caught by surprise when on 2 August 2006 a crowd of 500 job seekers appeared to protest and demanded jobs. The police used tear gas to disperse the demonstrators who fought back throwing stones. In the clash one peasant farmer was killed and many demonstrators were injured. In retaliation for the death, the next day angry residents blocked the road to Cajamarca and effectively paralyzed company operations. The police returned on 3 August to clear the road again, raising the possibility of more bloodshed. The timely intervention of an official from the Ministry of Mines and of the local Roman Catholic priest Marco Arana persuaded the police to pull back and to limit its activities to guarding only the mine installations.[44]

Over the coming weeks, inhabitants occasionally disrupted traffic on the road. More significantly, the nature of the conflict changed: "what began as protests over insufficient jobs at Yanacocha has evolved into an action against a mine expansion that peasant farmers believe will pollute and deplete their water supplies."[45] No less importantly, both private investors and the U.S. Embassy looked at Yanacocha as the first test case for García to prove his pro-business credentials; calls even appeared for promptly crushing the demonstrators.[46]

The first clash at Yanacocha had erupted just days after his inauguration, and García was not going to allow this social conflict to tarnish his reputation so early in his presidency. At first he hoped that a calming down period would gradually make the tension go away, but when on 23 August residents under the guidance of the priest Arana resumed the struggle and blocked completely the road to Cajamarca, the government took action. A high-level delegation went to negotiate with the demonstrators, and later the communities sent representatives to talk with Prime Minister Jorge del Castillo, who was the government's point man for dealing with social unrest. In an 11-point agreement with the protest leaders, the government and Newmont promised to build a road, to safeguard the water supply, and to create more jobs for locals. Satisfied that their demands were met, the protestors lifted the roadblocks, and the company was able to resume normal operations on 4 September 2006.[47]

The peaceful resolution of a potentially explosive conflict bolstered the prestige of the García presidency which continued to enjoy its honeymoon period. Unlike most political commentators, García did not worry at all about the upcoming regional elections of 19 November even when reliable polls showed that his party APRA would lose most of the regional governorships. In anticipation of this defeat, he announced on 18 October with great fanfare that he was transferring 20 key functions to the new regional authorities. This meant accelerating the timetable of three years that he had previously announced for these transfers. This action seemed to ratify his commitment to decentralization and also brought the political benefit of shifting blame for poor services to the regional authorities.[48]

Actually he viewed the 19 November 2006 regional elections not as an early referendum on his presidency but rather as an opportunity to increase his political power. Although APRA won only two governorships, the electoral defeats in the regional elections made him more powerful inside his own party. The fragmentation of political power among the many independent local candidates with no common views also confirmed him as the sole figure with national standing. The new regional governors and mayors had no choice but to turn submissively to the national government to plead for funds to finance their programs.[49]

As the year 2006 came to an end, amazed observers were surprised at the long duration of the honeymoon period. In spite of dire predictions to the contrary, the master political speaker had succeeded in convincing the majority of Peruvians that he really was working on their behalf.[50] He had achieved an impressive accomplishment often overlooked because of the later crises of his presidency. Everything indicated that had he remained as a sympathetic arbitrator among competing groups, Peru would have continued to enjoy peace and stability. But as happened to Hugo Chávez after his triumphal reelection in 2006, García overestimated his power and proceeded to embark on what ultimately turned out to be a path replete with strife and confrontation.

One issue he wanted to put to rest was decentralization. His desire to halt the shifting of authority away from Lima was not so much because his party, the APRA had done so poorly in the November 2006 regional elections, but mainly because independent local groups were rallying around the regional governorships to oppose foreign corporations. In a first indication of his reversal, on 25 January 2007 he abolished the National Council of Decentralization and merged it with the Council of Cabinet Ministers on the pretext of assigning more high-level attention to the process. But in reality "some observers emphasize the irony that the central government has reasserted control over a mechanism intended to distribute authority to regions and municipalities."[51]

The proof of the policy change over decentralization came with the failure to deliver on his promise to transfer 20 functions to the regional authorities. He had announced this action with great fanfare in October 2006, but the government transferred only six minor functions. One obstacle after another kept appearing to prevent the completion of the process. Very astutely García and his officials seized upon the lack of capabilities in the regional and municipal authorities as the real reason for announcing the impossibility of proceeding with decentralization. García, who since his first presidency had supported taking power away from Lima, astutely maintained his image as a champion of decentralization while at the same time killing any meaningful change more effectively than even the bitterest opponents of the proposal could ever have done.[52]

This first quiet victory for the president emboldened him to attack another irresistible and relatively easy target. As early as 2005 and before his election, García in private conversations promised that the second highest priority in his government would be improving the educational system. The failures of public education in Peru were well know, and in 2004 tests revealed that only 13 percent of sixth graders were able to write and read at minimal levels and that only 6 percent had basic arithmetic skills. The situation was not improving, because the results were practically identical to those in the previous national test of 1998. Not surprisingly, over 15 percent of Peruvians sent their children to private schools, and the percentage would have been higher had more parents been able to afford a private education for their children. Many teachers were poorly qualified, for example 47 percent were deficient in mathematics and 33 percent lacked basic reading skills.[53]

In this context, the educators became the ideal target for scapegoating. The participation of the Teacher's Union in the general strike of 2003 against Toledo had created considerable resentment among many families because children had remained without school during six weeks. Frustrated parents did not want their children to be without classes again, and public opinion easily shifted against the Teacher's Union. And the affiliation of the labor union to an extremist Maoist party made this political target even more attractive. This link gave the government the opportunity to use guilt by association to condemn the leftist group, even though it had openly clashed with the terrorist Shining Path of the same ideological inspiration.[54]

The Teacher's Union opposed the nationwide testing of teachers in January 2007 but left the decision to its members. Most educators complied because they were fearful of losing their jobs if they did not take the test. When the government decided to fire those who failed the test after three attempts, the Teacher's Union announced a strike to block the start of the school semester on 1 March 2007. Public opinion turned overwhelmingly against the teachers, and the union had no choice but to cancel the strike. President García had entered the fray as a way to win an easy victory, and he could not resist making biting comments about the labor leaders while his government in reprisal sharply cut back several union prerogatives.[55]

Another early indication of the commitment to capitalism of the García administration came when the government refused to nationalize the mining companies in Peru. Mining had been a source of constant clashes among communities, workers, and the companies. Neighboring Bolivia under its radical president Evo Morales had opted for nationalization as the only possible solution, but in Peru García refused to consider anything that would take natural resources out of the hands of private and usually foreign owners.[56]

By openly supporting free market and anti-union policies, García lost his political cover of governing from the middle. This was a particularly risky move on his part, because although he could show growth rates for the Peruvian economy, he was heading toward the same situation that had doomed his predecessor's presidency. The increase in wealth was not trickling down to the mass of the population and even less to the highlands and to southern Peru, traditionally the poorest areas of the country.[57]

March 2007 came to be the month of final warnings before the storm. In a series of meetings with government officials and even with diplomats in the U.S. Embassy in Lima, labor leaders warned that the direction García was taking the country could only lead to social conflicts. Organized labor felt betrayed by García who had campaigned on restoring the 1979 Constitution only to have him turn out to be more pro-business than Fujimori had been. The candidate had promised to renegotiate the Free Trade Agreement to protect the rights of vulnerable sectors such as domestic agricultural producers, but once in office he had forgotten his campaign pledges.[58]

Because García showed no intention of reversing his pro-business course, he ignored the warnings and in late April his honeymoon period came to an end. A small wave of protests broke out in several regions of the country, and initially the government through both soft and hard tactics was able to defuse the disturbances. Yet the unrest continued and Peru found itself in a situation reminiscent of the first wave of protests under the Toledo administration. The opposition groups were clearly of disparate origin and had vastly different demands. The coca growers (*cocaleros*) in Huánaco wanted freedom to grow their crops, while cotton and rice farmers in Piura wanted protection from U.S imports. In Iquitos a general strike of 48 hours demanded the hiring of 1000 more teachers, and grievances in the mining camps led to random outbreaks of violence against foreign companies. The government and the U.S. Embassy scrambled to find a common thread linking the protests, yet for part of the explanation García did not have to go beyond his own political party: APRA members were furious that he was not distributing patronage jobs to loyalists.[59]

Labor leaders had followed the campaign against the Teacher's Union and reached the conclusion that the events confirmed the pro-business bias of the administration. García received one last opportunity to mend fences with unions and to defuse social tensions when the Labor bill came to his desk for approval. In the capitalist system the firing of employees is a fundamental right of all employers, but in Peru unions had restricted considerably this power of employers. Actually both labor leaders and party stalwarts of APRA had wanted to return to the socialistic Constitution of 1979 and as a first step had negotiated the Labor bill in Congress to limit the authority of employers to fire their workers.[60]

Starting with the protracted parliamentary negotiations for the Labor bill in late 2006, García had taken a middle-of-the road position and urged both labor and business groups to seek common ground, but when the private sector felt the proposal was too hostile, he had no hesitation about vetoing the bill in mid–2007.[61] The veto of the Labor Bill, the defeat of the Teacher's Union, and the refusal to nationalize mining companies were unmistakable signs not just for organized labor but, increasingly also, for the public in general that this was a pro-business administration.

The combination of mounting tensions inside Peru and demands of the new Democratic majority in the U.S. Congress persuaded García that revising the Free Trade Agreement was the best way to regain his political standing. Although the amendments to the treaty restored some labor rights, domestic farmers were still left unprotected. At the last minute the government presented the proposed amendments to the Peruvian congress, which approved them 70 to 38 on 27 June 2007. The vote was less overwhelming than for the original treaty, and this seemed to indicate some disillusionment with the Free Trade Agreement. On the contrary, opinion polls showed that the public approval for free trade had actually increased by four percent to 59 percent in May 2007 compared to one year before, so the García administration confidently concluded that it had handled the mounting social tensions adequately.[62]

The confidence lacked foundation, because 35 serious social conflicts were raging at 16 of the 24 departments in Peru during June. The badly treated Teacher's Union joined forces with protesting mine workers and coca growers. Unlike the demonstrations in April, which had been only a preview, these were more intense and widespread. Very disturbing were the unlikely alliances spontaneously springing up in some parts of the country. For example, Pucallpa wanted to preserve its tax breaks, and to show massive popular support, the Chamber of Commerce recruited local Communist groups to fill the streets with protestors. At least three protesters died in disturbances across the country, but before the violence could intensify, this latest wave of social clashes came to an end by the start of July. Union leaders believed that an internal power struggle inside the Teacher's Union helped dampen the enthusiasm for continuing the protests.[63]

The fizzling out of the protests in July and the return to a modicum of calm counseled for using the pause to reverse the pro-business turn of the García administration. The president's poll numbers began to drop, and it was clear that he was headed for worse confrontations in 2008 unless he moderated his policies. But the president saw the protests of June as a predictable bump in the road and did not want to admit that he had suffered a setback as happened to Chávez in Venezuela. Because "García knows that the business community is watching closely to insure his economic policies stay on the straight and narrow path of economic orthodoxy,"[64] he refused to change course. His administration believed that only through slavish adherence to the free market could Peru reduce its poverty. He felt beholden only to the business community, and desperately seeking their constant approval, he decided to confirm his free market credentials by unilaterally removing many of the tariffs on imports into Peru. He had already issued an initial decree eliminating tariffs on nearly 3000 goods on 27 December 2006, and again in October 2007 he reduced the remaining ones to 5.8 percent from the previous 8 percent.[65] The optimism about the imminent entry into force of the Free Trade Agreement proved well founded. After approval by the U.S. Congress, the Free Trade Agreement became law on 14 December 2007.

By the unilateral tariff reductions, García opened up the Peruvian market to foreign competition before the Free Trade Agreement entered into force on 1 February 2008. Everyone knew that free trade was going to cause disruptions among producers supplying mainly the domestic market, but why the rush to begin this turmoil? Protected producers needed a gradual transition to adjust to the new intense competition, but speeding into the free market could only generate resentment, hostility, and confrontations.[66] These unilateral tariff reductions became the unsuspected culprits of what later became the first major crisis of the García presidency, as the next chapter will show. No less than in Venezuela, an exaggerated belief in the ability of the government to carry out vast transformations had led both Hugo Chávez and Alán García to try to seek overly ambitious goals. And with U.S. approval of the Free Trade Agreement, President García felt that he was in a much better position than his Venezuelan counterpart to face the mounting tide of social protest in Peru.

CHAPTER 13

Peru: The Self-Destruction of the Alán García Presidency

You have again forgotten, my friend, the intention of the legislator, who did not aim at making any one class in the State happy above the rest; the happiness was to be in the whole State, and he held the citizens together by persuasion and necessity, making them benefactors of the State, and therefore benefactors of one another.—Plato[1]

García championed businesses' agendas and markets arguably more so than Fujimori in the 1990s.—Moisés Arce[2]

The mounting popular resistance to the pro-business turn of President Alán García suggested caution before he embarked on any new extreme measures. The president had enjoyed an unexpectedly long honeymoon period after his inauguration as long as he appeared to be an honest and impartial broker among competing groups. But the more he acted as a free market zealot the more he distanced himself from the majority of Peruvians. Almost as if driven by hubris, he became even more determined to prove his capitalist credentials and eagerly sought to rush into a deadly confrontation.

New Outbreaks of Violence

In response to the impending approval of the Free Trade Agreement with the United States, already in March 2007 the country's leading labor confederation organized a political-social coordinator as a new steering body to galvanize public resistance to the free market preferences of the Alán García administration. This new body had learned from its participation in the July 2007 national protests and was planning a much larger general strike for July 8 and 9 of 2008. The goal was to unite the entire left in one general protest movement, which would then serve as the basis for launching a new political party. The political-social coordinator claimed to have the support of Nationalist Party leader Ollanta Humala and of eight regional governors (out of a total of 25). According to a police report, 38 groups were ready to participate in the general strike of July 8 and 9.[3]

The point man of the administration for dealing with the looming general strike was Prime Minister Jorge del Castillo. With the full blessing of President García, the prime minister adopted a divide and rule strategy of splintering the opposition. In negotiations with the member unions of the labor confederation, Castillo was able to buy some of them off with timely concessions. For the community leaders of shantytowns and slums, the prime minister gave money and gifts supposedly for improving the neighborhoods. And government employees who showed up for work on the days of the general strike received an additional payment.[4]

No disturbances or casualties occurred, and the general strike of July 8 and 9 remained relatively peaceful. For its part, the political-social coordinator acquired strong organizational abilities, and as one analyst told the U.S. Embassy, "this was the first national strike in a long time that successfully organized peaceful work stoppages and roadblocks in so many regions."[5] A large crowd gathered to protest in central Lima, but no serious disruptions occurred in the normal functioning of the capital. In several departments, most notably Ayacucho, Cuzco, and Puno, "strike and protests [...] slowed economic activity to a crawl." The divide and rule strategy of Prime Minister Castillo seemed to have worked, because the vast majority of Lima residents were more concerned about their daily lives than in participating in a national protest. Without admitting defeat, the leftist opposition began looking for other ways to block the free market reforms.

President García, counting on the imminent approval of the Free Trade Agreement, saw the opportunity to press forward and not give the opposition a moment's rest. In a most extraordinary move, he decided to express his preferences in three articles published in *El Comercio*, the leading daily newspaper of Peru. Starting with the first article on 28 October 2007, he drew on Aesop's fables to revive the story of the dog who did not eat and did not allow others to eat. He likened the dog to the Indians who blocked attempts to exploit the natural resources of the Amazon jungle. In a second article he expounded the extreme capitalist thesis that all obstacles impeding the operation of market forces had to be removed. The Indians felt insulted with these attacks, so in an attempt to calm their anger, the president wrote a final article on 2 March 2008. In a most condescending way, García tried to excuse the Indians by claiming it was not really their fault, because they could not understand or reason critically and thus were easily manipulated and duped by astute agitators.[6]

The third article incensed the already angry Indians even more, and confrontations over the natural resources of the Amazon were inevitable. Had President García been videotaped secretly making these statements to insiders or had he blurted out these comments in the heat of a spontaneous speech, he later could have issued apologies and retractions. A basic rule of politics is never to insult groups of citizens, but to have a sitting president make these outrageous accusations in premeditated articles with each word carefully selected was a baffling blunder and even more so when coming from a supposedly seasoned veteran politician. Clearly he was trying to gain momentum for his free market principles, but the risks seemed to outweigh the benefits. In reality, his main goal was to make a public profession of his newly found capitalist beliefs. As a recent convert to the virtues of the free market, he behaved as a true believer, and in particular he had to bury the flirting with socialism during his first presidency (1985–1990). He knew that Peruvian business and the international financial community were scrutinizing his every move for any hints of socialist or even populist tendencies. In contrast, his predecessor Alejandro Toledo had been a life-long believer in the virtues of the free market, and although he had done everything possible to advance the capitalist agenda, as born into the faith, he never felt the obligation to prove to anyone that he was a devout follower.[7]

Instead, President García constantly had to confirm his commitment to free market principles. The "dog in the manger" fable was the opening blast in a campaign to turn the Free Trade Agreement into a battering ram to shatter the non-capitalist elements present in the Peruvian economy. On 19 December, just five days after the U.S. ratification of the Free Trade Agreement on 14 December 2007, President García used the wave of euphoria to obtain from a pliant Peruvian congress authority to issue Decree Laws. The enabling power to legislate started on 1 January 2008 and lasted for a 180-day period ending on 28 June; as a safeguard, a simple congressional majority sufficed to repeal any decree. Supposedly the purpose of this broad authorization was to facilitate the implementation of the Free Trade Agreement, which was scheduled to enter into force on 1 February 2009. In reality all along the goal had been to give President García the authority to impose free market principles on all sectors of the economy, and not just those affected by the Free Trade Agreement as the Peruvian congress stipulated. Before the deadline to legislate expired, the government promulgated nearly 100 Decree Laws, only about 20 percent dealing with the provisions of the Free Trade Agreement. To sugarcoat the imposition of the free market principles, the government issued some measures protecting the environment. As many critics had feared, cabinet ministries drafted the texts of the Decree Laws with little or no popular participation in the process.[8]

The most flagrant violation of the legal obligation to consult with citizens came with the issuance of decrees adversely affecting Indians. Two Decree Laws (DL 1015 and 1073) were particularly harmful because they accelerated the disintegration of traditional Indian lands in the Amazon regions of Peru. Previously, any sale, lease, or partnership of community lands required the approval of two-thirds of the Indian members, but the two new Decree Laws reduced the percentage to only 50 percent. What investors were trying to do was to repeat an old maneuver dating back to the nineteenth century whereby illiterate Indians were tricked into selling small parcels for a pittance.[9] This had happened not just in Peru, but also in other countries such as Colombia and most recently in Mexico under the privatization campaign of President Carlos Salinas de Gortari. The village elders were well aware of the danger threatening their community lands: "One Embassy contact with ties to a key protest leader explained that for Amazonian communities, land is the only possession and it represents both their livelihood and their way of life. Communities will do anything to defend their land if they believe it is under threat. Our contact added that if the government sought to forcibly end the strike, it would only turn the protest leaders into martyrs."[10]

President García issued these Decree Laws in direct violation of the International Convention on Tribal and Indian Peoples of 1989. Peru had ratified this treaty in 1993, and by its clauses the government assumed the obligation of obtaining the approval of Indian communities before adopting any legislation affecting them. The failure to follow the proper legal procedure left no other alternative to AIDESEP (*Asociación Interétnica de Desarrollo de la Selva Peruana*), the organization representing the Amazon Indians, than to make an appeal on 9 August 2008 for a general strike to protect ancestral lands. Protesters in the departments of Loreto, Cuzco, and Amazonas set up road blocks, halted river navigation, and surrounded petroleum installations. These actions disrupted the activities of foreign extractive companies in the region. When the government refused to back down, the Indians resisted, injured several policemen, and took others hostage on 16 August. More clashes followed on 18 August, and in Puerto Maldonado the protest turned violent as the Indians burned down government offices. The conflict seemed to be spinning out of control, but the García administration did not back down and instead announced plans to deploy 1500 policemen and soldiers in the city to awe the protesters into submission.[11]

The unwillingness of the government to meet the demands of the protesters and pressure from organized labor and national organizations gave Peruvian legislators the opportunity to defuse the conflict. Because the congress retained the right to revoke any of the Decree Laws issued by President García, on 22 August the chamber decisively repealed DL 1015 and DL 1073 by a vote of 66 to 22. American diplomats supported this abrogation, because they had been from the start worried that the dispute over the ancestral lands might put at risk the entire Free Trade Agreement. Indian protest leaders took the repeal of the two Decree Laws as a significant first step and trusted that the congress would also undertake the process to revoke other Decree Laws affecting the Amazonian Indians. As calm returned to the Amazon, the public did not realize that the García administration had learned nothing from the episode and was as defiant as ever. Prime Minister Castillo, furious at the troublesome Indians, declared in a fit of anger that the government would do everything possible to nullify the rash congressional action.[12] Rather than cutting losses and moving on to other issues, the García administration stubbornly insisted on imposing its will in the Amazon, as the last section of this chapter will show.

The government was dealing not only with the conflictive situation in the Amazon but also with unforeseen costs of the decentralization campaign. As chapter 4 had explained, both Toledo and García never wavered in supporting decentralization as a fundamental solution for Peru's problems even though critics warned that the measure could only make worse the situation in Peru. The fears were confirmed by the clashes occurring in Moquegua and Tacna during 2008. The elected regional government of Moquegua shared mining royalties with Tacna to the south, and not satisfied with the amounts, staged violent demonstrations in the middle of June. When a police force tried to clear the streets on 16 June, the protesters took over 60 policemen hostage. Although the prisoners were released the next day, the police avoided additional clashes with demonstrators.[13] The only way to restore order was to call out the army, but as chapter 6 revealed, ever since the Arequipazo the generals had been most reluctant to use their soldiers to crush popular protests.

The tense situation seemed to have calmed down but exploded again on 28 October 2008 when protesters clashed with police over a key bridge in Moquegua. The confrontation became violent, and 71 protesters and policemen suffered serious injuries. To stop the outbreak from escalating, on 29 October the Peruvian congress passed a law increasing the percentage of royalties earmarked for Moquegua. Because this law meant reducing the royalties going to Tacna, the neighboring department exploded in violent protests on 30 October. Over 2000 demonstrators pushed aside the police and set two government buildings on fire. An uneasy truce followed in Tacna, but on 4 November a mob attacked police stations and a municipal building. By then the fury of the protest seemed to have spent itself, and the arrival of police reinforcements from nearby cities restored a tense calm to Tacna.[14] No doubt these regional disturbances would have continued to capture the attention of Lima, had not a major scandal appeared.

The Scandal of the Petro Audios

Even before the U.S. government ratified the Free Trade Agreement, an ideologically driven presidency could not wait to expose Peruvian producers to increased foreign competition. In a unilateral action in January 2007, the Alán García administration issued tariff reductions on a vast array of imported items. As a consequence, the possibility appeared that cement from Colombia and Mexico, in particular from the Mexican conglomerate CEMEX, could enter Peru and for the first time compete with local factories. Some executives in the Peruvian cement industry wanted advance notice of any imminent imports, and to provide this information the eavesdropping firm of Business Track emerged in 2007.[15]

Industrial espionage is nothing new or surprising in the private sector, and Business Track was just the latest of several private firms that had emerged after the fall of Vladimiro Montesinos to carry out eavesdropping and wiretapping. Trying to intercept phone calls was impossible without a court order or at least implicit government complicity, and how could a company secure official authorization for conducing espionage on private firms? The solution was to present Business Track as an undercover arm of Navy intelligence; a retired admiral headed the outfit, and naval personnel both retired and on active duty carried out the eavesdropping. The initial client was originally the Peruvian cement industry, but because Business Track proved to be such a lucrative activity, soon other private corporations, including a prominent bank, were paying for its services. Three executives ran Business Track, and one of them was a woman manager who discreetly peddled samples of recordings and made smooth power point presentations to prospective clients.[16]

The most important new client was Petro Tech Peruana, a mysterious petroleum holding company which had been incorporated under the lax rules of Delaware. Petro Tech had received most of the promising offshore blocks for drilling on Peruvian waters, but the government had not yet adjudicated some potentially very productive offshore areas. When a rival appeared also determined to obtain those same blocks, Petro Tech prepared to counter the move by first hiring Business Track to wiretap pertinent telephone conversations.[17]

In the murky world of petroleum leases, nothing is ever completely clear, and the rival was no less mysterious than Petro Tech. The new firm was Discover Petroleum International, a Norwegian company recently incorporated in 2005. Discover Petroleum did not own any producing wells, had a net worth of only $11,000,000, and already owed $13,000,000. A company with such a precarious financial situation could not possibly undertake even the simplest oil exploration on land. Aware of this weakness, Discover Petroleum justified its existence by a relationship with a technical company that supposedly had invented secret technology to carry out oil prospecting in deep offshore sites.[18]

Obviously Discover Petroleum was only an intermediary, but the unanswered question remained for whom. Perhaps it was already trying to sell the coveted offshore leases to prospective buyers who would then do the actual exploration in the blocks. Or perhaps it had been all along a shell outfit working for a major company that found it advisable to remain invisible until the leases had been formalized. Because Discover Petroleum was from Norway, it probably represented Norwegian investors who for unknown reasons preferred to remain concealed.

By April 2008 Discover Petroleum had put on its payroll Peruvian officials holding high-level positions. These individuals were supposed to lobby for offshore petroleum leases by securing access to key policy makers. Thanks to the lobbyists, Discover executives were able to meet with the minister of energy and then with Prime Minister Jorge del Castillo; the crowning achievement was the meeting with President Alán García on 26 April 2008. With the blessing of the highest figures in the government, the lobbyists, who had been generously "greasing" many officials with bribes, were in a great position to leverage the offshore blocks for Discover Petroleum. The recorded conversations revealed in fascinating detail how the lobbyists were maneuvering through the bureaucracy to carry out their criminal schemes. Already in May anonymous sources were denouncing these corrupt transactions to the country's leading newspaper, *El Comercio*, which previously had decided to start an investigation to uncover the illicit activities.[19]

The lobbyists, unaware that Business Track was secretly recording many of their conversations, concentrated on finding an ingenious solution for the vastly inadequate capital of Discover Petroleum. For over 18 years the state petroleum enterprise, PetroPeru, had not been involved in any oil extraction and had operated simply as a distribution, transportation, and refining company. Although PetroPeru barely escaped privatization, it did lose the authority to explore for petroleum deposits inside the country. Its officials and engineers wanted to reenter oil production, but the preference for foreign companies since Alberto Fujimori had deprived PetroPeru of any chance to participate in bidding for offshore blocks.[20]

In a brilliant strategic move, the lobbyists, by means of generous bribes, persuaded PetroPeru to become a partner with Discover Petroleum on 26 August 2008. The considerable assets on land of PetroPeru provided the net worth that the Norwegian company lacked, while the latter supposedly provided the offshore exploration expertise for the Peruvian company. As an indication that this was the crucial step to achieve success, the lobbyists received generous bonuses for having pulled off this coup.[21]

After this maneuver, only a few weeks later on 10 September 2008 the government awarded four offshore blocks and one in the Amazon jungle to the consortium of Discover Petroleum and PetroPeru. In response to the request of the consortium for two additional offshore blocks, the government postponed the decision for a later date. But first it was time to celebrate as the lobbyists with the Norwegians frequented the most exclusive clubs in Lima to throw wild parties.[22]

The lobbyists knew that their work was not yet completely done, and they diligently prepared to repeat the maneuver in order to bag the last two remaining offshore blocks still left unassigned. But on 8 September, two days before the government had announced the initial awards, *El Comercio* received copies of 50 e-mails of the lobbyists and the first batch of recorded telephone conversations; on 12 September the newspaper received the second group. Investigative journalists wanted to break the story, but the Board of Directors wanted no part of this political dynamite. As representatives of large corporations and the wealthy, they knew that the damage to the García presidency necessarily meant serious harm to private businesses. On one pretext after another such as turnover in personnel, seeking verification, and demanding to know the identity of the sources, *El Comercio* did not reveal the information either in print or through its two Television channels and radio stations during the rest of September. This desire to keep out of the public view any information critical of the free market presidency of García was in sharp contrast to the reckless behavior of the private media in Venezuela, where without any pretense of trying to seek confirmation, television and the press avidly competed to be the first to hurl the wildest accusations against the socialist government of Hugo Chávez.[23]

El Comercio was solidly defending its class interests even at the cost of sacrificing freedom of the press and possibly even its own profits. Once it became clear that the newspaper was not going to make the revelations, Petro Tech, the rival petroleum bidder, had the recordings sent to the television news program *The Fourth Estate*. The motive was clear, because unless Petro Tech acted fast, the consortium of Discover Petroleum and PetroPeru would receive the remaining two offshore blocks. A structural weakness of capitalism has been that the quest for profits has usually trumped the defense of class interests. The opportunity to see its ratings skyrocket was irresistible to the television program that on the night of 5 October 2008 delighted its viewers by playing excerpts of the intercepted telephone conversations among the Peruvian lobbyists.[24]

A political firestorm erupted and confirmed the worst fears about the dangers of capitalism in Peru. Since the start of the Free Trade Agreement negotiations under President Alejandro Toledo, critics had been warning that any expansion of the free market necessarily meant favoring the wealthy at the expense of the poor. This argument had been very persuasive when the Vladivideos of the Fujimori administration showed how businesses profited by corruption, but such graphic evidence had not yet tainted the Toledo and García administrations. *El Comercio*, faithful to its class interests, tried to contain the damage by minimizing its press coverage of the crisis. In a clever journalist move, the newspaper shifted the focus of its reporting to hackers such as Business Track and away from the criminals uncovered in the recordings. The low profile approach of *El Comercio* paralleled the efforts of the U.S. Embassy to downplay the incident. American diplomats were worried that the scandal might derail the Free Trade Agreement and in every way possible spread the word that this was just a media show to increase ratings and lacked any real substance.[25]

The efforts of the U.S. Embassy and of the majority of the media to contain the scandal gained time for the government to carry out damage control. The Petro Audios, as they came to be called, exposed a degree of corruption and favoritism not seen since the Fujimori-Montesino years. As a first step, President García accepted the resignations of all the high officials in the energy sector, including the minister of mines and the director of PetroPeru. But this was not enough to satisfy the public, and when Congress appointed a special commission to investigate the corruption scandal, the president had to jettison additional cabinet members, including his trusted confidante Castillo. The prime minister had been instrumental in facing the rising wave of protests, and with his departure, the president lost an effective and trusted collaborator. He did not heed demands for firing his entire cabinet, and in the resulting shuffle, he appointed only six new ministers and confirmed the remaining ten. He concluded that he had avoided the need to replace his entire cabinet by having picked a maverick as the new prime minister. Rather than appointing another trusted loyalist to this key position, he chose Yehude Simon, a reformed radical and regional governor of Lambayeque. Simon had been one of the few personal success stories of decentralization, and the efficient management of his department had earned him a favorable reputation across the country.[26]

García was taking a gamble with Simon who lacked national experience, but at least at the beginning he seemed to be handling the job well. To try to divert public attention away from the Petro Audios scandal, the government appointed a special commission on corruption, and the prime minister vigorously supported its activities. Skeptics wondered whether any commission could ever extirpate the deeply rooted official malfeasance in Peru, but at least the new prime minister offered hope about overcoming the mounting tide of social conflict in Peru.[27] His abilities were soon put to the test by the simmering problems with the Indians of the Amazon.

The Final Blow: The Bagua Massacre

The Petro Audios scandal inflicted permanent damage on the García presidency and sharply diminished its authority to govern. Wishfully the president believed that the cabinet shuffle of October 2008 and above all the appointment of Yehode Simon as the new prime minister had contained the damage from the crisis. In reality, the administration had only gained a chance to complete its term. A defiant García ignored the warnings and concluded that the government needed a dramatic show of force to regain its standing among the population. Believing that any concession was a sign of weakness, he arrogantly rejected the request of the Indians to repeal other Decree Laws affecting the Amazon. The government claimed that tampering with the remaining Decree Laws meant destroying the Free Trade Agreement, an opinion that not even the U.S. ambassador shared. Refusing to heed the demands of the Amazon was becoming politically costly, because in an infrequent occurrence, public opinion was shifting decidedly to the side of the Indians. When the Nationalist Party of Ollanta Humala became the first movement to express public support for the request of the Indians, the García administration mistakenly interpreted this warning as an opportunity to strike a blow against a political opponent.[28]

By late March 2009 the Indian communities reached the bitter conclusion that the García administration was not going to repeal the other Decree Laws affecting the Amazon. The Indians feared the destruction of their way of life, as had happened in bordering Ecuador once foreign corporations took over lands and contaminated the environment.[29] In Peru the Indian communities saw Decree Laws 1064 (on public lands) and 1090 (on forestry) as the most threatening, and in a last attempt to obtain their repeal, AIDESEP, the organization representing the native peoples of the Amazon, announced plans to launch another mobilization. This last warning did not budge the government, and consequently on 8 April 2009 AIDESEP convoked all Indian communities to a Second Amazonian General Strike beginning on 9 April. Gradually over the next week Indian and non–Indian communities joined the movement spreading from the Marañón River to the Ucayali River. The strong showing of support caught the government by surprise, and in a belated move, Prime Minister Yehode Simon, the chief damage control officer of the García administration, invited Indian leaders to participate in a series of emergency meetings. The Indians were waiting for action and not for talk, and any chance of a negotiated settlement ended when Prime Minister Simon insulted the Indian leaders of AIDESEP by calling them prone to whimsical behavior.[30]

As the Indian mobilization paralyzed most of the Amazon, protesters blockaded roads and prevented petroleum barges from navigating the rivers. The work stoppages did not appear across the Amazon all at once, because as each Indian community received the convocation of AIDESEP, its members slowly and carefully deliberated over the implications of joining the mobilization against Decree Laws 1064 and 1090. Many of the first protesters were Indians from the Cenepa River, the crucial strategic border zone that

Northern Peru

had been the site of the war with nearby Ecuador in 1981 and again in 1995. The unflinching support of the Cenepa Indians, both as soldiers and civilians, had been essential for Peruvian victory in those two wars, so in 2009 the Peruvian army was not going to do anything to antagonize these very loyal and militarily valuable Indians. Throughout the crisis the government issued resolutions authorizing and then ordering the entry of combat troops to stop the native mobilization, but the army commanders always found a way to avoid confrontations with the local communities.[31]

On 8 April the Cenepa Indians arrived at Pumping Station No. 6 next to the Marañón River, and their prestige as war veterans served as an example for the Awajún and Wampis tribes to join the mobilization on 16 April. Right away the Indians demanded that PetroPeru, the state petroleum enterprise, stop pumping Amazon crude through the pipeline. When the number of protesters reached menacing proportions, the company agreed to halt pumping on 24 April. To maintain the peaceful nature of the protest, the demonstrators pledged to stay out of the perimeter of Pumping Station No. 6 and to allow the rest of the installations, including the electric generator, to operate normally. The small police detachment on guard duty in the Pumping Station remained armed. Having stopped the pumping of the crude destined for export (not for the internal market as the government afterwards tried to claim), the protesters did not feel the need to block the road passing through the area.[32]

By the middle of May the number of protesters at Pumping Station No. 6 rose to 1,500 and on 20 May the number reached 2,500. Supporting this large number of Indians did not prove burdensome for the communities, because many were nearby residents who easily returned to their homes for food, refreshments, and shelter. The numerous Indian population in this area provided ample supplies for demonstrators coming from more distant regions. From the start it had become clear that any massive mobilization for the Second Amazonian General Strike meant that the village elders had to neglect their daily duties in the villages. As an alternative to the overburdened village elders, the communities created special "Struggle Committees" (*Comités de Lucha*) to lead the protests. In effect, control of the mobilization passed to young leaders, who lacked the experience, prestige, and authority of the village elders. This unfortunate decision was a major factor contributing to later tragic events.[33]

The Second Amazonian General Strike entered its final phase when on 20 May the Peruvian congress refused to repeal Decree Laws 1064 and 1090. This decision came as a complete surprise, because the previous day the congressional committee with jurisdiction over the matter had recommended unanimously the abrogation of the two Decree Laws. At the last moment APRA, the president's party, switched its position and voted against the repeal, and the Fujimorista party, which usually followed the lead of the government, did the same.[34]

The response of the Indian communities to this rebuff in the congress came soon. To increase the pressure on the government, the Struggle Committees decided to send most of the protesters from Pumping Station No. 6 to the road passing by Bagua. The Indians, many of whom were ex-servicemen and often veterans of the wars with Ecuador, picked the strategic spot of Curva del Diablo to set up a road block next to the Marañón River on 26 May. By the end of the month nearly 2000 protesters halted traffic on the road. Afterwards the government falsely claimed that the Indians had paralyzed the economic life of northern Peru, when in reality the road block adversely affected only truck tankers hauling fuel to the town of Tarapoto.[35]

And the Indians immediately discovered that feeding and supplying the nearly 2000 protesters at Curva del Diablo was much more difficult than at Pumping Station No. 6. Settlers of mostly Spanish origin occupied the area of Bagua, and although they sympathized with the Indian protest and provided assistance, they were not ready to supply all the needs of the protesters every day. The Indians had to truck the bulk of their supplies from their communities about 100 kilometers away at Pumping Station No. 6.[36]

On 27 May many organizations in Lima and other parts of the country began staging marches in support of the Indians in an indication that public sympathy was shifting in favor of the protesters; the Roman Catholic Church also came out strongly in defense of the Indians. As the spontaneous outpouring of national support grew, most Amazonian communities gradually concluded that the General Strike had achieved its goal, and they lifted road blocks and agreed to let activities return to normal. As May came to an end, rumblings to lift the road block at Curva del Diablo became more widespread.[37]

In all likelihood the Indians would have lifted the road block by the first few days of June, but unfortunately President García could not resist making more inflammatory comments on 31 May. In a speech he passionately defended Decree Law 1090 and stated that the Amazon belonged to all Peruvians and not just to some, a not too subtle jab at the Indians. The Indians considered the president's speech to be insulting and in a first reaction they delayed any evacuation from Curva del Diablo. But by 3 June the communities could no longer afford to supply the road block, and the next day at local assemblies all the protesters agreed to abandon the site. On 4 June leaders informed police of the intention to finish the withdrawal by the next day. The police commanders insisted on an immediate withdrawal, but the Indians refused saying that they preferred to die rather than flee like a bunch of scared rabbits. Already those Indians who lived nearby returned home on 4 June, but lack of trucks postponed the departure of the majority of Indians until 5 June.[38]

The García administration had no intention of allowing an orderly and peaceful evacuation of the road block and instead wanted to teach the Indians and the country a lesson. The ongoing Petro Audios scandal had caused enormous damage to the prestige of the government, and the president was determined to restore his authority with one dramatic show of force. But the army refused to send combat units to clear the road, and the Petro Audios revelations had so discredited the president that he could not take the risk of removing the generals in the high command. Even a failed coup attempt, such as had happened to Carlos Andres Pérez of Venezuela in 1989, could cause irreparable damage to an already weakened government. With difficulty García persuaded the generals to provide some supporting troops, but the orders became diluted as they went down the chain of command. And the reluctance was solidly based on the laws governing army relations with civilians, because officers knew that obeying orders meant breaking laws and possibly facing prosecution for violations of human rights.[39]

Inevitably the dirty work fell to the police, but in accordance with the preventive nature of that profession, police commanders preferred to wait for a negotiated solution rather than risk a violent clash. Because the Second Amazonian General Strike was rapidly winding down, the government knew that unless it acted quickly, there would be no demonstrators left to crush. The final barrier to taking action was Prime Minister Simon, who had been trying to negotiate a peaceful solution to the general strike with leaders of AIDESEP. These negotiations had no chance of success, because the prime minister was supposed to persuade the Indians to abandon completely and immediately their protest movement in exchange for nothing. The prime minister had to choose either siding with the administration on the use of force or resigning in protest, and in a decision that cost him his political career, at a cabinet meeting he agreed to join García and the hard liners. The prime minister and the entire cabinet gave full support to the minister of the interior, a passionate APRA loyalist, who almost immediately on 2 June fired the police director and carried out a wholesale replacement of high ranking officers, including those in charge of dealing with the Bagua sector. The new police director knew what his task was, and the next day he issued the orders to carry out the eviction of the protesters from Curva del Diablo.[40]

The police director set 4 June 2009 as the date for dislodging the protesters, but the new commander put in charge of the operation reported regretfully after arriving in the scene that the units could not be in place until dawn of 5 June. The government was upset when it learned about this postponement, and police officers, fearful of earning the wrath of the García administration by any additional delays, rushed to strike while they still had a target to hit. Not surprisingly, the commanders ignored the reports that the Indians were already evacuating Curva del Diablo and would all be gone by late afternoon on 5 June. Late on 4 June the police officers tried to coordinate with the commander of the nearby army garrison, but the general opposed the operation and ultimately did not deploy any troops.[41]

The lack of army support counseled against carrying out an operation estimated to require the deployment of at least several thousand policemen. The police commander in charge of the operation had previously dislodged protesters in urban rallies, but this experience was not exactly transferable to the countryside where military style movements were more appropriate. It is well recognized that soldiers trained to destroy their enemy are not suitable to carry out police functions, but no less true is the opposite principle that police commanders should not try to execute military operations, as the events at Bagua came to confirm.

The original attack plan, although unnecessary given that the Indians were evacuating, called for using trucks to carry personnel from the police base at Corral Quemado. The men were equipped with full riot gear, including shields and helmets, but to avoid bloodshed they were not armed and had to rely on tear gas to clear the protesters on the road. Police reserves were ready to send additional units of unarmed personnel, and if necessary large numbers of armed policemen were also ready to help the operation should it turn into combat. The likely outcome of the operation as originally planned was that the protesters, seeing this large force heading towards them, would either retreat to the east down the road or scatter most likely to the nearby hill; and, as good swimmers, some Indians probably would swim across the Marañón River.[42]

In spite of the rush to crush the protest swiftly, word about the impending operation leaked out. However, the Indians regarded the rumors as psychological warfare and refused to advance the date of their evacuation before 5 June. On principle, the Indians preferred to die as they stood their ground, because their core beliefs did not allow them to flee as cowards. The Indians were aware that the government might want to smash the road block and earlier had taken the precaution of posting observers in the hill overlooking the site. These sentries were under instructions to launch fireworks in case police personnel tried to occupy the top of the hill. Because many of the protesters had been soldiers in the army, they immediately realized that control of the hill was essential to prevent being trapped between a police column advancing along the road and units blocking the retreat through the hill. The fireworks (and not Rocket Propelled Grenades as malicious government propaganda later claimed) were necessary because the cellular phones of the Indians worked only at the top of the hill but not down in the road.

The first police force to leave the base of Corral Quemado at 0500 on 5 June was a unit of about 60 men riding on trucks. The policemen disembarked and in a flanking movement bypassed Curva del Diablo and began climbing up the hill which overlooked the road block. This deployment was not in the original plan, and nobody afterwards assumed responsibility for this maneuver almost guaranteed to provoke a violent reaction from the demonstrators. In a vicious and unfounded accusation, police generals later blamed Major Felipe Bazán, the second-in-command of the unit, for this modification of the original plan and also for arming the men with AK-47 automatic rifles and revolvers.[43]

Approximately at 0545 the policemen reached the summit of the hill and sat down to rest and also to use their cell phones which did work at this elevation. But already the Indian sentries had detected the approaching police unit and had fired off the first fireworks. The Indian leaders in the main camp feared that this was probably a diversion to lure them away from the road block and consequently allowed only about 250 Indians to climb up the hill while putting the rest of the nearly 2000 demonstrators on high alert to defend the barricades. It took the first wave of protesters about 15 minutes to cover the distance of one kilometer between the road block and the summit of the hill. The commander of the police unit interpreted the advance of the Indians as a hostile action and deployed his men in anti-riot formation. Once the 250 protesters reached the top of the hill, their appearance looked menacing to policemen who had never faced Indians before. All the Indians were bare chested and painted in their traditional colors, which the policemen, having seen perhaps too many Hollywood Western movies, interpreted as war paint. The Awajún and Wampis carried spears, their traditional tool, because unlike the inhabitants in most of the Amazon, they did not use bow and arrows for hunting and fishing. To face the shields of the police, the Indians crossed their spears on their chests, and this gesture seemed tremendously threatening to the policemen even though a distance of 30 meters still separated both groups. At 0615 the inevitable happened when policemen not in the line of contact with the Indians opened fire from the rear and wounded two protesters. Shortly after a third shot killed the first Indian.[44]

Without the presence of respected elders to control the situation, rage spread across the protesters, because according to the code of conduct of the Awajún and Wampis, when one of their tribe is killed, justice demands the death of a person of the opposite side. Outraged Indians rushed the police line while others, remembering their army training, went around to try to outflank the unit. For over half an hour ferocious combat ensued as the enraged Indians hurled themselves at the police and seized some of the AK-47s. By then the commander of the unit and some of his men were firing bursts of bullets from their rifles to cover their retreat down the hill along the path they had come. Those who did not retreat in time were caught between the Indians in front and those who appeared in the rear. In the final count, 11 policemen and 4 Indians died in the clash and many were wounded on both sides; the body of Major Bazán was the only one never found, and although he is presumed dead, officially he remains listed as missing in action.

As the survivors of the unit were fleeing from the hill top, the main police column finally began its advance along the road at 0630. Its departure nearly an hour after the small detachment had reached the summit of the hill revealed another major flaw in the operation. Seven kilometers separated the police base of Corral Quemado from Curva del Diablo, and at 0705 the vanguard of the advancing police column clashed with the Indian protesters who were ready and waiting. To overawe the Indians, commanders had placed at the head of the column armored vehicles, including a steel plated mine sweeper. The police did not make the required appeals by loudspeaker urging the protesters to clear the road and instead promptly tried to crash through the road block. Commanders were responding to the desperate pleas for help received by radio from the officer fleeing the hill, yet in spite of the urgency, the first attempt to clear the road failed, and soon gunfire broke out.[45]

The sequence of events in the road, in spite of videos and other visual images, is less clear than for the clash on the hill top, but apparently the Indians initially seized some of the tear gas guns from the police and turned them on the column. A police helicopter hovered overhead, at first launching tear gas canisters and then opening fire with an automatic weapon. The commander of the operation called in reinforcements from the police reserves, and gradually the column pushed its way through the protesters. The bursts from the police AK-47s were so intense, that the bullets set on fire the dry bush near the road. "The image is of total confusion with people running in every direction, while dust and smoke clouds increased the disorder by eliminating visibility."[46] Just as had happened on the hill top, Indians seized AK-47s and tear gas shotguns from the police; the dead and wounded on both sides received bullets only from the police AK-47s. Around 1100 the police finally cleared the road of demonstrators, but the fighting at

Curva del Diablo was still not over, because at 1230 an unknown assailant with his head covered hurled a hand grenade at one of the armored vehicles. The grenade rebounded from the vehicle and exploded nearby wounding several policemen. Because neither the police nor the Indians were known to carry hand grenades, its provenance remains a mystery.[47]

News of the clashes with police at Curva del Diablo almost immediately had direct repercussions in nearby areas. When the inhabitants of nearby towns such as Bagua heard the news on radio, riots broke out. Labor unions joined the violent protests, and soon several key buildings in the towns went up in flames, including the local headquarters of the APRA party. Looting was widespread, and in the riots in one town at least two residents died. The arrival of army troops at 1500 had an immediate calming effect upon demonstrators who promptly melted away, and the imposition of a curfew late in the afternoon completed the return to order.[48]

The most tragic consequence of the clashes at Curva del Diablo took place at Pumping Station No. 6, the original starting point of the Second Amazonian General Strike. A substantial contingent of Awajún and Wampis had remained at the PetroPeru installation to make sure that the pipeline did not carry crude. As soon as the radio broadcasts of the first clashes reached the Cenepa River, many enraged Indians who were former soldiers set out for the pumping station. By 0900 around 1500 Indians, including many females, were protesting outside the fence surrounding the installation. When the radio claimed that Indians had been killed at Curva del Diablo, the enraged protesters pushed their way through the gate at 1515. The Indians by then numbered 1800 and were shouting "kill them" in reference to the 38 policemen who had been doing guard duty at the pumping station for months.[49]

Fearing a massacre, police commander Miguel Montenegro did not allow his men to open fire on the advancing mob and instead constantly sought to negotiate a peaceful solution. The leaders of the Indians were unable to control the mob, and soon the protesters had disarmed the soldiers, took their boots away, and tied their hands with shoelaces. In reprisal for the tear gas hurled at the Indians at Curva del Diablo, the demonstrators threw an irritant substance in the eyes of the captives so that they would feel the same pain. At 1030 the Indians drove aboard a truck the 38 policemen to a large gathering at a nearby school. For the last time the leaders resisted the demands to kill all the hostages and instead convinced the mob to return them to a fenced-in area at the Pumping Station.

The crisis seemed to be over, but a disgruntled minority still clamored for justice. Led by the female Indians who considered themselves the guardians of their cultural traditions, the women demanded that the men follow their ancestral law that required one equivalent death for each Indian that had been killed at Curva del Diablo. The leaders tried to stop in vain the onrush, but they were not the village elders who had ample authority to check the passionate pleas of the shrieking women. Many of the Indians refused to participate in what was about to happen, but a small number remained determined to carry out their ghastly deed. At 1530 the Indians took away 18 captives, including Commander Montenegro, and soon after killed the first policeman. The Indians took only 18 of the 38 because according to erroneous radio broadcasts, that was the number of Indians who had died at Curva del Diablo. In the confusion of executing the prisoners, fortunately some of the designated victims were able to escape, so that the number of policemen executed in cold blood was only 11 out of the 18. Sadly, commander Montenegro did not escape alive.[50]

When news of the botched operation reached Lima, the García administration decided to depict the clash as a struggle of civilization against savage and primitive Indians. Released photographs showed the painted and bare-chested Indians brandishing spears and acting as barbarians when they dragged the bodies of dead policemen. Because the images still did not budge public opinion, government officials and President García accused the Indians of having decapitated the dead policemen and of having hurled others still alive from cliffs down to their death below in ravines, accusations without any foundation. Still insisting that the operation had been a complete success, the minister of interior in a public ceremony gave medals and awards to the police officers for having driven away these savage beasts. Already on 6 June arrest orders went out against the leaders of AISEDEP as the primary instigators of the bloody clash, when in reality these leaders had all been in Lima and had no role in the events unfolding in distant Amazon region.[51]

To avoid arrest, the Indians leaders sought asylum in a foreign embassy, and after careful consideration chose the embassy of Nicaragua. The choice of this country was particularly astute, because as part of the campaign to depict the Indians as savages, the government wanted to show that they were part of a foreign conspiracy orchestrated preferably by the Venezuela of Hugo Chávez yet the Bolivia of Evo Morales would do. No evidence of any foreign link ever appeared even after the most careful searches, and at least in this case, President Hugo Chávez prudently avoided making statements.[52]

Because neither the accusations of savage behavior or of foreign subversion were resonating with the Peruvian public, the García administration shifted direction slightly and decided to portray the Indians as childlike victims who had been fooled and manipulated by non–Indian groups, whether professional agitators or partisan recruiters. But it was the Indians who after careful and slow deliberation in many assemblies had taken the collective decisions about the Second Amazonian General Strike. Only Ollanta Humala's Nationalist Party had shown any sympathy for the Amazonian movement, but as quickly became clear, this party had not been involved in any of the steps that led to the confrontation in Bagua.[53]

Sensing that the blame for the Bagua incident was pointing towards the government, officials tried to shift the blame to the army. Here the García administration counted as unlikely allies the human rights activists who usually have a strong preference for condemning military institutions. Indeed human rights groups consider finding the army guilty of massacring civilians to be the gold standard of success. But not even hearsay could link soldiers to any of the bloody events, and the many photographs and videos depicting policemen firing at the Indians effectively erased any chance of scapegoating the army.[54]

In a last desperate attempt to escape the domestic and foreign condemnation rapidly closing in, the García administration tried to blame Catholic Church officials, including a bishop, as the instigators of the clashes. But the Catholic Church had been constantly trying to keep the Second Amazonian General Strike within peaceful channels and had made many pleas for the Indians to return home. The mediation of the Catholic clergy also had a positive effect in dissuading Indians from continuing the strike in Bagua.[55]

Police commanders, the new medals still shining on their chests, were the first to realize that the official version of events was crumbling. In an indication of how savage has been the competition for promotions and positions inside the institution, police officers decided to shift the blame for the botched operation on Major Felipe Bazán. In many ways he was an ideal scapegoat because he was dead and could not respond to the charges. The decision to continue listing him as missing in action rather than as killed helped feed the image that the Major had fled to avoid the disgrace of having planned the march to the hill top overlooking Curva del Diablo. Perhaps this line of argument might be persuasive inside the narrow confines of the police institution, but nobody else could find any merit in this preposterous claim about a person who had been only the second in command of this small unit.[56]

A wave of protests threatened to engulf the country and undermined the rapidly vanishing prestige of the García administration.[57] The scandal of the Petro Audios had never gone away and acquired a new significance with the Bagua clashes. Having the government send the police to crush Indians so that high officials could receive juicy bribes from foreign investors created the worst possible image in the minds of most Peruvians. The Amazonian Indians as the underdogs had gained the sympathy of vast sectors of the population, and the emerging alliance between Hispanic inhabitants and the Indian tribes was one of the most important legacies of the massacre. The U.S. Embassy in Lima accurately concluded that the event "represents the single greatest crisis faced by the García administration to date."[58]

The president was a sufficiently astute politician to realize that what was at stake was not his policy to hand over the Amazon to foreign investors but the survival of his administration. To save the sinking ship, he had to take drastic action, and in an amazing volte-face, he went on television on 17 June to announce that he had been wrong about refusing to consult with the Indian communities as required by the International Convention on Tribal and Indian Peoples. He promised to correct his Amazonian policy and announced that Prime Minister Simon was presenting a bill to congress to repeal Decree Laws 1064 and 1090.[59]

The Peruvian congress duly repealed the two Decree Laws the next day on 18 June, and with this action the Amazonian Indians pledged to remove any remaining road blocks and to return to normal activities. Because the cabinet had taken the original decision to send the police against the Indians, this crisis hit too close to the president. As an additional precaution to shield himself, García dismissed Simon as the prime minister, effectively ending the latter's career and incidentally also the efforts of the commission investigating systemic corruption.[60] With excessive optimism, the President initially believed that he had cut his losses and could resume his drive to bring the free market to other areas of Peru, as he had promised to do in his infamous newspaper articles on the "Dog in the Manger." But the crisis did not go away, and the combination of the Bagua crisis and the Petro Audios scandal permanently crippled his presidency. Worse than a lame duck, his last years in office resembled more an agonizing government struggling to survive until the day came to hand over the crushing burden to the next occupant of the presidential palace.

In a strangely cyclical way, Garcia found himself in the same situation where Toledo had been in his last years of the presidency. A simple nudge from García in May 2005 was all that was needed to prevent Toledo from finishing his term in office. Wisely García had resisted that temptation, but in 2010 it was he who was hanging in air by a thread; it was in the hands not of Toledo but of rising star Ollanta Humala to decide whether García would finish out his term. In an early indication that the radicalism of Humala had been vastly exaggerated, the candidate decided to focus his attention on the upcoming presidential election in June 2011 and not to attempt to topple the totally discredited government. Both Toledo and García had tried to push free market reforms for the benefit of a small privileged minority. But because the two presidents had gone beyond the views of the majority of the population, they both ended up badly bruised and barely surviving. From the experience of these two presidents Ollanta absorbed the lesson about the danger of overreaching, but as he entered the campaign for president, his real struggle was to convince a majority of Peruvian voters that unlike in his failed attempt of 2006, he was ready to govern at the pace of change that the country wanted.

CHAPTER 14

The Bolivarian Revolution on the Offensive, 2008–2011

Chávez is the hardest working politician in Venezuela.—U.S. diplomat Stephen McFarland[1]

After the shock of the defeat of the referendum on 2 December 2007, the Bolivarian Revolution regrouped and went on the offensive. The exhilarating sense of having regained the initiative persuaded Hugo Chávez to embark on even more dramatic transformations of Venezuela. The Bolivarian Revolution seemed capable of doing anything, and the headlong rush to reach new heights made for an exciting period beginning in 2008. But by 2011 it had become abundantly clear that the government had undertaken too many projects and often failed to bring them to a satisfactory conclusion. Worse, the Bolivarian Revolution exposed vulnerable flanks to a reinvigorated opposition avidly looking for the opportunity to halt the social experimentation.

PSUV, Nationalizations and Elections

Peruvian observers provided insightful comments about the defeat of the 2007 constitutional referendum. As almost everyone else, they were surprised that the electorate rejected the proposal, but they considered this only to be a "temporary setback" and saw "his acceptance of the vote as a tactical retreat that ironically boosts his democratic credibility as he plots to undermine the election results by other means."[2] In contrast to Alberto Fujimori, Chávez refused to steal the election and instead decided to modify his strategy to make sure that he again attracted a majority of voters to his banners. The next electoral contest was not coming until the elections on 23 November 2008 for governors and mayors, so that he had plenty of time to shape a campaign strategy. Even though he himself was not on the ballot in November, should his movement suffer another loss then his Bolivarian Revolution was likely headed for extinction.

The opposition could not stop gloating over its triumph of 2 December 2007, yet in many ways the celebrations were premature. In spite of having made strenuous efforts to bring citizens to the polls, the opposition was able to gain only 100,000 more votes over the 4.4 million candidate Manuel Rosales had received in the presidential election of 2006. The constitutional referendum failed by only 200,000 votes, and the real reason was that of the 7.3 million persons who voted for Chávez in 2006, only 4.4 million returned to vote in 2007. As the excitement of victory faded into the past, the opposition uneasily confronted the daunting task of trying to achieve the same success in the races for governors and mayors in late 2008.[3]

To lower the political tension, Chávez surprised the country by issuing on 31 December 2007 a very extensive amnesty for the participants in the April 2002 failed coup attempt. Although not all participants received immunity from criminal prosecution, the unexpected New Year's Eve amnesty was a welcome gift to the vast majority of citizens facing charges. The political calculation was astute in the extreme, because the main beneficiaries of this amnesty were the 360 signers of the Carmona decree of 12 April 2002. By this act, Chávez once again announced that he never intended to destroy the entire wealthy class but only those rich persons who had declared war on him. The implicit message was that the wealthy class, as long as it did not attack the government, was free to prosper in Venezuela.[4]

As a good politician, he knew that he needed to have a multi-class coalition supporting him. Having rejected expropriations and nationalizations as a universal formula, he always left the door open for wealthy individuals to collaborate or at least to tolerate the Bolivarian Revolution. An indispensable element for the construction of a multi-class coalition was the existence of a broad-based political party, in this case the Unified Socialist Party of Venezuela (*Partido Socialista Unificado de Venezuela*) or PSUV. No genius was needed to realize that the clumsy effort to convert Chávez's original party (the MVR) into the PSUV had been the real reason for the electoral debacle of 2 December 2007. Chávez himself, although never abandoning the insistence on the need for this party, even stated publicly that the attempt to create the PSUV in 2007 had been premature and a mistake. In politics timing is everything, and he realized that he should have gone to the constitutional referendum with the every effective electoral machinery of the MRV; only after winning should he have embarked on the process of persuading the people that the creation of the PSUV was the next logical step for the Bolivarian Revolution. Under no circumstances should he have tampered with the small pro–Chávez parties: they should be invited but not pressured to join and were free to remain independent entities in the electoral and legislative coalitions.[5]

In 2008 it was too late to go back to the MRV because a public reversal opened up the presidency to attacks besides revealing weakness. Chávez inaugurated the long-postponed founding congress of the PSUV on 19 January 2008, and the delegates gathered at least every weekend to discuss the structure of the party. One ugly episode occurred on 16 February when the party congress decided to expel Deputy Luis Tascón, one of the most dedicated Chavistas and who was famous for having posted the Tascón list on his website. He had denounced corruption possibly reaching Diosdado Cabello, one high-ranking official around whom controversy swirled during his entire career. The opposition media had a field day with the expulsion of Tascón and could not resist gloating on the theme of "the Revolution devours its children." The dispute was really another indication of the difficulties inherent in creating the new political party, but once the PSUV consolidated its structure, similar public disputes practically disappeared and the Revolution stopped devouring its children.[6]

The formal process of organizing the PSUV culminated with the closing ceremony for its founding congress on 2 March 2008. Chávez gave a lengthy speech broadcast on live television detailing the next steps to complete the organization of the party. The emphasis on "battalions" grouping militants continued, but what most intrigued members was the convocation of primaries on 1 May for choosing the party candidates for governors and mayors for the 23 November elections. His demand for primaries was quite remarkable, because in the previous elections for governors in October 2005 his original party MRV had won almost all the elections, so the need for change did not seem urgent. But he had apologized for not picking always the best candidates to run, and he felt that in the majority of cases a primary was a better way to select the most effective candidates. Chávez gave the marching orders to the delegates to advance rapidly on the consolidation of the PSUV as the only way to defeat the opposition in the November elections. As the delegates returned to their home states, Chávez followed their activities, and unlike in the previous year, this time he cut back on his international travels and personally intervened whenever difficulties appeared with the PSUV in Caracas and in the states.[7]

This hard and quiet work was indispensable for the success of PSUV but had the disadvantage of taking place largely out of the public view. And if, by neglect, Chávez abandoned the air waves to the opposition, he risked giving the image of a weakened leader who had never recovered from the defeat in the 2 December 2007 elections. He needed an issue that would capture public attention during the quiet period prior to the formal start of the campaigns for governors and mayors in late summer. He knew that a dynamic and forceful presidency provided the best wind for the PSUV candidates to defeat the opposition. And he also needed to distract public attention away from problems such as food shortages and rising crime.

Chávez proclaimed his "socialism for the twenty-first century" in January 2005, and he renewed his promise for nationalizations at the swearing-in ceremony of his new cabinet on January 2007. But as chapter 12 explained, after the purchase of the U.S.-owned Caracas electricity utility in February of that year, the drive toward state ownership seemed to have stalled. The next opportunity came when on 3 April 2008 in response to criticisms of a looming housing shortage, he announced the nationalization of the three foreign-owned cement factories; the largest firm, the Mexican Cemex, produced half of the country's supply. Blaming the foreign companies for exporting the cement rather than supplying the domestic market was an excellent way to increase the popularity of the government.[8]

In fact, shortage of cement was not among the complex reasons responsible for the housing shortage. The real economic reason for the nationalization was the refusal of the companies to produce the specialty cements that oil giant PDVSA needed for its operations. The state had purchased the rights to use the patents for these specialty cements, but when the companies refused, nationalization at a cost of nearly two billion dollars was the only way to break a bottleneck. Because the action resembled a similar response by the Cuban government in 1960 when American refineries refused to process Soviet crude, many observers expected cement to be the start of a drive to nationalize the entire private sector.[9]

A second significant nationalization followed on 9 April when at 1:20 a.m. Chávez decided to acquire a majority control of SIDOR, the huge steel mill of Venezuela. This company had been originally a state enterprise until 1997 when as part of the privatization campaign of the Fourth Republic, an Argentine company had acquired 60 percent of the shares. The state still had a minority stake of 40 percent, but buying out the Argentine company was estimated to cost at least two billion dollars. Rather than ideology, the real force behind the steel nationalization was once again PDVSA. Prior to privatization,

SIDOR had produced specialty steel products and petroleum piping for the oil company, but the new owners had shifted production to more profitable items. PDVSA was having to import at a much higher price those specialty metals it had previously purchased from SIDOR. Nationalizing the steel mill brought immediate savings to the oil giant which would recover in a few years the cost of nationalization.[10]

Thus, in both cases of steel and cement, no matter how Chávez explained the decision to maximum political advantage, sound business reasons had been the driving force behind these monumental nationalizations that by themselves were a lasting legacy of his presidency. In the third major takeover the business justification was largely absent. Because originally Chávez had dismissed the possibility of nationalizing firms in the financial sector, his announcement on 31 July that the government planned to purchase the Banco de Venezuela came as a surprise. The bank, founded in 1890, was one of the oldest institutions in the country and was widely respected. During the financial crisis of 1993–1994 the government had taken over the institution to prevent its collapse and in 1996 sold it to the Spanish conglomerate Banco de Santander. The Spanish firm decided to sell Banco de Venezuela early in 2008 and had accepted a higher bid by a rabid anti-Chávez banker.[11]

The sale normally would have occurred quietly, but because the Spanish Banco de Santander had rejected a lower bid by a group of Chavista investors, the latter turned to the government to block the sale. The maneuver confirmed that wealthy persons also belonged to the Chavista movement, but because the government could not legally force the Spaniards to accept the lower bid, the only option was to nationalize the Banco de Venezuela. With a touch of populism, Chávez explained that it was only natural that a bank named after Venezuela should belong to all the Venezuelan people, but he had another reason for wanting to acquire the bank in a rush. Control of the institution opened a channel to move funds quietly to states and municipalities facing hotly contested races in the November elections. Also, the government gained a place to shift the accounts of agencies away from hostile banks, thus punishing opponents and guaranteeing the success of the nationalized institution. The precaution was advisable, because unlike in neighboring Colombia where traditionally depositors have more confidence in state than in private banks, in Venezuela since the Fourth Republic citizens have preferred to keep their accounts in private banks.[12]

With the acquisition of the Banco de Venezuela, the government closed its cycle of nationalizations. In spite of constant accusations, Chávez had never intended to destroy private property; as an astute politician he felt that the nationalizations he did carry out could only take place under the political cover of "twenty-first-century Socialism." No matter what he said or did, the opposition was going to label him a socialist if not a Communist, so he might as well use the title proudly and move the population to accept government ownership as necessary in certain areas for the well-being of the country. He had many opportunities and excuses to purchase the automobile assembly lines of General Motors, Ford, and Chrysler, but he readily recognized the widely accepted truth that this was one of the most highly competitive industries in the world. When the number of automobile producers were shrinking to compete in price with economies of scale, for a country such as Venezuela to try to enter automobile production was nothing less than suicidal.[13]

After having captured the public attention with three major nationalizations, Chávez shifted his efforts in the summer to preparing for the November regional elections. The first act of the campaign started off with the primary elections on 1 June for PSUV candidates. Incumbents generally confirmed their popularity with voters, but the primary was also an opportunity for challengers to advance in the party hierarchy by proving their vote getting potential. When no clear winner emerged, then Chávez selected the most promising individual among the contenders, a less exhausting task than in the previous governors' race when he had to hand pick all the candidates. Because the opposition, riding on the wave of the recall victory, hoped to win ten of the 22 governorships, it was not immediately clear whether the primary system would help or weaken the PSUV candidates. A bad omen was the decision of bypassed candidates to run as dissidents, thereby splitting the PSUV vote and supposedly helping the opposition candidates.[14]

On 31 July, right before his authority under the Enabling Law expired, he issued 26 decree laws. Because that same day he also announced the nationalization of the Banco de Venezuela, the opposition was outraged and incorrectly saw the 26 decree laws as having the intention of completing the takeover of the private sector. But as explained earlier, different motivations were behind the acquisition of the Banco de Venezuela, which was the last nationalization of the year, while none of the 26 decree laws threatened the financial sector. Considerable study and effort had gone into drafting these texts, and even the U.S. Embassy admitted grudgingly that "some of the laws actually improve Venezuela's legal framework and, if implemented well, could improve its institutional and economic framework."[15]

Although 22 of the 26 decree laws dealt with economic matters, most of them were ineffective because they strove to enhance the role of the "communal councils," the latest attempt at creating a grassroots base for Chavismo. As will be recalled, the first experiment had been with the Bolivarian Circles, and as they disintegrated after 2004, the "battalions" of the PSUV vainly tried to fill the void. By pouring money and placing responsibilities on the communal councils, Chávez hoped that his latest attempt would be more successful, but their defeat in the constitutional referendum already showed that they enjoyed very limited popular appeal. Elected governors and mayors of all political stripes did not want the communal councils as rivals, and anti-Chavistas frequently infiltrated the new organizations.[16]

The weaknesses of the communal councils and the innocuousness of the 26 decree laws largely destroyed their value as campaign issues, yet by late September the opposition was so weak that it was scrambling to try to prevent another PSUV victory sweep in the 23 November elections. The lack of a unifying theme, as had been the case in the constitutional referendum, made it difficult to rally voters across the country, and very specific local issues of no interest outside of a particular state or municipality dominated the electoral contests. The opposition needed to frame the election as a repudiation of Chávez, and this possibility started to appear when defector and former general Raúl Baduel returned to the campaign to make this contest an opportunity to cast a vote against the president. As will be recalled from chapter 12, Baduel had been instrumental in securing that small margin of victory necessary to defeat the constitutional referendum on 2 December 2007. Many opposition leaders believed that he could repeat that feat and help them win their target of ten governorships. But before Baduel could have any impact, Chávez cut him off by allowing the attorney general to bring pending corruption charges against the former general. Baduel was arrested and eventually received a long prison term.[17]

In contrast, Chávez embarked on an intensive campaign tour throughout Venezuela almost as if he were running for office. He attended rallies in each state and in many of the municipalities. But his visits were not just a campaign tour, and in each locality he verified the effectiveness of the local PSUV organization, and if necessary he made changes in tactics and replaced personnel. His attention to detail, his immersion with crowds, and his close involvement with party operatives was in contrast to the largely distant approach he had followed during the failed constitutional referendum. His personal role was indispensable, because the PSUV had never been able to replicate the impressive electoral machinery of the defunct MRV, and until the party could stand on its own, only the commanding personality of Chávez could make possible a victory.[18]

The real fear in the 23 November regional elections was that the dissident candidates on the ballot would split the PSUV vote and bring many opposition victories. Doubtlessly that effect was present but not in a major way, because all the dissident candidates lost, while the opposition expanded its governorships from two to five, half of its stated goal of winning ten governorships. Even more interesting from the perspective of Chávez were the national vote totals. PSUV candidates received 5.5 million votes— a big jump from the 4.3 million the "yes" votes received on 2 December 2007; the opposition received basically the same 4.4 million votes in both elections, a number that had sufficed to defeat the constitutional referendum but not to sweep the regional elections.[19]

Chávez concluded that he had a superiority of a million votes over the opposition and that this adequate margin of victory gave him a good opportunity to try again to remove term limits from the presidency. The start of the world economic crisis as a result of the meltdown of financial institutions on Wall Street suggested that he might not have another opportunity to amend the 1999 Constitution; as the world entered into the Great Recession, the Venezuelan economy, in spite of its oil wealth, inevitably was going to suffer. As an incumbent he had to prepare for the negative consequences of economic decline, but stored up reserves gave him some time to maneuver and hopefully to secure the removal of term limits on the presidency. But he knew that the campaign was going to require that same attention to detail that had made success possible in the gubernatorial elections and that he could not delegate the task of winning to the PSUV.

Chávez took personal command of the new campaign, and this time he was not going to do anything that might endanger the outcome. His first order of business was to deal with the pro–Chávez independent parties; as will be recalled from chapter 12 he had arrogantly demanded their incorporation into the PSUV, and this divisive struggle had been a major reason why the constitutional referendum had failed in December 2007. Because the small independent parties had lost their governorships, it seemed that Chávez could safely ignore them, but he was not willing to take any chances. When the Communist Party of Venezuela and PPT (*Patria Para Todos*) announced that they were willing to support lifting term limits on all elected offices, Chávez did not lash out angrily as he had done in 2007 and instead welcomed the idea in 2009. By proposing to abolish all term limits, Chávez automatically gained the enthusiastic support of all incumbent office holders who in 2007 had only offered tepid support for a referendum that did nothing for them.[20]

At a strategy session at Fort Tiuna on 7 December, Chávez agreed with PSUV officials to begin a two-fold approach to eliminate all term limits. On 11 December he personally launched in Caracas the drive to obtain signatures from the public to convoke another vote; as had happened with the membership drive for the PSUV of the previous years, this new list provided an opportunity for followers to demonstrate their loyalty to Chavismo. Parallel to this process, on 18 December the National Assembly began discussions to authorize the referendum; according to the 1999 Constitution either the signature petition or the National Assembly approach sufficed to convoke a vote, but Chávez as a master politician saw a great opportunity to mobilize large numbers of citizens and also to focus public attention on the campaign to abolish all term limits. He was determined to take all precautions to make sure that this second attempt did not end in failure; as an additional reason, without the option of reelection, he was starting to feel that his immense powers were very slowly eroding as the public started to regard him as a lame-duck president.[21]

On 5 January 2009 he proposed changing the wording of the amendment to eliminate term limits for all positions; very astutely he framed the argument as a means to extend democratic practices by letting the people and not the constitution decide who could run for office. On 14 January the National Assembly by a nearly unanimous vote approved the amendment, and then the National Electoral Council set the date for the referendum on 15 February. But weeks before the formal approval, Chávez had been actively campaigning for the repeal of term limits. Red tents sprouted up in almost every neighborhood to collect signatures for the petition, and even after the National Assembly approved holding the referendum, the drive continued as a way to motivate supporters. The PSUV in early January seemed to have obtained at least five million signatures, and this large number also served to preempt any opposition attempt to start another recall vote in the middle of Chávez's presidential term.[22]

The opposition had been slow to mobilize against the referendum, and the first major effort came only on 13 January when the Roman Catholic bishops issued a statement strongly criticizing the proposed constitutional amendment. Just as in 2007 "the bishops stopped short of telling parishioners to vote NO."[23] The anti–Chávez parties tried to rally to this call, but they were "broke, tired, and disorganized"; in a fatal flaw, "the opposition was unable to connect with the lower socio-economic classes that made up the majority of Chavez's support."[24] Only university students continued their almost daily protest marches against the government, but this effort could well prove counterproductive.

By the end of January the student demonstrations turned into clashes with the police and with Chavista followers, must notably the colorful Lina Ron. Chávez saw the opportunity to present himself not just as above the fray but also as the only person who could restore peace and order to the country. He told followers such as Lina to avoid confrontations, thus leaving the students as the sole perpetrators of the violent clashes already irritating many citizens. Polls showed Chávez with a comfortable lead at the start of February, and as he began to feel confident of victory, he abandoned an earlier plan to frame the election again as a struggle between the United States and the Bolivarian Revolution. He dropped his plans for more diplomatic incidents when he decided to give president-elect Barack Obama a grace period to restore cordial relations with Venezuela.[25]

The opposition made a last minute push by convoking followers to participate in a march of 18 kilometers across Caracas on 7 February, just a week away from the referendum. At least 100,000 citizens joined in the march, the biggest one the opposition had been able to organize in two years. This outpouring was an indication that the NO vote was gaining ground, but it remained to be seen whether this big effort had come too late. Both sides realized that the outcome depended on voter turnout, and here the larger organization of the PSUV seemed to give the YES vote an advantage.[26]

The opposition could find comfort in its ability to deliver 5.2 million "no" votes on 15 February 2009, exceeding for the first time its usual range of four million votes. But even with this extraordinary effort, the YES vote still passed with 6.3 million votes. In the competition to get voters out to the polls, the electoral machinery of the PSUV had been much more efficient.[27] The obvious conclusion was that with both sides improving their abilities to bring voters to the polling places, each succeeding election was going to require even more strenuous efforts to achieve the margin of victory. Motivating the voter base, always a key component of Chavismo, became even more important for the survival of the Bolivarian Revolution.

2009: The Decisive Year

The approval of the referendum eliminating term limits in all elected offices guaranteed the political survival of Hugo Chávez and of his Bolivarian Revolution; without that victory, his movement risked disintegration and even defeat in the next presidential elections of 2012. Both foreign observers and opposition figures expected the government to use the victory of 15 February as a green light to radicalize the Bolivarian Revolution. Chávez himself promised to accelerate the pace of change, and he even went so far as to set December 15, the tenth anniversary of the promulgation of the 1999 Constitution, as the deadline to complete the next round of reforms.[28]

The exact nature of the new radical turn was unclear, but the government showed no hesitation about harassing and even persecuting political enemies. A favorite reprisal was to cut funds from states and municipalities that had elected candidates of rival parties. Officials also pressured media to end hostile coverage of the Bolivarian Revolution, and authorities even presented criminal charges against opposition figures. As chapter 7 explained, the refusal to arrest and prosecute the participants in the April 2002 coup attempt brought long-term adverse consequences for the government; however, to have authorities in 2009 go after political leaders who had not been directly involved in actions to overthrow Chávez seemed petty and belated, besides being counterproductive.[29]

The crucial dividing line was between those who advocated a change in policies by moving public opinion and winning elections versus those who actively conspired to use force to overthrow the government. Candidate Manuel Rosales, who had lost the presidential election of 6 December 2006, was in many ways an ideal opposition candidate. His proven contacts with American diplomats and the rumors that he intended to make the state of Zulia an independent republic left him vulnerable to attacks. Rather than keeping him as a punching bag, the government, in a political miscalculation, decided to bring old corruption charges against him. Rosales, after trying to defend himself, went into hiding and then appeared in Peru seeking political asylum. His escape worsened the already tense relations with Peru, but more importantly, allowed a real hard liner, Leopoldo López, to replace Rosales as a leader of the opposition.[30] López quickly gained a reputation as a firebrand who did not hesitate to incite crowds into violence, but the harmful consequences of the replacement of Rosales by López did not become obvious until 2014, as chapter 18 will explain.

The reprisals did not affect only the political opposition but also NGOs. Originally NGOs in Venezuela and elsewhere in the world had performed humanitarian, environmental, and human rights functions, but already in the late twentieth century the U.S.

government saw in NGOs the mechanism to influence politics and in particular to win elections in foreign countries. New NGOs operated mainly as a conduit of U.S. funding, and they had been instrumental in mobilizing support against the government during the April 2002 failed coup attempt. To control their activities, the National Assembly had previously passed a law requiring full disclosure of the origin of their funding. With around 20,000 NGOs existing in Venezuela, enforcement proved lax, and in 2009 as part of the reprisals against the opposition, the National Assembly intended to pass a bill—previously proposed in 2006—to require all funds for NGOs to pass through the national treasury for subsequent disbursement.[31]

Because governments in some countries have banned NGOs from receiving foreign funds and at times have outlawed those organizations altogether, at first sight it seemed like a good measure to weaken the opposition. But in Venezuela the proposed bill was of questionable benefit and could reinforce the image that the country was authoritarian. The CIA had never stopped disbursing funds and providing secret support to opposition groups, and if the government cut off financing through the NGOs, then the U.S. government simply would go back to the system of the 1960s of using only secret channels to fund opposition movements. Quiet lobbying by European Union diplomats persuaded the National Assembly to drop its plans to pass the bill imposing strict controls on foreign funding for NGOs.[32]

The recurrent harassment of anti–Chávez groups inevitably forced them to seek safety in numbers. Ever since the disintegration of the Coordinating Committee in late 2004, the opposition had lacked a single voice. Only with tremendous difficulty had the parties coalesced to present one candidate for the presidential elections, but for the other campaigns finding a consensus on supporting a single candidate for each of the other elected offices proved elusive. This fragmented opposition had been a major reason why Chavismo repeatedly had been able to sweep the legislative, state, and municipal elections. The traditional political parties, almost all dating back to the failed Fourth Republic, announced on 8 June 2009 that they were beginning the process to create a single political alternative eventually known as National Unity (*Unidad Nacional*). About 50 senior political leaders made the announcement, but only two females and no junior politicians were present at this event.[33]

Clearly the task of forging a unified opposition that would appeal to the majority of Venezuelans was going to be a difficult and long task. Only on 10 December 2009 after intense negotiations did National Unity announce a rough agreement to select the slate of candidates for the legislative elections in September 2010, but still a few leaders, including hard-liner Leopoldo López, did not support the agreement.[34] A more fundamental defect was the lack of grassroots support among the popular classes. The "United Socialist Party of Venezuela (PSUV) enjoys a virtual monopoly in Venezuela's countryside,"[35] and "the opposition has practically no presence in the barrios."[36] Unless the opposition could attract a majority of popular class voters, any challenge to Chávez was doomed to failure. Survival was the most pressing problem for the political parties, because in spite of their constant denunciations of the threat of Cuban socialism, private business largely had stopped making any contributions.[37] PODEMOS, the political party that once defiantly had split from Chávez in 2007 over the constitutional referendum, saw itself reduced to begging for U.S. help to survive in 2009.[38] PODEMOS requested U.S. money by playing up the danger of the Cuban and Iranian connections of the government, and "there was an element of panic in their appeal to the Embassy for assistance."[39] In still another country,

American officials once again found themselves in the predicament of having to finance an opposition that local citizens did not think deserved support.

The weakness and fragmentation of the opposition left the road clear for the Bolivarian Revolution, but as the country waited, not until 12 May 2009 did the government provide the first concrete indication of the nature of the coming changes. That day Chávez announced the signing of a new labor contract providing for salary raises and more stringent professional standards for both existing teachers and future hires who also were required to attend training sessions. Opposition leaders jumped to attack the contract as a clear attempt to convert teachers into political commissars whose sole function was not to teach but to indoctrinate children with the tenets of "twenty-first-century Socialism." The main teachers' union did not share these concerns, and a strike by a small number of dissident teachers quickly fizzled.[40]

The controversy over the new contract had been just the opening act of a much larger struggle over the educational bill that the National Assembly began to consider in May.[41] As chapter 4 explained, the protests of January 2001 against educational reform had been the first battle in the struggle that culminated in the coup attempt of April 2002. As far as the educational system, "despite local rumors of Cuban educational advisors and anti-capitalist and xenophobic additions to the curriculum, few significant nationwide curriculum changes appear to have occurred so far."[42] If in nearly ten years the government had made few modifications, then any new effort was sure to take as long to have any effect, because education officials were usually the slowest of bureaucrats to accept change. But the opposition refused to accept this reality and consequently began a furious campaign right after Chávez signed the new educational bill into law at a rally on 15 August.[43]

The opposition denounced the educational measure as a "birthday gift for Fidel Castro" and referred to it as the "Cuban Law," and on cue the Roman Catholic Church condemned the law for wanting to take God out of schools. Because the law also made changes to the public universities, the opposition hoped to galvanize many university students to form a resistance coalition with teachers, parents, and Catholics.[44]

A crescendo of protests culminated in a large march on 22 August, but the opposition had overestimated its strength. Teachers were largely satisfied with their recent salary increase, and the vast expansion of the educational system had filled the schools with many enthusiastic young Chavistas who supported the new law. The parents of children in private schools merely wanted to send a warning message to the government and had no desire for an angry confrontation.[45]

A special case was the Roman Catholic Church. The Catholic schools comprised the largest component of the private schools, and under special arrangements, the salaries of almost all the teachers in Catholic schools came out of the national budget; in addition the government paid for the teachers who provided the mandatory religious education in the public schools. In spite of all the official generosity, too many Church officials insisted on fighting the long defunct Cold War against Communism and insisted on angering Chávez by their repeated attacks on the government. But once the Catholic Church at last realized that the educational law did not modify the government largesse, its hostility to the measure dissipated.[46]

Protests continued after the large march on 22 August but gradually declined. A puzzled opposition, seeing the supposed anger melting away, believed that the start of the school year on 15 September meant a vast outpouring of crowds into the streets demanding the immediate repeal of the educational law. But when classes resumed at schools and universities, students, parents, and the teaching staffs found that nothing had changed. The new education law required regulations and bylaws for its implementation, but at the education ministry, traditionally among the most cumbersome in the entire bureaucracy, the process had not even begun. No sooner than the next school year some changes might start to trickle down to the students, but only in a piecemeal and fragmented way. The opposition could only watch helplessly as the new education law faded away as a source of controversy.[47]

Neither the opposition nor the government wanted to admit that the education law indicated that the Bolivarian Revolution was approaching its limits. The opposition had long been in intellectual bankruptcy, and with the effort to revive the nearly decade-old educational reform, the government was showing that it too was fast running out of new ideas or innovative proposals. The stage of experimentation was far from over, but almost imperceptibly the focus shifted in 2009 from making radical changes to preserving the gains of the Bolivarian Revolution. All revolutionary movements at some moment reach that phase, for example during the Cuban Revolution it can be dated to the early 1970s. As officials shifted the efforts to meeting the needs of the population, as the cases in the last section of this chapter show, the priority became to govern through existing channels rather than destroying and creating new structures.

The Great Recession did not spare Venezuela, and in 2009 its economy contracted by 2.9 percent. The government concentrated its efforts on isolating the population as much as possible from the adverse effects of the downturn in the world economy. The temporary decline in oil prices affected the country, but not as much as critics wanted to believe. A cherished assumption among foreign observers and opposition figures had been that as soon as oil prices fell, not only the economy but the regime would come crashing down. Analysts confidently predicted another "Caracazo," the popular upheaval of February1989 that had crippled the Fourth Republic. The conventional wisdom was that only enormous money transfers to the lower classes kept Chávez in power but that as soon as the oil faucet went dry, inevitably his presidency had to collapse.[48]

To the consternation of capitalist advocates, the Great Recession triggered not the fall of the government but the near collapse of the banking sector. An official bailout, however, was a real possibility; Chávez was personally grateful to bankers because they—in sharp contrast with the bank employees' union—had refused to support the strikes against his administration in 2002 and 2003. Until 2008, the banking sector in Venezuela "grew at a stunning rate in almost every indicator from 2004 through 2007."[49] In such booming times, not surprisingly bankers had no desire to overthrow the government and did not make contributions to the opposition parties. Meanwhile, the transfer of income to the popular classes enlarged domestic demand and gave many small businesses the opportunity to reap profits by taking out loans to expand their activities. About 50 small and middle-sized banks had emerged to meet the increased demand for financial services, and they complemented the five large institutions that held the majority of assets; of the five large ones, only Banco de Venezuela was state-owned.[50]

Just as for Wall Street, the economic expansion hid a multitude of sins, but "the bursting of Venezuela's economic bubble brought to light bad illegal, and/or unethical practices in the financial sector."[51] And just as in Wall Street, lax and haphazard regulation of financial institutions had made possible these abuses, the only difference being that while the Venezuelan opposition constantly condemned Chávez of imposing socialism, in the United States nobody made that charge against George W. Bush. When runs on deposits posed a real threat, Venezuelan authorities intervened the four most vulnerable banks on 20 November; the government could have nationalized or closed all of them, but wisely decided to take only this first step to determine whether they could be saved or not. Eventually the government intervened 11 banks, all in the small and medium range; the five large ones—including the state-owned Banco de Venezuela—were in solid condition and were in no risk of insolvency. In the United States the closing every year of a handful of the thousands of existing banks has over decades been such a routine activity that official web sites list the standard procedure to complete the process of their liquidation, but in Venezuela this is such a rare occurrence that the government had to devise a solution for the 11 failed banks.[52]

The Venezuelan financial world trembled when in a heated reaction Chávez on 29 November threatened to nationalize the entire banking sector for having violated Venezuela's laws. The specter of nationalization dissipated when on 6 December he specified that the government would purchase only those banks breaking the law and not the entire sector. These words calmed the markets because Chávez was performing the role not of radical socialist but of damage control officer.[53] He had a great excuse to nationalize the entire sector, but he had always been skeptical about state ownership as the sole solution to any country's problems; according to his beliefs, elites in state-owned entities could be as voracious as those of the private sector. And the start of the electricity outages (discussed in the next section) was a recent reminder that nationalization could easily make a problem worse, as had happened with the purchase of the U.S.-owned Caracas power utility in 2007.

The government closed the 11 intervened banks but not all of them permanently. Three of them merged with a small state-owned bank to form the new state-owned Banco Bicentenario, and others reopened but with the fear of a run on their deposits. In the process of shutting down the banks, officials discovered they held substantial assets in an insurance company also threatened with insolvency; in response the government nationalized this insurance company and reopened it as a state-owned Bolivariana de Seguros. As an additional precaution the government also acquired several brokerage and foreign exchange firms which were in danger of failing, and thus gained a minority stake in that branch of the financial sector. The government increased its ownership share in the banking sector in assets from 12 percent in January 2009 to 28 percent in January 2010.[54]

The fear that depositors would remove all their money from the reopened banks was real, and the authorities took additional steps to guarantee their soundness. Using a tool rarely available in the United States, the government shifted the accounts of many state-owned entities to the newly nationalized institutions. The official deposits gave the banks a solid base, and the next step was to reassure small depositors. Venezuela did have the equivalent of a Federal Deposit Insurance Company, but the amount guaranteed was rather small. The National Assembly passed a law not only tripling the amount of the coverage but also making it retroactive to those who had lost part of their deposits. The combination of all these measures restored trust in the banking system and showed a government more than willing to support private business and to protect the small depositors.[55]

The timely assistance to small depositors earned considerable good will for the government among the middle class and helped to restore the slipping prestige of the government in time for its next big electoral test in September 2010. As will be recalled, the opposition boycott of the 2005 elections gave the government control of almost all the seats in the National Assembly. The deputies served for five-year terms, and the 26 September 2010 elections were crucial to renew the legislative mandate of Chávez for another five years.

The Struggle to Safeguard Society

The indispensable obligation of any government is to guarantee access to those goods and services essential for the survival of the population. Whether the state, the private sector or most likely a combination of the two provides these goods and services has been an issue for each country to decide. But whatever the mix, the failure to provide any of the essential goods and services creates strains and eventually crises in the country. And if the government is unable to correct deficiencies only getting worse with the passage of time, society starts to disintegrate and the country itself can collapse, as has happened with the failed states in many parts of Africa and the Middle East.

Regimes carrying out revolutionary changes inevitably disrupt the supply of goods and the provision of services. A contributing factor always present is the replacement of the old management with new loyal followers who lack either the experience or the technical skills to run large institutions. But the question goes beyond having the right persons in the right positions, because revolutionary regimes are not content with replacing the "ins" with the "outs" but also want to convert into reality their ideal society. In the attempt to make the material world and human nature conform to revolutionary ideals, inevitably the production of goods and the provision of services suffers disruptions. Any society can withstand damage from occasional interruptions and can accommodate even moderate amounts of disorder, but past a breaking point, the country starts a downward spiral into collapse.

By its reliance on the disciplined military the Bolivarian Revolution was able to keep within manageable levels the disruptions resulting from its social transformations. But by 2007 even the talents inside the military were stretched too thinly across the country, and not only was corruption spreading among senior officers but combat capabilities were also declining. The previous section indicated that by then the government had exhausted its revolutionary initiatives. Several major problems affecting negatively the population increasingly were absorbing the attention of the government. Polls confirmed that citizens placed the crime wave and the food supply as their highest priorities, even though occasionally another issue, such as electricity outages, could become even more important.

Electricity Outages of 2009–2010 The Fourth Republic in its last years had privatized most of the utility companies of Venezuela. The Bolivarian Revolution decided to reverse this action and began buying the companies from investors; Hugo Chávez explained in military tones that electricity was a "strategic" sector that needed to be under state control. The plausible argument was that these usually foreign-owned utilities had neglected providing service to rural areas as being prohibitively expensive. Rural electrification obviously required subsidies to cover costs and did not seem such a pressing issue when around 90 percent of the population was urban. The tipping point came in 2007 with the costly nationalization of Electricidad de Caracas, a U.S.-owned firm that had provided excellent service to the huge population of the capital and to many surrounding regions. Not only did the Venezuelan government pay too high a price for this company, but the uncertainty about nationalization had persuaded management to defer the planned replacement of machinery in its generating stations. The company relied primarily on oil and gas-fired plants and only occasionally purchased hydroelectricity from the distant dams owned by the state.[56]

U.S. investors were pleased with the nationalization because they made a nice profit and recuperated their capital by selling outdated equipment at overvalued prices; no wonder investors have always been on the prowl for opportunities to engage in the admittedly risky business of privatization and nationalization of companies in Latin America. Senior executives and many mid-level managers left the utility, and the government filled the vacancies with throngs of Chavista followers with passionate commitment to the Bolivarian Revolution but usually short of the necessary operating skills. The new state enterprises soon were groaning under bloated bureaucracies, and a work force three or four times larger than that of the foreign-owned companies could produce at best only the same amount of electricity. And in May 2007 the government created the National Electric Corporation (*Corporación Eléctrica Nacional*) or CORPOELEC to administer the utilities, but this new agency just added an additional layer of bureaucracy to entangle operations. In the replacement and hiring of new personnel, the essential requirement that the nationalized utilities had to order immediately new Diesel and gas engines for its thermal plants slipped through the cracks.[57]

The urgency of expanding the capacity of the thermal plants in Caracas should have been obvious because since 1999 the redistributive policies of the Bolivarian Republic meant that consumption was rising at an annual rate of about 4.5 percent. Behind this increase in demand were falling poverty levels, low utility rates, and the rapid spread of air conditioning. Low tariffs on imported air conditioners allowed many citizens for the first time to enjoy this comfort often a necessity in the mainly tropical Venezuela. The only energy-saving measure came when, at the suggestion of Fidel Castro to Chávez, the government encouraged the widespread adoption of Compact Fluorescent light Bulbs (CFBs). With the cooperation of many Cuban advisers, thousands of volunteers knocked at the door of each household to seek permission to replace the inefficient incandescent light bulbs with the CFBs provided initially for free. The campaign had a lesser impact on shops and businesses because most already used fluorescent lighting.[58]

This lone energy conservation effort barely slowed the growth of consumption, so while demand rose by 43 percent between 1999 (the first year of the Chávez presidency) and 2008, installed capacity increased only by 19 percent. The obsolete thermal plants obviously could not increase their output, and CORPOELEC failed to order the new machinery; the neglect of routine maintenance also caused frequent interruptions in the supply of current. The easiest way to satisfy demand was to expand the installed hydroelectricity capacity of Venezuela, but this alternative came with serious disadvantages. Since the end of the Fourth Republic, 63 percent of the country's electricity had come from dams, and after nationalizations the share rose to 72 percent. Most of the hydroelectricity came from the southeastern part of Venezuela, particularly from the Guri dam, one of the largest reservoirs in the world, but the majority of the population lived in the northwestern part of the country, particularly in the Caracas metropolitan area. The original goal of the dams had been to provide cheap and abundant power for the industrial complexes appearing since the 1960s in the nearby Orinoco River basin, but sending the current across vast distances to the urban centers at the other end of the country did not seem to be the most optimal use of this resource.[59]

The long experience of countries heavily dependent on hydroelectricity, and most notably of bordering Colombia, had persuaded Venezuelan planners of the Fourth Republic to include droughts into the calculations of any dam project. In the most important case of Guri, the reservoir had been designed to store water on a two-year cycle, so that adequate water remained for normal generation even in a drought year. The margin of safety shrank starting in 2007 when thermal plants began failing and hydroelectricity filled the gap in supply. Because the decaying transmission network had never been designed to carry such large loads to the distant cities, frequent power outages in cities outside Caracas became the norm in 2007. The situation only worsened in 2008 when four widespread blackouts gripped the country as engineers scrambled to splice cables to replace the faltering output from thermal plants with hydroelectricity coming all the way from Guri.[60]

When the rains failed to arrive in October 2009 because of the weather phenomenon of El Niño, the outages outside Caracas became even more frequent, and an additional problem arose when the drought reduced the city's water supply. Shortages of water already were plaguing most cities in Venezuela, and on 26 October the government imposed rationing on Caracas; authorities were trying to prevent any neighborhood from being without water for more than 48 hours at a time. The government also announced plans to reduce electricity consumption, yet outages became more frequent across the country. In January 2010 CORPOELEC, fearing that Guri dam would not be able to make up the deficit indefinitely, imposed rolling blackouts.[61]

The situation continued to worsen, and on 8 February in a special radio broadcast Chávez declared an "electricity state of emergency" and imposed strict rationing to reduce demand. The regulations levied heavy fines on those who failed to reduce their consumption of electricity by at least 10 percent and gave discounts according to a sliding scale to those who reduced demand by 10 percent or more. A prohibition on billboards and public signs made Caracas look dark at nights, and the halt of all electric service on weekends and holidays became the normal practice. Shopping malls dimmed their lights and shut down escalators and elevators; without air conditioning the stuffy stores became unbearably hot. The government published the list of the 8000 largest buyers of electricity in Caracas, and soon officials were gluing large notices stating that these establishments had failed to reduce consumption by the required 10 percent; those who failed to comply faced additional fines and closings for 24 hours.[62]

The fines and the prohibitions were indispensable to prolong the life of the Guri reservoir, the source of nearly three-quarters of the country's electricity. Estimates for when the reservoir would exhaust its water ranged from between April to July 2010. The possibility of paralyzing the country was real, and the population watched with horror the water level at Guri gradually sink ever lower. When the water fell to 240 meters above sea level, the dam ceased to operate; on 1 November 2009 the reservoir stayed at 25 meters above that threshold level but by 1 February sank to 18 meters. One week later the reservoir level dropped another meter, and by 1 March was only 13 meters above the threshold. The imminence of a complete blackout and the acute shortages made the situation extremely bleak for the country. In one indication of the gravity of the crisis, American diplomats prepared to evacuate the U.S. Embassy, an action that inevitably indicated that the country was collapsing and rapidly heading to the status of a failed state. Even more ominous, predictions of another Caracazo, the violent popular upheaval of 1989, started to circulate.[63]

Throughout the crisis Chávez had demonstrated great leadership capacities as he repeatedly blamed the outages on El Niño and less accurately on capitalism. But he too knew who really ruled the destinies of humans, and starting in February, he called for the public to pray for rain; apparently he had an inside track to heaven when he claimed that "God was Bolivarian," and across the country electricity officials summoned the population to public prayer ceremonies.[64]

The Heavens showed compassion on the Bolivarian Revolution and the skies opened up to pour torrential rains over the Amazon basin; gradually as the rain clouds drifted north over Venezuela, the hemorrhage of water from Guri slowed down to a trickle by late March. The runoff water flowed into the reservoir and by the end of the summer the lake had reached record high levels. Gradually the government repealed rationing, beginning with the restoration of service on weekends and holidays; by late June the supply of both current and water had regained normal levels in almost all the country. Meanwhile CORPOELEC had launched a crash program to purchase new equipment for the expansion of its thermal generating plants, thereby reducing the dependence on hydroelectricity and easing the burden on the overstretched transmission network.[65]

Putting the blame on El Niño seemed to have worked politically, and the opposition did not make a campaign issue out of the electricity outages. The crime wave and food shortages, two problems that the Bolivarian Revolution had aggravated, provided more than ample opportunities to attack the government.

The Crime Wave During the Fourth Republic crime in Venezuela followed the Latin American pattern. The 18 to 20 homicides per 100,000 inhabitants were numbers similar to those of Mexico and Brazil yet over twice the world average. Personal safety remained an important concern throughout the Fourth Republic, and a crime wave provoked fear among citizens during several years. Authorities were not able to reduce the crime rate down to the world average mainly because of political decentralization; when the central government transferred most police functions to the states and municipalities in 1989, these entities were completely unprepared to assume this burden. The most important of these new agencies, the Caracas Metropolitan Police, also gained a reputation as a force riddled with corruption. Clearly the Bolivarian Republic inherited a daunting task.[66]

Perhaps inevitably, political considerations complicated the task of dealing with crime, but already in the first year of the Chávez presidency, it became clear that serious as were the political obstacles, ideological considerations were going to be the single most important barrier to solving the crime problem. Relishing the role of savior, Hugo Chávez implemented a penal code reform that promptly liberated 12,000 violent criminals from the country's overcrowded prisons. Supposedly their rehabilitation would continue under the supervision of parole officers, but in the political turmoil of 2001 to 2003, the breakdown in police institutions meant that many if not most of these individuals reverted to their criminal lifestyle.[67]

Chávez never regretted his decision to release these dangerous inmates because his action had not been a spontaneous outburst of mercy but reflected his deeply held belief that crime was the result of poverty. In common with many Liberals in the United States, Chávez stubbornly held to his simplistic explanation of the cause of crime. He even went so far as to state in his speeches and in his *Aló Presidente* TV program that if he were poor he too would engage in crime, thus taking to the extreme the cliché that criminals were "victims of society." This decriminalization of delinquency gave would-be criminals a justification and a green light to go out to commit robberies, kidnappings, and even murders.[68]

As chapter 5 explained, during the coup attempt of April 2002 the Caracas Metropolitan Police, the most corrupt of the country's police forces, had supported the Pedro Carmona regime. After the failed coup the Chávez administration began a long struggle to take control of the Caracas Metropolitan Police away from the city government. A military takeover in November 2002 prevented this force from supporting the petroleum strike. The legal and political struggle to gain control of the Caracas Metropolitan Police lasted for years, and the government had to be satisfied with disarming the state and municipal police forces as a way to limit their capacity to harm the Bolivarian Revolution. This disarmament made the outgunned police justifiably afraid to take on well-armed criminals, who increasingly realized that they enjoyed almost completely immunity to carry out their evil deeds.[69]

As homicides and other violent acts increased, crime became one of the two most important public issues during the Bolivarian Revolution. Worried citizens expressed their fears to their elected deputies, and in response the National Assembly passed in February 2005 a new Penal Code with harsh punishments for violent offenders. When this tough anti-crime bill reached the president's desk, Chávez for the first time faced the harsh reality that the policies of the Bolivarian Revolution had actually aggravated a problem. He had been reducing poverty and reducing the income inequality in the country, yet many individuals repaid this generosity by committing more crimes. Clearly he needed to discard his simplistic theory that crime was solely the result of poverty, but for the moment he stayed in denial and disingenuously claimed that he needed to intensify his social programs because the reduction in poverty had not been sufficiently large to lower the crime rate. But he needed some political cover, and he used the overcrowded prisons as the pretext to veto the tough anti-crime bill of the National Assembly.[70]

Nobody doubted that the prisons of Venezuela were in abysmal shape and that the inmates ran the establishments, but to say that lack of space was a valid reason for not arresting criminals was disingenuous at best. Chávez miscalculated when he concluded that the political costs from the rising crime wave did not really threaten the Bolivarian Revolution. The opposition picked up on crime as a campaign issue as early as 2005, but initially voters did not seem interested. And the defeat of the 2 December 2007 constitutional referendum, which contained amendments nationalizing the police forces, seemed to give indirect evidence that crime was not important to voters. Polls showed crime to be one of the two most important issues facing the country, but paradoxically citizens ignored the opposition's accusations and did not blame Chávez for the problem.[71]

The turning point came in 2008 when 14,589 homicides occurred in Venezuela (Table 2), and the rate of 52 per 1000 inhabitants made the country not only the most dangerous in Latin America but placed it among the most unsafe in the planet. Venezuelans adopted from Colombian criminals the practice of *sicariato* or murders on demand. Other indicators were as bad if not worse, such as the case of "express kidnappings," a modality also adopted from criminals in bordering Colombia whereby a person was released a few hours after the kidnappers had exhausted a victim's ATM account or credit card limit. Both wealthy and middle class families were afraid to go outside and lived like caged animals inside their homes. But the overwhelming majority of Venezuelans, with an excessively fatalistic attitude, accepted crime as just one of the inevitable calamities that occasionally and unpredictably afflicted inhabitants. And too many Venezuelans uncritically accepted the explanation of Chávez that the crime wave was really the spillover of the violence raging in Colombia.[72]

Table 2:
Venezuela: Homicides, 1990–2015

Year	*Number*	*Per 100,000 Citizens*
1990	2,474	12
1991	2,502	13
1992	3,366	16
1993	4,292	20
1994	4,733	22
1995	4,481	20
1996	4,961	22
1997	4,225	18
1998	4,550	20
1999	5,968	25
2000	8,022	33
2001	7,960	32
2002	9,617	38
2003	11,342	44
2004	9,719	37
2005	9,964	37
2006	12,257	45
2007	13,156	49
2008	14,589	52
2009	16,047	54
2010	17,600	57
2011	19,336	67
2012	21,692	73
2013	24,763	79
2014	24,980	82
2015	27,875	90

Sources: Venezuela, Instituto Nacional de Estadística; Observatorio Venezolano de Violencia; Roberto Briceño-León, "Violencia, ciudadanía y miedo en Caracas," *Foro Internacional* 47(2007): 559. Government officials consider many figures of the twenty-first century to be too high.

Chávez never found an explanation or at least a rationalization as to why no matter how much poverty declined, crime rates were going up faster. But he knew that total inactivity carried political risks, because at any moment the opposition could finally find the way to awake in citizens the fear of crime. A bill on police had been floundering in the National Assembly since July 2004, and his prompting persuaded the legislature to pass the bill in April 2008 which he signed into law. But it had not been just legislative laziness that had delayed passage of a bill trying to bypass but not to violate the 1999 Constitution. The new law created a new national Bolivarian police, which was closely patterned after the national police of Colombia. Just as in Colombia, the goal was to have a single unified and centralized police force, but while in Venezuela the government could create the new Bolivarian police, it could not take this attribute stipulated in the 1999 Constitution away from states and municipalities.[73]

The formal inauguration of the new Bolivarian National Police took place on 29

November 2009. The Chávez administration followed the dual approach of channeling resources to the new Bolivarian Police and of starving the state and municipal police forces of funding and luring away their personnel. Elected opposition officials bitterly resisted giving up control of their police forces and raised the accusations of excessive centralization. The majority of states and municipalities were in the hands of elected PSUV officials who were more than glad to have the national government take over their police obligations, but in reality the Bolivarian National Police was not going to be ready any time soon to assume these obligations.[74]

The police with its military appearance was for Chávez an intellectually satisfying solution for the crime wave. Once he learned that the international minimum standard was 3.5 police officers per 1000 inhabitants but that Venezuela had only 1.5 per 1000 inhabitants, he quickly calculated in front of television viewers that Venezuela had a shortfall of 70,000 police officers. For him increasing the number of police became the simplistic solution for the crime wave. As a general throwing more troops into a battle that he thinks can still be won, the military-sounding proposal of having 70,000 more loyal Chavistas in police uniforms was appealing to the president on many levels, not the least of which was not having to reexamine his assumption that poverty was the sole cause of crime.[75]

He was well aware that since the Fourth Republic corruption had plagued police in the country, and to avoid that danger the officers of the new Bolivarian National Police received salaries three times higher than those in the existing state and municipal forces. All qualified personnel first had to attend and pass a year-long training session, but even the higher salaries failed to attract adequate number of recruits. At speeches Chávez urged his political party and the communal councils to find persons suitable for the new force. The response was minimal, with initial applications numbering only 5,220, and only a fraction qualified for admission into the program. The number of recruits declined until only 947 graduated in December 2009. The small number of graduates postponed indefinitely any deployment of the officers of the initial graduating classes throughout the country. In 2013 the Bolivarian National Police had grown to around 15,000 police officers, far short of the required 70,000, and was deployed only in Caracas. By early 2015 units were stationed at six other states.[76]

The crime wave puzzled foreign observers, who dogmatically considered him a despot but could not explain how unlike real dictators he could not guarantee law and order. The creation of the Bolivarian National Police was the first major step to tackle the crime wave, and Chávez claimed early next year that as soon as the new officers began patrol duty, the crime rate dropped in those neighborhoods. While that may have been true, homicides in 2009 rose to a total of 16,047 or 54 per 100,000 inhabitants. The number of homicides continued to climb, and their increase reinforced the perception that crime was one of the most pressing problems facing the country.[77] With the population witnessing violent acts on an almost daily basis, the opposition seized upon crime as the most important issue to use in the next political campaigns.

Food Scarcity and Agriculture

After 2007 the other pressing issue constantly affecting citizens was food scarcity. Nobody ever went hungry, but all Venezuelans could expect to experience shortages of one or more basic foods on a regular basis. Prior to 2007 these shortages had been rare and of short duration, but starting in the middle of 2007, the struggle to find adequate food supplies became part of the daily ordeal for the majority of Venezuelans.[78] As discussed in chapter 1, the fertile soils and climate of the country are comparable to neighboring Colombia, which has traditionally been an exporter of agricultural products. Instead because of the "Dutch Disease" of petroleum, Venezuela in the middle of the twentieth century became a food importer. Not even massive expenditures by the Fourth Republic, in particular by the presidency of Carlos Andrés Pérez, had been able to make Venezuela self-sufficient in food.

As long as the Bolivarian Revolution maintained the agricultural policies of the Fourth Republic, the likelihood of achieving food independence remained a realistic goal. But when Chávez decided in 2005 to adopt socialism as the lodestar of his presidency, adverse consequences were not long in coming to the food supply of the country. To the original goals of agricultural self-sufficiency and low consumer prices for food he added the third goal of creating a socialist economy in the countryside. Reality forced him to temper his commitment to socialism in many other sectors of the economy, but in agriculture he found in Elías Jaua the perfect henchman to try to bring the entire food production chain of Venezuela under state control. His appointment as minister of agriculture in February 2006 marked the start of a series of disastrous policies that wrecked the agriculture of the country and at times threatened to bring the population to the verge of hunger. As an orthodox Marxist, Jaua was determined to impose a Cuban-style socialism on Venezuela, and Chávez gave him the opportunity to carry out this dangerous experiment. In contrast to the president's disruptive practice of making frequent cabinet changes, Jaua remained the czar of agriculture from February 2006 to October 2012 and in many ways he determined the political fortunes of the Bolivarian Revolution.[79]

The resounding reelection of Chávez in December 2006 gave a big boost to Jaua's drive to socialize Venezuelan agriculture. Nobody doubted the need for major changes, because serious complications were disrupting the supply of food to consumers. The country was importing at high prices large quantities of foodstuffs when its soils were easily capable of producing at lower cost those same items. At least 20 percent of the imports came from bordering Colombia, and this trade had become perverted beyond all logic. After the government purchased the Colombian products at high prices, the subsidized foodstuffs were then sold to the Venezuelan consumers at a sharp discount. In the states bordering Colombia the subsidized products were then smuggled back across the border for resale at a higher price to Colombian consumers. Smugglers earned a nice profit on these irrational exchanges made possible only by the huge petroleum revenues flowing into Venezuela.[80]

Minister Jaua imposed more price controls sometimes below the cost of production on many items grown in Venezuela, and not surprisingly food shortages began to appear across the country during the second half of 2007. Previous attempts to impose price controls had produced the same effects, so it was hard to understand why Minister Jaua repeated this failed policy again in 2007. A plausible hypothesis was that the government wanted to create these shortages in order to be able to justify to the public the nationalization in early 2008 of Polar, the largest food processor in the country. A combative Chávez boomed out that "it is not enough to close one store, and even less fair to close small businesses; no, we are going after the big ones. We are going to keep an eye on the big ones, that is where capitalism is at its fiercest, and the owners of these large chains

Western Venezuela

are members of the rancid anti–Bolivarian oligarchy."[81] But the defeat of the constitutional referendum on 2 December 2007 weakened the government and persuaded Chávez to shelve the nationalization of Polar at least for the moment. The more modest goal became to introduce socialism gradually to the food sector.[82]

The government urgently wanted to eliminate the food shortages, but the natural response of simply expanding the existing Mercal grocery stores was no longer adequate because many had become mired in corruption and inefficiency. The pool of skilled managers to run so many stores was too small, and the government was having a hard time restoring them to their original performance level. In order to tap into the management skills of PDVSA, in January 2008 Chávez entrusted to the state oil company the operation of a new discount chain. By April 2008 PDVSA had created a network of 210 stores, ten of which were megastores and the rest were small "7-Eleven" style stores many located next to the gasoline stations of the company. PDVSA purchased abroad most of the food sold at its retail subsidiary, and these imported products were also supposed to attract consumers from the middle class. The existing network of gasoline stations was a natural place to open food outlets for the entire population, and in this way the new PDVSA chain also supplemented the Mercal stores, which generally had not opened branches in affluent neighborhoods.[83]

The enthusiasm of creating a new government distributor for foodstuffs could not hide the reality of the chaotic policies of previous years. The minister of agriculture had raised the farm price of some products, in particular poultry, eggs, and milk but at the same time had authorized imports. The predictable result was a glut in the market, and producers dumped poultry into garbage dumps and poured milk into the streets. Chávez erupted in rage when he heard that PDVSA was importing foods from abroad rather than buying from domestic producers. The oversupply contrasted with acute shortages for other foodstuffs occurring at the same time because the bureaucrats kept purchase prices too low and failed to authorize sufficient imports.[84]

The most absurd case occurred with wheat. Traditionally Venezuela grew very little wheat and even before the oil boom had relied mainly on grain imports. It was a simple matter to calculate the consumption of wheat and then to authorize the corresponding amount of imports, but in late May 2009 bakeries and pasta factories were running out of flour and were on the point of stopping production of these basic items of the household basket. It turned out that the idea of food sovereignty had become the official party line, and nobody wanted to authorize wheat imports when Venezuela supposedly was set to become a wheat exporter. While revolutionary fervor fed these fantasies, without the permits to dock in Venezuelan ports, ships with cargoes of wheat stayed moored at U.S. ports and incurred high demurrage fees beginning on 14 May 2009. Only when bureaucrats finally admitted that no wheat was available in Venezuela did they authorize wheat imports and thus prevented the disappearance of bread and pasta from the household basket.[85]

The wheat episode exemplified incompetence and misguided revolutionary spirit. A different case was coffee, a product the country could produce and even export, but as mentioned before, only in the initial years of the Chávez presidency did the long and strenuous efforts of the Fourth Republic to attain self-sufficiency finally allow the country to cover its internal demand. Unfortunately the Ministry of Agriculture could not resist playing with the two variables involved in the coffee trade: the purchase price of the beans from growers and the sale price of the ground product to consumers.

By 2008 the result was an even greater distortion in the supply chain at huge costs to the government. Venezuelan growers smuggled their beans across the border for sale in Colombia at higher prices. The Colombian processors then sold ground coffee back to Venezuelan retailers who received a subsidy to keep low the price of the product. Then inevitably Colombian consumers crossed the border to buy this discounted ground coffee. The Venezuelan government incurred the huge costs of subsidizing the ground coffee, but local growers hesitated to expand production because they were afraid that the angry verbal clashes between Chávez and Colombian president Álvaro Uribe Vélez might interrupt trade with Colombia.[86]

For the majority of Venezuelans coffee was the most important non-alcoholic beverage, and rice was perhaps the most typical of food staples in the household basket. Venezuela possessed stupendous rice producing areas, particularly in Guárico State in the Orinoco River basin, and under the Fourth Republic the country was nearing self-sufficiency. Rice production depended on the upkeep of complex irrigation systems, and traditionally the government had collected fees from growers to maintain the network of the dikes, canals, and ditches. The appointment of employees of revolutionary fervor but doubtful competence brought the deterioration of the irrigation systems, and the drought of 2009–2010 reduced even more the rice harvests. Many growers shifted to growing other crops or simply abandoned agriculture altogether. As usual, the government solved its self-imposed problems by importing rice, with the principal supplier being the United States.[87]

Rice seeds required processing to make the grains suitable for human consumption, and specialized plants provided this service. But price controls forced processors to sell white rice at a loss, and not surprisingly the owners either stopped processing the raw rice or shifted to producing specialty varieties. White rice was disappearing from grocery shelves in 2009, and the government scrambled to provide consumers with ample supply at low prices. A power struggle erupted as the government pressured processors to sell rice at a price below production costs; analysts believed that the real target was Polar, because after the approval of the reelection referendum in February 2009, the Chávez administration felt emboldened to make another try to nationalize the largest food processor in the country.[88]

The unlikely pawn in this power struggle was Cargill, a multinational corporation and owner of a plant processing only parboiled rice. This type of rice was not covered under the price controls, but in February 2009 the Ministry of Agriculture told the company to bring the price of parboiled down to that of white rice. Cargill prepared to import the different machinery required to produce white rice, but before it could start the transition, on 4 March Chávez directed Minister Jaua to expropriate the plant because it had not shifted immediately to produce white rice. The action besides unexpected seemed unfair because in contrast to Polar, which actively supported the political opposition, Cargill had made sure not to antagonize or criticize the Chávez administration in any way. The company accepted a bad compensation deal on the parboiled plant in order to preserve its major presence in the Venezuelan economy. The rice plant had been only one of its 22 facilities in the country, and in contrast to its less than 3 percent share of the rice market, Cargill supplied 50 percent of the pasta, flour, and cooking oils in Venezuela and significant shares in other products such as grains, oils, and many animal feeds.[89]

After nationalization, the government kept the former Cargill plant processing parboiled rice rather than import the machinery to process white rice. Parboiled rice was a luxury product, and the nationalized company sold it at high price to the private supermarkets and at the low price of white rice to state stores such as Mercal, with the losses once again covered by subsidies. But the nationalization had never been about this one small rice plant but about sending a message to Polar and the other processors. Shortly after the government took over the Cargill plant in March 2009, the rest of the processors agreed to sell white rice at a loss at the price fixed by the government. Presumably these conglomerates covered their losses with profits from sales in other products. The difficulties of earning a return on investment in revolutionary Venezuela were not for the faint hearted, and unexpected blows at any moment could shatter profit calculations.[90]

A permanent obligation of American diplomats has been to find markets for U.S. products in foreign countries. In the case of rice in Venezuela, American diplomats found their efforts were unnecessary, because the self-destruction of that country's rice cultivation automatically guaranteed major markets for U.S. exporters. In 2008 almost all the imported rice had come from the United States, and even the Chávez administration realized the dangers of this political dependence by trying to buy rice from other countries. But diversification proved a failure, and the United States remained the primary source of rice imports for Venezuela, thus making it economically disastrous for the Chávez administration to seek any confrontation because of this economic lever.[91]

The United States became confirmed as the primary source of imported rice when on 1 August 2009 Chávez, in one of his quarrels with President Álvaro Uribe Vélez, decided to end all trade with Colombia. The bordering country had supplied rice and many other food items, including livestock and frozen meat, and each of those sectors suffered major losses when Venezuela imposed an embargo on trade with Colombia. Perhaps the most interesting was sugar, another basic staple of the diet and also subject to price controls. Sugar cane grows well in Venezuela's lush soils, and under the Fourth Republic 15 mills easily satisfied the demand for sugar in the country and occasionally generated small surpluses for export. As happened to many agricultural sectors, the land reform policies of the Bolivarian Republic disrupted sugar production, and soon Venezuela found itself importing growing quantities to cover the domestic market.[92]

The choke point in production was the supply of sugar cane. Property expropriations, land invasions, and the creation of rural cooperatives had sharply reduced the cane for the sugar mills, and without the raw material to grind, they faced imminent shutdown. The largest processor, Centro Azucarero Portuguesa (CAPSA) had read the political winds correctly and had become a strong supporter of the Bolivarian Revolution, but with insufficient cane to grind its output was declining. As a partial solution, the Chávez administration imported large amounts of raw sugar from Brazil, thus keeping the last stage of production, the refining of raw sugar into white sugar, in the Venezuelan mills. Because the white sugar was then sold at low prices to the public, a constant balancing act was required to make sure that the owners obtained the Brazilian raw sugar at a price low enough to keep the refining operation barely profitable. Needless to say, oil revenues covered the differences in prices, and the owners through their political contacts were able to secure from the bureaucracy the permits to import the required volume of raw sugar.[93]

The Táchira sugar mill—owned by Colombian owners—relied exclusively on abundant cane from Colombia for its raw material. Other sugar mills were complementing the insufficient Venezuelan supply with Colombian cane, but this alternative ended on 1 August 2009 when Chávez abruptly halted all trade with the neighboring country. When the Colombian owners suspended operations at the Táchira sugar mill, Chávez reacted by nationalizing this sugar mill and several others as well. After the expropriations, the state owned 6 out of the 15 sugar mills in Venezuela, but two of the nationalized mills were no longer operating. Output declined and once again the government turned to imports of refined sugar to supply the domestic market.[94]

By late 2009 it was clear that the official policies had left agriculture in shambles. Expensive food imports kept the shelves stocked most of the time, but the real danger existed of protests. To defuse the discontent nothing was better than a good show, and this Chávez provided with the nationalization of the Exito megastores (combination of supermarket and department store) in January 2010. Because its second largest owners were Colombians, Chávez justified this expropriation as part of his drive to halt all economic ties with the bordering country, but in reality the majority ownership belonged to the French company Casino. The six nationalized stores reopened in February under the name of "Bicentenario" and over the coming weeks Chávez was using his *Aló Presidente* TV program to announce bargains and special deals on appliances at the new Bicentenario stores as they ran down their inventories. He did not want to antagonize the Paris government, so the French owners received compensation, but the Colombian minority holders had to wait several years to receive any payment.[95]

The Exito/Bicentenario sideshow could not hide for long the mounting problems in agriculture and the persistent food shortages. Venezuela had never imported so many foodstuffs before, and not surprisingly the lack of experience in handling such large volumes led to considerable waste. The revelation in June 2010 that many containers were found full of rotting food provoked outrage when many store shelves were empty. Agricultural output declined as shortage of labor hindered farming and many landowners stopped producing because of fear of expropriations or land invasions.[96] In a first step to try to ease the food supply crisis, the government restored normal relations with Colombia in 2010, and soon products from the neighboring country were once again reaching the grocery shelves. In one of many possible examples, Venezuela resumed importing powdered milk from Colombia, in sharp contrast to the situation under the Fourth Republic when its then thriving dairy industry had been exporting large amounts of powdered milk to the neighboring country. The scarcity at times became so bad in Táchira state that residents avoided hunger only by crossing into Colombia to purchase in Cúcuta food items at prices three times higher than those in Venezuela.[97]

The more money the Chávez administration poured into agriculture and food imports, the worse the situation became in Venezuela. Food scarcities and the crime wave were two self-inflicted wounds that put the Bolivarian Revolution in peril. The unrealistic pursuit of unreachable ideals had brought enormous damage to the country, and only the ready availability of oil revenues kept the country from falling into disaster and chaos. Because the government showed no signs of wanting to moderate its idealistic policies, the danger of a societal collapse was real. On a political level, the food shortages and the crime wave provided on a silver platter the best opportunities in years for the opposition to mobilize public opinion against the Chávez presidency.

The End of the Offensive

The electricity blackouts from December 2009 through June 2010, the recurrent food shortages, and the crime wave confirmed the inability of the Chávez presidency to safeguard basic needs of the population. Although voters did not directly blame the government for the electricity shortages, the huge discomfort that households suffered made citizens more willing to criticize the Chávez administration about food scarcity and the crime wave. To regain its popularity, the government needed to take drastic action on these two vital issues, but partly because officials were afraid to be the bearers of bad news, Chávez took a long time to realize the gravity and urgency of the problems. Almost as if unaware of the mounting problems, he proclaimed on 30 December 2009 that 2010 would be a year of "Social Focus," and he trumpeted the resilience of the government in riding out the world financial crisis or Great Recession.[98]

He continued to pound away at his traditional theme of blaming capitalism for all the problems of his government and of Venezuela. But in his statements capitalism came out sounding as a synonym for greed, and it was unlikely that listeners made the distinction between an economic system based on private property and the moral vice of avarice. Because nobody was foolish enough to stand up to defend either greed or capitalism, the message seemed too vague to mobilize workers for the 26 September legislative elections, the next big hurdle for the Bolivarian Revolution.[99]

As explained before, the repeated mistakes of the opposition were mainly responsible for the majority of the electoral successes of Chávez. Perhaps the most egregious of several blunders was the boycott of legislative elections in 2005, thereby giving the government a rubber-stamp National Assembly composed exclusively of PSUV deputies and a minority of deputies from allied political parties. But in 2010 the five-year terms of the deputies ended, and this time the opposition decided to participate in the legislative elections. PSUV deputies, seeing their political future in danger, had taken the precaution of using redistricting to enhance the possibilities of retaining their seats.[100]

The worries about the future of PSUV candidates had reached Miraflores Palace, and as a way to improve the chances of candidates, the Chávez presidency decided to stifle opposition voices in the media. As narrated in chapter 12, in 2007 the government cancelled the license of RCTV to broadcast on the airwaves, but the television network continued to transmit by cable. This belated attempt to take RCTV out of the air provided a rallying point for the opposition which easily orchestrated a series of protests. The government had not learned the lesson of 2007 and repeated the same mistake when it announced on 23 January 2010 that RCTV and five other networks could no longer transmit by cable. As explained previously, the appropriate moment to close RCTV was right after the participation of the television station in the failed April 2002 coup, but once that opportunity had passed, any later attempt was bound to be counterproductive for the government.[101]

The return to cable service of three of the networks could not calm the demonstrators who continued to protest after RCTV ended its cable service permanently. The closing gave the opposition an issue that was ideal to galvanize the concerns of voters about food scarcity, electricity outages, and the crime wave. An unperturbed government pressed forward its campaign against the hostile media and obtained a great success when Globovisión, the last opposition network still broadcasting on the air waves, abandoned its hostility. Officials had not wanted to close this station and had recourse to financial pressures until the news broadcasts took a more acceptable center-left position.[102]

The elimination of savage criticism from television broadcasts gains time for this or any other government to solve the problems or issues originally feeding the discontent and the anger. Quite revealingly, the fears about negative results in the approaching legislative elections of 26 September were so intense, that the Chávez administration for the first time also targeted the print media. Venezuela has never been a country of widespread newspaper readership, and although flashy tabloids could reach substantial sales volumes, the classical newspapers were too stodgy for widespread circulation. *El Nacional* and *El Universal* had graced the tables of upper and middle-class homes, but perhaps because the latter had usually been the swing voting bloc in elections, the government decided to put pressure on the newspapers to tone down their articles. The most effective way to influence the coverage was by reducing advertisement revenue, and the order went out to state companies to buy commercial spaces only in pro–Chávez newspapers. The impact of this boycott increased as the government nationalized more companies; just the recent expropriation of Éxito megastores reduced the advertising revenue of *El Universal* by over 14 percent. In the case of *El Nacional*, the situation became so desperate that its owner asked the U.S. government for financial help to avert bankruptcy.[103]

Not even the most aggressive propaganda could compensate for the lack of many consumer products on the shelves and the mounting homicide rate. The electricity crisis had absorbed most of the attention of officials who had neglected the food shortages and the crime wave when the public expected concrete results about these last two pressing problems. Chávez was behaving in an erratic matter without really taking time to study the many pressing issues. An excellent example of this counterproductive behavior came when in one of his *Aló Presidente* television broadcasts he ordered the expropriation of La Francia, a historic ten-story building in downtown Caracas. The building was the diamond center of the country, and generations of Venezuelans had gone there to acquire their wedding rings. The president decided to include the structure among those slated for nationalization as part of the restoration of the historic center of Caracas. In reality the owner was the Universidad del Oriente, a state institution that received rental income from the diamond merchants. The sudden and unexpected disruption of this activity forced the merchants to find new places for their jewelry shops elsewhere in the city; more importantly the action created the image that no business was really safe from the whims of Chávez.[104]

In July 2010 he foolishly clashed again with the Roman Catholic Church when he made wild accusations against the hierarchy and came out looking as deranged. The timing of the clashes with the Catholic Church played right into the hands of the opposition on the eve of the legislative elections of 26 September. Chávez had repeatedly stated that his goal was a two-thirds majority for PSUV or a minimum of 110 of the 167 deputies. He did not plunge into the campaigns as he had done for the elections for governors and mayors, and many candidates floundered without the support from his magnetic personality. Once again, the involvement in foreign affairs, such as the crisis in Honduras, captured his attention and he neglected to put the necessary time and effort into the electoral campaign.[105]

The results of the 26 September legislative elections although disappointing were not at first glance as bad as many Chavistas had feared. The PSUV failed to win the 110 deputies needed for the two-thirds majority, but the 95 deputies seemed a respectable figure and guaranteed control of all leadership positions in the National Assembly. What was disturbing for the government was that the opposition received 52 percent of the votes, and only thanks to the redistricting was the PSUV able to retain control of the legislature. The opposition won the majority of seats in the six most populated states of the country and in the states bordering on Colombia; instead the rural districts gave the government the votes to retain control of the National Assembly. Some observers began to speak of the "ruralization" of the Bolivarian Revolution, and this electoral success in the countryside had the perverse effect of ratifying the socialist policies of Minister of Agriculture Elías Jaua. No matter how much damage the agriculture and the food supply suffered, the disastrous policies seemed to be delivering votes to the PSUV on Election Day.[106]

For the duration of the five-year terms of the deputies, the Bolivarian Revolution could no longer attempt to reshape the country. Initially it seemed that the failure to achieve a two-thirds majority in the National Assembly was a worse defeat than the rejection of the constitutional amendments on 2 December 2007. Chávez did not want to return to governing under the severe limitations of the early years of his presidency. After being able to legislate almost at will either through the compliant National Assembly or through the Enabling Law, he was not about to hammer agreements with the opposition to get legislation passed.

Perhaps Chávez was starting to realize that the best years of the Bolivarian Revolution lay not in the future but in the past. He had trapped himself into the corner of condemning capitalism and wanting to impose socialism, but his attempts had only disrupted the economic life of the country. A halt or a modification of the socialist policies and at the least certainly more care in their implementation seemed in order, but instead he decided to prolong artificially his unrestricted authority to make drastic changes. In December 2010, before the new National Assembly took office on 5 January 2011, he obtained from the outgoing deputies authorization to issue decree laws in a wide variety of areas for 18 months. This new Enabling Law was broader than previous ones and clearly aimed to sidestep the National Assembly should the minority opposition attempt to bloc legislation.[107]

The astute action was a clever legislative maneuver, but it was justified only if his administration had new ideas or proposals to put into effect. Lacking the authority to legislate is no less an efficient obstacle than lacking worthwhile proposals to convert into law. A profound reexamination of the nature of the Bolivarian Revolution was certainly necessary so that the government could determine the future direction of new policies, but it was not evident that Chávez was willing to take his government and the PSUV into a stage of self-criticism and reflection. And because a majority of voters had spoken on 26 September that they no longer supported this hard turn to socialism, once again the earlier decision of converting the Movement for the Fifth Republic (MVR) into the Unified Socialist Party of Venezuela (PSUV) came to haunt the electoral prospects of the government. Most Venezuelans still did not believe in a capitalism that they associated with greed and corruption, but before voters shifted their loyalty to socialism, they had to see the government resolve crucial problems, in particular the food shortages and the crime wave. Presumably those issues were going to be the top priority for the government in 2011, when early that year a totally unexpected situation shook the entire Venezuelan political system to its foundations.

CHAPTER 15

The Álvaro Uribe Presidency in Distress

Two fundamental principles are at play: the preservation of democratic institutions on the one hand, and the right of the people to decide their system of government on the other.—U.S. Ambassador Brownfield[1]

The Twilight of the Uribe Presidency

In his plan to restore peace and order to Colombia, Álvaro Uribe Vélez referred to the demobilization of the paramilitaries as a down payment on his promises to end the insurgency. But as explained in chapter 8 he had actually exaggerated the military importance of the paramilitaries in order to be able to show that his first term had achieved a real concrete victory. And by 2007 it was becoming clear that the demobilization of the paramilitaries had not been authentic, and that those illegal groups had simply metamorphosed into new criminal bands.

The incapacity of paramilitaries to engage guerrillas successfully in combat had largely passed unperceived by observers. Although the paramilitaries looked and dressed as combatants, they really were armed civilians who saw their weapons mostly as defensive. Even their counter insurgency sweeps had been exercises in social cleansing and had almost no effect on guerrillas. The paramilitaries had always preferred the killing of defenseless civilians to facing veteran guerrillas; initially the reluctance to engage in real combat had been explained away by their inferior armament, but by the mid–1990s the paramilitaries had acquired arsenals at least comparable to and often superior to those of the guerrillas. Not even mercenary soldiers, the paramilitaries were hired killers and armed thugs who preyed on civilians. Money had been their main motivation unlike the guerrillas who fought for a cause; not surprisingly the paramilitaries had been most reluctant to engage in any combat that might result in their death.

After demobilization in 2005, some paramilitaries saw the opportunity to return to civilian life, but the great majority did not know any other life and lacked the education or skills to transition to peaceful employment. Not surprisingly, many remained in violent activities, either individually or in groups. Extortion, kidnappings, and robberies remained lucrative sources of income, and new bands of criminals emerged. In some cases the paramilitary groups simply transitioned into criminal bands with a different name and sometimes even with the same name. The police estimated that by the end of

2006 at least 30 of these new criminal bands had emerged in Colombia. Those paramilitaries most closely involved in the drug trade simply continued their traditional activity, even without the political cover that their former organizations had offered. In the Caribbean coast of Colombia an urban mafia composed of former paramilitaries had extended a tight control over the region.[2]

At the individual level, former paramilitaries sometimes joined the ranks of hired killers or *sicarios*. The murder of rivals has been a very frequent occurrence in Colombia and offered occasional employment for those willing to earn extra money. While the *sicarios* might be hired to take care of personal, family, and love quarrels, most frequently they served wealthy persons who wished to terrorize poor peasants and workers. In response to this class warfare, specialized groups arose to kill labor and peasant leaders. Other criminal bands targeted human rights activists and political opponents of the regime. And during the presidential campaign of 2006, highly effective urban gangs made possible the president's resounding triumph in the election when they coerced many residents in the Caribbean region to vote for Uribe and thus eliminated the need for a runoff election.[3]

Outwardly the Uribe administration claimed to be making efforts to destroy these new criminal bands, and the law-enforcement task fell mainly to the rural mounted police or *carabineros*. This police group claimed to have reduced the number of criminal bands from 30 to 22 and to have arrested nearly 900 members and killed 150. The new bands were small and lacked the vulnerable central structures of AUC (*Autodefensas Unidas de Colombia*) and other defunct national organizations. Consequently, the new criminal bands were very difficult to infiltrate and to destroy. And if their members engaged in drug trafficking or formed part of the local governing structure in the countryside, it was practically impossible to dismantle them. But because they no longer claimed to have any role in national politics, the media was able to dismiss them as common criminals.[4] Colombians since the 1940s have been accustomed to endemic levels of violence in the countryside and too easily accepted the explanation that the large paramilitary organizations had degenerated into new criminal groups.

The official propaganda line that the Uribe presidency had achieved a huge success with the demobilization of the paramilitaries became harder to sustain and gradually faded from the political discourse. But because the demobilization was not really exposed as the fraud that it had been, the failure to end a non-existent security threat did not necessarily have to damage the reputation of the government. Uribe had been elected not to end the paramilitary threat but to destroy the insurgency. If he could eliminate guerrillas from Colombia, a grateful country should certainly reward him with a third term. In 2006 his argument that he needed a second presidential term to finish the task of eradicating the guerrillas had resonated with the public, and voters easily believed his claims that the destruction of the Revolutionary Armed Forces of Colombia (*Fuerzas Armadas Revolucionarias de Colombia*) or FARC was imminent.

Under his presidency Colombia had launched the largest and most continuous military offensive in its history against FARC. However as his first term gave way to the second, increasingly the Colombian army was replicating the experience of the U.S. army in the Vietnam War (1964–1973). The Colombian army, just as its role model, was winning every battle but seemed to be incapable of destroying the enemy. A perspective going beyond the battlefield is necessary to try to explain this apparently contradictory situation.[5] The Colombian army expanded to reach the largest size in its history, and

Southern Colombia

troops for the first time possessed not just adequate but also modern equipment and weapons. In particular, the new mobile brigades, well supported by air bombardment, proved instrumental in putting FARC on the defensive and keeping the guerrillas off-balance.

The wealth tax on the rich and modest U.S. financial and technical support had made possible the initial advances of the military, but perhaps because of the fascination with new shiny equipment and high-tech gear, the belief spread that a purely military solution to the insurgency was possible. In an insurgency, battlefield successes by themselves could not provide complete victory. In 2002 the Uribe administration took the strategic decision to favor the army over the police for expansion, and already by 2005 the consequences of this policy were starting to appear.

It was not that the military expansion had been too large but that the police expansion had been too small. Consequently, after army units cleared an area of guerrillas, a political vacuum ensued once the soldiers left to push deeper into the jungle. It was only a matter of time before the wily guerrillas returned and rebuilt their networks in the supposedly safe zones. U.S. officials were the first to detect this flaw in the offensive, and in response the U.S. government created the Police Reestablishment Program to assist the government in placing strong police forces in the areas cleared of guerrillas. But as U.S. funding for this program declined, the extent of the police presence diminished, and the detachments, rather than aggressively patrolling the countryside to detect any signs of a guerrilla return, ended up huddling inside barracks preparing to repel the next attack.[6]

Part of the problem was public perception, because citizens trusted the soldiers more than the police officers. Because of occasional corruption and other defects, try as hard as the police might, the institution could never inspire the same confidence as the army did among the population. This lack of trust was doubly unfortunate, because in Latin America the national police of Colombia ranks among the best and is a far cry from the proverbially inefficient and inherently corrupt Mexican police. But for Colombia an easy alternative was available, either in vastly enlarging the military police or in creating a gendarmerie-style body directly under the army. In what may appear confusing, although the national police was under the administrative control of the Ministry of Defense, institutionally it has remained a separate force not inside the chain of command of the army.

A great opportunity to create a new military police agency came when the army introduced its "Hometown Soldier" program for the new garrisons in former guerrilla areas. As locals, the assigned soldiers knew the residents in that town and were very effective in detecting any signs of guerrilla activity. But after a year or two the soldiers left either because their terms of enlistment were up or their units had been reassigned elsewhere, so the Hometown soldier program only had a short-term effect. Instead had these Hometown soldiers been recruited to serve in the same location as military police or gendarmes, their continued presence would have prevented guerrillas from returning.[7]

The recruitment of former soldiers into a growing police force also had an additional preventive effect. Guerrillas, the government, paramilitaries, and the successor criminal bands essentially had been recruiting from the same pool of unemployed young males in slums and poor rural areas. By providing jobs, first in the army and then long-term employment in police forces, the government was sending out the powerful message that opportunities for gainful employment and occasionally even for advancement existed inside the system. By draining the pool of recruits, the government could reduce the ranks of FARC more effectively than any military campaign trying to inflict casualties in the seemingly inexhaustible numbers of guerrillas.

A necessary complement to offering jobs in the army and the police to the unemployed was Civic Action or having the military provide economic and social services directly to the population in areas most influenced by the guerrillas. Under U.S. pressure, Colombia had adopted Civic Action in the 1960s, but by the initial years of the twenty-first century this tradition had practically disappeared. Once again it was American officials who pointed out this missing element, and the U.S. government agreed to support Civic Action in five localities. Although subsequently increased to seven areas, the small number was still woefully insufficient. The military needed to implement Civic Action in at least 100 conflict zones if the program was going to make any meaningful contribution to reducing the insurgency.[8]

Soldiers building schools, clinics, roads, and bridges showed residents the benefits of supporting the system, and the impact was even greater when the army hired some of the many unemployed inhabitants to work with the soldiers or under the direction of officers to carry out many public works projects in these otherwise abandoned communities. Civic Action was not just construction but also included providing health care and meals to locals, and also improving water, sewer, and electricity services. But Civic Action never took root during the Uribe administration and fierce bureaucratic fighting between the military, civilian agencies, and the office of the presidency plagued the few programs. Nothing even remotely comparable to what Hugo Chávez had done by sending out the army in his Plan Bolivar 2000 to help residents in poor rural areas and city slums ever occurred in Colombia. The absence of a comparable program of Civic Action was one major reason why the offensive against FARC ultimately failed to deliver major results.

In effect, FARC was a self-sustaining insurgency because it fed off the massive economic injustices rampant in Colombia; replacements were ready to fill any combat casualties. The Uribe administration repeatedly stated its preference for military expenditures over social programs. In its struggle with the insurgency, Colombia had reached the point of diminishing returns with the use of military force. Rather than fielding additional mobile brigades, the country needed to put more resources into land distribution and economic benefits for the rural population.[9] Without any improvement in the economic opportunities for its citizens and in particular for the rural population, the country could never find peace. The channel for expressing the violence did not really matter; whether crime waves, drug cartels, guerrillas, paramilitaries or criminal bands, the country seemed trapped in a destructive path and with no peaceful end in sight. The solution that Colombia adopted in the 1990s, privatization and the spread of free market principles, only made the situation worse. Starting with the presidency of César Gaviria (1990–1994) Colombia broke its traditional approach of turning to the state for solutions and instead entrusted the welfare of the country to market forces. The capitalist euphoria over the internal collapse of the Soviet Union fueled this mistaken conclusion, and Colombia eagerly plunged into privatization, much as was happening at the same time under Alberto Fujimori in Peru.

In Colombia the privatization proved less intense and was more gradual than in Peru, so that the already impoverished population had more time to absorb the harsh blows from the unleashed market forces. The upper class and corporations both foreign and domestic saw their incomes rise dramatically, as capitalism dutifully performed its inherent role of concentrating wealth in the top one percent of the population. Among the most dramatic examples was the unregulated banking sector, which earned record profits. Revenues from the Arauca petroleum fields cushioned the blow from privatization. Petroleum royalties became essential for the national budget government and also financed regional and municipal expenses. But the petroleum wealth never equaled that of neighboring Venezuela and could not soothe all of the many economic inequalities existing in the country. It is generally overlooked that the 1990s, the period of privatization and free market, coincided with the largest guerrilla offensive in the country's history; the situation was so desperate, that even U.S. officials began to fear a FARC victory during the Andrés Pastrana presidency.

The massive military offensive of 2002 to 2008 had put the guerrillas on the defensive but could not defeat a resilient FARC. It seemed hard to avoid the conclusion that without massive structural changes the endemic violence in Colombia could never end, even if by any chance the guerrillas agreed to demobilize. The example of El Salvador, whose guerrilla insurgency only gave way to a rampage of gang activities in that country, served as an eloquent warning. Yet the Uribe presidency remained adamant on pursuing a purely military solution to the insurgency in Colombia. He counted on voters giving him a third term to continue his military approach, but the appearance of three scandals seriously complicated the plans for another reelection.

Three Scandals

In October and November 2008 three scandals erupted nearly simultaneously, and the onset of the Great Recession in that year considerably diminished the gains from the previous economic expansion.

The economic growth at first sight seemed impressive, with an average annual expansion of 5 percent since 2003 and a record high of 7.5 percent in 2007. Despite this substantial growth, social protests steadily increased during the Uribe years for the simple reason that capitalism was performing its traditional function of concentrating income in the wealthiest sector of the population. The government did not pursue any redistributive policies and on the contrary Uribe usually pandered to the whims of the business class. The government insisted on completing the privatization of the remaining state assets. In spite of massive opposition, Uribe took a major step when he forced the state oil company Ecopetrol to sell a majority stake in the Cartagena refinery to the Swiss firm Glencore in 2006.[10]

The Uribe administration also wanted to complete the privatization of the Colombian banking sector. The underlying assumptions were that private ownership and deregulation were essential to bring prosperity to the country. Until the 1990s a large part of the Colombian banking sector had been state-owned. The service might not always have been as fast or efficient as in the private banks, but at least the majority of the population had access to financial services. But the privatization drive of the 1990s left the Agrarian Bank (*Caja Agraria*) as one of the few financial institutions that remained under state ownership. Its branches were usually located in the most remote rural regions of Colombia, and as a money-losing agency that subsidized poor farmers, private speculators were not eager to acquire the Agrarian Bank. Instead, the privatized banks located overwhelmingly in urban areas reaped record profits by serving only wealthy clients. Private management in the former state institutions used restrictions and high fees to purge the banks of poor and lower-middle class clients who had no other place to deposit their money or to carry out even the simplest of monetary transactions.[11]

In a glaring example of savage capitalism, the banks in the southwestern cities of Popayán, Pasto, Mocoa, Neiva, and to a lesser degree in Cali, were particularly aggressive in purging poor and lower middle class clients from their rosters. Shady speculators, in particular David Murcia Guzmán, soon realized that a great opportunity to make huge profits existed, and in the unregulated environment he opened bright offices pretending to be the equivalent of Savings and Loans Associations in the United States. Soon branches sprouted over southwestern Colombia and even in neighboring Ecuador. These establishments were in reality pyramid schemes, whereby the deposits of new clients financed high interest payments for earlier clients. The lack of requirements to open accounts attracted to these chains those persons shut out of the private banks. Constant publicity lured in many unsuspecting depositors who believed that this was a legitimate banking institution.[12]

The temptation for money-laundering was irresistible, and these new chains also served as conduits for transferring drug funds. Sudden infusions of cash from drug lords gave an unexpectedly long life to these institutions. But as with all pyramid schemes, the day of reckoning inevitably comes. On 17 November 2008 government officials raided and sealed the offices of the pyramid schemes; eventually David Murcia Guzmán was extradited to the United States and his associates ended up serving sentences either in Colombian or U.S. prisons.[13]

The political fallout from this first scandal was tremendous. On 17 November, the very day that authorities shut down the pyramid schemes, depositors began protests and marches against the government. The propaganda of the pyramid schemes had been so effective and seductive, that initially the depositors were angry at the government for having deprived them of the chance to earn high interest rates. When at last depositors realized that the whole scheme had been a gigantic fraud, they blamed authorities for having allowed these illegal activities to take place without any supervision or regulation. The same as happened in the United States prior to the Great Recession, the insistent pressure of the business and financial sectors had persuaded Colombia to eliminate nearly all regulation on the assumption that without controls the free market would miraculously bring great prosperity to the country.

The over half a million families ruined by the pyramid schemes demanded that the government refund their deposits. Riots broke out in southwestern Colombia in Neiva, Pasto, and Popayán; in the last city rioters broke into an office of Murcia Guzmán and frantically carried off every piece of movable property. The clashes in Mocoa turned out be particularly destructive, with 100 cars burned and many residents injured; the toll in southwestern Colombia included at least two deaths and many wounded. The violence threatened to spiral out of control, and as a precautionary move, in late November 2008 Ecopetrol halted pumping crude through its pipeline running through the turbulent areas. The state oil company resumed oil exports through that zone only in the first week of January 2009 when the situation had returned to a relative calm.[14]

The governors of the affected regions requested that the national government cover all the losses of the depositors, but Uribe was not willing to go so far. Because he realized that this scandal could make more difficult his drive to secure a third term in office, he promised to compensate depositors for their losses amounting to nearly half a billion dollars. Not surprisingly, as typically happens with Latin American politicians, his promises were empty words to calm a momentary political storm. After the sale of the few assets of the pyramid schemes, the depositors were lucky to recover ten cents on the dollar.[15] In a measure directed at preventing another crisis, the Uribe administration required banks to receive poor and lower-middle class persons as clients. Private institutions had learned nothing from the crisis and were outraged at this regulation; in particular "the mandatory removal of bank service charges represented a worrying precedent of Government of Colombia intervention into the free market."[16]

As the U.S. Embassy observed, "the scandal and protests could not have come at a worse time for Uribe"[17] who was struggling to get congressional approval as the first step to secure a third presidential term. The revelation that the two sons of Uribe had contacts with the pyramid scheme hurt the president's prestige, but even more damaging was confirmation that those same firms had been vigorously collecting signatures to obtain approval for a third term. This family and political involvement with the firms of the pyramid schemes was very threatening, and to contain the damage, Uribe had to modify his policies.[18]

Privatization was the real cause of the pyramid scheme, and as a first response, the government quietly abandoned plans for selling off any additional state assets. Incredible as it may seem, the government was still actively pursuing plans to privatize the Agrarian Bank, the only institution that had saved the agricultural sector from falling into the Great Recession. All agriculturalists had always bitterly opposed the privatization of the Agrarian Bank, and Uribe, not wishing to antagonize this influential sector while he was politically vulnerable, dropped the plans to sell off this indispensable institution of the Colombian countryside. The government kept this decision as quiet as possible, because any announcement risked scaring investors; privatization remained the litmus test for the many free market advocates in Colombia and Wall Street.[19]

Another case of failed privatization, the Cartagena refinery on the Caribbean coast, was too large and visible to keep out of the public view, and consequently the fallback position of the government was to resolve the matter as rapidly as possible. The story went back to 2006 when free market zealots had convinced the Uribe administration to sell a 51 percent stake in the Cartagena refinery of Ecopetrol to the Swiss firm of Glencore as the only way to expand the capacity of the installation. This sale provoked massive opposition from the region, the petroleum union, and the management of the state firm, but in spite of the political costs, Uribe preferred to follow the advice of the capitalists zealots who passionately argued that privatization no matter how rushed or badly handled was always better than the most efficient state firm. The forced sale to Glencore faced the additional objection that the coal-mining firm lacked any experience in the petroleum industry.[20]

Almost from the day it took over operations of the Cartagena refinery, Glencore ran into difficulties and fell behind on its contractual obligation to increase the capacity from the existing 80,000 barrels per day to 140,000. The corporation was really acting as an intermediary between foreign investors who had hoped to reap huge windfall gains from the privatization of the refinery. But when the Great Recession struck, financing for Glencore dried up and the company risked bankruptcy if it did not quickly end its participation in the Cartagena venture. Upon hearing the news, Ecopetrol jumped at the opportunity to regain its refinery. The state firm was earning record revenue for its petroleum exports because the actions of OPEC and Venezuela had raised world prices. With abundant cash reserves, the Colombian company on 3 March 2009 repurchased the 51 percent share in the Cartagena refinery and actually made a nice profit on the transaction by paying $109 million less than the sale price in 2006. Ecopetrol later secured adequate financing abroad and successfully completed the expansion in refining capacity.[21]

The behavior of Glencore had been so outrageous and irresponsible, that nobody questioned the nationalization of the Cartagena refinery. Even the U.S. Embassy normally hostile to any state enterprises accepted the solution as the best way for the Uribe administration to dispose speedily of a problem potentially damaging to the political prestige of the government. Indeed, Uribe could tap just a little into nationalistic feeling by restoring Colombian control over this installation vital to the economic life of the country.

From a broader perspective, the reacquisition of the Cartagena refinery closed the cycle of privatizations in Colombia begun in the 1990s. Although the nationalization lacked the drama and violence of the Arequipazo of 2002 in Peru, the Cartagena refinery had been the approximate equivalent of the aborted attempt to privatize the electric utility company in Arequipa.

The Uribe administration ably overcame the fiasco of the failed Cartagena privatization and handled the matter in a way that did not put into doubt its free-market credentials. Less effective had been its coping with the pyramid schemes, but at least the government had gradually tamped down the discontent and restored order to the most affected regions. The damage from the pyramid schemes cost the Uribe administration the loss of some political support but not enough to derail its plans for a third term. However, the nearly simultaneous appearance of a second political scandal permanently undermined his efforts to secure a third presidential term.

On 21 October 2008 the weekly newsmagazine *Semana* revealed that the FBI-like national security agency (*Departamento Administrative de Seguridad*) or DAS had without court authorization carried out surveillance of political opponents of the Uribe administration. Besides extensive reporting based on interviews, *Semana* also offered as proof two secret DAS documents. The same day that the magazine article appeared, DAS director María del Pilar Hurtado fired the author of one of the documents, hoping that this would quiet the scandal. But public outrage over the political eavesdropping did not diminish, and she had no choice but to resign herself the next day. Her departure and vigorous denials from the government quieted the uproar, and when most of the media rallied around Uribe, the story seemed to have died down.[22]

Actually, the government had only gained a breathing space while the media kept busy reporting on the pyramid schemes, a separate scandal that broke out on 17 November 2008. As officials scrambled to perform damage control on the pyramid scandal, they naively assumed that the controversy over domestic spying had been put to rest. In reality, the October revelations had not stopped illegal surveillance, and the agency continued to spy on independent journalists, human rights activists, political opponents, and even Supreme Court justices. Orders from the presidency made spying on the Supreme Court a high priority, and secret agents, unable to find any disreputable or shady actions, compiled lists of "likely lovers" of the justices to watch for possible blackmail threats in the future. Equally bad, DAS officials routinely sold classified information to drug lords and sometimes even to guerrilla groups. A culture of corruption prevailed in the agency, and because the Uribe administration failed to carry out a thorough house-cleaning and reorganization, conscientious whistleblowers were left with no other alternative than to leak materials to the independent press.[23]

The Uribe administration had no intention of dismantling the spy network because it had come to depend on political intelligence to stay one step ahead of the opposition. For government officials, the revelations of 21 October had been just a blip. A similar bump in the road had occurred in 2005; after a brief flurry over similar revelations the story died down and DAS resumed its political surveillance. At least since 2004 the agency had been conducting illegal domestic spying on a large scale; the recording of telephone conversations and interception of e-mail messages had become routine activities for DAS. But the agency did not merely collect information, it also engaged in a wide range of activities to destroy political opponents, union leaders, journalists, and human rights advocates. Sabotage, death threats, and blackmail were some of the methods

DAS used, and as a matter of fact the purpose of the surveillance had often been to gather information useful for shattering the lives of targeted individuals.[24] Official domestic spying for the purpose of taking action was in sharp contrast with the Petro Audios scandal in Peru where a private firm intercepted communications for the benefit of its clients.

On 21 February 2009 news magazine *Semana* revived the scandal by making new revelations about the very extensive spying operations of DAS. The article not only quoted many documents about specific cases of political surveillance but also confirmed that the agency had continued to spy without any interruption even after the October 2008 revelations. The charges were too serious to ignore, and in another attempt at trying to bury the controversy, the government announced on 26 February 2009 that it was transferring all intelligence gathering functions to the Colombian National Police, which also operated its own intercept programs under legal safeguards. But the record of the national police was far from unblemished because it too had engaged occasionally in illegal spying. And the oversight role of the national police was questionable, because the DAS teams would remain in place at their usual location and only report on paper to the commanders of the national police. The change was turning out to be nothing more than moving around boxes in an organization chart.[25]

The response was inadequate to calm the outrage over this continued political spying, especially when the media revealed that DAS had targeted for surveillance over 600 individuals. The public has traditionally loved spy stories, and news outlets such as *Semana* continued to feed the insatiable appetite for new revelations. The scandal became even more irresistible when listeners could hear on radio and television the leaked recordings of illegal intercepted telephone conversations. The voyeuristic appeal of listening to these recordings captivated audiences, while the print media kept the public well-supplied with a steady stream of revelations.[26]

The spy scandal had become a major problem for the Uribe administration, but it still could not bring itself to take the drastic step of abolishing DAS. Minister of Defense Juan Manuel Santos had already expressed publicly his view that the agency was a "sick patient" and he suggested that a "Christian burial" was probably the best solution.[27] When on 31 August 2009 *Semana* again reported that DAS was still carrying out illegal political surveillance, the Uribe administration pledged to dismantle the agency, but in reality the announcement was just another publicity trick to deflect the accusations. The political intelligence was so useful in the struggle to secure the third term for the president, that officials concluded that the benefits from the wiretaps far outweighed the bad publicity from the scandal. But for the U.S. Embassy the risks were too high. The United States had provided considerable training, assistance, and funds to the rogue agency, and eight American institutions worked closely with DAS. To avoid getting sucked into the scandal, American officials had begun as early as February 2009 to end their cooperation with the Colombian spy agency. The desire to cut all ties with DAS acquired additional urgency when a conversation between a U.S. embassy official and a Supreme Court justice was leaked to the media in September.[28]

In spite of the complications with the U.S. government, the Uribe administration still felt that it could contain the political damage long enough to push the third term proposal through congress. The risky political calculation was plausible, and had not a third scandal permanently undermined the credibility of the government, Uribe was still on track to secure authorization to run for a third term.

At least since the 1980s the Colombian army utilized the deceptive practice of counting civilian deaths as guerrilla casualties as a way to disguise "collateral damage" or the accidental killing of innocent peasants. The next step came in the last decade of the twentieth century when some officers had civilians killed and then counted them as guerrilla casualties. Because these executions were not widespread at that time, it remains unclear whether the Samper and Pastrana administrations knew about or tolerated this practice.[29]

By the time *Plan Patriota* (2002–2006) went into effect, the illegal practice had become widespread. Driving these crimes against humanity was the number-crunching that the Colombian army had learned from its U.S. counterpart. To show success in the counterinsurgency, officers had to report a high number of guerrillas killed in combat. These figures then fed into the promotion process, and officers assimilated the lesson that any advancement in rank required showing a large number of dead guerrillas. Because *Plan Patriota* in its initial years seemed to be yielding concrete victories such as the reoccupation of municipalities, the need to report many guerrilla casualties was not very pressing. But as the offensive bogged down in the Amazon jungle, officials desperate to show government successes incessantly reported large numbers of dead guerrillas.[30]

An indication of the shift toward numbers rather than victory was the Secret Directive of 17 November 2005 by which the Defense Ministry offered generous rewards for information about guerrillas, their equipment, and their weapons. Because this Secret Directive nicely complemented the existing network of informants President Uribe had created after his inauguration, it was inevitable that civilian and military personnel would cooperate to track down guerrillas in exchange for monetary rewards.[31]

The best known of the many criminal networks that proliferated under official encouragement during the Uribe presidency operated in Soacha, a suburb of Bogotá. Originally a separate town of 200,000 inhabitants in 1990, the arrival of displaced persons fleeing mainly the violence of the paramilitaries had increased its population to nearly half a million residents by 2008. The urban sprawl of the capital had by then linked up with Soacha and the town became a suburb or perhaps more accurately another slum of Bogotá. As a way station for people fleeing from the countryside or escaping the high cost of living in the capital, Soacha came to have a large floating population of drifters, homeless persons, and criminal elements. With the highest unemployment rate in Colombia, the town became a dumping ground for the flotsam of society. And because the majority of the population consisted of young males who constantly walked the streets in a desperate search for any type of employment, the presence of so many people roaming around sparked fear in the local authorities and in the minority of wealthy residents.[32]

To rid the streets of supposedly dangerous youngsters, social cleansing took root in Soacha perhaps more than in other communities. The killing of undesirables, social misfits, and drug addicts has a long history in Colombia, and these crimes had been a favorite activity of the paramilitaries. Social cleansing intensified under the Uribe administration particularly thanks to its paid network of informants. However, the disadvantage in Soacha and elsewhere was that the murderers received little or no recompense and bore all the risk should they be caught. Perhaps inevitably, it was only a matter of time before supply (the individuals targeted for elimination) caught up with the demand of the army for dead guerrillas. The criminal elements were the first to make the connection, because they realized that preying on poor people was not very lucrative and that the only valuable possession the poor youngsters possessed was their bodies.[33]

Criminal networks appeared in Soacha and elsewhere, and their primary task was to find candidates suitable to be labeled as guerrillas. During the initial years of the Uribe presidency the task was easy, because petty criminals, drug addicts, and homeless individuals were readily available in adequate numbers. Once the criminals had selected their candidates, dangling the bait of a job in another part of Colombia usually sufficed to lure the unsuspecting victims. The criminals then accompanied the youngsters in the trip supposedly to meet their new employers and then a day or two later handed over the unsuspecting victims to soldiers usually at what seemed to be a routine army checkpoint in the road. The transfer marked the end of the involvement of civilians who collected reward money of around $100 for each supposed guerrilla.[34]

The soldiers promptly asked the victims to hand over any identity documents in order to draw up their employment contracts. In the case of the Soacha 16, they were then taken to a site near Ocaña close to the border with Venezuela and promptly executed. The soldiers removed any clothing or any other signs that might identify the dead bodies and dressed the cadavers in guerrilla fatigues. The staging (*montaje*) of the crime scene had to be convincing, because officers always demanded photographs and sometimes might even come to inspect the "combat site." The soldiers placed in the hands of the dead guerrillas worn out and almost useless armament, usually a cheap rusted pistol or old hunting shotguns. And as final proof of the "combat" the soldiers scattered many empty cartridges from their automatic weapons. The best photographs went up the chain of command to impress superiors, while the numbers going into computer programs boosted the body counts of dead guerrillas and provided the supposedly irrefutable proof that FARC was on the way to defeat and extinction. Just like the officers, the rank and file were under great pressure to produce bodies of dead guerrillas. And the soldiers also knew that they were rewarded with days off and other material benefits for their hideous deeds.[35]

This practice of staging fake guerrilla deaths came to be known as the "False Positives" scandal. Because FARC continued to be active and vigorous, analysts and journalists remained baffled by the large number of reported guerrilla casualties. Some observers claimed that the high number of casualties was forcing FARC to recruit ill-trained youngsters into its ranks; other analysts assigned to FARC nearly miraculous powers to regenerate itself. Officials stuck resolutely to the official explanation that the guerrillas were doomed to extinction and that only more time, specifically a third term for Uribe, was needed to complete the mopping-up operations.[36] Truly Uribe was reaching the presidency by climbing upon the dead bodies of innocent victims.

The criminal farce could not be sustained indefinitely because of a weak link. Although the False Positives dovetailed perfectly with social cleansing, authorities had vastly exaggerated the number of misfits, undesirables and outcasts, even assuming that these marginal groups had really existed. Vicious violent acts such as those of the paramilitaries necessarily disrupted families and displaced many persons, but to call those individuals misfits is inaccurate when in reality they are internal refugees. A criminal element does exist, but ironically these were the ones who profited most from the False Positives, so that the goal of social cleansing was never achieved. Years before 2008 the criminals had exhausted the supply of drifters, drug addicts, and petty criminals in Soacha, just when the Uribe administration demanded more bodies of dead guerrillas.

The bands of recruiters from the start had taken the precaution of telling friends and relatives of the victims to forget about trying to find their loved ones, and these threats had worked or had proven unnecessary when the victims of the initial years had few if any acquaintances in Soacha. If the victims came from another part of the country, their relatives had a foggy notion of their whereabouts and at most knew that the youngsters had gone to Bogotá looking for employment. But by 2008 the recruiters in Soacha turned to luring typical youngsters who like almost all Colombians, had extensive family ties and usually were also well-known in their neighborhoods. The system of threats, and even occasionally murdering a relative simply could not keep quiet all the family members. Investigators confirmed that beginning in 2 January 2008 and continuing until 22 August of that year, recruiters lured away nine of the 16 youngsters aged from 16 to 32 with promises of jobs elsewhere; the exact ploy used for the rest remains unclear. The Soacha 16 all had mothers, most had brothers or sisters, and some were married; all were well-known in their neighborhoods. Another common thread running through the operation was that in spite of the efforts of the recruiters to keep the candidates isolated from the community, the victims managed to send a message to their families that they were leaving to accept a job; sometimes the youngster spoke to a friend on the street and in another case he make a quick call from a public telephone.[37]

When they failed to return, the relatives reported them missing, only to be met with icy indifference from the local authorities who refused to believe the accusations. Fortunately for the families of victims, so many persons had disappeared throughout the country that volunteers decided to organize a national missing persons' bureau. When this volunteer organization reported that the bodies of the Soacha 16 were probably those in a mass grave near Ocaña, one of the mothers traveled to that site. Upon arrival, government officials told her that her son Fair Leonardo Porras Bernal was the leader of a "narco-guerrilla" unit and that he had died in combat with a pistol in his right hand. The preposterous accusation was even more absurd when it was realized that the victim Leonardo, besides suffering from mental disability that would disqualify him to lead any guerrilla unit, was also paralyzed from birth in his right hand and thus unable to fire a pistol.[38]

In August 2008 right after the murder of the last of the Soacha 16, the government announced that this fearsome guerrilla band had been smashed near Ocaña. When photographs of the dead bodies became public, reporters asked questions about the young age of the individuals, and officers replied with the standard propaganda line that FARC was in such dire strait that it was forcing children into its ranks. The official story seemed to be holding, and President Uribe publicly ridiculed the youngsters when he said that they had not been there just to help gather the harvest in this coffee region.[39]

The disgraceful comments by the president could not prevent the cover story from unraveling, and on 29 September the government bowed to public pressure and appointed the first of several commissions to investigate the matter. Suspicion was emerging that this certainly had been a massacre, but the public took several weeks to recognize the deaths of the Soacha students as the first formal discovery of the False Positives. When an internal army investigation reported on 27 October to Defense Minister Santos and to President Uribe that this was not an isolated case but an endemic problem, the government knew that it had to respond forcefully to pacify the public anger. Since the start of the Uribe administration the media had glorified the army as the sacred instrument trying to rid the country of the scourge of insurgency, and yet here in September 2008 the army was systematically carrying out massacres that in a few years dwarfing anything that the guerrillas had ever done over decades. The formal term of "extrajudicial killings" of human rights organizations did not quite capture the cynicism and the barbarity of the False Positives.[40]

A first response came on 29 October 2009 when in a public announcement Uribe separated 27 officers from the army, including three generals, four colonels, and seven lieutenant colonels. Officers of this high rank had never before been dismissed in such a public manner by any Colombian government. It was clear that many officers had been involved in the crimes, but when Defense Minister Santos pushed for more firings, army commander Mario Montoya Uribe vigorously opposed the purge, and he too was dismissed. The friendly media celebrated the dramatic purge as the final step to bring the shameful episode to a close, but even normally pro-government newspapers such as *El Tiempo* asked for more drastic measures to root out the problem. The follow-up measures were not forthcoming, and not surprisingly the dismissal of the officers took a long time to execute. Actually those officers left the institution in the most favorable terms and did not face criminal charges. The most glaring example of justice denied was the dismissed army commander Montoya who received as a consolation prize the appointment as ambassador to the Dominican Republic.[41]

The scandal of the False Positives can be examined from several perspectives. The most disturbing was the confirmation that even after the public became aware of the scandals, the inhuman practice of killing civilians and dressing them up as guerrillas continued although in a more discreet manner. Against this backdrop of a pattern of illegal practices, the efforts to bring the perpetrators of these crimes against humanity have largely failed. The attention to just 16 deaths might seem exaggerated, but in reality these had not been the first crimes of this nature and were just the first ones to receive public attention in a media that normally blocked out any stories hostile to the government. As soon as the story of the Soacha 16 reached the public, the denunciations of similar cases drastically increased as relatives at last found the explanation for the disappearance of their loved ones. The number of confirmed False Positives has surpassed 5,000 and one estimate argues for 10,000 as a low figure. As the human toll mounted, human rights groups concluded that such a cold and calculating massacre of civilians for profit has no counterpart elsewhere in the world. The failure to obtain justice for the victims should not obscure the political impact of the False Positives, and this second perspective did have consequences for Colombia.[42]

The greatest effect of the False Positives was not to increase the awareness of the humanitarian crisis but to shatter the claims of military victory over FARC. The False Positives provided the real explanation for the high figures of guerrilla deaths and refuted the myth that an agonizing FARC was on the verge of collapse. With the army bogged down in the Amazon jungle, the failure of Uribe to deliver on his campaign promises to destroy the guerrillas could no longer be denied. Uribe had won his two presidential campaigns on the assumption that he was the only person who could deliver victory, but the False Positives proved that not only was he a liar but also a criminal. His actions placed Colombia among the countries with the worst human rights records on the planet, while the revenue from his taxes had gone not to defeat guerrillas but to fuel a well-organized machine for killing innocent civilians.

The False Positives also intensified the DAS scandal over political spying. That investigative agency had not only spied on political opponents but had also carried out actions against individuals perceived as hostile to the government. Most disturbing had been the political surveillance of justices, including those of the Supreme Court; the only difference that the threats and other reprisals against targeted figures had so far spared the justices. And the False Positives showed that once officials decided that lives could be sacrificed for private profit and political gains, it was only one more small step forward to start murdering influential officials on the grounds that they were guerrilla sympathizers. The triple blows of False Positives, DAS spying, and pyramid schemes sent the Uribe administration reeling and enormously complicated its efforts to obtain approval for a third presidential term.

The Third Term and the Presidential Election of 2010

The three scandals of the previous section should have sufficed to persuade Álvaro Uribe Vélez to abandon his bid for a third term, but his uncontrollable ambition and a sense of being the indispensable man in Colombia's history overcame any lingering notions about the public wellbeing. The three scandals resonated most with the Bogotá elite and confirmed the worst fears about him. Uribe had not been the first president to come from another region of Colombia but he had been the first in memory to jump from a governorship to the presidency. Previously natives of other regions had spent years if not decades gaining acceptance into the Bogotá elite, but Uribe Vélez had skipped that stage. Given the extraordinary circumstances of the security threat facing Colombia, this preferential treatment seemed justified. But once in office, he saw the presidential palace only as a hotel for week days because invariably he spent weekends and longer holidays travelling across the country. He thus avoided contact with the Bogotá elite during the weekend, and during the weekdays he never made time to attend the events that comprise the frantic pace in the social life of the capital.[43]

President Uribe knew that the intense work habits and tribal cohesion of natives of Antioquia like himself provoked considerable resentment if not envy among many Colombians. He rarely returned to his ranch so as not to make so blatant his regional origins, but in government the favoritism towards Antioquia was not so easily disguised. Again he took the precaution of appointing national figures and leaders from most regions of the country to his cabinet and other high-level positions. But in his palace team and at the sub-cabinet rank, persons from Antioquia predominated, in effect shutting out the Bogotá elite from the real corridors of power. At another level, the lack of opportunities to mingle with the Bogotá elite meant the absence of informal contacts to determine the prevailing moods and attitudes. Seeing Bogotá almost as a conquered territory populated with potentially hostile natives, the presidency became very keen in using the domestic surveillance of the spy agency DAS to find out what key leaders were thinking, as the previous section showed. But spying could never replace personal bonds, and increasingly the Bogotá elite felt ignored and excluded.[44]

Uribe believed that his unconditional support for the business leaders had won their support, and this strategy bore fruits when he secured his reelection in 2006. Although business leaders were an extremely influential component of the Bogotá elite, their enthusiasm for Uribe could not always guarantee adequate political support. The realization of the need for additional allies persuaded Uribe early in his first term to drop his demands for structural political reforms and instead to seek an accommodation with the traditional political leaders who controlled the congress. By operating as a traditional politician, the president learned how to obtain votes from the legislative body if he was willing to bargain away benefits and privileges. But the congress was largely an assembly of ambassadors from the provinces, who like Uribe himself also left the capital every weekend and normally stayed at hotels during weekdays before returning to their home districts. In spite of his apparent success in dealing with the political class of the country, he never had gained the acceptance of the Bogotá elite.

It is tempting to dissect the Bogotá elite to identify each of its constituent parts, but such an exercise is fundamentally flawed. The Bogotá elite is much more than the sum of its component and evolving groups: shared beliefs and accepted practices have been just as important as any numerical quantity or income characteristics. And even the traditional affiliation with the Liberal and Conservative parties was not an invariable requirement. Acting upon these shared assumptions, the scandals unfolding starting in 2008 persuaded the Bogotá elite that it was time to end the reign of Uribe and to bring to office one of its foremost representatives.

An essential feature of the Bogotá elite has been the existence of "presidential families" or dynasties. Expressed in the simplest terms, the political system of Colombia has come to depend on certain families to provide most of its presidents since the late nineteenth century. This phenomenon seems to be unique in Latin America and has certainly not happened in the large and best studied countries of the region. The closest example had been in Peru, but it is too early to tell whether Alán García or the Fujimori family will be able to return that country to a system similar to Colombia's. Membership in one of those exclusive families has not been a requisite for election as president, because the Bogotá elite has wisely left open several paths to the highest political position in the country. And of those new individuals who are elected president, some were successful in moving their families into this exclusive category, but for other presidents their families failed to enter the exclusive club or simply dropped out of politics altogether.

Once anointed as a presidential family, the descendants have the inside track to reenter politics. These presidential families are above and separate from the political class but as members of the Bogotá elite whenever they want they can rejoin the political class and automatically rise to leadership positions. A similar class of "senatorial" or cabinet families has existed to provide key officials for the legislative and executive branches, but once again, membership in these families has not been a requisite to hold those positions. Going down the hierarchy of the political class, the numbers of newcomers and outsiders dramatically increases, but always with the understanding that if a member of either senatorial or presidential families aspires to a political office, they enjoy preference over any newcomer.

Prior occupation of the presidency has not been an indispensable requirement to gain the status of a presidential family. The best example has been the Samper family, which qualified for that office since the middle of the nineteenth century, but only with Ernesto Samper Pizano finally occupied the presidency in 1986. His relatives and descendants remain presidential and could return to high office in the twentieth-first century. Perhaps the best known of these families have been the López, the Lleras, and the Pastrana families, each one providing two presidents for Colombia; their descendants could well aspire to provide a third president. But in 2010 it was the Santos family that was ready to occupy the presidency a second time.

Juan Manuel Santos had never hidden his life goal of becoming president of Colombia. As a very famous leader of the Liberal Party, in 2005 he was the ideal person to bring many Liberals into the new electoral vehicle of Uribe, the Social Party of National Unity or U Party as it was quickly named. As one of the most prestigious members of the Bogotá elite, he served as the ideal bridge between the provincial Uribe and the capital. Although

Uribe had the popular votes to win reelection in 2006, it is almost certain that without the active lobbying by Santos among former Liberal party members, the referendum proposal authorizing Uribe to run for a second term would not have been approved in time for the election. And the support of Santos made possible an Uribe victory by a huge margin in 2006 and without the need for a runoff.[45]

Uribe had appointed Santos to be defense minister partly as a reward for the latter's efforts but also to guarantee the success of the military offensive against the guerrillas. Uribe knew that ultimately the military victories of *Plan Patriota* had made possible his first reelection. By putting Santos in charge of the offensive, Uribe gained insurance: if the defeat of FARC was complete, Uribe could run for a third term, while if the military offensive failed, then both he and his defense minister were equally discredited and lost any chance to win the presidency. A marriage of convenience emerged between both men, but they could not forge a deep bond, because the social distance between the provincial rancher and the cosmopolitan urbanite was too wide to ever breach.[46] Santos was a man of his word, and in a country where political betrayals are routine, he never turned against Uribe.

Just as Santos had never hid his desire to be president, so Uribe even after his second inauguration did not keep secret his ambition to have a third term. And until early 2008, Uribe had every chance of achieving his goal. His approval ratings in April 2008 had reached the record-high figure of 84 percent. In March his followers easily gathered 260,000 signatures, almost twice as many as the 140,000 required to create an organizing committee for the amendment. This committee then launched a drive to collect signatures for a referendum to approve a constitutional amendment authorizing his third term. For this second drive, the committee needed to collect 1.4 million signatures, the equivalent of 5 percent of registered voters, before the congress could consider the matter. Uribe was so confident of winning approval for a third term that he engaged in the luxury of publicly clashing with the top courts in Colombia. Sparring between the president and the Supreme Court left a bitter taste, and it was obvious that Uribe resented having independent courts limiting his authority.[47]

These latest clashes with the judiciary finished poisoning relations with the judges, and the animosity came back next year to haunt Uribe. But it was not until the three scandals broke out in October 2008 that the campaign for the third term encountered serious resistance. Starting in early 2009, his approval ratings began to decline, and the first open indication that the third term campaign was in trouble came from the congress. In order to hold the referendum on amending the constitution, both houses had to approve the bill in four separate sessions. Because the time before the elections of May 2010 was insufficient to hold four regular sessions, Uribe convoked an extraordinary session on 16 November 2008 to obtain the second of the four approvals. This direct intervention speeded up the process and made obvious that the president, in spite of his denials, was keenly interested in a third term.[48]

Because Uribe continued to state in public that he had not made up his mind about a third term, cynics dismissed his statements as political theater while his loyalists emphasized the agonizing dilemma he was facing. All agreed that he did not have a political heir to continue his work once he left office, a typical situation with very authoritarian leaders who deliberately prevent the emergence of any possible political rivals. Precisely this independent streak ruled out Santos, who was not considered reliable and much less an insider of the presidential palace.[49] Uribe repeated the official line that he wanted the people to decide whether he should have a third term, and obviously it was very flattering for the ego of any politician to have the people consider him the indispensable ruler. Because he pressured legislators and bargained to obtain their votes, he justified his personal interventions as necessary to let the people's voice be heard, but in the process he revealed his own ambition. So why did he refuse to declare his candidacy? The explanation was rather simple and consisted in the difference between wanting something and being able to obtain it. He knew that he had made history by repealing the century-long prohibition on reelection, but as a gambler hesitant to roll the dice a second time, he was afraid of overreaching and ending his presidency in a shameful defeat.

The disastrous end to the Alberto Fujimori presidency in Peru in 2000 was a cautionary warning, but Uribe failed to heed the lessons of history. Selfishly he felt that if he could obtain the third term, he should take it. However, the real fear was that time was running out for the referendum. In the remote chance that the president could not run again, Uribe told Santos to go ahead and resign as minister of defense because cabinet ministers wanting to run for president had to leave office by May 2009. Santos became the head of the U Party and he would become its candidate for president in case that Uribe did not qualify to run again. But, both privately and publicly, Santos stated that under no circumstances would he run against Uribe should the referendum process authorize him to seek a third term.[50]

The matter was still in the hands of the congress because it had not yet given the fourth and final approval to the referendum proposal. Originally it had seemed that passage was a sure thing, but as the scandals eroded the popularity of the Uribe presidency, congressional support waned and the process dragged out. The smarter politicians had begun to rally around Santos as the more promising possibility for the future, but too many of the provincial politicians did not want to realize that the age of Uribe was nearing its end. After intense bargaining and the personal intervention of Uribe, final approval came when on 2 September 2009 the lower house passed by one vote the proposal for a referendum on the third term.[51]

Because polls showed that a majority of voters would approve the third term, the opposition began a campaign to urge people not to vote in the referendum. This was a repeat of the successful strategy that defeated the referendum of 2003 when the number of citizens who voted fell below the constitutional requirement of one-fourth of registered voters.[52] But before the proposal could appear on the ballot, the Constitutional Court had to give its approval. Originally the struggle of the executive branch had been mainly with the Supreme Court that did not have jurisdiction over the referendum, but the DAS spying had also led to clashes with the Constitutional Court which was the final authority on this issue.

Because Uribe had already appointed three loyalists to the Constitutional Court, the prevailing opinion was that it probably would approve the referendum. Yet even this body could not blatantly ignore the evidence presented and would be hard pressed to disregard a key decision by the National Electoral Council. This independent body ruled on 12 November that the signature drive was invalid because of illegal financing. The committee collecting the signatures could not explain the origin of most of its funds, and the sum had exceeded more than twice the legal limits. The public already knew that some of these funds had come from the pyramid scheme, so that this tainted money gave the whole campaign for the third term a foul smell.[53]

A rude awakening came in the first week of February 2010. Whether accidentally or intentionally done to prepare the public for its final decision, the 2 February draft by one of the judges of the Constitutional Court was leaked to the media. Several press outlets were quoting paragraphs and sentences, and this widespread diffusion suggested that the judges were trying to prepare public opinion by leaking this text arguing strongly against the referendum. Central to the argument was the decision of the National Electoral Council declaring the signature drive to be invalid. The leaked text practically shattered Uribe's dreams for a third term and left him no alternative but to summon Santos on 4 February 2010 for a meeting to state that the head of the U party had to prepare himself to become a presidential candidate.[54]

Santos dutifully declared to the public that he still supported the reelection of Uribe and refused to announce his candidacy as long as the Constitutional Court did not declare the referendum process invalid. But he had used his time wisely as president of the U party to gain the trust of many politicians. As mentioned earlier, the smart politicians had long since gravitated to his side, but younger and less experienced politicians were still under the spell of Uribe. A major reason for the difficulties with the third term campaign had been the refusal of Santos to lobby activity on Uribe's behalf as had been the case in the 2005–2006 reelection effort. And as head of the U party Santos was well positioned to shift the campaign away from Uribe and to himself.[55]

The Uribe presidency refused to die and desperately struggled to survive. In frantic and desperate last-minute attempts, the president's loyalists tried to pressure the judges of the Constitutional Court. Officials communicated with the judges and used every possible argument to try to persuade them to approve the referendum. Another indication that these judges were hostile came when it was learned that no alternative draft was circulating; without a text supporting the referendum, the judges would simply vote up and down; if they voted no, the process then dragged out until the judges came up with another draft approving the referendum. The danger of prolonging the agony must have weighed in the minds of the judges, who announced that the court would hand down a decision on 26 February 2010. As the deadline approached, speculation was rife in the country about the verdict; in a resemblance to guessing scores in a sports event, television and radio outlets amused the public with predictions about the tally of votes.[56]

Finally at 5:00 p.m. on 26 February the judges killed the referendum proposal by a margin of 7 to 2; only two of the three judges appointed by Uribe voted for approval. The Constitutional Court correctly argued that "the referendum accumulated a series of grotesque procedural flaws that severely compromised its nature as a popular initiative."[57] The central objection was the illegal use of money to finance the campaign for the third term; the organizers had exceeded by six times the spending cap and contributors had given sums more than 30 times larger than the legal amount. As mentioned earlier, even the pyramid schemes had generously contributed to the campaign for the third term. The referendum had turned out to be a classic test for democratic regimes between the popular will and the power of money; in an unlikely exception to the rule, wealth failed to carry the day.[58]

Without the approval of the referendum, Uribe could not run for a third term. The path was wide open for Santos to become the candidate of the U party. He already was the preferred choice for seasoned politicians and now the rest of the party members flocked to his side, including those who had been most reluctant to abandon Uribe. The nomination of Santos was inevitable, but for the election of 30 May he faced a crowded field of five major candidates. Analysts correctly predicted that a runoff election was inevitable, but some pollsters also believed that the eccentric former mayor of Bogotá, Antanas Mockus, might even be the top vote getter in the election.[59]

On 30 May as expected, Santos failed to win the required 50 percent of the votes, but his 46.5 percent more than doubled the 21.5 percent of his vaunted rival Mockus who came in second place. Pollsters quickly adjusted their estimates and now confidently predicted that Santos would be the winner in the 20 June runoff. However, many still expected Mockus to rise to a respectable second place and to garner at least 40 percent of the popular vote. Santos largely precluded this threat when he obtained the endorsement of two of the other presidential candidates including the third place winner; it was up to Mockus to counter this move by seeking an alliance with the main leftist movement, which could deliver as much as 20 percent of the popular vote. But a series of blunders during the Mockus campaign torpedoed his chances of forging an alliance with the left. Apparently many citizens in both elections had flirted with voting for Mockus, but increasingly voters of the left and the right saw him as too unpredictable and abandoned any thought of supporting his candidacy. Confirmation that Muckus was not prepared to be president came when in a silly mistake, he announced that Colombia should follow the example of Costa Rica in abolishing its army, a proposal that amounted to surrendering the country to the guerrillas.[60]

Mockus quickly reversed himself, but it was too late to save his campaign that more than anything else had provided comic entertainment to keep voters interested in the political process. Not surprisingly, on 20 June 2010 Santos received 69.1 percent of the vote and left his rival badly trailing with barely 27.5 percent. Although Santos had not been able to win in the first round, he now more than compensated by receiving the highest percentage of votes any president had received in the history of the country. Clearly the Colombian people had given Santos an overwhelming mandate to continue the policies of his predecessor. In a noble gesture characteristic of the Bogotá elite, Santos during the victory celebrations announced that his victory was also a recognition to his predecessor Uribe. In his inaugural speech on 7 August 2010, Santos expanded on his appreciation of the work done by the outgoing president and thus openly reaffirmed the continuity in policies to the people.[61] It remained to be seen whether Uribe, who had never accepted the rejection of his third term, would exit gracefully from the political stage as past presidents had done and would let Santos govern Colombia.

Chapter 16

Peru: The Nationalist Reaction

Declaring himself a nationalist, not a leftist, Humala said that he represents the pragmatic change that Peru needs.—U.S. Ambassador P. Michael McKinley[1]

The Presidential Campaign of 2011

No sooner had the presidential election of 2006 ended than the campaign for 2011 began in Peru. Ollanta Humala could not believe that he had finished in second place in the runoff election in June 2006, when he had won by a clear majority in April. Carefully he scrutinized and analyzed the voting results for each district to try to understand the reasons for his upset defeat. The numbers showed that he had lost the coastal regions and every voting district in Lima. Because the majority of Peru's population was located in the coastal region, no candidate could hope to win a national election without making significant gains among these voters.[2]

Gradually the defeated candidate identified three main reasons for his electoral loss and then he prepared to correct each one. The first had been his failure to stay away from Hugo Chávez. Alán García with little effort had been able to create in the minds of many coastal Peruvians the image that Humala was a puppet of the Venezuelan ruler. To correct this perception, Humala frequently emphasized that Peru had nothing to learn from the vastly different Venezuelan experience. Above all, he avoided any contact with Chávez and never again repeated the disastrous Caracas trip of January 2006.[3]

Fortunately for Humala, the Venezuelan president willingly cooperated and learned to keep quiet about Peruvian politics. But the opposition had no intention of letting pass such an easy way to smear Humala as an extremist leftist as had happened before in the election of 2006. Thus eliminating Chávez did not suffice to remove the label of radical leftist from the Peruvian candidate. Identifying this second cause of the electoral failure was easy, but finding a solution was not so simple.

The structural reality was that without the votes of leftist groups, Humala could not run a good campaign or even hope to win the presidential election. If he moved to the right, then he lost the votes of the left that he needed to make it into the runoff election. If he moved to the right, well-established candidates with impeccable pro-business and pro–U.S. credentials already crowded the field and inevitably placed him in the fringe of the more than 20 marginal candidates vying for the presidency in the first round of the elections in April 2011. The electoral mathematics was going to be very close, so he first had to tilt to the left for the first round and then move firmly to the right for the runoff. Could he carry out this delicate and shifting balancing act? For the first round he followed a two-track strategy. He kept his personal statements relatively moderate even though he went on the campaign trail accompanied by well-known leftist personalities. At the same time, he had his Nationalist Party issue a campaign platform containing many of the traditional socialist formulas. By not sounding personally too extremist, he hoped to reassure voters on the coast while with the more radical written statements he intended to keep satisfied voters in the highlands.[4]

The third reason for the electoral defeat of Humala in 2006 had been his failure to realize that any candidate to be successful needed the approval of the U.S. Embassy. This third reason was related to his links with Chávez and the left. The U.S. government did not necessarily decide the outcome of the election but simply required that the winner had to come from a slate of pro-American candidates. In 2006 Humala had failed to make the case that he was not hostile to the United States, and consequently the Embassy did not want to run risks with him and on the contrary undermined his campaign. But in spite of the hostility, the U.S. Embassy continued to struggle to understand Humala and remained baffled about his true views. Almost as poker players with a likely winning hand, American diplomats did not wish to take risks but were afraid to miss a great opportunity. Embassy doors remained open to Humala, and between 2006 and 2011 a steady stream of surrogates reassured American diplomats about his beliefs. Soon the candidate himself joined the ranks of office seekers throughout the Caribbean and Central America who go personally to secure the approval of U.S. embassies. Humala sensed the ambivalence of American diplomats about him, and as a final move, during his visits in 2009 he repeatedly stated his intention to visit Washington to talk to high officials. Gradually the U.S. Embassy concluded that he qualified to join the growing list of acceptable candidates vying for the position of president of Peru.[5]

The second most important individual in the presidential election of 2011 was not even on the ballot. Outgoing President Alán García was ineligible to run for reelection, but he had already set his sights on the then still distant presidential election of 2016. Wisely he had not tried to authorize his reelection by amending the constitution as President Álvaro Uribe Vélez had done in Colombia. The only threat to García's ambitions was relatively simple: as long as he remained the head of the APRA as ex-president, he could guarantee his nomination for the 2016 election. Instead, should another APRA insider become president in 2011, the nomination of García would be at risk. Not surprisingly, the different attempts to nominate an APRA candidate in 2011 foundered, and without a viable candidate promising a direct continuity with the outgoing García presidency, the field was left wide open for another candidate of the right to fill the gap.

Among the first to sense the opening was former president Alejandro Toledo who promptly launched his candidacy for reelection. He clearly had name recognition, but was remembered mostly for the failures and scandals of his administration. His entry into the field had the effect of splintering the vote on the right among several other candidates, including Keiko Fujimori, the daughter of deposed and imprisoned dictator Alberto Fujimori. The Fujimoristas had been quietly building a support base over the years, had already gained a substantial delegation to congress, and in 2011 decided to make an attempt to win the presidency.

As the 10 April election approached, Humala was the clear front runner but still unable to gain over 50 percent of the vote in the first round. Sensing that he was going to have to pivot to the right in order to win the runoff, he abandoned the long leftist platform of his Nationalist Party even before the election. The shift was not hard to do, because officially he was not running under the label of his Nationalist Party. Technical difficulties had forced him in 2006 to run under the cover of a mini-party. This anomaly actually turned out to give the candidate considerable flexibility in his 2006 campaign, and he decided to repeat the tactic in 2011 by running as the candidate of an electoral vehicle destined to die after the campaign.[6]

The first round of elections on 10 April 2011 yielded some surprising results. Keiko Fujimori had made the best impression on right-wing voters and emerged in second place with 23.5% of the votes. As expected, Humala came in clear first place with 31.7 percent of the votes. The most startling result was the poor showing of Alejandro Toledo; his disappointing fourth place finish with only 15.6 percent of the vote seemed to have ended his political career. That the legacy of dictator Fujimori was more popular than democratic Toledo spoke volumes about the future of popular regimes in Peru.[7]

The challenge for both Humala and Keiko was to attract the center without alienating too many voters of the left and the right. Keiko hoped to repeat the maneuver of Alán García who had catapulted from second place to winner in the 2006 election. But she was facing a more experienced and wiser Humala who was not going to be shut out of the presidential palace again. The conventional wisdom was that neither candidate could win with just their bases on the left and the right, but Humala was having a hard time retaining his support from the left while the right effortlessly gravitated to Keiko. Clearly fear of the left was a more vital concern to private business than the risk of returning to an authoritarian regime.

The U.S. Embassy remained largely neutral in this election and simply enjoyed watching with curiosity to see which one of the two acceptable candidates won the runoff. So unlike in 2006 when the U.S. Embassy had undermined Humala, this time around American diplomats stayed neutral. But because he realized that Peru's elite was still running scared about his supposed desire to redistribute wealth, he needed to find some way to ease the fears. After extensive negotiations, Humala was able to secure the backing of Toledo. If the presidency of Toledo had not been so discredited, this in itself should have been more than adequate to win the election. But even if all the citizens who voted for Toledo in the first round moved over to Humala, the latter still fell short of the majority needed to win the runoff.[8]

The most powerful ally of Keiko was the media, led by the print and television conglomerate of *El Comercio*. This once respected newspaper became a public relations machine for Keiko; its director, an open supporter of her candidacy, used the media outlets to hurl every conceivable attack against Humala. The virulent hostility of news media in Peru paralleled that of their counterparts in Nicaragua and Venezuela as its owners spared no effort to denigrate leftist candidates in the most extreme way possible. The power of the media was so strong, that the campaign of *El Comercio* should have been successful if Keiko did not have to carry the baggage of her authoritarian father.[9]

Nobel laureate Mario Vargas Llosa came at the precise moment to turn the tide in the last week of May 2011. He was a well-known critic of socialism who however had an even greater fear of dictatorship. Although residing mainly in Europe, with his visits and in particular through his syndicated column appearing weekly in *El Comercio*, he remained in contact with the Peruvian public. In a very effective publicity stunt, Vargas Llosa stopped writing his column in protest at the newspaper's transformation into a propaganda vehicle for the Keiko campaign. He made the announcement with great flair, and the media sensation filled television broadcasts for many days.[10]

The intervention of Vargas Llosa came just at the right moment, because until then most polls said that the election was too close call, and some even reported Keiko pulling ahead with a lead of 1 to 2 percent. On 5 June 2011, early results gave Humala a slightly wider lead than in the final tabulations where he dropped to 51.4 percent of the vote, compared to 48.6 percent for Keiko. A margin of less than one and a half percent had decided the winner in this election.[11]

The analysis of the voting results yields many insights, some with great implications for the future. The right and pro-business groups have so captured the imagination of the Peruvian public, that in the foreseeable future any candidate who does not espouse free market views stands almost no chance of becoming president of Peru. Humala just barely squeaked by: as in 2006, he again lost Lima and his need to retain leftist voters had almost cost him the election. The ease with which right-wing voters accepted Keiko confirmed that they feared socialism more than a return to dictatorship.[12] So entrenched have become the pro-capitalist views among many sectors of the population, that the situation remains ripe for an ambitious pro-business ruler to gain power and possibly even to establish another regime in the style of Fujimori-Montesinos.

Equally fascinating has been the ability of the small minority benefitting from the free market to captivate a majority of Peruvians. At most 20 percent of the population and more likely less than 10 percent have been direct beneficiaries of the income from the export-led growth of the Peruvian economy. But this small percentage of the population has persuaded the inhabitants of the coast and in particular those in Lima to support free market policies. This was notably the case in the 2006 elections, and the maneuver to sway voters almost succeeded another time in 2011.

Admittedly the prospects for the left gaining power in Peru are bleak and dim for the foreseeable future. But a fundamental structural flaw of capitalism always leaves open a door to starting a socialist transition. In savage capitalism, economic activity inevitably concentrates wealth in the hands of the top 10 percent of the population and particularly in the top 1 percent. The growing income inequality provides the opportunity to carry out peaceful or violent transformations, and possibly even the extreme case of a real revolution. In Western countries many redistributive mechanisms channel income back to other social classes in this way constantly postponing the day of reckoning. But in underdeveloped countries such as Peru, the growing concentration of wealth advances relentlessly, and the privileged minority uses all the means at its disposal to preserve its status. Not only does defending free market policies become a prerequisite for national politicians wishing to win election, but to govern a country the support of the business sectors remains indispensable, as Ollanta Humala found out even before his formal inauguration.

Ollanta Humala: Defining the Presidency

The day after the elections of 5 June the stock market in Lima lost 12 percent of its value and the exchange rate for the Peruvian currency had the single largest one day drop since 2009. The Peruvian economy seemed to be in a free fall as panicky investors pulled their capital out of the country. To try to stem the losses, president-elect Ollanta Humala made a public profession of his strong belief in the free market and promised to encourage private investments. But the business community was not satisfied and insisted on knowing immediately the names of his principal economic officials. Correctly he explained to the public that never before had a president-elect been pressured to name his close collaborators just two days after the elections, and mistakenly he assumed that the best way to let this turmoil calm down was to go on a South American trip to meet with his counterparts. On 9 June he departed Lima for a trip beginning in Brazil and taking him to Paraguay, Uruguay, and Argentina, with a final stop in Chile.[13]

Quite deliberately Venezuela did not appear in his itinerary to avoid inflaming the fears of Peruvian business groups. Because the pressure from the private sector did not let up, he felt it necessary to declare that he was not planning to carry out nationalizations as his idol General Juan Velasco had done in 1968–1975. The APRA congressional delegation very diplomatically announced that it was eager to work with Humala in passing bills to help private investors and in general to strengthen the free market; implicit in the offer was the warning that if he tried to do anything against the powerful economic groups, he could expect furious opposition from APRA.[14]

The APRA offer had been in reality a shot over the bow, and because Humala did not accept the offer immediately, the pressure on the president-elect increased. APRA, the mouthpiece of its leader, ex-president Alán García, introduced a bill to prevent relatives by blood or by marriage of an outgoing president from running for the office. This bill was aimed at keeping Nadine Herrera, the popular and very efficient wife of Humala, from trying to succeed her husband; the bill also aimed to prevent the less likely candidacy of his controversial brother Antauro. An implicit message in the bill was the subtle threat that if the opposition could prevent Humala from running relatives as successors, so it could prevent him from finishing his presidential term.[15]

Upon his return from the South American trip, the president-elect found unbearable the pressure to announce his appointments for economic positions. And he discovered that his every appointment was going to be closely scrutinized and possibly also opposed. The first fight arose over the head of Peru's Central Bank. Humala's preferred choice was not an extremist but a former head of the Central Bank, a candidate that should have been acceptable. But the private sector was enchanted with Julio Velarde, the outgoing director, and wanted him reappointed. This was a major decision, because unlike cabinet ministers who served at the pleasure of the president, the head of the Central Bank served for five years and could not be replaced until his term was over. The appointment of the head of the Central Bank became a tug of war with the business community and only ended when Velarde was ratified for another five-year term. Humala tried to appoint two leftist-leaning economists to the Board of Directors of the Central Bank, but the business did not grant him even this consolation prize, and the president-elect had to back down after suffering these serious defeats.[16]

The most important economic appointment was finance minister, and Humala originally had in his short list two university professors with Ph.Ds from U.S. universities. In response to strong pressure from business groups, the position went to Luis Miguel Castilla, who almost from his first day in office supported free market policies even more extreme than those of the outgoing García administration. Castilla was actually closer to Humala's wife Nadine, who wielded almost as much influence in the government as her husband. Humala felt that by giving the choicest positions to defenders of the free market, the business community would let him govern. He did not realize that appeasing the right is impossible, and that the more a ruler grants the more the right demands.[17]

After giving up so much to the right, Humala knew that he had to placate the left so that he could present to the public a cabinet representing the major political currents in Peru. His choice for prime minister was a close collaborator, the well-known leftist Salomón Lerner. But as a wealthy and successful businessman, his leftist views were very mild, and Humala all along counted on him to craft alliances with the right. The high visibility of the office of prime minister, supposedly a surrogate for the president, seemed to be an open affirmation of the campaign promise to help the majority of Peruvians left behind in poverty during the economic expansion. But in reality, the prime minister was left hanging virtually in air; he had only token support from Humala while very conservative representatives controlled the real levers of economic power in the Ministry of Finance and the Central Bank. It would take incredible feats of magic for Lerner to pull off this balancing act. And for Humala, any opportunity of doing even minimal transformations in the Peruvian economy simply vanished even before he had taken office.[18]

After completing his other cabinet appointments to the relative satisfaction of the principal political groups, Humala prepared for his inauguration on 28 July 2011. He had raised great expectations among many Peruvians who hoped to receive support from the new government. How to find a way to reconcile the aspirations of millions of Peruvians with the demands of wealthy groups became the most challenging task of the incoming Humala administration.

The Ongoing Struggle Over the Conga Mining Project

During the presidential campaign, "Ollanta Humala promised to walk the finest line in Peruvian politics: maintaining the flow of mining and gas investment while placating the social movements that oppose such industries."[19] A poll showed that 78 percent of the population of Cajamarca opposed any expansion of gold mining, and consequently when Newmont Corporation announced in July 2011 that it was starting a massive gold mining project at Conga 24 kilometers to the north of its existing installations at Yanacocha, a bitter clash became inevitable.[20] As will be recalled from a previous chapter, Denver-based Newmont had been involved in frequent conflicts over its open-pit mining at Yanacocha. Because of the contamination of water supplies, opposition had coalesced under the leadership of Catholic priest Marco Arana. In spite of repeated attempts to try to shut down the entire mine, the local inhabitants most grudgingly accepted the gold extraction in exchange for promises to safeguard the water supply and additional money for community projects in Cajamarca.

The Cajamarca region contained at least five major mining projects in different stages of development. Inhabitants had never accepted the reality of having mining companies extract huge profits while leaving behind environmental disasters in the impoverished region. And when Newmont announced in July 2011 the start of the Conga project, the resentment of most residents turned to outrage because the mining project threatened to contaminate many more rivers reaching as far as the basin of the Marañón River. Conga called for an investment of nearly five billion dollars and the project would be three to four times larger than Yanacocha. Conga was also the test case for future foreign investment in the mining sector, and gullible officials enthusiastically claimed that Peru could receive as much as 50 billion dollars from these supposedly fabulous projects. The Peruvian media wholeheartedly supported Conga mine and carefully distributed only favorable news. In the tradition of the by then infamous "Dog in the Manger Syndrome" articles of former president Alán García, the press did everything possible to denigrate and ridicule the opponents of the project.[21]

In contrast to the highly influential *El Comercio* conglomerate and other Peruvian news organizations, the foreign media was not always sympathetic to Conga. But Newmont had more to worry about than occasional hostile articles appearing abroad. Leadership of the opposition had passed from the priest Arana to respected local leaders. Cajamarca was the home of the officially recognized night watches (*Rondas campesinas*), armed groups that since 1976 had been patrolling the region to provide basic security services. The night watches had participated in earlier demonstrations including the Bagua mobilization of 2009; in 2011 under their leader Idelso Hernández they were well organized and ready to oppose Newmont. And in an unforeseen consequence of decentralization, the elected regional governor of Cajamarca, Gregorio Santos, emerged as the leader of the opposition. The situation was much more complex than in the 2006 protests (chapter 12), because with legally constituted and elected officials leading the opposition, neither the government nor Newmont could claim to be facing lawless mobs.[22]

A town mayor began the struggle when he led peasants to block temporarily the road from Cajamarca to Bambamarca on 14 October 2011. Governor Santos called a one-day work stoppage in Cajamarca on 9 November, and occasional incidents clashes occurred until 24 November when regional governor Santos called for the first indefinite strike, which was promptly heeded by peasants and then gradually spread to the city. Demonstrators shouted the slogan "Yes to Water, No to Gold," and soon had brought all activities in Cajamarca to a halt, including businesses, public transport, and schools. The response from Lima was confused, because the Humala administration was going through the first of several identity crises. In a first indication of future direction, leftist presidential advisor Carlos Tapia and the vice-minister of Mines and Energy, the two officials who sympathized the most with the protest, lost their positions. Sensing that the Humala administration was not yet in any condition to crush the protest, Newmont decided to gain time to prepare a counter blow. In a temporary tactical withdrawal, the American company announced on 29 November the suspension of the start of the Conga mining project. The decision defused the confrontation and arrived barely just in time, because on 30 November the government flew in over 500 soldiers in Antonov cargo planes to reinforce the local garrison, and the added army presence raised fears of repression and bloodshed. The general strike had already left 18 injured among protesters and police.[23]

The company announcement persuaded the opposition to end the general strike that had lasted for six days. Calm returned to the city, but regional governor Santos and other opposition leaders emphasized that the real goal of the protest was to cancel the Conga project completely. Santos went so far as to have the regional government issue an ordinance prohibiting the company from using any additional land for the extraction of gold, but as expected, the ordinance soon faced many constitutional challenges about having usurped the authority of the central government.[24]

Prime Minister Salomón Lerner, the most prominent leftist in the cabinet, had gone to negotiate some compromise between the company and the opposition, but because no immediate solution appeared, the president declared a 60-day state of emergency on 4 December. With these extraordinary powers, the police gained the authority to suspend all constitutional guarantees. An outraged prime minister tried to reverse this path toward confrontation, but only achieved his dismissal on 11 December 2011. The remaining leftist cabinet ministers soon after departed, and their exit confirmed the turn to the right of the Humala administration. As additional indication of the conservative shift, the president appointed Óscar Valdés, a retired army officer who had been a professor of Humala at the military academy, to be the new prime minister. Although the trend toward more pro-business policies was unmistakable, some observers mistakenly interpreted the appointment of Valdés as the militarization of a presidency eager to adopt harsh repression against protesters in Cajamarca. As a first indication of the new hard line against the Conga protesters, the government tried to file criminal charges against regional governor Santos.[25]

Although the dispute over the Conga mine seemed to be over, the outbreak of future clashes became inevitable when the new Prime Minister Valdés promised to maintain the pro-mining policies of the previous García presidency. Cajamarca realized that it needed national support to make the gains permanent, and the leaders organized a protest march to Lima. This National March for Water lasted from 1 to 10 February and generated sympathy for Cajamarca across the country. Inhabitants of other regions shared the stories of their struggles against similar mining projects, and a Lima increasingly sympathetic to environmental movements welcomed the marchers; almost imperceptibly, public opinion was shifting to the side of Cajamarca in spite of the constant barrage of propaganda from the mainstream media outlets.[26]

The increased public awareness still could not budge the Humala administration. Several mobilizations kept the issue before the public, and on 31 May Cajamarca announced a second indefinite strike. In spite of these concrete actions, the government believed that the dispute had died down and foolishly announced on 23 June 2012 the resumption of operations in Conga. Not surprisingly, bloody confrontations injured many and killed five during 3–5 July, and the area remained paralyzed. Belatedly Humala realized that he was repeating the same mistake of García in the Bagua dispute and that he had to back down before the situation became worse. When Prime Minister Valdés failed to reach an agreement with regional governor Santos, Humala changed his cabinet again to give it a more centrist orientation. The new prime minister, Juan Jiménez, announced a two-year suspension in the Conga mine project, and it seemed that this long cooling-off period might allow both sides to reach a compromise.[27]

How the government's position of "gold and water" could be reconciled with the opposition's slogan of "either gold or water" remained unclear. In reality both the government and Newmont were doing everything possible to undermine the opposition to the Conga mining project. As before, the private news organizations and in particular the media conglomerate of *El Comercio* carried out a relentless media campaign to portray the opponents of Conga as primitives and tried to reduce to the minimum the reporting on the real concerns about the quality of water in Cajamarca.[28] In spite of the constant media barrage against the opponents of Conga mine, the adverse publicity had no effect on Cajamarca and was even backfiring in Peru with polls reporting that 74 percent of the public supported the demonstrators.[29]

The government turned to repression as a supposedly more effective instrument to control the unrest, and the police continued its traditional practice of persecuting the political opponents of whatever government happened to be in power. If anything, the practice of criminalizing dissent became more widespread and the police arbitrarily detained a large number of protesters. Already over 300 persons faced criminal charges for participating in the Conga clashes, but this intimidation was not sufficient to silence the leaders. Local inhabitants knew all too well the harsh police response with arrests and beatings, but the degree of extensive surveillance did not become public knowledge until hackers broke into official databases. Among the targets of police surveillance had been regional governor Santos and chief of the night watches Hernández. Undercover agents also infiltrated the meetings of night watches to report any plans to disrupt the operations of Newmont and also to collect incriminating evidence to file criminal charges. Because the flimsy evidence could not support prosecution, detectives dug into the past of many of these leftist leaders with the hope of trying to link them with Shining Path, the Maoist organization universally despised in Peru. Guilt by association would be a powerful tool to smear the leaders, but the detectives came up empty handed in their wild goose chase.[30]

In the meantime Newmont had been busy applying pressure to try to divide the opposition. Late in 2013 the company met with carefully selected members of 32 areas to secure their support and also to make an attempt to undermine the leadership of Governor Santos and the heads of the night watches. It soon became clear that these individuals did not represent their communities and were social outcasts because they had sold lands to the company.[31] Newmont had caused deep divisions inside communities as "families who sell land to the company do so at the risk of retribution and personal harm,"[32] but the company failed to stop a new wave of demonstrations from erupting in January 2014. Newmont had no choice but to postpone again the start of Conga mine beyond 2014, and the reelection by large margins of governor Santos and other regional officials left no doubt that the majority of the population was determined to stop this foreign company from expanding its operations in Cajamarca.[33]

Chapter 17

Transitions in Venezuela and Colombia

For virtue is more persecuted by the wicked than loved by the good.—Miguel de Cervantes Saavedra[1]

Unexpected changes in the rulers of these two countries began transitions at first imperceptible in their political systems. In Venezuela no one doubted that things could not be the same without the charismatic presence of Hugo Chávez. In Colombia the departure of Álvaro Uribe Vélez allowed the government for the first time to embark on new policy initiatives.

The Agony of the Hugo Chávez Presidency

The Enabling Law of December 2010 giving the president authority to legislate at will had been a masterful political stroke on the part of Hugo Chávez, who during 18 months could issue new decree laws to radicalize his Bolivarian Revolution. Unexpectedly these extraordinary powers proved unnecessary, because Chávez had little opportunity to legislate and he was unable to complete his project to transform Venezuela.

Observers had missed early hints of what was coming, and their oversight was understandable because Chávez himself ignored the warning signs. On 30 May 2009 he did not show up for the last two days of a four-day television marathon commemorating the tenth anniversary of his *Aló Presidente* show; he also broke his promise to attend the presidential inauguration of the leftist Mauricio Funes in El Salvador. His absence triggered widespread speculation about his health or about other possible explanations for his behavior. When he reappeared on 2 June, Chávez sensed a propaganda opportunity to attack the CIA by claiming that he had been hiding to escape an assassination attempt. A more credible explanation was that he had suffered a bout of the intestinal disorders so common in tropical Venezuela.[2] Even his absence once again confirmed his commanding presence: "interestingly, even when the usually loquacious Venezuela president disappears from public view, he still dominates the local news."[3]

Cynics dismissed the episode as a slick publicity ploy to stay in the public view, when in reality the absence disguised a real health problem. Like many Latin Americans of his and previous generations, he distrusted doctors and did not follow their advice to undergo routine medical checkups. A more poignant exclamation came in April 2010 when in the closing speech at the convention of his Unified Socialist Party of Venezuela

(*Partido Socialista Unificado de Venezuela*) or PSUV, after saying that the Bolivarian Revolution was taking a life of its own, he somewhat cryptically told his followers "that I am still needed."[4] Outwardly he was trying to persuade party faithful who needed no convincing, but inwardly he was trying to make a case with God to give him more time on earth to complete his work.

By spring 2011 he felt weak and tired, and occasionally he needed a crutch to walk around; but both he and officials blamed temporary ailments. A clear reminder of mortality came in March 2011, when Lina Ron, the colorful female motorcyclist and leader of a Chavista political party suddenly died of heart attack at age 53. With long blond hair streaming from under her helmet, she and her motorcycle gangs (*colectivos*) had been a fixture at many rallies, and Chávez gave a very emotional speech at her funeral. But it was mentor Fidel Castro who at last overcame the resistance of Chávez to taking a thorough physical examination. During a trip to Cuba, the Castro brothers prevailed upon the Venezuelan president to undergo treatment, and on the last day of June 2011 in a broadcast from Havana, he told the Venezuelan public about the presence of cancerous cells in his body and that surgeons had extirpated a pelvic cancer.[5]

The possibility of losing their leader plunged millions of Venezuelans into despair, and to reassure them, officials and Chávez claimed that with treatments such as chemotherapy, the president was expected to make a full recovery and return to his usual active lifestyle. A doctor of the Chávez family who knew some of the medical history broke with the party line and stated to the press that in his medical opinion the disease was terminal and that the treatments could only prolong the life of the president for a maximum of two years. This revelation caused an uproar, and in the rush to punish the messenger, the harassment became so dangerous that for his own safety the doctor moved to Spain.[6]

Almost as if making a deathbed confession, on August 2011 Chávez admitted that his lack of attention to details and weak follow-up had resulted in many failures in political, economic, and social matters. Many of his programs and ideas were very meritorious had they been properly implemented, but his preference had been to jump constantly to a new issue rather than stay solving a particular problem. In reality, his confession of errors was the opening shot of his campaign for the presidential reelection on 7 October 2012. He had struggled so hard to eliminate term limits that he was not going to let the opposition deprive him of reelection.[7]

The August 2011 confession laid out the theme that he had made mistakes but that the people needed to give him another chance to make things right. So as not to leave any doubts about his intentions, he stated that his only error about socialism was not having embarked on this path from the first years of his presidency. It was impossible not to realize that whatever the outcome of the October 2012 elections, the person driving the changes in the future could not be Chávez. There was still time to have the PSUV run another candidate, and an orderly transition with the inauguration of the new president in January 2013 offered the best chance to preserve the Bolivarian Revolution, which no less than Chávez, was fighting for its survival.

Following the example of the PSUV, the opposition held a single nationwide primary to pick the presidential candidate. On 12 February 2012 Henrique Capriles, with the support of rising star Leopoldo López, won the opposition primary and assumed the staggering task of trying to unseat the extremely popular Chávez. Capriles correctly chose to attack the government on crime, but his proposed solution of decentralizing police forces seemed hollow and unconvincing. As part of the crime issue, he denounced the deplorable conditions in the prisons, but Chávez countered with a humane proposal to have inmates serve out part of their prison terms in community work. Capriles tried to market himself as being center-left on the political specter so as not to reduce his appeal among a population increasingly absorbing socialist ideas, but the evidence mounted that his position was really to the right and that he was an unabashed supporter of the free market.[8]

When it became known that private investors were eagerly awaiting a Capriles presidency to reap huge profits as they had done in the best days of the Fourth Republic, whatever appeal the opposition candidate might have enjoyed among undecided voters rapidly evaporated.[9] His candidacy seemed to get a boost when the horrific explosion of the Amuay refinery at dawn on 25 August 2012 wounded over 150, killed 42, and ignited a ferocious fire that raged for three days until finally extinguished in the morning of 28 August. The opposition candidate recycled the old accusations of the petroleum strike of 2002–2003 that the destruction of the meritocracy at PDVSA had wrecked the company and produced this unnecessary disaster. The refinery resumed operations three days later, and once it was clear that the country had not suffered any interruptions in gasoline and fuel services, the public largely accepted the official explanation that the petroleum sector was in sound condition and that the Amuay explosion had been a freak accident.[10]

The voters were too mesmerized by the fate of their ruler to pay much attention to specific issues such as economic inefficiency and the crime wave; meanwhile the opposition candidate planted seeds of doubt in the minds of many Venezuelans. Capriles struggled to find some argument to counter the outpouring of public sympathy for Chávez, and any candidate would have been hard pressed to find anything capable of matching this groundswell of human emotions for the ailing president. The health relapses of Chávez and his return to Cuba for more treatment triggered even more sympathy for the leader. Not just the early polls but later surveys were giving Chávez a solid lead, yet a determined Capriles soldiered on, at some moment realizing that this campaign was a practice run for another presidential contest in the not too distant future.[11]

Chávez closed his campaign with in a massive public rally in Caracas on 4 October 2012. In the perhaps largest ever gathering in the history of the country, hundreds of thousands turned out under the rain to see their leader. The political significance in this last rally to get out the vote was obvious, but most participants sensed that this demonstration also was a final farewell to their president. The strategy of running Chávez and not another individual as candidate seemed to be working and certainly mobilized 8.1 million voters to go to the polls, the largest number that Chávez received. The victory margin on 7 October 2012 of 11 percent over the 44 percent of Capriles was an impressive achievement for a candidate so seriously ill.[12]

Another test of the strategy of keeping Chávez in office came in the upcoming regional elections of 16 December 2012. The prospects were good for the PSUV gubernatorial candidates, because Capriles had lost in 22 of the 24 states of Venezuela, and if the citizens who chose Chávez on 7 October could be persuaded to vote for his party on 16 December, the Bolivarian Revolution stood to solidify its continuity in the life of the country. Even more significantly, the regional elections helped to legitimize the succession that Chávez was preparing as he increasingly confronted the reality that his participation in the political life of Venezuela was rapidly approaching its end.[13]

Should anything incapacitate Chávez, the next in succession was Vice President

Elías Jaua, who as discussed in chapter 14 had been instrumental in wrecking agriculture and creating food shortages. His loyalty and orthodox Marxism had kept him in high government positions, but he clearly was not the person to engineer a smooth transition, as his post-election appeals to radicalize the Bolivarian Revolution confirmed. He also lacked an independent power base and could easily be manipulated by other stalwarts in the party, in particular the brusque and tough Diosdado Cabello. Just a few days after his electoral victory, Chávez announced that Jaua was leaving high national office to run for the governorship of Miranda against Capriles, who was trying to regain his old post after his resignation from the governorship as required to run for president. Although the PSUV and the government put all their resources behind this campaign, it was really a mission impossible for Jaua and was more a way to discredit his standing among high party circles.[14]

In that same announcement, Chávez appointed Nicolás Maduro as Jaua's successor in the vice presidency. Since the failed April 2002 coup Maduro had earned a reputation as a passionate supporter who was always ready to try to keep the Bolivarian Revolution moving on a steady keel. He had earned the president's trust as someone ready and able to solve some of the many self-inflected problems of the government and had always lurked as a possible successor. Insiders and close observers realized immediately that Maduro was the heir apparent, even though Chávez had not formally anointed him as the chosen successor. And, as an added sign of confidence, Chávez also kept him as foreign minister, a post Maduro had held since August 2006. None of these appointments could console the new vice president, who could not imagine a life without his mentor and leader. He had assumed that Chávez would be around for at least another decade and maybe two, and it was too much for Maduro to accept that his mentor was leaving this earth.[15]

In late November Chávez flew to Cuba for more treatments and then returned to support the PSUV candidates in the gubernatorial campaigns and also to announce his final intentions before the elections. On 8 December he made the long anticipated declaration that if he could no longer participate in politics, he urged his followers to vote for Maduro. By making this announcement Chávez gave the regional elections an added significance as a way to validate his choice of successor, and by not waiting any longer, he also hoped to give Maduro time to consolidate his position in the government and in the party. The reality was that as Chávez' health declined, so did his political influence, and in the ensuing vacuum Maduro had to move fast on his feet to prevent rivals from pushing him aside.[16]

The regional elections were a resounding triumph, and the PSUV swept almost all the governorships; the biggest exception was the defeat of Jaua who lost to the heavy favorite Capriles. The reasons for the victory, however, were not always well understood, and in particular the reliance of Chávez on retired military officers to run for governors revealed an emerging trend. The PSUV was going back to its military origins in the MVR (Movement for the Fifth Republic) and the preference of Venezuelans for military figures was too obvious to deny. Because Maduro had never been a military officer, this was not a good omen for his future presidency.[17]

Chávez could not savor his victory for long, and he was soon back in Cuba for a final treatment. In spite of claims of a miraculous recovery, the cancer had advanced relentlessly, and without any medical breakthroughs, his time allotted on earth dwindled irreversibly. As a major indication of the rapidly approaching end, he was unable to return in January 2013 for his inauguration, and perhaps for the first time in the history of Latin America, a president in absentia assumed his duties. Early in the morning of 18 February 2013, he made his final return trip to Venezuela after the Cuban doctors admitted to having exhausted all existing medical treatments. He had come home to die in the native country that he had passionately loved so hard. After weeks of painful suffering, God released him from the intense torment and Chávez died at 4:25 p.m. on 5 March 2013.[18] Immediately Maduro assumed the powers of the presidency, and the country and the world waited with expectation to see if a new age in the history of Venezuela was beginning.

Course Corrections in Colombia

Juan Manuel Santos both in his victory speech and in his inaugural oration had thanked effusively outgoing president Álvaro Uribe Vélez. But even before taking office on 7 August 2010, the new ruler of Colombia had taken actions promising a different direction for the country. The choice of labor leader Angelino Garzón as vice presidential running mate had irked the followers of Uribe who could not accept having a dark-skinned person of low class origin in the second highest office in the country. Yet for Santos, having the labor leader balanced the ticket and helped contribute to the overwhelming victory in the runoff election of 20 June 2010. Even more repulsive was the invitation to Hugo Chávez to attend the inauguration. Under Uribe relations with Venezuela had become so bitter, that Chávez routinely denounced Colombia for wanting to stage a U.S.-led invasion to destroy the Bolivarian Revolution. Instead Santos by this opening gesture secured the reestablishment of trade relations with the neighboring country, and he obtained $600 million as compensation for Colombian businesses whose properties had been nationalized in Venezuela during the Uribe administration.[19]

In politics Santos stated his desire to have a "National Unity" government composed of representatives of the main parties. Eventually 80 percent of political groups came to support his administration in exchange for high positions; some leftist parties joined his coalition, but even those that stayed outside agreed to engage in conversations with officials over policies. Santos seemed to have been so successful in forging a consensus that for a few brief months the fear arose that he was trying to create a single-party system such as the PRI in twentieth-century Mexico. Actually in a foreshadowing of later events, it was Uribe's followers who were most disgruntled with these moves, even though they occupied a privileged position inside the government. Uribe himself was furious that some of his most bitter personal enemies had landed high positions in the Santos administration; in particular he considered an affront the appointment of Germán Vargas Lleras, who had led the fight against the third term, as interior minister. The friendly visits of Santos to the Supreme Court and in particular to the Constitutional Court that had killed the third term also enraged the former president.[20]

Santos had optimistically concluded that if he could have in his cabinet Vargas Lleras who had been a rival candidate in the 2010 election, then Uribe could also forget past quarrels with the Supreme Court and the Constitutional Court. The president also balanced his cabinet appointment between technocrats and professional politicians of all tendencies. What was amply clear to the country was that Santos "set a new tone of government, the arrival of consensual politics to replace Uribe's more confrontational style."[21]

Having a national coalition yielded important benefits for the Santos administration. A major step came when on 16 March 2011 the congress gave enabling power to the president to restructure the Colombian state through the issuance of decrees having the force of law. For a period of six months Santos could abolish, create, merge or modify in any ways the institutions and agencies of the state, including the cabinet ministries. For politicians this was a fearsome power to delegate to the president, because theoretically he could deprive them of their ability to give jobs and benefits to their followers. The methodical negotiation between the president and legislative leaders inspired confidence in the latter that these enabling powers would not hurt politicians and were necessary to correct defects in the operations of the government. The bill was ready to be voted on, when at the last minute deputies as an additional precaution against presidential overreach inserted a final clause giving a congressional committee authority to repeal any decree issued under the enabling authority. Santos agreed to the measure, but the oversight proved unnecessary because the president had intended all along to consult with congress before issuing any of the decrees. He also enjoyed a large majority in the oversight committee, and in practice it found nothing to reject in the president's decrees.[22]

The restructuring of the state was long overdue and began with the abolishment of certain failed entities. The dismantling of the secret spying agency DAS, which had been mired in scandal after scandal as discussed before, was a foregone conclusion. Santos distributed the functions of DAS among several ministries and to the National Police; however the conclusion that the government had ended illegal eavesdropping turned out to be premature. Legislators were delighted when Santos decided to reinstate three previously existing cabinet ministries, which Uribe had merged in order to save money for the military offensives. Separating Justice from the Interior Ministry was the most important step, and in all three new ministries the politicians gained a large number of jobs and benefits to distribute among their followers.[23]

Another major accomplishment was the successful struggle in congress to obtain passage of the Victims' Law. This bill aimed to restore to their rightful owners land seized by armed groups whether guerrillas or paramilitaries. When restitution was not feasible, the bill then provided monetary compensation to the original proprietors. Uribe violently condemned the bill because for the first time it gave legal recognition to the insurgency when instead he had always denounced the guerrillas as "terrorists"; on a more practical level, he also feared that the bill would expose the many links between his administration and paramilitaries. The opposition of Uribe had blocked passage of similar legislation during his years in office, but the incoming Santos presidency in one of its first acts promptly presented congress with a new version which went farther than the original draft. The new bill also initiated a policy of expanding land ownership among peasants. Although it was only an initial step and a comprehensive agrarian reform law was still needed in the future, for the first time the Colombian government was starting to treat the insurgency not just as a military problem but also as an economic issue. Congress carefully and slowly studied and modified the bill, and it became the Victims' Law on 10 June 2011.[24]

By late 2010 Uribe felt that his legacy was under threat and already in April 2011 he demanded right-wing measures from Santos. The president, who felt that he had placated the left, decided to meet some of the demands of the hard-core followers of Uribe. The president was playing the risky game of "triangulation": by granting some things to the left and then balancing them with other measures to the right, he hoped to increase his power and maintain his popularity at high levels. In mid–January 2011 rumors began to circulate that the government intended to abolish fixed fees for transporting cargo aboard trucks; henceforth the market forces of supply and demand would determine the prices. The Uribe administration had already clashed with truck drivers over this issue, but no final showdown had occurred.[25]

The ability of the truck drivers to paralyze the economy made any tampering with the system of fees a very risky proposition for the government, and Santos had made a major political mistake in using this issue as a way to appease the right. Once the government confirmed that decrees lifting price controls would soon be published, the truck drivers feared that they would lose their jobs. In response their labor union announced a strike for 2 February 2011, and the business group of truck owners also supported the work stoppage but less enthusiastically. In reality, the struggle against the government mirrored a parallel struggle inside the ranks of truck owners. At one level were the large fleets of corporations and on another side were the small proprietors who generally owned at most one truck. This latter group could consist of a single owner, of family members who owned a truck, or of a pool of drivers who each held a share of the vehicle. The abolishment of fixed fees meant the elimination of the small owners and the creation of an oligopoly among a few large trucking firms. Not surprisingly the small owners were determined to protect their livelihood at all costs and launched the first strike against the Santos administration on 2 February.[26]

Soon cargo backed up in farms and warehouses throughout the country while store shelves gradually emptied of merchandise. Colombia, in one of its structural flaws, lacks a well-developed railroad network, and cargo inside the country moves primarily aboard trucks; this is particularly true for bringing agricultural products to the cities. As companies exhausted their inventories and supermarkets ran out of food, the popular pressure for a solution intensified. Cargo was also piling up in the international borders with Ecuador and Venezuela, the country was losing foreign currency, and the Colombian economy was suffering massive damages. So as not to inflame the situation, officials held off issuing the decrees, but the truck drivers insisted that the strike would not end until the government pledged not to destroy the system of fixed fees.[27]

So far the strike had been a work stoppage, but the refusal of the government to modify its position forced the drivers to escalate the pressure, and starting on Monday, February 14, they placed their trucks in key intersections to block the passage of all traffic. Often the trucks were chained together making their removal difficult for the police. Violence frequently erupted when the drivers defended their trucks, and the police began arresting the strikers in a futile attempt to clear the roads. The union of the truck drivers agreed to enter into negotiations with the government to lift the strike, but many workers still wanted to continue the struggle. The participation of vice president Garzón, himself a former labor leader, proved instrumental in persuading the drivers to accept the government's promise to maintain the existing system of fixed fees. After 15 days of work stoppage, truck traffic returned to normal on 19 February 2011.[28]

The truck strike had been a serious blow to free market advocates and clearly showed that the population of the country had reached a saturation point about capitalism. The collapse of the Soviet Bloc in 1989 seemed to have condemned socialism, yet two decades later many Colombians were getting tired of waiting for the extraordinary benefits that unbridled competition and the search for profits was supposed to bring. The trucking strike was also significant because it began a period of protests and popular mobilizations in Colombia, comparable to what the Arequipazo had triggered in Peru. At least initially, the Santos administration failed to recognize in the truckers' strike the start of a period of protests against free market initiatives. The political priority of the Santos presidency was to satisfy the demands of the right-wing faction in his coalition. He had failed to deliver the trucking sector to the free market advocates, and he now hoped to appease the right wing of his coalition by delivering nothing less than the privatization of higher education in Colombia.

This project dated back to the Uribe administration, which had been quietly working on how to incorporate the state universities into the prevailing free market ideology. The two main elements of the proposal were bringing private investment into the over 30 state universities in the country and opening up the educational sector to the entry of foreign capitalists who would establish for-profit universities. The proposed transformation was of a fascinating dimension, because it meant a paradigm shift: higher education no longer was an essential human right but become simply another source of profit for investors. The proposal seemed to clash with the clauses of the Constitution of 1991, and court challenges were inevitable, but the government trusted the doubtful legal argument that simply proposing a new piece of legislation sufficed to replace the previous Law 30 of 1992. Government officials, in particular Minister of Education María Fernanda Campo, launched a publicity campaign claiming that the university system had to be fixed because it was broke and could not provide the professional personnel the country desperately needed. A more accurate explanation for the deficiencies was inadequate funding at a time when government spending on the military more than tripled expenditures on education in 2009.[29]

For the Santos administration, the privatization of universities seemed to solve many problems. Foreign investors provided the capital to expand higher education, while the gradual privatization of state universities guaranteed a supply of graduates suitable to be cogs in the capitalist system rather than critical questioners of the Colombian reality. Politically, Santos placated his right wing and repaired the fallout from the flop of the truck driver's strike. And lurking behind, Wall Street was sure to be very pleased with this additional proof that Colombia was extending the profit motive throughout the country. The rosy panorama sounded too good even for Santos, and his political instincts told him to keep a low profile on the matter; if everything turned out well as his capitalist advisors promised, he could always step in at the end to take full credit, but if things did not go according to plan, he was a sufficiently detached observer who could step in to defuse any crisis.

Hoping to regain political momentum, on 10 March 2011, just weeks after the fiasco with the truck drivers, Santos made a speech formally launching the initiative to turn higher education into a source of profit for private business. He entrusted the implementation of the proposal to Education Minister Campo, who was supposed to secure passage for the bill in congress. The administration began its campaign with a massive publicity blitz, and for days television broadcasts praised the benefits of the changes and also ominously warned citizens not to be misled by possible troublemakers. If this initiative was going to have any chance of approval, it needed the full support of university administrators, yet in a few days hostile comments appeared in newspapers and sometimes in television broadcasts. University presidents came out against the proposal, and the president of the National University of Colombia, the largest in the country, repeatedly published articles in the press denouncing the proposed changes. The Association of

Colombian Universities, the main lobbying group representing both public and private institutions, reported that none of their members had been consulted. Unanimously the presidents of state institutions condemned the proposal, and the heads of several private universities also expressed serious objections; almost nobody came out to advocate for privatization.[30]

Faculty unions were vehement in condemning the proposal, and soon students formed a steering body to lead the struggle against privatization. The lack of response from the government brought many student leaders to the realization that street action was necessary to obtain changes. On 7 April 2011 the students carried out a massive nation-wide protest against the proposal; the demonstrations in almost all the state institutions spread even to some private universities. Having tens of thousands protesting was already impressive, but what worried the government most was that other groups had joined demonstrations that could easily get out of hand and turn into a general strike. The Gay, Lesbian, and Transgender community participated in the protests, and so did ethnic minorities such as Africans and Indians. Feminist groups also rallied to the demonstrations as did labor unions in some cities. Officials realized that the danger of a national coalition emerging was real and that they had to do something to lower the tensions. Then President Santos intervened in the controversy on 23 August to announce that he was withdrawing the provision about bringing private investment into state universities, thus supposedly ending the danger of privatizing the existing institutions.[31]

By this modification he largely eliminated the opposition from the heads of state universities, and he also hoped to keep the students away from other groups hostile to the free market agenda. He justified the modification on the grounds that the original draft obviously had not emerged out of a consensus. Having removed what he felt was the sole obstacle to approval, he then assigned to Education Minister Campo the task of obtaining legislative approval for the shortened bill. The students however, were still not convinced, and the more they scrutinized the remainder of the proposal, the more they became disgusted. What Minister Campo was still proposing was to allow the entry of foreign investors who would create new private universities and charge high tuition. Obviously the students could not afford the expensive payments, so financial institutions stood ready to make loans at high interest rates. For the private sector, the profits would come both from the tuition and from the interest payments on the loans, and many a speculator was itching at the chance to become a millionaire by extracting profits from the loan money of students who were condemned for the rest of their lives to debt slavery.[32]

At the same time in Chile the university students were leading a similar struggle to stop the privatization of education, and their efforts served as a stimulus for the Colombian students to continue fighting the government. When the new semester started, university associations became active in organizing protests and used social networks to bring students together. Whether through cell phones or personal computers, this extensive use of digital media to communicate among themselves was a significant difference from the university protests of the twentieth century. Students who did not know each other and lived in distant regions learned that they shared the same ideas and could coordinate actions simultaneously across the country. These social networks made possibly going beyond the twentieth-century formula of gathering in assemblies and organizing rallies in one university; students in 2011 could schedule those traditional meetings to occur simultaneously across the country in all the state universities.[33]

As a result of the social networking, students shut down the state university at Pereira on 8 September and this work stoppage gradually spread to several other universities. As the national steering group deliberated on the next step to take, the students under the guidance of faculty advisors reached the conclusion that a national work stoppage was their most effective weapon to force a Santos administration, always worried about its reputation, to shelve the proposal. The students announced that on October 3, the day that the executive branch presented the formal bill to the congress, activities on all campuses would stop. Those state universities still open began shutting down, first just certain schools and then the whole campus until the entire higher education system was practically paralyzed.[34]

The students also organized a series of marches and local rallies until the movement climaxed in nation-wide protests in November. What was distinctive about the marches was that students deliberately went out of their way to avoid violence and destructive acts. As a matter of fact, they drew on the "make love and not war" tradition of the 1960s to portray their demonstrations not as fear-inspiring events but as love feasts in which everyone was hugging and kissing each other. The press was soon publishing photographs of the students hugging and embracing rather than hitting and throwing rocks at the police. Public opinion massively shifted to the side of the students, and the citizens knew that the future of their children was at stake.[35]

Through social media the students organized rallies simultaneously in 31 cities, and over half a million citizens marched on the streets on 3 November to defend the not-for-profit nature of all universities. The students had also announced the "taking of Bogotá" for 10 November when many students from the whole country would march to the capital to defend their movement. On 9 November, the day before the flood of students was supposed to arrive in Bogotá, President Santos caved in to the pressure of parents who did not want their children to lose an academic semester and thus be unable to graduate on time. He announced to the country that he was withdrawing the proposed educational bill from congress and was asking the students to return to their classes.[36]

The students were extremely happy with the presidential announcement, but prudently fearing that this was just a trick, still decided to hold the "taking of Bogotá" on 10 November. This was the most colorful event of the entire protest movement, and the students came from many regions to participate in the festive atmosphere to the sounds of music in an almost carnival spirit. The students avoided any confrontation with the police and profusely hugged each other and danced. For female students, this was a coming-of-age experience; many women painted their breasts in the national colors and paraded bare chested to the immense delight of the male participants. The rivers of students pouring into the city dispelled any lingering notions the government might have had about proceeding with some variation of privatization.[37]

The congress had never shown any interest in the privatization of the universities and had always regarded the proposal as something imposed by the executive branch in response to pressure from international organizations such as the World Bank and foreign corporations. On 16 November the committee of the house with jurisdiction over the matter voted unanimously to withdraw the proposal to privatize higher education. The students wildly celebrated their successful preservation of the not-for-profit status of all higher education in Colombia, but for the Santos administration this had been a very public and embarrassing defeat.[38]

Public opinion welcomed the decision, but it was a different matter with those right-wing politicians closely associated with former president Uribe. The somewhat sudden reversal of the Santos administration reflected the power struggle raging inside the National Unity coalition of the government. The left wing always had opposed the privatization proposal, and its most visible leader Minister of Interior Germán Vargas Lleras had even gone so far as to express sympathy for the student movement.[39] Once the whole university sector was paralyzed, Santos had no choice but to abort the attempt to convert the universities into sources of profit. However, abandoning the bill for higher education meant that he had not done anything to satisfy the demands of the extreme right wing in his coalition, and this after having failed to lift the price controls from the trucking sector. His strategy of governing by "triangulation," that is standing as an umpire between the conflicting demands of the right and the left was not working.

The Free Trade Agreement with the United States gave a temporary respite to Santos. Both countries had signed the original draft on 24 August 2006, but congressional opposition in Washington had blocked ratification of the treaty during the Uribe administration. Democrats felt that the draft did not include adequate guarantees for union activities. Colombia had earned the fearful reputation of being one of the countries in the world with the largest number of murdered labor leaders. What finally broke the logjam in the U.S. Congress was the executive agreement Santos signed with President Barack Obama; by this measure, the Colombian government provided extensive protections to labor leaders. After intense Colombian lobbying in Washington, D.C., the U.S. congress finally passed the Free Trade Agreement on 12 October 2011, and President Barack Obama signed it into law on 21 October. The agreement entered into force on 15 May 2012, months sooner than expected. Santos believed that he had ratified his capitalist credentials and also hoped to appease Uribe by attaining a fundamental goal of the previous presidency. An open break between the two leaders might have yet been averted, had not Santos rejected the fundamental policy of the Uribe presidency.[40]

After taking office, Santos had made conciliatory statements suggesting peace talks with the guerrilla groups. Supposedly rebel leaders contacted him first about the possibility of holding secret talks to end the insurgency. Irrespective of who initiated the contacts, by early 2012 the Santos administration was engaged in conversations with FARC leaders. A first public indication that something was taking place came on 26 February 2012 when Timochenko Jiménez, the head of FARC, declared that his group was abandoning the practice of kidnappings. Confirmation of this promise had already come when over the previous months the guerrillas gradually had been releasing their kidnapped hostages and imprisoned soldiers. Speculation was rife about why FARC was taking these unilateral actions, and soon leaks suggested that the changes were the result of conversations with the government. Apparently sooner than he would have liked, the threat of more leaks pressured Santos to declare on 27 August 2012 that the government was entering negotiations to bring the insurgency to an end.[41]

The formal meetings began in Oslo, Norway, in October 2012, but the long distance from Colombia suggested a closer place as more suitable. Cuba offered to host the delegations, and in November Havana became the new venue. Both sides agreed to negotiate over six issues, the two most important being agrarian reform and political participation for guerrillas. The other four issues were the drug trade, demobilization, the rights of victims, and mechanisms for implementing the accord. Great expectations existed that an accord could be reached in months, but the talks soon slowed down to a crawl. Only in May 2013 did the Colombian government announced that agreement had been reached on most of the aspects of the agrarian reform and that some progress had taken place about the other five points.[42]

Colombians began to doubt that a peace accord was possible, and even Santos admitted that the process had been slower than he expected. But the lack of progress did not stop Uribe from condemning the Santos administration for caving in to the left. Particularly offensive was the resumption of normal relations with neighboring Venezuela, a country Uribe had always denounced as the primary backer of FARC. The former president fanned the fear that Santos would give away too much to the rebel group, while the wave of social protests in Colombia seemed to create the impression that the government was losing control of the country. The message was clear that Colombia needed new leadership, and already on 5 July 2012 Uribe bolted from the party of the U and created a new rump group. He decided to run only for the senate, and he had his new political group nominate his former treasury minister, Óscar Iván Zuluoga, to run in the presidential election of May 2014. Uribe incessantly bashed the Santos administration for having betrayed the country, and he hoped that his attacks would persuade the president to abandon any plans to run for a second term in office.[43]

Chapter 18

The Closing of a Period

The best thing for a republic or a monarchy is not to have someone in charge who governs well for as long as he lives; it is better to have someone who organizes the state so that when he dies it will continue without him.—Niccolò Machiavelli[1]

Colombia: The Struggle for Peace

The speculation about whether Juan Manuel Santos would run for reelection came to an end on 20 November 2013 when he officially declared himself a candidate. As will be recalled from chapter 11, President Álvaro Uribe Vélez had amended the Constitution of 1991 to allow any incumbent to run for a second consecutive presidential term, and Santos availed himself of that opportunity to present his candidacy to the Colombian people. He was well aware that his campaign automatically provoked the wrath of Uribe who would do everything possible to defeat Santos.[2]

As discussed in the previous chapter, both men had been openly clashing, and Santos knew that he had to take precautions to avoid a humiliating defeat at the hands of the voters. It was clear that most right-wing elements were rallying to the siren calls of former president Uribe, so Santos felt that he had no choice but to rely on the left if he was going to have any chance of winning reelection. First order of business was to rearrange his ticket. Vice President Angelino Garzón, the former labor leader, had been a loyal and effective collaborator, but large segments of the population had never been able to accept a dark-skinned person of low social origin in such a high position. Garzón was costing likely voters, and Santos needed to cut losses and convert the liability into an asset. He reached into his cabinet and selected Germán Vargas Lleras, who had been Minister of Interior, to be his new vice presidential running mate. Vargas Lleras was a veteran politician who had a national following, and although representing the left, he was the leftist-leaning candidate most acceptable to many Colombians. In retrospect, his addition to the ticket proved essential for the campaign of Santos.

By then Uribe had become an extremely angry opponent, and this hostility of a former president to his successor was something that had never before occurred in the history of Colombia. As will be recalled, Uribe had tried to stop passage of the Victims' Law of June 2011, a refusal that might seem odd because his main constituency were landowners. By opposing the Victims' Law, Uribe revealed his true colors as a defender of large landowners, but only if they still owned land; in the Uribe movement there was no room either for small land owners or for previous owners of large landed estates. The Santos administration had planned on a ten-year period for the restitution of land and the compensation payments; consequently, all those citizens who hoped to benefit realized that continuity of policies in the government was indispensable. The obvious conclusion was that Santos needed to be reelected, while on the contrary the election of any Uribe surrogate meant dashing any hopes for restitution. The Victims' Law besides signifying the definite break with the Uribe movement also gained a solid block of citizens determined to vote for the reelection of Santos.[3]

On the negative side, the Santos presidency faced an increasing number of social protests in Colombia. It was not just the case that the tensions repressed under Uribe were coming out under the more open Santos administration. As may be recalled, the business conglomerates had given almost propaganda-like media coverage to the Uribe presidency, and in particular they had minimized and underreported the many social protests taking place during those years. The media never shifted to hostile reporting on Santos, but the pressure to provide the most favorable coverage disappeared, and increasingly the public could learn for the first time about many of the social conflicts that had been occurring across the country. The public gained the mistaken impression that the country was on the verge of a breakdown when in reality the situation was only slightly more turbulent than under Uribe. Perhaps inevitably, conservative groups began longing for the supposedly quieter days of the Uribe presidency, and this idea that Santos was losing control of the country threatened to undermine fatally the reelection campaign.[4]

Clearly his campaign was in trouble, but in a first indication that the left was starting to accept Santos, on 16 May 2014 peace negotiators in Havana reached agreement on the need to wage a relentless effort against the cocaine trade. The government accepted the request of FARC (*Fuerzas Armadas Revolucionarias de Colombia*) to assist coca growers in their transition to other crops and also agreed to end the aerial fumigation of coca fields. Under strong U.S. pressure Colombia was the only country still carrying out aerial fumigation in South America, yet the supply of cocaine did not decline. Worse, the herbicides were harming food crops and leaving soils unsuitable for cultivation for many years. As will be recalled, reaching agreement on the drug trade was one of the six points FARC and the government had established as the basis for reaching peace accords.[5]

The announcement on 16 May came just in time to save the reelection. Nobody had expected Santos to win 50 percent of the vote in the first round, but his second-place finish among five candidates on 25 May was particularly embarrassing. The lackluster Óscar Iván Zuluaga, the anointed candidate of Uribe, came in at first place with 29.2 percent of the vote compared to the 25.6 percent of incumbent Santos. And it was obvious that unless something dramatic occurred, the president would not be reelected in the runoff election of 25 June.[6]

The possibility of Uribe destroying the political career of Santos was too much for the sitting president, and much against his capitalist beliefs, he regretfully concluded that only by aggressively appealing to the left did he stand a chance of winning the runoff. Even though Zuluaga was such a poor candidate that Uribe had to accompany him on most campaign stops to rally the faithful, it was clear that the two men had already cornered most of the right. It was too late for Santos, after having advanced so far in the peace talks, to go back to the failed Uribe formula of labeling the guerrillas as terrorists and insisting on an unrelenting war against FARC.[7] Santos reached out to the left, including its candidates of the first round. One of the most striking characteristics in Colombian politics for decades has been the preference of voters for candidates who will worsen income inequality and do little or nothing to improve the situation of the lower and middle classes. A major reason for the success of this formula to persuade citizens to vote against their own material welfare and economic benefits has been the constant demonization of the left as sympathizers of the terrorist FARC. Uribe perfected this ability to a fine art, and his portrayal of the guerrillas as inhuman monsters conveniently served to tar all leftists as closet guerrillas associated with the worst crimes imaginable.

The fragmentation and petty ideological disputes among leftist groups in Colombia are legendary, but by 2014 the realization was taking root that the armed guerrillas rather than helping were hurting any chances to bring real progressive policies to the country. If FARC remained engaged in combat, then candidates in the Uribe mold would continue to win elections by scaring the Colombian electorate and thus perpetuate the policies favoring exclusively the wealthy elite. To break this cycle, the insurgency had to end, yet the only leader who had staked his political future on negotiating a peace accord was Santos. His past lurches to the right when he tried to impose market forces into the trucking and education sectors made this a hard choice to swallow, but the left had no other alternative if it ever wanted to have its ideas influence the policies of the coming decades. And because Santos could not afford to alienate all right-wing voters, he continued with his platitudes about the wondrous benefits of the free market and free trade, although not as frequently and enthusiastically as before. These reassurances and the experience of his first term persuaded most business groups to remain solidly behind the president. Triangulation between the right and the left was giving way to a marriage of convenience between Santos and the left, with each side retaining considerable independence and flexibility.[8]

Labor unions, leftist groups, and educators declared their support for the reelection of Santos. Leftist candidate Clara López, who had received 15 percent of the popular vote in the first round of 25 May, came out openly in favor of the president. The elected leftist mayors of large cities also urged their followers to vote for Santos. The endorsement by Gustavo Petro, was particularly valuable and not just because he was the mayor of Bogotá. As a former guerrilla leader, his support already carried considerable weight and was significant because his previous relationship with the president had been very rocky. Petro's decision to forget past quarrels and to support Santos sent a powerful message that the only realistic option for the left was the reelection of the president and that this was the only way to secure an opening for progressive measures in future decades.[9]

In the runoff election of 15 June, Santos won with a margin of 51 percent compared to Zuluaga's 45 percent. In vote counts, Santos received 900,000 more votes than his rival, a sharp reversal from the 25 May first round when Zuluaga had received 500,000 more votes than the president. Geographically, the winning strategy consisted in taking a ten-point lead among the leftist-leaning electorate of Bogotá and gaining overwhelming majorities in the Caribbean coast; in this region the political bosses who controlled blocks of votes had pinned their political future on a Santos victory.[10]

The reelected president did not want to repeat the failed peace process of the Andrés Pastrana administration. The usual approach of ending wars with a sudden cessation of hostilities was certainly more dramatic but was not the best way to have the combatants return to civilian life. Instead if the levels of violence and combat gradually declined, guerrillas would be more likely to make a smoother and hopefully imperceptible transition away from combat into peace. As a move in this direction, Santos announced on

14 January 2015 that "we are seeking to de-escalate the intensity of the conflict,"[11] but he again emphasized that a full halt to combat depended on the formal signing of a peace accord. FARC had announced a unilateral cease fire in December 2014, and the president was considering how to respond to this gesture. After intensive consultation, in March he announced the end of air strikes against the guerrillas, a move that Uribe and his followers promptly and loudly condemned.[12]

At this critical juncture Santos received much needed support when the U.S. government in March 2015 pledged to back the peace process; to stress its commitment to the negotiations, Washington appointed a special envoy to the talks. Although the senior American diplomat did not participate directly in the negotiations, he stood ready to help facilitate the process. U.S. support was tested when in May 2015 the Santos administration implemented its earlier promise to stop aerial fumigation of coca plants. Anti-drug officials were understandably upset with this measure, yet the action did not make the Barack Obama administration waver in its support for seeking a negotiated end to the war.[13]

The peace process seemed to collapse on 14 April when a guerrilla unit ambushed an army patrol, killed a dozen soldiers, and wounded another twenty near the village of La Esperanza in Cauca Department. FARC had promised in December to use force only in self-defense, but this well-planned and carefully executed ambush was clearly an offensive action; in response the Santos administration resumed air strikes against guerrillas. The ambush was the last major clash of the insurgency, and apparently local commanders carried out the operation without the approval of the Secretariat, the governing body of FARC. Perhaps hard-liners in the guerilla organization wanted to continue the insurgency; another possible explanation was that discipline was disintegrating inside the FARC as local units acted independently to survive. This last consideration had serious implications for the long-term prospects for law and order in Colombia, because it could mean that even when a peace accord is reached, splinter groups may want to remain independent and evolve into criminal groups. This happened first with dissident factions of the guerrillas who demobilized in 1991 and more recently with many paramilitaries who drifted into criminal activities after 2005.[14]

The ambush of 14 April certainly delayed any agreement, and only after many intensive conversations did both sides agree to a partial cease fire on 20 July 2015. By this agreement, both sides promised not to engage in attacks or any type of offensive action but retained the right to use force in self-defense. The most important consequence of this cease fire came just days later when on 25 July the president announced the suspension of air strikes against the guerrillas. If the armed forces felt that an air strike was necessary to disrupt any concentration of FARC units, only the president could give final approval. And under no circumstances could warplanes bomb any areas near urban centers.[15] Santos claimed that the country could not afford to waste this last opportunity to reach a successful conclusion; philosophically he claimed that as the peace process neared its end "it is necessary to be changing strategies, mental attitudes, and behavior."[16]

After the inevitable harsh denunciations from Uribe who claimed that Santos was cuddling terrorists, the long-expected breakthrough came on September 23 when the president flew to Havana to participate in a decisive event. In a photograph that went around the world, Santos shook hands with the FARC negotiator while in the middle stood a smiling President Raúl Castro who placed his hands above those of the Colombians. What persuaded Santos to fly to Havana was a decisive breakthrough: for the first time both sides pledged to complete a peace accord in six months on 23 March 2016. In an additional stipulation, the guerrillas promised to demobilize sixty days after the signing of the final peace accord. The participants had been able to set these two deadlines for ending the war because they had also made considerable progress on the outstanding issues.[17]

Of the six issues subject to negotiation, the most contentious remained prison sentences for crimes committed by guerrillas. Large segments of the population and human rights groups demanded harsh punishment for those who committed horrible crimes and in particular for the perpetrators of inhuman kidnappings. For FARC negotiators the precedent was the immunity from prosecution that the Central American peace accords of the 1990s had given to guerrillas. The Colombian government and human rights groups argued that international law had evolved and no longer considered acceptable that hideous crimes remain unpunished. On the practical side, the cost of incarcerating tens of thousands of prisoners for long sentences was prohibitive. The government agreed to amnesty the rank and file combatants, provided that they had not personally committed atrocities. If guerrilla commanders confessed to all their crimes then they qualified for special treatment and would receive maximum prison sentences ranging from 5 to 8 years; however if the guerrilla commanders did not make a full confession before a special tribunal, then the government would prosecute them to the full extent of the law and sentence them to the maximum prison terms then in the penal code. The confession was the rough equivalent to the "plea bargains" in the United States and seemed more than reasonable when in Colombia the overwhelming majority of major crimes not only go unpunished but are not even prosecuted. But those who wanted the war to remain a permanent part of Colombian life were outraged by the compromise, and Uribe denounced the agreement as a "sell-out."[18]

In an attempt to reconcile Uribe to a possible peace agreement, Santos started trying to make contacts with the former president, but the latter refused and insisted on denouncing the government for having sold out to "Castro-Chavismo ." By February 2016 it had become clear that settling the differences between Uribe and Santos was going to be harder than making peace with the guerrillas.[19]

A no less serious threat to the peace process came from the revelation that the Colombian National Police had been deeply involved in domestic spying. As will be recalled from the previous chapter, Santos had hoped to avoid these political scandals by abolishing the secret-service agency (DAS) and by transferring all intelligence functions to the National Police. But by late 2015 leaks indicated that domestic spying had never stopped. The revelations have not been as extensive as during the Uribe presidency, but more than ample evidence came out to show that the National Police, the body that supposedly had the primary responsibility for enforcing any peace agreement, was extremely politicized and seemed incapable of maintaining the rule of law in a post-conflict Colombia.[20]

The situation became even worse when additional leaks confirmed that domestic spying tied in with a parallel process of malfeasance in the National Police. Illegal eavesdropping discovered the sexual preferences of many politicians, and at least since 2013 the national police orchestrated a bizarre prostitution network to satisfy the erotic fantasies of members of congress. At the beginning officers selected the most beautiful females in the ranks and ordered them to provide sexual favors to key political leaders, presumably in exchange for approving funds and legislation favorable to the institution.

By late 2015 the practice extended to servicing the needs of homosexual members of congress, and officers ordered attractive policemen to become male prostitutes. This arrangement was known by the code name of the "Fellowship of the Ring." The president had stood behind the institution during the initial revelations about the domestic spying, but the networks of male and female prostitution was too much, and on 17 February 2016 General Rodolfo Palomino was forced to resign as head of the National Police.[21]

These scandals weakened the institution that was supposed to have a major role in guaranteeing peace and order in a post-conflict Colombia, and not surprisingly the peace negotiations slowed to a crawl. FARC and the government jointly appealed to the United Nations to take charge of the implementation of any peace accord, and in a unanimous vote the Security Council approved the request in January 2016. Last-minute complications threatened to derail the process, but both sides realized that ending the talks was worse than postponing the deadline. In spite of having reached agreement on the great majority of issues, the two sides could not solve several small points. President Santos on 9 March announced that the deadline of 23 March needed to be postponed. He stated his preference to waiting a bit longer for the best possible agreement rather than signing a bad deal on the deadline of 23 March. FARC spokespersons ratified the demand for more time to hammer out a complete agreement. The United Nations, the European Union, and the United States sympathized with the need to extend the deadline.[22]

Two main differences had prevented both parties from announcing an agreement by the self-imposed deadline of 23 March 2016. The first was the sharp divergence over the number of zones for demobilizing the guerrillas. In the initial bargaining positions of 2015, the guerrillas demanded seventy and the government offered only seven— the exact number of combat "blocs" existing in the FARC military structure. By March 2016 the government had accepted the figure of 14 zones while the guerrillas had lowered their demand to 60. Because several aspects of implementation of an accord depended on the number of zones, the remaining gap of 46 impeded the conclusion of a final peace agreement. The expectation was that the intervention of United Nations negotiators—as authorized by the Security Council—could help to overcome this obstacle.[23]

The second disagreement was about the final disposition of the guerrilla arsenals. The government wanted all arms melted down in a furnace as soon as demobilization took place, but FARC insisted on preserving them in some form as a homage to its many fallen followers. Also, rank-and-filed combatants were emotionally and psychologically attached to their small arms; the sense of empowerment was vital to the peasant recruits of FARC, for otherwise they felt themselves unable to cope with the complexities of post-industrial society. The government agreed to begin destroying the heavy weapons first and to leave the rifles of the guerrillas for last. But beyond this point the negotiators could not budge. The guerrillas proposed disabling the rifles by removing key parts; another idea surfaced to weld the rifles into monuments commemorating the fallen insurgents, but the Colombia military was totally opposed to any solution glorifying in any way the guerrillas.[24]

These two remaining disputes did not seem insurmountable, especially after both sides had reached agreement on all the fundamental issues concerning the economic and political systems. However, in a strange twist, another matter unexpectedly came to take center stage in the process to reach a peace agreement in Colombia. On 22 September 2015 the Colombian government, in what initially seemed a wise move, had submitted to the congress a constitutional proposal for implementing the peace accord; once legislators passed the bill, it needed voter approval to enter into force. The government had presented this proposal just the day before the historic photograph of Santos shaking hands with his FARC counterpart under the approving smile of President Raúl Castro in Havana. As Santos later explained, no obligation existed to pursue the referendum, because ample legal authorization already existed to conclude a peace agreement with FARC.[25]

Because the Santos administration enjoyed overwhelming majorities in both houses of congress, ratification did not seem a problem, but as the negotiations in Havana dragged on, legislators could not resist tampering with the original proposal. The core element of giving the president extraordinary powers to issue decrees with the force of law during 180 days remained in place. However, the lower chamber rejected the idea of having a "mini-congress" (*congresito*) legislate on demobilization and instead gave congress expedited authority to issue laws. The real surprise was the amendment stating that the constitutional reform including the referendum vote could take place only after the peace accords had been signed. In effect, by this amendment the lower house postponed completion of the peace process until 2017.[26]

Another complication arose when Álvaro Uribe Vélez used every step of the legislative process to vent virulent hostility toward the peace negotiations. But controlling only a small minority of legislators, the disgruntled and embittered former president could do nothing to stop the steady progress of the constitutional proposal through both houses of congress. It took eight roll-call votes to defeat the obstructionist attempts by Uribe's followers, but even after the senate gave its final approval on 14 June 2016 the struggle was far from over.[27]

Already on June 4 Uribe had begun collecting signatures in Medellín for a ten-part manifesto denouncing the entire peace process. He pledged to collect signatures until August 4 and subsequently extended the deadline until September 11. He claimed to have opened one hundred tables to collect signatures from citizens in thirty Colombian cities and even in some foreign countries. The purpose of this signature collecting campaign was two-fold. First, by obtaining the names of millions of citizens, he hoped to persuade the Constitutional Court to declare the proposal invalid. As may be recalled, this Court has the final word on whether reforms to the Constitution could be presented to the voters. A second purpose of the signature drive was to start mobilizing citizens to vote against the referendum, which all observers expected to take place sometime in late 2016.[28]

The attempt to persuade the Constitutional Court to block the proposal seemed to have failed when it became known that at least five of the nine judges supported sending the constitutional reform to the voters. But the judge who circulated the draft of the decision approving the constitutional referendum already inserted a crucial and possibly fatal requirement. The draft stipulated that voters needed to see the final text of the peace agreement no less than thirty days before the referendum took place. By this change, the Constitutional Court converted the referendum on giving special powers to the government into a vote on the peace agreement itself. In Central America the peace agreements had never been submitted to the voters, and this change opened the possibility that the referendum could fail and not just because a majority voted against it. Absenteeism in elections and even more shamefully in congress has become rampant in Colombia and the possibility existed that the number of voters might fall below the minimum percentage of the electorate.[29] FARC had promised to begin demobilization sixty days after the proclamation of the peace agreement, but if voters rejected the constitutional proposal, did this mean that the peace agreement was no longer binding?

Both the Colombian government and FARC realized that they were losing control over the peace process. In an attempt to regain the initiative, Santos and the guerrilla leader decided to sign a cease fire in Havana on 23 June 2016 again with the enthusiastic blessing of a radiant Raúl Castro. In reality, the landmark text was both less and more than a cease fire. The complete cessation of hostilities would begin only on 20 July when the final peace accords were signed, but at the same time the 23 June 2016 text already contained some of the provisions of the final peace agreement. The failure to halt combat immediately was less significant than it seemed, because as mentioned before, both sides had agreed to a partial cease fire in July 2015 and had limited their operations to only defensive actions; as a result, combat engagements had practically disappeared by the end of 2015.[30]

What was new in the 23 June 2016 text was the announcement that the demobilization would take place during the six months following the signing of the accord on 20 July and that the guerrillas would congregate in 23 zones. The dispute over the number of zones had earlier threatened to block the peace agreement, but the intervention of U.N. negotiators proved decisive in reaching agreement. U.N. officials acting under the mandate of the Security Council were in charge of supervising the demobilization and disarmament of FARC guerrillas.[31] In the case of Colombia, the United Nations had stepped in to fill the vacuum left by the weak regional body, the Organization of American States.

The overwhelming desire for an end to the conflict was so intense in congress, in the Constitutional Court, and in the great majority of the Colombian people that the demobilization of FARC seems inevitable in 2017. The long dragged-out nature of the process, rather than being surprising, actually corresponded with the way the insurgency began. The military campaign against Marquetalia during 1962–1964, the real start of this guerrilla movement, had not occurred in one day but over several years, and perhaps it was inevitable that the end of FARC should likewise take place in gradual steps over several years.[32]

And the transition from violence to peace was certain not to be complete, because already in 2016 signs abounded that as FARC contingents prepared psychologically to demobilize, their authority over regions was starting to erode. Without the restraining force of FARC, some guerrilla militants who saw their way of life coming to an end were searching for profitable alternatives and new employment opportunities.[33] A similar process had taken place with the supposed demobilization of paramilitary groups during 2003–2005 when many former paramilitaries became members of criminal bands still afflicting many regions of Colombia. Although formal guerrilla warfare in all probability will come to an end during 2017, the violence and crime endemic in the country's history will certainly continue in the foreseeable future.

Peru: Trapped in Conflicts

In the presidential campaign of 1990 Alberto Fujimori began the pattern of candidates promising populist and leftist solutions but then turning to the right with a pro-capitalist agenda once they took office. The pattern reappeared in the administrations of Alejandro Toledo, Alán García, and could not be different under Ollanta Humala. Admittedly these presidencies were not carbon copies of the Fujimori model, yet they adopted the common strategy of disguising their intentions during an initial honeymoon period. In contrast Fujimori already in his first month in office shocked Peru with a drastic austerity package. Almost as if performing a carefully choreographed dance, these three other presidents initially lulled the population into a false sense of security before striking hard and fast at the unsuspecting victims.

Humala followed the script, but he showed himself to be the ruler most hesitant to use force and repression to impose capitalist measures. Repeatedly he went to the brink but backed off before inflicting another Arequipazo on the country. He tried to push the capitalist agenda forward through a combination of bluffs and force demonstrations, but when confronted with widespread and determined popular resistance, he inevitably found a way to defuse or at least postpone the confrontation.

The shift from left to right seemed ironic because Wall Street and Peruvian business initially were terrified that as a former Lieutenant Colonel like the dreaded Hugo Chávez, Humala intended to follow the example of Venezuela. As chapter 16 showed, even before he took office in 2011 he already had caved in to the demands of Wall Street and Peruvian business. Full recognition of his status came during his visit to Washington D.C. in June 2013 when U.S. business leaders and President Barack Obama welcomed him as someone who was bucking the socialist tendency in neighboring countries.[34] For Humala, the shift to a pro-capitalist position had not been a very huge jump, because all along he had held only the mildest of leftist views. As explained in previous chapters, at most he espoused a very narrow nationalism, but this belief was rapidly emerging as mere words disconnected from the material poverty so many Peruvians were having to suffer.

Beginning with the Fujimori administration but in particular since the Toledo presidency, figures showing rapid economic growth had fueled the belief that capitalism was the solution for Peru's endemic problems. This mistaken illusion wounded the Toledo administration that barely limped to the end of its term and almost destroyed the García presidency. If the annual growth figures were as spectacular as economists enthusiastically claimed did not matter, because it was impossible to deny the increasing concentration of wealth in the hands of a very small privileged minority, in particular the top 1 percent of society. Income inequality intensified as the economy supposedly grew, and the geographical disparity inside the country also worsened, with the coastal zone receiving most of the benefits and the highlands in the Andes Mountains bearing most of the costs. Because the prosperity of Peru came mainly from mineral exports, principally gold and copper, and also lead and zinc, the resource-rich areas suffered the ravages of mining in order to benefit small privileged groups in the coastal zones.[35]

President Humala had to decide between supporting the popular protests or the foreign mining corporations. The decision became a litmus test for Peruvian business leaders, who although rarely involved in mining, saw in mineral exports the basis for their prosperity. An effective alliance between foreign corporations, Wall Street, and Peruvian business created a formidable barrier to any president who dared to sympathize with the demands of protestors in mining areas. Humala, in spite of the broken promises during his campaign, became a resolute supporter of the mining enterprises in Peru. Once his decision became public knowledge, not surprisingly his approval ratings began dropping and continued to do so until the end of his term. Humala joined the list of presidents who again had sacrificed the interests of the Peruvian people for the sake of supporting capitalism.[36]

The demand for profits is insatiable, and this greed means that no matter how much

Humala or any other president did for corporations, additional demands were inevitable. Business groups knew that to have a docile and obedient population, they needed to have the full support of the media. During the years of Fujimori his infamous associate Vladimiro Montesinos had bribed reporters, television stations, and other press outlets to assure a steady stream of propaganda for the dictatorship and its pro-business policies, but how could Peru find an institutional substitute? Capitalism provided the solution with its inherent monopoly trends, a characteristic intimately linked to the concentration of wealth in the hands of a small minority.

Each sector of the economy gradually fell under the control of one or a few large enterprises, and this phenomenon likewise happened in the outlets of the press, television, and radio. As will be recalled, the newspaper *El Comercio* had tried to destroy the campaign of Humala, and yet at that time it only controlled about 50 percent of the media. The independent newspaper *La Republica* was left with a measly share of 17 percent after it had lost the struggle with wealthier *El Comercio* to acquire a rival outlet. Without a need for the criminal practices of Montesinos, the business community acquired a near monopoly on the media in Peru. But in contrast to the foreign denunciations against the Bolivarian Revolution for reducing press freedom, the business takeover in Peru rarely merited a mention and much less any analysis.[37] And when Humala in one of his last acts of defiance stated that this concentration of media ownership was bad for the country, the leading business group promptly slapped him down and warned him that statements like these "are harming business confidence and worsening the climate for investments."[38]

Humala dropped any plans to ask congress for legislation preventing concentration of ownership in the media, yet not even a constant barrage of propaganda could persuade the inhabitants of the highlands to accept the massive mining projects threatening their communities. After the suspension of the Conga project in Cajamarca Department in January 2014, the next big test for the pro-business credentials of Humala came with the Tía María copper mine in the extreme southern tip of Arequipa Department. The Southern Copper Corporation wanted to dig open pit mines, and the proximity of the mineral deposits to the sea made the site particularly attractive for exporting the ore. This Mexican firm in a drive to maximize profits decided to use the scarce fresh water in the agricultural region rather than the desalinated water from the nearby ocean. In a reaction similar to that experienced during the Lime War in Piura Department in the northern coast region of Peru, the farmers saw their ancestral livelihood threatened and bitterly opposed the start of operations. In a referendum in late 2009 the inhabitants voted overwhelmingly against mining in their province, but the national government routinely ignored these ballot initiatives.[39]

Two violent work stoppages and road blocks in April and November 2010 failed to stop the exploratory work. A third violent strike in March 2011 ended with the death of four farmers, and when a report from an agency of the United Nations validated the environmental concerns of the inhabitants, the government wisely decided to postpone work on the open pit mine. The simultaneous outbreak of the struggle over the Conga mine monopolized the attention of the government, and when protesters succeeded in blocking the start of the expansion of gold mining operations, the Humala administration began looking for other ways to increase mineral exports.[40]

The Great Recession brought a decline in mineral prices, and the Humala administration saw in the revival of the Tía María copper mine an easy way to increase proceeds from exports. To try to assuage the concerns of local inhabitants, Southern Copper

Corporation promised to obtain all its water from a desalination plant on the Pacific Coast. As environmental experts observed, had the company promised in 2009 not to use local waters, it might just have secured local tolerance for the project, but after the bloodshed of the previous clashes, the community was dead set against the project. Anti-mining activists from the Conga gold mine came to Tía María to share their tactics with the locals who already were determined to block the start of exploration.[41]

On 23 March 2015 the inhabitants began daily protests against Southern Peru Corporation, and the demonstrations only became worse when in April Humala publicly announced his full support for the mining project. In an attempt to awe the protestors into submission, the government sent 4,000 police into the region. In addition the army deployed 1,000 troops to guard some of the crossings and bridges in the strategic area near the border with Chile. The inhabitants set up barricades and burned tires to block the roads not just near Tía María but also throughout southern Peru. The culminating confrontation came when residents of Arequipa tore cobblestones from the central plaza and hurled them at police. In the clashes two protesters and one policeman died.[42]

Humala announced that the government could not unilaterally halt the project out of fear of very costly lawsuits and that any cancellation also hurt the image of Peru as a friendly place for foreign investors. However, in behind the scenes negotiations with the Mexican company, community leaders and government officials quietly argued for a voluntary withdrawal. Southern Copper realized that without at least the tolerance of the inhabitants operations were impossible and on 15 May 2015 it announced a suspension of the project for sixty days. This face-saving device allowed the situation to return to normal in Arequipa department. However, investigative reporters discovered that in early 2016 the company was conducting behind-the-scenes maneuvers to obtain authorization from the outgoing Humala administration to authorize the mining project.[43]

Meanwhile the public's attention shifted to the presidential campaign, with the first polls of voters' intentions coming out in July 2015. As will be recalled, Humala had narrowly defeated Keiko Fujimori in the runoff election of 5 June 2011, and not surprisingly she loomed as the candidate most likely to win in 2016. Beginning with the first polls in July 2015 and continuing until March 2016, she consistently emerged in first place with at least 30 percent of voter preferences, although only rarely did she reach the high of one-third of the electorate. She formally announced her candidacy on 4 December 2015, but whether she won the presidency ultimately depended on the appeal of the candidates running against her.[44]

Peru had no shortage of candidates for the first round of elections on 10 April 2016, but for months it was not clear who would be her rivals. By the end of 2015 the number of candidates rose to 19, and the inevitable fragmentation of the electorate guaranteed a runoff election. Among the candidates were the two former presidents Alejandro Toledo and Alán García, but they were so discredited that they lacked any chance to win. The most serious contender to Keiko was the economist Pedro Pablo Kuczynsky, who during 2015 was consistently polling around 15 percent of voter preference, considerably below her but higher than the other candidates. His initial rise was hard to understand, because the 77-year-old lacked charisma and did not have any following outside Lima. And as a former prime minister and finance minister of Toledo, he also was tarnished by his close association with some of the worst capitalist policies of that disastrous presidency.[45]

In January 2016 voters suddenly abandoned Kuczysky and shifted their preferences to a new face, the economist Julio Guzmán who was also closely connected to international financial institutions. Keiko continued to lead with her 31 percentage preference with voters, "nevertheless the big surprise was the surge of Julio Guzmán,"[46] who rose to second place. People were attracted to him because he was a fresh new face and not connected to the scandals of the past, while his innate conservatism reassured the business sector. Nobody could win the first round, but Guzmán had emerged as the first real rival to Keiko. And as recently as 2006, García, the second-place winner in the first round, had gone on to win the presidential election, so a repeat of this maneuver was possible for Guzmán in 2016.[47]

Just as the presidential campaign of 2016 was heating up to become a real contest between an outsider and traditional politicians, a totally unforeseen and unique event occurred. On 9 March 2016, the Electoral Board disqualified two of the 19 candidates. The five board members unanimously decided to disqualify one candidate when he was taped buying votes in a public square, but only three voted to remove Guzmán from the list of candidates. Claiming that the candidate had not met all the filing requirements, the Electoral Board singled him out for punishment when in reality other candidates had also failed to meet those same requisites. Had this decision occurred in late 2015, it might have been justified, but the timing just one month before the first round in 10 April 2016 was completely unacceptable. The maneuver reeked of the worst intrigues of the Fujimori administration, and was an action Vladimiro Montesinos would have been proud to author.[48]

With the elimination of Guzmán, who had been the most dangerous rival in the 2016 campaign, the road was clear for the election of Keiko. The return to the shady deals of her father's administration reinforced the underlying unease about her possible presidency. Because polls showed that she still kept a lead of at least five percent in voter preference over Kuczynski, Keiko emerged as the favorite for the 5 June runoff election. Her popularity reflected both the gratitude many poor people felt for her father who had distributed funds to many of the lower class during his presidency of 1990–2000 and also the failure of the administrations of Toledo, García, and Humala to improve substantially the standard of living of most Peruvians. Over-idealization of her father's legacy was propelling Keiko to the presidency, even though she knew that her father had exhausted the supply of readily available funds to distribute to the lower class.[49]

Candidate Kuczynski immediately after the first round turned to the left for support. He knew that he had to secure the votes of the left, particularly of all those citizens who had voted for the third-place winner. Even though the capitalist ideology of Kuczynski was anathema to leftists, they valiantly swallowed their pride and decided that preventing the revival of a Fujimori dictatorship was the immediate and more urging task. As leftists slowly took the agonizing decision of supporting a right-wing candidate they truly despised, the poll numbers of Keiko began to fall, and her voter preference dropped to less than five percent over Kuczynski. Because the party of Keiko had already won in the congressional elections a clear majority in the National Assembly (73 out of 130 seats), her campaign failed to realize the dangers in her gradual descent in the polls. However, so many of her associates had been involved in the scandals of her father's administration that she could not send surrogates to praise her virtues on prime time television, and usually she was left as the sole visible spokesperson of her campaign.[50]

Ten days before the election it still looked that she might limp to the finish line but without the large victory margin she had originally expected. But then her campaign received an unexpected blow when the Drug Enforcement Agency (DEA) announced in late May 2016 the investigation of one of her campaign advisors on charges of money laundering. The media ran with the story and with relentless reporting focused the attention of the public on this new scandal so similar to those of her father. The money-laundering accusations revived the fears about the corruption and favoritism of the Fujimori years, and Keiko could not find a way to distance her campaign from the hostile media coverage. Other major political figures and Nobel winner Mario Vargas Llosa also urged citizens to vote for Kuczynski.[51]

In such a confused situation, when Peruvians went to vote on Sunday 5 June 2016, not surprisingly the initial results were so close that no clear winner emerged immediately. Peru had not experienced such a close election in recent history, and citizens waited anxiously for the electoral authorities to declare a winner. But already in the early results with many districts still not reporting, Keiko was trailing behind Kuczynski. As the numbers came in from the remaining districts, the margin widened slightly, until it became clear that Peru had experienced a political upset: the underdog Kuczynski had defeated the favorite Keiko.[52]

The victory margin was small, with Kuczynski receiving 50.12 percent of the popular vote compared to 49.88 percent for Keiko. In actual numbers, the winner received 49, 597 more votes out of the 17 million persons who participated in this election. Analysts immediately worried about gridlock because Keiko controlled a majority in the national assembly, but in reality both candidates were staunch supporters of capitalism so these concerns were unfounded. The Fujimori bloc in the congress traditionally had supported the most extreme free market policies which happened to coincide with the views of Kuczynski, a private banker with deep links to the international financial community.[53]

The real losers in the presidential elections of 2016 were the Peruvians, because at the end the choice was down to picking between two candidates of the right. Once again powerful economic groups both foreign and domestic had shown that through elections they could gain control of the structures of the national government. While analysts needlessly worried about how Kuczynski was going to get approval from the Fujimori bloc for legislation, the real question was whether he was going to continue imposing a capitalist and free trade agenda on the country. Two alternatives lay before the new president. He could follow the measured and moderate path of Ollanta Humala and thus gradually end this period of social conflict in the history of Peru. Or to the contrary he could insist on imposing privatization and foreign mining as Toledo and García had attempted to do even in the face of massive resistance. The experience of the first fifteen years of the twenty-first century showed that the latter path could only lead to renewed social conflict and intensified clashes throughout the country.

Venezuela: The Bolivarian Revolution on the Defensive

Trying to Fill the Shoes of Hugo Chávez The death of Hugo Chávez on 5 March 2013 was the only instance in the period covered in this book when an acting president died in office. Under the best of circumstances any transition to a new government had to be difficult and rife with mistakes as a new team tried to assume the functions of ruling a country. In the case of Venezuela, two additional factors made the transition even harder. The 1999 Constitution called for new elections to choose the next president 30 days later, so that the interim regime had to cope with the burdens of both ruling a country and winning an electoral campaign. Secondly, at stake was not just finding a successor to Chávez but also deciding upon the fate of his legacy. The election of 14 April was really about whether voters wanted to preserve the Bolivarian Revolution or return to the failed Fourth Republic of the twentieth century.

Everything indicated that the overwhelming majority of voters were totally opposed to returning to the corrupt Fourth Republic and that consequently Nicolás Maduro, the handpicked successor of Chávez, could expect an easy victory. Opposition leader Henrique Capriles wrestled with this conundrum and concluded that the only way to defeat Maduro was to take Chávez out of the election. The first hint of this strategy had come in the gracious concession speech after the 7 October 2012 presidential election, a campaign he had considered a practice run for the real contest against Maduro. In a televised speech in April 2013 Capriles explained that he was not running against Chávez; he was perhaps the first opposition leader to realize that the only way to win an election was to persuade Chavista voters to defect. Actually, his most difficult task was not to lure away Chavista voters but to persuade opposition voters to abandon their public hatred of the deceased president. And unless the rival candidate neutralized the sympathy vote after the magnificent state funeral for Chávez and the mass outpouring of emotions, Capriles knew that he had no chance of defeating Maduro who initially was leading in the polls by a wide margin.[54]

Ever since his election in 1998, a steady stream of increasingly virulent anti–Chávez statements had been the only factor uniting the opposition. Many upper and middle class voters, long accustomed to Chávez bashing, could not accept the image of a wise and well-intentioned ruler. But this rehabilitated image was indispensable to lure Chavistas in sufficient numbers away from Maduro. Once Chávez was out of the race, then the task of portraying his anointed successor as vastly inferior was relatively easy. The opposition repeatedly emphasized that Maduro, a former bus driver who had not completed his high school education, lacked the credentials of the well-educated Chávez who besides graduating from the military academy had completed an advanced degree; because Venezuelans have always been attracted to military figures, the subliminal message that Maduro was just a civilian also diminished his appeal. To try to counter the gap the opposition was creating between him and Chávez, Maduro embraced more desperately the image of the deceased president. He cited Chávez at least 7000 times in his campaign speeches, and no rally was complete without extended homage to huge portraits of the former president. In death Chávez was visible even more than he had been in life.[55]

Pundits dismissed Maduro's embrace of Chávez as pure theater, when in reality the candidate had never psychologically recovered from the unexpected departure of his mentor. The message that Chávez had been a great president whose only mistake was his choice of successor was starting to resonate with Chavista voters and even with Maduro who never had considered himself able to replace the deceased leader. And if the followers did not always detect the differences in the educational level of Chávez and Maduro, the latter's inability to whip up a crowd clearly revealed an inferior performance. This was not the first electoral campaign for Maduro who previously had been elected a deputy to the National Assembly, but it was one thing to campaign as a native son in a small familiar area and another to replicate the excitement that Chávez always created by his mere appearance. The impassioned and fiery rhetoric was missing, and as Maduro struggled to connect with voters, many started to believe the opposition's claims that Chávez had picked the wrong person to succeed him.[56]

In a longer campaign Maduro certainly would have found his stride, but in the short period of weeks he necessarily struggled when at the same time he had to cope with rivalries inside his own party. The two finalists for receiving the blessing of Chávez had been Maduro and the president of the National Assembly, Diosdado Cabello. Except for the latter's absolute loyalty to Chávez, he had always been an enigmatic figure bordering on the shady. The Cubans had correctly urged Chávez to select Maduro, but the open question remained whether Cabello could shift his loyalty from Chávez to the new president. With tremendous influence inside the Unified Socialist Party of Venezuela (*Partido Socialista Unificado de Venezuela*) or PSUV, all that Cabello had to do was to sit out the campaign, and without the enthusiastic support of his followers most likely Maduro would lose the election. But sometime during the brief presidential campaign Cabello redid his political calculations and concluded that for him an opposition win was a lot worse than a Maduro victory. Before the end of the campaign Cabello was working hard to save the new president.[57]

In April 2013 Cabello was just starting to rally to Maduro's side, while Capriles was still having trouble persuading all opposition figures to stop attacking Chávez and to concentrate on the deficiencies of Maduro. Chávez had won his last presidential election on 7 October 2012 with a margin of 10 percent over Capriles, but on 14 April Maduro running against the same opposition candidate barely squeezed by with a margin of less than 2 percent or just 262,000 votes. In another confirmation that the essence of democratic elections had failed to take root in Venezuela, the opposition, rather than accepting completely the clear results, concluded that Maduro was weak and vulnerable to being pushed out of office. The opposition had learned nothing and, just like after the 49 decrees of November 2001, began to look for ways to remove the elected president from office. Calls again surfaced not just to use the recall mechanism of the 1999 Constitution but also to approve an amendment for new presidential elections. And lurking behind was the possibility of creating so much disorder that Maduro would have to resign from office, possibly in response to pressure from disgruntled military officers.[58]

The narrow victory on 14 April came as a shock to the Maduro administration, and officials feared that this apparent weakness might persuade opposition leaders to try something extreme. Officials quickly put a stop to reprisals by zealous supporters who began to fire employees at government institutions. The most obvious cases came at the nationalized Banco de Venezuela, where not all employees had embraced the Bolivarian Revolution and many individuals still remained deeply attached to the old capitalist ways. But without anything comparable to the Tascón list to determine who was in the opposition, any widespread reprisal attempts could turn into a witch hunt targeting innocent people; apparently several hundred individuals suffered some penalties before the government prohibited this type of punishment.[59]

The narrow electoral victory persuaded the Maduro administration that it could no longer afford the luxury of having a hostile television station broadcasting on air waves. In February 2010 Globovisión had changed its broadcasts from violent attacks to a more moderate centrist position, but the Maduro administration concluded that it needed to go farther. The government brought extreme pressure on the owners who in early May sold the television station to a group of investors closely connected to the Maduro administration. The tone of the broadcasts became upbeat, even though the TV network occasionally still provided healthy and useful criticism of the government.[60]

Advocates of the press saw the change in Globovisión as another restriction on freedom of expression, when in reality it was one more step in persuading business groups to accept the Bolivarian Revolution. The message was clear: those businessmen who supported the Maduro administration received benefits, but those who joined the opposition suffered penalties and in extreme cases could even be nationalized. The financial calculations of a positive bottom line trumped any ideological preferences for the free market, and Maduro was able to seal an alliance with the leading businessman of Venezuela, Lorenzo Mendoza, the owner of Polar the second biggest corporation in the country (state oil corporation PDVSA was the largest). Both the government and Polar needed each other, but in the past personal animosity between Mendoza and Chávez had been so bitter that the government even considered nationalizing the private company. Maduro was a new face, and without the baggage of previous hostility he could seek a reconciliation.[61]

Polar was best known as the largest brewery in the country, although it also produced basic food products such as the flour for the corn patties (*arepas*) and many other household items in the family shopping basket. The sale of beer was the biggest source of revenue for the company, and restrictions on imported whiskey increased its revenues. No policy of supplying foodstuffs to consumers and supporting domestic agriculture could be successful without the participation of Polar that stood to gain enormous benefits. Shortly after the election Maduro invited Mendoza to a private meeting at Miraflores Palace as a first step toward ironing out differences. This meeting helped increase the perception among private businesses that if profits were the real goal, then cooperation rather than confrontation with the government was the best alternative. Businessmen had learned the lesson that having FEDECAMARAS and other trade groups openly clash with the government was counterproductive; most private businesses refused to support the opposition politicians who seemed intent on repeating the costly and failed attempts of the first decade of the twenty-first century.[62]

Looking for another way to weaken the political opposition, in early October Maduro sought authorization from the National Assembly to issue decrees with the force of law. Here he was following the example of Hugo Chávez who had several times received similar authorization, and on 19 November the legislature under the leadership of Cabello approved an enabling law giving the president the authority to legislate during the next twelve months. Within the PSUV the fear was that Maduro planned to use this extraordinary power to move Venezuela into the direction of a Cuban-style socialism, but the real risk was that the move might drive opposition politicians to seek extremist solutions.[63]

The first use of the enabling law was more for electoral gimmickry than socialist transformation. As the municipal elections of December 8 approached, Maduro wanted to show that the PSUV enjoyed much more support than had appeared in the presidential contest of April 14. The Christmas shopping season came early to Venezuelans in late November when "in what amounted to a nationwide fire sale, huge crowds have been descending on retailers across the country for weeks, after President Nicolás Maduro ordered discounts on everything from clothing and cellphones to car parts and home supplies."[64] The trick seemed to have aroused the latent sympathy of many voters for the Bolivarian Revolution, and in the municipal elections of December 8 the PSUV won in two-thirds of municipalities. Equally revealing, the percentage of victory of the PSUV rose to a margin of nearly 10 percent over the rival coalition.[65]

The municipal elections should have dispelled the idea that the Bolivarian Revolution no longer enjoyed overwhelming support from the population. However, opposition politicians insisted on believing that Maduro was simple unable to replace Chávez. As a supposedly weak and inept president, the politicians saw Maduro as vulnerable, but they disagreed on the best way to drive him from office.

Violent Protests: February—April 2014 After the presidential election of April 2013 the opposition fell into two main groups. Those preferring violent demonstrations and street clashes were in the camp of Leopoldo López and Marina Corina Machado, while those seeking a peaceful solution had Henrique Capriles as their leader. The priorities were not absolute, because both groups were sometimes willing to combine peaceful with violent actions. Those opposition figures seeking a peaceful solution suffered a severe setback in the mayoral elections of 8 December 2013. The shattering of the myth that a majority of Venezuelans were just waiting to repudiate the Bolivarian Revolution meant that Nicolás Maduro was very likely to finish his six-year presidential term.[66] No realistic option existed to remove Maduro from office until the opposition gained control of the National Assembly in the legislative elections of December 2015 and then only with a two-thirds majority.

The faction of Capriles tried to keep alive illusions such as anticipating presidential elections and another recall vote. In response to their bases, hard-liners López and Machado were hungrily looking for an opportunity to drive Maduro from office through a mass mobilization. But they needed an issue to galvanize public attention, and it at last appeared when the government in January 2014 announced its intention to increase gradually the price of gasoline from 5 cents a gallon to around 17 cents. The last increase in price had occurred in 1996, and Venezuela was long overdue for at least this modest increase. The low price created serious distortions in the economy, and among other imbalances, supported massive smuggling of gasoline across the border into Colombia. Gasoline stations no longer bothered to post prices, and the low price was a permanent source of losses for PDVSA.[67]

Because the government planned to continue subsidizing public transportation, the lower class, which did not own many vehicles, was largely spared of any negative effects. The brunt of the blow of any increase in gasoline prices fell hardest on the middle class, the group that comprised the largest percentage of automobile owners in the country. Also adversely affected were the smugglers who sold gasoline to Colombia from the bordering states.[68]

López and Machado convoked their followers to a demonstration on 12 February 2014 not so much to protest the gasoline increase as to demand the resignation or what came to be known as "the exit" (*la salida*) of Nicolás Maduro. López participated personally in the march and openly incited the crowds to engage in acts of violence against the government. Street clashes turned bloody, with at least three deaths and dozens more injured; the opposition gained its first martyrs, and 12 February became the official start date of the violent demonstrations to drive Maduro from office. Because similar protests had driven out governments from office in other countries, most recently in Ukraine, the foreign media enthusiastically reported the unfolding events and confidently expected the fall of another supposedly corrupt and dictatorial regime.[69]

The gendarmerie of Venezuela (National Guard) was trying to control the continuing protests, and the next day on 13 February the government issued an arrest warrant for López, who went into custody on 18 February. Because U.S. consular officials had been in contact with university students, Maduro had the perfect opportunity to denounce

American involvement. On 17 February he ordered the expulsion of three U.S. consular officials, and this fanning of anti-American sentiment helped to discredit the protests. Deprived of the leadership of López the street marches were starting to die down, and it seemed that the government had overcome this latest obstacle from the divided opposition.[70]

Capriles had not supported the 12 February protest demonstration, but the outcry to avenge the fallen martyrs made him reconsider his position. The imprisonment of López gave Capriles the opportunity to become the single undisputed leader of the opposition provided he preempted Machado. In a remarkable turnaround, on 21 February Capriles decided to call on his supporters for a massive demonstration on Saturday 22 February. In a first very public sign of U.S. support, Secretary of State John Kerry made a statement defending the right of Venezuelans to protest. The march was tremendously successful, with possibly over a hundred thousand persons participating; the opposition had not had this level of popular participation since the massive protest that had launched the coup attempt of 11 April 2002. Opposition leaders, quick to draw false analogies, concluded that the opportunity to overthrow the government had presented itself again.[71]

The massive 22 February demonstration marked the start of a new phase in the campaign to drive Maduro from office. The next day on Sunday protestors showed up in smaller numbers, and very ominously a retired army general incited the population to defy the government. Did the statements of the retired general represent a lone voice or did they reflect wider concerns among the military? Would the protests of 2014 be the cue to trigger a previously planned military coup as happened in April 2002? Many protestors felt that if the confrontation dragged on, the generals necessarily had to force Maduro to leave office. On Monday 24 February the protestors had already made up their mind, and no longer did they go on the streets just to protest; in a very dangerous escalation, they established road blocks in key streets and began to set up barricades in many neighborhoods.[72]

Up to this moment the National Guard had been able to contain the demonstrations, but the road blocks and the barricades complicated the task of clearing the streets. Not wishing to use excessive force, the government tolerated a certain stalemate in Caracas as protestors standing behind barricades stared down the National Guard. The protests were no longer just in the capital city but also spread to the regions bordering Colombia, particularly Táchira. With the aim of lowering tensions, on 27 February Maduro offered to negotiate with the opposition, but the hard liners saw this offer as a sign of weakness and refused to participate. In an attempt to reduce the confrontations, on February 26 Maduro declared the next two days national holidays so that Venezuelans could go to the seashore to celebrate the carnival. The government added many bus routes so that Venezuelans could go to the beaches and enjoy the carnival season and let off some tension.[73]

The violence did diminish, but after the carnival most protestors returned to their barricades and once again faced off the police at the road blocks. March was shaping up to be the decisive month to determine the outcome of the demonstrations, and in preparation protestors set up residential camps in several places to confirm their determination to stay until the end. The authorities knew that before striking, the protest movement needed time to lose its initial energy. The government was confident that it enjoyed the luxury of riding out the storm, because the location of the protests and barricades largely in middle and upper class neighborhoods persuaded the Maduro administration that the popular sectors of the population were still solidly loyal.[74]

The government could afford to wait out the violent opposition, while the National Guard kept open the principal avenues in Caracas. Clearing the many road blocks required the use of troops, but the president did not want to call on the army. As a partial alternative, motorcycle gangs (*colectivos*) of Chavistas under Lino Pinto began attacking protestors; these were the same *colectivos* that had been largely under the control of the colorful female personality Lina Ron before her death. While the opposition later demonized the *colectivos*, they were involved at most in a third of the violent clashes with demonstrators.[75] Besides their actual effect on scattering demonstrators, the *colectivos* served as reminder to the middle class that large numbers of militants were willing to take any action to defend the Bolivarian Revolution.

The cracks inside the opposition became deeper, beginning with the willingness of Capriles to start negotiating with the government. He had viewed the successful rally of 22 February as a demonstration of popular strength to obtain concessions from an administration desperate to return peace to the country, but the hardliners insisted on seeing that rally as the beginning of a violent insurrection to topple Maduro. Whether the violence came from the protestors or the *colectivos* became irrelevant to many middle class individuals who were increasingly disenchanted with violence as a means to obtain political change. Within the opposition the demand for a return to peaceful activities increasingly contrasted with the cries of hardliners to convert the demonstrations into an armed resistance on the style of insurrectionary movements.[76]

Toward the end of March, residents in many middle class neighborhoods wanted the nightmare of protests to finish. While services and shops functioned normally in the popular neighborhoods in the west, middle class residents could not reach their supermarkets that were poorly stocked for the first time because of the road blocks and the barricades. The foreign media, eagerly looking for the fall of the government, rarely mentioned that by the end of March clashes had broken out inside middle class neighborhoods between residents who wanted to dismantle the barricades and extremists who insisted on attacking the National Guard and the *colectivos*. For its part, on 24 March the government arrested three generals suspected of plotting, thereby eliminating any illusion about a military coup, and the next day the National Assembly expelled deputy Machado for having incited the people to revolt.[77]

Sensing the opposition weakening, Capriles insisted on his original position of holding negotiations, and both sides agreed to talks on 10 April. In a major concession, the government authorized the live broadcasting of the talks on television channels. The extremists and the student activists, however, refused to participate in the dialogue, so in a sense the government was negotiating with those groups that had already abandoned the protests but not with those still on the streets. Maduro had timed perfectly the right moment to clear the streets, and the authorities had already identified the few remaining strongholds of the violent demonstrators. The talks of 10 April were stretching late into the night when many units of the National Guard swooped down and overran the camps of protestors and removed the last remaining barricades. The operation had been so swift and unexpected, that the drowsy protestors had little time to respond before they either fled or were arrested.[78]

For all practical purposes the talks on 10 April and the subsequent raids shattered the protest movement. Extremists were angry with moderate leaders for having engaged in negotiations with officials on live TV, and the whole episode created deep splits inside the opposition. The raids revealed that the protestors could not count on support even in the neighborhoods of the middle class. Die-hard demonstrators could only rally small numbers of supporters for protest marches over the coming days, and by the end of April the protests fizzled out.[79]

The movement to overthrow Maduro never had a chance to succeed because of the lack of popular support, and the street protests lasted only until the middle class turned against the demonstrators. The massive international coverage on television and newspapers, however, had gained the demonstrators foreign support. The victory of the Republican Party in the midterm elections in the United States brought back a hawkish tone to relations with Venezuela, even though the Maduro administration struggled to prove U.S. involvement in the protest movement. The examination of diplomatic cables released by Wikileaks left no doubt about the hostility of the Bush administration, but proving that in 2014 the U.S. government wanted to overthrow Maduro was not so easy. But the need to find evidence disappeared when on 21 May Secretary of State John Kerry publicly threatened U.S. sanctions against Venezuela and later the Republican-controlled U.S. Congress passed them. In a contrast with the Bush administration in 2002 that had generally kept its preferences quiet while actively trying to overthrow Chávez, the Obama administration was openly declaring its hostility.[80]

The U.S. sanctions bolstered the popularity of the Maduro presidency by arousing Venezuelan nationalism. The government easily wrapped itself as the defender of Venezuela against the empire of the north, a strategy that Chávez had utilized to great effect on many occasions. The violent protests of February-April 2014, rather than weakening the Maduro administration, had actually made it stronger and reaffirmed its credentials as a nationalistic defender of the legacy of Hugo Chávez. The victory over the protestors confirmed an earlier confidential analysis of the opposition that not only "is Chavismo actually a stable political regimen, sustained by a complex of its own institutions" but "it is also independent of the personal will of the leader and has its own dynamic force."[81]

The Continuing Confrontation The fall in petroleum prices in 2015 posed a different set of challenges for the Maduro administration, which was slow to respond. As imports declined and lines formed outside grocery stores, Maduro finally asked the National Assembly for enabling authority to issue decrees with the force of law. An internal struggle inside the administration failed to reach a consensus on what measures were needed, and as the economic situation worsened, the approval ratings of the government fell. A new test loomed ahead for the Bolivarian Revolution in late 2015 with the legislative elections, but the administration could not decide to use its enabling authority to counterbalance the deteriorating conditions. Oil prices continued to fall, and the government did little to deal with the economic problems facing the population under the assumption that any rash measures would hurt its chances to retain control of the National Assembly in the elections of 6 December 2015.[82]

The opposition at last saw an opportunity to strike a major blow against the Bolivarian Revolution. In an unprecedented feat, the over 20 opposition political parties united to run a single slate for all deputies to the National Assembly. Not even this unexpected show of force could prod the government into action, and the result was a near landslide victory for the loose coalition in the legislative election of 6 December 2015. For the first time the Bolivarian Revolution lost control of the National Assembly, and preliminary results suggested that the opposition had gained a two-thirds majority that would allow it to repeal many populist and socialist features.[83]

The opposition fed the illusions of foreign critics that this sharp turn to the right in the legislative body would persuade the government to abandon its socialist policies and to support a pro-capitalist agenda. Such an illusion assumed that Maduro lacked any firm convictions and that he would cave in as had happened with presidents in the United States as soon as conservatives gained control of the congress. The response in Venezuela was precisely the opposite, because the electoral outcome, where two million former Chavistas shifted their votes to the opposition, conclusively proved that the response of doing very little about the deteriorating economic situation had been a complete failure. The setback shocked the Maduro administration into a frantic pace of countermeasures. A galvanized government proceeded with a two-fold strategy first of damage control to limit the harm the hostile National Assembly could do and then of adopting new measures to deal with the economic hardships that the fall in petroleum prices had created for Venezuela.[84]

The outgoing National Assembly remained in office until 15 December, and Maduro rushed through a whole series of judicial appointments through the legislative body; he also named loyalists to all unfilled executive positions requiring congressional confirmation. A decisive action came on 31 December, when the Supreme Court blocked three deputies from taking office because of irregularities in their elections; without these three deputies, the opposition fell short of the two-thirds majority needed to approve major legislative bills such as constitutional amendments and recall measures.[85]

The firm alliance between the executive and judicial branches put the National Assembly on the defensive early in 2016. As he had done in the past, Maduro asked the deputies to grant him enabling authority to issue laws to deal with the economic crisis. The slim hope existed that the deputies would listen more to their voters who wanted concrete solutions to their economic problems, but the opposition preferred to score an easy victory by defeating the request for enabling authority. This was the first big mistake of an opposition that began gaining the image of being more interested in scoring political points than in solving the problems of the country. The field was wide open for Maduro to declare on 14 January 2016 that because of the emergency the country faced, he could no longer wait for legislators to make up their mind, and consequently he was assuming emergency powers, initially for a sixty-day period. Promptly the National Assembly appealed this decision to the Supreme Court, which on 11 February completely ratified the president's authority as long as the emergency situation existed.[86]

This was the most important of several major victories that reduced the power of the National Assembly by March 2016. Once the opposition realized that it lacked any real powers, it turned to its traditional occupation of planning the overthrown of the government. Ever since 2001 the most extremist elements in the opposition had never abandoned the idea of driving the president from power. All efforts against Chávez had failed, but the opposition believed that a weaker and less charismatic Maduro was a much easier target. So as not to fail this time, the leaders planned a three-fold strategy in the hope that at least one of the alternatives would succeed.[87]

A first alternative was to pass a constitutional amendment shortening the presidential term from six to four years and thus force Maduro to face voters for his ultimate electoral defeat. Without the control of the judiciary branch, this alternative was impossible to attain and was struck down by the Supreme Court in April 2016. Another proposal was to stage a recall of the president after he had completed half his term. This procedure already existed in the 1999 Constitution, but required collecting a huge number of signatures and then getting a majority of citizens to vote for the recall. The hurdles seemed large, and the initiative might just fail as had happened with the recall attempt against Chávez in 2004. The worst alternative was to start a series of escalating protests and street rallies until a defeated Maduro finally resigned from office. This formula was a repetition of the 2014 protests that ultimately contributed to strengthening the government and did not seem very likely to succeed in 2016.[88]

The Opposition's Spring Offensive: April–June 2016 Gaining control of the National Assembly paradoxically came to weaken the opposition, which now fractured into three main groups: the followers of jailed leader Leopoldo López, the supporters of defeated presidential candidate Henrique Capriles, and the new rulers of the legislative branch. The three-fold division made seeking consensus harder among opposition groups, and at first they did not unite to pursue any of the three alternatives aggressively. The National Assembly did not offer constructive criticism as the loyal opposition does in Western countries and instead concentrated all its efforts on removing Maduro from office. At the same time, the anti–Maduro coalition let precious months slip by without taking any decisive action to carry out a change of government.[89]

Low petroleum prices eventually falling below $20 a barrel fueled the discontent in the country, and just like the Bolivarian Revolution had assumed that high oil prices would last forever, so the opposition believed that low prices would last indefinitely. The idea of waiting for the Maduro presidency to become so weakened that only a slight push was needed to provoke its downfall was very alluring. The moment to strike seemed to have come with the return of El Niño in late March when electricity shortages plunged Venezuela into the dark. Chapter 14 showed that the power blackouts of 2009–2010 had created a major political crisis for Hugo Chávez. In 2016 without his charismatic leadership and without ample petroleum revenues, the opposition believed that a vulnerable Maduro was ready to be overthrown. And as an additional incentive, on 5 April the opposition gained the support of the Secretary General of the Organization of American States (OAS) to try to achieve a negotiated change of government.[90]

In April the opposition decided to launch a drive to collect signatures for the recall of Maduro, but by then precious months had passed on an effort that should have begun in January. Beginning in April meant that only under the best of circumstances could the opposition hope to complete the process of collecting signatures for the recall election. Maduro could easily delay the recall election until 10 January 2017, and after that date even if he lost, the vice president automatically replaced him and the Bolivarian Revolution could continue until the end of his term in 2019. Maduro had shown himself to be a masterful fighter, and since January 2016 he had already used all the means at his disposal to block the initiatives of the hostile National Assembly. In particular, the president had crafted an alliance with the Supreme Court to declare unconstitutional any laws threatening the principles of the Bolivarian Revolution.[91]

Many observers considered the president to lack the charisma of his illustrious predecessor, and be that as it may, the opposition failed to recognize in Maduro a fearsome adversary and a born fighter who was determined to struggle as hard as necessary to save the Bolivarian Revolution. Falling oil prices meant food shortages in supermarkets, and to avoid hoarding and price gouging by distributors, in March 2016 Maduro created thousands of Supply Committees (*Comités locales de abastecimiento y producción*) or CLAPs starting in the Chavista neighborhoods of the country. These committees, whose leaders were appointed by the local branch of the Unified Socialist Party of Venezuela (PSUV), were the latest attempt of the Bolivarian Revolution to fill the need for a grassroots organization similar to the Committees for the Defense of the Revolution in Socialist Cuba. The absence of neighborhood institutions with strong links to the people had always been a weakness of the Chávez presidency, and Maduro hoped to remedy that gap with the spread of the CLAPs. However, the creation of these Supply Committees came too late to head off the looting and occasional riots that took place as angry residents, particularly in the states bordering Colombia, broke into grocery stores and sometimes seized food trucks.[92]

The specter haunting the Maduro administration was extremely serious and steadily became worse as the reality of electricity shortages sank in. But this time the government promptly admitted that a problem existed and took immediate steps to counter the shortfall. As is often the case in times of crisis in Venezuela, Maduro appointed a general, Luis Motta, as Minister of Electricity to spearhead the effort against the looming power shortages. Actually the situation was not as bad as in 2009–2010 because Venezuela had expanded its capacity of oil and gas-burning plants to offset declines in the output of hydroelectricity; what was new was the unusual severity of El Niño. According to the best predictions, the severe drought, which was also causing water shortages in the cities, was supposed to end with abundant rains in late May. The government announced crash measures to allow the country to survive through the worst days of the drought. Rationing began on 6 April and by 22 of that month had become rolling blackouts spreading across the country. Starting on 26 April all government offices opened only on Monday and Tuesday. On 9 May the government shortened the academic week by having all schools close on Fridays.[93]

The electricity and water shortages combined with the looting of food stores made Venezuela appear to be on the verge of collapse, an apocalyptic image that the opposition purposely exaggerated in the foreign media. The Barack Obama administration had not made any real effort to use the weakened state of Venezuela to press for the removal of Maduro, but not all sectors of the U.S. government were as complacent. In a briefing to reporters, two U.S. intelligence officials said that Venezuela faced a "meltdown … you can hear the ice cracking. You know there is a crisis coming."[94] Such closed-door briefings have been a traditional tool used by one part of the bureaucracy to influence U.S. foreign policy, but in this case the maneuver backfired. The Obama administration, saddled with the legacy of interventions in the Middle East, was not about to embark upon another foreign adventure, while the Maduro presidency seized on these statements as a life raft to mobilize nationalistic feeling against an impending U.S. invasion. The Venezuelan government now had the proof that Washington saw the country as ripe for the taking, and once again as Chávez had done several times, Maduro rallied nationalists to support his faltering regime.

The most important audience for the nationalistic campaign was the military. Up to this moment in the spring 2016 crisis the armed forces had not really made a clear statement of support for Maduro, but at the same time opposition leaders were trying to establish links with officers for a possible coup to remove the president from office. Since 2001 the opposition had no hesitation about using any means to destroy the Bolivarian Revolution, but the chance of a military coup ended when opposition leaders foolishly announced that they would punish all those officers supporting Maduro. All of a sudden the positions of all high-ranking officers were in danger, and fearing a purge should the opposition come to power, the generals publicly demonstrated their support not just in statements but in very showy parades and military maneuvers. Maduro himself appeared inside a tank, and his review of soldiers marching in lockstep in front of him left no doubt for the population that the military solidly supported the government. Whether the public believed the accusations of an impending U.S. invasion did not matter, because the military support bolstered Maduro's standing and imperceptibly made large segments of the population hesitant to mount an all-out challenge to the government.[95]

The decisive show of force by the military in late May was just the first of a series of events that forcefully strengthened the government. In the first days of June, the attempt by the Secretary General of the Organization of American States (OAS) to support the opposition gradually fizzled out when he found himself not just lacking support from Latin American countries but even from the United States. Even more decisively, as the rains arriving in late May replenished the Guri dam, electricity blackouts became rare during early June and rationing formally ended on 4 July. Without shortages of electricity and water, the opposition lost some of the vital issues to attack the government. Then the rise of petroleum prices to over $40 a barrel provided the biggest boost of all to the Maduro administration. The government was now able to authorize food processor Polar and the auto assembly plants to obtain foreign credits to finance the purchase of much needed raw materials to resume their production. With the additional oil revenue, the government could now engage in extensive purchases of food abroad, and as these imports reached the country, the worst of the food shortages passed. Trinidad and Tobago because of its geographical proximity proved a very convenient source of foodstuffs, and the cargoes usually came by ship but in some urgent cases even by plane into Venezuela.[96]

The opposition incessantly attacked the Supply Committees for favoring Chavistas, and only gradually did residents realize that they had to organize their own committees to be first in line to receive the food imports. The upper and middle class neighborhoods dependent on supermarkets were the hardest hit, and it was not clear when food distribution to all social classes would reach normal levels.[97]

As the Maduro government recovered its vital life forces, it felt emboldened to take a hard line with the recall vote and did everything possibly to block this maneuver. Going on the offensive, the police began occasional arrests of activists whom the government claimed to be inciting crowds to engage in looting of grocery stores. And perhaps the boldest move of all was the proposal to dissolve the National Assembly. Chavista leaders claimed in late June 2016 that the legislature had exceeded its constitutional authority and that the citizens did not really know what they were voting for when they gave the opposition a majority in the legislative elections of 6 December 2015.[98] By having new elections, the people supposedly were sure to renew their support for the socialist candidates; the real challenge was not in dissolving the existing National Assembly but in making sure that the official candidates won. Should the economic outlook continue to improve in Venezuela, at the very least Maduro will remain in the presidency, and the real possibility existed of regaining control of the National Assembly from the divided opposition. On those crucial economic and political tests hung the future survival of the Bolivarian Revolution.

Chapter Notes

Chapter 1

1. David Eugene Blank, *Venezuela: Politics in a Petroleum Republic* (New York: Praeger Publishers, 1984), p. 129.

2. Luis José Silva Luongo, *De Cipriano Castro a Carlos Andrés Pérez, 1899–1979* (Caracas: Monte Ávila, 2005), p. 597; Alfredo Peña, *Conversaciones con Carlos Andrés Pérez*, 2 vols. (Caracas: Ateneo de Caracas, 1979), 2: 67; René De La Pedraja, *Wars of Latin America, 1948–1982: The Rise of the Guerrillas* (Jefferson, NC: McFarland, 2013), pp. 184–185.

3. Gregory Wilpert, *Changing Venezuela by Taking Power: The History and Policies of the Chávez Government* (London: Verso, 2007), pp. 105–115; Blank, *Petroleum Republic*, p. 192.

4. Jonathan Di John, "The Political Economy of Industrial Policy in Venezuela," in Ricardo Hausmann and Francisco Rodríguez, eds., *Venezuela before Chávez: Anatomy of an Economic Collapse* (University Park: Pennsylvania State University Press, 2014), pp. 353–359; Silva Luongo, *De Cipriano Castro a Carlos Andrés Pérez*, p. 731; Blank, *Petroleum Republic*, pp. 180–186.

5. Wilpert, *Changing Venezuela*, pp. 69–72; Silva Luongo, *De Cipriano Castro a Carlos Andrés Pérez*, p. 726.

6. Blank, *Petroleum Republic*, p. 126.

7. Carlos Andrés Pérez, *Memorias proscritas* (Caracas: El Nacional, 2007), pp. 223–228; Blank, *Petroleum Republic*, pp. 123–124.

8. Stephen G. Rabe, *The Road to OPEC: United States Relations with Venezuela, 1919–1976* (Austin: University of Texas Press, 1982), pp. 185–186; Blank, *Petroleum Republic*, p. 145; Silva Luongo, *De Cipriano Castro a Carlos Andrés Pérez*, pp. 785–786; Peña, *Conversaciones con Carlos Andrés Pérez*, 2:60–61; Project Management Institute, "The Guri Dam," George Washington University, 2006.

9. Silva Luongo, *De Cipriano Castro a Carlos Andrés Pérez*, pp. 804–808; Rabe, *The Road to OPEC*, p. 186; Blank, *Petroleum Republic*, pp. 145–147, 150. The full name was Petróleo de Venezuela, Sociedad Anónima, and for a short time the company used the name of PETROVEN. However, the respect for private property rights was so great, that when it was discovered that a small firm had already copyrighted that acronym, the state-owned company adopted PDVSA (pronounced *PeDeVeSa*) as its official designation.

10. Bernard Mommer, "Subversive Oil," in Steve Ellner and Daniel Hellinger, eds., *Venezuelan Politics in the Chávez Era: Class, Polarization, and Conflict* (London: Lynne Rienner Publishers, 2003), p. 132; Pérez, *Memorias proscritas*, pp. 228–229; Blank, *Petroleum Republic*, pp. 156–158; Rabe, *The Road to OPEC*, pp. 185–186.

11. Peña, *Conversaciones con Carlos Andrés Pérez*, 2:41–42; Pérez, *Memorias proscritas*, pp. 261–262.

12. Peña, *Conversaciones con Carlos Andrés Pérez*, 2:42–43, 60–63; Pérez, *Memorias proscritas*, pp. 261–263.

13. Jason Seawright, *Party-System Collapse: The Roots of Crisis in Peru and Venezuela* (Stanford: University Press, 2012), pp. 67–68; Wilpert, *Changing Venezuela*, p. 84.

14. Leslie C. Gates, *Electing Chávez: The Business of Anti-Neoliberal Politics in Venezuela* (Pittsburgh: University Press, 2010), p. 65; Julia Buxton, "Economic Policy and the Rise of Hugo Chávez," in Ellner and Hellinger, eds., *Venezuelan Politics in the Chávez Era*, pp. 115–116; Seawright, *Party-System Collapse*, p. 68; Rabe, *The Road to OPEC*, p. 188; Wilpert, *Changing Venezuela*, pp. 84–85.

15. Buxton, "Economic Policy and the Rise of Hugo Chávez," pp. 117–119; Blank, *Petroleum Republic*, pp. 129–130; Pérez, *Memorias proscritas*, pp. 252–253; Silva Luongo, *De Cipriano Castro a Carlos Andrés Pérez*, pp. 600, 784.

16. Wilpert, *Changing Venezuela*, pp. 107–109; Seawright, *Party-System Collapse*, pp. 68–69; Samuel Freije, "Income Distribution and Redistribution in Venezuela," in Ricardo Hausmann and Francisco Rodríguez, eds., *Venezuela before Chávez: Anatomy of an Economic Collapse* (University Park: Pennsylvania State University Press, 2014), pp. 220–224.

17. Gates, *Electing Chávez*, pp. 72–74, 65–69; Blank, *Petroleum Republic*, pp. 123, 126, 129; Guillermo García Ponce, *El golpe del 11 de abril*, 2nd Ed. (Caracas: Alcaldía, 2002), p. 95.

18. Blank, *Petroleum Republic*, pp. 124, 127–128.

19. For a brief account of the decline and bitter end of the state-owned shipping company CAVN, See René De La Pedraja, *Latin American Merchant Shipping in the Age of Global Competition* (Westport, CT: Greenwood Press, 1999), pp. 87–94 and in particular pages 130–131.

20. Blank, *Petroleum Republic*, p. 155.

21. Mommer, "Subversive Oil," p. 131; Blank, *Petroleum Republic*, pp. 156–158.

22. "Interpelación al militar Carlos Aguilera," Caracas, 15 May 2002, www.urru.org; Mommer, "Subversive Oil," pp. 134–135.

23. Mommer, "Subversive Oil," pp. 132, 134–135, 137; Pérez, *Memorias proscritas*, pp. 231–232.

24. *Los Angeles Times*, 4 March 1989; Blank, *Petroleum Republic*, p. 164.

25. "PDVSA: Operation Morrocoy Update," Cable from U.S. Embassy, Caracas, 15 March 2002, U.S. Department of State Freedom of Information Act (henceforth Dept State FOIA).

26. "Interpelación al militar Carlos Aguilera," Caracas, 15 May 2002, www.urru.org.

27. Daniel Ellinger, "Political Overview: The Break-

down of *Puntofijismo* and the Rise of Chavismo," in Ellner and Ellinger, eds., *Venezuelan Politics in the Chávez Era*, p. 31; Bart Jones, *¡Hugo! The Hugo Chávez Story from Mud Hut to Perpetual Revolution* (Hanover, NH: Steerforth Press, 2007), p. 111.

28. Pérez, *Memorias proscritas*, pp. 329, 331–332.

29. *Los Angeles Times*, 3 March 1989; *Washington Post*, 1 March 1989; Jones, *Hugo*, pp. 115–116.

30. Mommer, "Subversive Oil," pp. 136–137; *Washington Post*, 1 March 1989; Jones, *Hugo*, p. 116; Pérez, *Memorias proscritas* , p. 337.

31. Margarita López Maya, "The Venezuelan Caracazo of 1989: Popular Protest and Institutional Weakness," *Journal of Latin American Studies* 35 (2003):134; Jones, *Hugo*, p. 117. Pérez blames the police for having incited (*estimulado*) the disorders, a false accusation that reflects his attempts to shift blame away from himself. See, Pérez, *Memorias proscritas*, p. 335.

32. López Maya, "The Venezuelan Caracazo of 1989," p. 121; Jones, *Hugo*, p. 116; Roberto Briceño-León, "Violencia, ciudadanía y miedo en Caracas," *Foro Internacional* 47(2007): 557–558.

33. López Maya, "The Venezuelan Caracazo of 1989," pp. 123–124; Jones, *Hugo*, p. 117.

34. *Washington Post*, 1 March 1989; López Maya, "The Venezuelan Caracazo of 1989," pp. 124–125.

35. *Washington Post*, 1 March 1989.

36. López Maya, "The Venezuelan Caracazo of 1989," pp. 125–126; Jones, *Hugo*, pp. 117–120.

37. López Maya, "The Venezuelan Caracazo of 1989," pp. 127–128; Jones, *Hugo*, pp. 120–122; Pérez, *Memorias proscritas*, pp. 335–336; Briceño-León, "Violencia, ciudadanía y miedo en Caracas," p. 558.

38. *Los Angeles Times*, 3 March 1989; Jones, *Hugo*, p. 125; Pérez, *Memorias proscritas*, pp. 337–340.

39. Francisco Monaldi and Michael Penfold, "Institutional Collapse: The Rise and Decline of Democratic Governance in Venezuela," in Hausmann and Rodríguez, eds., *Venezuela before Chávez*, p. 304; Seawright, *Party-System Collapse*, pp. 68–70; Jones, *Hugo*, pp. 128–129.

40. *Los Angeles Times*, 4 March 1989; Jones, *Hugo*, pp. 127–128.

41. Margarita López Maya, "Venezuela after the Caracazo: Forms of Protest in a Deinstitutionalized Context," *Bulletin of Latin American Research*, 21 (2002): 202–204; Jones, *Hugo*, p. 128; *New York Times*, 21 January 1992.

42. Marta Harnecker, ed., *Hugo Chávez Frías: un hombre, un pueblo* (Havana: Editorial de Ciencias Sociales, 2002), pp. 18–19; Jones, *Hugo*, pp. 122, 125–127.

43. Harnecker, ed., *Hugo Chávez Frías*, pp. 26–27. The reporting of Jones, *Hugo* p. 167 has Luis Miquilena coming to meet Chávez for the first time in prison. In reality, Miquilena "met Chávez and took him under his wing" years before and had participated closely with Chávez in the February 1992 coup attempt; See, "Biographic Report: Luis Miquilena: Political Godfather to Hugo Chávez," Cable from U.S. Embassy, Caracas, 27 October 1998, Wikileaks.

44. "Spot Report Venezuela Coup Attempt," 4 February 1992, Dept State, FOIA; Jones, *Hugo*, pp. 130–134, 138–139; Harnecker, ed., *Hugo Chávez Frías*, pp. 32–33.

45. "After the Coup Attempt: Chronology of Events February 3–4," Cable from U.S. Embassy, Caracas, 7 February 1992, Dept State FOIA; Jones, *Hugo*, pp. 141–148; Wilpert, *Changing Venezuela*, p. 17.

46. "After the Coup Attempt: Chronology of Events February 3–4," Cable from U.S. Embassy, Caracas, 7 February 1992, Dept State FOIA; Jones, *Hugo*, pp. 148–156.

47. "After the Coup Attempt: Chronology of Events February 3–4," Cable from U.S. Embassy, Caracas, 7 February 1992, Dept State FOIA; Jones, *Hugo*, pp. 156–158; Wilpert, *Changing Venezuela*, p. 17.

48. "Reactions to Release of February 1992 Coup Leader Hugo Chávez," Cable from U.S. Embassy, Caracas, 6 April 1994, Wikileaks; Harnecker, ed., *Hugo Chávez Frías*, pp. 42–43, 64–67; Daniel Hellinger, "Political Overview: The Breakdown of *Puntofijismo* and the Rise of Chavismo," in Ellner and Hellinger, *Venezuelan Politics in the Chávez Era*, p. 32.

49. "Reactions to Release of February 1992 Coup Leader Hugo Chávez," Cable from U.S. Embassy, Caracas, 6 April 1994, Wikileaks.

50. Harnecker, ed., *Hugo Chávez Frías*, pp. 31–32; Jones, *Hugo*, pp. 187–189. The financial crisis was triggered by the collapse of Banco Latino, the second largest in the country; See, *New York Times*, 16 May 1994 and Gates, *Electing Chávez*, pp. 69–71, 111–121.

51. "Hugo Chávez Celebrates Day of Dignity," Cable from U.S. Embassy, Caracas, 25 February 1998, Wikileaks; Jones, *Hugo*, pp. 186–189.

52. Harnecker, ed., *Hugo Chávez Frías*, pp. 19–20, 30–31; Jones, *Hugo*, p. 191.

53. "Biographic Report: Luis Miquilena: Political Godfather to Hugo Chávez," Cable from U.S. Embassy, Caracas, 27 October 1998, Wikileaks.

54. "Castro Greets Former Coup Leader Chávez," Cable from U.S. Embassy, Caracas, 18 December 1994, Wikileaks; Jones, *Hugo*, pp. 191–192.

55. "Castro Greets Former Coup Leader Chávez," Cable from U.S. Embassy, Caracas, 18 December 1994, Wikileaks.

56. Jones, *Hugo*, pp. 195, 198–199; Harnecker, ed., *Hugo Chávez Frías*, pp. 28, 45–46.

57. Jones, *Hugo*, pp. 202–203; Harnecker, ed., *Hugo Chávez Frías*, p. 28; Margarita López Maya, "Hugo Chávez Frías: His Movement and His Presidency," in Ellner and Hellinger, eds., *Venezuelan Politics in the Chávez Era*, p. 82.

58. Harnecker, ed., *Hugo Chávez Frías*, pp. 23–25, 30–31; López-Maya, "Venezuela after the Caracazo," *Bulletin of Latin American Research* 21(2002): 204.

59. Steve Ellner, *Rethinking Venezuelan Politics: Class, Conflict, and the Chávez Phenomenon* (Boulder, CO: Lynne Rienner, 2008), pp. 100–101, 103; Harnecker, ed., *Hugo Chávez Frías*, p. 33; Jones, *Hugo*, pp. 195–196, 202–203; López Maya, "Hugo Chávez Frías," p. 83; Hellinger, "Political Overview," p. 34.

60. Harnecker, ed., *Hugo Chávez Frías*, pp. 33–36; Jones, *Hugo*, pp. 203–204.

61. Harnecker, ed., *Hugo Chávez Frías*, pp. 33–35; Jones, *Hugo*, pp. 196–198, 214; López Maya, "Hugo Chávez Frías," pp. 83–84.

62. Jones, *Hugo*, pp. 217–218; "Taking Another Step in Our Dialogue with Hugo Chávez," Cable from U.S. Embassy, Caracas, 22 September 1998, Dept State FOIA; "Ambassador Meets with Hugo Chávez," Cable from U.S. Embassy, Caracas, 25 September 1998, Wikileaks.

63. Harnecker. ed., *Hugo Chávez Frías*, pp. 19–20, 30–31; Hellinger, "Political Overview," p. 38.

64. Gates, *Electing Chávez*, pp. 85–88; Jones, *Hugo*, p. 219; "Taking Another Step in Our Dialogue with Hugo Chávez," Cable from U.S. Embassy, Caracas, 22 September 1998, Dept State FOIA; "Ambassador Meets with Hugo Chávez," Cable from U.S. Embassy, Caracas, 25 September 1998, Wikileaks. Some might argue that Chávez was not being truthful with U.S. diplomats, but their only concern was that "we will have problems with Chavez, however, around the issue of the Constitutional Assembly." In reality his statements were genuine expressions of his core beliefs. He remained skeptical about state ownership and repeatedly showed a reluctance to nationalize private firms.

65. Jones, *Hugo*, pp. 205–211, 216–217, 220; Hellinger, "Political Overview," pp. 38–39.

66. López Maya, "Hugo Chávez Frías," p. 84; Jones,

Hugo, pp. 220–223; Hellinger, "Political Overview," pp. 40, 42–43; "Scene Setter for Your Visit to Venezuela," Cable from U.S. Embassy, Caracas, 26 October 1998, Dept State FOIA; "Hugo Chávez Wins in a Landslide," Cable from U.S. Embassy, Caracas, 7 December 1998, Wikileaks.

67. Jones, *Hugo*, p. 223.

68. "Hugo Chávez Wins in a Landslide," Cable from U.S. Embassy, Caracas, 7 December 1998, Wikileaks; Jones, *Hugo*, p. 223.

Chapter 2

1. Alfonso W. Quiroz, *Corrupt Circles: A History of Unbound Graft in Peru* (Washington, D.C.: Woodrow Wilson Center Press, 2008), p. 421.

2. Cynthia McClintock and Fabián Vallas, *The United States and Peru: Cooperation at a Cost* (New York: Routledge, 2003), pp. 49–50; René De La Pedraja, *Wars of Latin America, 1948–1982: The Rise of the Guerrillas* (Jefferson, NC: McFarland, 2013), pp. 198–202; José Ugaz, *Caiga quien caiga: la historia íntima de cómo se desmontó la mafia fujimontesinista* (Lima: Planeta, 2014), pp. 124–125. Although Vlaldimiro Montesinos frequently is referred to as the Peruvian Rasputin, a more accurate historical analogy is to Thomas Cromwell, the infamous prime minister of Henry VIII in Britain. In reality none of the historical analogies capture the unique and symbiotic bond with Fujimori. As far as inspiration for his actions, Montesinos diligently practiced the precepts that Niccolò Machiavelli recommended in the *Prince*.

3. Quiroz, *Corrupt Circles*, 361–362; McClintock and Vallas, *The United States and Peru*, pp. 44, 55. The question of whether Vladimiro Montesinos was an asset or "source" for the CIA in the 1970s remains unresolved. The normal operating procedure for handling assets is that they report secretly to CIA officers; the station chief then decides what portions of this information—including the identity of the source—to share with the embassy and with headquarters at Langley. But Montesinos spent considerable time with political officers of the embassy, and he was instrumental in letting them know the attitudes of the military government. Even more intriguing, he was carrying out this function with the blessing of his Peruvian superiors. The above does not rule out receiving payments from the CIA, but in that case he would have been a most unusual "source" or asset. See, "FY—76 IV Nomination," Cable from U.S. Embassy, Lima, 8 January 1976, National Security Archive (henceforth NSA); "Detention of Vladimiro Montesinos," Cable from U.S. Embassy, Lima, 4 April 1977, NSA.

4. McClintock and Vallas, *The United States and Peru*, p. 54.

5. "FY-76 IV Nomination," Cable from U.S. Embassy, Lima, 8 January 1976, NSA; Peru, Congress, *En la sala de la corrupción: Videos y audios de Vladimiro Montesinos 1998–2000*, 6 vols. (Lima: Fondo Editorial del Congreso del Peru, 2004), 5: 2579, 2589.

6. "Comments on Fujimori, Montesinos," Cable from U.S. Embassy, Lima, 22 January 1993, U.S. State Department, Freedom of Information Act (henceforth Dept State FOIA); Peru, Comisión de la Verdad y de la Reconciliación (henceforth CVR), *Informe final*, 9 vols. (Lima: Comisión de la Verdad y de la Reconciliación, 2003), 2: 298.

7. McClintock and Vallas, *The United States and Peru*, p. 56; Quiroz, *Corrupt Circles*, 363; "Comments on Fujimori, Montesinos," Cable from U.S. Embassy, Lima, 22 January 1993, Dept State FOIA.

8. "Cayara: No Bodies Left," Cable from U.S. Embassy, Lima, 1 June 1988, and "Government of Peru Quashes the Cayara Massacre Report," Cable from U.S. Embassy, Lima, 10 November 1988, NSA; Quiroz, *Corrupt Circles*, p. 364; "Comments on Fujimori, Montesinos," Cable from U.S. Embassy, Lima, 22 January 1993, Dept State FOIA; Charles D. Kenney, *Fujimori's Coup and the Breakdown of Democracy in Peru* (Notre Dame: University of Notre Dame Press, 2004), pp. 110–111. For the start of the Shining Path insurgency, See, De La Pedraja, *Wars of Latin America, 1948–1982*, pp. 291–297.

9. Ugaz, *Caiga quien caiga*, pp. 117, 120–121; Fernando Rospigliosi, *Montesinos y las Fuerzas Armadas* (Lima: Instituto de Estudios Peruanos, 2001), p. 18; Luis Felipe Gamarra, *Pequeños dictadores: Todo dictador necesita pequeños dictadores* (Lima: MR, 2009), pp. 134–135, 147.

10. This paragraph and the next draw on Ugaz, *Caiga quien caiga*, pp. 124–125; Gamarra, *Pequeños dictadores*, pp. 119, 131–133.

11. "Comments on Fujimori, Montesinos," Cable from U.S. Embassy, Lima, 22 January 1993, Dept State FOIA; Barry S. Levitt, *Power in the Balance: Presidents, Parties, and Legislatures in Peru and Beyond* (Notre Dame, IN: University of Notre Dame Press, 2012), pp. 59–60.

12. Catherine M. Conaghan, *Fujimori's Peru: Deception in the Public Space* (Pittsburgh: University of Pittsburgh Press, 2005), pp. 16–17; Mario Vargas Llosa, *El pez en el agua; Memorias* (Bogotá: Seix Barral, 1993), pp. 262–264, 351–355, 449–454; Quiroz, *Corrupt Circles*, p. 358.

13. Kenney, *Fujimori's Coup*, pp. 94, 106, 111; Levitt, *Power in the Balance*, pp. 112–113; Quiroz, *Corrupt Circles*, pp. 358–359; Conaghan, *Fujimori's Peru*, p. 18. Actually, Alberto Fujimori had been running for a senate seat and merely was using the presidential race as a great way to gain exposure for his senate campaign; at that time under the 1979 Constitution a candidate could run simultaneously for two elected positions.

14. McClintock and Vallas, *The United States and Peru*, pp. 49–50, 56; Rospigliosi, *Montesinos y las Fuerzas Armadas*, pp. 16, 18; Vargas Llosa, *El pez en el agua*, p. 509.

15. Conaghan, *Fujimori's Peru*, pp. 20, 25; Rospigliosi, *Montesinos y las Fuerzas Armadas*, pp. 18–19, 21; Kenney, *Fujimori's Coup*, pp. 107–109.

16. Kurt Weyland, "The Rise and Decline of Fujimori's Neopopulist Leadership," in Julio E. Carrión, ed., *The Fujimori Legacy: The Rise of Electoral Authoritarianism in Peru* (University Park: Pennsylvania State University Press, 2006), p. 21; Conaghan, *Fujimori's Peru*, p. 264n35; McClintock and Vallas, *The United States and Peru*, p. 94; CVR, *Informe final*, 3:69.

17. "Reported Secret Annex to National Pacification/Human Rights Plan," Secret No Forn Cable from U.S. Embassy, Lima, 23 August 1990, Dept State FOIA; Carlos Iván Degregori, *La década de la antipolítica: Auge y caída de Alberto Fujimori y Vladimiro Montesinos*, 2nd ed. (Lima: Instituto de Estudios Peruanos, 2012), p. 51.

18. Gamarra, *Pequeños dictadores*, pp. 217–218; CVR, *Informe final*, 3: 130, 142–159.

19. Keeney, *Fujimori's Coup*, pp. 90–92; CVR, *Informe final*, 2: 338; Levitt, *Power in the Balance*, pp. 64–65. Besides being indirect proof that the corruption of the Fujimori presidency had begun in its initial months, the agreement giving immunity from prosecution for Alán García also helped to bolster the precedent that the incoming administration did not investigate the previous one.

20. Weyland, "The Rise and Decline of Fujimori's Neopopulist Leadership," pp. 21–22; Degregori, *La década de la antipolítica*, pp. 31–32; CVR, *Informe final*, 2: 345.

21. Kenney, *Fujimori's Coup*, p. 199; Ugaz, *Caiga quien caiga*, p. 39; Degregori, *La década de la antipolítica*, pp. 37–38; CVR, *Informe final*, 2: 337; Conaghan, *Fujimori's Peru*, pp. 85–86.

22. McClintock and Vallas, *The United States and Peru*, p. 56; CVR, *Informe final*, 3:78; Raspigliosi, *Montesinos y las Fuerzas Armadas*, p. 23.

23. Quiroz, *Corrupt Circles*, pp. 413–414; McClintock

and Vallas, *The United States and Peru*, pp. 56–57; Raspigliosi, *Montesinos y las Fuerzas Armadas*, pp. 26–27.

24. Degregori, *La década de la antipolítica*, p. 62; McClintock and Vallas, *The United States and Peru*, pp. 56–57; CVR, *Informe final*, 2:352; Raspigliosi, *Montesinos y las Fuerzas Armadas*, p. 29.

25. Quiroz, *Corrupt Circles*, p. 365.

26. McClintock and Vallas, *The United States and Peru*, pp. 44, 55; Raspigliosi, *Montesinos y las Fuerzas Armadas*, p. 38; Gamarra, *Pequeños dictadores*, p. 167.

27. Kenney, *Fujimori's Coup*, pp. 12, 116; Degregori, *La década de la antipolítica*, p. 38; CVR, *Informe final*, 2: 329.

28. Kenney, *Fujimori's Coup*, pp. 202–204; Degregori, *La década de la antipolítica*, pp. 32–33, 56; Conaghan, *Fujimori's Peru*, pp. 27–28; Quiroz, *Corrupt Circles*, p. 370; CVR, *Informe final*, 2: 346–347, 3: 83.

29. "Superintendent of Banking on Implications of Coup," Cable from U.S. Embassy, Lima, 8 April 1992, Dept State FOIA; Kenney, *Fujimori's Coup*, pp. 205–206; Weyland, "The Rise and Decline of Fujimori's Neopopulist Leadership," p. 22; Conaghan, *Fujimori's Peru*, pp. 28–30; Degregori, *La década de la antipolítica*, pp. 33, 34, 39.

30. McClintock and Vallas, *The United States and Peru*, pp. 138–139; Conaghan, *Fujimori's Peru*, pp. 36–41.

31. McClintock and Vallas, *The United States and Peru*, p. 62; Conaghan, *Fujimori's Peru*, pp. 41–42; Quiroz, *Corrupt Circles*, pp. 366, 372.

32. Ugaz, *Caiga quien caiga*, p. 60; Conaghan, *Fujimori's Peru*, pp. 66–67; Quiroz, *Corrupt Circles*, 366, 372; Rospigliosi, *Montesinos y las Fuerzas Armadas*, pp. 129–131.

33. René De La Pedraja, *Wars of Latin America, 1982–2013: The Path to Peace* (Jefferson, NC: McFarland, 2013), pp. 175–176.

34. "Fujimori Took Refuge in Japanese Ambassador's Residence," Cable from U.S. Embassy, Lima, 20 November 1992, Dept State FOIA; Conaghan, *Fujimori's Peru*, p. 55; Degregori, *La década de la antipolítica*, p. 280; McClintock and Vallas, *The United States and Peru*, p. 52; Rospigliosi, *Montesinos y las Fuerzas Armadas*, p. 35.

35. Kenney, *Fujimori's Coup*, pp. 225–226, 241–242; Degregori, *La década de la antipolítica*, pp. 42, 61.

36. José I. Távara, "The Regulation of Market Power in a Democratic Transition," in John Crabtree, ed., *Making Institutions Work in Peru* (London: Institute for the Study of the Americas, 2006), p. 212; Javier Diez Canseco Cisneros, ed., *Decretos secretos y mal uso de fondos públicos: El Perú bajo el Fujimorismo* (Lima: Biblioteca del Congreso del Perú, 2003), pp. 23–31; McClintock and Vallas, *United States and Peru*, pp. 90–91, 98.

37. Távara, "The Regulation of Market Power," p. 212.

38. Francisco Durand, "The Problem of Strengthening Business Institutions," in Crabtree, *Making Institutions Work in Peru*, p. 192. For similar conclusions, See also, McClintock and Vallas, *The United States and Peru*, pp. 99–101.

39. Conaghan, *Fujimori's Peru*, p. 121. PetroPeru did not escape unscathed from the rush to privatize. It lost its right to drill for petroleum to a new agency Perupetro in August 1993; See Article 6 of Law No. 26221 of 19 August 1993. Perupetro was soon abusing its authority to grant oil concessions to foreign companies, and the most notorious episode occurred with the scandals of the Petro-Audios in 2008 (see chapter 13).

40. "The Ccd, Poverty, and the Sendero," Cable from U.S. Embassy, Lima, 4 January 1993, Wikileaks; Conaghan, *Fujimori's Peru*, p. 55l; CVR, *Informe final*, 3:102.

41. Weyland, "The Rise and Decline of Fujimori's Neopopulist Leadership," p. 24; Degregori, *La década de la antipolítica*, p. 43; Levitt, *Power in the Balance*, p. 69; Conaghan, *Fujimori's Peru*, pp. 56–57.

42. Weyland, "The Rise and Decline of Fujimori's Neopopulist Leadership," p. 24.

43. Levitt, *Power in the Balance*, pp. 69–71; Degregori, *La década de la antipolítica*, p. 43.

44. Conversations with officials of *Defensoria del Pueblo*, Lima, July 2015.

45. Levitt, *Power in the Balance*, pp. 70–71; Degregori, *La década de la antipolítica*, pp. 43–44; Conaghan, *Fujimori's Peru*, pp. 64, 78–79.

46. Pedro Francke, "Institutional Change and Social Programmes," in Crabtree, *Making Institutions Work in Peru*, pp. 95–96; Conaghan, *Fujimori's Peru*, pp. 42, 79; Quiroz, *Corrupt Circles*, p. 400; Carol Wise, "Against the Odds: The Paradoxes of Peru's Economic Recovery in the 1990s," in Carrión, *Fujimori Legacy*, p. 217.

47. The two quotes in this paragraph come from Weyland, "The Rise and Decline of Fujimori's Neopopulist Leadership," p. 26.

48. Patricia Oliart, "Alberto Fujimori: The Man Peru Needed?" in Steve J. Stern, ed., *Shining and Other Paths: War and Society in Peru, 1980–1995* (Durham: Duke University Press, 1998), pp. 415–421; Degregori, *La década de la antipolítica*, pp. 45–46; Levitt, *Power in the Balance*, p. 70; Conaghan, *Fujimori's Peru*, pp. 79, 82; Quiroz, *Corrupt Circles*, p. 400.

49. Conaghan, *Fujimori's Peru*, pp. 94–96; McClintock and Vallas, *The United States and Peru*, p. 142; Umberto Jara, *Historia de dos aventureros: La política como engaño* (Lima: n.p., 2005), pp. 54–55.

50. Conaghan, *Fujimori's Peru*, pp. 95–96; St. John, *Toledo's Peru*, pp. 15–16.

51. St. John, *Toledo's Peru*, p. 16; Jara, *Dos aventureros*, pp. 62–63.

52. Conaghan, *Fujimori's Peru*, pp. 94–95; Oliart, "The Man Peru Needed," pp. 421–423.

53. De La Pedraja, *Wars of Latin America, 1948-1982*, pp. 297–304; CVR, *Informe final*, 2: 367–369.

54. Conaghan, *Fujimori's Peru*, pp. 98–99; Maxwell Cameron, "The Rise and Decline of Fujimori's Neopopulist Leadership," in Carrión, *Fujimori Legacy*, pp. 24–27; Enrique Obando, "Civil-Military Relations in Peru, 1980–1996: How to Control and Coopt the Military," in Stern, *Shining and Other Paths*, pp. 400–401; McClintock and Vallas, *The United States and Peru*, p. 142.

55. "Amnesty Law in Peru: Analysis and Recommendations," Cable from U.S. Embassy, Lima, 15 June 1995, Dept State FOIA; Conaghan, *Fujimori's Peru*, pp. 105–107; Degregori, *La década de la antipolítica*, p. 69; CVR, *Informe final*, 3: 105.

56. Durand, "Business Institutions," pp. 201–203; Wise, "Against the Odds," p. 214.

57. Conaghan, *Fujimori's Peru*, pp. 121, 123; Diez Canseco, *Decretos secretos*, pp. 24–25, 187; Quiroz, *Corrupt Circles*, pp. 399–400; Catherine M. Conaghan, "The Immoral Economy of Fujimorismo," in Carrión, *The Fujimori Legacy*, p. 107.

58. "Peru: Freefall," Top Secret Report, 31 July 1997, NSA.

59. McClintock and Vallas, *The United States and Peru*, pp. 52–53; Degregori, *La década de la antipolítica*, p. 72; Jara, *Dos aventureros*, p. 55; "Peru: Freefall," Top Secret Report, 31 July 1997, NSA; Maxwell Cameron, "Text, Power and Social Exclusion: From Colonialism to the Crisis of *Criollo* Republicanism," in John Crabtree, ed., *Fractured Politics: Peruvian Democracy Past and Present* (London: Institute for the Study of the Americas, 2011), p. 43.

60. Conaghan, *Fujimori's Peru*, pp. 120–122; McClintock and Vallas, *The United States and Peru*, p. 144.

61. Gamarra, *Pequeños dictatores*, p. 125; Degregori, *La década de la antipolítica*, p. 71; Quiroz, *Corrupt Circles*, p. 414.

62. Conaghan,"The Immoral Economy of Fujimo-

rismo," p. 115; Degregori, *La década de la antipolítica*, p. 72; Gamarra, *Pequeños dictatores*, p. 126; Quiroz, *Corrupt Circles*, pp. 384, 414. For the Roman Catholic Church, Bishop (later cardinal) Luis Cipriani was the Peruvian equivalent of the infamous Cardinal Ignacio Velasco in Venezuela. Both men were examples of the high church officials Pope John Paul II appointed to fight the anti-Communist war of Eastern Europe and who did immense harm to Latin America.

63. Raspigliosi, *Montesinos y las Fuerzas Armadas*, 278–282.

64. Cameron, "Text, Power and Social Exclusion," pp. 43, 45; "Peru: Freefall," Top Secret Report, 31 July 1997, NSA; McClintock and Vallas, *The United States and Peru*, p. 144; Conaghan, *Fujimori's Peru*, pp. 126–130.

65. McClintock and Vallas, *The United States and Peru*, p. 75; Gamarra, *Pequeños dictatores*, pp. 179–180; Diez Canseco, *Decretos Secretos*, pp. 219–224.

66. Gamarra, *Pequeños dictatores*, pp. 180–182; Quiroz, *Corrupt Circles*, p. 408.

67. Fernando Rospigliosi, "The Blocking of Reform in the Security Services," in Crabtree, *Making Institutions Work in Peru*, p. 88n36. Vladimiro Montesinos was grooming his brother-in-law General Luis Cubas Portal to be the commander in chief of the army in late 2000, See Rospigliosi, *Montesinos y las Fuerzas Armadas*, pp. 41–42.

Chapter 3

1. Carlos Iván Degregori, *La década de la antipolítica: Auge y huída de Alberto Fujimori y Vladimiro Montesinos* (Lima: Instituto de Estudios Peruanos, 2012), p. 291.

2. Alfonso W. Quiroz, *Corrupt Circles: A History of Unbound Graft in Peru* (Washington, D.C.: Woodrow Wilson Center Press, 2008), pp. 410–413. For a good example of Mexican drug lords paying authorities to arrest rivals, See, René De La Pedraja, *The United States and the Armed Forces of Mexico, Central America, and the Caribbean, 2000–2014* (Jefferson, NC: McFarland, 2014), p. 71.

3. David Scott Palmer, "The Often Surprising Outcomes of Asymmetry in International Affairs: United States–Peru Relations in the 1990s," in Julio F. Carrión, ed., *The Fujimori Legacy: The Rise of Electoral Authoritarianism in Peru* (University Park: Pennsylvania State University Press, 2006), p. 236; Cynthia McClintock and Fabián Vallas, *The United States and Peru: Cooperation at a Cost* (New York: Routledge, 2003), p. 86. No reason exists to doubt the statement of U.S. ambassador John Hamilton that Vladimiro Montesinos was not a CIA agent in the 1990s; See, John R. Hamilton, "The Fall of Fujimori: A Diplomat's Perspective," *The Fletcher Forum of World Affairs* 30(2006): 193.

4. "D/ONDCP Visit—the Montesinos Factor," Cable from U.S. Embassy, Lima, 22 July 1999, U.S. Department of State Freedom of Information Act (henceforth Dept State FOIA); Quiroz, *Corrupt Circles*, p. 412.

5. Catherine M. Conaghan, "The Immoral Economy of Fujimorismo," in Carrión, *The Fujimori Legacy*, pp. 103, 109–113; Javier Diez Canseco Cisneros, ed., *Decretos secretos y mal uso de fondos públicos: El Perú bajo el Fujimorismo* (Lima: Biblioteca del Congreso del Peru, 2003), p. 217; Gustavo Gorriti, *Petroaudios; políticos, espías y periodistas detrás del escándalo* (Lima: Planeta, 2009), pp. 12–13.

6. Diez Canseco, *Decretos secretos*, p. 217.

7. Most of the equipment and weapons purchased could not be salvaged or put to any good use. However, because the MIG-29 was actually a superb warplane, Russia (which had not sold the plane) agreed to service the fleet and to upgrade its weapon systems in 2007. Russia was trying to restore its influence to the level that it had enjoyed during the Peruvian military regime of 1968–1980. See René De La Pedraja, "Statesmen and Airpower in Latin America, 1945–2010," in Robin Higham and Mark Parillo, eds., *The Influence of Airpower upon History: Statesmanship, Diplomacy, and Foreign Policy since 1903* (Lexington: University of Kentucky Press, 2013), p. 167.

8. José Ugaz, *Caiga quien caiga: la historia íntima de cómo se desmontó la mafia fujimontesinista* (Lima: Planeta, 2014), pp. 215–218; "Declaración testimonial de Carmen de Guadalupe Delgado Méndez," Lima, 28 November 2000, Dept State FOIA; McClintock and Vallas, *The United States and Peru*, pp. 86–87.

9. Ugaz, *Caiga quien caiga*, pp. 219–220; Ronald Bruce St. John, *Toledo's Peru: Vision and Reality* (Gainesville: University Press of Florida, 2010), p. 25; Quiroz, *Corrupt Circles*, p. 416; McClintock and Fabián, *The United States and Peru*, p. 87.

10. "Peru: Fujimori Leading in Controversial Presidential Race," Secret Intelligence Report, CIA FOIA.

11. Catherine M. Conaghan, *Fujimori's Peru: Deception in the Public Sphere* (Pittsburgh: University of Pittsburgh Press, 2005), pp. 169, 172, 187; St. John, *Toledo's Peru*, p. 19; Umberto Jara, *Historia de dos aventureros* (Lima: n.p. 2005.), pp. 163–164.

12. "The State of the Military on the Eve of Elections," Cable from U.S. Embassy, Lima, 7 April 2000, Dept State FOIA; St. John, *Toledo's Peru*, p. 181; Conaghan, *Fujimori's Peru*, p. 165.

13. "The State of the Military on the Eve of Elections," Cable from U.S. Embassy, Lima, 7 April 2000, Dept State FOIA.

14. St. John, *Toledo's Peru*, pp. 19–20; Jara, *Historia de dos aventureros*, p. 164; Conaghan, *Fujimori's Peru*, p. 194. For the 9 April 2000 election different figures exist for the percentages; because of fraud the correct numbers will probably never be known.

15. Jara, *Historia de dos aventureros*, pp. 165–166; Ugaz, *Caiga quien caiga*, pp. 55–56; St. John, *Toledo's Peru*, p. 19.

16. Jara, *Historia de dos aventureros*, pp. 166–167.

17. Conaghan, *Fujimori's Peru*, p. 209; Jara, *Historia de dos aventureros*, pp. 74–77.

18. Conaghan, *Fujimori's Peru*, pp. 196–198; Jara, *Historia de dos aventureros*, pp. 179–180; McClintock and Vallas, *The United States and Peru*, p. 151; St. John, *Toledo's Peru*, pp. 20–21 provides the explanation Toledo constructed to account for his campaign maneuverings, but a major flaw in this version is that it assumed that Toledo knew that Fujimori would not complete his third term.

19. Conaghan, *Fujimori's Peru*, pp. 202–204, 211–212; Quiroz, *Corrupt Circles*, pp. 385–386.

20. Conaghan, "The Immoral Economy of Fujimorismo," p. 111; Cameron, "The Vladivideo and the Fall of Peru's Fujimori," pp. 276–277; Jara, *Historia de dos aventureros*, p. 173; Quiroz, *Corrupt Circles*, p. 386. In an indicator of their respective worth in Peruvian society, generals cost millions of dollars, while judges, district attorneys and politicians cost tens of thousands of dollars.

21. Henry Pease García, *Por los pasos perdidos: El Parlamento peruano entre el 2000 y el 2005* (Lima: Fondo Editorial del Congreso del Perú, 2006), pp. 48–49.

22. Conaghan, *Fujimori's Peru*, p. 219. For Plutarco Elías Calles in Mexico, See, René De La Pedraja, *Wars of Latin America, 1899–1941* (Jefferson, NC: McFarland, 2006), pp. 298–308.

23. Conaghan, *Fujimori's Peru*, pp. 209, 215; Degregori, *La década de la antipolítica*, pp. 215–216, 307, 328; St. John, *Toledo's Peru*, pp. 23–24.

24. Degregori, *La década de la antipolítica*, pp. 217–218, 307; Conaghan, *Fujimori's Peru*, pp. 215–216; Pease, *Los pasos perdidos*, p. 50.

25. Degregori, *La década de la antipolítica*, p. 328; Conaghan, *Fujimori's Peru*, pp. 216–218; Pease, *Los pasos perdidos*, p. 50.

26. Jara, *Historia de dos aventureros*, pp. 79, 216; Ugaz, *Caiga quien caiga*, p. 125.

27. Jara, *Historia de dos aventureros*, p. 216; Ugaz, *Caiga quien caiga*, p. 125.

28. Palmer, "United States–Peru Relations in the 1990s," in Carrión, *Fujimori Legacy*, p. 237; Jara, *Historia de dos aventureros*, pp. 192–193; Ugaz, *Caiga quien caiga*, pp. 221–222. A good example of how the U.S. government strives to keep Latin American countries out of each other's affairs was the U.S. opposition to a Panamanian request for Colombian help in December 2009; See, De La Pedraja, *The United States and the Armed Forces of Mexico, Central America, and the Caribbean*, pp. 219–221. According to Washington, any intervention by another country necessarily means a corresponding reduction of U.S. influence in that Latin American country. It has been extremely difficult and usually impossible to persuade imperial U.S. officials to abandon their view of international relations as a zero-sum game.

29. Ugaz, *Caiga quien caiga*, p. 223; René De La Pedraja, *Wars of Latin America, 1982–2013: The Path to Peace* (Jefferson, NC: McFarland, 2013), pp. 202–207.

30. Quiroz, *Corrupt Circles*, p. 403.

31. Conaghan, *Fujimori's Peru*, pp. 225–226; Degregori, *La década de la antipolítica*, p. 332; Jara, *Historia de dos aventureros*, pp. 194–195; Quiroz, *Corrupt Circles*, p. 418; McClintock and Vallas, *The United States and Peru*, p. 87; Peru, Comisión de la Verdad y de la Reconciliación, *Informe final*, 9 vols. (Lima: Comisión de la Verdad y de la Reconciliación, 2003), 2:376.

32. Hamilton, "Fall of Fujimori," pp. 195–196; Conaghan, *Fujimori's Peru*, p. 226; Jara, *Historia de dos aventureros*, pp. 195–196. Although Secretary of State Madelaine Albright had made a career of denouncing the interference of the Soviet Union in Eastern Europe (McClinctock, *United States and Peru*, pp. 45–46), she had no hesitation about practicing similar interventions in Latin America. Whether the specific pretext happens to be human rights, democracy, or workers' solidarity does not really matter, because Great Powers prefer to cloak coercion with more noble goals.

33. Palmer, "United States–Peru Relations in the 1990s," pp. 237–238; Maxwell A. Cameron, "Endogenous Regime Breakdown: The Vladivideo and the Fall of Peru's Fujimori," in Carrión, ed., *The Fujimori Legacy*, pp. 281–283. One of the major revelations in the Wikileaks diplomatic cables has been the realization that the final service of American officials consists in disguising the U.S. informal empire; consequently, scholars must be extremely skeptical when using interviews of usually all too friendly American officials as their main source. Cf. McClintock and Vallas, *United States and Peru*, p. 153.

34. Luis Felipe Gamarra, *Pequeños dictadores: Todo dictador necesita pequeños dictadores* (Lima: MR, 2009), pp. 138–140. Matilde Pinchi Pinchi in her first deposition claimed that she released the video to stop Montesinos from going in the wrong direction of ordering murders of his rivals, but the special prosecutor rejected the explanation that she was really trying to save or "help" Montesinos. In later accounts, she claimed that she released the video when she overheard him arranging her murder because security guards accused her of being untrustworthy, but even then her own confession that Montesinos took a long time to realize that she was the traitor refutes her claim. In 2000 and again in his 2014 memoirs, the impartial special prosecutor found no evidence that Montesinos had ever ordered rivals to be murdered and concluded that the real reason for the release of the video was the angry jealousy of Pinchi Pinchi at the mistress of Montesinos.

35. "El Vladivideo que marcó el fin del régimen de Fujimori, doce años después," *El Comercio*, 14 September 2012; Ugaz, *Caiga quien caiga*, p. 123; Jara, *Historia de dos aventureros*, pp. 218–220.

36. Cameron, "The Vladivideo and the Fall of Peru's Fujimori," pp. 275–276; Ugaz, *Caiga quien caiga*, pp. 123–124. Germán Barrera kept the original video recordings and had sold only copies. Later Matilde Pinchi Pinchi bought back the originals from Barrera for $50,000 dollars so that she could prove to the authorities without any doubt that she had been the source of the video that toppled Montesinos.

37. "El Vladivideo que marcó el fin del régimen de Fujimori, doce años después," *El Comercio*, 14 September 2012; Gamarra, *Pequeños dictadores*, pp. 140–143.

38. Cameron, "The Vladivideo and the Fall of Peru's Fujimori," pp. 277–283; Gamarra, *Pequeños dictadores*, pp. 114–116; Degregori, *La década de la antipolítica*, p. 278; Quiroz, *Corrupt Circles*, p. 231.

39. Jara, *Historia de dos aventureros*, p. 198; Palmer, "United States–Peru Relations in the 1990s," p. 237; Gamarra, *Pequeños dictadores*, pp. 142–143; "Montesinos Video," Secret Cable from U.S. Embassy, Lima, 15 September 2000, Dept State FOIA.

40. Conaghan, *Fujimori's Peru*, p. 232.

41. "Guidance on Peru Policy," Secret cable from State Department, 20 September 2000, Dept State FOIA; Cameron, "The Vladivideo and the Fall of Peru's Fujimori," pp. 276–279; Jara, *Historia de dos aventureros*, pp. 198–199; Degregori, *La década de la antipolítica*, pp. 279–280; Conaghan, *Fujimori's Peru*, p. 230.

42. "Guidance on Peru Policy," Secret cable from State Department, 20 September 2000, Dept State FOIA; Palmer, "United States–Peru Relations in the 1990s," p. 237; Jara, *Historia de dos aventureros*, pp. 201–202; Conaghan, *Fujimori's Peru*, p. 235.

43. Conaghan, "The Immoral Economy of Fujimorismo," p. 108; Jara, *Historia de dos aventureros*, pp. 201–203; Ugaz, *Caiga quien caiga*, pp. 131–132; Cameron, "The Vladivideo and the Fall of Peru's Fujimori," p. 283; Quiroz, *Corrupt Circles*, pp. 398, 418. In a blatantly illegal action Alberto Fujimori took the fifteen million dollars for the severance payment of Vladimiro Montesinos from official Peruvian funds; the president avoided prosecution for this breach by placing back in the budget fifteen million in unmarked U.S. bills of unknown provenance.

44. McClintock and Vallas, *United States and Peru*, p. 154; Ugaz, *Caiga quien caiga*, p. 132; Jara, *Historia de dos aventureros*, pp. 203–204.

45. Hamilton, "Fall of Fujimorli," pp. 202–203; Conaghan, *Fujimori's Peru*, p. 236; Pease, *Pasos perdidos*, pp. 55, 57.

46. Conaghan, *Fujimori's Peru*, p. 237; Jara, *Historia de dos aventureros*, pp. 205–206; Ugaz, *Caiga quien caiga*, p. 132.

47. Hamilton, "Fall of Fujimori," p. 204; Conaghan, *Fujimori's Peru*, pp. 237–238, 297n49; Ugaz, *Caiga quien caiga*, p. 132; Quiroz, *Corrupt Circles*, 401; TV news broadcasts of Univisión, October 25–30, 2000.

48. Hamilton, "Fall of Fujimori," p. 205; Peru, Congress, *En la sala de la corrupción: Videos y audios de Vladimiro Montesinos 1998–2000*, 6 vols. (Lima: Fondo Editorial del Congreso del Peru, 2004), 6: 3113; Jara, *Historia de dos aventureros*, pp. 203, 212–213; Palmer, "United States–Peru Relations in the 1990s," p. 237; Conaghan, *Fujimori's Peru*, p. 238.

49. Ollanta Humala, *De Locumba a candidato a la presidencia* (Mexico: Ocean Sur, 2009), pp. 72–109; *La República*, 23 August 2011; Luis Vásquez Medina "Shining Path Inside Peruvian Army: Colonel Humala's Strange

Revolt," *EIR* vol. 27, No. 47, 1 December 2000, p. 33; *Washington Post*, 21 May 2006; Neydo Hidalgo Chronology, 14 September–20 November 2000, Internet. Vladimiro Montesinos made some false and self-serving accusations about the Ollanta Humala revolt perhaps in an attempt to gain sympathy from Alán García. For a conclusive refutation, See, Maxwell A. Cameron, "Analysis of Audio Tape by Vladimiro Montesinos Concerning Ollanta Humala," 20 May 2006, Internet.

50. Conaghan, *Fujimori's Peru*, p. 238. It is not clear whether Vladimiro Montesinos asked his official mistress to come aboard the sailing boat or whether she declined to follow him on his secret escape. As for Montesinos, Matilde Pinchi Pinchi betrayed him again by revealing his location in Venezuela; he was arrested in Venezuela in April 2001 and then deported to Peru where he was tried and sentenced to life imprisonment.

51. Ugaz, *Caiga quien caiga*, pp. 9–18; Gamarra, *Pequeños dictadores*, pp. 115, 125.

52. Conaghan, *Fujimori's Peru*, p. 239; Ugaz, *Caiga quien caiga*, pp. 9–18; Quiroz, *Corrupt Circles*, p. 418.

53. Ugaz, *Caiga quien caiga*, pp. 19–27. The discovery of the Swiss bank accounts was fortuitous and reflected another miscalculation on the part of Vladimiro Montesinos. He had been stashing away his ill-gotten gains mainly in offshore banks in Panama and Cayman Islands. He also had deposits in the United States, but he knew that large sums in New York banks were sure to call the attention of American officials. When an intermediary said the chance existed of opening accounts in Switzerland in Montesinos's name, he decided to diversify his deposits. A Swiss banker was eager to obtain funds for his institution, and he believed the intermediary's lie that Montesinos was a wealthy fishing magnate. But Switzerland, in an attempt to erase its image as a safe haven for the stolen money of corrupt officials, had imposed on bankers the requirement to verify the origin of the funds. Had the Swiss banker merely telephoned Peru, he easily would have learned the real occupation of the depositor. Once world news reported on the predicaments of Montesinos in Peru, a scared Swiss banker promptly reported the deposits to authorities in the hope of escaping prosecution.

54. Gamarra, *Pequeños dictadores*, pp. 115–116; Neydo Hidalgo Chronology, 14 September–20 November 2000, Internet. Blanca Nélida Colán subsequently was sentenced to ten years in prison and ordered to pay a large fine. After six years of imprisonment and when she had reached the age of 72, her lawyers successfully petitioned to have her complete the remainder of the sentence under house arrest. The request was based on the Peruvian law that established the possibility that persons 70 and over may serve the prison term in their homes.

55. Ugaz, *Caiga quien caiga*, pp. 59–61.

56. *Ibid.*, p. 70.

57. *Ibid.*

58. Congress of Peru, *En la sala de la corrupción*, 1: xxi; Ugaz, *Caiga quien caiga*, pp. 70–72.

59. Conaghan, *Fujimori's Peru*, pp. 239–240; Ugaz, *Caiga quien caiga*, p. 72; Congress of Peru, *En la sala de la corrupción*, 1: xxi.

60. McClintock and Vallas, *United States and Peru*, pp. 163–164; Conaghan, *Fujimori's Peru*, p. 240; Ugaz, *Caiga quien caiga*, pp. 74–75.

61. Congress of Peru, *En la sala de la corrupción*, 1: xii–xiii; St. John, *Toledo's Peru*, p. 26.

62. Degregori, *La década de la antipolítica*, pp. 277–279.

63. Gamarra, *Pequeños dictadores*, p. 121; Ugaz, *Caiga quien caiga*, p. 79.

64. Pease, *Pasos perdidos*, pp. 55–56.

65. Hamilton, "Fall of Fujimori," p. 207; Conaghan, *Fujimori's Peru*, p. 240; Pease, *Pasos perdidos*, pp. 56–57; Ugaz, *Caiga quien caiga*, p. 87.

66. Conaghan, *Fujimori's Peru*, p. 240; Degregori, *La década de la antipolítica*, p. 335; Ugaz, *Caiga quien caiga*, p. 87.

67. Pease, *Pasos perdidos*, p. 57.

68. Levitt, *Power in the Balance*, p. 77; Pease, *Pasos perdidos*, p. 57.

69. Hamilton, "Fall of Fujimori," p. 208; Levitt, *Power in the Balance*, p. 76; Pease, *Pasos perdidos*, p. 57.

70. St. John, *Toledo's Peru*, p. 27; Pease, *Pasos perdidos*, p. 58; Levitt, *Power in the Balance*, p. 76; Humala, *De Locumba*, pp. 109–111.

71. Pease, *Pasos perdidos*, pp. 58–60; Levitt, *Power in the Balance*, p. 77.

72. "Ollanta Humala: Keys to his Character, Likely Attitude toward the U.S.," Cable from U.S. Embassy, Lima, 23 January 2006, Wikileaks; Pease, *Pasos perdidos*, p. 73; Quiroz, *Corrupt Circles*, pp. 419–420; Humala, *De Locumba*, pp. 113–117.

73. Conaghan, *Fujimori's Peru*, p. 243; Ugaz, *Caiga quien caiga*, pp. 79–80.

74. St. John, *Toledo's Peru*, pp. 27–28; Levitt, *Power in the Balance*, p. 132.

75. Carlos Soria, "Los Cuatro Suyos no terminan en Arequipa," in DESCO, *Perú hoy; Toledo: a un año de gobierno* (Lima: DESCO, 2002), p. 79; St. John, *Toledo's Peru*, p. 29.

76. Levitt, *Power in the Balance*, p. 132; St. John, *Toledo's Peru*, p. 29.

77. Levitt, *Power in the Balance*, pp. 78, 132; St. John, *Toledo's Peru*, p. 30.

78. Levitt, *Power in the Balance*, pp. 131–135.

79. Coletta A. Youngers, "Promoting Human Rights: NGOs and the State in Peru," in John Crabtree, ed., *Makings Institutions Work in Peru* (London: Institute for the Study of the Americas, 2006), pp. 177–178, 183n24.

80. St. John, *Toledo's Peru*, p. 31.

Chapter 4

1. Aristotle, *The Politics*, trans. H. Rackham (London: William Heinemann, 1932), p. 279.

2. Rodolfo Sanz, *Dialéctica de una victoria* (Caracas: Nuevo Pensamiento Crítico, 2003), p. 21; Bart Jones, *¡Hugo! The Hugo Chávez Story from Mud Hut to Perpetual Revolution* (Hanover, NH: Steerforth Press, 2007), p. 226.

3. Sanz, *Dialéctica de una victoria*, p. 23; "Chávez Takes Office, Asks for Forgiveness, Convokes a Constitutional Referendum, and Lays Out His Agenda," Cable from U.S. Embassy, Caracas, 9 February 1999, U.S. Department of State, Freedom of Information Act (henceforth Dept State FOIA); Jones, *Hugo*, pp. 226–227.

4. Sanz, *Dialéctica de una victoria*, p. 25; "Chávez Takes Office, Asks for Forgiveness, Convokes a Constitutional Referendum, and Lays Out His Agenda," Cable from U.S. Embassy, Caracas, 9 February 1999, Dept State FOIA; Venezuela, *Aló presidente 1999* (Caracas: Imprenta Nacional, 2014), p. 26.

5. René De La Pedraja, *The United States and the Armed Forces of Mexico, Central America, and the Caribbean, 2000–2014* (Jefferson, NC: McFarland, 2014), pp. 26–27; Gregory Wilpert, *Changing Venezuela by Taking Power* (London: Verso, 2007), pp. 40–41.

6. "Venezuelan Soldiers Leave their Barracks to Implement Chavez's Civil-Military Public Works Program," Cable from U.S. Embassy, Caracas, 8 March 1999, Dept State FOIA; De La Pedraja, *United States and Armed Forces, 2000–2014*, p. 27.

7. "Venezuelan Soldiers Leave their Barracks to Implement Chavez's Civil-Military Public Works Program,"

Cable from U.S. Embassy, Caracas, 8 March 1999, Dept State FOIA.

8. De La Pedraja, *United States and Armed Forces, 2000–2014*, pp. 27–28; Wilpert, *Changing Venezuela*, pp. 50–51.

9. "Maritza Izaguirre to Continue as Finance Minister" Cable from U.S. Embassy, Caracas, 13 January 1999, Dept State FOIA; "Scene Setter for Your Visit to Venezuela," Cable from U.S. Embassy, Caracas, 12 March 1999, Dept State FOIA; Jones, *Hugo*, pp. 230, 236; Steve Ellner, *Rethinking Venezuelan Politics: Class, Conflict, and the Chávez Phenomenon* (Boulder, CO: Lynne Rienner, 2008), pp. 110–112.

10. "Maritza Izaguirre to Continue as Finance Minister" Cable from U.S. Embassy, Caracas, 13 January 1999, Dept State FOIA; "Chávez after Five Weeks," Cable from U.S. Embassy, Caracas, 10 March 1999, Wikileaks; Ellner, *Rethinking Venezuelan Politics*, p. 110.

11. "Chávez after Five Weeks," Cable from U.S. Embassy, Caracas, 10 March 1999, Wikileaks.

12. "Chávez Victory Lap Around the Region," Cable from U.S. Embassy, Caracas, 23 December 1998, Wikileaks; "Maritza Izaguirre to Continue as Finance Minister" Cable from U.S. Embassy, Caracas, 13 January 1999, Dept State FOIA.

13. "Chávez after Five Weeks," Cable from U.S. Embassy, Caracas, 10 March 1999, Wikileaks; Jones, *Hugo*, pp. 228, 234–236; "Scene setter for Visit to Washington of President-Elect Hugo Chávez," Cable from U.S. Embassy, Caracas, 20 January 1999, Dept State FOIA; Venezuela, *Aló Presidente 1999* , p. 47.

14. "Scene Setter for Your Visit to Venezuela," Cable from U.S. Embassy, Caracas, 12 March 1999, Dept State FOIA; Jones, *Hugo*, pp. 240–247.

15. De La Pedraja, *United States and Armed Forces, 2000–2014*, pp. 27–28; Wilpert, *Changing Venezuela*, pp. 40–41.

16. Sanz, *Dialéctica de una victoria*, pp. 27, 64; "Chávez Takes Office, Asks for Forgiveness, Convokes a Constitutional Referendum, and Lays Out His Agenda," Cable from U.S. Embassy, Caracas, 9 February 1999, Dept State FOIA; Vladimir Chelminski, director of Caracas Chamber of Commerce to Constitutional Convention, 17 September 1999, Vladimir Chelminski Papers, Hoover Institution, Stanford, California.

17. Jones, *Hugo*, pp. 240–247; Wilpert, *Changing Venezuela*, pp. 29–31.

18. From a public relations angle, just delaying the closing of the convention until after the New Year would have given the more forward sounding title of 2000 Constitution as more appropriate for the twenty-first century rather than 1999 Constitution implying the last gasp of the previous century.

19. "Chávez to Run After All," Cable from U.S. Embassy, Caracas, 22 November 1999, Wikileaks.

20. Jones, *Hugo*, pp. 274–275; Wilpert, *Changing Venezuela*, pp. 21–22; Noam Lupu, "Who Votes for Chavismo? Class Voting in Hugo Chávez's Venezuela," *Latin American Research Review* 45(2010): 17, 22.

21. Nikolas Kozloff, *Hugo Chávez: Oil, Politics, and the Challenge to the United States* (New York: Palgrave, 2006), p. 24; Jones, *Hugo*, pp. 278–280; Wilpert, *Changing Venezuela*, pp. 96–97.

22. Jones, *Hugo*, pp. 281–283; Kozloff, *Oil*, pp. 24–25; Orlando J. Pérez, "U.S. Security Policy and U.S.-Venezuelan Relations," in Brian Loveman, ed., *Addicted to Failure: U.S. Security Policy in Latin America and the Andean Region* (London: Rowman & Littlefield, 2006), p. 84.

23. Jones, *Hugo*, pp. 284–286; Wilpert, *Changing Venezuela*, pp. 93-94; Kozloff, *Oil*, pp. 25–26.

24. Jones, *Hugo*, pp. 286–290; Kozloff, *Oil*, p. 25; Pérez, "U.S.-Venezuelan Relations," p. 84.

25. Wilpert, *Changing Venezuela*, p. 121–124; "Thousands protest against Chávez's Education Reforms in Venezuela," CNN, 19 January 2001; Venezuela, *Aló Presidente 1999*, p. 28.

26. "Venezuelan Soldiers Leave their Barracks to Implement Chavez's Civil-Military Public Works Program," Cable from U.S. Embassy, Caracas, 8 March 1999, Dept State FOIA; Wilpert, *Changing Venezuela*, pp. 121–124.

27. Sandra La Fuente and Alfredo Meza, *El acertijo de abril: Relato periodístico de la breve caída de Hugo Chávez* (Caracas: Debate, 2003), p. 33; Sanz, *Dialéctica de una victoria*, pp. 66–67; Jones, *Hugo*, pp. 291–292.

28. "Bolivarians Readying New Attack on Education," Cable from U.S. Embassy, Caracas, 19 June 2006, Wikileaks; Jones, *Hugo*, pp. 291–292; La Fuente and Meza, *El acertijo de abril*, p. 33. In one of many clear links between the educational protests of January 2001 and the 2002 April coup attempt, Leonardo Carvajal, a major organizer of the January 2001 demonstrations, received the appointment of Secretary of Education under the regime of Pedro Carmona; See, Ernesto Villegas Poljak, *Abril, golpe adentro* (Caracas: Correo del Orinoco, 2012), pp. 159–160, 419.

29. Sanz, *Dialéctica de una victoria*, p. 67; "Thousands protest against Chávez's Education Reforms in Venezuela," CNN, 19 January 2001.

30. "Bolivarians Readying New Attack on Education," Cable from U.S. Embassy, Caracas, 19 June 2006, Wikileaks; Jones, *Hugo*, p. 293.

31. Ellner, *Rethinking Venezuelan Politics*, p. 112; Jones, *Hugo*, pp. 297–302; Pérez, "U.S.-Venezuelan Relations," pp. 86–87.

32. Jones, *Hugo*, pp. 302–304; Pérez, "U.S.-Venezuelan Relations," p. 86; Eva Gollinger, *The Chávez Code: Cracking U.S. Intervention in Venezuela* (Northampton, MA: Olive Branch Press, 2006), pp. 37–41.

33. Jones, *Hugo*, pp. 296–297; Gollinger, *The Chávez Code*, pp. 57–65.

34. Ellner, *Rethinking Venezuelan Politics*, pp. 152–153; "Labor Situation in Venezuela," circa October 2001, Dept State FOIA; Sanz, *Dialéctica de una victoria*, pp. 61–62.

35. Ellner, *Rethinking Venezuelan Politics*, pp. 153–155; "Labor Situation in Venezuela," circa October 2001, Dept State FOIA; Sanz, *Dialéctica de una victoria*, pp. 62–63; "Venezuela," circa December 2001, Dept State FOIA.

36. Ronald Bruce St John, *Toledo's Peru: Vision and Reality* (Gainesville: University Press of Florida, 2010), p. 31; Cynthia McClintock and Fabián Vallas, *The United States and Peru: Cooperation at a Cost* (New York: Routledge, 2003), p. 161.

37. Francisco Durand, "The Problem of Strengthening Business Institutions," in John Crabtree, ed., *Making Institutions Work in Peru* (London: Institute for the Study of the Americas, 2006), p. 200; Carlos Soria, "Los Cuatro Suyos no terminan en Arequipa," in DESCO, *Perú Hoy; Toledo: A un año de gobierno* (Lima: DESCO, 2002), pp. 68, 71.

38. St John, *Toledo's Peru*, p. 65.

39. Henry Pease García, *Por los pasos perdidos: El parlamento peruano entre el 2000 y el 2006* (Lima: Fondo Editorial del Congreso, 2006), pp. 96–118.

40. Crabtree, "Political Parties and Intermediation in Peru," in Crabtree, *Making Institutions Work in Peru*, pp. 33-37; Soria, "Arequipa," pp. 69–70.

41. Manuel González Prada, *Sobre el militarismo; Bajo el oprobio* (Lima: Editorial Horizonte, 1978), p. 95.

42. Stephanie McNulty, *Voice and Vote: Decentralization and Participation in Post-Fujimori Peru* (Stanford: Stanford University Press, 2011), p. 56; St. John, *Toledo's Peru*, pp. 30–31, 88. In 2002 the government attempted to rename the departments "regions" but the new term

caught on only when referring to officials, in particular the new elected regional governors.

43. Carlos Casas Tragodara, *Avances y perspectivas del proceso de descentralización en el Perú* (Lima: Universidad del Pacífico, CIES, 2005), p. 2; Carlos Monge Salgado, "Decentralisation: An Opportunity for Democratic Governance," in Crabtree, *Making Institutions Work in Peru*, p. 48.

44. Casas Tragodara, *Descentralización en el Perú*, pp. 2, 5, 7.

45. Barry S. Levitt, *Power in the Balance: Presidents, Parties, and Legislatures in Peru and Beyond* (Notre Dame, IN: University of Notre Dame Press, 2012), p. 137; St. John, *Toledo's Peru*, pp. 87–88; Moisés Arce, *Resource Extraction and Protest in Peru* (Pittsburgh: University Press, 2014), pp. 32, 55. Toledo was disingenuous when he claimed (McNulty, *Voice and Vote*, p. 56) that he set an early date for the regional elections in response to political pressure from main opposition leader and former rival candidate Alán García. In reality the latter was just exploiting the growing discontent with the Toledo administration.

46. Presidencia del Consejo de Ministros, "Consejo Nacional de Descentralización," 26 June 2002; Casas Tragodara, *Descentralización en el Perú*, pp. 6–8, 13. In a belated attempt to salvage the regional elections, in 2010 the government introduced the requirement that a 30 percent plurality was needed to win the election; See, Arce, *Resource Extraction*, p. 55.

47. McNulty, *Voice and Vote*, pp. 53, 173n1; Casas Tragodara, *Descentralización en el Perú*, p. 12; "Decentralization: Making Democracy Work in Peru, Pt 1," Cable from U.S. Embassy, Lima, 27 October 2005, Wikileaks.

48. Casas Tragodara, *Descentralización en el Perú*, p. 11.

49. McNulty, *Voice and Vote*, pp. 72–78; Levitt, *Power in the Balance*, p. 84.

50. Quoted in McNulty, *Voice and Vote*, p. 74.

51. "Decentralization: Making Democracy Work in Peru, Pt 1," Cable from U.S. Embassy, Lima, 27 October 2005, Wikileaks; "Perú: riesgos de la descentralización," *La tercera*, 14 June 2014; Arce, *Resource Extraction*, pp. 54, 56.

52. Levitt, *Power in the Balance*, p. 84; "Decentralization: Making Democracy Work in Peru, Pt 1," Cable from U.S. Embassy, Lima, 27 October 2005, Wikileaks. The willingness of Alán García to follow the views of American diplomats about drug eradication was an early factor persuading the U.S. Embassy to shift its attitude toward him from hostility to sympathetic support as the 2006 presidential campaign neared.

53. "Former President Alán García Talks Politics, Trade with Ambassador," Cable from U.S. Embassy, Lima, 9 March 2005, Wikileaks; "Decentralization: Making Democracy Work in Peru, Pt 1," Cable from U.S. Embassy, Lima, 27 October 2005, Wikileaks.

54. "Former President Alán García Talks Politics, Trade with Ambassador," Cable from U.S. Embassy, Lima, 9 March 2005, Wikileaks; "President of Congress Flores-Araoz Tells Ambassador His Hat Is in the Ring," Cable from U.S. Embassy, Lima, 15 March 2005, Wikileaks; Pease, *Pasos perdidos*, p. 310.

55. "Decentralization: Making Democracy Work in Peru, Pt 2," Cable from U.S. Embassy, Lima, 27 October 2005, Wikileaks; "Attempt to Facilitate Passage of Macro-Region Referenda Fails in Congress," Cable from U.S. Embassy, Lima, 28 October 2005, Wikileaks; Pease, *Pasos perdidos*, pp. 370–371.

56. "Decentralization: Making Democracy Work in Peru, Pt 2," Cable from U.S. Embassy, Lima, 27 October 2005, Wikileaks.

57. St. John, *Toledo's Peru*, pp. 89–90; "Decentralization: Making Democracy Work in Peru, Pt 2," Cable from U.S. Embassy, Lima, 27 October 2005, Wikileaks; "Macro-Region Referenda Fail—Decentralization Process to be Rethought," Cable from U.S. Embassy, Lima, 31 October 2005, Wikileaks.

58. "Ambassador Discusses Humala, Development Issues in Arequipa," Cable from U.S. Embassy, Lima, 30 December 2005, Wikileaks; *La República*, 1 November 2005.

Chapter 5

1. Niccoló Machiavelli, *The Prince*, trans. W.K. Marriott (London: Everyman's Library, 1908), pp. 48–49.

2. Bart Jones, *¡Hugo! The Hugo Chávez Story from Mud Hut to Perpetual Revolution* (Hanover, NH: Steerforth Press, 2007), pp. 294–295; Interpelación of Diosdado Cabello, 15 May 2002, www.urru.org.

3. Jones, *Hugo*, p. 305; Sandra La Fuente and Alfredo Meza, *El acertijo de abril: Relato periodístico de la breve caída de Hugo Chávez* (Caracas: Debate, 2003), p. 33; "Chronology of Dept of State Activities and the Venezuelan Coup Attempt," 15 May 2002, U.S. State Department, Freedom of Information Act (henceforth Dept State FOIA).

4. Gregory Wilpert, *Changing Venezuela by Taking Power* (London: Verso, 2007), pp. 110–111; Jones, *Hugo*, pp. 306–308; "Venezuelan Leader's Land Law Raises Wrath of Private Sector," *Houston Chronicle*, 8 December 2002.

5. Wilpert, *Changing Venezuela*, pp. 111–113; Jones, *Hugo*, pp. 306–308; "Venezuelan Leader's Land Law Raises Wrath of Private Sector," *Houston Chronicle*, 8 December 2002.

6. Jones, *Hugo*, p. 305; Wilpert, *Changing Venezuela*, p. 23.

7. "Chronology of Dept of State Activities and the Venezuelan Coup Attempt," 15 May 2002, Dept State FOIA; Jones, *Hugo*, p. 306; Wilpert, *Changing Venezuela*, pp. 23, 94.

8. "Business Associations Stop Communication with Government of Venezuela," Cable from U.S. Embassy, Caracas, 19 November 2001, Dept State FOIA; La Fuente and Meza, *El acertijo de abril*, pp. 34–35.

9. Wilpert, *Changing Venezuela*, p. 23; "Business Associations Stop Communication with Government of Venezuela," Cable from U.S. Embassy, Caracas, 19 November 2001, Dept State FOIA; "The Shutdown," Cable from U.S. Embassy, Caracas, 30 November 2001, Dept State FOIA; La Fuente and Meza, *El acertijo de abril*, pp. 34–35; Leslie C. Gates, *Electing Chávez: The Business of Anti-Neoliberal Politics in Venezuela* (Pittsburgh: University Press, 2010), pp. 91–93.

10. "The Shutdown: Petroleum Sector Rapprochement with National Assembly," Cable from U.S. Embassy, Caracas, 7 December 2001, Dept State FOIA; Rodolfo Sanz, *Dialéctica de una victoria* (Caracas: Nuevo Pensamiento Crítico, 2003), pp. 81–82. Besides being a mentor and close friend of Hugo Chávez, the departure of Luis Miquilena deprived the administration of an element of efficiency and continuity. The void was only partially filled when Miquilena's friend and loyal Chavista José Vicente Rangel became vice president in May 2002.

11. "National Work Stoppage a Success," Cable from U.S. Embassy, Caracas, 10 December 2001, Dept State FOIA.

12. "Land Reform: Chávez Plays to the Crowd," Cable from U.S. Embassy, Caracas, 12 December 2001, Dept State FOIA; Sanz, *Dialéctica de una victoria*, pp. 78–79.

13. "Venezuela Opposition Marches to Challenge Chávez," Otto J. Reich to Secretary of State, Washington, D.C., 27 January 2002, Dept State FOIA; Sanz, *Dialéctica de una victoria*, pp. 96–99.

14. "Scene Setter for Your Visit to Venezuela," Cable

from U.S. Embassy, Caracas, 26 October 1998, Dept State FOIA; Marta Harnecker, ed., *Hugo Chávez Frías: Un hombre, un pueblo* (Havana: Editorial de Ciencias Sociales, 2002), pp. 75–76, 84; René De La Pedraja, *The United States and the Armed Forces of Mexico, Central America, and the Caribbean, 2000–2014* (Jefferson, NC: McFarland, 2014), pp. 11–12, 26–28.

15. "Active Mourning March Set for February 27; General Strike in March," Cable from U.S. Embassy, Caracas, 25 February 2002, Dept State FOIA; Interpelación of Minister of Interior Ramón Rodríguez Chacín, 6 May 2002, www.urru.org; De La Pedraja, *The United States and the Armed Forces, 2000–2014*, pp. 221–222.

16. Interpelación of Ramón Rodríguez Chacín, 6 May 2002, www.urru.org; "Fourth Venezuelan Military Officer Demands Chávez Resign," Afternoon Brief, 26 February 2002, Washington D.C. Dept State FOIA; La Fuente and Meza, *El acertijo de abril*, p. 32.

17. "Generales que estorban a Chávez fueron enviados a Washington," *El Nacional*, 27 January 2002; Interpelación of Ovidio Poggioli, 17 May 2002, www.urru.org; Interpelación of Carlos Aguilera, 15 May 2002, www.urru.org; Harnecker, *Hugo Chávez Frías*, pp. 77–78.

18. Interpelación of General Wilfredo Silva, 23 May 2002, www.urru.org; Interpelación of General Jorge Luis García Carneiro, 22 May 2002, www.urru.org; Interpelación of General Efraín Vásquez Velasco, 17 May 2002, www.urru.org; Marta Harnecker, ed., *Militares junto al pueblo: Entrevistas a nueve comandantes venezolanos que protagonizaron la gesta de abril de 2002* (Caracas: Vadell Hermanos Editores, 2003), pp. 41, 286.

19. "Ambassador Shapiro's Meeting [of April 4] with Rodríguez Chacín," Cable from U.S. Embassy, Caracas, 24 May 2002, Dept State FOIA.

20. Jones, *Hugo*, pp. 302–303.

21. "PDVSA in Revolt," Cable from U.S. Embassy, Caracas, 28 February 2002, Dept State FOIA; "PDVSA: Operación Morrocoy Update," Cable of U.S. Embassy, Caracas, 15 March 2002, Dept State FOIA; Gregory Wilpert, "The 47-Hour Coup that Changed Everything," 14 April 2012, Venezuelanalysis.com; Frederick Klindt M. "February Newsletter," 10 March 2002, E.B. Brossard Papers, Box 22, Hoover Institution, Stanford, California (henceforth Hoover); Nikolas Kozloff, *Hugo Chávez: Oil, Politics, and the Challenge to the United States* (New York: Palgrave Macmillan, 2006), pp. 26, 87; Interpelación of Carlos Aguilera, former director of secret police, 15 May 2002, www.urru.org.

22. "Labor, Business, and Church Announce Transition Pact," Cable from U.S. Embassy, Caracas, 5 March 2002, Dept State FOIA; Venezuela, Asamblea Nacional, *Informe de la Comisión Parlamentaria Especial para investigar los sucesos de abril de 2002*, p. 15.

23. "PDVSA Begins Slowdown Action," Cable from U.S. Embassy, Caracas, 13 March 2002, Dept State FOIA; "PDVSA: First Blood," Cable from U.S. Embassy, Caracas, 27 March 2002, Dept State FOIA; "PDVSA Workers Begin Shutdowns," Cable from U.S. Embassy, Caracas, 4 April 2002, Dept State FOIA.

24. "PDVSA: More Suspensions," Cable from U.S. Embassy, Caracas, 8 April 2002, Dept State FOIA; "PDVSA: The Heavy Hand of Hugo Chávez," Cable from U.S. Embassy, Caracas, 9 April 2002, Dept State FOIA. Of the executives, seven were fired, another twelve were forced into early retirement, and five were demoted.

25. "PDVSA: More Suspensions," Cable from U.S. Embassy, Caracas, 8 April 2002, Dept State FOIA; "Ambassador Shapiro's Meeting [of April 4] with Rodríguez Chacín," Cable from U.S. Embassy, Caracas, 24 May 2002, Dept State FOIA.

26. "Venezuela's April 9 Work Stoppage, T Minus 12 Hours—Economic Considerations," Cable from U.S. Embassy, Caracas, 9 April 2002, Dept State FOIA; "PDVSA: The Heavy Hand of Chávez," Cable from U.S. Embassy, Caracas, 9 April 2002, Dept State FOIA; Interpelación of General Efraín Vásquez Velasco, 17 May 2002, www.urru.org; Interpelación of General Manuel Rosendo, 10 May 2002, www.urru.org; Brian A. Nelson, *The Silence and the Scorpion: The Coup against Chávez and the Making of Modern Venezuela* (New York: Nation Books, 2009), pp. 17–23.

27. La Fuente and Meza, *El acertijo de abril*, pp. 126–126, 133–134; De La Pedraja, *The United States and Armed Forces, 2000–2014*, pp. 17–18.

28. Interpelación of Freddy Bernal, 3 May 2002, www.urru.org; Interpelación of General Manuel Rosendo, 10 May 2002, www.urru.org.

29. La Fuente and Meza, *El acertijo de abril*, pp. 52–53; Interpelación of General Jorge Luis García Carneiro, 22 May 2002, www.urru.org.

30. "Tale of Two Cities—The March on Miraflores Palace," Cable from U.S. Embassy, Caracas, 12 April 2002, Dept State FOIA. In this cable, the U.S. Embassy reported a two-hour meeting of the Coordinating Committee for Democracy and Liberty" taking place at FEDECAMARAS in the morning of 11 April right before Carmona, Ortega, and Lameda addressed the crowd at PDVSA headquarters. At this meeting "The Coordinating Committee decided to go for broke—to seek the immediate departure of President Chávez by popular acclamation." Because secret police agents reported this decision from the meeting also at FEDECAMARAS the night before on 10 April, the diplomats might have confused the dates. Thus, the morning meeting on 11 April might not have taken place, although another meeting on the morning of 11 April to confirm details of the planned march cannot be ruled out. Likewise, the possibility exists that hostile U.S. diplomats already were trying to create a narrative sympathetic to the coup and wanted to move forward to 11 April the date of the decision to march to Miraflores to demand the resignation of Chávez; by moving the date forward the actions did not appear as planned but as a nearly spontaneous outpouring of the popular will.

31. Interpelación of Carlos Aguilera, 15 May 2002, www.urru.org; Interpelación of General Manuel Rosendo, 10 May 2002, www.urru.org.

32. Interpelación of General Francisco Belisario Landis, 13 May 2002, www.urru.org; Interpelación of General Carlos Rafael Alfonzo Martínez, 11 May 2002, www.urru.org; Interpelación of General Manuel Rosendo, 10 May 2002, www.urru.org.

33. La Fuente and Meza, *El acertijo de abril*, p. 58; De La Pedraja, *The United States and Armed Forces, 2000–2014*, p. 14.

34. Interpelación of General Wilfredo Silva, 23 May 2002, www.urru.org; De La Pedraja, *The United States and Armed Forces, 2000–2014*, pp. 14–15; Ernesto Villegas Poljak, *Abril, golpe adentro* (Caracas: Ediciones Correo del Orinoco, 2012), p. 56.

35. La Fuente and Meza, *El acertijo de abril*, p. 58; De La Pedraja, *The United States and Armed Forces, 2000–2014*, pp. 15–16.

36. Interpelación of General Jorge Luis García Carneiro, 22 May 2002, www.urru.org; Harnecker, *Militares junto al pueblo*, p. 70; Interpelación of General Wilfredo Silva, 23 May 2002, www.urru.org; Guillermo García Ponce, *El golpe del 11 de abril*, 2nd. Ed. (Caracas: Alcaldía, 2002), p. 27.

37. "Transcripción de comunicación de Tiburón 1" 11 April 2002, www.urru.org; Interpelación of General Wilfredo Silva, 23 May 2002, www.urru.org; Interpelación of General Manuel Rosendo, 10 May 2002, www.urru.org;

Harnecker, *Militares junto al pueblo*, pp. 42–43, 71; García Ponce, *El golpe del 11 de abril*, pp. 31–32.

38. Jones, *Hugo*, pp. 322–326; Nelson, *Coup against Chávez*, pp. 291–293 devotes an appendix to "the sniper riddle."

39. Jones, *Hugo*, pp. 327–330; La Fuente and Meza, *El acertijo de abril*, p. 115.

40. "Venezuela's General Strike as of 11:00 P.M. April 11," Cable from U.S. Embassy, Caracas, 12 April 2002, Dept State FOIA; La Fuente and Meza, *El acertijo de abril*, pp. 115–116; García Ponce, *El golpe del 11 de abril*, pp. 38, 44–45.

41. Interpelación of General Wilfredo Silva, 23 May 2002, www.urru.org; Harnecker, *Militares junto al pueblo*, 46, 50, 72.

42. De La Pedraja, *The United States and Armed Forces, 2000–2014*, pp. 16–17; Villegas, *Abril*, p. 107.

43. Interpelación of Coronel Jesús Morao Gardona, 21 May 2002, www.urru.org; Interpelación of General Manuel Rosendo, 10 May 2002, www.urru.org; Harnecker, *Hugo Chávez Frías*, pp. 92, 178–179.

44. Villegas, *Abril*, p. 107; La Fuente and Meza, *El acertijo de abril*, pp. 60–61; Interpelación of Héctor Ramírez Pérez, 16 May 2002, www.urru.org; Interpelación of Coronel José Gregorio Montilla Pantoja, 21 May 2002, www.urru.org; Interpelación of General Manuel Rosendo, 10 May 2002, www.urru.org.

45. La Fuente and Meza, *El acertijo de abril*, pp. 115–117.

46. Harnecker, *Hugo Chávez Frías*, pp. 81–82; La Fuente and Meza, *El acertijo de abril*, pp. 126–127.

47. Rafael Arreaza Padilla, "Acta de entrevista," 27 September 2004, in Villegas, *Abril*, p. 424; Interpelación of Coronel José Gregorio Montilla Pantoja, 21 May 2002, www.urru.org.

48. La Fuente and Meza, *El acertijo de abril*, pp. 125–127.

49. Rafael Arreaza Padilla "Acta de entrevista," 27 September 2004; José Gregorio Vásquez, "Mi paso por un gobierno breve," www.urru.org; "PDVSA: Back to Normal," Cable from U.S. Embassy, Caracas, 12 April 2002, Dept State FOIA; Harnecker, *Militares junto al pueblo*, p. 149; Kozloff, *Oil*, p. 29.

50. Gregorio Vásquez, "Mi paso por un gobierno breve"; La Fuente and Meza, *El acertijo de abril*, pp. 129–131, 189–196.

51. "PDVSA: Back to Normal," Cable from U.S. Embassy, Caracas, 12 April 2002, Dept State FOIA; Villegas Poljak, *Abril*, pp. 131–133; Kozloff, *Oil*, pp. 29–30.

52. Gregorio Vásquez, "Mi paso por un gobierno breve"; La Fuente and Meza, *El acertijo de abril*, p. 131; Sanz, *Dialéctica de una victoria*, pp. 152–153; Villegas, *Abril*, pp. 136–138.

53. La Fuente and Meza, *El acertijo de abril*, pp. 130–134; Stratfor, "Venezuela: Carmona Out, Chávez Back—But for How Long?" E.B. Brossard Paper, Box 15, Hoover.

54. Ceremonia con motivo de la Constitución del Gobierno de Transición Democrática y Unidad Nacional," 12 April 2012, Live televisión broadcast reprinted in Sanz, *Dialéctica de una victoria*, pp. 320–331; Villegas, *Abril*, pp. 177–182; Rafael Arreaza Padilla, "Acta de entrevista," 27 September 2004; Gregorio Vásquez, "Mi paso por un gobierno breve."

55. "Chronology of Dept of State Activities and the Venezuelan Coup Attempt," 15 May 2002, Dept State FOIA; Harnecker, *Militares junto al pueblo*, p. 47; Stratfor, "Venezuela: Carmona Out, Chávez Back—But for How Long?" E.B. Brossard Papers, Box 15, Hoover.

56. Villegas, *Abril*, 229–233; De La Pedraja, *The United States and Armed Forces, 2000–2014*, p. 24; La Fuente and Meza, *El acertijo de abril*, pp. 151–153; Interpelación of General Efraín Vásquez Velasco, 17 May 2002, www.urru.org; Interpelación of General Manuel Rosendo, 10 May 2002, www.urru.org; Interpelación of Vice Admiral Héctor Ramírez Pérez, 16 May 2002, www.urru.org.

57. Harnecker, *Militares junto al pueblo*, pp. 149–150; Interpelación of Coronel Jesús Morao Gardona, 21 May 2002, www.urru.org.

58. Gregorio Vásquez, "Mi paso por un gobierno breve"; La Fuente and Meza, *El acertijo de abril*, pp. 154–155; Interpelación of Ovidio Poggioli, 17 May 2002, www.urru.org.

59. Harnecker, *Militares junto al pueblo*, pp. 151–152; Interpelación of Coronel Jesús Morao Gardona, 21 May 2002, www.urru.org.

60. Interpelación of Coronel José Gregorio Montilla Pantoja, 21 May 2002, www.urru.org; Interpelación of General Jorge Luis García Carneiro, 22 May 2002, www.urru.org; Interpelación of General Wildredo Silva, 23 May 2002, www.urru.org. The best epitaph for the Carmona regime came from Stratfor analysts: "Carmona's short-lived interim presidency unraveled when the political coalition that negotiated his appointment collapsed due to efforts by extreme right-wing civilian and military groups to hijack his transition government." Stratfor, "Venezuela: Carmona Out, Chávez Back—But for How Long?" E.B. Brossard Papers, Box 15, Hoover.

61. Harnecker, *Hugo Chávez Frías*, pp. 179–182; Stratfor, "Venezuela: Carmona Out, Chávez Back—But for How Long?" E.B. Brossard Papers, Box 15, Hoover.

62. Sanz, *Dialéctica de una victoria*, pp. 177–180, 211; Interpelación of Coronel José Gregorio Montilla Pantoja, 21 May 2002, www.urru.org; Harnecker, *Hugo Chávez Frías*, pp. 183–187.

Chapter 6

1. Cable from U.S. Embassy, Bogotá, 6 March 2002, U.S. Department of State, Freedom of Information Act (henceforth Dept State FOIA).

2. René De La Pedraja, *Wars of Latin America, 1982–2013* (Jefferson, NC: McFarland, 2013), chapter 10; Harvey F. Kline, *Showing Teeth to the Dragons: State Building by Colombian President Álvaro Uribe Vélez, 2002–2006* (Tuscaloosa: University of Alabama Press, 2009), pp. 18–22.

3. Since the 1980s analysts have correctly concluded that a peace agreement with FARC automatically compelled ELN to end its limited activities. Because over 90 percent of Colombia's counterinsurgency efforts targeted FARC, it was an easy matter for the government to redeploy overwhelming forces to smother the few ELN strongholds.

4. De La Pedraja, *Wars of Latin America, 1982–2013*, p. 202; Kline, *Showing Teeth to the Dragons*, p. 22.

5. De La Pedraja, *Wars of Latin America, 1982–2013*, pp. 203–207; Kline, *Showing Teeth to the Dragons*, p. 23; Paola Fajardo-Heyward, "Understanding the Effect of Security Assistance on Human Rights: The Case of Plan Colombia," *The Latin Americanist*, June 2015, pp. 7, 11.

6. "Costly Losses: Repercussions of Petroleum," Cable from U.S. Embassy, Bogotá, 2 May 2001, Dept State FOIA; *El Tiempo*, 4 November 2001.

7. "Costly Losses: Repercussions of Petroleum," Cable from U.S. Embassy, Bogotá, 2 May 2001, Dept State FOIA; "Notes from the Field: Paramilitaries Challenge Guerrillas in Arauca," Cable from U.S. Embassy, Bogotá, 23 October 2001, Dept State FOIA; "Early Efforts in Arauca Paying Off," Cable from U.S. Embassy, Bogotá, 3 January 2003, Dept State FOIA; *El Tiempo*, 29 June 1998.

8. "Scene setter: New Challenges and Opportunities for Colombia," Cable from U.S. Embassy, Bogotá, 2 August

2002, Dept State FOIA; Ana María Bejarano, "Politicizing Insecurity: Uribe's Instrumental Use of Populism," in Carlos de la Torre and Cynthia J. Arnson, eds., *Latin American Populism in the Twenty-First Century* (Washington, D.C.: Woodrow Wilson Center Press, 2012), pp. 340–341; Laura Wills-Otero, "Colombia: Analyzing the Strategies for Political Action of Álvaro Uribe's Government, 2002–2010," in Juan Pablo Luna and Cristóbal Rovira Kaltwasser, eds., *The Resilience of the Latin American Right* (Baltimore: Johns Hopkins Press, 2014), p. 199.

9. "Weathering the Storm: Colombia in the Coming Months," Cable from U.S. Embassy, Bogotá, 6 March 2002, Dept State FOIA; "Scene setter: New Challenges and Opportunities for Colombia," Cable from U.S. Embassy, Bogotá, 2 August 2002, Dept State FOIA; Bejarano, "Politicizing Insecurity," pp. 328–329; Colombia, *Constitución Política de Colombia* (Bogotá: Editorial Temis, 1991), article 190.

10. "Weathering the Storm: Colombia in the Coming Months," Cable from U.S. Embassy, Bogotá, 6 March 2002, Dept State FOIA; "Scene setter: New Challenges and Opportunities for Colombia," Cable from U.S. Embassy, Bogotá, 2 August 2002, Dept State FOIA; Kline, *Showing Teeth to the Dragons*, pp. 3–4, 22–23.

11. "Weathering the Storm: Colombia in the Coming Months," Cable from U.S. Embassy, Bogotá, 6 March 2002, Dept State FOIA; Wills-Otero, "Colombia," p. 198.

12. "Weathering the Storm: Colombia in the Coming Months," Cable from U.S. Embassy, Bogotá, 6 March 2002, Dept State FOIA.

13. "Notes from the Field: Paramilitaries Challenge Guerrillas in Arauca," Cable from U.S. Embassy, Bogotá, 23 October 2001, Dept State FOIA; *El Tiempo*, 14 November 1999.

14. Witness for Peace, "The Real Cost of Pipeline Security in Colombia: Corporate Welfare with Deadly Consequences," Report of July 2002; *El Tiempo*, 2 July 1998. For excellent reporting on the Santo Domingo bombing of civilians, See, "A Colombian Town Caught in a Cross-Fire," *Los Angeles Times*, 17 March 2002. At least since early 2002 a bilateral working group headed by the vice minister of defense and the deputy chief of mission of the U.S. Embassy had been shaping policies to protect the Arauca pipeline; See, "Department of State Report to Congress on Caño Limón Pipeline, December 2002."

15. "Costly Losses: Repercussions of Petroleum," Cable from U.S. Embassy, Bogotá, 2 May 2001, Dept State FOIA; "Government of Colombia Justice Program in Arauca a Model for Other Conflictive Zones," Cable from U.S. Embassy, Bogotá, 2 January 2003, Dept State FOIA; "Uribe's Democratic Security Strategy: Impact in Arauca Department," Cable from U.S. Embassy, Bogotá, 26 June 2003, Dept State FOIA; Witness for Peace, "Pipeline Security"; "Department of State Report to Congress on Caño Limón Pipeline, December 2002."

16. "Government of Colombia Justice Program in Arauca a Model for Other Conflictive Zones," Cable from U.S. Embassy, Bogotá, 2 January 2003, Dept State FOIA; "Early Efforts in Arauca Paying Off," Cable from U.S. Embassy, Bogotá, 3 January 2003, Dept State FOIA.

17. *El Tiempo*, 30 October 2002; "Uribe's Democratic Security Strategy: Impact in Arauca Department," Cable from U.S. Embassy, Bogotá, 26 June 2003, Dept State FOIA.

18. Moisés Arce, "The Repoliticization of Collective Action after Neoliberalism in Peru," *Latin American Politics and Society* 50(2008): 51.

19. Carlos Soria, "Los Cuatro Suyos no terminan en Arequipa," in DESCO, *Perú hoy; Toledo: A un año de gobierno* (Lima: DESCO, 2002), pp. 68, 71; Francisco Durand, "The Problem of Strengthening Business Institutions," in John Crabtree, ed., *Making Institutions Work in Peru* (London: Institute for the Study of the Americas, 2006), p. 200.

20. Soria, "Arequipa," p. 71; Eduardo Ballón E., "El toledismo y el movimiento social," in DESCO, *Perú hoy; Toledo: A un año de gobierno* (Lima: DESCO, 2002), p. 26; Ronald Bruce St. John, *Toledo's Peru: Vision and Reality* (Gainesville: University Press of Florida, 2010), p. 40.

21. Ulises Humala, "Globalizando al Perú," in DESCO, *Perú hoy*, p. 182; Gabriela Carrasco, "Cronología de movilizaciones y debates en torno a las acciones del gobierno," in DESCO, *Perú hoy*, p. 221.

22. José Luis Vargas Gutiérrez, "¡Erupcionó Arequipa!" *Quehacer*, no. 136 (2002), p. 77; Arce, "Collective Action," p. 50.

23. Carrasco, "Cronología de movilizaciones," pp. 221–222; Vargas Gutiérrez, "Arequipa," p. 73; St. John, *Toledo's Peru*, p. 40; Henry Pease García, *Por los pasos perdidos: El parlamento Peruano entre el 2000 y el 2006* (Lima: Fondo Editorial del Congreso, 2006), p. 125.

24. Carrasco, "Cronología de movilizaciones," pp. 222–223; Arce, "Collective Action," p. 50.

25. Vargas Gutiérrez, "Arequipa," p. 73; Arce, "Collective Action," p. 51.

26. Vargas Gutiérrez, "Arequipa," p. 74. The original Spanish was "solo unos muertos de hambre" which has been translated as "beggars" but I feel that "deadbeats" better captures the intention. By the way, Minister of Interior Fernando Rospigliosi later denied having made the statement, but this rectification is irrelevant for explaining the historical process, because the protestors believed that he had uttered those words. This is another case in the classic principle of appearance being as important as reality. Similarly, during the start of the French Revolution it did not matter whether it was true that Marie Antoinette had said "let them eat cake," because the people believed that she had made the statement.

27. Carrasco, "Cronología de movilizaciones," p. 223; Vargas Gutiérrez, "Arequipa," pp. 73–74.

28. Vargas Gutiérrez, "Arequipa," pp. 74–75.

29. Fernando Rospigliosi, "The Blocking of Reform in the Security Services," in John Crabtree, ed., *Making Institutions Work in Peru* (London: Institute for the Study of the Americas, 2006), p. 73; Carrasco, "Cronología de movilizaciones," p. 224.

30. Vargas Gutiérrez, "Arequipa," p. 75; Carrasco, "Cronología de movilizaciones," pp. 223–225; Pease, *Pasos Perdidos*, p. 126.

31. St. John, *Toledo's Peru*, p. 40; Soria, "Arequipa," pp. 63, 72; Arce, "Collective Action," p. 52.

32. "Teacher's Union Takes it on the Chin over Test Results," Cable from U.S. Embassy, Lima, 6 March 2007, Wikileaks; Arce, "Collective Action," p. 44; St. John, *Toledo's Peru*, pp. 41–42.

33. Moisés Arce, *Resource Extraction and Protest in Peru* (Pittsburgh: University Press, 2004), pp. 69–72, 80; Defensoría del Pueblo, *Ante todo, el diálogo: Defensoría del Pueblo y conflictos sociales y políticos* (Lima: Defensoría del Pueblo, 2005), pp. 62–63.

34. Arce, *Resource Extraction*, pp. 74–75; Seo Ji-Hyun, "Neoliberal Extractivism and Rural Resistance: The Anti-Mining Movement in the Peruvian Northern Highlands, Cajamarca (2011–2013)," Ph.D. Dissertation, University of Liverpool, 2014, pp. 212–213. It should be noted that the Lime War began years *before* the decentralization of Toledo went into effect. This early starting date refutes the claim of some critics who blame decentralization for sparking the unrest in the provinces, when in reality the protest movements used whatever institutions were available to channel the discontent.

35. Congress of Peru, "Informe Final sobre los sucesos

de la provincia del Collao," 2004, pp. 33, 51; Defensoría del Pueblo, *Ante todo, el diálogo*, p. 38.

36. Congress of Peru, "Informe Final," pp. 52–58, 96; Defensoría del Pueblo, *Ante todo, el diálogo*, pp. 40–41; St. John, *Toledo's Peru*, p. 43.

37. "Tangled Strands in Fight over Peru Gold Mine: The Cost of Gold; Treasure of Yanacocha," *New York Times*, 25 October 2005; Iván Salas Rodríguez, *Quilish hora cero: Cajamarca, la lucha de un pueblo que defiende su vida y dignidad* (Cajamarca, Peru, 2006), p. 171; Arce, *Resource Extraction*, p. 81.

38. "Peru's Mines Dig Deep at Local Discontent," *Washington Post*, 17 December 2004; Ji-Hyun, "The Anti-Mining Movement in Cajamarca," p. 172.

39. Arce, *Resource Extraction*, pp. 74–75, 90–91; Ji-Hyun, "The Anti-Mining Movement in Cajamarca," p. 174; Salas, *Quilish hora cero*, pp. 36, 38.

40. Arce, *Resource Extraction*, pp. 92–93; Salas, *Quilish hora cero*, pp. 47–48.

41. Ji-Hyun, "The Anti-Mining Movement in Cajamarca," p. 175; Salas, *Quilish hora cero*, pp. 40–41, 57. Documents such as the Newmont letter of 26 February 2002 threatening Peru with losing its foreign investment are infrequent precisely because they are unnecessary. When capitalist zealots are in control of the government as was the case under the Toledo presidency, these officials share the same free market ideology as the company executives. So in other cases in Peru and elsewhere the absence of similar documents should not be used as "evidence" to prove the lack of collusion when the ideological affinity guaranteed a stanchly pro-business position.

42. "Tangled Strands," *New York Times*, 25 October 2005; Salas, *Quilish hora cero*, pp. 66, 68–70.

43. Ji-Hyun, "The Anti-Mining Movement in Cajamarca," p. 175; Salas, *Quilish hora cero*, pp. 74, 76–77.

44. Arce, *Resource Extraction*, pp. 97–98; "Tangled Strands," *New York Times*, 25 October 2005; *Denver Post*, 14 September 2004; Salas, *Quilish hora cero*, pp. 83–85; Ji-Hyun, "The Anti-Mining Movement in Cajamarca," p. 175.

45. Arce, *Resource Extraction*, p. 98; *Denver Post*, 19 September 2004; Salas, *Quilish hora cero*, p. 85; Ji-Hyun, "The Anti-Mining Movement in Cajamarca," p. 176.

46. Defensoría del Pueblo, *Ante todo, el diálogo*, p. 57n27; Congress of Peru, "Informe Final," p. 45; "Former Interior Minister Rospigliosi Worried about Ollanta Humala," Cable from U.S. Embassy, Lima, 29 November 2005, Wikileaks; Ollanta Humala, *De Locumba a candidato a la presidencia* (Mexico: Ocean Sur, 2009), pp. 132, 135.

47. Defensoría del Pueblo, *Ante todo, el diálogo*, p. 57; Rospigliosi, "The Blocking of Reform," p. 74; Ollanta, *De Locumba*, pp. 140–141.

48. Defensoría del Pueblo, *Ante todo, el diálogo*, pp. 57–58; Rospigliosi, "The Blocking of Reform," pp. 74–75; "Supreme Court Decides That Rebel Leader Antauro Humala Should Be Tried in Andahuaylas, Not Lima," Cable from U.S. Embassy, Lima, 22 September 2005, Wikileaks; Ollanta, *De Locumba*, pp. 133, 138.

Chapter 7

1. Niccolò Machiavelli, *The Prince* (London: Everyman's Library, 1908), p. 121.

2. Speech of Hugo Chávez upon return to Miraflores Palace, 14 April 2002.

3. "Venezuela Political Update, May 5, 2002," Cable from U.S. Embassy, Caracas, 5 May 2002, U.S. State Department Freedom of Information Act (henceforth Dept State FOIA); Rodolfo Sanz, *Dialéctica de una victoria* (Caracas: Nuevo Pensamiento Crítico, 2003), pp. 195–196; Bart Jones, *¡Hugo! The Hugo Chávez Story from Mud Hut to Perpetual Revolution* (Hanover, NH: Steerforth Press, 2007), pp. 368–369.

4. Guillermo García Ponce, *El golpe del 11 de abril*, 2nd Ed. (Caracas: Alcaldía, 2002), pp. 99–100; Sanz, *Dialéctica de una victoria*, pp. 182–185; Jones, *Hugo*, pp. 369, 374.

5. Sanz, *Dialéctica de una victoria*, p. 184.

6. Venezuelan-American Chamber of Commerce to Hugo Chávez, 26 April 2002 in Sanz, *Dialéctica de una victoria*, pp. 337–339. U.S. ambassador Charles Shapiro had urged the Venezuelan-American Chamber of Commerce to enter into dialogue with the government; "Chronology of Department of State Activities and the Venezuelan Coup Attempt," 15 May 2002, Secret/NoForn, p. 61, Dept State FOIA.

7. "FEDECAMARAS Conference—Venezuela's Business Community Confronts Chávez," Cable from U.S. Embassy, Caracas, 9 October 2002, Dept State FOIA; Sanz, *Dialéctica de una victoria*, p. 202; Gregory Wilpert, *Changing Venezuela by Taking Power: The History and Policies of the Chávez Government* (London: Verso, 2007), p. 72.

8. "Political Update: August 6–7, 2002," Cable from U.S. Embassy, Caracas, 8 August 2002, Dept State FOIA; "Varios oficiales de la Fuerza Armada de Venezuela, Pronunciamiento" Caracas, 22 October 2002, www.urru.org; "Chávez Purging Military after Coup," *Miami Herald*, 19 May 2002; "Más de 42 por ciento de los generales de la FAV permanece sin cargos," *El Nacional*, 6 May 2002.

9. In reality, the distinction between destroying the old army and just replacing generals was blurry and not as sharp as it might seem. Mexico abolished the old federal army in 1914, yet countless federal officers eventually ended up serving in the new army emerging after 1920. Nicaragua abolished the despised Guardia Nacional of Dictator Anastasio Somoza in 1979 and still recycled thousands of former Guardia Nacional members (soldiers, NCOs, and junior officers) into the new Sandinista army.

10. García Ponce, *El golpe del 11 de abril*, pp. 40–42; Sanz, *Dialéctica de una victoria*, pp. 216–217.

11. "Ambassador's Courtesy Call on President of Supreme Tribunal of Justice," Cable from U.S. Embassy, Caracas, 29 May 2002, Dept State FOIA; "No Military Rebellion: Analyzing How the Supreme Court Ruled," Cable from U.S. Embassy, Caracas, 26 August 2002, Dept State FOIA; Sanz, *Dialéctica de una victoria*, pp. 205–208.

12. "Political Update—June 20, 2002," Cable from U.S. Embassy, Caracas, 20 June 2002, Dept State FOIA; Sanz, *Dialéctica de una victoria*, pp. 185–187, 218–219.

13. "Government of Venezuela Takes Over Metropolitan Police," Cable from U.S. Embassy, Caracas, 19 November 2002, Dept State FOIA; Nelson, *Coup against Chávez*, p. 267; Sanz, *Dialéctica de una victoria*, pp. 229–231.

14. "FEDECAMARAS Conference—Venezuela's Business Community Confronts Chávez," Cable from U.S. Embassy, Caracas, 9 October 2002, Dept State FOIA; "Venezuela's Strike Continuing to December 3," Cable from U.S. Embassy, Caracas, 2 December 2002, Dept State FOIA; Rodolfo Sanz, *Dialéctica de una victoria* (Caracas: Nuevo Pensamiento Crítico, 2003), pp. 225–226.

15. "FEDECAMARAS Conference—Venezuela's Business Community Confronts Chávez," Cable from U.S. Embassy, Caracas, 9 October 2002, Dept State FOIA; "October 10 Opposition March Sitrep No.2," Cable from U.S. Embassy, Caracas, 10 October 2002, Dept State FOIA.

16. "Varios oficiales de la Fuerza Armada de Venezuela, Pronunciamiento" Caracas, 22 October 2002, www.urru.org; Jones, *Hugo*, pp. 372–373; Stratfor, "Storm Clouds Again Forming over Venezuela," 7 June 2002, E. B. Brossard Papers, Box 35, Hoover Institution, Stanford, California (henceforth Hoover).

17. "Varios oficiales de la Fuerza Armada de Venezuela, Pronunciamiento" Caracas, 22 October 2002, www.urru.

org; Jones, *Hugo*, pp. 373–374; Sanz, *Dialéctica de una victoria*, pp. 223–224.

18. Speech of Alí Rodríguez, CEO of PDVSA, 9 December 2002, in Sanz, *Dialéctica de una victoria*, pp. 340–341; Steve Ellner, *Rethinking Venezuelan Politics: Class, Conflict, and the Chávez Phenomenon* (Boulder, CO: Lynne Rienner, 2008), p. 119; Rory Carroll, *Comandante: Hugo Chávez's Venezuela* (New York: Penguin, 2014), p. 158. As one former PDVSA executive explained about Alí Rodríguez, "His ideology is of full State ownership and control. He has always been a Communist in his beliefs. The only thing is that he is a smooth and nice Communist, contrary to the S.O.B. that Chávez appointed prior to the strike," Evanan Romero to Scott, 24 April 2002, E. B. Brossard Papers, Box 30, Hoover.

19. "Venezuela's Strike Continuing to December 3," Cable from U.S. Embassy, Caracas, 2 December 2002, Dept State FOIA; "PDVSA and the General Strike," Cable from U.S. Embassy, Caracas, 2 December 2002, Dept State FOIA; "Government of Venezuela Hangs in as Economy Grinds to a Halt," Cable from U.S. Embassy, Caracas, 11 December 2002, Dept State FOIA.

20. "PDVSA and the General Strike," Cable from U.S. Embassy, Caracas, 2 December 2002, Dept State FOIA; Sanz, *Dialéctica de una victoria*, pp. 237, 242–244.

21. "PDVSA on Day Four of the General Strike," Cable from U.S. Embassy, Caracas, 5 December 2002, Dept State FOIA; Jones, *Hugo*, pp. 375–376; Sanz, *Dialéctica de una victoria*, pp. 262–263.

22. "Strike Day Five: Looking for Ways Out?" Cable from U.S. Embassy, Caracas, 6 December 2002, Dept State FOIA; "Government of Venezuela Hangs in as Economy Grinds to a Halt," Cable from U.S. Embassy, Caracas, 11 December 2002, Dept State FOIA.

23. "PDVSA: Day Five of the General Strike," Cable from U.S. Embassy, Caracas, 6 December 2002, Dept State FOIA; "Political Sitrep: December 9, 1:00 P.M.," Cable from U.S. Embassy, Caracas, 9 December 2002, Dept State FOIA; "PDVSA: Running on Empty," Cable from U.S. Embassy, Caracas, 9 December 2002, Dept State FOIA; "Government of Venezuela Hangs On as Economy Grinds to a Halt," Cable from U.S. Embassy, Caracas, 11 December 2002, Dept State FOIA; Sanz, *Dialéctica de una victoria*, pp. 247–250.

24. "Energy Sector: Strike Day 12," Cable from U.S. Embassy, Caracas, 13 December 2002, Dept State FOIA; Jones, *Hugo*, pp. 376–380.

25. Marta Harnecker, ed., *Militares junto al pueblo* (Caracas: Vadell Hermanos Editores, 2003), pp. 248–252; Jones, *Hugo*, pp. 380–382.

26. "Venezuela Strike: The Shipping Stand-off After *Pilín León*," Cable from U.S. Embassy, Caracas, 24 December 2002, Dept State FOIA; Harnecker, *Militares junto al pueblo*, pp. 245–246; Jones, *Hugo*, pp. 379–380.

27. "Strike Day 25: PDVSA Touts Impending Normalization," Cable from U.S. Embassy, Caracas, 26 December 2003, Dept State FOIA; Jones, *Hugo*, pp. 379–380; Harnecker, *Militares junto al pueblo*, pp. 245–246; Sanz, *Dialéctica de una victoria*, pp. 262–263.

28. "Strike Day 25: PDVSA Touts Impending Normalization," Cable from U.S. Embassy, Caracas, 26 December 2003, Dept State FOIA; "Political Update: December 30, 2002," Cable from U.S. Embassy, Caracas, 30 December 2002, Dept State FOIA; Sanz, *Dialéctica de una victoria*, pp. 263–264.

29. "Strike Day 25: PDVSA Touts Impending Normalization," Cable from U.S. Embassy, Caracas, 26 December 2003, Dept State FOIA; "Political Update: December 30, 2002," Cable from U.S. Embassy, Caracas, 30 December 2002, Dept State FOIA; Jones, *Hugo*, pp. 383–384; Harnecker, *Militares junto al pueblo*, pp. 83–84, 305; Sanz, *Dialéctica de una victoria*, pp. 240, 245.

30. "Government of Venezuela Hangs On as Economy Grinds to a Halt," Cable from U.S. Embassy, Caracas, 11 December 2002, Dept State FOIA; "Venezuela: Energy Update January 9, 2003," Cable from U.S. Embassy, Caracas, 9 January 2003, Dept State FOIA; "Venezuela: Political Update January 14, 2003" Cable from U.S. Embassy, Caracas, 14 January 2002, Dept State FOIA; "Venezuela: The Strike in Week Eight," Cable from U.S. Embassy, Caracas, 24 January 2002, Dept State FOIA; Jones, *Hugo*, p. 383.

31. "Venezuela: Political Update January 14, 2003" Cable from U.S. Embassy, Caracas, 14 January 2002, Dept State FOIA; "Venezuela Resumes Oil Shipments to Cuba," Cable from U.S. Embassy, Caracas, Dept State FOIA; "Venezuela: The Strike in Week Eight," Cable from U.S. Embassy, Caracas, 24 January 2002, Dept State FOIA; Jones, *Hugo*, p. 384.

32. "Venezuela's General Strike: Looking for New Weapons," Cable from U.S. Embassy, Caracas, 9 January 2003, Dept State FOIA; "Venezuela: The Strike in Week Eight," Cable from U.S. Embassy, Caracas, 24 January 2002, Dept State FOIA; "Venezuela: Political Update: January 27, 2003," Cable from U.S. Embassy, Caracas, 27 January 2003, Dept State FOIA; Jones, *Hugo*, pp. 384–386; "Lavando los trapos sucios," 14 February 2003, E. B. Brossard Papers, Box 26, Hoover.

33. Ellner, *Rethinking Venezuelan Politics*, p. 119.

34. Jones, *Hugo*, p. 387.

Chapter 8

1. Álvaro Uribe Vélez statement to Collin Powell in "Secretary's December 4 Meeting with President Uribe," Secret Cable from U.S. Embassy, Bogotá, 10 December 2002, U.S. Department of State, Freedom of Information Act (henceforth Dept State FOIA).

2. "Staffdel Cardenas," Cable from U.S. Embassy, Bogotá, 5 June 2002, Dept State FOIA.

3. Harvey F. Kline, *Showing Teeth to the Dragons: State Building by Colombian President Álvaro Uribe Vélez 2002–2006* (Tuscaloosa: University of Alabama Press, 2009), pp. 40, 45; "Scene Setter: New Challenges and Opportunities for Colombia," Cable from U.S. Embassy, Bogotá, 2 August 2002, Dept State FOIA.

4. René De La Pedraja, *Wars of Latin America, 1982–2013: The Path to Peace* (Jefferson, NC: McCarland, 2013), pp. 224–226; Kline, *Showing Teeth to the Dragons*, pp. 39–41; "Why January 2006 Is Different from January 2005," Cable from U.S. Embassy, Bogotá, 6 January 2006, Wikileaks; Paola Fajardo-Heyward, "Understanding the Effect of Security Assistance on Human Rights: The Case of Plan Colombia," *Latin Americanist*, 2015 June, p. 11.

5. De La Pedraja, *Wars of Latin America, 1982–2013*, p. 226; Kline, *Showing Teeth to the Dragons*, p. 46; "A General Overview of Colombia's Security Situation," Cable from U.S. Embassy, Bogotá, 16 April 2004, Wikileaks; *El Tiempo*, 5 February 2006.

6. "FARC attempts Major Kidnapping in Huila Department," Cable from U.S. Embassy, Bogotá, 27 February 2004, Wikileaks; De La Pedraja, *Wars of Latin America, 1982–2013*, p. 226.

7. Kline, *Showing Teeth to the Dragons*, p. 47; De La Pedraja, *Wars of Latin America, 1982–2013*, p. 227; "Codel First's Meetings in Bogotá," Cable from U.S. Embassy, Bogotá, 7 January 2004, Wikileaks.

8. *El Tiempo*, 5 February 2006; De La Pedraja, *Wars of Latin America, 1982–2013*, p. 227; Kline, *Showing Teeth to the Dragons*, p. 47.

9. Laura Wills-Otero, "Colombia: Analyzing the Strategies for Political Action of Álvaro Uribe's Government, 2002–2010," in Juan Pablo Luna and Cristóbal Rovira Kaltwasser, eds., *The Resilience of the Latin American Right*

(Baltimore: Johns Hopkins Press, 2014), pp. 198–199; Ana María Bejarano, "Politicizing Insecurity: Uribe's Instrumental Use of Populism," in Carlos de la Torre and Cynthia J. Arnson, eds., *Latin American Populism in the Twenty-First Century* (Washington, D.C.: Woodrow Wilson Center Press, 2012), pp. 340–341; "Scene Setter: New Challenges and Opportunities for Colombia," Cable from U.S. Embassy, Bogotá, 2 August 2002, Dept State FOIA; Kline, *Showing Teeth to the Dragons*, p. 64.

10. Wills-Otero, "Colombia," pp. 204–205; Jasmin Hristov, *Blood and Capital: The Paramilitarization of Colombia* (Athens: Ohio University Press, 2009), pp. 46–49; María Jimena Duzán, *Así gobierna Uribe* (Bogotá: Planeta, 2004), pp. 103–107; "Scene Setter: New Challenges and Opportunities for Colombia," Cable from U.S. Embassy, Bogotá, 2 August 2002, Dept State FOIA; Fajardo-Heyward, "Security Assistance," pp. 11–12.

11. Wills-Otero, "Colombia," pp. 204–205.

12. Bejarano, "Politicizing Insecurity," p. 343. The paragraph also draws on *Ibid.* and Duzán, *Así gobierna Uribe*, pp. 85–93.

13. Kline, *Showing Teeth to the Dragons*, pp. 39–40; "Staffdel Cardenas," Cable from U.S. Embassy, Bogotá, 5 June 2002, Dept State FOIA; "Colombia: Under Secretary of State's Inaugural Visit—Looking at the Human Cost of FARC Violence," Cable from U.S. Embassy, Bogotá, 9 August 2002, Dept State FOIA.

14. Kline, *Showing Teeth to the Dragons*, pp. 37, 43; "Colombia: Under Secretary of State's Inaugural Visit—Looking at the Human Cost of FARC Violence," Cable from U.S. Embassy, Bogotá, 9 August 2002, Dept State FOIA.

15. Kline, *Showing Teeth to the Dragons*, pp. 43–44; "Colombia: Under Secretary of State's Inaugural Visit—Looking at the Human Cost of FARC Violence," Cable from U.S. Embassy, Bogotá, 9 August 2002, Dept State FOIA.

16. Kline, *Showing Teeth to the Dragons*, p. 44; Duzán, *Así gobierna Uribe*, pp. 125–129; Colombia, *Constitución Política de Colombia* (Bogotá: Editorial Temis, 1991), articles 377–378.

17. Hristov, *Blood and Capital*, pp. 74–77; Carlos Miguel Ortiz Sarmiento, *Urabá: pulsiones de vida y desafíos de muerte* (Bogotá: La Carreta Social, 2007), p. 157; René De La Pedraja, *Wars of Latin America, 1982–2013: The Path to Peace* (Jefferson, NC: McFarland, 2013), pp. 89–93.

18. Juan Carlos Garzón, "La complejidad paramilitar: Una aproximación estratégica," in Alfredo Rangel, ed., *El poder paramilitar* (Bogotá: Planeta, 2005), pp. 69, 81; William Ramírez Tabón, "Autodefensas y poder local," in Rangel, *El Poder paramilitar*, pp. 165, 167, 175; De La Pedraja, *Wars of Latin America, 1982–2013*, pp. 135–137.

19. Hristov, *Blood and Capital*, pp. 90–92; Garzón, "Una aproximación estratégica," pp. 69–72; Ortiz Sarmiento, *Urabá*, pp. 154–156.

20. "Ambassador's Meeting with ICRC Head of Delegation," Cable from U.S. Embassy, Bogotá, 2 April 2004, Wikileaks; De La Pedraja, *Wars of Latin America, 1982–2013*, pp. 217–221. In Urabá the demobilization in March 1991 of a third guerrilla group, the Maoist ELP, had left an opening for FARC and the paramilitaries to try to fill the resulting power vacuum in the region. But as the text states, a strong army presence and fierce local hostility against FARC were the real reasons for the failure of the guerrillas to enter the area.

21. Hristov, *Blood and Capital*, pp. 70–72, 94, 96, 80–81; Ramírez Tabón, "Autodefensas y poder local," pp. 143, 147; Garzón, "Una aproximación estratégica," pp. 69–72; Fernando Cubides Cipagauta "Narcotráfico y paramilitarismo: ¿Matrimonio indisoluble?" in Rangel, *El Poder paramilitar*, p. 236; "Carlos Castaño Goes Prime time," Cable from U.S. Embassy, Bogotá, 6 March 2000, Dept State FOIA; "Who Are the Paramilitary Commanders?" Cable from U.S. Embassy, Bogotá, 23 September 2004, Wikileaks; Mauricio Aranguren Molina, *Mi confesión; Carlos Castaño revela sus secretos* (Bogotá: Oveja Negra, 2002), pp. 201–202.

22. Garzón, "Una aproximación estratégica," pp. 80–81, 101; De La Pedraja, *Wars of Latin America, 1982–2013*, pp. 202–203; Aranguren Molina, *Carlos Castaño revela sus secretos*, pp. 261–285.

23. "Carlos Castaño Goes Prime time," Cable from U.S. Embassy, Bogotá, 6 March 2000, Dept State FOIA; Garzón, "Una aproximación estratégica," pp. 79–80; Aranguren Molina, *Carlos Castaño revela sus secretos*, pp. 9–16.

24. "Carlos Castaño Goes Prime time," Cable from U.S. Embassy, Bogotá, 6 March 2000, Dept State FOIA; Aranguren Molina, *Carlos Castaño revela sus secretos*, pp. 327–343.

25. "North Coast Businessmen View Political and Economic Situation," Cable from U.S. Embassy, Bogotá, 25 September 2000, Dept State FOIA; Kline, *Showing Teeth to the Dragons*, p. 23; Hristov, *Blood and Capital*, pp. 79–80; Fajardo-Heyward, "Security Assistance," pp. 11–12.

26. Kline, *Showing Teeth to the Dragons*, pp. 71–72, 77–78.

27. Ramírez Tabón, "Autodefensas y poder local," p. 147; Kline, *Showing Teeth to the Dragons*, pp. 71, 78; "Interagency Delegation Discusses AUC Demobilization Plan," Cable from U.S. Embassy, Bogotá, 10 February 2002, Wikileaks.

28. Alfredo Rangel, "¿A dónde van los paramilitares?" in Rangel, *El poder paramilitar*, p. 16; Kline, *Showing Teeth to the Dragons*, pp. 78–79; Hristov, *Blood and Capital*, p. 146.

29. "Who Are the Paramilitary Commanders?" Cable from U.S. Embassy, Bogotá, 23 September 2004, Wikileaks; Kline, *Showing Teeth to the Dragons*, pp. 79, 82; Hristov, *Blood and Capital*, pp. 70–71.

30. "Paramilitary Peace Difficulties," Secret/NoForn Cable from U.S. Embassy, Bogotá, 2 March 2004, Wikileaks; "Castaño's Fate Unknown," Cable from U.S. Embassy, Bogotá, 23 April 2004, Wikileaks; "Next Steps in Paramilitary Peace Process," Cable from U.S. Embassy, Bogotá, 17 May 2004, Wikileaks.

31. "Paramilitary Peace Difficulties," Secret/NoForn Cable from U.S. Embassy, Bogotá, 2 March 2004, Wikileaks; "Peace Commissioner Describes Demobilization Details," Cable from U.S. Embassy, Bogotá, 2 November 2002, Wikileaks; Kline, *Showing Teeth to the Dragons*, pp. 84–85; Garzón, "Una aproximación estratégica," pp. 106–107.

32. "Government of Colombia Hard Line on Demobilization Makes Narcoterrorists Uneasy," Cable from U.S. Embassy, Bogotá, 2 March 2004, Wikileaks; "Government of Colombia Continuing to Confront Paramilitaries," Cable from U.S. Embassy, Bogotá, 2 March 2004; "Staffdel Meeting with Vice President Santos," Cable from U.S. Embassy, Bogotá, 2 August 2002, Dept State FOIA; Kline, *Showing Teeth to the Dragons*, pp. 80–81; Garzón, "Una aproximación estratégica," pp. 100, 102–104, 112. Females comprised no more than 2 percent of the paramilitaries, in contrast to making up a fifth to a fourth of guerrilla units; in another difference with the guerrillas, minors under 18 were a very small percentage.

33. Hristov, *Blood and Capital*, pp. 147–148; Kline, *Showing Teeth to the Dragons*, pp. 64–65, 80.

Chapter 9

1. "Making Sense of Venezuela's Polls," Cable from U.S. Embassy, Caracas, 12 August 2004, Wikileaks.

2. "Government of Venezuela Hangs in as Economy Grinds to a Halt," Cable from U.S. Embassy, Caracas, 11 December 2002, Department of State Freedom of Information Act (henceforth Dept State FOIA); "Energy Sector: Strike Day 12," Cable from U.S. Embassy, Caracas, 13 December 2002, Dept State FOIA; "Fired Workers Languish in the Political Crossfire," Cable from U.S. Embassy, Caracas, 18 September 2003, Dept State FOIA; Nikolas Kozloff, *Hugo Chávez: Oil, Politics, and the Challenge to the United States* (New York: Palgrave Macmillan, 2006), pp. 32–33.

3. "Venezuela's Quick Recovery Surprises Experts," *Miami Herald*, 29 May 2009; Kozloff, *Chávez and Oil*, p. 33; Bart Jones, *!Hugo¡ The Hugo Chávez Story from Mud Hut to Perpetual Revolution* (Hanover, NH: Steerforth Press, 2007), pp. 382–383.

4. "Fired Workers Languish in the Political Crossfire," Cable from U.S. Embassy, Caracas, 18 September 2003, Dept State FOIA; "Government of Venezuela Denies Labor Claims of Ex-Oil Workers," Cable from U.S. Embassy, Caracas, 8 September 2004, Wikileaks; Mark P. Sullivan, "Venezuela: Political Conditions and U.S. Policy," 10 October 2008, Congressional Research Service, Wikileaks.

5. Rodolfo Sanz, *Dialéctica de una victoria* (Caracas: Nuevo Pensamiento Crítico, 2003) pp. 282–284; "Chavez Switches His Game Plan," Cable from U.S. Embassy, Caracas, 15 May 2003, Dept State FOIA; Jones, *Hugo*, p. 386.

6. "Chávez Maintains Popularity, But Still Vulnerable on Recall," Cable from U.S. Embassy, Caracas, 2 January 2004, Wikileaks.

7. Gregory Wilpert, *Changing Venezuela by Taking Power; The History and Policies of the Chávez Government* (London: Verso, 2007), pp. 34–35; Jones, *Hugo*, pp. 402–404; Sullivan, "Venezuela Political Conditions."

8. Jones, *Hugo*, pp. 403–404; Sullivan, "Venezuela Political Conditions."

9. "Venezuela on the Verge of a Purge," Cable from U.S. Embassy, Caracas, 19 March 2004, Wikileak; Wilpert, *Changing Venezuela*, p. 148.

10. Jones, *Hugo*, pp. 408–409; Wilpert, *Changing Venezuela*, p. 26.

11. This quotation and the next from "The Tropical Unity of the Opposition," Cable from U.S. Embassy, Caracas, 12 February 2004, Wikileaks. The same idea about the incompetence of the opposition is in Norman F. Carnahan to Emma Brossard, 17 August 2004, E.B. Brossard Papers, Box 38, Hoover Institution, Stanford, California (henceforth Hoover).

12. "Weekend of Conflict in Caracas, No CNE Decision Yet," Cable from U.S. Embassy, Caracas, 1 March 2004, Wikileaks; "Opposition Governors, Mayor: A Snapshot of Venezuela's Crisis," Cable from U.S. Embassy, Caracas, 24 March 2004, Wikileaks.

13. Steve Ellner, *Rethinking Venezuelan Politics; Class, Conflict, and the Chávez Phenomenon* (Boulder: Lynne Rienner, 2008), pp. 119–120; Jones, *Hugo*, pp. 404–405.

14. "Venezuela: Two Polls Confirm Polarization," Cable from U.S. Embassy, Caracas, 11 May 2004, Wikileaks; "Venezuela's Power Sector: Heading for Another Crisis," Cable from U.S. Embassy, Caracas, 12 May 2004, Wikileaks; Sullivan, "Venezuela Political Conditions"; Wilpert, *Changing Venezuela*, p. 27; Ellner, *Rethinking Venezuelan Politics*, p. 121.

15. "Chávez: Coup Attempt Averted with Arrest of Paramilitaries," Cable from U.S. Embassy, Caracas, 11 May 2004, Wikileaks; "Paramilitaries Update," Cable from U.S. Embassy, Caracas, 17 June 2004, Wikileaks.

16. "The Tropical Unity of the Opposition," Cable from U.S. Embassy, Caracas, 12 February 2004, Wikileaks; "What's Next for Chávez," Cable from U.S. Embassy, Caracas, 3 June 2004, Wikileaks.

17. "Chávez Agrees to Recall Referendum," Cable from U.S. Embassy, Caracas, 4 June 2004, Wikileaks; "Venezuela Referendum: Recall or Ratification?" Cable from U.S. Embassy, Caracas, 9 June 2004, Wikileaks.

18. "Minimum Wage Increase," Cable from U.S. Embassy, Caracas, 12 May 2004, Wikileaks; "New Referendum Polling Figures," Cable from U.S. Embassy, Caracas, 25 June 2004, Wikileaks; "Opposition Launches National Consensus Plan," Cable from U.S. Embassy, Caracas, 15 July 2004, Wikileaks.

19. "Chávez versus Chávez: What's His Plan?" Cable from U.S. Embassy, Caracas, 25 June 2004, Wikileaks; "Comando Maisanta: A Mid-Campaign Update," Cable from U.S. Embassy, Caracas, 27 July 2004, Wikileaks; "Chávez Pads Votes with Naturalization and Identity Cards," Cable from U.S. Embassy, Caracas, 2 July 2004, Wikileaks.

20. "Lack of Funding Worries Venezuelan Opposition," Cable from U.S. Embassy, 21 July 2004, Wikileaks: "Economy on Upswing as Referendum Draw Near," Cable from U.S. Embassy, Caracas, 4 August 2004, Wikileaks: "Ambassador's Views on Venezuela's Referendum," Cable from U.S. Embassy, Caracas, 12 August 2004, Wikileaks; Norman Carnahan to Emma Brossard, 17 August 2004, E.B. Brossard Papers, Box 38, Hoover.

21. "Chávez Declares Referendum Victory—So Does Opposition," Cable from U.S. Embassy, Caracas, 16 August 2004, Wikileaks.

22. Wilpert, *Changing Venezuela*, p. 27; "Venezuela: No Closer to Acceptance of Government Victory by Opposition," Cable from U.S. Embassy, Caracas, 16 August 2004, Wikileaks.

23. "Venezuela: Why Chávez Won," Cable from U.S. Embassy, Caracas, 19 August 2004, Wikileaks; Sullivan, "Venezuela Political Conditions."

24. "Venezuelan Business Adjusts to Chávez's Victory," Cable from U.S. Embassy, Caracas, 19 August 2004, Wikileaks.

25. Sanz, *Dialéctica de una victoria*, pp. 283–284; Jones, *Hugo*, pp. 404–405; "Venezuelan Business Adjusts to Chávez's Victory," Cable from U.S. Embassy, Caracas, 19 August 2004, Wikileaks.

26. "Rocky Start to Business-Government Dialogue," Cable from U.S. Embassy, Caracas 8 September 2004, Wikileaks.

27. "Venezuelan Business Adjusts to Chávez's Victory," Cable from U.S. Embassy, Caracas, 19 August 2004, Wikileaks; Ernesto Villegas Poljak, *Abril, golpe adentro* (Caracas Correo del Orinoco, 2012), pp. 182–184. Luis Enrique Ball, the president of the Venezuelan-American Chamber of Commerce had foolishly signed the Carmona decree of 12 April 2002, and soon after the failure of the coup he was replaced by a less tainted figure able to resume the usual discussions with the government over practical issues affecting businesses.

28. "Rocky Start to Business-Government Dialogue," Cable from U.S. Embassy, Caracas 8 September 2004, Wikileaks.

29. "Venezuelan Business Adjusts to Chávez's Victory," Cable from U.S. Embassy, Caracas, 19 August 2004, Wikileaks.

30. "Chavistas Win Big in Regional Elections," Cable from U.S. Embassy, Caracas, 1 November 2004, Wikileaks.

31. "Red Map in Venezuela: What Chávez won in the Regionals," Cable from U.S. Embassy, Caracas, 5 November 2004, Wikileaks.

32. "Venezuelan Prosecutor Investigates 400 for Rebellion," Cable from U.S. Embassy, Caracas, 19 October 2004, Wikileaks; Ministerio Público, "Balance Informaciones sobre sucesos abril de 2002," 8 April 2005, www.urru.org.

33. "Venezuelan Prosecutor Investigates 400 for Rebel-

lion," Cable from U.S. Embassy, Caracas, 19 October 2004, Wikileaks.

34. The fullest available list of names is "Los Carmona-firmantes," in Villegas Poljak, *Abril, golpe adentro*, pp. 413–417. Because some participants signed directly under the text of the Carmona decree while others wrote on blank sheets of papers that secretaries were badgering citizens to sign, the task of putting together a complete list of all the names has proved difficult. As could be expected, after the failure of the coup the signers of the blank sheets claimed that they were only confirming their attendance in the event and thus should not be included among those citizens ratifying the Carmona decree. Some signatures were illegible (a possible precaution?); and one signer wrote only his first name "Rodolfo" and declined to give his last name, thus sparing himself from prosecution and reducing the number of identified signers from 361 to 360. An analysis of each of the names will probably reveal that peer pressure compelled many participants to sign, and that besides writing illegibly, they also protected their identities by writing down fake names or those of relatives. See also, Interpelación of Diosdado Cabello, 5 May 2002, www.urru.org.

35. "Killing of Political Prosecutor," Cable from U.S. Embassy, Caracas, 19 November 2004, Wikileaks.

36. Ministerio Público, "Balance Informaciones sobre sucesos abril de 2002," 8 April 2005, www.urru.org; "Update on Anderson Investigation," Cable from U.S. Embassy, Caracas, 6 December 2004, Wikileaks. The reluctance of Chávez to pursue the intellectual authors of the Anderson murder was a major lost opportunity for his presidency. If he had hoped that by going easy on the upper class he would gain their support or at least tolerance, he clearly had miscalculated.

37. "Chavistas Get Tough: Venezuela's Penal Code Amendments," Cable from U.S. Embassy, Caracas, 19 January 2005, Wikileaks; "Chávez Vetoes Penal Code Reform,"Cable from U.S. Embassy, Caracas, 11 February 2005, Wikileaks.

38. Jones, *Hugo*, pp. 241–242; "Revolutionary Justice: Changes in Venezuela's Top Court," Cable from U.S. Embassy, Caracas, 11 February 2005, Wikileaks; "April 11 Revisited: Venezuelan Supreme Court Overrides Itself," Cable from U.S. Embassy, Caracas, 17 March 2005, Wikileaks.

39. Jones, *Hugo*, pp. 449–450; "Chávez Calls for End to Black Listing; Opposition Does Not Buy It," Cable from U.S. Embassy, Caracas, 4 May 2005, Wikileaks; "Venezuelan Judicial Purges: Ending Corruption or Opposition?" Cable from U.S. Embassy, Caracas, 17 May 2005, Wikileaks.

40. "Why the Opposition Withdrawal Surprised Observers," Cable from U.S. Embassy, Caracas, 9 December 2005, Wikileaks; Sullivan, "Venezuela Political Conditions."

41. "Venezuela Political Update: December 5," Cable from U.S. Embassy, Caracas, 5 December 2005; Sullivan, "Venezuela Political Conditions."

42. "Why the Opposition Withdrawal Surprised Observers," Cable from U.S. Embassy, Caracas, 9 December 2005, Wikileaks.

43. "Chávez Gives Marching Orders for the Revolution," Cable from U.S. Embassy, Caracas, 23 December 2004, Wikileaks; "Chávez Bolivarian Business Models: The Triumph of Ideology," Cable from U.S. Embassy, Caracas, 5 May 2006, Wikileaks; "Laboring under Chavez Economic Planning," Cable from U.S. Embassy, Caracas, 17 August 2007, Wikileaks.

44. Wilpert, *Changing Venezuela*, pp. 111–113.

45. "Chávez Gives Marching Orders for the Revolution," Cable from U.S. Embassy, Caracas, 23 December 2004, Wikileaks.

46. "Problems with Venezuelan Cooperatives," Cable from U.S. Embassy, Caracas, 27 June 2005, Wikileaks; Wilpert, *Changing Venezuela*, pp. 110–111.

47. Jones, *Hugo*, pp. 438–440; Wilpert, *Changing Venezuela*, pp. 113.

48. "Venezuelan Agrarian Land Reform: Ambitious Goals Mask Different Agenda," Cable from U.S. Embassy, Caracas, 8 February 2006, Wikileaks.

49. "Chávez Ushers in New Wave of Land Expropriations," Cable from U.S. Embassy, Caracas, 29 March 2007, Wikileaks; Wilpert, *Changing Venezuela*, p. 115.

50. "Venezuelan Agrarian Land Reform: Ambitious Goals Mask Different Agenda," Cable from U.S. Embassy, Caracas, 8 February 2006, Wikileaks.

51. "Chávez Ushers in New Wave of Land Expropriations," Cable from U.S. Embassy, Caracas, 29 March 2007, Wikileaks.

52. "Venezuelan Cattleman's Association Views on Expropriations, MERCOSUR," Cable from U.S. Embassy, Caracas, 17 May 2006, Wikileaks.

53. "Land Reform Fits and Starts," Cable from U.S. Embassy, Caracas, 15 March 2005, Wikileaks.

54. "Food Vulnerabilities: Bolivarian Republic Policy Responses Crack under Rolling Shortages," Cable from U.S. Embassy, Caracas, 20 December 2007, Wikileaks.

55. "Venezuela Wakes Up and Smells the Coffee," Cable from U.S. Embassy, Caracas, 16 February 2006, Wikileaks.

56. "Venezuela Wakes Up and Smells the Coffee," Cable from U.S. Embassy, Caracas, 16 February 2006, Wikileaks.

57. "Leviathan's Return: Chavez's New Economic Bureaucracies," Cable from U.S. Embassy, Caracas, 16 November 2004, Wikileaks; "Food Vulnerabilities: Bolivarian Republic Policy Responses Crack under Rolling Shortages," Cable from U.S. Embassy, Caracas, 20 December 2007, Wikileaks.

58. "Through Discount Chain, the State Takes over Much of Food Distribution," Cable from U.S. Embassy, Caracas, 23 February 2005, Wikileaks.

59. Observations and conversations during study trip to Venezuela of June 2007; "Mercal: The Bolivarian Republic of Venezuela's Most Popular Mission," Cable from U.S. Embassy, Caracas, 23 June 2005, Wikileaks; Jones, *Hugo*, p. 395.

60. Observations and conversations during study trip to Venezuela of June 2007; "Mercal: The Bolivarian Republic of Venezuela's Most Popular Mission," Cable from U.S. Embassy, Caracas, 23 June 2005, Wikileaks.

61. Jones, *Hugo*, pp. 11, 432, 469.

62. "Chávez Gives Marching Orders for the Revolution," Cable from U.S. Embassy, Caracas, 23 December 2004, Wikileaks; Jones, *Hugo*, pp. 433, 437; Wilpert, *Changing Venezuela*, pp. 105–106 and especially 236–240.

63. "Problems with Venezuelan Cooperatives," Cable from U.S. Embassy, Caracas, 27 June 2005, Wikileaks.

64. "Problems with Venezuelan Cooperatives," Cable from U.S. Embassy, Caracas, 27 June 2005, Wikileaks.

65. "Venezuelan Urban and Rural Expropriations Continue (Part 2 of 2)" Cable from U.S. Embassy, Caracas, 6 April 2004, Wikileaks; "Problems with Venezuelan Cooperatives," Cable from U.S. Embassy, Caracas, 27 June 2005, Wikileaks.

66. "Chávez Bolivarian Business Models: The Triumph of Ideology," Cable from U.S. Embassy, Caracas, 5 May 2005, Wikileaks; Wilpert, *Changing Venezuela*, pp. 77–78; Ellner, *Rethinking Venezuelan Politics*, pp. 186–187.

67. Rory Carroll, *Comandante: Hugo Chávez's Venezuela* (New York: Penguin, 2014), pp. 216–217; "Chávez Bolivarian Business Models: The Triumph of Ideology," Cable from U.S. Embassy, Caracas, 5 May 2005, Wikileaks; Wilpert, *Changing Venezuela*, pp. 78, 82–83.

68. "Chávez Bolivarian Business Models: The Triumph

of Ideology," Cable from U.S. Embassy, Caracas, 5 May 2005, Wikileaks; Wilpert, *Changing Venezuela*, pp. 78–79; Jones, *Hugo*, p. 437; Ellner, *Rethinking Venezuelan Politics*, pp. 187–188.

69. "Chávez Bolivarian Business Models: The Triumph of Ideology," Cable from U.S. Embassy, Caracas, 5 May 2005, Wikileaks; Wilpert, *Changing Venezuela*, pp. 81–82; Jones, *Hugo*, p. 437.

Chapter 10

1. U.S. Ambassador Struble in "Cabinet Crisis an Intergovernmental Affair for Now, but Future Consequences Remain Unclear," Cable from U.S. Embassy, Lima, 12 August 2005, Wikileaks.

2. Ronald Bruce St. John, *Toledo's Peru: Vision and Reality* (Gainesville: University Press of Florida, 2010), p. 54.

3. "Economic Expansion Beginning to Reduce Poverty," Cable from U.S. Embassy, Lima, 4 November 2005, Wikileaks; "Poverty in Peru Decreasing Substantially," Cable from U.S. Embassy, Lima, 4 September 2008, Wikileaks.

4. St. John, *Toledo's Peru*, p. 44.

5. "Peru LNG: New Pipe, But No New Jungle Pipeline," Cable from U.S. Embassy, Lima, 17 May 2007, Wikileaks; St. John, *Toledo's Peru*, p. 44.

6. "Camisea Scorecard: Toledo's Great Legacy," Cable from U.S. Embassy, Lima, 15 September 2006, Wikileaks; *Toledo's Peru*, p. 47.

7. "Camisea II Promises Job Growth and Export Revenues," Cable from U.S. Embassy, Lima, 24 February 2006, Wikileaks; "Government of Peru Investigating Camisea Pipeline Ruptures," Cable from U.S. Embassy, Lima, 10 March 2006, Wikileaks; Henry Pease García, *Por los pasos perdidos; El parlamento peruano entre el 2000 y el 2006* (Lima: Fondo Editorial del Congreso del Peru, 2006), pp. 375, 377; St. John, *Toledo's Peru*, p. 47.

8. "Camisea II Promises Job Growth and Export Revenues," Cable from U.S. Embassy, Lima, 24 February 2006, Wikileaks; "Peru's LNG's Agricultural Community Social Responsibility Projects," Cable from U.S. Embassy, Lima, 25 June 2008, Wikileaks.

9. "Camisea Scorecard: Toledo's Great Legacy," Cable from U.S. Embassy, Lima, 15 September 2006, Wikileaks; St. John, *Toledo's Peru*, p. 45.

10. This paragraph and the next two draw on: "Peru Energy: Shifting from Oil to Natural Gas," Cable from U.S. Embassy, Lima, 20 May 2006, Wikileaks; "Camisea Scorecard: Toledo's Great Legacy," Cable from U.S. Embassy, Lima, 15 September 2006, Wikileaks; St. John, *Toledo's Peru*, p. 45.

11. "Peru Energy: Shifting from Oil to Natural Gas," Cable from U.S. Embassy, Lima, 20 May 2006, Wikileaks.

12. American diplomats wrote that "Peru's poor, middle class, large industries and entrepreneurs have gotten cheaper, cleaner energy from the Camisea project. [. . .] For a country desperately in need of job creation, poverty alleviation, affordable energy and improved health, there has been no benefit as great as the environmentally friendly energy self-sufficiency that Camisea will bring." Cable from U.S. Embassy, Lima, 15 September 2006, Wikileaks.

13. Gustavo Ávila, Claudia Viale, and Carlos Monge, "Extractive Industries and Their Imprint," in John Crabtree, ed., *Fractured Politics: Peruvian Democracy Past and Present* (London: Institute for the Study of the Americas, 2011), p. 163; St. John, *Toledo's Peru*, p. 49; "Poverty in Peru Decreasing Substantially," Cable from U.S. Embassy, Lima, 4 September 2008, Wikileaks.

14. Congressional Research Service, "A Free Trade Area of the Americas: Major Policy Issues and Status of Negotiations," 15 July 2008, Wikileaks.

15. "Peru: 2005 ATPDEA Eligibility Report," Cable from U.S. Embassy, Lima, 21 March 2005, Wikileaks.

16. Humberto Campodónico, "Deshojando el TLC," *Quehacer* No. 161, July-August 2006; "Peru: 2005 ATPDEA Eligibility Report," Cable from U.S. Embassy, Lima, 21 March 2005, Wikileaks.

17. Congressional Research Service, "A Free Trade Area of the Americas: Major Policy Issues and Status of Negotiations," 15 July 2008, Wikileaks.

18. René De La Pedraja, *The United States and the Armed Forces of Mexico, Central America, and the Caribbean, 2000–2014* (Jefferson, NC: McFarland, 2014), p. 260.

19. "Peru's 2006 National Trade Estimate Report," Cable from U.S. Embassy, Lima, 22 November 2005, Wikileaks; St. John, *Toledo's Peru*, p. 52.

20. "FTA and Culture: Peruvian Response," Cable from U.S. Embassy, Lima, 15 March 2005, Wikileaks; "Andean FTA: Lima Round Scene Setter for Regina Vargo," Cable from U.S. Embassy, Lima, 13 April 2005, Wikileaks; "Visit of Peruvian Ministers to Discuss FTA," Cable from U.S. Embassy, Lima, 17 June 2005, Wikileaks.

21. St. John, *Toledo's Peru*, p. 84; Peru, Comisión de la Verdad y de la Reconciliación (henceforth CVR), *Informe final*, 9 vols. (Lima: Comisión de la Verdad y de la Reconciliación, 2003), vols. 1 and 2.

22. St. John, *Toledo's Peru*, p. 87; CVR, *Informe final*, vols 1 and 8.

23. "Toledo at the Helm," Cable from U.S. Embassy, Lima, 19 June 2001, Wikileaks.

24. "Ambassador and Diplomatic Corps Show Public Support for Truth and Reconciliation Commission," Cable from U.S. Embassy, Lima, 24 October 2005, Wikileaks; St. John, *Toledo's Peru*, pp. 85–86; CVR, *Informe final*, vol. 8.

25. "President of Congress Flores-Araoz Tells Ambassador His Hat is in the Ring," Cable from U.S. Embassy, Lima, 15 March 2005, Wikileaks; "Finance Minister on the Current Situation and his Political Prospects," Cable from U.S. Embassy, Lima, 21 March 2005, Wikileaks.

26. "Former President Alan García Talks Politics, Trade with Ambassador," Cable from U.S. Embassy, Lima, 9 March 2005, Wikileaks; "Finance Minister on the Current Situation and his Political Prospects," Cable from U.S. Embassy, Lima, 21 March 2005, Wikileaks; "Government of Peru Responds Quickly to *Campesino* Unrest in Andahuaylas," Cable from U.S. Embassy, Lima, 5 April 2005, Wikileaks; Pease, *Pasos perdidos*, p. 310.

27. "Strikes by Agricultural Producers Affect Ten Regions," Cable from U.S. Embassy, Lima, 25 May 2005, Wikileaks; "GOP Response to Agricultural Strike! Promises, Promises, Promises!" Cable from U.S. Embassy, Lima, 7 June 2005, Wikileaks; Pease, *Pasos perdidos*, pp. 310–311; "Request for Pl-480, Title I Program for Peru," Cable from U.S. Embassy, Lima, 3 November 2005, Wikileaks. Promoting the consumption of U.S. wheat in underdeveloped countries has long been a normal activity of American diplomats. The economic benefits to American farmers of increased wheat exports are clear, but no less important are the political advantages: U.S. embassies gain another lever to pressure local governments on other issues. However, the attachment of the majority of Peruvian consumers to their native potatoes and corn crippled the wheat campaign which had only a very modest effect.

28. "Finance Minister on the Current Situation and his Political Prospects," Cable from U.S. Embassy, Lima, 21 March 2005, Wikileaks; "GOP Response to Agricultural Strike! Promises, Promises, Promises!" Cable from U.S. Embassy, Lima, 7 June 2005, Wikileaks; Pease, *Pasos perdidos*, pp. 310–311.

29. "Andean FTA: Lima Round Scene Setter for Regina

Vargo," Cable from U.S. Embassy, Lima, 13 April 2005, Wikileaks; The Toledo-Uribe Meeting and Peru's Game Plan for U.S.-Andean FTA," Cable from U.S. Embassy, Lima, 8 September 2005, Wikileaks; "Trade Minister Foreshadows FTA Red Lines," Cable from U.S. Embassy, Lima, 30 September 2005, Wikileaks.

30. "Party Registration Scandal Continues to Hound President Toledo," Cable from U.S. Embassy, Lima, 22 March 2005, Wikileaks; "Fe de erratas" to Villanueva Commission Report, 4 May 2005; Pease, *Pasos perdidos*, pp. 223–224, 319; *Caretas*, 31 March 2005.

31. "Party Registration Scandal Continues to Hound President Toledo," Cable from U.S. Embassy, Lima, 22 March 2005, Wikileaks; St. John, *Toledo's Peru*, pp. 66, 71.

32. "Former President Alan García Talks Politics, Trade with Ambassador," Cable from U.S. Embassy, Lima, 9 March 2005, Wikileaks; "Party Registration Scandal Continues to Hound President Toledo," Cable from U.S. Embassy, Lima, 22 March 2005, Wikileaks; Barry S. Levitt, *Power in the Balance: Presidents, Parties, and Legislatures in Peru and Beyond* (Notre Dame, IN: University of Notre Dame Press, 2012), pp. 88–89; *Caretas*, 31 March 2005.

33. "Congressional Committee Report on Forged Signatures Scandal Remains Mired in Controversy," Cable from U.S. Embassy, Lima, 4 May 2005, Wikileaks. For this paragraph, See also, Levitt, *Power in the Balance*, p. 89; "Fe de erratas" to Villanueva Commission Report, 4 May 2005; *La Republica*, 3 May 2005.

34. "Opposition Leaders Tell Ambassador They Will not Spark Constitutional Crisis," Cable from U.S. Embassy, Lima, 19 May 2005, Wikileaks.

35. "Is It Peru's Turn to Have a Constitutional Crisis?" Cable from U.S. Embassy, Lima, 18 May 2005, Wikileaks; "Opposition Leaders Tell Ambassador They Will not Spark Constitutional Crisis," Cable from U.S. Embassy, Lima, 19 May 2005, Wikileaks.

36. "Fe de erratas" to Villanueva Commission Report, 4 May 2005; "Opposition Leaders Tell Ambassador They Will not Spark Constitutional Crisis," Cable from U.S. Embassy, Lima, 19 May 2005, Wikileaks.

37. "Congress Avoids Vote on Proposed Toledo Sanctions, Passes Villanueva Documents to Public Ministry," Cable from U.S. Embassy, Lima, 20 May 2005, Wikileaks; Levitt, *Power in the Balance*, p. 89; Pease, *Pasos perdidos*, p. 322.

38. "Visit of Peruvian Ministers to Discuss FTA," Cable from U.S. Embassy, Lima, 17 June 2005, Wikileaks; "Trade Minister Foreshadows FTA Red Lines," Cable from U.S. Embassy, Lima, 30 September 2005, Wikileaks; "The Peruvian Election Campaign Baseline: Humala Surging Forward But There Is still a Long Way to Go," Cable from U.S. Embassy, Lima, 16 December 2005, Wikileaks; "Peruvians Want Quick Congressional Vote on U.S. Trade Agreement," Cable from U.S. Embassy, Lima, 16 December 2005, Wikileaks.

Chapter 11

1. U.S. Ambassador Struble in "Countering Chávez in Peru," Cable from U.S. Embassy, Lima, 22 November 2005, Wikileaks.

2. Laura Wills-Otero, "Colombia: Analyzing the Strategies for Political Action of Álvaro Uribe's Government, 2002–2010," in Juan Pablo Luna and Cristóbal Rovira Katlwasser, eds., *The Resilience of the Latin American Right* (Baltimore MD: Johns Hopkins University Press, 2014), pp. 204–205; "Staffdel Cardenas," Cable from U.S. Embassy, Bogotá, 5 June 2002, U.S. Department of State, Freedom of Information Act (henceforth Dept State FOIA); Paola Fajardo-Heyward, "Understanding the Effect of Security Assistance on Human Rights: The Case of Plan Colombia," *The Latin Americanist*, 2015 June, pp. 11–12.

3. Jasmin Hristov, *Blood and Capital: The Paramilitarization of Colombia* (Athens: Ohio University Press, 2009), pp. 46–47; Wills-Otero, "Colombia," pp. 204–205.

4. *El Tiempo*, 5 February 2006; René De La Pedraja, *Wars of Latin America, 1982–2013: The Path to Peace* (Jefferson, NC: McFarland, 2013), p. 227.

5. All quotations in paragraph from "Colombia Security Update, First Quarter 2006," Secret Cable from U.S. Embassy, Bogotá, 1 May 2006, Wikileaks.

6. "Why January 2006 Is Different from January 2005," Cable from U.S. Embassy, Bogotá, 6 January 2006, Wikileaks; *El Tiempo*, 5 February 2006. For the Marquetalia military campaign of 1964, See, René De La Pedraja, *Wars of Latin America, 1948–1982: The Rise of the Guerrillas* (Jefferson, NC: McFarland, 2013), pp. 128–134.

7. "Will Congress Come Through for Uribe?" Cable from U.S. Embassy, Bogotá, 2 March 2004, Wikileaks; María Jimena Duzán, *Así gobierna Uribe* (Bogotá: Planeta, 2004), pp. 125–129.

8. "Will Congress Come Through for Uribe?" Cable from U.S. Embassy, Bogotá, 2 March 2004, Wikileaks; Duzán, *Así gobierna Uribe*, pp. 170–171; Wills-Otero, "Colombia," pp. 204–205.

9. "Presidential Reelection Passes First Test," Cable from U.S. Embassy, Bogotá, 6 May 2004, Wikileaks; Duzán, *Así gobierna Uribe*, pp. 161–163.

10. "New Developments on Reelection," Cable #12860 of December 2004, Wikileaks; "Update on Reelection: Thinking of Plan B," Cable from U.S. Embassy, Bogotá, 30 September 2005, Wikileaks; "Court Says Constitution Has Been Reformed to Allow Reelection," Cable from U.S. Embassy, 20 October 2005, Wikileaks.

11. "President Uribe Wins Reelection in Landslide," Cable from U.S. Embassy, Bogotá, 29 May 2006, Wikileaks; Harvey F. Kline, *Showing Teeth to the Dragons; State Building by Colombian President Álvaro Uribe Vélez* (Tuscaloosa: University of Alabama Press, 2009), pp. 64–65, 80.

12. "President Uribe Wins Reelection in Landslide," Cable from U.S. Embassy, Bogotá, 29 May 2006, Wikileaks; Ana María Bejarano, "Politicizing Insecurity: Uribe's Instrumental Use of Populism," in Carlos de la Torre and Cynthia J. Arnson, eds., *Latin American Populism in the Twenty-First Century* (Washington, D.C.: Woodrow Wilson Center Press, 2013), pp. 330–331.

13. "WHA/and Director's Meetings with Leading Presidential Candidates," Cable from U.S. Embassy, Lima, 24 October 2005, Wikileaks; Maxwell A. Cameron, "The Left Turn That Wasn't," in Steven Levitsky and Kenneth M. Roberts, eds., *The Resurgence of the Latin American Left* (Baltimore: The Johns Hopkins University Press, 2011), p. 384.

14. "Far Left, Inspired by Chávez, Seeking to Ride Ollanta Humala's Coat Tails into Congress," Cable from U.S. Embassy, Lima, 22 September 2005, Wikileaks; Felipe Nesbet-Montesinos, "Humala antes de Ollanta: Evolución política del nuevo presidente peruano," *Revista Europea de Estudios Latinoamericanos y del Caribe*, no. 91 (2011), p. 82; Cynthia McClintock, "Populism in Peru: From APRA to Ollanta Humala," in Torre and Arnson, eds., *Latin American Populism*, p. 232; Ollanta Humala, *De Locumba a candidato a la presidencia* (Mexico: Ocean Sur, 2009), pp. 118–124.

15. "The Peruvian Election Campaign Baseline: Humala Surging Forward but There is Still a Long Way to Go," Cable from U.S. Embassy, Lima, 16 December 2005, Wikileaks; "Ex-Candidate Paniagua on Political Scene," Cable from U.S. Embassy, Lima, 23 May 2006, Wikileaks.

16. "Far Left, Inspired by Chávez, Seeking to Ride Ollanta Humala's Coat Tails into Congress," Cable from U.S.

Embassy, Lima, 22 September 2005, Wikileaks; Gustavo Gorriti, *Petroaudios; políticos, espías y periodistas detrás del escándalo* (Lima: Planeta, 2009), pp. 119–120.

17. "Humala Feints to the Center, but Continues to Flirt with the Far Left," Cable from U.S. Embassy, Lima, 15 November 2005, Wikileaks.

18. "The Peruvian Election Campaign Baseline: Humala Surging Forward but There is Still a Long Way to Go," Cable from U.S. Embassy, Lima, 16 December 2005, Wikileaks. This paragraph also draws on this cable.

19. "Former Interior Minister Rospigliosi Worried about Ollanta Humala," Cable from U.S. Embassy, Lima, 29 November 2005, Wikileaks. When in a private meeting on 17 May 2006 Humala confronted the U.S. Ambassador about accusations of U.S. involvement in the electoral campaign, the latter was suspiciously evasive in the denials; See, "PDAS Shapiro/Ambassador Meet with Humala," 23 May 2006, Cable from U.S. Embassy, Lima, 23 May 2006, Wikileaks.

20. "The Peruvian Election Campaign Baseline: Humala Surging Forward but There is Still a Long Way to Go," Cable from U.S. Embassy, Lima, 16 December 2005, Wikileaks.

21. This was an example of using AID (Agency for International Development) as a mechanism to intervene in the internal politics of foreign countries in a blatant distortion of its original intent to finance economic projects. This early case went largely unperceived in the mass media, unlike the now infamous Zunzuneo project of AID designed to overthrown the Cuban government. See, René De La Pedraja, *The United States and the Armed Forces of Mexico, the Caribbean, and Central America, 2000–2014* (Jefferson, NC: McFarland, 2014), pp. 264–265.

22. The U.S. Embassy struggled to define Humala, as the many analytical reports on him-some quite long- illustrate. A good example is: "Ollanta Humala: Keys to his Character, Likely Attitude toward the U.S.," Cable from U.S. Embassy, Lima, 23 January 2006, Wikileaks.

23. "Chávez, Evo Morales back Humala at Caracas Meeting," Cable from U.S. Embassy, Lima, 4 January 2006, Wikileaks; "Ollanta Humala: Keys to his Character, Likely Attitude toward the U.S.," Cable from U.S. Embassy, Lima, 23 January 2006, Wikileaks.

24. "Chávez, Evo Morales back Humala at Caracas Meeting," Cable from U.S. Embassy, Lima, 4 January 2006, Wikileaks; "Why García Won and Humala Lost," Cable from U.S. Embassy, Lima, 9 June 2006, Wikileaks.

25. "Business Sector's Analyst Foresees Humala Victory," Secret Cable from U.S. Embassy, Lima, 20 March 2006, Wikileaks. Peruvian voters living abroad disregarded the Lesbian accusations; See, Angeles Escrivá et al. "Migration, Gender, and Politics: The 2006 Peruvian Elections Abroad," *Latin American Perspectives* 37(2010): 110–111.

26. Cameron, "The Left Turn That Wasn't," p. 387. In an interesting outcome, Flores won 58.2 percent of the votes cast by all Peruvians living abroad, and a whopping 70.8 percent of Peruvians living in the United States voted for her. Scholars have provided explanations for the lopsided result among the 48,000 Peruvian voters in Spain, and they seem applicable as well for Peruvians living in the United States (the largest number at 70,000) and Argentina (the second largest number at 51,400, See, Escrivá et al., "The 2006 Peruvian Elections Abroad," pp. 111–118. By law all votes of Peruvians living abroad are counted as belonging to the Lima metropolitan area, thus maximizing the already large percentage Lourdes enjoyed in the capital.

27. "Humala Dogged by Allegations of Human Rights Violations," Cable from U.S. Embassy, Lima, 6 February 2006, Wikileaks; Gorriti, *Petroaudios*, pp. 87–88, 120–121.

28. Cameron, "The Left Turn That Wasn't," p. 386.

29. "Business Sector's Analyst Foresees Humala Victory," Secret Cable from U.S. Embassy, Lima, 20 March 2006, Wikileaks.

30. "WHA/and Director's Meetings with Leading Presidential Candidates," Cable from U.S. Embassy, Lima, 24 October 2005, Wikileaks; "Scene Setter for Visit of Secretary of State Condoleezza Rice," Secret/NoForn Cable from U.S. Embassy, Lima, 3 March 2006, Wikileaks; "Alán García's Economic Plan," Cable from U.S. Embassy, Lima, 23 March 2006, Wikileaks. The crucial statement in the decision to support García came in the "Ambassador's Comment" in the Cable from U.S. Embassy, Lima, 9 March 2005. As I have observed in another book, "Ambassador's Comments" are very rare in the quarter million Wikileaks diplomatic cables and appear only in cases of extreme importance; See, De La Pedraja, *United States and Armed Forces*, p. 279n31.

31. "Humala's Liaison to Business Sector Meets with the Ambassador," Cable from U.S. Embassy, Lima, 30 March 2006, Wikileaks; "New Vice-Foreign Minister Lobbies Ambassador for Humala," Cable from U.S. Embassy, Lima, 7 April 2006, Wikileaks.

32. "PDAS Shapiro/Ambassador Meet with Humala," 23 May 2006, Cable from U.S. Embassy, Lima, 23 May 2006, Wikileaks.

33. "Scene Setter for Visit of Secretary of State Condoleezza Rice," Secret/NoForn Cable from U.S. Embassy, Lima, 3 March 2006, Wikileaks.

34. "Chávez Fuels More Contretemps with Peru," Cable from U.S. Embassy, Lima, 2 May 2006, Wikileaks.

35. "Why García Won and Humala Lost," Cable from U.S. Embassy, Lima, 9 June 2006, Wikileaks; "Taking the Bait: Chávez Creates Another International Row," Cable from U.S. Embassy, Lima, 3 May 2006, Wikileaks.

36. McClintock, "Populism in Peru," p. 230; "Why García Won and Humala Lost," Cable from U.S. Embassy, Lima, 9 June 2006, Wikileaks.

37. Cameron, "The Left Turn That Wasn't," p. 387.

Chapter 12

1. Ralph D. Sawyer, trans., *One Hundred Unorthodox Strategies for the Everyday Warrior* (Boulder, CO: Westview Press, 1996), p. 155.

2. "Chávez Celebrates Seven Years in Power, Goes for Fourteen More," Cable from U.S. Embassy, Caracas, 6 February 2006, Wikileaks; "Chávez versus Bush 2006," Cable from U.S. Embassy, Caracas, 13 March 2006, Wikileaks; Conversations during my study trip to Caracas of June 2007.

3. "What to Expect from Chávez's Presidential Campaign," Cable from U.S. Embassy, Caracas, 21 February 2006, Wikileaks; "Chávez Pushes a Step Closer to President for Life," Cable from U.S. Embassy, Caracas, 24 February 2006, Wikileaks.

4. Conversations during my study trip to Caracas of June 2007; "What to Expect from Chávez's Presidential Campaign," Cable from U.S. Embassy, Caracas, 21 February 2006, Wikileaks; "Chávez Pushes a Step Closer to President for Life," Cable from U.S. Embassy, Caracas, 24 February 2006, Wikileaks.

5. "Viva Zulia—Chávez again Hits Rosales," Cable from U.S. Embassy, Caracas, 7 March 2006, Wikileaks; Mark P. Sullivan, "Venezuela: Political Conditions and U.S. Policy," 10 October 2008, Congressional Research Service, Wikileaks; Bart Jones, *!Hugo¡ The Hugo Chávez Story from Mud Hut to Perpetual Revolution* (Hanover, NH: Steerforth Press, 2007), p. 446.

6. "Carrier Visit to Benefit U.S. Policy toward Venezuela," Secret Cable from U.S. Embassy, Caracas, 23 March 2006, Wikileaks. For the 3 December 2006 presidential election, See: René De La Pedraja, *The United States and*

the Armed Forces of Mexico, Central America, and The Caribbean, 2000–2014 (Jefferson, NC: McFarland, 2014), pp. 34–37.

7. "What to Expect from Chávez's Presidential Campaign," Cable from U.S. Embassy, Caracas, 21 February 2006, Wikileaks; "Opposition Candidate Manuel Rosales's Inner Circle," Cable from U.S. Embassy, Caracas, 20 October 2006, Wikileaks; "United Nations Security Council Defeat: Chávez Trying to Save Face," Cable from U.S. Embassy Caracas, 6 November 2006, Wikileaks.

8. "Presidential Election: Winners and Losers," Cable from U.S. Embassy, Caracas, 8 December 2006, Wikileaks; Sullivan, "Venezuela Political Conditions"; De La Pedraja, *United States and Armed Forces*, p. 37.

9. "Time to Redouble our Pro-Democracy Efforts in Venezuela," Cable from U.S. Embassy, Caracas, 5 December 2006, Wikileaks.

10. Julio Escalona, "La agresión de Estados Unidos usando a Colombia como base," 17 February 2008, Venezuelan ambassador Freddy Balzán emails, Wikileaks; "Venezuela: The Best Is Yet to Come," Cable from U.S. Embassy, Caracas, 19 December 2006, Wikileaks; "Venezuela: Constitutional Reform Back to Front Burner for Now," Cable from U.S. Embassy, Caracas, 17 July 2007, Wikileaks; Rory Carroll, *Comandante: Hugo Chávez's Venezuela* (New York: Penguin, 2014), p. 139; Javier Corrales and Michael Penfold, *Dragon in the Tropics: Venezuela and the Legacy of Hugo Chávez*, 2d ed. (Washington, D.C.: Brookings Institute, 2015), p. 34.

11. "Venezuela: The Best Is Yet to Come," Cable from U.S. Embassy, Caracas, 19 December 2006, Wikileaks.

12. "Ending 2006 on a High," Cable from U.S. Embassy, 3 January 2007, Wikileaks. Actually, the policies of Chávez had major differences with the Import-Industrialization-Substitution of the 1960s; See, Corrales and Penfold, *Dragon in the Tropics*, pp. 64–65.

13. "Ending 2006 on a High," Cable from U.S. Embassy, 3 January 2007, Wikileaks; "Venezuela: The Best Is Yet to Come," Cable from U.S. Embassy, Caracas, 19 December 2006, Wikileaks.

14. Corrales and Penfold, *Dragon in the Tropics*, p. 60.

15. "Chávez Announces Plans to Nationalize Strategic Sectors," Cable from U.S. Embassy, Caracas, 9 January 2007, Wikileaks; "Economic Ramifications of Chávez's Enabling Law: Is Atlas Shrugging," Cable from U.S. Embassy, Caracas, 22 January 2007, Wikileaks.

16. "Chávez Swearing In: Socialism or Death," Cable from U.S. Embassy, Caracas, 10 January 2009, Wikileaks; "Chávez's Way Ahead: Words to Deeds," Cable from U.S. Embassy, Caracas, 12 January 2007, Wikileaks.

17. "Meeting with Electricidad de Caracas on Nationalization Announcement," Cable from U.S. Embassy, Caracas, 22 January 2007, Wikileaks; *El Nacional*, 2 February 2007.

18. "AES and Bolivarian Republic of Venezuela Reach Agreement on Electricidad de Caracas Sale," Cable from U.S. Embassy, Caracas, 12 February 2007, Wikileaks. Chávez promised the 48,000 investors who owned 18 percent of Electricidad de Caracas that their shares were safe, See, *El Nacional*, 2 February 2007.

19. "Venezuela's Power Sector: Heading for Another Crisis?" Cable from U.S. Embassy, Caracas, 12 May 2004, Wikileaks; "Lights Out in Caracas," *Wall Street Journal*, 5 February 2007.

20. "Economic Ramifications of Chávez's Enabling Law: Is Atlas Shrugging?" Cable from U.S. Embassy, Caracas, 22 January 2007, Wikileaks; "IMF and World Bank: So Long and Thanks for the Memories," Cable from U.S. Embassy, Caracas, 3 May 2007, Wikileaks.

21. "Chávez Working on Many Fronts, Slow to Use Enabling Law," Cable from U.S. Embassy, Caracas, 22 May 2007, Wikileaks.

22. Escalona, "EEUU y la agresión a Venezuela," 17 February 2008, Venezuelan ambassador Freddy Balzán emails, Wikileaks; "Chávez Announces Intention to Create a Single Revolutionary Party," Cable from U.S. Embassy, Caracas, 11 October 2006, Wikileaks.

23. "Chávez Pressing Ahead with a Single Revolutionary Party," Cable from U.S. Embassy, Caracas, 5 January 2007, Wikileaks; Escalona, "EEUU y la agresión a Venezuela."

24. "Pro-Chávez Parties Put Brakes on Formation of a Unified Socialist Party," Cable from U.S. Embassy, Caracas, 15 March 2007, Wikileaks; "PPT: What Doesn't Destroy Us, Makes Us Stronger," Cable from U.S. Embassy, Caracas, 24 May 2007, Wikileaks.

25. "Chavez Single Party: By Uniting He Divides," Cable from U.S. Embassy, Caracas, 26 April 2007, Wikileaks.

26. "Chávez New Party: Inflated Numbers and Deep Divisions," Cable from U.S. Embassy, Caracas, 12 June 2007, Wikileaks; Corrales and Penfold, *Dragon in the Tropics*, p. 28.

27. Escalona, "EEUU y la agresión a Venezuela"; "Chávez New Party Plagued by Organizational Problems," Cable from U.S. Embassy, Caracas, 22 August 2007, Wikileaks; "Chávez's New Party: Disciplining Discussion," Cable from U.S. Embassy, Caracas, 7 September 2007, Wikileaks.

28. "Opposition Severely Challenged, Looking Long Term," Cable from U.S. Embassy, Caracas, 30 January 2007, Wikileaks.

29. Sullivan, "Venezuela Political Conditions"; Carroll, *Comandante*, p. 112.

30. "Venezuela: Constitutional Reform Back to Front Burner for Now," Cable from U.S. Embassy, Caracas, 17 July 2007, Wikileaks; Escalona, "EEUU y la agresión a Venezuela"; Freddy Baptista to Hugo Chávez, Caracas, 23 July 2007, Venezuelan ambassador Freddy Balzán emails, Wikileaks; Sullivan, "Venezuela Political Conditions."

31. "Chávez Proposes Socialist Constitutional Changes," Cable from U.S. Embassy, Caracas, 16 August 2007, Wikileaks; Sullivan, "Venezuela Political Conditions."

32. "Chávez Constitution Rewrite: Battle Lines Forming," Cable from U.S. Embassy, Caracas, 14 August 2007, Wikileaks; "Round One of Constitutional Reform Debate," Cable from U.S. Embassy, Caracas, 28 August 2007, Wikileaks; "Pro-Chávez Party Criticizes Chávez's Constitutional Proposal," Cable from U.S. Embassy, Caracas, 11 September 2007, Wikileaks; "FEDECAMARAS Speaks Out Against Constitutional Reform," Confidential/NoForn Cable from U.S. Embassy, Caracas, 6 November 2007, Wikileaks.

33. "Chavez Constitutional Package: Opposition Divided (Again)," Cable from U.S. Embassy, Caracas, 27 September 2007, Wikileaks.

34. "Legislature Passes Chávez's Constitutional Package," Cable from U.S. Embassy, Caracas, 2 November 2007, Wikileaks; Sullivan, "Venezuela Political Conditions."

35. "Legislature Passes Chávez's Constitutional Package," Cable from U.S. Embassy, Caracas, 2 November 2007, Wikileaks.

36. "Bolivarian Republic of Venezuela Derides Baduel, Opposition Reacts Slowly," Cable from U.S. Embassy, Caracas, 9 November 2007, Wikileaks; Carroll, *Comandante*, pp. 146–147; Sullivan, "Venezuela Political Conditions."

37. "Constitutional Referendum: Keller Poll Says No Vote Gaining Ground," Cable from U.S. Embassy, Caracas, 19 November 2007, Wikileaks; "Chávez Electoral Machine Kicks into High Gear," Cable from U.S. Embassy, Caracas, 23 November 2007, Wikileaks; Sullivan, "Venezuela Political Conditions."

38. "Chávez Loses Constitutional Referendum," Cable from U.S. Embassy, Caracas, 3 December 2007, Wikileaks; Sullivan, "Venezuela Political Conditions."

39. "President-Elect García Wants the U.S.-Peru Free Trade Agreement," Confidential/No Forn Cable from U.S. Embassy, Lima, 9 June 2006, Wikileaks.

40. "President's García's First Message to the Nation," Cable from U.S. Embassy, Lima, 2 August 2006, Wikileaks; "García's Promise of Water for Everyone," Cable from U.S. Embassy, Lima, 10 August 2006, Wikileaks.

41. Maxwell A. Cameron, "Peru: The Left Turn That Wasn't," in Steven Levitsky and Kenneth M. Roberts, eds., *The Resurgence of the Latin American Left* (Baltimore: The Johns Hopkins University Press, 2011), pp. 376–377.

42. "García Names Famous Economist," Cable from U.S. Embassy, Lima, 21 August 2006, Wikeleaks; "Assistant U.S. Trade Representative," Cable from U.S. Embassy, Lima, 14 September 2006, Wikileaks.

43. "García's Economic Priorities," Cable from U.S. Embassy, Lima, 26 June 2006, Wikileaks.

44. *Washington Post*, 17 February 2004; "Yanacocha Mine Closes, Reopening after Protests," Cable from U.S. Embassy, Lima, 31 August 2006, Wikileaks; *Denver Post*, 29 August 2006; *Global Information Network*, 21 September 2006. The refusal to give any names of persons, institutions, and sometimes even of places—an axiom of social sciences studies—drastically limits the usefulness of reports such as Caroline Rees, Deanna Kemp and Rachel Davis, *Conflict Management and Corporate Culture in the Extractive Industries: A Study in Peru* (Cambridge, MA: Kennedy School of Government, Harvard University, 2012). The scholar is left floundering trying to match the general attitudes with a specific historical event occurring in only one place; however, in *Ibid.*, pp. 17–20 the coincidence with Yanacocha is clear.

45. *Denver Post*, 30 August 2006.

46. *Financial Times*, 31 August 2006; "Yanacocha Mine Closes, Reopening after Protests," Cable from U.S. Embassy, Lima, 31 August 2006, Wikileaks; *Denver Post*, 30 August 2006; "Cajamarca and Regional Unrest," Cable from U.S. Embassy, Lima, 19 December 2006, Wikileaks.

47. "Yanacocha Mine Closes, Reopening after Protests," Cable from U.S. Embassy, Lima, 31 August 2006, Wikileaks; *Global Information Network*, 21 September 2006; "Mining Conflict: The View from Cajarmarca," Cable from U.S. Embassy, Lima, 12 September 2007, Wikileaks; *New York Times*, 29 August 2006. On the priest Marco Arana, who was instrumental in the protest mobilizations, See, Fabiana Li, "Relating Divergent Worlds: Mines Aquifers, and Sacred Mountains in Peru," *Anthropologica* 5(2013): 402–403. This excellent and insightful study also provides a glimpse into the prevailing attitudes in the field of anthropology, when its author is apologetic about not having been able to interview informants in their native Indian languages because "the influence of Spanish colonialism" left Spanish as virtually the only language spoken in Cajamarca, See, *Ibid.*, pp. 403 and 410n.3.

48. "Government of Peru Decentralization Shock a Necessary but Incomplete Step Forward," Cable from U.S. Embassy, Lima, 29 November 2006, Wikileaks; Eduardo Ballón Echegaray, *Balance del proceso peruano de descentralización desde los gobiernos regionales* (Lima: EED, 2008), p. 13.

49. Barry S. Levitt, *Power in the Balance: Presidents, Parties, and Legislatures in Peru and Beyond* (Notre Dame, IN: University of Notre Dame Press, 2012), p. 137; "Regional Elections: APRA Down and Humala Out," Cable from U.S. Embassy, Lima, 21 November 2006, Wikileaks; Moisés Arce, *Resource Extraction and Protest in Peru* (Pittsburgh: University Press, 2014), pp. 32–33, 55; Ballón Echegaray, *Balance de descentralización*, pp. 14–18.

50. "Peru: President García at 100 Plus Days," Cable from U.S. Embassy, Lima, 7 December 2006, Wikileaks.

51. "García Recentralizes Decentralization," Cable from U.S. Embassy, Lima, 2 February 2007, Wikileaks. See also for this paragraph, Ballón Echegaray, *Balance de descentralización*, p. 22.

52. "Decentralization: Government Ambivalence and Regional (In)capacity," Cable from U.S. Embassy, Lima, 11 June 2007, Wikileaks; Ballón Echegaray, *Balance de descentralización*, pp. 19–21.

53. "García Gears Up to Take On Powerful, Left-wing Teacher's Union," Cable from U.S. Embassy, Lima, 5 January 2007, Wikileaks; "Former President Alán García Talks Politics, Trade with Ambassador," 9 March 2005, Wikileaks. He also wanted schools in Peru to intensify the teaching of English as a necessary tool to advance in the world economy. Before the election, García claimed that his highest priority was agriculture, but other than supporting agricultural exports from coastal Peru to the United States under the Free Trade Agreement, he largely ignored this promise and did practically nothing for peasant farmers in the highlands and in the Amazon region.

54. "Government of Peru Wins Battle against Radical Teacher's Union," Cable from U.S. Embassy, Lima, 22 January 2007, Wikileaks; "Teacher's Union Takes It on the Chin over Test Results," Cable from U.S. Embassy, Lima, 6 March 2007, Wikileaks; "Labor Leaders Skeptical about García, Free Trade Agreement, Labor Law," Cable from U.S. Embassy, Lima, 21 March 2007, Wikileaks; Moisés Arce, "The Repoliticization of Collective Action after Neoliberalism in Peru," *Latin American Politics* 50 (2008): 45. In a survey of 2003, 84 percent supported the Teacher's strike, but in 2007 the public was no longer sympathetic. The change in attitude reflected the fact that in 2003 the Peruvian population had already repudiated the discredited government of Alejandro Toledo; instead in 2007 the clash with the Teacher's union came when the public was still in the last stage of the honeymoon period with President García.

55. "Government of Peru Wins Battle against Radical Teacher's Union," Cable from U.S. Embassy, Lima, 22 January 2007, Wikileaks; "Teacher's Union Takes It on the Chin over Test Results," Cable from U.S. Embassy, Lima, 6 March 2007, Wikileaks.

56. "Scene Setter for Secretary Paulson," Cable from U.S. Embassy, Lima, 1 March 2007, Wikileaks.

57. "Labor Leaders Skeptical about García, Free Trade Agreement, Labor Law," Cable from U.S. Embassy, Lima, 21 March 2007, Wikileaks; "Scene Setter for Secretary Paulson," Cable from U.S. Embassy, Lima, 1 March 2007, Wikileaks.

58. "Labor Leaders Skeptical about García, Free Trade Agreement, Labor Law," Cable from U.S. Embassy, Lima, 21 March 2007, Wikileaks; "Deputy U.S. Trade Representative Veroneau with Peru's President García on Trade and Regional Developments, March 12–13," Confidential/No-Forn Cable from U.S. Embassy, Lima, 27 March 2007, Wikileaks.

59. "García Government: Honeymoon Over, Time for Results," Cable from U.S. Embassy, Lima, 11 May 2007, Wikileaks.

60. "Congress Labor Committee Bullish on Labor Law," Cable from U.S. Embassy, Lima, 1 December 2006, Wikileaks; "Peru: Labor Reform Inches Forward," Cable from U.S. Embassy, Lima, 29 January 2007, Wikileaks.

61. "García's Dog Days—Polls Down, But Economy Up," Cable from U.S. Embassy, Lima, 30 July 2007, Wikileaks; "Congress Labor Committee Bullish on Labor Law," Cable from U.S. Embassy, Lima, 1 December 2006, Wikileaks.

62. "Peru's Congress Approves Amendments to Free

Trade Agreement," Cable from U.S. Embassy, Lima, 28 June 2007, Wikileaks.

63. "Peru's Season of Protest," Cable from U.S. Embassy, Lima, 6 July 2007, Wikileaks; "Peru Faces a Tornado of Protest," Cable from U.S. Embassy, Lima, 13 July 2007, Wikileaks.

64. "García's Dog Days—Polls Down, But Economy Up," Cable from U.S. Embassy, Lima, 30 July 2007, Wikileaks.

65. "Peru Lowers Tariffs Again, Unilaterally," Cable from U.S. Embassy, Lima, 26 October 2007, Wikileaks; "Peru Eliminates Tariffs on 2,894 Items," Cable from U.S. Embassy, Lima, 8 January 2007, Wikileaks.

66. "Peru Lowers Tariffs Again, Unilaterally," Cable from U.S. Embassy, Lima, 26 October 2007, Wikileaks.

Chapter 13

1. Plato, *Republic*, trans. Benjamin Jewett (Oxford: University Press, 1888), p. 220.

2. Moisés Arce, *Resource Extraction and Protest in Peru* (Pittsburgh: University Press, 2014), p. 104.

3. "National Strike on July 8 and 9," Cable from U.S. Embassy, Lima, 7 July 2008, Wikileaks.

4. "National Strike Mostly Peaceful, Strongest in Unrest-Prone Regions," Cable from U.S. Embassy, Lima, 14 July 2008, Wikileaks; "National Strike on July 8 and 9," Cable from U.S. Embassy, Lima, 7 July 2008, Wikileaks.

5. "National Strike Mostly Peaceful, Strongest in Unrest-Prone Regions," Cable from U.S. Embassy, Lima, 14 July 2008, Wikileaks.

6. Edgar Reymundo Mercado y Róger Nájar Kokally, *Más allá de la Curva del Diablo; Lecciones de Bagua* (Lima: Fondo Editorial del Congreso del Perú), pp. 71–72. The three articles of Alán García are: "El síndrome del perro del hortelano," *El Comercio*, 28 October 2007, "Receta para acabar con el perro del hortelano," *El Comercio*, 29 November 2007, and "El perro del hortelano contra el pobre," *El Comercio*, 2 March 2008. For the reaction of the Amazon Indians, See, Comisión Especial para Investigar y Analizar los Sucesos de Bagua, *Informe Final Diciembre 2009* (henceforth Bagua, *Informe Final*), p. 27 and Comisión Especial para Investigar y Analizar los Sucesos de Bagua, *Informe en Minoría April 2010* (henceforth Bagua, *Informe en Minoría*), pp. 30–31.

7. "García's Dog Days—Polls Down, But Economy Up," Cable from U.S. Embassy, Lima, 30 July 2007, Wikileaks; Maxwell A. Cameron, "Peru: The Left Turn That Wasn't," in Steven Levitsky and Kenneth M. Roberts, eds., *The Resurgence of the Latin American Left* (Baltimore: The Johns Hopkins University Press, 2011), pp. 387–388; Arce, *Resource Extraction*, pp. 104–106.

8. Bagua, *Informe Final*, p. 28; Bagua, *Informe en Minoría*, pp. 16–17; "Deluge of Decrees for FTA Implementation and Consequences," Cable from U.S. Embassy, Lima, 1 July 2008, Wikileaks; Mercado and Nájar, *Curva del Diablo*, pp. 72–73. The muted objections to the enabling power García received to legislate in Peru sharply contrasted with the vociferous outrage in Venezuela and abroad whenever the National Assembly granted Hugo Chávez a similar authority to issue decree laws. What opponents considered to be granting dictatorial powers in Venezuela was acceptable in Peru.

9. Arce, *Resource Extraction*, pp. 107–108; Mercado and Nájar, *Curva del Diablo*, pp. 74–78.

10. "Indigenous Strikes in the Amazon," Cable from U.S. Embassy, Lima, 19 August 2008, Wikileaks.

11. Arce, *Resource Extraction*, pp. 106–109; Bagua, *Informe en Minoría*, pp. 23–24; Bagua, *Informe Final*, pp. 29–30; Arce, *Resource Extraction*, p. 108; "Indigenous Strikes in the Amazon," Cable from U.S. Embassy, Lima, 19 August 2008, Wikileaks.

12. "Indigenous Strikes Suspended," Cable from U.S. Embassy, Lima, 25 August 2008, Wikileaks; Bagua, *Informe Final*, p. 30; Bagua, *Informe en Minoría*, pp. 18–19; Arce, *Resource Extraction*, pp. 109–110; Mercado and Nájar, *Curva del Diablo*, pp. 88–90.

13. "Protests in South Hit Two Regions," Cable from U.S. Embassy, Lima, 17 June 2008, Wikileaks.

14. "More Social Conflict in Provinces," Cable from U.S. Embassy, Lima, 31 October 2008, Wikileaks; ""Government of Peru Declares Emergency to Quell Violent Protests in South," Cable from U.S. Embassy, Lima, 7 November 2008, Wikileaks.

15. Gustavo Gorriti, *Petroaudios; periodistas, espías y periodistas detrás del escándalo* (Lima: Planeta, 2009), p. 37; "Caso Petroaudios: Nuevo Giro," *Caretas*, 19 November 2008; Fernando Ampuero, "El laberinto de los audios," *Quehacer*, no. 172 (2008 Oct-Dec), pp. 4–5, 9; José Alejandro Godoy, "Petroaudios en preguntas y respuestas," 13 April 2010, Desde el Tercer Piso.

16. "Marinos confesaron ser los chuponeadores de los petroaudios," 24 January 2009, peru21.pe; Godoy, "Petroaudios," 13 April 2010, Desde el Tercer Piso; "Eavesdropping Scandal Drags on, but no Smoking Gun," Cable from U.S. Embassy, 11 February 2009, Wikileaks; Gorriti, *Petro Audios*, pp. 17–18, 49–51, 118.

17. "Más sorpresas de Petro-Bill," *Caretas*, 21 May 2009.

18. Pablo O'Brien, "Los petroaudios y la cultura de negocios," *Semana económica*, November 2009.

19. Ampuero, "El laberinto de los audios," pp. 5–6; Pablo O'Brien, "Los petroaudios y la cultura de negocios," *Semana económica*, November 2009; Gorriti, *Petroaudios*, pp. 23, 34.

20. Pablo O'Brien, "Los petroaudios y la cultura de negocios," *Semana económica*, November 2009.

21. "Corruption Scandal Puts Government on the Defensive," Cable from U.S. Embassy, Lima, 8 October 2008, Wikileaks; Pablo O'Brien, "Los petroaudios y la cultura de negocios," *Semana económica*, November 2009.

22. Gorriti, *Petroaudios*, pp. 65–67; Pablo O'Brien, "Los petroaudios y la cultura de negocios," *Semana económica*, November 2009.

23. Gorriti, *Petroaudios*, pp. 25–43; Ampuero, "El laberinto de los audios," pp. 3, 5–6, 8; Francisco Miró Quesada Rada, "Chuponeados y chuponeadores," *Quehacer*, no. 172 (2009 January-March), pp. 9, 14; "Caso Petroaudios: Nuevo Giro," *Caretas*, 19 November 2008.

24. Gorriti, *Petroaudios*, pp. 5, 41–43; Quesada Rada, "Chuponeados y chuponeadores," *Quehacer*, no. 172 (2009 Jan-March), pp. 10, 14; "Marinos confesaron ser los chuponeadores de los petroaudios," 24 January 2009, peru21.pe.

25. Quesada Rada, "Chuponeados y chuponeadores," *Quehacer*, no. 172 (2009 Jan-March), p. 12; "Corruption Scandal Puts Government on the Defensive," Cable from U.S. Embassy, Lima, 8 October 2008, Wikileaks; "Eavesdropping Scandal Drags on, but no Smoking Gun," Cable from U.S. Embassy, 11 February 2009, Wikileaks; Gorriti, *Petroaudios*, p. 6.

26. "Peru's New Prime Minister: Reformed Radical, Yehude Simon," Cable from U.S. Embassy, Lima, 14 October 2008, Wikileaks; "Peru Cabinet Shuffle: Less than a Clean Break," Cable from U.S. Embassy, Lima, 15 October 2008, Wikileaks; Gorriti, *Petroaudios*, p. 6.

27. "Peru's New Prime Minister: Reformed Radical, Yehude Simon," Cable from U.S. Embassy, Lima, 14 October 2007, Wikileaks.

28. "Indigenous Strikes Suspended," Cable from U.S. Embassy, Lima, 25 August 2008, Wikileaks; Bagua, *Informe en Minoría*, pp. 18–19; Bagua, *Informe Final*, pp. 32–33.

29. For a good summary, See Paul M. Barrett, "A Way to Settle Ecuador's Oil Mess," *Bloomberg Business News*, 22 September 2014.

30. Mercado and Nájar, *Curva del Diablo*, pp. 78–80, 98–99; Bagua, *Informe Final*, pp. 34–38. Established in 1980, AIDESEP (*Asociación Interétnica de Desarrollo de la Selva Peruana*) from its headquarters building in Lima vigorously advocated for vital Indian concerns; See, Shane Greene, "Getting over the Andes: The Geo-Eco-Politics of Indigenous Movements in Peru's Twenty-First Century Inca Empire," *Journal of Latin American Studies* 38(2006): 341–348.

31. Bagua, *Informe en Minoría*, p. 50; Bagua, *Informe Final*, pp. 39–40.

32. Bagua, *Informe en Minoría*, pp. 92–93, 94n277, 97n291.

33. Bagua, *Informe en Minoría*, pp. 48, 93–94.

34. "Amazon Protests Spark Debate over Decrees," Cable from U.S. Embassy, Lima, 1 June 2009, Wikileaks; Bagua, *Informe Final*, p. 41; Mercado and Nájar, *Curva del Diablo*, pp. 101–103. Because both APRA and the Fujimoristas shared the same assumptions about the free market and the benefits of the free trade agreement, the similarity of their voting in congress was not surprising. In general the differences between the two parties were about the tactics to achieve the free market goals rather than about fundamental assumptions.

35. Bagua, *Informe Final*, p. 42; Bagua, *Informe en Minoría*, pp. 54n124, 58, 93n272.

36. Bagua, *Informe en Minoría*, pp. 57–58.

37. Mercado and Nájar, *Curva del Diablo*, pp. 99–100, 219–222; Bagua, *Informe Final*, pp. 49–50; Bagua, *Informe en Minoría*, pp. 58–62.

38. Bagua, *Informe Final*, pp. 42–43, 49; Bagua, *Informe en Minoría*, pp. 58–59, 61; "Amazon Decrees Spark Debate over Decrees," Cable from U.S. Embassy, Lima, 1 June 2009, Wikileaks.

39. Bagua, *Informe en Minoría*, pp. 51–55, 103–104.

40. "Clash Leaves Nine Police, Eleven Protesters Dead," Cable from U.S. Embassy, Lima, 5 June 2009, Wikileaks, "Amazon Protests: State of Play," Cable from U.S. Embassy, Lima, 9 June 2009, Wikileaks; Mercado and Nájar, *Curva del Diablo*, p. 84, and Arce, *Resource Extraction*, p. 112.

41. Bagua, *Informe en Minoría*, pp. 53–54; Bagua, *Informe Final*, pp. 48–49.

42. Bagua, *Informe en Minoría*, pp. 51–56.

43. Mercado and Nájar, *Curva del Diablo*, pp. 103–104; Bagua, *Informe Final*, pp. 51–53; Bagua, *Informe en Minoría*, p. 64.

44. This paragraph and the next rely on the detailed account in Bagua, *Informe en Minoría*, pp. 71–78 and also Mercado and Nájar, *Curva del Diablo*, pp. 103–104, and photograph in p. 266.

45. Bagua, *Informe Final*, pp. 54–56; Bagua, *Informe en Minoría*, pp. 82–85.

46. Bagua, *Informe en Minoría*, p. 86.

47. Bagua, *Informe Final*, p. 57; Bagua, *Informe en Minoría*, p. 87. Most likely a protester captured the grenade from a policeman. The chief objection to this explanation is that none of the inventories of armament issued to the policemen included hand grenades. But the investigative commissions confirmed that policemen during the clash had used some weapons not in the official inventories. Other explanations are possible. While in the army, Indians occasionally were known to report weapons as lost but then to take them secretly back home after their term of service was over. Also, members of the Self-Defense Committees of Cajamarca strongly sympathized with the Indian protest and may have slipped a grenade as a token of support. But then grenades were almost never the usual armament for Self-Defense Committees. And of course anybody with close links to the drug trade, perhaps a coca grower (*cocalero*), could have obtained the hand grenade.

48. Mercado and Nájar, *Curva del Diablo*, pp. 104–107, 234–238; Bagua, *Informe Final*, pp. 57–58; Bagua, *Informe en Minoría*, pp. 103–111.

49. This paragraph and the next draw on Bagua, *Informe Final*, pp. 58–60, Bagua, *Informe en Minoría*, pp. 95–96, 98–99, and Mercado and Nájar, *Curva del Diablo*, pp. 104–105.

50. Bagua, *Informe Final*, pp. 60–62; Bagua, *Informe en Minoría*, pp. 96–101.

51. "Clash Leaves Nine Police, Eleven Protesters Dead," Cable from U.S. Embassy, Lima, 5 June 2009, Wikileaks; "Bloody Bagua Photo Highlights Unresolved Issues," Cable from U.S. Embassy, Lima, 8 January 2010, Wikileaks; Bagua, *Informe en Minoría*, pp. 100, 119, 125.

52. "Amazonian Violence: Confusion about Details," Cable from U.S. Embassy, Lima, 8 June 2009, Wikileaks; "Amazon Protests: State of Play," Cable from U.S. Embassy, Lima, 9 June 2009, Wikileaks; Arce, *Resource Extraction*, pp. 112–113.

53. Bagua, *Informe en Minoría*, p. 118; Arce, *Resource Extraction*, p. 113.

54. "Amazon Protests: Update on June 5 Violence and Aftermath," Cable from U.S. Embassy, Lima, 11 June 2009, Wikileaks.

55. Mercado and Nájar, *Curva del Diablo*, pp. 114–119, 219–233; Bagua, *Informe en Minoría*, pp. 111, 120; Bagua, *Informe Final*, pp. 48–49.

56. "Bloody Bagua Photo Highlights Unresolved Issues," Cable from U.S. Embassy, Lima, 8 January 2010, Wikileaks; Bagua, *Informe en Minoría*, pp. 62–67.

57. "Congress Suspends Decrees to Defuse Protests," Cable from U.S. Embassy, Lima, 10 June 2009, Wikileaks; "Protests Peaceful, Nationalist Congressmen Suspended," Cable from U.S. Embassy, 12 June 2009, Wikileaks.

58. "Bloody Bagua Photo Highlights Unresolved Issues," Cable from U.S. Embassy, Lima, 8 January 2010, Wikileaks.

59. "President Calls for Reconciliation, Congress Repeals Decrees," Cable from U.S. Embassy, Lima, 18 June 2009, Wikileaks; Bagua, *Informe Final*, pp. 66–68.

60. "Government of Peru Signs Agreement with Indigenous Leaders," 15 June 2009, Cable from U.S. Embassy, Wikileaks; Mercado and Nájar, *Curva del Diablo*, p. 123; Arce, *Resource Extraction*, p. 114.

Chapter 14

1. U.S. diplomat Stephen McFarland in "Chávez Gives Marching Orders for the Revolution," Cable from U.S. Embassy, Caracas, 23 December 2004, Wikileaks.

2. "Peruvians Welcome Venezuela Referendum Results as Positive Sign for Democracy," Cable from U.S. Embassy, Lima, 5 December 2007, Wikileaks.

3. "Chávez Loses Constitutional Referendum," Cable from U.S. Embassy, Caracas, 3 December 2008, Wikileaks; "Constitutional Referendum: Winners and Losers," Cable from U.S. Embassy, Caracas, 7 December 2007, Wikileaks; "Opposition Looks Toward 2008," Cable from U.S. Embassy, Caracas, 18 December 2007, Wikileaks.

4. "Chávez Decrees Partial Amnesty Law for Events of 2002," Cable from U.S. Embassy, Caracas, 3 January 2008, Wikileaks.

5. "Chávez Reiterates Intention to Run Again," Cable from U.S. Embassy, Caracas, 28 May 2008, Wikileaks; "Chávez Fills in PSUV Party Structure," Cable from U.S. Embassy, Caracas, 4 April 2008, Wikileaks; Julio Escalona, "La agresión de Estados Unidos usando a Colombia como base," 17 February 2008, Venezuelan ambassador Freddy Balzán emails, Wikileaks.

6. "PSUV Founding Congress: Delays and an Expulsion," Cable from U.S. Embassy, Caracas, 22 February 2008, Wikileaks; Mark P. Sullivan, "Venezuela: Political Conditions and U.S. Policy," 10 October 2008, Congressional Research Service, Wikileaks; Rory Carroll, *Comandante: Hugo Chávez's Venezuela* (New York: Penguin, 2014), pp. 175–179. After Luis Tascón died of colon cancer in August 2010 at the relatively young age of 41, he was "rehabilitated" as a revolutionary.

7. "Chávez Puts Finishing Touches on His PSUV Party," Cable from U.S. Embassy, Caracas, 3 March 2008, Wikileaks; "Chávez Fills in PSUV Party Structure," Cable from U.S. Embassy, Caracas, 4 April 2008, Wikileaks.

8. "Chávez to Nationalize Venezuelan Cement Industry," Cable from U.S. Embassy, Caracas, 8 April 2008, Wikileaks; *Los Angeles Times*, 4 May 2007.

9. "Chávez to Nationalize Venezuelan Cement Industry," Cable from U.S. Embassy, Caracas, 8 April 2008, Wikileaks.

10. "Chávez to Nationalize Latin American Steel Leader SIDOR," Cable from U.S. Embassy, Caracas, 16 April 2008, Wikileaks.

11. "Chávez Announces Intention to Nationalize Banco de Venezuela," Cable from U.S. Embassy, Caracas, 31 July 2008, Wikileaks; *Financial Times*, 1 August 2008, 23 May 2009.

12. "Chávez Announces Intention to Nationalize Banco de Venezuela," Cable from U.S. Embassy, Caracas, 31 July 2008, Wikileaks; *Financial Times*, 1 August 2008, 23 May 2009.

13. "GM Faces Continued Labor Problems," Cable from U.S. Embassy, Caracas, 21 August 2008, Wikileaks.

14. "Chávez Loyalists Win PSUV Primary," Cable from U.S. Embassy, Caracas, 2 June 2008, Wikileaks; "Pro-Chávez Forces Still Divided (Not Just Opposition)," Cable from U.S. Embassy, Caracas, 1 August 2008, Wikileaks.

15. "Chávez Economic Decrees Strengthen Executive Control," Cable from U.S. Embassy, Caracas, 12 August 2008, Wikileaks; Carroll, *Comandante*, pp. 254, 257.

16. "Chávez Economic Decrees Strengthen Executive Control," Cable from U.S. Embassy, Caracas, 12 August 2008, Wikileaks. The benefits from these feeble 26 decrees were so small and the criticism of the Enabling Law as a naked dictatorial power grab was so strong, that Chávez should not have wasted political capital to secure the authorization to legislate.

17. "General Baduel Arrested," Cable from U.S. Embassy, Caracas, 7 October 2008, Wikileaks; Carroll, *Comandante*, pp. 146–147.

18. "Chávez Fills in PSUV Party Structure," Cable from U.S. Embassy, Caracas, 4 April 2008, Wikileaks; "Chávez Fires Up the Base," Cable from U.S. Embassy, Caracas, 18 November 2008, Wikileaks.

19. "Chávez Spins Electoral Results Underscoring the PSUV's Dominance," Cable from U.S. Embassy, Caracas, 25 November 2008, Wikileaks; "State and Local Elections" Winners and Losers," Cable from U.S. Embassy, Caracas, 28 November 2008, Wikileaks. The PSUV also won 265 of the 328 municipalities.

20. "Chávez Spins Electoral Results Underscoring the PSUV's Dominance," Cable from U.S. Embassy, Caracas, 25 November 2008, Wikileaks; "Chávez Moving Forward to Remove Term Limits," Cable from U.S. Embassy, Caracas, 5 December 2008, Wikileaks.

21. "Chávez Dual Tracks Re-election Initiative," Cable from U.S. Embassy, Caracas, 8 December 2008, Wikileaks; "Chávez Personalizing Amendment Proposal," Cable from U.S. Embassy, Caracas, 16 December 2008, Wikileaks; "Presidential Term Limits Referendum: What's at Stake," Cable from U.S. Embassy, Caracas, 20 January 2009, Wikileaks.

22. "Chávez Broadens Amendment Language; Opposition Finally Begins to React," Cable from U.S. Embassy, Caracas, 15 January 2009, Wikileaks; "Chávez's Campaign: I Am the Revolution," Cable from U.S. Embassy, Caracas, 21 January 2009, Wikileaks.

23. "Catholic Bishops Criticize Indefinite Reelection Proposal," Cable from U.S. Embassy, Caracas, 15 January 2009, Wikileaks.

24. "Opposition Lackluster While Students March Forward with NO Campaign," Cable from U.S. Embassy, Caracas, 28 January 2009, Wikileaks.

25. "Chávez Broadens Amendment Language; Opposition Finally Begins to React," Cable from U.S. Embassy, Caracas, 15 January 2009, Wikileaks; "Chávez Sharply Criticizes New U.S. President," Cable from U.S. Embassy, Caracas, 20 January 2009, Wikileaks; "Attacks on Opposition by Pro-Government Groups Supporting Referendum," Cable from U.S. Embassy, Caracas, 21 January 2009, Wikileaks; "Chávez Maintains Maneuvering Room Regarding Obama and New Administration," Cable from U.S. Embassy, Caracas, 29 January 2009, Wikileaks; "Tensions Mounting with Two Weeks to Go," Cable from U.S. Embassy, Caracas, 30 January 2009, Wikileaks.

26. "Referendum Update–Five Days Out," Cable from U.S. Embassy, Caracas, 9 February 2009, Wikileaks.

27. "Venezuelans Approve Elimination of Term Limits," Cable from U.S. Embassy, Caracas, 17 February 2009, Wikileaks; "February 15 Referendum—Winners and Losers," Cable from U.S. Embassy, Caracas, 17 February 2009, Wikileaks.

28. 'The Bolivarian Revolution Advances: What's Next?" Cable from U.S. Embassy, Caracas, 27 February 2009, Wikileaks; "Chávez Determined to Accelerate His Revolution," Cable from U.S. Embassy, Caracas, 28 July 2009, Wikileaks.

29. "Chávez Concentrates More Power at the Expense of Opposition State and Local Governments," Cable from U.S. Embassy, Caracas, 16 March 2009, Wikileaks; "Chávez Continues Attacks on the Opposition and Includes some (Formerly) Party Faithful," Cable from U.S. Embassy, Caracas, 29 April 2009, Wikileaks; "Venezuelan Government Targets More Political Opponents," Cable from U.S. Embassy, Caracas, 11 May 2009, Wikileaks.

30. "Opposition Leader Rosales Still in Hiding as Charges Mount," Cable from U.S. Embassy, Caracas, 6 April 2009, Wikileaks; "Government of Venezuela Recalls Ambassador from Peru," Cable from U.S. Embassy, Caracas, 29 April 2009, Wikileaks; "As Chávez Expands Control, Opposition Implodes," Cable from U.S. Embassy, Caracas, 18 March 2009, Wikileaks.

31. "Request for Additional Funds to Help Strengthen Local Governments and Civil Society Group," Cable from U.S. Embassy, Caracas, 27 March 2009, Wikileaks; "National Assembly Poised to Silence Independent NGOs," Cable from U.S. Embassy, Caracas, 16 April 2009, Wikileaks.

32. "International Community working Quietly to Stop NGO Law," Cable from U.S. Embassy, Caracas, 11 Mary 2009, Wikileaks; "Explaining Venezuelan Acquiescence," Cable from U.S. Embassy, Caracas, 5 June 2009, Wikileaks.

33. "Opposition Announces Newest Unity Effort," Cable from U.S. Embassy, Caracas, 10 June 2009, Wikileaks; "Explaining Venezuelan Acquiescence," Cable from U.S. Embassy, Caracas, 5 June 2009, Wikileaks; Comisión para la Estrategia de la Mesa de la Unidad Democrática, "Informe Final," 28 December 2012, www.urru.org.

34. "Opposition Unity Table Approves Candidate Selection Process," Cable from U.S. Embassy, Caracas, 22 December 2009, Wikileaks; Comisión para la Estrategia de la Mesa de la Unidad Democrática, "Informe Final," 28 December 2012, www.urru.org.

35. "Explaining Venezuelan Acquiescence," Cable from U.S. Embassy, Caracas, 5 June 2009, Wikileaks.
36. "View from the Barrios: Caritas Explains Chávez Continued Appeal," Cable from U.S. Embassy, Caracas, 20 October 2009, Wikileaks.
37. "Explaining Venezuelan Acquiescence," Cable from U.S. Embassy, Caracas, 5 June 2009, Wikileaks.
38. "Venezuelan Government Targets More Political Opponents," Cable from U.S. Embassy, Caracas, 11 May 2009, Wikileaks.
39. "Opposition Party PODEMOS Asks for U.S. Assistance to Counter Chávez," Cable from U.S. Embassy, Caracas, 14 September 2009, Wikileaks.
40. "Teachers Call New Contract Ideological," Cable from U.S. Embassy, Caracas, 27 May 2009, Wikileaks.
41. "Chávez Determined to Accelerate His Revolution," Cable from U.S. Embassy, Caracas, 28 July 2009, Wikileaks.
42. "Teachers Call New Contract Ideological," Cable from U.S. Embassy, Caracas, 27 May 2009, Wikileaks.
43. "Education Law Promulgated, Opposition Calls for a Referendum," Cable from U.S. Embassy, Caracas, 17 August 2009, Wikileaks.
44. "National Assembly Approves Education Law, Legislator Calls it "Birthday Gift for Fidel Castro," Cable from U.S. Embassy, Caracas, 15 August 2009, Wikileaks.
45. "Opposition Mounts Impressive Protest Against Education Law, Chavez Attacks United States," Cable from U.S. Embassy, Caracas, 24 August 2009, Wikileaks.
46. "Schools on Alert, No Implementation Yet of Education Law," Cable from U.S. Embassy, Caracas, 1 October 2009, Wikileaks; "Teachers Call New Contract Ideological," Cable from U.S. Embassy, Caracas, 27 May 2009, Wikileaks.
47. "Schools on Alert, No Implementation Yet of Education Law," Cable from U.S. Embassy, Caracas, 1 October 2009, Wikileaks.
48. "Venezuela: The Revolution Accelerates as the Economy Heads South," Cable from U.S. Embassy, Caracas, 1 July 2009, Wikileaks; "Venezuela's Financial Sector: Fragility Grows, But neither Complete Nationalization nor Systemic Crisis Likely," Cable from U.S. Embassy, Caracas, 19 February 2010, Wikileaks.
49. "Venezuela's Financial Sector: Fragility Grows, But neither Complete Nationalization nor Systemic Crisis Likely," Cable from U.S. Embassy, Caracas, 19 February 2010, Wikileaks.
50. "Venezuelan Government Takes Over Three Additional Banks," Cable from U.S. Embassy, Caracas, 7 December 2009, Wikileaks; *Wall Street Journal*, 29 January 2008; Matías Braun, "Understanding Economic Growth in Venezuela, 1970–2005: The Real Effects of a Financial Collapse," in Ricardo Hausmann and Francisco R. Rodríguez, eds., *Venezuela before Chávez: Anatomy of an Economic Collapse* (University Park: Pennsylvania State University Press, 2014), pp. 161–162, 177–178.
51. "Venezuela's Financial Sector: Fragility Grows, But neither Complete Nationalization nor Systemic Crisis Likely," Cable from U.S. Embassy, Caracas, 19 February 2010, Wikileaks.
52. "Venezuelan Government Takes Control of Four Private Banks," Cable from U.S. Embassy, Caracas, 20 November 2009, Wikileaks; *Asia News Monitor*, 1 December 2009; *Wall Street Journal*, 5 December 2009.
53. "Venezuelan Government Shuts Four Banks," Cable from U.S. Embassy, Caracas, 1 December 2009, Wikileaks; "Venezuelan Government Takes Over Three Additional Banks," Cable from U.S. Embassy, Caracas, 7 December 2009, Wikileaks; *Wall Street Journal*, 8 December 2009.
54. "Venezuelan Government Takes Over Three Additional Banks," Cable from U.S. Embassy, Caracas, 7 December 2009, Wikileaks; "Venezuela: Banco Bicentenario Opens, But Is the Banking Episode Over?" Cable from U.S. Embassy, Caracas, 23 December 2009, Wikileaks. "Venezuela's Financial Sector: Fragility Grows, But Neither Complete Nationalization Nor Systemic Crisis Likely," Cable from U.S. Embassy, Caracas, 19 February 2010, Wikileaks.
55. "Venezuela's Financial Sector: Fragility Grows, But neither Complete Nationalization nor Systemic Crisis Likely," Cable from U.S. Embassy, Caracas, 19 February 2010, Wikileaks; *Wall Street Journal*, 8 December 2009.
56. "Chávez Announces Plans to Nationalize Strategic Sectors," Cable from U.S. Embassy, 9 January 2007, Wikileaks; *El Nacional*, 2 February 2007; "Lights Out in Caracas," *Wall Street Journal*, 5 February 2007.
57. "Government of Bolivarian Republic of Venezuela Imposes Water and Electricity Rationing Through the End of 2009," Cable from U.S. Embassy, Caracas, 23 October 2009, Wikileaks; "Lights Out in Caracas," *Wall Street Journal*, 5 February 2007. In René De La Pedraja, *Energy Politics in Colombia* (Boulder CO: Westview Press, 1989), a book also widely available in a Spanish translation, I had repeatedly emphasized the risks that overreliance on hydroelectricity brought, but obviously not all Venezuelan planners had assimilated this lesson fully.
58. "Venezuela: Looming Power Blackouts," Cable from U.S. Embassy, Caracas, 14 October 2009, Wikileaks; "Venezuela: Deciphering the Current Electricity Crisis," Cable from U.S. Embassy, Caracas, 20 November 2009, Wikileaks; Telemundo, daily news broadcasts, 2009.
59. "Venezuela: Deciphering the Current Electricity Crisis," Cable from U.S. Embassy, Caracas, 20 November 2009, Wikileaks; Javier Corrales and Michael Penfold, *Dragon in the Tropics: Venezuela and the Legacy of Hugo Chávez*, 2d ed. (Washington, D.C.: Brookings Institution, 2015), p. 69.
60. "Venezuela: Looming Power Blackouts," Cable from U.S. Embassy, Caracas, 14 October 2009, Wikileaks; *El Tiempo*, 9 January 2010.
61. "Venezuela: Government Imposes Water and Electricity Rationing Through the End of 2009," Cable from U.S. Embassy, Caracas, 23 October 2009, Wikileaks; Carroll, *Comandante*, pp. 180–181; *El Tiempo*, 9 January 2010; *Wall Street Journal*, 30 January 2010.
62. "Venezuela: Chávez Declares Electricity State of Emergency," Cable from U.S. Embassy, Caracas, 11 February 2010, Wikileaks; *El Tiempo*, 10 February, 10 March 2010.
63. "Venezuela's Economy in 2010: A Difficult and Uncertain Year," Cable from U.S. Embassy, Caracas, 22 January 2010, Wikileaks; *El Tiempo*, 9 February 2010: "Tripwires for Authorized and Ordered Departure in the Event of Catastrophic Failure of Electricity and Water Supply," Cable from U.S. Embassy, Caracas, 25 February 2010, Wikileaks; Corrales and Penfold, *Dragon in the Tropics*, p. 70.
64. *El Tiempo*, 10, 11, 14 February, 10 March 2010.
65. Carroll, *Comandante*, p. 208; *El Tiempo*, 19 May, 8, 16 June 2010. Although the expansion of the thermal electricity plants was the right response in the short run, the development of alternate energy sources provided the only environmentally acceptable long-term solutions. The brisk winds blowing from the Caribbean Sea seemed ideal for wind turbines, while the scorching sun for a country so near the equator made solar energy another natural choice.
66. Luis José Silva Luongo, *De Cipriano Castro a Carlos Andrés Pérez (1899–1979); Hechos, vivencias y apreciaciones* (Caracas: Monte Ávila Editores, 2005), pp. 701–703; Allan R. Brewer-Carías, "Centralized Federalism in Venezuela," *Duquesne Law Review* 43(2005): 632; "Rampant Crime in Venezuela—Chávez's Achilles Heel?" Cable from U.S. Em-

bassy, Caracas, 24 August 2009, Wikileaks; *El Tiempo*, 3 January 2010.

67. "Rampant Crime in Venezuela—Chávez's Achilles Heel?" Cable from U.S. Embassy, Caracas, 24 August 2009, Wikileaks; "High Crime Affects Voters but Spares Candidates," Cable from U.S. Embassy, Caracas, 24 November 2008.

68. "Rampant Crime in Venezuela—Chávez's Achilles Heel?" Cable from U.S. Embassy, Caracas, 24 August 2009, Wikileaks.

69. "Homicide: Life on the Streets of Caracas," Cable from U.S. Embassy, Caracas, 28 April 2008, Wikileaks; "Rampant Crime in Venezuela—Chávez's Achilles Heel?" Cable from U.S. Embassy, Caracas, 24 August 2009, Wikileaks; Carroll, *Comandante*, pp. 233–234. As late as 2013 Chavista officials claimed that the bad habits of the old Caracas Metropolitan Police still survived; See, "Transcripción de la grabación de Mario Silva," *El Nacional*, 20 May 2013.

70. "Urgent Venezuelan National Police Law Delayed Again," Cable from U.S. Embassy, Caracas, 25 April 2006, Wikileaks; Carroll, *Comandante*, pp. 236–240.

71. "High Crime Affects Voters but Spares Candidates," Cable from U.S. Embassy, Caracas, 24 November 2008, Wikileaks; Carroll, *Comandante*, pp. 234–240.

72. "Rampant Crime in Venezuela—Chávez's Achilles Heel?" Cable from U.S. Embassy, Caracas, 24 August 2009, Wikileaks; "High Crime Affects Voters but Spares Candidates," Cable from U.S. Embassy, Caracas, 24 November 2008, Wikileaks; *El Tiempo*, 3 January 2010.

73. "Urgent Venezuelan National Police Law Delayed Again," Cable from U.S. Embassy, Caracas, 25 April 2006, Caracas, Wikileaks.

74. "Chávez Tackles Rising Crime with the Bolivarian National Police," Cable from U.S. Embassy, Caracas, 26 January 2010, Wikileaks; "Chávez Concentrates More Power at the Expense of Opposition State and Local Governments," Cable from U.S. Embassy, Caracas, 16 Mach 2009, Wikileaks.

75. "Chávez Tackles Rising Crime with the Bolivarian National Police," Cable from U.S. Embassy, Caracas, 26 January 2010, Wikileaks; *El Tiempo*, 19 February 2012.

76. "Chávez Tackles Rising Crime with the Bolivarian National Police," Cable from U.S. Embassy, Caracas, 26 January 2010, Wikileaks; "Maduro moves to Address Security Situation," *Oxford Analytica Daily Brief Service*, 3 June 2013; U.S. Department of State, "Venezuela 2015 Crime and Safety Report," 19 February 2015.

77. "Chávez Tackles Rising Crime with the Bolivarian National Police," Cable from U.S. Embassy, Caracas, 26 January 2010, Wikileaks; *El Tiempo*, 20 August 2010, 6 January, 19 February 2012.

78. "Food Vulnerabilities: Bolivarian Republic Policy Responses Crack under Rolling Shortages," Cable from U.S. Embassy, Caracas, 20 December 2007, Wikileaks; "Venezuela's 2009 Economic Outlook: Grim to Dire," Cable from U.S. Embassy, Caracas, 22 January 2009, Wikileaks.

79. Carroll, *Comandante*, pp. 119–120; "Ascension of Agriculture Minister to Vice Presidency Bodes Ill for Agriculture," Cable from U.S. Embassy, Caracas, 4 February 2010, Wikileaks. Elías Jaua left a protégé as minister of agriculture from July 2010 until January 2012 when he again held that position until October of that year; then his protégé again occupied the position.

80. "Bolivarian Republic of Venezuela Consumed with Normalizing Venezuelan Food Supply," Cable from U.S. Embassy, Caracas, 23 January 2008, Wikileaks; "Colombian Beef Is Not What Is for Dinner," Cable from U.S. Embassy, Caracas, 17 August 2009, Wikileaks.

81. "Chávez Threatens to Expropriate Large Food Distributors," Cable from U.S. Embassy, Caracas, 7 February 2008, Wikileaks.

82. "Polar Still Skating on Thin Ice," Cable from U.S. Embassy, Caracas, 17 March 2008, Wikileaks.

83. "Bolivarian Republic of Venezuela Consumed with Normalizing Venezuelan Food Supply," Cable from U.S. Embassy, Caracas, 23 January 2008, Wikileaks; "PDVAL: The Venezuelan Government's Newest Food Distributor," Cable from U.S. Embassy, Caracas, 4 April 2008, Wikileaks.

84. "The Food Shortage Saga Continues: The Supermarket Chapter," Cable from U.S. Embassy, Caracas, 19 March 2008, Wikileaks; "Venezuelan Market Interference Leads to Both Food Oversupply and Shortages," Cable from U.S. Embassy, 1 August 2008, Wikileaks.

85. "President Makes Importing Food More Difficult, Especially for Selected Companies," Cable from U.S. Embassy, Caracas, 4 June 2009, Wikileaks.

86. "There's Trouble Brewing: Venezuelan Coffee Industry under Attack," Cable from U.S. Embassy, Caracas, 7 August 2009, Wikileaks.

87. "Venezuela's Rice Availability Diminishing," Cable from U.S. Embassy, Caracas, 8 December 2009, Wikileaks; "Venezuela's Rice Industry Threatened for Political Gain," Cable from U.S. Embassy, Caracas, 3 March 2009, Wikileaks.

88. "Venezuelan Government Threatens to Expropriate a U.S. Multinational's Plant," Cable from U.S. Embassy, Caracas, 5 March 2009, Wikileaks; "Venezuelan Government Versus U.S. Company Cargill," Cable from U.S. Embassy, Caracas, 20 March 2009, Wikileaks.

89. "Venezuelan Government Threatens to Expropriate a U.S. Multinational's Plant," Cable from U.S. Embassy, Caracas, 5 March 2009, Wikileaks; "Venezuelan Government Hits the Accelerator on Intervention in the Economy," Cable from U.S. Embassy, Caracas, 10 March 2009, Wikileaks; "Venezuelan Government Versus U.S. Company Cargill," Cable from U.S. Embassy, Caracas, 20 March 2009,Wikileaks.

90. "Cargill Takes a Hit to Protect Larger Interests," Cable from U.S. Embassy, Caracas, 27 January 2009, Wikileaks; "Not a Good Idea but It Is the Law," Cable from U.S. Embassy, Caracas, 26 March 2009, Wikileaks.

91. "Venezuela's Rice Industry Threatened for Political Gain," Cable from U.S. Embassy, Caracas, 3 March 2009, Wikileaks; "Venezuela's Rice Availability Diminishing," Cable from U.S. Embassy, Caracas, 8 December 2009, Wikileaks. Once again, Colombia was the only other nearby country able to replace the United States as the sole supplier of rice. Although the bordering country normally exported modest amounts of rice to Venezuela, most Colombian rice growers were hesitant to make the permanent investments necessary to expand their production because of the political uncertainties of the Bolivarian Revolution.

92. "Colombian Beef Is Not What Is for Dinner," Cable from U.S. Embassy, Caracas, 17 August 2009, Wikileaks; "Sugar Processors are Bolivarian Republic of Venezuela Favorites," Cable from U.S. Embassy, Caracas, 5 October 2009, Wikileaks; "Chávez Expropriates Two Sugar Mills," Cable from U.S. Embassy, Caracas, 26 October 2009, Wikileaks.

93. "Sugar Processors are Bolivarian Republic of Venezuela Favorites," Cable from U.S. Embassy, Caracas, 5 October 2009, Wikileaks; Carroll, *Comandante*, pp. 216–217.

94. "Colombian Beef Is Not What Is for Dinner," Cable from U.S. Embassy, Caracas, 17 August 2009, Wikileaks; "Chávez Expropriates Two Sugar Mills," Cable from U.S. Embassy, Caracas, 26 October 2009, Wikileaks; *El Tiempo*, 14, 15 January 2010. Once relations returned to normal,

the nationalized sugar mills had no choice but to resume importing sugar cane from Colombia for the 2011 harvest season; See, *El Tiempo*, 14 August 2010.

95. "Chávez Seizes Éxito," Cable from U.S. Embassy, Caracas, 27 January 2010, Wikileaks; *El Tiempo*, 12 January, 3 September 2010.

96. "Bolivarian Aggressive Land Interventions Benefit Selected Officials to the Country's Cost," Cable from U.S. Embassy, Caracas, 25 November 2009, Wikileaks; "Ascension of Agriculture Minister to Vice Presidency Bodes Ill for Agriculture," Cable from U.S. Embassy, Caracas, 4 February 2010, Wikileaks; "Venezuelans Struggle to Cope with Soaring Food Prices, Inflation Tops Latin America," Associated Press, 30 May 2011; *El Tiempo*, 2, 29 June 2010; Carroll, *Comandante*, pp. 216–217; Corrales and Penfold, *Dragon in the Tropics*, p. 60.

97. *El Tiempo*, 14 August 2010, 26 September, 7 October 2012. During the Fourth Republic, canned powdered milk was one of the few Venezuelan products to enjoy a good reputation among Colombian consumers.

98. "Chávez Asserts 2009 Ended Well," Cable from U.S. Embassy, Caracas, 15 January 2010, Wikileaks.

99. "Chávez Promotes Transition to Socialist Economy, Threatens Foreign Automakers," Cable from U.S. Embassy, Caracas, 29 December 2009, Wikileaks; *El Tiempo*, 9 April 2010.

100. "Opposition Committed to Elections Despite Challenges," Cable from U.S. Embassy, Caracas, 12 February 2010, Wikileaks.

101. "RCTV Closed; Protests Erupt," Cable from U.S. Embassy, Caracas, 25 January 2010, Wikileaks; *El Tiempo*, 23, 25 January 2010; *Washington Post*, 25 January 2010.

102. Julio Escalona, "La agresión de Estados Unidos usando a Colombia como base," 17 February 2008, Venezuelan ambassador Freddy Balzán emails, Wikileaks; "RCTV Closed; Protests Erupt," Cable from U.S. Embassy, Caracas, 25 January 2010, Wikileaks; "Globovisión Owners Acknowledge Defeat; *El Nacional* on the Ropes?" Secret Cable from U.S. Embassy, Caracas, 23 February 2010, Wikileaks; "Three Cable Stations Reopen, Student Protests Continue," Cable from U.S. Embassy, Caracas, 28 January 2010.

103. "Globovisión Owners Acknowledge Defeat; *El Nacional* on the Ropes?" Secret Cable from U.S. Embassy, Caracas, 23 February 2010, Wikileaks. Presumably the request to assist *El Nacional* went to the CIA that could draw on its secret funds.

104. "La agonía de La Francia, famoso centro joyero de Venezuela," *El Tiempo*, 15 February 2010. I visited La Francia during my study trip to Caracas in 2007 and was well impressed by the ornate building. Because 60 percent of the diamond merchants were of Jewish origin, some denounced this nationalization as anti-Semitic and as a way for Chávez to win favor with Muslim countries, but this accusation seems unlikely because La Francia lacked an obvious Jewish image.

105. *El Tiempo*, 20, 28 July 2010; "Expectations for Chavez's Electoral Strategy," Cable from U.S. Embassy, Caracas, 13 February 2010, Wikileaks.

106. *El Tiempo*, 27, 28 September, 2 October 2010.

107. *Christian Science Monitor*, 23, 27 December 2010; *El Tiempo*, 15, 24 December 2010.

Chapter 15

1. U.S. Ambassador Brownfield in Cable from U.S. Embassy, Bogotá, 8 October 2009, Wikileaks.

2. "New Criminal Groups are Law Enforcement Threat, Shadow of Ex-Paramilitaries," Cable from U.S. Embassy, Bogotá, 13 February 2007, Wikileaks; Jasmin Hristov, *Blood and Capital: The Paramilitarization of Colombia* (Athens: Ohio University Press, 2009), pp. 148–149; "Caramagna Says DeParamilization of Regions Possible," Cable from U.S. Embassy, Bogotá, 16 May 2007, Wikileaks.

3. "New Criminal Groups Remain Decentralized," Cable from U.S. Embassy, Bogotá, 23 March 2007, Wikileaks; Hristov, *The Paramilitarization of Colombia*, pp. 155–158, 167–168; Philip Alston, *Report of the Special Rapporteur on Extrajudicial, Summary, or Arbitrary Executions; Mission to Colombia* (New York: United Nations General Assembly, 2010), pp. 22–23, 35–36.

4. Hristov, *The Paramilitarization of Colombia*, pp. 159, 161–163, 173–175; René De La Pedraja, *Wars of Latin America, 1982–2013: The Path to Peace* (Jefferson, NC: McFarland, 2013), pp. 228, 230; "New Criminal Groups Remain Decentralized," Cable from U.S. Embassy, Bogotá, 23 March 2007, Wikileaks; "Colombia's New Criminal Groups: The Drug Trade's New Generation," Cable from U.S. Embassy, Bogotá, 13 August 2007, Wikileaks.

5. For a detailed account of the campaigns of the Colombian army, See, De La Pedraja, *Wars of Latin America, 1982–2013*, pp. 224–229.

6. "Colombia National Police Presence in Conflictive Areas: Mission Accomplished," Cable from U.S. Embassy, Bogotá, 4 February 2004, Wikileaks; "A General Overview of Colombia's Security Situation," Cable from U.S. Embassy, Bogotá, 16 April 2004, Wikileaks; De La Pedraja *Wars of Latin America, 1982–2013*, pp. 226, 228, 230.

7. Harvey F. Kline, *Showing Teeth to the Dragons: State-building by Colombian President Álvaro Uribe Vélez, 2002–2006* (Tuscaloosa: University of Alabama Press, 2009), pp. 41–42; "Minister of Defense Defends Colombian Demobilization and Reinsertion Strategy," Cable from U.S. Embassy, Bogotá, 1 September 2004, Wikileaks; "Colombia's Hometown Soldiers Program," Cable from U.S. Embassy, Bogotá, 13 September 2004, Wikileaks.

8. "Government of Colombia Initiates Interagency Social Assistance Projects," Cable from U.S. Embassy, Bogotá, 18 May 2004, Wikileaks; "Scene setter for Chairman of the Joint Chiefs of Staff General Myers," Cable from U.S. Embassy, Bogotá, 7 April 2005, Wikileaks; René De La Pedraja, *Energy Politics in Colombia* (Boulder, CO: Westview Press, 1989), pp. 205–207.

9. "Colombia's Economy in 2004 Looked Strong, But," Cable from U.S. Embassy, Bogotá, 7 January 2005, Wikileaks.

10. "Social Protests—Why Now?" 30 October 2008, Cable from U.S. Embassy, Bogotá, 30 October 2008, Wikileaks; "Colombian Economic Outlook: What a Difference a Year Makes," Cable from U.S. Embassy, Bogotá, 5 January 2009, Wikileaks; "Ecopetrol Buys Back Cartagena Refinery; Looks for New Partners," Cable from U.S. Embassy, Bogotá, 5 March 2009, Wikileaks. For the history of the Cartagena refinery, See, De La Pedraja, *Energy Politics in Colombia*, pp. 56–58.

11. "Strong Performance in the Colombian Banking Sector," Cable from U.S. Embassy, Bogotá, 14 September 2004, Wikileaks; "Government of Colombia Arrests Alleged Pyramid Ringleaders amid Protest," Cable from U.S. Embassy, Bogotá, 21 November 2008, Wikileaks; "Agriculture Sector Bracing for Tumultuous 2009," Cable from U.S. Embassy, Bogotá, 28 January 2009, Wikileaks; *The Guardian*, 13 November 2008.

12. "Government of Colombia Arrests Alleged Pyramid Ringleaders amid Protest," Cable from U.S. Embassy, Bogotá, 21 November 2008, Wikileaks; "Los Secretos de DMG," *Semana*, 22 November 2008; "Pyramid Schemes in Colombia," *Americas Quarterly*, 6 January 2009.

13. "Government of Colombia Arrests Alleged Pyramid Ringleaders amid Protest," Cable from U.S. Embassy, Bogotá, 21 November 2008, Wikileaks; "Extradition Ap-

proved for Pyramid Scheme Mastermind," Cable from U.S. Embassy, Bogotá, 15 October 2009, Wikileaks; "Los Secretos de DMG," *Semana*, 22 November 2008; "Colombia Scam Mastermind Jailed," *BBC News*, 17 December 2009.

14. "Fallout from Pyramid Scheme Continues to Shake Colombia," Cable from U.S. Embassy, 28 November 2008, Wikileaks; "Turmoil from Pyramid Scheme Curbs Southern Oil Production," Cable from U.S. Embassy, Bogotá, 7 January 2009, Wikileaks; *The Guardian*, 13 November 2008; *Telegraph*, 13 November 2008; Mónica Pachón, "Colombia 2008," *Revista de Ciencia Política* 29(2009): 344–345.

15. "Pyramid Schemes in Colombia," *Americas Quarterly*, 6 January 2009; "Ponzi Scheme DMG to Compensate Investors $11.7 million," *Colombia Reports*, 30 November 2011.

16. "Fallout from Pyramid Scheme Continues to Shake Colombia," Cable from U.S. Embassy, 28 November 2008, Wikileaks.

17. "Government of Colombia Arrests Alleged Pyramid Ringleaders amid Protest," Cable from U.S. Embassy, Bogotá, 21 November 2008, Wikileaks.

18. "Los Secretos de DMG," *Semana*, 22 November 2001; "Colombia Reels after Investment Schemes," *Washington Post*, 5 December 2008. "Government of Colombia Arrests Alleged Pyramid Ringleaders amid Protest," Cable from U.S. Embassy, Bogotá, 21 November 2008, Wikileaks.

19. "Agriculture Sector Bracing for Tumultuous 2009," Cable from U.S. Embassy, Bogotá, 28 January 2009, Wikileaks.

20. "Ecopetrol Buys Back Cartagena Refinery; Looks for New Partners," Cable from U.S. Embassy, Bogotá, 5 March 2009, Wikileaks.

21. "Construction in Colombia," *Hydrocarbon Engineering*, September 2010; "Ecopetrol Buys Back Cartagena Refinery; Looks for New Partners," Cable from U.S. Embassy, Bogotá, 5 March 2009, Wikileaks; "Colombia's Energy Sector to Expand with Exim Financing," Cable from U.S. Embassy, Bogotá, 18 November 2009, Wikileaks; "Despierta la refinería de Cartagena," *Semana*, 17 October 2015.

22. "DAS Director Resigns over Opposition Spying Scandal," Cable from U.S. Embassy, Bogotá, 24 October 2008, Wikileaks; Fundación para la Libertad de Prensa, *Espionaje contra periodistas: La justicia tiene la palabra*, Report of 3 December 2010, Bogotá, p. 4.

23. "DAS Continues Domestic Spying," Cable from U.S. Embassy, Bogotá, 23 February 2009, Wikileaks; "El espionaje era peor," *Semana*, 25 April 2009; "Bitácora del espionaje del DAS," *El Espectador*, 2 March 2015; Libertad de Prensa, *Espionaje contra periodistas*, p. 12.

24. "[Attorney General Office's] Investigation into Illegal DAS Surveillance," Cable from U.S. Embassy, Bogotá, 23 June 2009, Wikileaks; "Bitácora del espionaje del DAS," *El Espectador*, 2 March 2015; Libertad de Prensa, *Espionaje contra periodistas*, pp. 4–5, 9; "A Case of Aid Gone Bad in Colombia," *Washington Post*, 21 August 2011.

25. "Uribe Restricts DAS Intelligence Operations in Reaction to Eavesdropping Scandal," Secret Cable from U.S. Embassy, Bogotá, 2 March 2009, Wikileaks; Federación Internacional de Derechos Humanos, *Colombia: Actividades ilegales del DAS*, Report of 2010, Paris, p. 8.

26. "Bitácora del espionaje del DAS," *El Espectador*, 2 March 2015; Derechos Humanos, *Actividades ilegales del DAS*, p. 8.

27. "Uribe Restricts DAS Intelligence Operations in Reaction to Eavesdropping Scandal," Secret Cable from U.S. Embassy, Bogotá, 2 March 2009, Wikileaks.

28. "Ambassador and VP Santos Discuss Response to DAS Scandals," Secret Cable from U.S. Embassy, Bogotá, 16 September 2009, Wikileaks; Derechos Humanos, *Actividades ilegales del DAS*, pp. 38–39; "A Case of Aid Gone Bad in Colombia," *Washington Post*, 21 August 2011.

29. René De La Pedraja, *The United States and the Armed Forces of Mexico, Central America, and the Caribbean, 2000–2014* (Jefferson, NC: McFarland, 2014), pp. 109, 111; Fundación para la Educación y el Desarrollo, *Soacha: La punta del iceberg, falsos positivos e impunidad* (Bogotá: Ediciones Ántropos, 2010), p. 49; Alston, *Mission to Colombia*, pp. 8–9.

30. Observatorio de derechos humanos y derecho humanitario, *Informe final de la Misión Internacional sobre Ejecuciones Extrajudiciales e Impunidad en Colombia* (Bogotá: Coordinación Colombia-Europa-Estados Unidos, 2008), p. 11; Hristov, *The Paramilitarization of Colombia*, pp. 50–52; De La Pedraja, *U.S. and Armed Forces*, pp. 110–111; Alston, *Mission to Colombia*, p. 12.

31. Izagirre, "Así se fabrican guerrilleros muertos"; Secret Directiva Ministerial Permanente No. 29, Bogotá, 17 November 2005; Hristov, *The Paramilitarization of Colombia*, pp. 55–56; Alston, *Mission to Colombia*, p. 13.

32. Izagirre, "Así se fabrican guerrilleros muertos"; FEDES, *La punta del iceberg*, pp. 22, 43.

33. Hristov, *The Paramilitarization of Colombia*, pp. 55–56, 92–94; FEDES, *La punta del iceberg*, pp. 22, 34–35.

34. Izagirre, "Así se fabrican guerrilleros muertos"; FEDES, *La punta del iceberg*, pp. 34–35, 52; Alston, *Mission to Colombia*, p. 8.

35. Hristov, *The Paramilitarization of Colombia*, pp. 46–47; Observatorio de derechos humanos, *Informe final sobre ejecuciones extrajudiciales*, pp. 10, 35–36, 57; *El Tiempo*, 23 May 2009; Alston, *Mission to Colombia*, pp. 8, 14.

36. De La Pedraja, *U.S. and Armed Forces*, p. 112.

37. Observatorio de derechos humanos, *Informe final sobre ejecuciones extrajudiciales*, pp. 11, 37–39, 42, 76; Izagirre, "Así se fabrican guerrilleros muertos."

38. FEDES, *La punta del iceberg*, pp. 11, 52–57, 73; Izagirre, "Así se fabrican guerrilleros muertos"; Observatorio de derechos humanos, *Informe final sobre ejecuciones extrajudiciales*, pp. 10–11.

39. Izagirre, "Así se fabrican guerrilleros muertos"; De La Pedraja, *U.S. and Armed Forces*, pp. 112.

40. "Special Prosecutor's Team to Investigate Soacha Deaths," Secret Cable from U.S. Embassy, Bogotá, 7 October 2,008, Wikileaks; Hristov, *The Paramilitarization of Colombia*, pp. 48–49.

41. "Colombian Military Commander Montoya Resigns," Secret Cable from U.S. Embassy, Bogotá, 6 November 2008, Wikileaks; "Government of Colombia Fires 27 Military Officials for Links to Extrajudicial Killings," Cable from U.S. Embassy, Bogotá, Wikileaks; Izagirre, "Así se fabrican guerrilleros muertos"; "Purga histórica," *El Tiempo*, 29 October 2008.

42. De La Pedraja, *U.S. and Armed Forces*, pp. 113–114, 288n10; Izagirre, "Así se fabrican guerrilleros muertos"; CINEP, *Informe especial: Falsos positivos, balance del segundo semestre de 2008* (Bogotá: CINEP, 2009), pp. 5, 7; Alston, *Mission to Colombia*, pp. 9–11, 14–16.

43. María Jimena Duzán, *Así gobierna Uribe* (Bogotá: Planeta, 2004), pp. 23–25; "Colombia in the Political Doldrums," Cable from U.S. Embassy, Bogotá, 17 November 2009, Wikileaks; Felipe Botero, "Flash Report: A Key Decision in Colombia," March 2010, Centre for the Study of Democratic Institutions, The University of British Columbia.

44. "Colombia in the Political Doldrums," Cable from U.S. Embassy, Bogotá, 17 November 2009, Wikileaks; Duzán, *Asi gobierna Uribe*, pp. 103–109, 178–194.

45. "Defense Chief Hopes to Lead Colombia; Santos Quits for Possible Run in 2010," *Washington Post*, 19 May 2009.

46. "Colombia's New Leader Seen as Good for U.S.," *Washington Post*, 17 December 2010; Eduardo Posada-Carbó, "Colombia after Uribe," *Journal of Democracy* 22(2011): 147.

47. "Uribe's 84 Percent Approval Rating Spurs Re-Election Strategy," Cable from U.S. Embassy, Bogotá, 14 March 2008, Wikileaks; "No End in Sight to Uribe-Supreme Court Power Struggle," Cable from U.S. Embassy, Bogotá, 15 August 2008, Wikileaks; Colombia, *Constitución Política de Colombia* (Bogotá: Editorial Temis, 1991), Title 13.

48. "Third Term Referendum Takes a Second Small Step Forward," Cable from U.S. Embassy, Bogotá, 17 December 2008, Wikileaks; Botero, "Flash Report."

49. "Uribe Third Term Issue Dominates Reform Effort, Presidential Contender Plans, and Scandals," Cable from U.S. Embassy, Bogotá, 17 June 2008, Wikileaks; "Juan Manuel Santos Discusses Presidential Prospects with Ambassador," Cable from U.S. Embassy, Bogotá, 27 October 2009, Wikileaks.

50. "Defense Chief Hopes to Lead Colombia; Santos Quits for Possible Run in 2010," *Washington Post*, 19 May 2009; "Santos Eager to Assume Uribe's Mantle, But Uribe Still Kicking," Cable from U.S. Embassy, Bogotá, 12 February 2010, Wikileaks; "Juan Manuel Santos Discusses Presidential Prospects with Ambassador," Cable from U.S. Embassy, Bogotá, 27 October 2009, Wikileaks; Posada-Carbó, "Colombia after Uribe," p. 139.

51. "Uribe Keeps Them Guessing on Possible Third Term," Cable from U.S. Embassy, Bogotá, 5 September 2008, Wikileaks; Botero, "Flash Report"; "Congress Approves Reelection Referendum, But Hurdles Remain," Cable from U.S. Embassy, Bogotá, 3 September 2009, Wikileaks; "The Uribe Coalition: Less than Solid," Cable from U.S. Embassy, Bogotá, 15 July 2009, Wikileaks; "Reelection Effort Running out of Stream—and Time," Cable from U.S. Embassy, Bogotá, 4 August 2009, Wikileaks.

52. "Third Uribe Term Increasingly Likely," Cable from U.S. Embassy, Bogotá, 3 February 2010, Wikileaks.

53. Botero, "Flash Report"; "Uribe Reelection Bid Hits another Speed Bump," Cable from U.S. Embassy, Bogotá, 13 November 2009, Wikileaks.

54. "Santos Eager to Assume Uribe's Mantle, But Uribe Still Kicking," Cable from U.S. Embassy, Bogotá, 12 February 2010, Wikileaks.

55. "Defense Chief Hopes to Lead Colombia; Santos Quits for Possible Run in 2010," *Washington Post*, 19 May 2009; "The Uribe Coalition: Less than Solid," Cable from U.S. Embassy, Bogotá, 15 July 2009, Wikileaks.

56. "Court Rules Uribe Third Term Referendum Unconstitutional," Cable from U.S. Embassy, Bogotá, 26 February 2010, Wikileaks; Botero, "Flash Report"; "Santos Eager to Assume Uribe's Mantle, But Uribe Still Kicking," Cable from U.S. Embassy, Bogotá, 12 February 2010, Wikileaks.

57. Botero, "Flash Report."

58. "Court Rules Uribe Third Term Referendum Unconstitutional," Cable from U.S. Embassy, Bogotá, 26 February 2010, Wikileaks. Another major objection to the referendum was that the government had convoked the extraordinary session of congress illegally in December 2008. For an incisive discussion of the flaws in the referendum proposal, See, Botero, "Flash Report."

59. *Los Angeles Times*, 31 May 2010; *Washington Post*, 31 May 2010; *Wall Street Journal*, 1 June 2010; "The Uribe Coalition: Less than Solid," Cable from U.S. Embassy, Bogotá, 15 July 2009, Wikileaks; "Reelection Effort Running out of Steam—and Time," Cable from U.S. Embassy, Bogotá, 4 August 2009, Wikileaks.

60. Posada-Carbó, "Colombia after Uribe," pp. 144–146; Laura Wills-Otero and Christian Iván Benito, "De Uribe a Santos: Cambios y continuidades de la política colombiana en 2011," *Revista de Ciencia Política* 32(2012): 94–95; *Los Angeles Times*, 21 June 2010; *New York Times*, 21 June 2010.

61. Wills-Otero and Benito, "De Uribe a Santos," p. 96; Ligia Yamila Villarraga, "Análisis del discurso de posesión de Juan Manuel Santos: La ideología de la Unidad Nacional," *Forma y Función* 25(2012): 48–40; *Washington Post*, 21 June 2010.

Chapter 16

1. "Ollanta Humala Claims He Can Save Peru from Extremists," Cable from U.S. Embassy, Lima, 26 June 2008, Wikileaks.

2. "Ambassador Meets with Ollanta Humala," Cable from U.S. Embassy, Lima, 4 May 2009, Wikileaks.

3. "Peru's Presidential Race Very Tight: Polls," 29 May 2011, Reuters; Jo-Marie Burt and Coletta A. Youngers, "Peru: What's Next for Humala?" 17 June 2011; "Peru—In Latest Polls Fujimori Only Has 1–1.5 Percent Lead over Humala," 29 May 2011, Stratfor Global Intelligence Files, Wikileaks; *New York Times*, 6 June 2011.

4. "Ambassador Meets with Ollanta Humala," Cable from U.S. Embassy, Lima, 4 May 2009, Wikileaks; "Humala: Hedging Bets in Run Up to Elections," Cable from U.S. Embassy, Lima, 21 October 2009, Wikileaks; "Humala Cabinet Picks Will Test Lula-Like Reinvention to Calm Peru Markets," 7 June 2011, Bloombergnews.

5. "Ambassador Meets with Ollanta Humala," Cable from U.S. Embassy, Lima, 4 May 2009, Wikileaks; *New York Times*, 6 June 2011.

6. "Humala Cabinet Picks Will Test Lula-Like Reinvention to Calm Peru Markets," 7 June 2011, Bloomberg news.com; "PUP Brief," 7 June 2011, Stratfor Global Intelligence Files, Wikileaks.

7. Burt and Youngers, "Peru: What's Next for Humala?" 17 June 2011; "Peru 2011," 13 April 2011, World Elections, Word Press.

8. *Los Angeles Times*, 2 June 2011; "Neptune for Internal Comments," 31 May 2011, Stratfor, Global Intelligence Files, Wikileaks.

9. *Los Angeles Times*, 2 June 2011; *Washington Post*, 4 June 2011.

10. "Good Story on Infighting in Peru," 2 June 2011, Stratfor Global Intelligence Files, Wikileaks; *Los Angeles Times*, 2 June 2011.

11. "Peru's Presidential Race Very Tight: Polls," 29 May 2011, Reuters; "In Latest Polls Fujimori Only Has 1–1.5 Percent Lead over Humala," 29 May 2011, Stratfor Global Intelligence Files, Wikileaks; "Peru—Election Results," 6 May 2011, 5 June 2011, Stratfor Global Intelligence Files, Wikileaks.

12. Burt and Youngers, "Peru: What's Next for Humala?" 17 June 2011.

13. "Venezuela," 31 May 2011, "PUP Brief" 7 June 2011, and "PUP Brief," 9 June 2011, Stratfor Global Intelligence Files, Wikileaks; Burt and Youngers, "Peru: What's Next for Humala?" 17 June 2011.

14. "Humala Says Apply Open market Economy to Strengthen the Internal Market," 6 June 2011, and "PUP Brief" 7 June 2011 and 10 June 2011, Stratfor Global Intelligence Files, Wikileaks.

15. "PUP Brief," 9 June 2011, 14 June 2011, Stratfor Global Intelligence Files, Wikileaks.

16. "PUP Brief," 10 June 2011, "PUP Brief," 14 June 2011, "PUP Brief," 17 June, and" Quarterly Bullets for Comment," 14 June 2011, Stratfor Global Intelligence Files, Wikileaks; Francisco Durand, "El Señor," *Quehacer*, no. 185 (2012 January-March), pp. 20–21.

17. Francisco Durand, "Humala: entre la izquierda y la derecha," *Quehacer*, no. 194 (2014 April-June 2014), p. 7.

18. Durand, "El Señor," pp. 19–20; Durand, "Humala: entre la izquierda y la derecha," pp. 8–9.

19. "Honeymoon over," *The Economist*, 19 November 2011.

20. Lynda Sullivan, "Getting to the Bottom of Extractive Capitalism: A Case Study of Open Pit Mining in Cajamarca, Peru," *Policy and Practice—A Development Education Review* 19(2014): 4; Seo Ji-Hyun, "Neoliberal Extractivism and Rural Resistance: The Anti-Mining Movement in the Peruvian Northern Highlands, Cajamarca, 2011–2013," p. 190; "Honeymoon over," *The Economist*, 19 November 2011.

21. Gustavo Ávila, Claudia Viale, and Carlos Monge, "Extractive Industries and their Imprint," in John Crabtree, ed., *Fractured Politics: Peruvian Democracy Past and Present* (London: Institute for the Study of the Americas, 2011), pp. 162–163; Sullivan, "Extractive Capitalism: Open Pit Mining in Cajamarca," 19(2014): 8; Catherine Cheney, "Peru's Humala Prioritizes Foreign Investment with Cabinet Reshuffle," *World Politics Review*, 14 December 2011; Ji-Hyun, "The Anti-Mining Movement in Cajamarca," pp. 193, 229.

22. "Sociológico/ minero; Nota de información No. 2535," 15 November 2013, *La República*, 26 December 2013; Sullivan, "Extractive Capitalism: Open Pit Mining in Cajamarca," pp. 5–6; Ávila *et al*, "Extractive Industries and Their Imprint," pp. 167, 183. For a brief account of the night watch, See, René De La Pedraja, *Wars of Latin America, 1982–2013: The Path to Peace* (Jefferson, NC: McFarland & Co., Publishers, 2013), pp. 98, 100; for a book-length study See, Orin Starn, *Nightwatch: The Politics of Protest in the Andes* (Durham, NC: Duke University Press, 1999).

23. *El Comercio*, 9 November 2011; Deborah Poole and Gerardo Rénique, "Peru: Humala Takes Off His Gloves," *NACLA Report on the Americas* 45(Spring 2012): 4–5; "Peru: Cajamarca Protests Continue as Conga Gold Mine Awaits Green Light," *Upside Down World*, 29 March 2012; "Yanacocha suspende proyecto en mina Conga y da paso al diálogo," *La República*, 30 November 2011; *Americas*, 29 November 2011; Ji-Hyun, "The Anti-Mining Movement in Cajamarca," pp. 194. Bloggers also reported the arrival of the soldiers: "Peru: Blogs de Cajamarca reportan sobre conflicto por mina Conga," 3 December 2011, es.globalvoicesonline.org.

24. "Cajamarca Protests Continue," *Upside Down World*; "Yanacocha suspende proyecto en mina Conga y da paso al diálogo," *La República*, 30 November 2011; Deanne Kemp et al., *Listening to the City of Cajamarca* (Queensland, Australia: Centre for Social Responsibility in Mining, 2013), pp. 5, 18.

25. Cheney, "Peru's Humala Prioritizes Foreign Investment," *World Politics Review*, 14 December 2011; "Peru Declares Emergency over Disputed Mine," Al Jazeera, 6 December 2011; "Yanacocha suspende proyecto en mina Conga y da paso al diálogo," *La República*, 30 November 2011; Ji-Hyun, "The Anti-Mining Movement in Cajamarca," pp. 194–195, 248; Kemp et al., *Listening to Cajamarca*, pp. 5–6.

26. Ji-Hyun, "The Anti-Mining Movement in Cajamarca," pp. 195, 218–220.

27. "Peru suspende la mina Conga," *El Espectador*, 23 July 2012; "Humala Changes Six Ministers after Mine Turmoil Turn Deadly," Bloomberg News, 24 July 2012; Kemp et al., *Listening to Cajamarca*, p. 6; Ji-Hyun, "The Anti-Mining Movement in Cajamarca," pp. 197, 249.

28. Sullivan, "Extractive Capitalism: Open Pit Mining in Cajamarca," p. 8; Ji-Hyun, "The Anti-Mining Movement in Cajamarca," p. 229; "Peru: Blogs de Cajamarca reportan sobre conflicto por mina Conga," 3 December 2011, es.globalvoicesonline.org.

29. "Humala Takes Off His Gloves," p. 3.

30. "Sociológico/ minero; Nota de información No. 2535," 15 November 2013, "Sociológico; Nota de información, 26 November 2013," *La República*, 26 December 2013; "Un Wikileaks peruano revela secretos del gobierno de Humala," *El País*, 28 December 2013; Kemp et al., *Listening to Cajamarca*, p. 11; Ji-Hyun, "The Anti-Mining Movement in Cajamarca," pp. 201–202.

31. *El Comercio*, 28 December 2013, 17 January 2014.

32. Kemp et al., *Listening to Cajamarca*, p. 9.

33. *El Comercio*, 17 January 2014; RadioPeru Noticias, 22 May 2014; *Wall Street Journal*, 6 October 2014.

Chapter 17

1. Miguel de Cervantes Saavedra, *Don Quixote de la Mancha*, trans. John Ormsby, 4 vols. (London: Smith, Elder & Co., 1885), 2: 327.

2. "Chávez Back in Public View, Claims CIA Assassination Plot," Cable from U.S. Embassy, Caracas, 4 June 2009, Wikileaks.

3. "Where's Hugo?" Cable from U.S. Embassy, Caracas, 3 June 2009, Wikileaks.

4. *El Tiempo*, 26 April 2010.

5. Telemundo, daily news broadcasts, June 2011; Rory Carroll, *Comandante: Hugo Chávez's Venezuela* (New York: Penguin, 2014), pp. 270–271; *El Tiempo*, 7 March 2011.

6. Carroll, *Comandante*, p. 272; *El Tiempo*, 17 October 2011; *Wall Street Journal*, 5 July 2011.

7. *El Tiempo*, 8 August 2011 for this and the next paragraph.

8. *Business Bloomberg Week*, 21 May 2012; *Washington Post*, 9 February 2012; *El Tiempo*, 25 January, 12, 13 February, 22 August, 15 September, 7 October 2012; *Pittsburgh Post-Gazette*, 2 July 2012; Comisión para la Estrategia de la Mesa de la Unidad Democrática, "Informe Final," 28 December 2012, www.urru.org.

9. *El Tiempo*, 19 September 2012.

10. Centro de Orientación en Energía, "Informe de investigación sobre la explosión e incendio ocurrido en la Refinería de Amuay el 25 de agosto de 2012," Caracas, 25 August 2003; *El Tiempo*, 26, 27 August, 1 September 2012.

11. *El Tiempo*, 18 July, 10 October 2011, 23 February, 28 March 2012.

12. *Time*, October 2012; Carroll, *Comandante*, pp. 284–286; *El Tiempo*, 4 October 2012.

13. *New York Times*, 17 October 2012; *El Tiempo*, 9, 12 October 2012.

14. "Ascension of Agriculture Minister to Vice Presidency Bodes Ill for Agriculture," Cable from U.S. Embassy, Caracas, 4 February 2010, Wikileaks; Carroll, *Comandante*, pp. 286–287; *El Tiempo*, 10 October 2012; *New York Times*, 12 June 2012.

15. *El Tiempo*, 10, 13, 14 October, 10 December 2012; Carroll, *Comandante*, p. 287; Javier Corrales and Michael Penfold, *Dragon in the Tropics: Venezuela and the Legacy of Hugo Chávez*, 2d ed. (Washington, D.C.: Brookings Institution Press, 2015), pp. 161, 163. On ideology, Elías Jaua was the official nearest to the Cuban Revolution. However, partly because of the very close working relationship of the Foreign Minister Nicolás Maduro with the Cuban ambassador to Venezuela, the Cubans persuaded Chávez to replace Jaua with pragmatic Maduro as the official best capable of preserving the Bolivarian Revolution.

16. Telemundo, daily news broadcasts, December 2012 and January 2013; *Wall Street Journal*, 10 December 2012; *El Tiempo*, 28 November, 7, 9 December 2012; *Washington Post*, 11 December 2012.

17. *El Tiempo*, 16, 17 December 2012; Corrales and Penfold, *Dragon in the Tropics*, pp. 174–175.

18. *Wall Street Journal*, 20 December 2012; *El Tiempo*, 10 December 2012; Carroll, *Comandante*, pp. 287–289; *Washington Post*, 6 January, 9 March 2013; *New York Times*, 16 January 2013.

19. Eduardo Posada-Carbó, "Colombia after Uribe," *Journal of Democracy* 22(2011): 148–149; *Washington Post*, 21 June 2010; *Wall Street Journal*, 7 July 2011; Ligia Yamila Villarraga, "Análisis del discurso de posesión de Juan Manuel Santos: La ideología de la Unidad Nacional," *Forma y Función* 25(2012): 48–49.

20. Posada-Carbó, "Colombia after Uribe," pp. 148–149; Laura Wills-Otero and Christian Iván Benito, "De Uribe a Santos: Cambios y continuidades de la política colombiana en 2011," *Revista de Ciencia Política* 32(2012): 102.

21. Posada-Carbó, "Colombia after Uribe," p. 148.

22. Wills-Otero and Benito, "De Uribe a Santos," p. 93; José Manuel Mejía V. and Juan Carlos López G., "¿Reestructuración del Estado o captura de la burocracia estatal?" *Revista Andina de Estudios Políticos*, No. 4, March 2011.

23. Juan Manuel Santos, *Informe al congreso 2012* (Bogotá: Imprenta Nacional, 2012), pp. 9, 139–141; Wills-Otero and Benito, "De Uribe a Santos," p. 93; Mejía V. and López G., "Reestructuración del Estado."

24. Lina Forero-Niño, "Colombia's Historic Victims and Land Restitution Law," *Law and Business Review of the Americas* 18(2012): 97–100; Wills-Otero and Benito, "De Uribe a Santos," p. 93; Silla Brodzinski, "How Colombia's President Santos Aims to Tackle Decades of Violent Land Disputes, *Christian Science Monitor*, 4 October 2010; Santos, *Informe al congreso 2012*, pp. 9, 124.

25. José Manuel Mejía, "Movilización con inmovilización: ¿La génesis de un año de tensión socio—política para el gobierno de Santos?" *Revista Andina de Estudios Políticos*, No. 3, February 2011; José Manuel Mejía, "Santos cerca de la independencia: preámbulo a la desintegración de la Unidad Nacional," *Revista Andina de Estudios Políticos*, No. 5, April 2011.

26. *Semana*, 18 February 2011; Mejía, "Movilización con inmovilización"; Wills-Otero and Benito, "De Uribe a Santos," p. 88.

27. Mejía, "Movilización con inmovilización"; *Semana*, 18 February 2011.

28. Mejía, "Movilización con inmovilización"; Wills-Otero and Benito, "De Uribe a Santos," p. 88; *Semana*, 18 February 2011.

29. Mónica Rivera Valencia, "Marcos de interpretación en las protestas estudiantiles de 2011 en Colombia," Thesis, Universidad del Valle, Cali, 2014, pp. 22, 28, 30, 43, 50, 70; Paola Montilla, "Colombia: ¿Hacia una reestructuración del sistema político?" *Revista de Ciencia Política* 34(2014): 111; Wills-Otero and Benito, "De Uribe a Santos," p. 88.

30. Rivera Valencia, "Protestas estudiantiles de 2011," pp. 34–41; Edwin Cruz Rodríguez, "La MANE y el paro nacional universitario de 2011 en Colombia," *Ciencia Política*, no. 14, July-December 2012, pp. 143–144; Wills-Otero and Benito, "De Uribe a Santos," p. 88; Colombia, Presidencia de la República, "Resumen del día de las actividades del Presidente Juan Manuel Santos 10 de marzo de 2011," YouTube.

31. Rivera Valencia, "Protestas estudiantiles de 2011," pp. 41–43, 46, 66; Cruz, "Paro nacional universitario de 2011," pp. 144–145; Humberto Vélez Ramírez, "Idearios universitarios, reforma de la Ley 30 y neoliberalismo académico," *Atisbos Analíticos*, No. 133, November 2011.

32. Rivera Valencia, "Protestas estudiantiles de 2011," p. 47; Cruz, "Paro nacional universitario de 2011," pp. 143, 147; Wills-Otero and Benito, "De Uribe a Santos," p. 88; Vélez Ramírez, "Idearios universitarios, reforma de la Ley 30."

33. Rivera Valencia, "Protestas estudiantiles de 2011," pp. 61–64; *Semana*, 15 November 2011.

34. Cruz, "Paro nacional universitario de 2011," p. 147; Rivera Valencia, "Protestas estudiantiles de 2011," pp. 31, 58.

35. Montilla, "Sistema político," p. 111; Rivera Valencia, "Protestas estudiantiles de 2011," pp. 61–64.

36. "Declaración del Presidente Juan Manuel Santos sobre proyecto de reforma a la educación superior," 9 November 2011; Cruz, "Paro nacional universitario de 2011," pp. 150–151; Rivera Valencia, "Protestas estudiantiles de 2011," pp. 32, 76.

37. Rivera Valencia, "Protestas estudiantiles de 2011," pp. 32, 76; "Estudia y desobedece," 23 November 2011; Enrique Santos Calderón, "De cocteles Molotov a senos al aire," *El Tiempo*, 27 noviembre 2011; Humberto Vélez Ramírez, "Constituyente universitaria, congreso nacional universitario y proyecto alternativo de educación superior," *Atisbos Analíticos*, No. 134, November 2011.

38. Rivera Valencia, "Protestas estudiantiles de 2011," pp. 33, 76; Wills-Otero and Benito, "De Uribe a Santos," p. 88.

39. Rivera Valencia, "Protestas estudiantiles de 2011," p. 44.

40. M. Ángeles Villareal, *The U.S.-Colombia Free Trade Agreement: Background and Issues* (Washington, D.C.: Congressional Research Service, 2014), p. 1; Cato Institute, *Free Trade Bulletin*, No. 44, 15 February 2011; "Colombia Agrees to Protect Unions," *Washington Post*, 7 April 2011; Jonathan D. Rosen, "Plan Colombia and Beyond: Pastrana to Santos (2000 to 2012)," Ph.D. Dissertation, University of Miami, 2012, pp. 117–121.

41. *Wall Street Journal*, 9 June 2014; Wills-Otero and Benito, "De Uribe a Santos," p. 91; René De La Pedraja, *Wars of Latin America, 1982–2013: The Path to Peace* (Jefferson, NC: McFarland, 2013), p. 232.

42. *Wall Street Journal*, 24 September 2015; Montilla, "Sistema político," pp. 112–113; De La Pedraja, *Wars of Latin America, 1982–2013*, pp. 232–233.

43. Margarita Battle and Gustavo Duncan, "Colombia: un panorama menos confuso," *Revista de Ciencia Política* 33(2013): 104; Montilla, "Sistema político," pp. 108–109, 111; *Washington Post*, 6 October 2013; *Wall Street Journal*, 5 August, 20 November 2013.

Chapter 18

1. Niccolò Machiavelli, *Selected Political Writings: The Prince, Selections from the Discourses, Letter to Vettori*, trans. David Wootton (Indianapolis: Hackett Publishing, 1994), p. 116.

2. *Wall Street Journal*, 20 November 2013.

3. Lina Forero-Niño, "Colombia's Historic Victims and Land Restitution Law," *Law and Business Review of the Americas* 18(2012): 102–103.

4. Paola Montilla, "Colombia: ¿Hacia una reestructuración del sistema político?" *Revista de Ciencia Política* 34(2014): 108–109, 111; *Wall Street Journal*, 20 August 2013; *Los Angeles Times*, 3 March 2013.

5. *Wall Street Journal*, 17 May 2014; Jonathan D. Rosen, "Plan Colombia and Beyond: Pastrana to Santos," Ph.D. Dissertation, University of Miami, 2012, pp. 129–132.

6. *New York Times*, 16 May 2014; *Washington Post*, 26 May 2014.

7. *The Economist*, 31 May 2014; *Wall Street Journal*, 2, 9 June 2014.

8. *Los Angeles Times*, 16 June 2014; *Portafolio*, 17 June 2014.

9. *Washington Post*, 16 June 2014; *Los Angeles Times*, 16 June 2014; *Economist*, 31 May 2014.

10. *Wall Street Journal*, 16 June 2014; *Washington Post*, 16 June 2014.

11. *New York Times*, 16 January 2015.

12. *El Espectador*, 15 April 2015; *New York Times*, 16 January 2015.
13. *New York Times*, 9 March, 14 May 2015.
14. *El Espectador*, 15 April 2015.
15. *El Espectador*, 25 July 2015; "FARC ordenan a sus tropas el cese de las acciones violentas a partir de este lunes," BBC Mundo, 20 July 2015; "Presidente de Colombia suspende bombardeos a campamentos de las FARC," 26 July 2015.
16. *El Espectador*, 25 July 2015.
17. *El Espectador*, 9 September 2015; *Wall Street Journal*, 24 September 2015; *New York Times*, 24 September 2015.
18. "Santos y sus intentos de reconciliarse con Uribe," *El Espectador*, 12 February 2016; *Wall Street Journal*, 24 September 2015; *New York Times*, 26 September 2015.
19. "Santos y sus intentos de reconciliarse con Uribe," *El Espectador*, 12 February 2016.
20. *El Espectador*, 8, 12 December 2015, 16, 20 February 2016.
21. "Chief of Colombia's National Police Resigns amid Prostitution Ring Allegations," CNN, 17 February 2016; *El Espectador*, 21 December 2015, 16, 20 February 2016.
22. "U.N. Can Seal the Peace in Colombia," editorial, *New York Times*, 23 January 2016; "Por cumplir una fecha, no voy a firmar un mal acuerdo," BBC Mundo, 9 March 2016; El Espectador, 10 March 2016.
23. "Turbulencia antes del Día D del proceso de paz," *Semana*, 11 June 2016; "Sin humo blanco en La Habana sobre cese al fuego bilateral," *Semana*, 3 June 2011.
24. "Turbulencia antes del Día D del proceso de paz," *Semana*, 11 June 2016; "¿Niebla en la Habana?" *Semana*, 15 June 2016. For the intimate bonds between guerrillas and their rifles, particularly the Kalashnikovs, See, René De La Pedraja, *Wars of Latin America, 1982–2013: The Path to Peace* (Jefferson, NC: McFarland Publishers, 2013), pp. 204–205.
25. "Quiero entregarle la paz al pueblo: Santos," *Semana*, 26 May 2016; "Lista conciliación del acto legislativo para la paz," *Semana*, 14 June 2016.
26. "¿Niebla en la Habana?" *Semana*, 15 June 2016; "El último round del acto legislativo por la paz," *Semana*, 14 Junio 2016.
27. "Lista conciliación del acto legislativo para la paz," *Semana*, 14 June 2016.
28. *El Espectador*, 5 June 2016; "Uribe recoge firmas en contra de acuerdos de paz con las FARC," *Semana*, 4 June 2016; "Proceso de paz: la batalla por la opinión," *Semana*, 18 June 2016.
29. "Le dimos confianza jurídica a la paz," *El Espectador*, 18 June 2016; "Al menos cinco magistrados aprobarían plebiscito por la paz," *Semana*, 19 June 2016.
30. "Esto significa el fin de las FARC como grupo armado: Santos," *El Espectador*, 23 June 2016; "Colombia and FARC Rebels Reach Definitive Cease Fire Deal," Reuters, 22 June 2016.
31. "Colombia's President: Making Peace with Rebels is a Good Investment," National Public Radio, 29 June 2016; "Colombia and FARC Rebels Reach Definitive Cease Fire Deal," Reuters, 22 June 2016.
32. For the Marquetalia campaign, See, René De La Pedraja, *Wars of Latin America, 1948–1982, The Rise of the Guerrillas* (Jefferson, NC: McFarland Publishers, 2013), pp. 128–134.
33. See, "En las entrañas del Catatumbo," *Semana*, 28 May 2016 for a typical case of how the receding authority of FARC is opening the door for criminal groups to expand illicit activities such as drugs and smuggling.
34. *Wall Street Journal*, 11 June 2013.
35. Ronald Bruce St. John, *Toledo's Peru: Vision and Reality* (Gainesville: University Press of Florida, 2010), pp. 52–55; *New York Times*, 20 August 2013.
36. *Chicago Tribune*, 11, 12 August 2013.
37. *Wall Street Journal*, 3, 13 January 2014.
38. *Wall Street Journal*, 13 January 2014.
39. Moisés Arce, *Resource Extraction and Protest in Peru* (Pittsburgh: University of Pittsburgh Press, 2014), pp. 82, 122, 124. In early 2016 the likelihood of gold mining in Conga seemed slim; See Cecilia Jamasmie, "Community Opposition Forces Newmont to abandon Conga Project in Peru," 18 April 2016, www.mining.com.
40. *Wall Street Journal*, 17 April 2015; Arce, *Resource Extraction*, p. 123.
41. *Wall Street Journal*, 17 April, 15 May 2015.
42. *Financial Times*, 12 May 2015; *Wall Street Journal*, 16 May 2015.
43. *Wall Street Journal*, 27 March, 15, 16 May 2015; "Tía María: El tajo que divide el sur del Perú," *La República*, 3 April 2016.
44. "Candidates Jockey for Position ahead of 2016 Elections," EIU Views Wire, 15 July 2015; "Peru's Keiko Fujimori Launches Presidential Bid," *Asia News Monitor*, 8 December 2015.
45. "Elecciones 2016: Las hojas de vida de los 19 candidatos a la presidencia," *Gestión*, 14 January 2016; "Keiko Fujimori Clear Favorite in Peru Election Poll," *Asia News Monitor*, 17 December 2015; "Who's Running in the 2016 Presidential Election," Explainer, 8 March 2016.
46. *La República*, 1 February 2016.
47. *El Comercio*, 9 March 2016; *Wall Street Journal*, 10 March 2016; *La República*, 1 February 2016; "Elecciones 2016: Las hojas de vida de los 19 candidatos a la presidencia," *Gestión*, 14 January 2016.
48. *Wall Street Journal*, 10 March 2016; "Who's Running in the 2016 Presidential Election," Explainer, 8 March 2016.
49. "Kuczynski, presidente de Perú por la mínima," *El Espectador*, 10 June 2016; "Peru's Elections: Keiko Fujimori Trails Pedro Pablo Kuyczynski," *The Washington Post*, 6 June 2016.
50. "Kuczynski, presidente de Perú por la mínima," *El Espectador*, 10 June 2016; *The Guardian*, 10 June 2016.
51. "Peru's Keiko Fujimori Trails in Early Returns in Presidential Election," *Los Angeles Times*, 5 June 2016; "Peru's Elections: Keiko Fujimori Trails Pedro Pablo Kuczynski," *The Washington Post*, 6 June 2016; David Dudenhoefer, "After Narrow Win in Peru, Kuczynski Must Still Contend with Fujimori," *World Politics Review*, 14 June 2016.
52. "Peru's Keiko Fujimori Trails in Early Returns in Presidential Election," *Los Angeles Times*, 5 June 2016; Daily TV news broadcasts of BBC, June 6 to 10, 2016.
53. "Keiko Fujimori Concedes Defeat to Pedro Pablo Kuczynski in Peru Election," *The Guardian*, 10 June 2016; Dudenhoefer, "Narrow Win in Peru," *World Politics Review*, 14 June 2016.
54. Rory Carroll, *Comandante: Hugo Chávez's Venezuela* (New York: Penguin, 2014), pp. 289–291; *Christian Science Monitor*, 9, 12 March 2013; *Washington Post*, 9 March 2013.
55. Comisión para la Estrategia de la Mesa de la Unidad Democrática, "Informe Final," 28 December 2012; Carroll, *Comandante*, pp. 290–291.
56. Javier Corrales and Michael Penfold, *Dragon in the Tropics: The Legacy of Hugo Chávez* (Washington, D.C.: Brookings Institution Press, 2015), pp. 163, 167; *New York Times*, 16 April 2013; Telemundo, daily news broadcasts, April 2013; Carroll, *Comandante*, pp. 290–291.
57. "Allegations of Minister Diosdado Cabello's Corruption Expanding to Financial Sector," Cable from U.S. Embassy, Caracas, 20 July 2009, Wikileaks; *Wall Street Journal*, 6 March 2013; *El Tiempo*, 8 March 2012; Corrales and Penfold, *Dragon in the Tropics*, pp. 161–162.
58. Carroll, *Comandante*, p. 291; *New York Times*, 15,

16 April 2013; "Transcripción de la grabación de Mario Silva," *El Nacional*, 20 May 2013; Corrales and Penfold, *Dragon in the Tropics*, pp. 161–162.

59. *Wall Street Journal*, 15, 27 April 2013; *New York Times* 16 April 2013.

60. "Globovisión Owners Acknowledge Defeat; *El Nacional* on the Ropes?" Secret Cable from U.S. Embassy, Caracas, 23 February 2010, Wikileaks; *Chicago Tribune*, 16 May 2013; *Los Angeles Times*, 15 May 2013.

61. *Financial Times*, 24 September 2013; "The Bolivarian Revolution Advances: What's Next?" Cable from U.S. Embassy, Caracas, 27 February 2009, Wikileaks. The relationship of Lorenzo Mendoza with Nicolás Maduro remained rocky, and by the end of 2015 the business leader was again attacking the Bolivarian Revolution; Telemundo daily news broadcasts.

62. *Financial Times*, 24 September 2013; "Polar Still Skating on Thin Ice," Cable from U.S. Embassy, Caracas, 17 March 2008, Wikileaks.

63. *Wall Street Journal*, 9 October, 20 November 2013; *Oxford Analytica Daily Brief Service*, 25 November 2013.

64. *Christian Science Monitor*, 29 November 2013.

65. *Economist*, 14 December 2013; *Christian Science Monitor*, 9 December 2013; *Oxford Analytica Daily Brief Service*, 10 December 2013.

66. *Christian Science Monitor*, 9 December 2013; *Wall Street Journal*, 14 August 2014.

67. *Washington Post*, 20 January 2014.

68. "Chávez Promotes Transition to Socialist Economy, Threatens Foreign Automakers," Cable from U.S. Embassy, Caracas, 29 December 2009, Wikileaks; *Washington Post*, 20 January 2014.

69. *Wall Street Journal*, 13 February 2014; *Christian Science Monitor*, 13 February 2014.

70. *Wall Street Journal*, 21 February 2014; *New York Times*, 18 February 2014; *Christian Science Monitor*, 13 February 2014.

71. *Wall Street Journal*, 22 February 2014; *Christian Science Monitor*, 13, 18 February 2014.

72. *Wall Street Journal*, 24 February 2014; *New York Times*, 25 February 2014.

73. Telemundo, daily news broadcasts, February 2014; *Wall Street Journal*, 28 February 2014; *New York Times*, 25 February 2014.

74. *Chicago Tribune*, 14 March 2014; *Christian Science Monitor*, 6 March 2014; *NACLA Report on the Americas*, 47(fall 2014): 14–18.

75. *Wall Street Journal*, 21 February, 6 May 2014; *Washington Post*, 8 May 2014.

76. *Christian Science Monitor*, 13 February, 6 March 2014; *Washington Post*, 29 March 2014.

77. *NACLA Report on the Americas*, 47(fall 2014): 14–18; *Wall Street Journal*, 26 March 2014; Telemundo, daily news broadcasts, March 2014.

78. *Americas Quarterly*, 8(summer 2014): 48–53; *Christian Science Monitor*, 10 April 2014; *Washington Post*, 10 April 2014; *New York Times*, 11 April 2014.

79. *NACLA Report on the Americas*, 47(fall 2014): 14–18; *Wall Street Journal*, 14 August 2014.

80. Telemundo, daily news broadcasts, May-June 2014; *Washington Post*, 21 May 2024; *Wall Street Journal*, 14 August 2014.

81. Comisión para la Estrategia de la Mesa de la Unidad Democrática, "Informe Final," 28 December 2012.

82. "Emergencia económica en Venezuela," BBC Mundo, 22 January 2016.

83. "Cuatro retos de la oposición de Venezuela tras su victoria en las elecciones parlamentarias," BBC Mundo, 9 December 2015; Telemundo daily news broadcasts, December 2015.

84. "Cuatro retos de la oposición de Venezuela tras su victoria en las elecciones parlamentarias," BBC Mundo, 9 December 2015; "The Last Days of Nicolás Maduro," Foreign Policy, 22 February 2016.

85. "Cuatro retos de la oposición de Venezuela tras su victoria en las elecciones parlamentarias," BBC Mundo, 9 December 2015; "The Last Days of Nicolás Maduro," Foreign Policy, 22 February 2016; "Cómo el Tribunal Supremo de Venezuela le quita poder a la Asamblea Nacional," BBC Mundo 3 March 2016.

86. "The Last Days of Nicolás Maduro," Foreign Policy, 22 February 2016; "Venezuela Opposition Begins Campaign to Oust President Nicolás Maduro," Reuters, 8 March 2016.

87. "Los planes de la oposición de Venezuela para tratar de sacar a Maduro del poder antes que acabe el año," BBC Mundo, 8 March 2016; "Cómo el Tribunal Supremo de Venezuela le quita poder a la Asamblea Nacional," BBC Mundo 3 March 2016; "Venezuela Opposition Begins Campaign to Oust President Nicolás Maduro," Reuters, 8 March 2016.

88. "Los planes de la oposición de Venezuela para tratar de sacar a Maduro del poder antes que acabe el año," BBC Mundo, 8 March 2016; "Venezuela Opposition Begins Campaign to Oust President Nicolás Maduro," Reuters, 8 March 2016; "You Won't Get Rid of Me! Venezuela's Maduro Tells Foes," Reuters, 10 March 2016; "Venezuela Court Blocks another Opposition Tactic to Oust Maduro," Reuters, 25 April 2016.

89. "Drive to Oust Venezuela's Maduro Returns Old Foe to Front Line," Reuters, 1 June 2016; "A Venezuelan Dissident Speaks Out from Jail," *Bloomberg Business Week*, 25 January 2016; "Venezuela Security Forces Block New Anti-Maduro Protest," Reuters, 7 June 2016.

90. "Venezuela Announces Daily, Nationwide Power Cuts on Drought," Reuters, 21 April 2016; "La tensa relación entre Almagro y Venezuela," *El Espectador*, 4 June 2016.

91. "Cómo el Tribunal Supremo de Venezuela le quita poder a la Asamblea Nacional controlada por la oposición," BBC Mundo, 3 March 2016; "Así es el largo y difícil camino hacia el revocatorio contra Maduro," *El Espectador*, 1, 20 June 2016; "Venezuela Court Blocks Another Opposition Tactic to Oust Maduro," Reuters, 25 April 2016; "How Much Time Does Maduro Have?" *Bloomberg Business Week*, 7 March 2016; Corrales and Penfold, *Dragon in the Tropics*, pp. 160–162.

92. "You Won't Get Rid of Me! Venezuela's Maduro Tells Foes," Reuters, 10 March 2016; "Shortage-Plagued Venezuela Puts Socialist Committees in Charge of Selling Food," Reuters, 9 June 2016; "En Venezuela se dan las condiciones para un estallido social," *El Tiempo*, 16 June 2016; "Todos los días hay saqueos en Venezuela," *El Espectador*, 15 June 2016. Smugglers in the western states of Venezuela, who were furious that the government was restricting their lucrative trade with Colombia, were responsible for most of the looting of grocery stores and food trucks.

93. "Drought-Hit Venezuela Awaits Rain at Crucial Guri Dam," Reuters, 12 April 2016; "Forty Days of Blackouts Hit Venezuela amid Economic Crisis," CNN Money, 22 April 2016; "Venezuela Drifts into New Territory: Hunger, Blackouts and Government Shutdown," *International New York Times*, 28 May 2016. As part of the energy-saving measures, Maduro also reversed the decision of Chávez who had set clocks back 30 minutes in 2007. Originally the measure was intended to prevent children from having to wake up in the dark to go to school, but having the extra half-hour in the evening saved electricity because people did not have to turn on lights and air-conditioning so soon upon returning home. See, "Venezuela Scraps Half-Hour Time Difference Set by Chávez," Reuters, 15 April 2016.

94. "U.S. Concern Grows over Possible Venezuela Meltdown: Officials," Reuters, 16 May 2016.

95. "Venezuela's Military in the Spotlight," *International New York Times*, 24 May 2015; "Venezuela Crisis Puts Influential Military in Spotlight," Reuters, 20 May 2016; "Venezuela Leaders Says U.S. Dreams of Dividing Loyal Military," Reuters, 22 May 2016.

96. "Polar adquirió millonario préstamo para reanudar producción cervecera en Venezuela," *El Espectador*, 1 June 2016; "The Only Number That Matters in Venezuela Is This One," *The Washington Post*, 3 June 2016; "La tensa relación de Almagro y Venezuela," *El Espectador*, 4 June 2016; "Venezuela Eases Power Rationing, Ends Two-Day Working Week," Reuters, 13 June 2016; "Empleados públicos venezolanos volverán a trabajar cinco días por semana," *El Espectador*, 14 June 2016; "Venezuela evaluaría dolarizar para salvar industria automotriz," *El Espectador*, 23 June 2016; "Venezuela inició importación masiva de alimentos desde Trinidad y Tobago," *El Espectador*, 23 June 2016; "Venezuela's Maduro Ends Power Rationing as Drought Eases," Reuters, 1 July 2016.

97. "Venezuelans Ransack Stores as Hunger Grips the Nation," *International New York Times*, 19 June 2016; "Venezuelans Are Storming Supermarkets and Attacking Trucks as Food Supplies Dwindle," *The Washington Post*, 28 June 2016.

98. "Venezuela Indicts Opposition Activists amid Recall Effort," Reuters, 22 June 2016; "Chavismo planea pedir la disolución de Parlamento opositor en Venezuela," *El Espectador*, 28 June 2016.

Annotated Bibliography

The following are books and reports available in English

Alston, Philip. *Report of the Special Rapporteur on Extrajudicial, Summary, or Arbitrary Executions; Mission to Colombia.* New York: United Nations General Assembly, 2010. This perceptive and authoritative account places the "False Positives" in the context of the lawlessness in Colombia; highly recommended.

Arce, Moisés. *Resource Extraction and Protest in Peru.* Pittsburgh: University of Pittsburgh Press, 2014. Detailed statistics on mobilization protests and careful analysis make this book indispensable to understand social conflict in Peru. See also Ji-Hyun, Seo.

Carrión, Julio F., ed. *The Fujimori Legacy: The Rise of Electoral Authoritarianism in Peru.* University Park: Pennsylvania State University Press, 2006. Leading scholars analyze the principal aspects of the Fujimori regime.

Carroll, Rory. *Comandante: Hugo Chávez's Venezuela.* New York: Penguin, 2013. In spite of extreme hostility, this book concentrating on the later years of the presidency of Hugo Chávez has valuable insights; not as detailed as Jones, Bart.

Conaghan, Catherine M. *Fujimori's Peru: Deception in the Public Sphere.* Pittsburgh: University of Pittsburgh Press, 2005. A book-length study on the manipulations of Vladimiro Montesinos and Fujimori.

Corrales, Javier, and Michael Penfold. *Dragon in the Tropics: Venezuela and the Legacy of Hugo Chávez.* Second Edition. Washington, D.C.: Brookings Institution Press, 2015. Hostility to Chávez did not prevent the authors from providing valuable insights into the Bolivarian Revolution; the book also covers the first two years of the Nicolás Maduro presidency. Should be contrasted with Wilpert, Gregory.

Crabtree, John, ed. *Fractured Politics: Peruvian Democracy Past and Present.* London: Institute for the Study of the Americas, 2011. Contains studies of the same high quality as the previous volume by the same editor.

_____. *Making Institutions Work in Peru.* London: Institute for the Study of the Americas, 2006. Excellent studies by leading scholars, covering both political and economic institutions; highly recommended.

De La Pedraja, René. *The United States and the Armed Forces of Mexico, Central America, and the Caribbean, 2000–2014.* Jefferson, NC: McFarland, 2014.

_____. *Wars of Latin America, 1982–2013: The Path to Peace.* Jefferson, NC: McFarland, 2013.

Degregori, Carlos Iván. *La década de la antipolítica: Auge y huída de Alberto Fujimori y Vladimiro Montesinos.* Lima: Instituto de Estudios Peruanos, 2012. A scholar-observer provides an insightful examination of the Fujimori regime.

Ellner, Steve. *Rethinking Venezuelan Politics: Class, Conflict, and the Chávez Phenomenon.* Boulder: Lynne Rienner, 2009. This is the best scholarly study available to understand the movement of Chávez; highly recommended.

Gates, Leslie C. *Electing Chávez: The Business of Anti-Neoliberal Politics in Venezuela.* Pittsburgh: Pittsburgh University Press, 2010.

Hausmann, Ricardo and Francisco R. Rodríguez, eds. *Venezuela before Chávez: Anatomy of an Economic Collapse.* University Park: Pennsylvania State University Press, 2014.

Hristov, Jasmin. *Blood and Capital: The Paramilitarization of Colombia.* Athens: Ohio University Press, 2009. This book is much broader than its title suggests. The author draws on extensive field work in Colombia to paint a devastating view of the abuses in the political system.

Isacson, Adam. *Consolidating "Consolidation."* Washington, D.C.: Washington Office on Latin America, December 2012. A reliable and very careful study.

Ji-Hyun, Seo. "Neoliberal Extractivism and Rural Resistance: The Anti-Mining Movement in the Peruvian Northern Highlands, Cajamarca (2011–2013)." Ph.D. Dissertation, University of Liverpool, 2014. Available on Google Scholar, this meticulous researched study is the result of field work and observation in Peru. Should be read after Arce, Moisés.

Jones, Bart. *¡Hugo! The Hugo Chávez Story from Mud Hut to Perpetual Revolution*. Hanover, NH: Steerforth Press, 2007. The best and most detailed study of the Bolivarian Revolution covers events until the end of 2006; clearly written and scrupulously fair; highly recommended. For the final years of the Chávez presidency, see Carroll, Rory.

Kenney, Charles D. *Fujimori's Coup and the Breakdown of Democracy in Peru*. Notre Dame: University of Notre Dame Press, 2004. This very detailed study of the 1992 coup is a welcome addition. For subsequent events of this presidency, see Carrión and Conaghan.

Kline, Harvey F. *Showing Teeth to the Dragons: State Building by Colombian President Álvaro Uribe Vélez, 2002–2006*. Tuscaloosa: University of Alabama Press, 2009. This very careful scholarly study is indispensable to understand the first term of the Uribe presidency.

Levitt, Barry S. *Power in the Balance: Presidents, Parties, and Legislatures in Peru and Beyond*. Notre Dame: University of Notre Dame Press, 2012. By studying the neglected topic of legislatures, this book illuminates many aspects of the political process in Peru.

Nelson, Brian A. *The Silence and the Scorpion: The Coup against Chávez and the Making of Modern Venezuela*. New York: Nation Books, 2009. This account hostile to Hugo Chávez contains useful information on the April 2002 coup attempt.

Quiroz, Alfonso W. *Corrupt Circles: A History of Unbound Graft in Peru*. Washington, D.C. Woodrow Wilson Center Press, 2008. An encyclopedic if depressing autopsy of an endemic vice in Peru.

Peru. Comisión de la Verdad y la Reconciliación. *Informe Final*. 9 vols. Lima: Comisión de la Verdad y la Reconciliación, 2003. Offers a wealth of information on Peru.

St. John, Ronald Bruce, *Toledo's Peru: Vision and Reality*. Gainesville: University Press of Florida, 2010. This authorized biography contains extensive information and covers all the main issues.

Sullivan, Mark P. "Venezuela: Political Conditions and U.S. Policy." Congressional Research Service, 10 October 2008, Wikileaks. This leaked document provides a useful factual survey.

Trinkunas, Harold A. *Crafting Civilian Control of the Military in Venezuela: A Comparative Perspective*. Chapel Hill: University of North Carolina Press, 2005. This very meticulous scholarly study is indispensable to understand the military of Venezuela.

Wilpert, Gregory. *Changing Venezuela by Taking Power: The History and Policies of the Chávez Government*. London: Verso, 2007. This very sympathetic account captures the excitement about the limitless possibilities for social transformation during the first half of the Hugo Chávez presidency. Should be contrasted with Corrales, Javier and Michael Penfold.

Index

absenteeism 278
accounting 9
AD (Venezuela) 11
Aesop's Fables 187
Afghanistan 68
Agrarian Bank (Colombia) 236, 238
agricultura: Colombia 3, 236, 238; Venezuela 3–4, 141–142, 221–227
AIDESEP (Peru) 188–189, 193–200, 320*n*30
air conditioning 216–217, 330*n*93
air forcé: Colombia 99; Venezuela 15, 90
airports 24, 103, 156
AK-47s 197–197; *see also* Kalashnikovs
Albright, Madelaine 46, 302*n*32
Alfonzo, Gen. Carlos 89
Allende, Salvador 83, 89
Aló Presidente (Venezuela) 118, 123, 134, 137, 142, 146, 179, 218; anniversary 260; and Castro 66; and 2002 coup 77, 84–85
Altamira Plaza (Caracas) 114
aluminum 4, 63, 141
Amazon region (Peru) 23; *see also* Bagua; Iquitos
Ambassador's Comment 316*n*30
ambition 245
amnesty 35, 57, 204
Andahuaylas Province (Peru) 109, 156
Andean Trade Promotion Act 153–154
Andean Trade Promotion and Drug Eradication Act 153–154, 158, 168
Anderson, Danilo 138–139
anthropology 318
Antioquia (Colombia) 129, 245
anti-politics 97, 122
appliances, household 12–13
APRA (Peru) 58–59, 168, 179, 181–182, 195, 252; in congress 255, 320*n*34; and Fujimori 26, 31–32; and Toledo 72–76, 158
Arana, Marco 181, 256–257
Arauca (Colombia) 97–100, 121
Arauca City (Colombia) 99–100
Arequipa (Peru) 22, 33, 76, 101–104, 239
Arequipa Department (Peru) 281–282
Arequipazo 100–104, 197, 239
Argentina 143, 154, 205
Arias Cárdenas, Francisco 15, 18, 64–65
armed forces 1–2; Colombia 120–121; Peru 54, 155; Venezuela 61, 111–112, 294–295
army (Colombia) 232–235
army (Peru) 22; and Arequipazo 104; and Bagua 194, 196, 198, 200; and Conga 257; counter coup 30, 35; election of 2000 41–42; war with Ecuador 34, 194; and Yanacocha 108
army (Venezuela): and Caracazo 13–14
army coup of 1968 (Peru) 22, 32
army coup of 1992 (Venezuela) 15–16
Arreaza Padilla, Rafael 91–92
arrest warrants 51–52, 132
Asia 55
asparagus 153
assassinations 139
Association of Colombian Universities 267–268
asylum 132
ATMs 219
Attorney General's Office *see* Office of Attorney General
AUC (Colombia) 99, 126, 232; *see also* paramilitaries
austerity and austerity programs: Peru 26; Venezuela 12–14, 17, 19
automobile assembly plants 206
Awajún (Peru) 194
Ayacucho (Peru) 187
Aznar, José María 86, 92

babies 17
Baduel, Gen. Raúl 82, 90, 94, 178–179, 207
Bagua (Peru) 193–202, 257
Ball, Luis Enrique 312*n*27
Bambamarca (Peru) 257
banana republics 25, 29, 46, 52, 59
bananas 124
Banco de la Nación (Peru) 44
Banco de Santander 206
Banco de Venezuela 206, 213, 286
bank employees union (Venezuela) 116–118
bank robberies 129, 231
banks: Colombia 235–238; foreign 20, 52; offshore 9, 40; Venezuela 17, 80, 116, 213–214; *see also* Wall Street
Barinas (Venezuela) 80
Barquisimeto (Venezuela) 12–13
Barrera, Germán 47
barricades 103, 197, 282, 289–290
barrios (Caracas) 13–14
Barrios Altos (Lima) 26, 28
Bases for a Democratic Accord (Venezuela) 84
Bazán, Maj. Felipe 197–201
beauty queens 116, 119
Belgian 102
beret, red 16–17, 62
Bicentenario stores (Venezuela) 227
blacklisting 132
blackmail 239
blacks 124
Bogotá 121, 241, 245–247
Bolívar, Simón 93
Bolívar Avenue (Caracas) 88
Bolivarian Circles 77, 85, 93, 207
Bolivarian National Police 220–221
Bolivarian Republic 64, 93
Bolivarian Revolution *see* Chávez, Hugo
Bolivarian schools 67
Bolivia 33, 105, 166
bombs 100
bosses, political 74, 274
Brazil 48, 118, 143, 153–154
brewery 287
bribes 6, 23–24, 27, 34, 40, 191; of Peruvian deputies 43, 47
bridge in Maracaibo 117–118
Britain and British 142
Brunei 55–56
budgets: Peru 70, 73; Venezuela 6
bus fares 12
bus owners 12
Bush, George H.W. 63

Bush, George W. 59, 69; and Chávez 63, 65, 67, 83, 88, 93, 146, 160; and Colombia 120
business and business leaders (Colombia) 98, 122, 124, 236, 245, 273–274
business and business leaders (Peru) 24, 70; and Fujimori 30, 32, 35–36; and García 58–59; and Humala 165; and Toledo 102
business and business leaders (Venezuela) 7, 287; and Chávez 111; and 1998 presidential election 20; and 1999 Constitution 63
Business Track (Peru) 190–192

Cabello, Diosdado 204, 263, 286
CAFTA-DR 154
Caguán Valley (Colombia) 96–99
Cajamarca City 106–107
Cajamarca Department (Peru) 106–107, 181, 256–259
Caldera, Rafael 3–4, 16–17, 19, 62
Cali (Colombia) 236
Callao (Peru) 72
Calles, Plutarco Elías 44
Camet, Jorge 35
Camisea gas project 150–154
Campo, María Fernanda 267
Canada and Canadians 104–105
cancer 261
Caño Limón oil field (Colombia) 97
capitalism 1, 11, 13, 23, 71, 109; concentration of wealth 106, 235; savage 101; and socialism 20, 24–25, 62–63; weakness 192; *see also* free market
Capriani, Bishop Luis 36
Capriles, Henrique 261–263, 285–286, 288–290, 293
car bombs 30, 139
Caracas 138; disturbances 12–14, 288–290; OPEC Summit 65–66; protests 67
Caracas Metropolitan Police 2, 87, 89, 93, 113, 218–219
Caracazo (1989) 12–14, 15, 61
Caracol of Colombia 94
Cargill 225–226
Caribbean 46
Carmona, Pedro 79, 83–84, 86–87, 90–95, 114, 304*n*28
Carmona decree 92–94, 110, 137–139, 171, 312*n*27; amnesty 204
carnival 289
Cartagena (Colombia) 236, 238–239
Carter, Jimmy 132
Carvajal, Leonardo 304*n*28
casino stores (France) 227
Castaño, Carlos 126–129
Castilla, Luis Miguel 255
Castillo, Jorge del 181, 186–187, 189, 191–192
Castro, Fidel 16–18, 20, 66–67, 89, 109, 261
Castro, Raúl 18, 275, 278–279
cattle 78
CAVN 8
Cayara, Ayacucho 23
cease fires 128, 275, 279
cement: Peru 190; Venezuela 5, 205
CEMEX 190, 205
Cenepa River (Peru) 193, 199
census 62
Central Banks: Peru 255; Venezuela 112
Central University of Venezuela 12
centralism (Peru) 71–72
Centro Azucarero Portuguesa 226
ceviche (Peru) 105
Chacao (Caracas) 21
Chacín, Rodríguez 83
Chávez, Hugo 1, 60–68, 170–179; and coup of April 2002 77–95; final years 260–264; and Fourth Republic 4, 6–7, 10–11, 14–21; and Humala 165–166, 168, 251; and Maduro 284–288, 291–294; and petroleum strike 110–119; and recall 131–136
chicken pox 14–15
children 17
Chile 5, 23, 31, 268
Chinese jewelry 24
Chorrillos base 25
Chorrillos military academy 22, 42
Christmas 115
Chuao (Caracas) 86
CIA (Central Intelligence Agency) 39, 67, 211, 299*n*3, 324*n*103
Cipriani, Cardinal Luis 301*n*62
Círculo Militar (Lima) 25
civic-action 66, 234–235
class warfare 13; *see also* lower class; middle class
climate 79
Clinton, Bill 28–29, 62, 65, 67
CNN of Atlanta 94
coca growers 74, 165, 183, 273
cocaine 39–40, 273
coffee 143–144, 224–225
Colina Group (Peru) 26, 29, 35
Colombia 1, 17, 21, 36, 118, 96–100, 120–130, 160–164, 222, 231–250, 264–271, 272–279; and crime in Venezuela 219–220; and Montesinos 45–46, 48; and sugar 226–227; war with Peru 121
Colombian embassy 28
Colombians 135, 171
co-management 147
Comando Maisanta 135
El Comercio (Lima) 187, 191–192, 281; and Keiko 253; and mining 257–258
communal councils (Venezuela) 207, 221
Communist Party and Communists 175, 178, 184, 208
community or communal lands 188–189
commuters 12
compensation 5, 264
competition 5
computers 19, 268
Conga mine (Peru) 256–259, 329*n*39
conglomerates 5
congress (Colombia) 123–124, 162–163; 245–248; absenteeism 278; and prostitutes 276–277; and universities 269–270
congress (Peru) 26–28, 31–32, 35–36; and decentralization 72–75; and Fujimori 43, 49, 54–57, 59; *see also* National Assembly
congress (Venezuela) 4, 16; and petroleum 5; and PDVSA 9; *see also* National Assembly
Conservative Party (Colombia) 97, 122, 163–164, 246
conspicuous consumption 6
constituent or constitutional conventions 20, 28, 31, 60–61, 63, 68, 77
Constitution of 1961 (Venezuela) 60; suspension of 13
Constitution of 1979 (Peru) 25, 28, 32, 70, 183
Constitution of 1991 (Colombia) 17, 20, 98, 124, 162, 267
Constitution of 1993 (Peru) 32, 36, 70, 72, 74, 64
Constitution of 1999 (Venezuela) 64–66, 68, 77–78, 81, 93, 95, 112, 284; and recall 132–136; and reelection 170, 208
Constitutional Courts: Colombia 162–163, 248–249, 264, 278; Peru 107
cooperatives (Venezuela) 141, 145–147, 226
Coordinating Committee for Democracy and Liberty (Venezuela) 86–87, 116–117, 119, 132–136; end 137–138, 211
copper 5, 104–105, 280
CORPOELEC (Venezuela) 216–218
Corral Quemado (Peru) 197–198
corruption (Colombia) 239
corruption (Peru) 27, 38, 40, 48, 57–58, 193; in departments 74; and drugs 27, 36; in judiciary 54; and petroleum 190–193; and political parties 20
corruption (Venezuela): in Fourth Republic 6–7, 63–65, 67; in judiciary 113
counter coup (Peru) 30, 35
counter rally 80
credit cards 45, 219
crime and criminals 139
crime wave (Venezuela) 218–221
criminal bands 231–232
CTV (labor confederation) 63, 68, 80, 83–84, 91; and petroleum strike 114–115, 133
Cuba 16–18, 20, 66, 78, 316*n*21; exile in 90; and peace talks 270; petroleum for 92, 119

Cubans in Venezuela 66–67, 216
Cubas Portal, Gen. Luis 38, 301*n*67
Cudemus, Alberto 136–137
curfew 13
currency and controls 6–7, 254
Curva del Diablo (Peru) 195–199, 202
Cuzco (Peru) 33, 74, 187–188

dams 4
Dañino, Roberto 69, 101, 104
dark skin 264
DAS (Colombia) 239–240, 265, 276
Davos, Switzerland 15
DEA Drug Enforcement Agency (U.S) 39–40, 283–284
death squads 26, 29, 35
decentralization: Peru 70–76, 180–182, 192, 308*n*34; Venezuela 218
Decree Laws 1015 and 1073 (Peru) 188–189
Decree Laws 1064 and 1090 (Peru) 193–201
Decree 1011 (Venezuela) 67
Defensoría del Pueblo see Ombudsman
deficits: budget 5; trade 6
demobilizations 129, 231–232, 277, 279
democratic security (Colombia) 98, 100, 181
demonstrations: Colombia 268–269; Peru 35, 105–106, 179; Venezuela 15, 19
departments (Peru) 71; *see also* decentralization
deregulation 213, 235–238
dictatorship 22–38
Discover Petroleum 190–192
dress 33, 41
dropout rates 6
Drug Enforcement Agency *see* DEA
drug lords 23, 27, 237, 239
drug traffickers 23, 36, 126, 237
"Dutch Disease" 4, 8, 222

economic growth 149–150, 236
economists and economics 71, 75–76
Ecopetrol 100, 236–238
Ecuador 34–35, 40, 49, 108, 194
education, public: Peru 182–183; Venezuela 3, 6, 66–67, 212–213
EGASA (Peru) 101
EGESUR (Peru) 101
18th Brigade (Colombia) 99
El Niño 217–218, 293–295
elections (Colombia): 2002 presidential 97–99
elections (Peru): 1990 presidential 15; 1995 presidential 33–35; 2000 presidential 40–43, 56–59; 2016 presidential 282–284
elections (Venezuela): 18; 1998 congressional 21; 1998 presidential 16, 19–21; 2010 legislative 228–231; 2013 presidential 285–286; 2015 legislative 291
Electricidad de Caracas 173
electricity 4, 101, 134, 293–294; in Peru 151–152; in Venezuela 215–216
electroshocks 36
elites 7, 59, 22, 93
ELN (National Liberation Army) 96, 97, 100, 126–127, 307*n*3
employment 8
enabling authority: Colombia 265; Peru 26–27, 188–189, 319*n*8; Venezuela 4, 77–78, 173, 207, 260, 321*n*16
Energy Crisis of 1973 4
engineers 61, 118 , 217
English language 318
environment and environmental 106–107, 152, 182, 188, 256
envy 2, 235
EPL (People's Liberation Army) 96, 311*n*20
Española de Televisión 94
Éxito megastores (Venezuela) 227, 229
extortion 99, 124, 128, 231
extradition 237
Europe 68–69
European Union 4, 74, 277
Exxon 5

F-16s 15
False Positives (Colombia) 242–244
FARC (*Fuerzas Armadas Revolucionarias de Colombia*) 40–41, 45–46, 48, 96–100; and False Positives 242–244; offensive against 120–122, 126–127, 161–162, 232–236; peace talks 270–271, 273–279
fax 51, 56
FEDECAMARAS (Venezuela) 111, 132, 136–137, 177, 287; and coup of 2002 79–81, 83–84, 87, 91; and petroleum strike 114–115
FEDEPETROL (Venezuela) 68, 84–85, 115–116, 132
Fellowship of the Ring (Colombia) 277
feminists 268
Fernández, Carlos 114, 116, 136
Ferrero, Carlos 158
5th Mobile Brigade (Colombia) 99
Fifth Republic (Venezuela) 20; *see also* Venezuela
financial crisis of 1994 (Venezuela) 17
firing of employees 8
Fisheries Law (Venezuela) 78
Flores, Lourdes 58, 75, 158, 164–168, 316*n*26
FONCODES (Peru) 32–33
food and foodstuffs 11–12, 61, 78, 221–227, 293–294; *see also* agriculture
food imports 143; *see also* agriculture
food sovereignty 141, 143, 224
foreign aid 1, 166, 314*n*27
foreign capital 1
foreign debt 5, 14
foreign investment 5, 7, 20, 31, 111
Foreign Ministry (Peru) 29, 48
Fort Tiuna (Venezuela) 82, 88, 90, 93; summit 142, 146, 208
fortune teller 51
49 decree laws (Venezuela) 78–81, 111
Fourth Estate (Peru) 192
Fourth Republic (Venezuela) 3–21, 60, 62–63, 79, 92; and agriculture 143–144, 222–227; privatizations 205, 215; *see also* Venezuela
France 227
free trade 1; *see also* capitalism
Free Trade Agreement (Colombia) 270
Free Trade Agreement (Peru) 153–154, 156, 158, 165, 167, 179–180, 183–187, 193
Free Trade Agreement of the Americas 111, 143, 153
Fujimori, Alberto 22–38, 39–59, 69–70; legacy 100–101
Fujimori, Keiko 252–254, 282–284
Fujimori, Santiago 30, 36
Fujimorista party 195, 284, 320*n*34
fumigation 271, 275
Funes, Mauricio 260
furniture 12

gangs 126, 232
García, Alán 11, 24–28, 58–59, 71–76; and Humala 255, 279–280, 282–283; presidency 179–185, 186–202; and Toledo 157–158; 2006 campaign 164–168; 2016 campaign 282–284
García Carneiro, Gen. Jorge 88, 94
Garzón, Angelino 264, 266, 272
gas, natural 150–153
gasoline 12, 116–118, 288
gasoline or service stations 31, 116–118, 151–152, 224
Gaviria, Carlos 163
Gaviria, César 48–49, 235
gays 268, 277
Gechen Turbay, Eduardo 98
general strikes 108, 114–117, 183, 186–189, 257; in Amazon 188–189, 193–201
generals 112; Colombia 127, 244; Peru 27, 42, 45, 50, 54, 164; Venezuela 16, 19, 91
George Washington, U.S.N. 171
Giusti, Luis 10
Glencore 236, 238
Globovisión 228, 286
God 261
gold 69, 104–107, 181, 256–259, 280
governorship 245
Great Betrayal (Venezuela) 12

Great Recession 208, 213, 228, 236–238, 281
greed 40, 280
grocery stores 12, 144–145, 224, 291–292
growth, economic 14
Guarenas (Venezuela) 12
Guárico State (Venezuela) 225
Guaviare River (Colombia) 121
Guayaquil (Ecuador) 49
guerrillas: Colombia 17, 96–100, 120–122, 124, 126–127, 129–130; Peru 37; Venezuela 3, 17–19; *see also* FARC; Shining Path
Guillén, Juan Manuel 102
Guri dam 4, 173, 216–218, 295
Guzmán, Abimael 22
Guzmán, Julio 282–283

Haiti 81
Harvard University 33–34
Havana 17–18, 261, 270, 273–275, 278
health care (Venezuela) 3, 6
helicopters 99, 198
Hermoza, Gen. Nicolás 27–28, 35–38, 40
Hernández, Idelso 157, 259
higher education *see* students; universities
Higuchi, Susana 25, 27–28
history and historians 1, 75–76
homeless persons 241–242
Hometown soldiers (Colombia) 234
homicides 218–220
Hotel Bolívar (Lima) 47
Hotel Crillón (Lima) 25, 30
housing 173, 205
Huallaga River (Peru) 36
Huamán, Col. Roberto 50
Humala, Antauro 50–51, 108–109, 256, 255
Humala, Nadine Herrera 166, 168, 255
Humala, Ollanta 108–109, 179, 186; and Fujimori 50–51, 56–57; and García 201; presidency 251–259, 279–284; 2006 campaign 164–169
human rights 23, 26, 59, 65, 154–155, 196; activists 135, 167, 200, 232, 239
Hurtado, María del Pilar 239
Hussein, Saddam 14, 65
Hydrocarbon Law (Venezuela) 79, 111
hydroelectricity (Venezuela) 4, 173, 216–217
Ilave (Peru) 105–106

IMF *see* International Monetary Fund
Import-Substitution-Industrialization (ISI) 3, 172–173, 317*n*12
imports (Venezuela) 3–5, 7
income inequality 14, 149–150, 280
independence 103, 171, 210
Indians and Indian appearances 41, 59, 62, 104–107, 124, 268, 318*n*47; in Amazon 187–188, 193–202
industry and industrialists 111, 141, 172–173, 216
inefficiency of state enterprises 8
inflation 28
informants 27, 40–41, 241
Inter-American Development Bank 73
internally displaced persons 124
International Convention on Tribal and Indian Peoples 188, 201
International Labor Organization 68
International Monetary Fund (IMF) 11–12, 19, 26, 32; withdrawal of Venezuela 174
Interpol 52
Iquitos (Peru) 183
Iran 65
Iraq War 14, 65
ISI *see* Import-Substitution Industrialization

Japan and Japanese 25, 54, 56, 59
Japanese ambassador's residence 37
Japanese embassy 30
Jaua, Elías 222, 225, 230, 262–263, 327*n*15
Jesus Christ 173
jewelry shops 229
Jews 324*n*104
Jiménez, Juan 258
Jiménez, Timochenko 270
Jordan 41, 45–46
judges 23, 25, 51–52, 54, 112; Venezuela 139–140
judiciary branch 28–29, 52; *see also* judges

Kalashnikov rifles 41, 45, 329*n*24; *see also* AK-47s
Karp, Eliane 42, 44, 157
Kerry, John 289, 291
kidnappings 124, 219, 231, 270
Kuczynksi, Pedro Pablo 69, 101, 104, 282–284
Kuori, Alberto 43, 47, 54
Kuwait 14

labor, organized: Colombia 99, 126, 232, 266; Peru 183–184, 186
labor unions (Venezuela) 15, 63, 68
La Cantuta University (Peru) 29
La Esperanza (Colombia) 275
La Francia building (Caracas) 229
Lake Maracaibo 116–119
Lambayeque (Peru) 73, 192
Lameda, Guaicaipuro 83, 87, 91, 93
Land Law (Venezuela) 78, 80, 137, 141–142, 146–147
La Orchila Island (Venezuela) 90, 95, 110
lawyers 22–23
left and leftists (Colombia) 272–274
left and leftists (Peru) 24, 186–187, 251–252; and 2016 campaign 283–284; weakness 254
left and leftists (Venezuela) 15, 17, 19
Leoni, Raúl 3
Lerner Salomón 256–257
lesbian 167, 268, 316*n*25
"Let's Save PDVSA" 83–84, 131–132, 140
Liberal Party (Colombia) 98, 122, 163–164, 246
Libertad I (Colombia) 121
Libya 4
liquidation 8
Lima 71
Lima international airport 24
Lime War (Peru) 104–105, 308*n*34
Locumba (Peru) 50–51
looting 123, 294–295, 330*n*92
López, Capt. Carlos 117
López, Clara 274
López, Leopoldo 210–211, 261, 288, 293
lower class: Colombia 236, 264; Venezuela 6, 14

M-19 (Colombia) 17, 96
Machado, Marina Corina 288, 290
machismo 13
Madrid 86
Maduro, Nicolás 63, 85, 263–264, 284–295, 327*n*15, 330*n*61
maleness *see* machismo
managers of PDVSA 9, 131–136
Manhattan Minerals Corporation 104–105
manifesto 51, 84, 109, 114, 137
manufacturing (Venezuela) 3, 141
Maoists 23, 26, 154, 183, 311*n*20
Maracaibo 15, 18, 115
Maracay 82, 83
Marañón River (Peru) 194–200, 256
March of the Four Corners (Peru) 44–45, 58
marches 209, 212, 258, 269
markets, popular 61; *see also* Mercal
mass (Roman Catholic) 51
massacres 13, 23, 26, 61, 126, 193–202, 243
McCaffrey, Barry 40
meat 4
medallion 53
Medellín (Colombia) 129, 278
media (Colombia) 122–124, 160–161, 239, 244, 273
media (Peru) 40, 44, 100–101; and Keiko 253
media (Venezuela) 5, 9; hostility to Hugo Chávez 18, 20, 67
Medina Gómez, Gen. Enrique 111
mega-elections (Venezuela) 64–65
Mendoza, Lorenzo 287, 330*n*61

Mercal (Venezuela) 144–145, 224, 226
MERCOSUR 143, 156
mercury 106
Mexican Revolution 84
Mexico 8–9, 11, 44, 205; and petroleum 65
middle class (Colombia) 98, 236
middle class (Peru) 24
middle class (Venezuela) 6, 14, 20, 112, 134, 229; and coup of 2002 81, 93; and education 66
MIG-29 40, 301*n*7
military academy 22
military attachés 82, 109
military-civilian alliance 62
milk 227, 324*n*97
minimum wage 84, 134–135
mining 73, 104–105, 181, 280; *see also* specific mineral
minister of defense, civilian 113
Ministry of Defense (Colombia) 234, 241
Ministry of Energy (Venezuela) 9
Ministry of the Presidency (Peru) 33
Miquilena, Luis 15–17, 61, 63, 80, 89, 95, 112, 177, 298*n*43, 305*n*10
Miraflores Presidential Palace 15, 80, 85–90, 110, 228
Miranda State (Venezuela) 263
Miss Universe 21
mistresses and lovers 24, 45, 49, 239, 303*n*50
Mobil 5
Mockus, Antanas 250
Mocoa (Colombia) 236–237
Molotov cocktails 134
Moncada attack (Cuba) 16, 109
monopolies 7, 281
Montenegro, Commander Miguel 199
Montesinos, Vladimiro 22–38, 39–59, 100–101, 106, 281; wife of 52–53; *see also* mistress
Montilla Pantoja, Col. José Gregorio 94–95
Moquequa Department (Peru) 50–51, 189
Mora, Omar 139
Morales, Evo 166, 200
morals and morality 22
Morocco 49
Motta, Luis 2949
Mount Ávila (Venezuela) 64, 154
Mount Quilish (Peru) 106–107
MRTA (Peru) 37
municipalities: Colombia 121–122, 241; Peru 71, 73, 182; Venezuela 218, 287
Muñoz, Albis 136
Murcia Guzmán, David 236–237
murders 99, 219, 232
MVR (Venezuela) 140, 175–176, 179, 204, 230, 263
mysticism 95, 173

El Nacional (Caracas) 229, 324*n*103
NAFTA 153–154
National Assembly (Peru) 157–158 , 283–284
National Assembly (Venezuela) 63, 77–78, 92–95, 229–230; and crime 139, 218–220; and Maduro 285–287, 295; and opposition 292–293; and referendum 173–175, 178
National Council of Decentralization 73, 182
National Decentralization Commission 72–73
National Electoral Council 133–136, 248
National Endowment for Democracy 67–68
National Guard (Venezuela) 87, 89, 288–290
National Liberation Army *see* ELN
National Unity (Venezuela) 211
nationalism and nationalists (Colombia) 238
nationalism and nationalists (Peru) 34, 40, 50–51, 105, 151–152, 165–166, 169
nationalism and nationalists (Venezuela) 5, 111, 115, 171–172, 291
Nationalist Party (Peru) 108–109, 186, 252–253
nationalizations: Colombia 238; Venezuela 5, 7, 20
naturalizations 135, 171
navy 15; Peru 25, 167, 190; Venezuela 90, 94, 117–118
Neiva (Colombia) 121
Nélida Colán, Blanca 29–30, 36, 48, 51–52
Neo-Conservatives (U.S) 67
New Rich 6
New Year's 57, 109, 204
New York City 62
Newmont Mining Corporation 106–107, 181, 256–259
newspapers 9; Caracas 229; Lima 28; provincial 18
NGOs (Non-Governmental Organizations) 71, 105, 123, 210–211
night watches (*rondas campesinas*) 257, 259
9/11 terrorist attacks 120
Non-Governmental Organizations *see* NGOs
Norway 270

Obama, Barack 209, 270, 275, 280, 294
Ocaña (Colombia) 242–243
Office of the Attorney General (Peru) 23, 28–29, 59, 158
officers: Colombia 241, 244; Peru 22–23, 30, 37; Venezuela 15, 63, 81, 114–115, 134, 215, 263
offshore banks *see* banks
oligarchy and oligarchs 5, 6–7, 9
oligopoly 5, 7
Ombudsman (*Defensoría del Pueblo*) 32, 48
OPEC (Organization of Petroleum Exporting Countries) 10, 65, 141
Operation Guarimba (Venezuela) 134–136
Operation Recruitment (Peru) 43
optimism 6
Opus Dei lay fraternity 93
Organization of American States (OAS) 48, 132, 293–295
Orinoco River (Venezuela) 225
Orinoco Steel Company *see* SIDOR
Ortega, Carlos: and coup of 2002 80, 83–84, 86–87, 90–91; and petroleum strike 114–118, 132
Oxy petroleum 100

Palace of Justice (Lima) 28, 44
Panama 49
Paniagua, Valentín 55–57, 59, 75, 101, 104, 154, 164–165
parachute 41
parades 77, 295
paramilitaries 99, 124, 126–130, 231–231; in Venezuela 134
paratroopers 16, 62, 82
Parque del Este (Caracas) 86
Parra Luzardo, Gastón 83–85, 87, 110
parties, political: Peru 70; Venezuela 11, 20–21; *see also* indvidual parties
Pasto (Colombia) 236–237
Pastrana, Andrés 96–99, 120, 127–128, 235
patron-client relationship 1
patronage 20, 162–163, 184
payroll 8
PDVSA (*Petróleos de Venezuela Sociedad Anónima*) 5, 8–11, 14, 141, 287; and Chávez 62, 65–66; and coup of 2002 83–84, 91–93; and grocery stores 22; and labor 68; and petroleum strike 110–119, 131–133; and royalties 79; and social production enterprises 147–148
peasants 23, 78, 106–107, 124, 126; land for 265; murder of 232, 241
PEMEX 8–10
pensions and pension funds 31, 35, 70, 78
Pereira (Colombia) 269
Pérez, Carlos Andrés 4–6, 8, 11–17, 19, 62
Pérez de Cuéllar, Javier 33–35, 57
Pérez Jiménez, Marcos 19
Pérez Recao, Isaac 90
Peru 1, 11, 22–38, 39–59, 68–76, 100–109, 149–159, 164–169, 179–185, 186–202, 251–259, 279–284; example 61
Perupetro 300*n*39
Peter the Brief 90–95
petitions 83–84, 86, 92, 105, 131–132
Petro, Gustavo 274

petroleum (Venezuela) 4, 65–66; for Cuba 66, 92
petroleum strike (Venezuela) 114–119, 131–132
Petro Tech Peruana 190–192
PetroPeru 31, 35, 154, 191, 300*n*39; and Bagua massacre 194; and gas 150, 152
photographs 241
Pilín León 116, 119
Pinchi Pinchi, Matilde 23–24, 45, 47, 302*n*34, 303*n*50
Pinochet, Augusto 23
Pinto, Lino 290
pipelines: in Colombia 97–100, 121, 237; in Peru 150–151, 194, 199; in Venezuela 9;
Pisco (Peru) 49, 50
Piura Department (Peru) 104–105, 183
Plan Ávila 13, 88
Plan Bolívar 61–62, 66, 81
Plan Patriota (Colombia) 121, 161–162, 241
PODEMOS (Venezuela) 175–178, 211
Poggioli, Ovidios 82, 94
Polar (Venezuela) 222, 224–226, 287, 295
police (Colombia) 120–122, 265; and criminal bands 232; and FARC 233–234; and paramilitaries 231–232; and wiretapping 240, 276
police: and Bagua massacre 196–201; Peru 103, 109, 258–259; Venezuela 12, 220–221
Police Reestablishment Program 234
politicians: Colombia 98, 122–124, 162–163, 249, 265; Peru 24, 48, 76; Venezuela 9, 20–21, 63–64, 79, 178
polls: Colombia 98–99, 248; Peru 28, 34, 43, 157, 166–167, 184, 282–283; Venezuela 21, 133–135, 179, 209, 215, 219, 262
Popayán (Colombia) 236–237
pork and pork producers 136–137, 143
Porras Bernal, Fair Leonardo 243
ports (Venezuela) 6
potatoes 154, 314*n*27
poverty and crime 218–219; Peru 70, 149–150, 152; Venezuela 6, 218
PPT (Venezuela) 175–176, 208
presidential families 246
presidential guard 87, 89, 91, 94
price controls 112, 143, 222, 225, 227
prices: gasoline 12; petroleum 4, 10–11, 14, 141, 291–292
primaries 205, 207, 261
prison sentences 276
prisons 38–39, 218–219
privatization: Colombia 98, 235–236, 267–269; Peru 27–28, 30–31, 35, 101–104, 150, 156, 191; Venezuela 17, 20, 62–63, 77–78, 141
profits 9–11, 34; hiding 116; and sacred mountain 107
promotions (military) 22, 63, 81, 241; police 200
prosecutors 23, 29, 51, 54
prostitutes 41–42, 58, 276–277
protection payments 97
protectionism 7
protests 37, 114, 123, 155, 236–237
provinces and provincials 22
PSUV 175–176, 178–179, 204–205, 207–211, 263, 286; convention 260–261; and food supply 293–294; and police 221; and 2010 legislative elections 228–231
Pucallpa (Peru) 184
Puerto Maldonado (Peru) 189
Pumping Station No. 6 (Peru) 194–195, 199
Puno (Peru) 33, 105–106, 187
purges 29–30
pyramid schemes 237, 248

race *see* Indians; dark skinned
radio 16, 18, 49
rains and rainfall 134, 216–218
ranching and ranchers 78, 124, 143
Rangel, José Vicente 82, 112, 137–138, 305*n*10
RCTV 176–177, 228–229
recall 64, 113
redistricting 229
reelections 31–31, 37, 64, 130, 170–172, 174
referendums 123–124, 248–249, 278–279; Peru 32, 75–76, 281; Venezuela 60, 208–209
refineries: Colombia 236, 238–239; Peru 31, 156; Venezuela 9, 116–118
Reich, Otto 83
reporters and journalists 5, 9, 40, 239, 282
repression 13–14, 258–259
La República (Lima) 281
reserves of petroleum 10
Revolutionary Military (Peru) 22–23, 61
rice 156, 225–226, 323*n*91
rifles 41, 45
riots 12
rising expectations 6
road blocks 105, 134, 156, 188–189, 257, 266, 281; *see also* demonstrations; protests
Rodríguez, Alí 65, 115, 117–118, 131, 310*n*18
Rodríguez, Carlos 132
Rodríguez, Isaías 92–93
Roman Catholic Church: Colombia 128; Peru 50, 104, 18, 1951; Venezuela 64, 84, 95, 110, 177, 209, 212, 229
Romero, Daniel 90, 93–94
Ron, Lina 209, 261, 29
rondas campesinas *see* night watches
Rosales, Manuel 138, 171–173, 203
Rosendo, Gen. Manuel 88, 90
Rospigliosi, Fernando 102–104, 308*n*26
royalties 79, 99–100, 152, 235, 189
Russia 44–45, 47, 301*n*7

sabotage 117, 239
sacred mountain 107
Sáez, Irene 20–21
salaries: of PDVSA 9–10; of Venezuelan military 15
Salas Römer, Henrique 21
Salinas de Gortari, Carlos 11
San Jorge Valley (Colombia) 124
Santo Domingo (Colombia) 99
Santos, Gregorio 257, 259
Santos, Juan Manuel 230, 243–244; campaign 246–250; presidency 264–271, 272–279
satyriasis 22, 24, 45
Saudi Arabia 14, 65
scandals 75, 236–245
schools, private (Venezuela) 6
schools, public (Venezuela) 6, 61, 66
search warrant 52–53
secrecy and secrets 5, 9, 22
Secret Directive (Colombia) 241
secret police 18, 83, 87, 89, 94; *see also* SIN
Self-coup of 1992 28
Semana (Bogotá) 239–240
senate (Peru) 74–75
Shining Path (*Sendero Luminoso*) 22–23, 26–27, 29–30, 54, 59, 154–155, 183
shock program 25
sicarios 219, 232
SIDOR (Orinoco Steel Company) 4, 205–206
signatures: Colombia 238, 247, 278; scandal of forged 75, 157–158; Venezuela 133, 208–209, 292–293
Silva, Gen. Wildredo 88
Simón, Yehude 73, 192–193, 196, 201
SIN (*Servicio de Inteligencia Nacional*) 23–27, 33–34, 39–46
Sinú valley (Colombia) 124
slums: Bogotá 241; Caracas 19; Colombia 127–128, 234; Peru 33; Venezuela 66
smog 152
smuggling and smugglers 222, 288, 330*n*92
Soacha (Bogotá) 241–243
social cleansing 241–242
social networks 268–269
social pages 9
Social Party of Social Unity *see* U Party
social production enterprises (Venezuela) 147–148
social security 30–31, 35, 63, 78
social welfare (Venezuela) 3, 6
socialism 13; rejection 11, 20; *see also* 21st century socialism

Soto, Hernando de 180
soup kitchens 33
Southern Copper Corporation 281–282
Soviet Union and Soviet bloc 24–25, 30, 62, 66, 101, 235
Spain and Spaniards 48, 86, 142
spears 198, 200
speculators 105, 142–143
spies and espionage 27, 100, 239, 276; industrial espionage 190–192; *see also* DAS; SIN
squatters 142
state enterprises (Venezuela) 7, 20; *see also* individual companies
steel 4, 205–206
stimulus package 70, 101
stock market 254
Stop Chávez movement 21
strikes 104; *see also* general strike; petroleum strike
students, university: Colombia 268–269; Peru 37, 103, 107–108; Venezuela 12, 19
subsidies 7
suffrage to soldiers 63
sugar 226–227
supermarkets 12, 118–119, 144–145, 227, 293, 295
Supply Committees 293–295
Supreme Court: Colombia 124, 239–240, 247, 264; Peru 37, 74, 106; Venezuela 60, 92, 112, 139–140, 292–293
survey 19, 21
suspension of constitutional guarantees 13
Switzerland 52, 303*n*53

Táchira 289
Táchira sugar mill 226–227
Tacna (Peru) 101, 189
Talara (Peru) 156
Tambogrande (Peru) 104–105
tankers 116
tanks 88
Tapia, Carlos 168, 257
Tarapoto (Peru) 195
tariffs 185; *see also* Free Trade Agreements
Tascón, Luis 133, 140, 204, 321*n*6
Tascón List 140, 176, 286
taxes 7, 35, 70, 119, 152; evasion 24; war tax 120, 128, 233
teachers 104, 182–184, 212
technology 7, 190–191
telephones 63, 239–240, 268–269
television (Cuba) 18
television (Peru): and Montesinos 40, 47, 50, 53; and petroleum 192; and self-coup of 1992; and 2006 election 165–168
television (Venezuela) 228–229; and Caracazo 13; and Chávez 66, 78; and coup attempt of 1992 15–16; and coup of 2002 84–86, 88–90, 92, 94; and petroleum strike 114, 116–118
terrorism and terrorists 26, 30
Tía María mine (Peru) 281–282
El Tiempo (Bogotá) 160, 244
Tokyo 56
Toledo, Alejandro 33–34, 41–44, 56–59, 252–253; and Humala 279–280, 282–283; presidency 68–76, 149–159, 164; 2016 campaign 282–283
Toledo, Margarita 157
Toquepala 51
torture 36
tour, campaign 16–17
town hall meetings 63, 123
Tractabel 102
triangulation 265, 274
Trinidad and Tobago 118, 295
triumvirate (Peru) 27, 37–38
trucks 12, 266
Trujillo (Peru) 74
Truth and Reconciliation Commission (Peru) 59, 154–155
tugboats 117–118
21st century socialism 146, 172, 179, 205, 206

U party (Colombia) 246, 248–249, 271
Ucayali River (Peru) 193
Ugaz, José 51–52, 57
unicameral legislatures 32
uniforms 16–17, 62, 90
unions *see* labor, organized
United Nations 46, 171, 277, 279
United States: and Peru 28–29, 39–59, 68–69, 74; and Venezuela 52–63, 65–68
U.S. AID 166, 316*n*21
U.S. Congress 153–154, 180, 184–185, 270; and Venezuela 291
U.S. embassies 1–2; Caracas 211, 217; Lima 52, 56, 74, 76, 158, 252
U.S. Navy 171
U.S. Southern Command 50
El Universal (Caracas) 229
Universidad del Oriente (Venezuela) 229
universities 267–269
upper class 14, 20, 127–128, 138–139, 172, 235; Venezuela 204, 229, 313*n*36
Urabá (Colombia) 124, 126
Uribe Vélez, Álvaro 96–100, 120–130, 160–164, 231–250; and Santos 264–267, 270–273, 275–276, 278
Uruguay 156
utility companies 101–104

Valdés, Óscar 258
Valdivia, Gen. José 23
vanity 37
Vargas Lleras, Germán 264, 270, 272
Vargas Llosa, Mario 24–26, 30, 33; and Keiko 253–254, 284
Vargas Ruiz, Archbishop Fernando 104
Vásquez Velasco, Gen. Efraín 82–83, 88–89, 94
Vaticano (Demetrio Chávez) 23, 36, 39
Velarde, Julio 255
Velasco, Card. Ignacio 84, 93, 95, 110, 116, 301*n*62
Velasco, Gen. Juan 6, 152
VENALUM 141
Venezuela 1, 3–21, 50–68, 110–119, 131–148, 170–179, 260–264, 284–295
Venezuelan-American Chamber of Commerce (VENAMCHAM) 137, 312*n*27
vengeance 110
Verizon 173
VIASA 8
Victims' Law 265, 272–273
videos 30, 43, 47–48, 50–51, 53–54, 57, 108; of Toledo 41–42, 58, 157; of Venezuela 89
Villa El Salvador (Lima) 33
village elders 195
Villanueva, Edgar 157–158
violence 1, 14; in Colombia 96, 126, 129–130, 232, 235, 266; Venezuela 133–134, 290
visas (U.S.) 17
Vladivideos 47–48, 50–51, 53–54, 57–58, 108
voter fatigue 171

wages *see* salaries
Wall Street 1, 213, 267; and Peru 25–26, 28, 69, 101; and Venezuela 62
Wampis (Peru) 194, 198–199
water supply 107, 181, 217, 257–258, 281–282, 294–295
wheat 156, 224, 314*n*27
whiskey 14, 112, 172, 287
white and whites 58–59, 93
Wikileaks 1
wiretaps 18; Colombia 239–240; Peru 25, 190–192
witch 42, 51, 53
women 44–45, 119, 164; and FARC 311*n*32; Indian 199; in Shining Path 30
work stoppage 80, 84, 86, 101–102, 257, 266, 281; *see also* general strikes
workers 10, 232
World Bank 11–12, 26, 32–33, 35, 69; and decentralization 73; withdrawal of Venezuela 173

Yanacocha (Peru) 69, 106–107, 181, 256

Zorba the Greek video 30
Zulia state 18, 138, 171, 210
Zuluaga, Óscar Iván 271, 273–274
Zunzuneo (Cuba) 316*n*21

www.ingramcontent.com/pod-product-compliance
Ingram Content Group UK Ltd.
Pitfield, Milton Keynes, MK11 3LW, UK
UKHW051929100926
8556IPUK00022B/1453

9 780786 499298